ONE WEEK LOAN

This book is accompanied by _|_ CD-ROM(s)
Check on Issue and Return

ABAP® Objects

 **PRESS**

SAP PRESS is a joint initiative of SAP and Galileo Press. The know-how offered by SAP specialists combined with the expertise of the publishing house Galileo Press offers the reader expert books in the field. SAP PRESS features first-hand information and expert advice, and provides useful skills for professional decision-making.

SAP PRESS offers a variety of books on technical and business related topics for the SAP user. For further information, please visit our website: *www.sap-press.com.*

Ulli Hoffmann
Web Dynpro for ABAP
2006, 359 pp.
ISBN 978-1-59229-078-9

Brian McKellar, Thomas Jung
Advanced BSP Programming
2006, 492 pp.
ISBN 978-1-59229-049-9

Horst Keller
The Official ABAP Reference
2005, 1216 pp.
ISBN 978-1-59229-039-0

Tobias Trapp
XML Data Exchange Using ABAP
2006, 121 pp.
SAP PRESS Essentials 13
ISBN 978-1-59229-076-5

Horst Keller, Sascha Krüger

ABAP® Objects

ABAP Programming in SAP NetWeaver™

Galileo Press

Bonn · Boston

ISBN   978-1-59229-079-6

2nd edition 2007

Translation Lemoine International, Inc., Salt Lake City, UT
Editor Florian Zimniak
Copy Editor Nancy Etscovitz, Boston, MA
Cover Design Silke Braun
Layout Design Vera Brauner
Production Iris Warkus
Typesetting SatzPro, Krefeld
Printed and bound in Germany

© 2007 by Galileo Press
SAP PRESS is an imprint of Galileo Press,
Boston, MA, USA
Bonn, Germany

Contents at a Glance

Contents

3 Basic Principles of ABAP 141

5 Basic ABAP Language Elements 225

6 Advanced Concepts in ABAP Objects 341

Foreword

This book is the sequel to *ABAP Objects: An Introduction to Programming SAP Applications* from the SAP PRESS series. Instead of producing a reworked second edition of the Introduction, we have written a new book that is based, in part, on the manuscript for the previous book.

The earlier book was the first ABAP book in the SAP PRESS series and was intended to serve both as an introduction to ABAP Objects as well as a general overview of the ABAP language and SAP Basis. Since then, however, SAP PRESS has published dedicated introduction and practice books, as well as a comprehensive ABAP reference book, which is complemented by an ABAP quick reference guide to provide a quick overview. This has allowed us to take a new direction in the current book. This book is much less of a reference guide than its predecessor. Instead, it is intended to function as the programming handbook in the series of ABAP books that have previously appeared at SAP PRESS, grouped between introductory practical books and ABAP reference guides.

In this book, we are therefore offering our readers a compendium of modern ABAP programming and of the key possibilities of the ABAP Application Server in SAP NetWeaver. Modern ABAP programming means programming with ABAP Objects. Contrary to the previous book, ABAP Objects are no longer treated as an addition to classical ABAP, but rather as the underlying programming model. Consistent with all books on object-oriented programming languages, the presentation of the ABAP language in Chapter 4 begins this time with "Classes and Objects." From the start, we have integrated the description of the Class Builder into the description of classes and objects. All remaining language elements and tools have been presented in the same way that they are used in ABAP Objects to implement classes. The classical concepts of ABAP are mentioned where they are still used. We no longer discuss obsolete concepts; and if we do, we only touch on them very briefly.

Whereas in the previous book, we dealt mainly with elementary ABAP language topics, in this book we have also included—in addition to the many new developments that the ABAP language has seen in the meantime—additional topics that are essential for the programming of the ABAP Application Server in SAP NetWeaver. In fact, we devote an entire chapter to the error handling reaching from exception classes to assertions, offer an introduction to Web Dynpro for ABAP, provide a separate chapter on dynamic programming including Run Time Type Creation, and a chapter on the external communication and data interfaces from RFC over ICF to XML, and also provide an overview of all possible tools to use for testing quality assurance.

Because of the large number of new topics, the scope of this book has now passed the magical 1000-page milestone. Therefore, we will at least try to keep the foreword brief, albeit without neglecting to extend our thanks to all of the people who have helped, directly or indirectly, to produce this book.

First we must mention our colleagues in the department "SAP NetWeaver Foundation ABAP." While this organizational unit had a different name in all of the other books that have appeared to date, it is essentially still the "ABAP Language" group, which develops the ABAP language and the ABAP tools, and which now also encompasses the groups "ABAP Workbench" and "ABAP Connectivity." This group's work is the foundation of everything that is described in this book, and we do not exaggerate when we say that the output of this group is the basis of any ABAP developments internationally. In appreciation of all of this team's members, we would here again like to thank the Vice President Andreas Blumenthal, who has supported this book from the very beginning and provided the necessary resources to make it become a reality.

We would specifically like to thank the following colleagues who have made special contributions to producing this book: Kai Baumgarten (information and corrections on Shared Objects), Thomas Becker (information on qRFC), Joachim Bender and Michael Schmitt (proofreading of the section on Web Services), Dirk Feeken and Manfred Lutz (publication of the AS ABAP Trial Version on DVD), Eva Pflug (help in setting up the AS ABAP trial version as a translation system, to ensure that the examples also work when users log on in English), Susanne Rothaug and Volker Wichers (support with testing the ABAP Web Services on another J2EE Server), Klaus-Dieter Scherer (help and information on ALV print lists), Stefan Seemann (hooked the MaxDB that failed when we tried to install a parallel J2EE Server backup to the AS ABAP trial version), Markus Tolksdorf (information and corrections on JCo), and Doris Vielsack (information and corrections on dynpros).

As a further new feature, this issue of the ABAP Objects book is also based on texts from authors who are responsible for *one* particular contribution: Stefan Bresch (object services), Rupert Hieble (XML), Anne Lanfermann (Web Services), Frank Müller (RFC and ICF), and Stefanie Rohland (Web Dynpro). We would like to thank these authors for their readiness to assist with this project, in addition to their normal responsibilities. The authors' bios are provided at the end of this book.

We would like to thank the publishers at Galileo Press for their collaboration, which was, as always, excellent. Alexandra Müller and Florian Zimniak did an outstanding job correcting and editing the manuscript, even going so far as to find formal errors in the code. For the production, we would like to thank Iris Warkus (Galileo Press) and Dirk Hemke (SatzPro), most especially for the fact that right from the first typesetting for this book, we found nothing of note to grumble about. For the English edition, the authors want to express their gratitude to Nancy Etscovitz from Wellesley Information Services, who did a terrific job in editing the translation, and to Snezhina Gileva from SAP Labs Sofia for proof reading the final manuscript.

Sascha Krüger would especially like to thank his wife Katja for so many things too numerous to mention, both big and small, such as keeping him free from any "distractions," loads of understanding, constant encouragement and motivation, lots of free space, more than a little coffee, and so much more. In this way, she ultimately played a large part in the production of his share of the manuscript.

Horst Keller would like to thank his wife Ute, as always, who again supported the creation of this book with her considerable patience and understanding. Despite the promises made after every previous book—that next time things would be easier—this book, in particular, again proved that such promises cannot always be kept, and consequently much joint free time during the first half of 2006 had to be sacrificed. The fact that Ute never once questioned this project, but just looked forward with Horst to meeting the deadline, proved to be invaluable.

Walldorf, February 2007
Horst Keller
Sascha Krüger

"A journey of a thousand miles starts with a single step."
—Lao-Tse

1 Introduction

We would like to invite you to embark on a fascinating journey that spans more than a thousand pages through the world of ABAP. We will start with a brief overview explaining our reasons for undertaking this journey, that is, ABAP and its significance for programming in today's SAP environment. Then, we will turn our attention to our destination and prepare you for the stops that we shall make along the way. Lastly, in this chapter, we will discuss how you can actively contribute to making this journey a success.

1.1 What Is ABAP?

ABAP (*Advanced Business Application Programming*) is a programming language that was developed by SAP for developing commercial applications in the SAP environment.

1.1.1 The Evolution of ABAP

The development process of ABAP went through the following evolutionary stages:

▶ In the early days (i. e., the 1970s), ABAP stood for "Allgemeiner Berichts-Aufbereitungs Prozessor" ("*Generic Report Generation Processor*"). ABAP in this stage was implemented as a macro assembler under R/2, and, as the name implies, was used exclusively for creating reports. R/2

▶ By the mid-1980s, ABAP had become an interpreter language. It was now an established part of the R/2 system, and was powerful enough to be used to create business application programs. In particular, it could be used to program dialog-controlled transactions.

R/3 ▸ In the early 1990s, the SAP R/3 system was born, and ABAP became ABAP/4 or Advanced Business Application Programming, a fourth-generation (4GL) programming language. Far from just being an "add-on" to R/3, it now formed the technical and software basis of the entire system. Apart from the system core, which was programmed in C, all SAP application modules, R/3 Basis system components, and even the development environment were now created in ABAP/4.

ABAP Objects ▸ At the end of the 1990s, there was a new addition in the form of ABAP Objects. From this point on, the language was again known as "ABAP" (without the "/4"). ABAP Objects is an object-oriented language extension that implements all the important concepts of the object-oriented programming paradigm, such as encapsulation, inheritance, and polymorphism. Thus, in this book, we speak of "ABAP" when we mean the entire ABAP language, and "ABAP Objects" when we are referring to its object-oriented aspects only.

Unicode ▸ At the beginning of this century, ABAP programs were made Unicode-compatible in order to optimally support the internationalization of the SAP system. With Unicode-compatible programs and Unicode programs, stricter Unicode checks are used for syntax checking, and some statements use different semantics to non-Unicode programs. This kind of program usually delivers the same results in both Unicode and non-Unicode systems. A Unicode system is one in which all possible characters are encoded in a single code page using the Unicode character set. Unicode systems replace the earlier MDMP (*multi-display, multi-processing*) systems, and can run only Unicode programs.

SAP NetWeaver ▸ With the new positioning of the SAP technology platform under the name "SAP NetWeaver," ABAP became the programming interface of the SAP NetWeaver Application Server ABAP (AS ABAP for short), which replaced the earlier SAP Basis and has also become known as SAP Web Application Server. AS ABAP is a highly efficient, robust, scalable infrastructure, and is available in SAP NetWeaver alongside AS Java. Both versions are mutually callable and are therefore interlinked. An installation of SAP NetWeaver Application Server ABAP is the prerequisite for using the ABAP programming language. AS ABAP provides interfaces to dialog users, external programs, and the Internet.

1.1.2   Scope of ABAP

ABAP is essentially still a 4GL language that was specifically devel-   4GL
oped for mass data processing in commercial applications. Compared
to elementary languages, it contains many language elements that
are usually stored in libraries. These kinds of language elements
encapsulate the underlying technology, thus ensuring the platform-
independence of the application development. The advantages of
integrating these functions into the language instead of storing them
in libraries are that it enhances program performance and makes
static checking easier. ABAP also contains considerably more language elements than elementary programming languages. In Appendix A.1, we provide a complete list of the ABAP statements that are
available for use.

The following are examples of ABAP language elements that are typ-   Language elements
ical of 4GL:

▶ Integrated database access in the form of Open SQL

▶ Performance optimization of database access integrated into the
  ABAP runtime environment using SAP buffering

▶ Internal tables for dynamic storage and processing of tabular mass
  data in the memory

▶ The *online transaction processing* (OLTP) concept is integrated into
  the ABAP runtime environment via SAP LUW. OLTP allows multiple users to simultaneously access the central database.

▶ Integrated interface to other programming environments via
  remote function call (RFC)

▶ Integrated interface to XML

Besides the functions that are directly integrated into the language,   System library
the classes and interfaces in the system library also provide access to
the ABAP runtime environment functions. Examples include:

▶ Administration of and access to shared objects in shared memory

▶ Administration of and access to persistent objects in the database

▶ Access to the Internet

▶ Access to user interfaces

ABAP programs can be programmed completely independently of   Multilingualism
natural languages: language-specific program components are kept

separate from the source code, and are loaded in accordance with the current language when the program is executed. A "text environment" determines the specific behavior of the program at runtime, such as the order that is used to sort texts. ABAP supports Unicode, and older installations still support code pages for single-byte code and double-byte code.

1.1.3 ABAP Development Environment

ABAP programs are developed in a development environment that is integrated into the AS ABAP of SAP NetWeaver. Besides the actual programs, all the development objects that are required for an ABAP application are also created and managed in this environment. This functionality comprises everything from defining database tables in an ABAP dictionary to creating and publishing Web Services. The development environment supports "early prototyping"; in other words, development objects can be tested directly in their own environment, without the need to carry out an explicit "deployment" or to restart the server. The integrated correction and transport system is then used to deploy a finished piece of programming work.

1.1.4 ABAP Programming Model

ABAP supports a hybrid programming model, composed of the following:

ABAP Objects
- An object-oriented programming model that is based on classes and interfaces of ABAP Objects
- A procedural programming model that is based on procedure calls and system event handling

Both models are interoperable, that is, you can call classes from classic procedures, and you can call classic procedures from methods. The classic programming model is still supported for the sake of compatibility, but we recommend that you use ABAP Objects.

Why Use ABAP Objects?

ABAP Objects supports object-oriented programming. Object-oriented programming is the recognized programming model for solving complex problems. The object-oriented programming model using ABAP Objects is superior to the classic procedural programming model for the following reasons:

1. ABAP Objects classes implement an advanced data encapsulation technology that increases the ease of maintenance and stability of programs. In the procedural model, the status of a program is represented by its global data. In object-oriented programming, on the other hand, individual classes and objects encapsulate their own status. Because object-oriented programming differentiates between publicly visible and private components, access to the components of an object can be explicitly controlled. Even without extensive object-oriented modeling, it is still better to use classes, as it is virtually impossible to control the status of a large program that is defined only by its own global data.

   Data encapsulation

2. ABAP Objects enables you to create multiple instances of a class using explicit statements. Every object of this kind has its own status, and can change this status using its own methods. Automatic garbage collection ensures that objects that are no longer required are deleted from the memory. Procedural models do not provide multiple instantiation, which is why they force you to use stateless functions on separately stored data.

   Instantiation

3. ABAP Objects enables you to reuse code from existing classes by means of inheritance. The inheritance concept is an integral property of the object-oriented programming paradigm. It allows programmers to derive classes with special characteristics from generic classes while re-implementing only the new code. In the procedural model, the rule is "all or nothing." You either use the existing functions exactly as they are, or create new ones.

   Inheritance

4. ABAP Objects allows developers to access objects via independent interfaces. This means that the user does not have to worry about the implementation details behind the interface, and providers can modify implementations transparently without the users noticing and without having to modify the interface itself. The procedural model, on the other hand, does not have a concept of independent interfaces.

   Interfaces

5. ABAP Objects makes it easier to implement event-driven program flows. A *publish-and-subscribe* mechanism can loosely link applications, without the trigger of an event having to know anything about any handlers that may exist. This allows for greater flexibil-

   Events

ity than the procedural approach, which uses much stronger linkage and thus, has a much more strictly-defined program flow.

In addition to these reasons, which are all related to the object-oriented programming model, there are also other, ABAP-specific reasons for using ABAP Objects instead of procedural ABAP:

Orthogonal concepts

▶ ABAP Objects is more explicit than classic procedural ABAP, and is therefore easier to learn and use. ABAP Objects contains a small number of closely defined, mutually orthogonal, fundamental concepts, which makes it more reliable and less error-prone. Classic procedural ABAP, on the other hand, is dominated by implicit behaviors in which programs are controlled by implicit events in the runtime environment and via global data.

Syntax cleansing

▶ ABAP Objects contains cleansed rules for syntax and semantics. Classic procedural ABAP is a language that has evolved over time, and contains several obsolete and overlapping concepts. In ABAP Objects—that is, inside classes and methods—most obsolete and error-prone language constructs are simply forbidden. Also, questionable and potentially faulty data accesses are checked more closely and may also be forbidden. This syntactical and semantic cleansing was taken to the next stage with the introduction of Unicode-compatible programs. Syntax cleansing forces the developer to use the ABAP language in the way that is recommended outside classes (but cannot be enforced there due to compatibility issues).[1]

New technologies

▶ ABAP Objects is the only way of using new ABAP technologies. For example, GUI controls, Web Dynpro ABAP, Run-Time Type Services, and the *Internet Communication Framework* (ICF) provide exclusively class-based interfaces. Using ABAP Objects only is also recommended for clients of these services, rather than using services from inside the procedural model. Otherwise, the programming models would be mixed unnecessarily, leading to increased complexity.

For these reasons, we recommend that you use ABAP Objects wherever possible. In practice, this means that data should be declared only in global or local program classes, and all functional ABAP code should be implemented in class methods. Exceptions to this rule are

---

1 There are more than 200 million lines of productive ABAP code that must continue to function even after the introduction of ABAP Objects.

the reuse of services that are located in procedures of the procedural model, and new classic procedures that are created for technical reasons. Examples of the latter are function modules for RFC, updates, or handling non-object-oriented user interfaces (dynpros). We will strictly adhere to this recommendation in this book.

When implementing methods, you have the invaluable advantage of unrestricted use of all the strengths of a programming language that is focused on the development of business client-server applications (see Section 1.1.2). However, in a method, you must always make sure to use only the language elements that are appropriate to that method.

1.1.5   ABAP and SAP NetWeaver

ABAP is the programming interface of SAP NetWeaver Application Server ABAP (AS ABAP for short). AS ABAP is an integral component of the application server (AS) of SAP NetWeaver. It is the result of a process of evolution from the SAP Basis of the R/3 system, to the SAP Web AS, to today's AS ABAP. The most far-reaching technical change was made in Release 6.10/6.20, when the introduction of the *Internet Communication Manager* (ICM) enabled the existing SAP Basis and its ABAP programs to communicate with the Internet via the HTTP, HTTPS, and SMTP protocols, thus turning it into a web server. Nothing has essentially changed since then. Today's more general name "AS ABAP" only expresses more succinctly that this technology is the ABAP version of the AS of SAP NetWeaver, which can function as a server for many different clients, only one of which is the web.

SAP NetWeaver Application Server

ABAP is a programming language that was developed to meet the requirements of business data processing inside an ERP system (R/3), and was further developed as requirements changed. Before the introduction in Release 6.20 of Java as a language of equal status, and J2EE technology for handling business problems within SAP NetWeaver, all application programs of an SAP AS that accessed the server database were written in ABAP. Today, ABAP is still the most widely-used language within SAP for services that execute database accesses, while Java has established itself more in the presentation area (for the programming of portals, for example).

Within SAP NetWeaver, ABAP must fulfill two basic requirements:

Enterprise SOA/ESI ▸ It must meet all present and future requirements in terms of application server technology, which are embodied in keywords such as enterprise SOA and ESI (enterprise service-oriented architecture and enterprise services infrastructure).

ERP ▸ The AS ABAP is still the technology platform for ERP-like systems that use ABAP reporting and classic transaction programming, and it also has to support the requirements of these systems.

Service orientation Both requirements can be met if a strictly service-oriented type of programming is used. This programming type even allows reusable services to be provided for both the ABAP and the Java "worlds." Services can be both business services and technical services. While business services can be relatively stable and reusable, a technical service is dependent on its real-world environment. In classic dialog programming, for example, a piece of ABAP code that reacts to user input is a technical service.[2] In the enterprise SOA world, this task could be carried out via a Web Service. Both variants have to access a suitable business service in order to perform the required task. For a business service to be reusable, it has to be kept strictly separate from technical services.

1.1.6 ABAP or Java?

Since Release 6.20 of what was then known as SAP Web Application Server (now SAP NetWeaver Application Server), SAP has provided its AS Java alongside AS ABAP as a development platform for the Java-based J2EE technology.

Technology platform Although ABAP has been a real success story inside SAP and among its customers from the start, before the introduction of SAP NetWeaver, SAP had no ambitions to market ABAP and the ABAP Workbench as a self-contained technology platform. In most cases, the SAP Basis and later, the SAP Web Application Server ABAP, were delivered only as part of SAP applications. The ABAP world was made up of its own ecosystem, which was, to a larger extent, available only to SAP application developers and SAP customers.

---

2 Those of you who are already familiar with ABAP can consider this as the description of a dialog module.

When SAP began its initiative to market SAP NetWeaver as a self-contained, comprehensive technology platform, it had to face the challenge that while its in-house ABAP technology was technically mature and perfectly suited to SAP's own requirements, it was basically unknown outside the SAP world.

There was also the fact that the Java and J2EE technologies had meanwhile established themselves as the widely accepted standards in the non-SAP business software market. The target market of SAP NetWeaver was twofold, and SAP had to satisfy these dual requirements. While the two concepts of ABAP and Java are quite different, each has sufficient benefits to ensure that there is no danger of one squeezing the other out of the market. It therefore made sense for SAP to integrate both concepts into SAP NetWeaver.

J2EE

1.1.7 ABAP and Java!

In SAP NetWeaver, SAP provides two application server programming environments that are of equal importance and provide basically the same functionality. While there is usually no alternative to using ABAP for further developing existing applications, the decision about which programming environment to use for *new development* depends on a number of factors. The following tendencies are likely to arise:

► Developers and developer teams who have experience and knowledge of ABAP and already work with ABAP-based systems are likely to continue to work with the familiar tool. ABAP is developed on an ongoing basis to enable such developers to continue to work in the SAP NetWeaver environment. Web Dynpro and Web Services for ABAP are examples for the ongoing support of ABAP in the new environment.

► Developers and development teams who have no SAP or ABAP experience and who are used to working in the standardized J2EE world will most likely want to stay in this environment rather than switch over to ABAP.

► Developers and development teams who either have experience in both worlds, or are unfamiliar with both, have to decide which programming environment will suit them best. When making this decision, they will have to take into account the expected costs of training their developers in the new technology, the likely efficiency of development work, and maintenance costs.

Integration
The main strength of the SAP NetWeaver Application Server is that nobody is forced to work with a technology that he or she does not know or (for whatever reason) like; instead, both technologies are supported in equal measure. This is particularly welcome among customers who use Java-based solutions alongside their existing ABAP-based business software. SAP NetWeaver now provides the framework for integrating both technologies within a single application server.

In terms of this book, the focus is on demonstrating what the AS ABAP has to offer application developers. For more information on the AS Java, we recommend the book *Programming with the SAP Web Application Server*.[3] To give you a better understanding of the differences between the ABAP and Java worlds, we will highlight some differences as they arise in the course of this book, albeit from our own ABAP-oriented viewpoint.

"Look and Feel" of ABAP and Java

A factor that should not be underestimated in evaluating and selecting a programming language is the impression that it makes on the user, or the "look and feel" of the language—keeping in mind, of course, this can also be influenced by the user's own taste and habits.

Figures 1.1 and 1.2 compare the implementation of a bank application program in ABAP and in Java.

Both programs contain the definition of a class called account as a template for account objects. The classes in both languages have the same functionality—they contain methods for deposits, withdrawals, and transfers, and can trigger exceptions.

---

3 Kessler, Karl; Tillert, Peter; Dobrikov Panayot: *Java Programming with the SAP Web Application Server*. SAP PRESS, Bonn 2005.

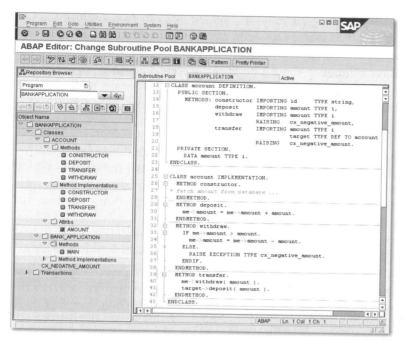

Figure 1.1 Account Class for Bank Application in ABAP

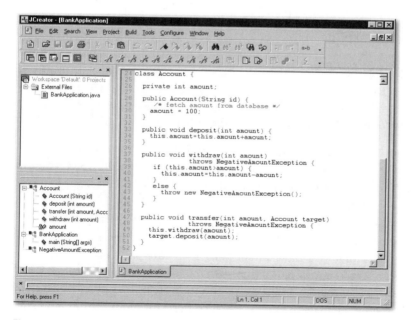

Figure 1.2 Account Class for Bank Application in Java

Development
environment

At first glance, both versions look almost identical. Both programs are developed in a source-code editor that is embedded in a development environment and displays the components of the development project on the left-hand side of the screen. The ABAP development environment is the ABAP Workbench, which comes with every AS ABAP delivery. The Java development environment is freely available and can be downloaded on the Internet.

On closer inspection of the source code, we see that Java uses less text in favor of curly brackets. Although this makes very little difference to the programmer, because the ABAP Editor provides programming aids such as patterns and code completions, we note that the Java source code appears to be leaner and thus more modern. ABAP is clearly a language that has evolved over many years, which is also why the class is divided into two separate parts for declaration and implementation. It would certainly be conceivable to give the ABAP syntax a facelift in order to make it look more like Java. For the moment, however, lovers of curly brackets have to do without these in ABAP, or else try their hand at Java.

After all, the syntax of a language is largely a matter of taste and habit. The main consideration is how a language expresses a particular solution to a problem.

Scope of ABAP and Java

In terms of the scope of each language—that is, the question of how many keywords each has—there is a world of difference. Java has approximately 50 keywords, while ABAP has more than 700!

Keywords

There is a single, direct equivalent in ABAP for most of the 50 Java keywords. As we can see from the examples above, in ABAP you can create classes with attributes and methods, execute basic operations in the methods, and trigger exceptions, just like in Java. The reason for the large number of remaining ABAP keywords is that ABAP is a 4GL language that evolved over time. Almost every important functionality that you have to specially load into Java in the form of a library is already contained in ABAP. Therefore, several ABAP statements resemble an interface to the underlying C kernel more than they do a language element. Because the ABAP application language is separate from the C technology language, ABAP automatically contains a level of abstraction that does not exist in the Java environment, where both application and technology are programmed using the same language.

This applies in particular to the functions that are so important for business applications, such as database access and mass data processing. For these purposes, ABAP provides concepts that are embedded in the language, such as Open SQL and internal tables, which enable programmers to write robust, high-performance applications. Static checking of syntax and types ensures the robustness of the applications, while performance is optimized in the C kernel itself in a process that is invisible to the ABAP developer.

The wide range of the language is often said to make ABAP difficult to learn. This is worth thinking about, because ABAP is actually intended to be a simple language that enables the application developer to concentrate on his or her main task, that is, creating solutions to business problems.

Ease of learning

In terms of Java, however, we must point out that this supposedly ABAP-specific problem also occurs in Java, except that in Java, it occurs in the libraries rather than directly in the language. Consequently, instead of a plethora of language elements and their documentation,[4] in Java you have to deal with an even greater number of interfaces and classes and their interface descriptions. The complexity of application development, and the tools thus required, are determined by application requirements in the business area. Moreover, this complexity is not usually reduced by using a simple language with only a few language elements. It is simply because of its origins as the programming language of the Internet that Java has a "cool" image, as it has outsourced to its libraries the "uncoolness" that necessarily comes with being a framework for business applications. ABAP, a language that is oriented towards business applications, does not have this positive side effect, and so it is seen as being "uncool." Nevertheless, we must mention that this accusation never comes from the users for whom it is individually customized, that is, application programmers in the classic SAP environment.

Libraries

Since much of the fundamental functionality of ABAP is implemented in the language itself and not in libraries, it has the following

Obsolete language elements

---

4 After all, in ABAP, the documentation is promptly available for each language element by pressing a key.

disadvantage: As older concepts were superceded by new developments in the course of ABAP's evolution, the principle of strict downward compatibility dictated that the older concepts could not be removed. This means that the scope of ABAP has grown constantly and the language now contains a relatively large number of obsolete language elements. These elements are no longer supposed to be used, but create the impression that ABAP contains a glut of competing and overlapping concepts. In fact, ABAP Objects, the object-oriented extension of ABAP, provides the best example. While in Java, you can program only in classes, ABAP still contains the earlier, procedural, event-oriented programming model. So, today, you can use the modern and service-oriented ABAP Objects on the one hand, and still run reports that were used in the R/2 system on the other.

Downward compatibility The reason for this is that ABAP has more than 200 million lines of production application code in use by SAP customers worldwide, and SAP guarantees its customers that this code will remain executable under new versions of the language.[5] Unfortunately, this situation is often abused, and obsolete language constructs are still sometimes used in new development work.

A lean language like Java does not have this problem. Even for the libraries it uses, downward compatibility is not such a major issue as it is with ABAP. In this case, new versions are usually rolled out and changes are communicated without any guarantee that existing code will be usable with the new version. This freedom stems from the fact that Java and its libraries are relatively independent of any applications that are based on them, while ABAP, as the programming language of the earlier R/3 and today's AS ABAP, is still an integral part of a greater whole.

In this book, it makes sense for us to describe ABAP from today's viewpoint only. In other words, we will describe only the recommended procedures for the latest release, and will not discuss obsolete concepts, or only refer to them very briefly.

---

5 Only genuine error corrections or the prohibition of language constructs whose use has caused errors are excluded from the strict concept of downward compatibility. But even in those cases, the syntax check will generate only warnings for a certain period of time, but does not regard the error in question as a real syntax error during that period.

Availability of ABAP and Java

Another factor in the ease of learning and enforceability of a programming language is its availability. It is clear that Java, an elementary language with a compiler that can be downloaded from the Internet, has a major advantage in this regard.

Programmers who want to learn to use ABAP, the programming interface of the AS ABAP, require a complete AS ABAP installation. As recently as 10 years ago, this kind of application server, in the form of the then SAP Basis, was usually available only as a component of a complete R/3 system. For that reason, it was possible to access ABAP only through companies or universities that ran an SAP system. Since then, there has been a fundamental change. Since the first edition of this book, which initially included a "Mini Basis" on CD, SAP began providing a test version of AS ABAP with every release for installation on personal computers. Today the latest version of AS ABAP can be downloaded free of charge as a *SAP NetWeaver 2004s ABAP Trial Version* from the SAP Developer Network, and of course, also comes with this book. ABAP is thus de facto freely available.

AS ABAP

A possible objection is that it is a little over-the-top to have to install a complete application server in order to learn a programming language. Consequently, programmers who want to learn ABAP must also become somewhat familiar with administrating the server. The clear response to that objection is that ABAP programming is useful only on the AS ABAP. But this is merely a truism, because ABAP is the language of the AS ABAP and is not intended to be used for other programming tasks. It would be just as much of a mistake to try to program SQL without a database.[6]

You should note that in no way does the easy availability of Java mean that everyone who learns Java[7] is automatically a proficient business application programmer. Java programmers also need an infrastructure,[8] which has the same requirements as ABAP in terms of space, complexity, and the time and effort required to learn it. In fact, in some cases, it even exceeds the requirements of ABAP; for

---

6 Of course, ABAP is much more powerful than SQL!
7 To put it succinctly, we mean everyone who has programmed an applet.
8 Unless you want to write everything by yourself.

example, the current size of the download file for the complete *SAP NetWeaver 2004s Java Trial Version* is three times that of the ABAP version!

Organizing Development in ABAP and Java

Another factor that the success of application development depends on is the software logistics that the programming environment provides. With its mature and well established technology, this is an area in which ABAP shines:

▶ Application program development is carried out in a development environment that is integrated into the AS ABAP. Application programs are part of AS ABAP. They can be executed and tested in their natural environment during the development phase, without the need for formal deployment.

Correction and transport system

▶ The ABAP development environment contains a sophisticated, integrated correction and transport system. Multiple development projects can be carried out concurrently by one or more teams on an AS ABAP that has been set up as a development system. This development work can be imported in the form of transports into AS ABAPs that are set up as test or production systems, and the work is then available immediately. New development work or corrections can even be imported into an AS ABAP during productive operations.

▶ The SAP Service Marketplace (*http://service.sap.com*) provides comprehensive support for ABAP programs delivered by SAP. For example, it enables service staff and application developers to analyze errors in customer systems and to make the necessary corrections using remote connections.

Based on its many years of experience with the AS ABAP, SAP has developed its own Java application programming platform, the AS Java, that is similarly easy to use.

Regardless of the programming language that a developer uses, she should be able to concentrate primarily on the logical programming tasks without having to pay undue attention to the architecture of the application server.

Standardization of ABAP and Java

One argument that is often made against ABAP and in favor of Java is that ABAP is proprietary, while the J2EE environment for business programming in Java uses open standards. For example, it should always be possible in principle to migrate any existing J2EE application to an AS Java without encountering any major problems.

On the other hand, through its widespread distribution in the SAP application systems, ABAP has made its name as the nearest thing to an industry standard for business application programming, and its proprietary nature has not proved to be a disadvantage in this regard. Also, thanks to the aforementioned transport mechanisms, in theory there are no difficulties with transporting applications from one AS ABAP to another. An *independent software vendor* (ISV), for example, can develop an application or an extension to an existing application for SAP NetWeaver and sell it on the market equally well using either an AS ABAP or an AS Java.

ABAP: almost an industry standard

The standard for the ABAP programming language and its environment is controlled by SAP. This can have distinct advantages. SAP builds solutions for special technical tasks directly into the language, thus ensuring that SAP developers can react to current and future requirements of business application programming. This is done without adversely affecting investments already made in existing code. In the Java camp, on the other hand, one or several solutions may emerge from a large pool of concepts. Unlike with ABAP, in theory, every member of the Java community can personally affect any development and provide his own solutions to a particular problem. An example of this is the handling of persistent data in a database. In ABAP, Open SQL is directly integrated into the language, providing a robust interface that is specifically designed for business applications on an application server. Java, on the other hand, offers several generic and competing persistence frameworks, and the individual developer has to select the most suitable for his purposes.

Standards control

Conclusion

ABAP is a comprehensive, proprietary language that is tailored by SAP to meet the requirements of the business software that it provides, and is further developed in accordance with these requirements. Java, on the other hand, is a lean language that can be extended in any direction via libraries that are contributed by a large community. Creating business software is only one of the many possible uses of Java.

With AS ABAP, SAP enables developers to access its well established business programming language, ABAP, whereas with AS Java, SAP has opened itself to the Java community. Both approaches are equal pillars of a unique product—the SAP NetWeaver Application Server. Ultimately, it is irrelevant to a user of this application server which language or which server is used for the service she is requesting, as long as it works, is robust, and performs well.

1.2 The Objective of This Book

The objective of this book is to provide an overview of ABAP programming within the framework of ABAP Objects and to introduce the reader to the possibilities offered by the AS ABAP on SAP NetWeaver. It shows that with relatively little effort and in a user-friendly development environment, you can create the widest range of services for business applications, the basis of which is the consistent processing of data in a database.

In this book, we deal with the fundamental concepts of ABAP programming, though without going into too much detail. We have strived to present each topic thoroughly, using consistent terminology, so that even readers who are new to ABAP (though not always only these readers) can understand its unique "language," which can often seem impenetrable. For more detailed information, we suggest that you refer to *The Official ABAP Reference*[9] and to the Online Help of the AS ABAP.

1.2.1 Target Audience

This book is intended for all developers who come into contact with ABAP in their work. This includes both beginners and experienced ABAP programmers who want to obtain a thorough overview of programming SAP NetWeaver using ABAP and ABAP Objects. The book is also aimed at project team members and consultants who work in the area of ABAP technology. Students and other interested parties

---

9 Keller, Horst: *The Official ABAP Reference*. 2nd Edition. SAP PRESS, Bonn 2005.

will also gain a more in-depth insight into SAP programming using ABAP from the book. If you are an ABAP training course participant, you are in possession of the right book for supporting you in the learning process and expanding on what you learn in the course.

In your ABAP development work, you are sure to encounter the following situations, among others:

- You decide or your company decides to develop a complete application in ABAP.

- You adapt to your own requirements ABAP applications that are already in use.[10]

- You program a service in ABAP and make it generally available.

- You want to use a service that is programmed in ABAP and gain a better understanding of its functions.

When developing applications on the basis of the AS ABAP, knowledge of the ABAP language and its environment is essential. It is also extremely likely that any developer working in the SAP area will encounter ABAP sooner or later. Even Java programmers who work in the SAP area often have to come to grips with ABAP at some time; for example, if they "inherit" ABAP programs in their subject area and need to be able to understand these programs.

We assume that the readers of this book have basic programming knowledge. Therefore, for example, we will not explain what a loop is, but only how it is implemented in ABAP. While it is not imperative that you know ABAP and object-oriented programming in order to use this book and gain an understanding of ABAP Objects, prior familiarity with the subject matter will make getting started considerably easier.

Programming knowledge

1.2.2 Structure of this Book

The structure of this book is primarily linear, leading from basic topics to more specialized ones. Earlier chapters contain a lot of information that is a prerequisite for understanding later chapters. Chap-

---

10 At this point, we should mention that in this edition of the book we will not deal with the frameworks for extensions and modifications of existing applications. We will primarily describe the basic principles of programming with ABAP that you must, of course, master as well if you want to extend and modify an application.

ter 9 and subsequent chapters, in particular, deal with specialized topics that are quite independent of each other. Therefore, we recommend that you read the earlier chapters consecutively,[11] and you can then approach the later chapters as your own particular interest dictates.

The following overview of the individual chapters will give you a clearer idea of the structure of this book:

- ▶ **Chapter 2, A Practical Introduction to ABAP**
  Although, as we mentioned already, this book is not intended to be a practical trainer for ABAP, a basic introduction is nonetheless contained also in this new edition. This chapter is intended for anyone who would like to get an insight into how to program a small but complete ABAP application in SAP NetWeaver before moving on to more theoretical considerations in the next chapter. It was written both for beginners and for classic ABAP programmers who have not had much experience with ABAP Objects. In this chapter, we develop a program for rental car reservations, starting with creating suitable database tables, moving on to programming the GUI, and ending with creating exception and application classes, all in the form of a guided tour through the ABAP Workbench. You will encounter many of the most important basic elements of an ABAP Objects application. You will also learn the basics of using the ABAP Workbench, and be introduced to more advanced concepts, such as the package concept and the correction and transport system. These topics are not addressed in the rest of the book.

- ▶ **Chapter 3, Basic Principles of ABAP**
  With only two programming examples, this chapter is probably the least practice-oriented in the book. Nonetheless, it lays the groundwork for understanding the general subject of ABAP programming in SAP NetWeaver. It guides you from the AS ABAP to the general properties[12] of ABAP programs to their internal memory organization. Despite its mainly theoretical emphasis, you should still read this chapter carefully, as it introduces you to and explains many ABAP terms that are essential for understanding subsequent chapters.

---

11 Or at least browse through their pages.
12 Perhaps even peculiarities.

▶ **Chapter 4, Classes and Objects**

This book focuses on programming with ABAP Objects. Programming with ABAP Objects means implementing application logic in classes and creating objects of these classes. Thus, complementing the more technical fundamentals described in the previous chapter, this chapter sets the formal scope for all subsequent chapters. In it, you will learn how to create and use classes and objects. You will not be able to program in ABAP Objects if you are not familiar with the content of this chapter.

▶ **Chapter 5, Basic ABAP Language Elements**

This chapter familiarizes you with all the basic language elements that can be used in your classes in order to implement their functions. The ABAP type concept, operations, expressions, and control structures are only some of the topics that we address. For introductory purposes, we first deal with processing character strings and internal tables. The language elements in this chapter are usually required by every ABAP program, regardless of its individual purpose.

▶ **Chapter 6, Advanced Concepts of ABAP Objects**

Chapter 4 covered the framework for using language elements, and Chapter 5 explained the most important of those elements. Now, Chapter 6 deals with the elements that make the object-oriented approach of ABAP Objects so powerful. Here, we deal in detail with the ABAP Objects concepts of inheritance, interfaces, polymorphism, and events. Furthermore, the section on *shared objects* introduces you to the topic of shared memory programming in the AS ABAP. In short, this chapter is the basis of advanced programming in ABAP Objects.

▶ **Chapter 7, Classic ABAP—Events and Procedures**

As we mentioned in Section 1.1.1, the development process of ABAP was evolutionary. The previous programming model of ABAP Objects, which we refer to as "classic ABAP," can still be used. Some aspects of classic ABAP, such as its program execution functions, are still required in ABAP Objects. Also, much existing functionality is based on classic concepts such as services that are available as function modules. This chapter presents classic ABAP with the appropriate brevity and the recommendations on how it should be used with ABAP Objects.

▶ **Chapter 8, Error Handling**

This chapter deals with a topic that is often neglected, but fundamental: how to deal with errors in a program. We discuss measures for avoiding errors, and how to properly handle errors that, in the worst-case scenario, could cause the program to terminate. Most of this chapter is dedicated to describing class-based exceptions that you can trigger yourself or use to avoid program terminations. We also mention the predecessor technology of class-based exceptions: classic exceptions. Finally, we touch on the subject of assertions, which you can use to ensure that a program is running smoothly.

▶ **Chapter 9, GUI Programming with ABAP**

This chapter presents the most important tools that enable you to communicate with the user in an ABAP program. A large part of the chapter deals with classic techniques such as dynpros, selection screens, and lists, as these are closely linked to the ABAP language and are still widely used today. We show how these non-object-oriented techniques can be used with ABAP Objects, and how they may be superceded, as in the case of classic lists. This chapter ends with a description of Web Dynpro for ABAP, the successor technology to classic dynpros, using two practical examples. Although the current trend is to program ABAP in a service-oriented way—that is, to create functional units without a direct user interface—this chapter is by far the most extensive of the book.

▶ **Chapter 10, Working with Persistent Data**

Almost no ABAP program can work without processing persistent data. The main consideration here is accessing the central database of an AS ABAP. This chapter then deals with all statements for read and write database access and provides tips for using them effectively. We also explain the concept of the SAP LUW as the basis of consistent data retention. With the following introduction to handling persistent objects in a database using the associated object services, we bridge the gap between the relational world of databases and the object-oriented world of ABAP Objects. In this chapter, we also consider the most important aspects of file access, and discuss working with the ABAP-specific data clusters technology. The chapter concludes with a summary of the topic of authorization checks in AS ABAP.

▶ **Chapter 11, Dynamic Programming**

One of the main strengths of ABAP is that it enables you to write relatively generic programs whose behavior develops dynamically when the programs are executed. This chapter introduces you to all language elements that are required for dynamic programming, in their own context. Based on dynamic data access using field symbols, and data references and the *Run Time Type Services* (RTTS) to dynamically specify and define type properties, it presents dynamic token input and dynamic procedure calls, the most important dynamic language elements in ABAP. The chapter ends with a look at dynamic program generation, which generates and executes complete ABAP programs without any static checking.

▶ **Chapter 12, External Interfaces**

While Chapter 9 describes the programming of interfaces for human users of the AS ABAP, this chapter deals with the far-reaching topic of communication with other systems. We focus here on the role of the AS ABAP as both a server and a client, presenting Remote Function Call (RFC), the classic communication channel of ABAP to external systems, and the Internet Communication Framework (ICF), the basis of all communication between ABAP programs and the Internet. We also provide an example of how to directly access the ICF. In practice, however, you will use wrappers for this purpose, such as Web Services for ABAP, which are also addressed in this chapter. Lastly, in this chapter, we look at how to work with XML in ABAP programs. XML has clearly become *the* data exchange format, and ABAP provides several ways of using this format.

▶ **Chapter 13, Testing and Analysis Tools**

In this final chapter, we deal with the often unpopular, but nonetheless important topic of program quality. We introduce the main tools that are used for quality assurance, which ensure, among other things, functional correctness, adherence to standards, and program performance in terms of memory usage and runtime. Specifically, this chapter looks at the main features of the following tools: static program analysis using syntax checking and the Code Inspector; the functional test tools ABAP Debugger and ABAP Unit; and performance tests using the Memory Inspector and runtime analysis. The chapter closes with a brief look at other test tools, such as the Coverage Analyzer.

▶ **Appendix**

The Appendix includes an overview of all ABAP statements, system fields, ABAP program types, ABAP naming conventions, and selectors. It also contains the code of an auxiliary class for simple text output, some web references, and tips on installing the *SAP NetWeaver 2004s ABAP Trial Version*, which are contained on a DVD that comes with this book.

We hope that while using this book, you will see that, despite its considerable capabilities, ABAP is not difficult to learn. On the contrary, several language elements have been added over the years to make your work easier, and ultimately, to enable you to create stable, powerful applications.

1.2.3 Observing Programming Guidelines

While this book was being written, the January-February, March-April, and May-June 2006 editions of the *SAP Professional Journal* (*http://www.sappro.com*) featured a three-part article on ABAP programming guidelines, of which one of the authors of this book was an author. The fundamental rules, formal criteria, and best practices described in this article are used wherever possible as a basis for the information presented in this book. The most important programming guidelines can be summarized as follows:

▶ Create only Unicode programs.

▶ Use only the functions of ABAP Objects for structuring your programs, and implement your functionality in methods only.

Separation of concerns
▶ Separate your presentation logic from your application logic. For example, a method that responds to user input as part of a framework for user input (such as Web Dynpro ABAP) should never directly access a database table.[13] Instead, it should call an appropriate wrapper service. Conversely, this kind of service cannot directly contain a user dialog.

▶ Use only the latest language constructs, and correspondingly, avoid old and obsolete constructs wherever possible.

▶ Ensure the quality of your programs by testing them with all the available test tools, both during and after the development process.

---

13 Even though there might be nothing else more tempting!

One consequence of adhering to these guidelines is that we don't need to go into any more detail on the differences between Unicode and non-Unicode programs in this book. Therefore, just as ABAP Objects is the better programming model, these guidelines assume that Unicode programs are the better programs. We will therefore create only Unicode programs and deal with the rules that apply in this case.

In addition to providing you with a general overview of ABAP, another explicit goal of this book is guiding you through the jungle of possibilities of the language. With this book, we hope to give you not only the basic knowledge required for working with ABAP, but also the tools for creating robust, comprehensible, and easy-to-maintain programs.

1.2.4 Syntax Conventions

In this book, we use simple syntax diagrams to introduce you to the most important ABAP statements. In doing so, we purposely do not list all the variants and extras of a statement, as *The Official ABAP Reference* already fulfills this purpose. Similarly, we do not show complete syntax diagrams, as these are available in *The ABAP Quick Reference*.[14] In our diagrams, we simply demonstrate the most important versions of each statement. Of course, we adhere to the same conventions that are used in the ABAP reference works and the ABAP keyword documentation of the AS ABAP. These conventions are shown in Table 1.1.

Convention	Description
ABAP	All ABAP words—that is, keywords and additions—are displayed in uppercase letters and bold typeface.
operand	Operands are displayed in lowercase letters.
. : , ( )	Periods, colons, commas, and parentheses are part of the syntax.
+ − * / ...	Operators are part of the syntax and are displayed as normal.
[ ]	Square brackets indicate that you can, but do not have to, use the parts of the statement that they contain. Ensure that you don't use the square brackets themselves.

Table 1.1 Syntax Conventions

---

14 Keller, Horst: *The ABAP Quick Reference*. SAP PRESS, Bonn 2005.

Convention	Description
|	A vertical bar between two statements means that you can use only one of the two statements.
{}	If the statements separated by the vertical bar | are not clearly distinguishable, they are enclosed in curly brackets. Curly brackets are not part of the ABAP syntax.
...	Three consecutive periods mean that you can insert any elements here that suit the current context.

Table 1.1 Syntax Conventions (cont.)

As well as the syntax diagrams, the many source code examples in this book also demonstrate how to use most of the statements. Once you gain access to these examples in your ABAP Editor by importing a transport or installing an up-to-date version of the *SAP NetWeaver 2004s ABAP Trial Version*, simply call the [F1] Help for each statement used there to view full syntax diagrams and the relevant information.

1.3 How Can I Use This Book on a Practical Level?

Although this book is not intended to be a practical training guide, it is clearly impossible to learn a programming language simply by reading a book straight through, just as it is impossible to learn a natural language in this way. Practice is the only way to progress—that is, to analyze existing programs and to closely study and implement the examples of specific problems. For this reason, we have placed great value on providing comprehensive usage examples of the concepts we describe.

1.3.1 Creating the Examples

AS ABAP
Trial Version

All the examples used here were programmed and tested exclusively for this book on a 1.59-GHz laptop with 1.0 GB RAM under Microsoft Windows XP, Service Pack 2, with an installation of *SAP NetWeaver 2004s ABAP Trial Version* and user BCUSER. Performance in all cases was satisfactory. When installing the trial version, we followed the installation instructions strictly and did not make any other changes to the computer. We installed the trial version exclusively in order to write this book, and did not undertake any changes or development work other than those described in this book. All the development objects that were created for this book are contained in a package called Z_ABAP_BOOK, which is also available as an online addition to this book in the form of transport files at *http://www.sap-press.com* or *http://www.sap-press.de/1210*.

1.3.2 Goal of the Examples

Our goal is that everyone who has an installation of SAP NetWeaver 2004s ABAP Trial Version or another AS ABAP should be able to recreate the examples contained in this book in that system. However, this book certainly does not claim to be an easy path through the aforementioned jungle. Apart from the practical introduction, this book provides little in the way of step-by-step instructions for creating the examples. That would be beyond the scope of this book, especially in light of the sheer volume of material. Rather than going into the minor details and secondary considerations, such as the maintenance of program attributes for every individual sample program, we explain only what is essential for each example. Therefore, the reader is challenged to think a little "outside the box" in each example.

1.3.3 Using the Examples

The installation files of a trial version of the AS ABAP, on which all examples are pre-installed, are contained on a DVD that comes with this book. If you install this version, you can use the BCUSER user to gain development authorization to the examples[15] and can thus modify them, although you will have to create a transport request to do this. To restore the initial state, re-install the system or import the transport files listed in Section 1.3.1.

DVD

To program the examples yourself from scratch—which we recommend, especially for Chapter 2—the best way to proceed is to create your own package, as described in that chapter, and store your development objects there. Regarding a naming convention, we recommend that you simply replace the Z in the examples given with a Y, so that, for example, your package is then called Y_ABAP_BOOK instead of Z_ABAP_BOOK.

---

15 From the point of view of the system, the BCUSER user is simply the "author" of the examples!

1.3.4 Releases Described

In using an AS ABAP of Release SAP NetWeaver 2004s, we cover all the functionality of this release plus all previous releases. Thus, with some restrictions, it should be possible to execute many of the examples as far back as SAP Basis Release 4.6. As of SAP Web Application Server Release 6.20/6.40, almost all the examples can be executed, with the exception of the very latest developments such as regular expressions. The ABAP keyword documentation contains an overview of all release-independent changes in ABAP. Because the follow-on release for the next release of SAP NetWeaver was being developed as the manuscript for this book was being prepared, we have been able to alert you of the most important new developments (see the footnotes).

1.3.5 Database Tables Used

In the practical introduction (Chapter 2), we will create our own database tables and fill them with data. However, because we cannot assume that every reader will recreate the examples from the introduction, or will have ongoing access to a trial version with the pre-installed examples, we will rarely use these database tables again in subsequent chapters. Instead, as with most examples in this book where we access the AS ABAP database, we use the SAP flight data model, which is also used in SAP's ABAP training courses and in the ABAP documentation for the purposes of demonstration and exercises. Many readers may already be familiar with this model. It has proven itself to be a useful didactic concept and we therefore see no reason to discard it.

SAP flight data model

The SAP flight data model is a simplified model of a flight booking system. It models flights, flight connections, bookings, and so on, mainly using a set of relational database tables that are interlinked via foreign key relationships. These tables are delivered with every AS ABAP and come populated with data in the AS ABAP Trial Version. You can also use Transaction BC_DATA_GEN to regenerate the data records in every system and in different sizes, as many times as you like.

Figure 1.3 shows in the form of a SERM (*structured entity relationship model*) diagram the database tables that we use for the flight data model. You can view the definitions of the individual tables at any time in your AS ABAP using the ABAP Dictionary tool (transaction SE11).

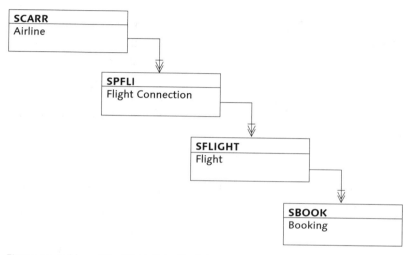

Figure 1.3 Tables of the Flight Data Model

"Experience is perception understood."
—Immanuel Kant

2 A Practical Introduction to ABAP

This chapter is a guided tour or tutorial of the important tools and concepts of the ABAP Workbench and the ABAP programming language. In this chapter, you will create a small but complete application, including the corresponding database tables. Existing data is not a prerequisite for this tutorial. All you'll need is access to an Application Server ABAP (SAP NetWeaver) or a Web Application Server ABAP at Release 6.20 or higher, and developer authorization to the server. The program shown here was developed on a laptop with a fresh installation of *SAP NetWeaver 2004s ABAP Trial Version*, and the screenshots were taken there as well. A copy of the SAP NetWeaver 2004s ABAP Trial Version, which already contains all the examples presented here, accompanies this book. However, the tutorial has been structured in such a way that it can be run without limitations on a Mini Web Application Server (Mini Web AS) at Release 6.20 or 6.40, which was attached to earlier books from SAP PRESS.[1] Some of the syntax used, however, like method calls without the CALL METHOD language element, is only available from Release 6.10/6.20 on, and must therefore be adapted when the tutorials are executed on a 4.6 system.

We want to create a rudimentary reservation system for rental cars. There is no need for this application to be mature, or even to be the optimal solution for the task at hand. Rather, the goal of this tutorial is to cover as many important concepts of the ABAP language as possible, which will then be introduced systematically in later chapters. Many concepts in the ABAP Workbench will only be covered in this tutorial, since the focus of this book is on the programming language itself.

---

1 You can run the examples in this book on any full installation of a Web or NetWeaver Application Server, too.

Note   This practical introduction is not intended to be simple, nor is it intended to be a complete introduction to the ABAP Workbench. Rather, it is an introductory tour with a lot of room for individual initiative. We aren't going to specify exactly where to click your mouse every time; instead, we'll let you discover whether you want to use this or that function.

2.1   Functionality of the Sample Application

The main task of applications written on SAP NetWeaver in ABAP is to process business data, which is generally stored in different database tables in a central database. Therefore, an ABAP program must do the following:

- Read data
- Analyze and modify data
- Pass the data in a suitable form to a presentation layer, or retrieve it from that layer
- Store data

Functionality   In this practical introduction, we want to demonstrate these aspects of ABAP. We will program a small rental car application that accesses data in three database tables: a customer table, a rental car table, and a reservation table. The program should allow you to make one or more rental car reservations for a customer in different categories on one screen. To achieve this, the main tasks are to check the availability of a rental car of the requested category in the time period specified, and then to store the reservation in the reservation table.

2.2   Getting Started with the ABAP Workbench

The development environment for ABAP programs and all their components is the *ABAP Workbench*. In order to write an ABAP program, you must therefore open the ABAP Workbench of AS ABAP. The ABAP Workbench is a component of SAP NetWeaver AS ABAP, and is available in every ABAP-based SAP system. However, you need an authorization as a developer to your NetWeaver AS in order to work with the ABAP Workbench. By the way, the ABAP Workbench is itself completely written in ABAP.

In addition to developer authorization, you must also have a developer key. This key is registered with SAP through SAPNet and allows the assignment of a developer to any modified original objects of the ABAP system. Even though we won't be making changes to original objects in the context of this book, you must still be registered as a developer. In the SAP NetWeaver 2004s ABAP Trial Version, the specified user is automatically registered as a developer.

This section will do the following:

▶ Show you how to access the tools of the ABAP Workbench after logging on to an AS ABAP

▶ Introduce the Object Navigator as a general startup tool

If you're already familiar with these topics, you can skip this section.

2.2.1 Entry through SAP Easy Access

After logging into an AS ABAP (see Section 3.1.3), you are usually in SAP Easy Access, which is a startup program that automatically starts after login and shows a starting menu for AS ABAP. By default, the starting menu is an *SAP menu* specified by SAP, or a *user menu*. The latter includes all functions needed by a user, and is assigned to the user by the system administrator according to the user's role. In addition, every user can define his own Favorites menu. Figure 2.1 shows SAP Easy Access after the user BCUSER has logged into SAP NetWeaver 2004s ABAP Trial Version.

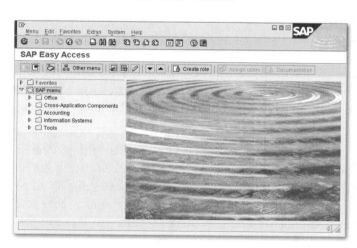

Figure 2.1 SAP Easy Access

There are no entries in the Favorites menu yet. The menu **Extras • Settings** can be used to change the display (see Figure 2.2).

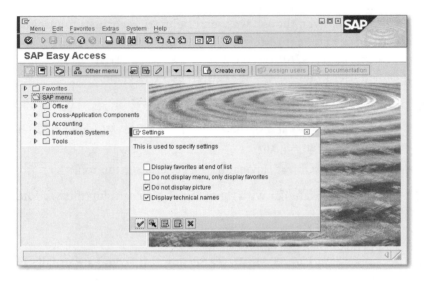

Figure 2.2 Settings in SAP Easy Access

We recommend that developers select the **Display technical names** option in order to have the transaction code displayed before every entry. A transaction code is the technical name, which can be used to call any program in an ABAP system. If you select this option, and then open the **Development** node under **Tools • ABAP Workbench** in the SAP menu, you will find a list of different important ABAP Workbench programming tools, like the *ABAP Editor* you can use to edit ABAP programs, the *Screen Painter* and *Menu Painter* you can use to build the screens of the SAP GUI, and also the *Function Builder* and *Class Builder* with which you can program special ABAP programs like function groups and global classes, or the *Dictionary*, which you use to write global data declarations in the ABAP Dictionary (see Figure 2.3).

Tools
The abbreviations, like SE11, SE38, and so on, are the aforementioned transaction codes of the individual tools (see Section 3.2.3 for more information). The wide variety of tools indicates that an ABAP program is composed of many components, like source code and presentation components, and that there are different types of program editing (i. e., for functions and classes).

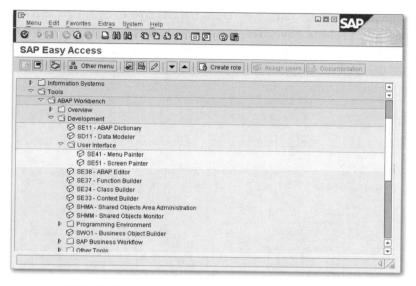

Figure 2.3 ABAP Workbench Tools with Transaction Codes

We could start the ABAP Editor in this list, for instance, to create an ABAP program or to edit an existing program, but then we could only edit one component of the program at a time, namely the source code, and in this case, we wouldn't have an overview of the other components of the program, such as its screens. So this option of entering through the tools is preferable when you already know the program and the components that you want to edit, and you want to be able to access them quickly and directly.[2]

2.2.2   The Object Navigator

First, let's look at the general entry point into ABAP programming, the Object Navigator. Open the **ABAP Workbench • Overview** node. There you will find the **Object Navigator** entry (see Figure 2.4).

The Object Navigator is the main entry point to the ABAP Workbench. If you have not already done so, we recommend that you create an entry for the Object Navigator in the **Favorites** menu. To do

---

2   If you edit a development object directly through a tool, you can always get to the associated context via **Utilities • Object list.** The object list is then shown on the right-hand side in the tree structure, like the Repository Browser of the Object Navigator.

this, position your cursor on **Object Navigator** in SAP Easy Access and select **Add to Favorites**, or select **Favorites • Insert transaction** and then enter the transaction code "SE80".[3] Then you will always see the **Object Navigator** node at the highest level under **Favorites** in your SAP startup screen.

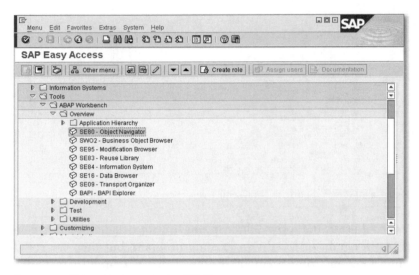

Figure 2.4 Object Navigator in the SAP Menu

SE80 This allows you to call the Object Navigator directly at any time after logging into AS ABAP, by selecting this node. You can also call the Object Navigator like any other program whose transaction code you know, by entering "/n" or "/o" followed by the transaction code—in this case "/nse80"—into the entry field in the standard toolbar[4] from any SAP screen. For "/o", in contrast to "/n", a new window is opened, while "/n" uses the current window, canceling the running program.

---

3 We will often use the terms "selection" or "select." Depending on the context, this may mean a double-click with the mouse, pressing a key, clicking on an icon or a menu item, etc. The AS ABAP user interface normally provides many different selection options for a function, which we will not list individually. The most important functions can generally be selected using icons on the upper edge of the screen and simultaneously using the function keys on the keyboard. All functions of the SAP GUI can be reached via menu items. In this book, you will learn how you can define these functions for your own programs.

4 The entry field in the standard toolbar is not always displayed by default, but can be opened by clicking on the small triangle in the standard toolbar.

Directly after its first start, the Object Navigator is displayed as shown in Figure 2.5.

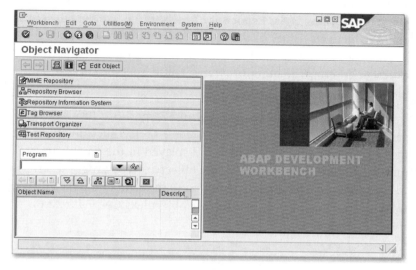

Figure 2.5 Initial Screen of the Object Navigator

The Object Navigator is a development environment for the central editing of development objects, which are any objects that can be edited with the ABAP Workbench tools. We call these objects *repository objects*. This includes all ABAP programs of AS ABAP and all their components. However, there are many other repository objects, such as global data definitions in the ABAP Dictionary, or XSLT programs. Together, these development objects in the ABAP Workbench form a so-called *repository*. This repository is a special part of the database content of the central database, which, instead of customer data, comprises the programs of AS ABAP itself.

Repository object

The Object Navigator displays repository objects as nodes in different tree displays (browsers), like the *Repository Browser*, the repository information system, and the enhancement information system, in the navigation area on the left-hand side. From there, they can be edited in the tool area on the right using forward navigation.[5]

---

5 "Forward navigation" is a technique within the ABAP Workbench to move into the appropriate editing tool of a repository object. The cursor must be positioned on the object's name and the object must be selected.

Repository
browser The buttons in the upper part of the navigation area allow the selection of a browser. Which browsers are presented for selection with buttons can be configured in **Utilities • Settings**. The browser we will generally be using is the **Repository Browser**. It is the default setting of the Object Navigator and also the most generic browser, which provides an overview of all important repository objects sorted by different criteria. The other browsers handle special tasks for particular topics.

Access to repository objects through the Repository Browser is organized using so-called *object lists*. You must select such an object list in the dropdown list box, which is displayed in the navigation area under the buttons. In Figure 2.5, the object list type **Program** is set as the default type. The input help button to the right of the field can be used to display a list of other possible object lists (see Figure 2.6).

Figure 2.6 Object Lists of the Repository Browser

2.3   Packages

One possible object list in the Repository Browser is **Package**. Packages are used to organize development objects and handle their connection to the AS ABAP software logistics. All repository objects, that is, all objects which can be changed using the ABAP Workbench, are part of a package. Therefore, when developing an application, you must assign each component you create to a package. When you specify a package as an object list type in the Repository Browser, all the objects of that package are displayed.

This section will do the following:

▶ Show you a package for pure test developments

▶ Introduce packages for transportable development objects

▶ Show how a package is created

▶ Give a short overview of the transport mechanisms of AS ABAP

The contents of Section 2.3.1 are enough to proceed with the practical introduction; however, we recommend executing the other steps as well, since we will not be covering packages any further in the other chapters of this book.

2.3.1 Package for Local Development Objects

Every AS ABAP contains a predefined package named $TMP, in which you can create local practice and test programs, which shouldn't be transported to other systems.

If you select **Local Objects** in the Repository Browser (see Figure 2.7), enter "BCUSER" in the input field under the dropdown list box, and press ⌈Enter⌉, the Repository Browser displays all the development objects in this special package, which were created under your user name.

Local objects

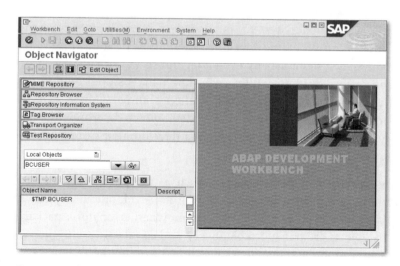

Figure 2.7 Object List of Local Objects

Figure 2.7 shows that no development objects exist yet for user BCUSER in SAP NetWeaver 2004s ABAP Trial Version directly after installation. If you want, you can always create the sample application from our practical introduction in the predefined $TMP package. To do this, continue directly with Section 2.4, but whenever the system asks for a package, always enter "$TMP" or click on the **Local Object** button. Of course, local objects can always be assigned to different packages later.

2.3.2   Packages for Transportable Development Objects

Since Release 6.10, packages replace the so-called *development classes*. Development classes were used to group repository objects and connected them to the change and transport system. Packages include this functionality of development classes, and provide some other features, like the nesting of packages and control of the use of the repository objects they contain by defining package interfaces and visibility. Usage control is currently done only statically using special check programs. The verification of package interfaces at program runtime is in preparation for the next release of SAP NetWeaver.

Change and Transport System

Besides the organization of development projects and usage control, the connection of development objects to the *SAP Change and Transport System* (CTS) is an important property of packages. The CTS regulates the transport of repository objects between different ABAP-based SAP systems. Application development, of course, never takes place in a production system, but rather in a development system. The application programs developed there must be transported into a production system, usually even after transport, into other consolidation or test systems, while accounting data is stored only in the production system. With CTS, so-called *transport layers* can be defined for every ABAP-based SAP system, which determine the target systems into which material from a development system should be transported.

Transport Organizer

Every package can be assigned to such a transport layer, thereby determining transport properties for all its development objects. A naming convention is used to determine whether or not a package and its objects are transportable. Every package starting with the "$" character cannot be transported, and it may also not be assigned to a transport layer. The predefined $TMP package mentioned earlier is a good example. Every other package must be assigned to a transport layer and its development objects are therefore subject to the CTS. Changes to transportable packages are organized into tasks and are only performed in the context of *transport requests* or *change requests*, which are managed using the Transport Organizer of the ABAP Workbench.

2.3.3 Creating a Package

Packages themselves are also repository objects, which can be edited using the ABAP Workbench. We want to create a separate package for our sample application. To do this, we select the **Package** object list in the Repository Browser again, and enter the name "Z_ABAP_BOOK" into the input field below. Note that repository objects created for customers in customer systems have different naming conventions than those that apply to SAP's own programs: A customer must use "Y" or "Z" for the first letter, or the abbreviations reserved by SAP for the customer's company. SAP NetWeaver 2004s ABAP Trial Version is set up as a customer system in which the user BCUSER is registered as a customer.

Namespace

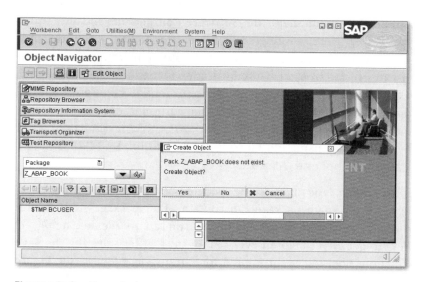

Figure 2.8 Creating a Package

When you confirm the entry with ⎡Enter⎤, the dialog window shown in Figure 2.8 displays. If you click on **Yes** here, another dialog window appears in which you can define the package properties (see Figure 2.9).

Figure 2.9 Defining Package Properties

Package properties
In addition to a suitable short description, you must specify the **Application Component**, the **Software Component**, and the **Transport Layer**. Here, we select suitable entries from the selection list, which is displayed after pressing the input help key F4. These values are created by system administration when the system is created. The software component "HOME", for example, is equipped with all the tools available for transportable customer development. For more information, refer to the book *SAP R/3 System Administration* by Sigrid Hagemann and Liane Will (2nd Edition, SAP PRESS 2003), which still applies to AS ABAP.

The **Package Type** must also be specified. We select **Not a Main Package**, since a main package can contain other packages, but cannot directly contain development objects. You can use the field help (F1 key) to get direct help on every input field. After selecting the **Save** function, you will be prompted for a transport request (see Figure 2.10).[6] This shows that your package is now a development object managed by the CTS.

---

6 If the **Request** input field already contains an existing request, create a new request for the programs in this book.

To create this kind of request, select **Create Request**, enter a short description into the dialog window that displays (see Figure 2.11), and select **Save**.

Figure 2.10 Prompt for Transport Request

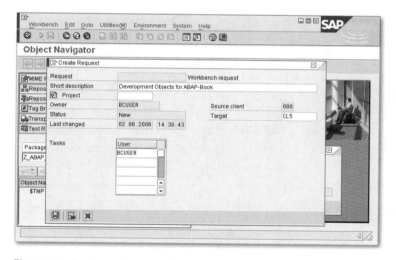

Figure 2.11 Creating a Transport Request

Now you can assign the package to the transport request, whose code is generated by the CTS, as shown in Figure 2.12. This kind of assignment to a transport request must later be performed for all repository objects that are part of this package. You can only skip this step for non-transportable packages with names starting with "$".

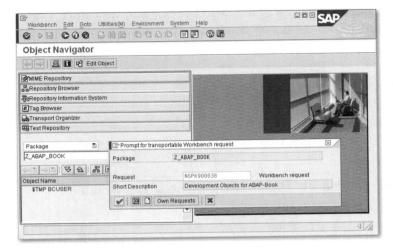

Figure 2.12 Assigning a Transport Request

After this organizational work, the new package is created, and the Repository Browser shows you the package properties in the Package Builder tool, if you double-click on the name "Z_ABAP_BOOK" (see Figure 2.13).

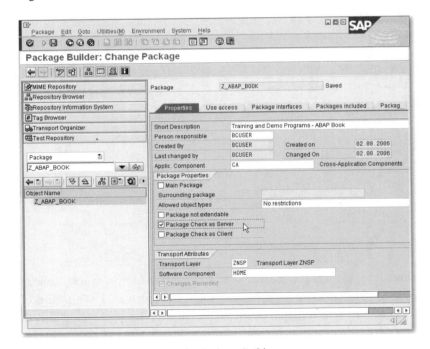

Figure 2.13 Package Properties in the Package Builder

So that the package will not simply serve as a sort criterion for associated repository objects and their assignment to a common transport path, we switch to change mode using **Display <-> Change**, and then check the **Package Check as Server** field. This ensures that only objects declared in the package interface of the package can be addressed from other transportable packages. These usages are determined statically using an extended program check and are flagged as errors (see Section 13.1.2). Then we save the package with **Save**.

2.3.4 Calling the Transport Organizer

If you click on the **Transport Organizer** button in the Object Navigator, you can check the inclusion of our package into the CTS (see Figure 2.14). You can see that the system has also created a task under the transport request from Figure 2.12, in which the package appears. A transport request can contain multiple tasks for one or more developers. All the tasks must be released before a transport request can be issued at the end of a development. During the development of our sample application, you should check the Transport Organizer to see how the other development objects are inserted into the transport request.

Transport Organizer

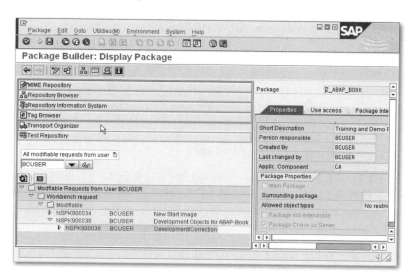

Figure 2.14 Transport Organizer

Now the preparation for our development project is complete. It may well be that you find this section about packages and transports

Software logistics

a little too detailed. We could have made our lives much easier simply by using the existing package $TMP for our development objects without connecting to the CTS. The use of a transportable package, however, is intended to demonstrate that the software logistics tools, which are necessary for the creation of large-scale industrial applications, are fully integrated into the ABAP Workbench and are easy to use. In your everyday work, you will have to rely on using these tools for any application that goes beyond mere testing. Next, we finally want to begin creating the data storage for our application.

2.4 Database Tables

Database tables are by far the most common data storage for applications written in ABAP. In fact, even all system settings are stored as the contents of so-called *customizing tables*, and nearly all ABAP development objects in the ABAP Repository are stored in database tables. This section will create three separate database tables for our application: a customer table, a rental car table, and a reservation table.

While creating the database tables, you should note the following:

▶ You will get to know the ABAP Dictionary

▶ You will discover that a database table for AS ABAP is more than a tabular storage

▶ You will learn the two-phased domain concept consisting of a data element and a domain for the typing of database fields.

2.4.1 Creating a Customer Table

Return to the Repository Browser and, as shown in Figure 2.15, select **Create · Dictionary Object · Database Table** from the context menu, which you can display by right-clicking on the package name.

First, let's create the customer table. Enter the name "ZCUSTOMERS" in the **Table Name** field which displays (see Figure 2.16) and confirm your entry with ⌞Enter⌟.

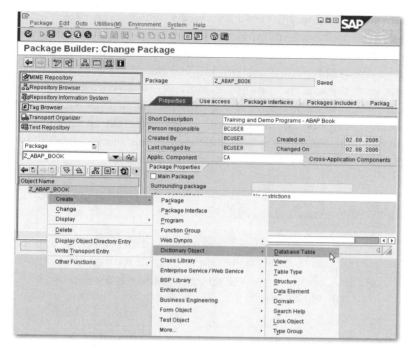

Figure 2.15 Creating a Database Table

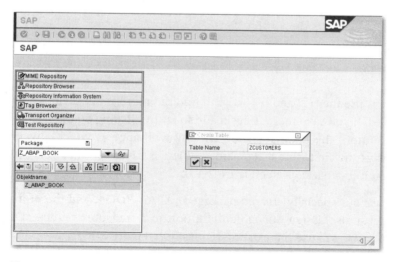

Figure 2.16 Entering the Table Name

This takes you to the display of the tool for the *ABAP Dictionary* on **ABAP Dictionary** the right-hand side. The ABAP Dictionary is a storage for data types that can be used in all repository objects, which have access to the associated packages. An important feature of the ABAP Dictionary is that structured types can be instantiated as database tables in the central database of the ABAP system, and that the structure of a database table in ABAP can also simply be addressed as a type. Correspondingly, the table maintenance tool is provided, in which we first enter a short description and **A** to denote a **Delivery Class** and determine how the table content may be handled in the *data browser* (see Figure 2.17).

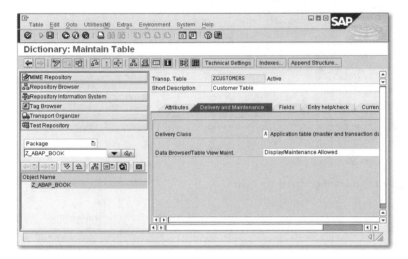

Figure 2.17 Initial Screen of Table Maintenance

Always use the [F1] and [F4] keys to find out more about the possible entries. If you save the settings made so far by clicking on the respective button, the familiar dialog window will appear, which always displays the first time a repository object is saved, so that you can assign it to a package (see Figure 2.18).

We use our specially created package Z_ABAP_BOOK, and therefore we must also assign our table definition to a transport request. Of course, we will use the existing request (see Figure 2.19).

You can see that a table definition is a transportable repository object like any other development object edited in the ABAP Workbench. The dialog from Figures 2.18 and 2.19 must be executed for every repository object we will create, and we will not mention it explicitly again.

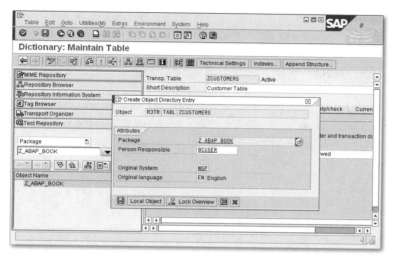

Figure 2.18 Assigning the Table to a Package

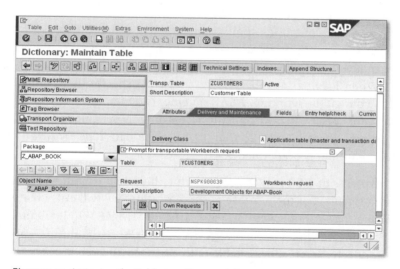

Figure 2.19 Assigning the Table to a Transport Request

Next, we will define the structure of the table. To do this, select the **Fields** tab and fill in the first three lines, as shown in Figure 2.20.

The entries in the **Field** column are the names of the columns in the database table, a checkmark in **Key** defines the table key whose content is used for the unique identification of table rows, and entries under **Data element** determine the data type of the columns.

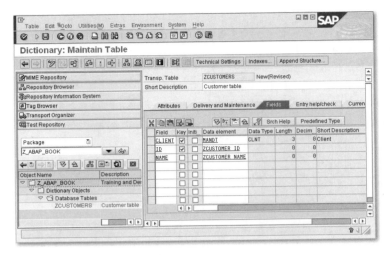

Figure 2.20 Fields of the Customer Table

Client

The entry in the first line, "CLIENT", is an SAP-specific feature for database tables containing application data. This is the so-called *client field* for the entry of a three-character client ID. A client is an area with independent application data within an ABAP-based SAP system. When logging into the system, you must specify the client in which you will be working. ABAP statements (Open SQL) that work with client-specific tables implicitly access only those table rows with the current client ID (see Section 10.1.2). The data type "MANDT" for a client field is predefined.

The two entries "ID" and "NAME" define the actual columns of our customer table. For the purpose of simplification, we will only create a unique, one-column key "ID" and a name "NAME". In an actual application, we would probably specify an address with multiple columns, or refer to an address table with a foreign key dependency.

2.4.2 Creating a Data Element

Forward navigation

Next is the question of the data type of our columns. We want to use types specific to our application, so under **Data element** we enter the names "ZCUSTOMER_ID" and "ZCUSTOMER_NAME". From the naming convention, you can already see that these data elements are probably repository objects that we haven't yet created. Reusing suitable existing data elements (selected using ⌗F4⌗) is also an option under certain circumstances. Double-click on the entry "ZCUSTOMER_

ID". Selecting a repository object in a particular place (particularly in ABAP source code) activates forward navigation, which can jump to the corresponding tool. If the ABAP Workbench cannot find a matching repository object for the name selected, it generally displays a dialog window in which you can create it (see Figure 2.21). If you confirm that you want to create the data element, the tool for data element maintenance appears on the right-hand side of the Repository Browser (see Figure 2.22).

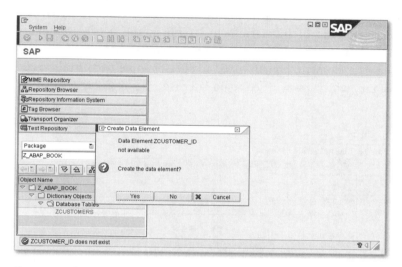

Figure 2.21 Creating a Data Element

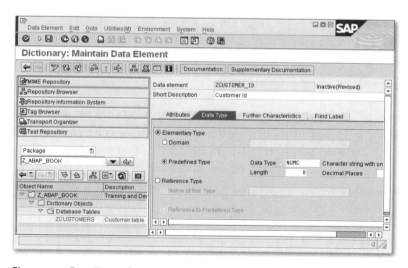

Figure 2.22 Data Type of a Data Element

Data element   A data element is a repository object in the ABAP Dictionary that defines an elementary data type. Besides the technical properties of a database field, it also describes its semantic meaning, that is, it contains headings for tabular displays and documentation texts. Properties such as its actual data type, length, and so on, are either defined using **Predefined Type** in the data element, or are copied from so-called *domains*.

We specify the data type directly as "NUMC" with a length of 8 characters. NUMC (numerical text which may only contain digits) is a predefined type of indeterminate length in the ABAP Dictionary (again, see the [F1] help or the [F4] help).[7] To conclude the definition of the data element, we still need to specify some texts in the **Field Label** tab, which we will see again later (see Figure 2.23).

Figure 2.23 Field Label of a Data Element

Activation   Now the data element is complete. To release it for use, you must activate it by selecting the function **Activate**. You generally need to do this for nearly every repository object that you create or modify. Inactive repository objects are essentially unknown to the system. During activation, the system creates active versions that can be used

---

7 As an alternative to using a data element, elementary data types like NUMC can also be specified directly in Figure 2.20 using the **Predefined Type** button, but then the semantic properties are lost.

by other repository objects; for example, ABAP programs are compiled into executable byte code during activation.

The dialog window shown in Figure 2.24 displays during the activation of repository objects. Here you can find lists of your inactive repository objects. In our case, the transportable objects that have existed up to now are the table definition and the data element. Since we haven't yet created the table, let's just activate the data element for now. If the activation fails, you will get a corresponding error message that will indicate the cause.

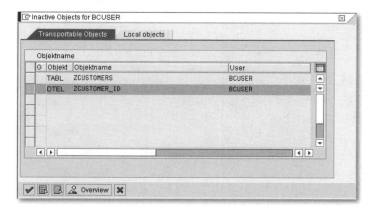

Figure 2.24 Activating Repository Objects

2.4.3 Creating a Domain

After the activation is complete, navigate back to table maintenance by selecting **Back** or by selecting the table name in the Repository Browser, and then create the data element ZCUSTOMER_NAME in the same way. The data type of the name should simply be a character string of fixed length. We could use a predefined type CHAR with a length specification in data element maintenance again, but in this case we'd like to demonstrate the use of a domain.

A *domain* is a repository object in the ABAP Dictionary that describes the technical properties of data elements, such as the data type or value range and can be linked to any number of data elements. The data type of a database field can therefore be defined in two phases. The text in the data element defines the semantic properties of the type, while the domain determines the technical properties. As shown in Figure 2.25, we enter the predefined domain "CHAR20"

Technical properties of the data element

75

that defines the data type of the data element as a character string of length 20. If you want to learn more about a specific domain, you can double-click on it to navigate to its definition in the domain maintenance.

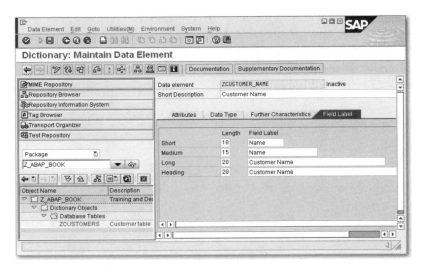

Figure 2.25 Specifying a Domain

2.4.4 Completing the Customer Table

After entering the field labels, saving, and activating the data element, you can complete your database table. To do this, in table maintenance (Figure 2.20), to where you can return by selecting the **Back** function, select the **Technical settings** function, in which suitable values for the configuration of the database in the database system and for the handling of tables in the database interface of the ABAP system must be specified. Enter the settings as shown in Figure 2.26, save them, and return to table maintenance.

Enhancement category

In Release 6.40 systems and later, the so-called *enhancement category* must also be managed under **Extras • Enhancement category … .** This classification is used during a program check to generate an appropriate warning in all places where later structural extensions could cause syntax errors or a changed program behavior. Here, select **not extensible**, which makes the structure stable and usable in ABAP programs according to its type without limitation, at the cost of later extensibility.

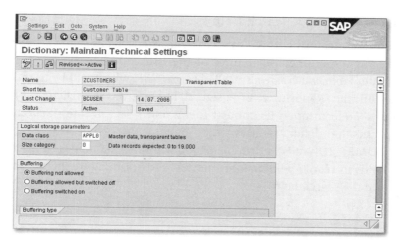

Figure 2.26 Technical Settings of a Database Table

Now you can activate the table. To be on the safe side, use **Check** to verify that you made no errors, and click on the button to activate the table. The activation causes the table to be created in the database, and it can be used immediately by other repository objects, particularly ABAP programs. The result of our work so far is displayed in the Repository Browser (see Figure 2.27). The table and the data elements are listed under our package in their active versions. Inactive objects are displayed in a different color.

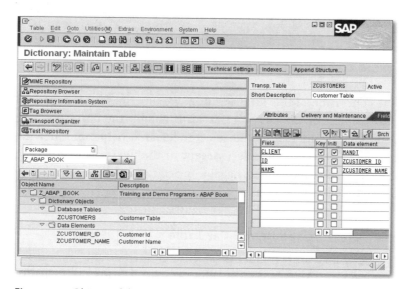

Figure 2.27 Objects of the ABAP Dictionary in the Repository Browser

2.4.5 Creating a Search Help

Before we create the other two tables in the same way, let's look briefly at some other capabilities of the ABAP Dictionary. For the customer table, we create a so-called *search help*, which will be useful later. In the Repository Browser, right-click on the **Dictionary Objects** node to open its context menu and select **Create · Search help**. In the dialog window that opens, enter the name "Z_CUSTOMER_ID" and confirm the dialog windows that appear. Fill in the fields in search help maintenance, as shown in Figure 2.28, and activate the search help.

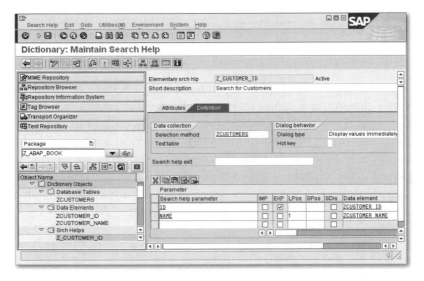

Figure 2.28 Creating a Search Help

At the conclusion of this little addition, we link the search help with the **ID** column of the customer table. Highlight the corresponding row in table maintenance, and select the **Search help** tab. Enter the name of the search help, select **Accept** in the next dialog window, and activate the database table again. In Section 2.7.4, you'll see how the search help can be used.

2.4.6 Creating the Rental Car Table

Next, we will create a rental car table ZCARS. To do this, repeat the procedure for ZCUSTOMERS step by step, by creating the fields for the table as shown in Figure 2.29.

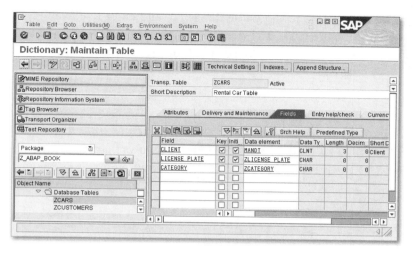

Figure 2.29 Fields for the Rental Car Table

You create the data element ZLICENSE_PLATE analogously to Figures 2.22 and 2.23, using a predefined data type CHAR with length 10. For the data element ZCATEGORY, enter a domain "ZCATEGORY" as in Figure 2.30 and use forward navigation to move to domain management to create it. In the **Definition** tab, enter the data type as shown in Figure 2.31.

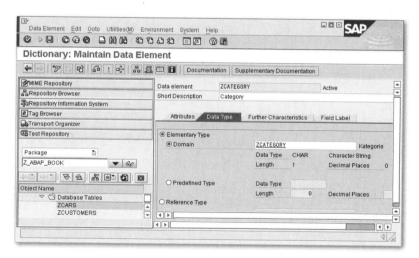

Figure 2.30 Data Element for Rental Car Category

The reason we want to create a separate domain here is that we want to be able to limit our rental car categories to a set of specific values.

Fixed values

To do this, switch to the **Value Range** tab and enter fixed values, as shown in Figure 2.32. The domain can then be activated. You will also see the effect of these fixed values in Section 2.7.4.

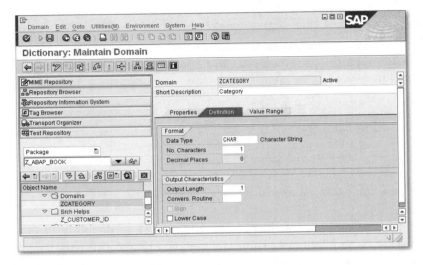

Figure 2.31 Data Type of a Domain

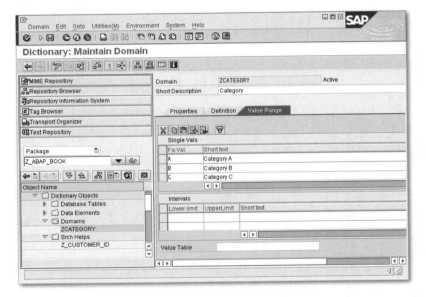

Figure 2.32 Value Range of a Domain

Activate the domain, the data element, and the rental car table.

2.4.7 Creating the Reservations Table

For the final table, we will now create a reservations table ZRESER-VATIONS, with fields as shown in Figure 2.33. For the fields CUSTOMER_ID and LICENSE_PLATE, use the already defined data elements. For the fields RESERVATION_ID, DATE_FROM, and DATE_TO, create data elements analogous to Figures 2.22 and 2.23, with properties as shown in Figure 2.33. Activate the data elements and the reservations table.

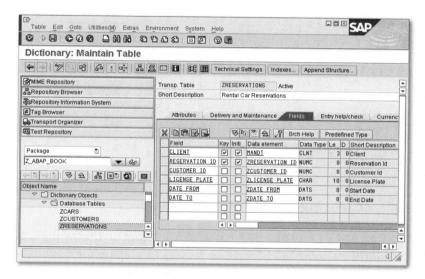

Figure 2.33 Fields of the Reservations Table

If you select the rows for CUSTOMER_ID or LICENSE_PLATE in table maintenance for the reservations table and select the function **Foreign key**, you can link these fields with the matching fields in the ZCUSTOMER and ZCARS tables (see Figure 2.34). The ZRESERVA-TIONS table thus becomes a foreign key table in which the fields CUSTOMER_ID and LICENSE_PLATE are foreign keys connected with check tables. These kinds of foreign key dependencies can be used for value checks (see Section 9.1.12).

Foreign key

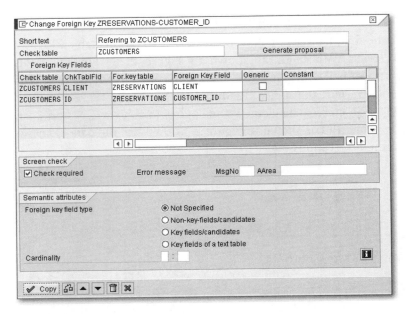

Figure 2.34 Creating a Foreign Key

2.5 Creating an ABAP Program

Our first ABAP program will be an auxiliary program for the population of the customer and rental car tables. To prepare for this auxiliary program, we will introduce you to the following:

- Properties of ABAP programs
- ABAP Editor
- ABAP syntax
- Structure of ABAP programs
- Syntax check
- Execution of programs
- Copying of programs

2.5.1 Creating an Auxiliary Program

To create the program, in the Repository Brower right-click on our package and in the context menu, select **Create · Program**. Fill out the dialog window as shown in Figure 2.35. For the time being, do not select the checkbox **With TOP INCL.**

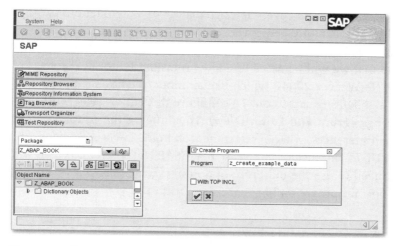

Figure 2.35 Creating an ABAP Program

You can define the properties of the new program in the next dialog window (see Figure 2.36). This is an important step, since the program properties determine the execution of the program in the ABAP runtime environment. One of the most important program properties of an ABAP program is its type. From the list provided, we want to select the type **Executable program** for our simple auxiliary program, and no other properties. In particular, ensure that the properties **Unicode checks active** and **Fixed point arithmetic** are selected. In this book, we only cover Unicode programs (see Section 3.2.5).

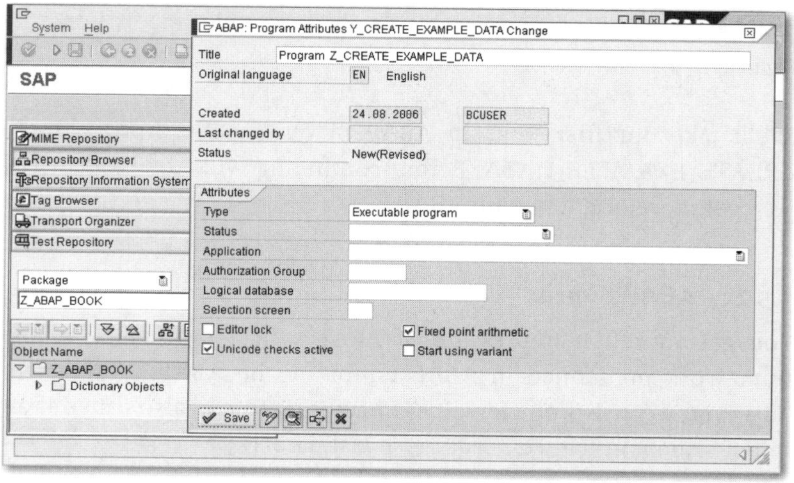

Figure 2.36 Properties of an ABAP Program

ABAP Editor If you now click on **Save**, the usual dialog for assignment to package and transport request displays, and you are then rewarded for your efforts with the appearance of the ABAP Editor (see Figure 2.37). Note that we will be using the new Front-End Editor available as of SAP NetWeaver 2004s, which like all modern editors supports syntax highlighting and so on. To configure this editor, select **Utilities · Settings · Front-End Editor (New)**. To configure the editor for your own preferences, you can select the icon in the lower right-hand corner. Up to and including Release 6.40 (SAP NetWeaver 04), you will still need to use the old Front-End Editor, which provides a lot less support for programming.

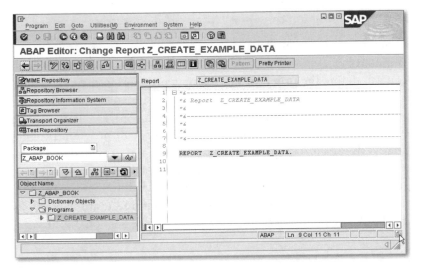

Figure 2.37 The ABAP Editor

We'll take our first steps in ABAP in our auxiliary program Z_ CREATE_EXAMPLE_DATA. Before continuing with the work itself, let's get more oriented with ABAP.

2.5.2 ABAP Syntax

You get your first impression of ABAP syntax by looking at the framework predefined in ABAP Editor by the ABAP Workbench. This syntax consists of a few lines of comments, and also contains an initial statement named REPORT (see Listing 2.1).

Listing 2.1 Program Lines Predefined by the Workbench

```
*&---------------------------------------------------------------------*
*&  Report Z_CREATE_EXAMPLE_DATA                                       *
*&                                                                     *
*&---------------------------------------------------------------------*
*&                                                                     *
*&                                                                     *
*&---------------------------------------------------------------------*

REPORT Z_CREATE_EXAMPLE_DATA.
```

The first seven lines are comment lines, and the eighth line is a statement. This already demonstrates the basic syntax rule of ABAP: Every ABAP program consists of comments and statements.

Comments

Comment lines are introduced by an asterisk * in the first position. The rest of the line is arbitrary and is shown in a different color by the editor. To mark only the final portion of a line as a comment, you can use the character **"**. You can place this character (**"**) in any position (including the first). All characters in a line with an asterisk * in the first position, and all characters after a **"** are ignored by the compiler.

Comment line

Statements

Statements are composed of so-called *tokens* and are terminated by a period. Possible tokens include ABAP words, operands, operators, and a few special characters. ABAP words are either ABAP keywords or additions to keywords. Most ABAP applications are introduced by a keyword. In our case, the keyword is REPORT and the operand is Z_CREATE_EXAMPLE_DATA. Tokens must be separated from one another by at least one space. This applies particularly to operators like plus (+) and minus (-) signs, or special characters like parentheses ( ), which must also be separated from their operands by spaces. Beyond these rules, there are no specific limitations regarding the formatting of source code. There may be more than one statement on a program line, and one statement may extend over multiple program lines.

ABAP statement

The ABAP compiler does not differentiate between uppercase and lowercase letters, so REPORT is just as correct as report or RePort. For

Pretty Printer

better readability, however, all ABAP keywords and their suffixes are written in capital letters in this book, while all operands are always written in lowercase. The ABAP Editor supports us with this decision with its *Pretty Printer* functionality. To configure the pretty printer to suit your own preferences, you can select **Utilities • Settings** in the ABAP Editor, and then the **Pretty Printer** tab. Now you can configure the pretty printer as shown in Figure 2.38.[8]

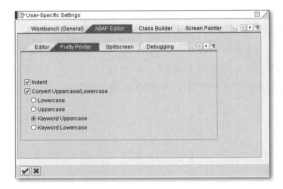

Figure 2.38 Pretty Printer Settings

If you then click on the **Pretty Printer** button in the ABAP Editor, the ABAP statement in our program changes, as shown in Listing 2.2.

Listing 2.2 Effect of the Pretty Printer

```
REPORT z_create_example_data.
```

Moreover, when using the settings we chose, the Pretty Printer also improves the program layout by indenting the code according to the program structure. From this point on, we will show all sample programs in this book as they are formatted by the Pretty Printer, and we recommend that you execute this function often.

2.5.3 General Program Structure

Every standalone ABAP program, that is, all types of programs except for so-called *include programs*, start with an introductory statement.

---

8 Thanks to syntax highlighting, the configuration of uppercase/lowercase is no longer so critical in the new ABAP Editor. By not using this setting, mixed cases are allowed, which are common in Java, for instance.

All subsequent statements therefore belong to this program. Unless you reference include programs (see Section 3.3.1), you will always see all the statements in an ABAP program in the ABAP Editor.

In our first program, the introductory statement is REPORT. This designation is historical and expresses the fact that an executable program was once exclusively used for reporting. As you will see later (see Section 7.1.1), executable programs still support reporting, but they can also be used for other purposes. At this time, however, it suffices to know that our first statement introduces the program z_create_example_data.

After the introductory statement, every ABAP program follows a fixed program structure that divides it into two parts:

▶ a global declaration part
▶ a procedural part

In the *global declaration part*, which directly follows the introductory statement, declarative statements can be used for definitions and declarations, which will be visible and applicable throughout the entire ABAP program. Examples of objects that can be declared or defined are data types, classes, and data objects. For larger programs, these declarations are generally made in a special include program, the "top include," which is supported by the ABAP Workbench and inserted at this position.

Declaration part

After the global declaration part comes the implementation part, in which the actual processing logic of the ABAP program is implemented. The implementation part is divided into individual procedural units that are referred to as *processing blocks*. Every ABAP statement that is not part of the global declaration part always belongs to exactly one processing block. The statements within a processing block are processed sequentially. The arrangement of processing blocks in the implementation part is not significant for program execution. The order in which processing blocks are executed during the execution of the ABAP program is controlled by calls or by the ABAP runtime environment.

Implementation part

To keep an ABAP program readable and simple, we recommend that you select a semantically relevant program structure, and then make that structure visible using comment lines, particularly if no top include or other includes are used.

2.5.4 Two "Hello World" Programs

As in earlier editions of this book, we cannot omit the usual "Hello world!" from this book, and so we will go through this little exercise for anyone who is completely new to ABAP. If you already have some experience, feel free to go directly to Section 2.6. For the first "Hello world" program, type the source code shown in Listing 2.3 into the ABAP Editor.

Listing 2.3 The First "Hello World" Program

```
*&---------------------------------------------------*
*& Report Z_CREATE_EXAMPLE_DATA                      *
*&---------------------------------------------------*

REPORT z_create_example_data.
*&---------------------------------------------------*
*& Global Declarations                               *
*&---------------------------------------------------*
DATA text TYPE string VALUE `Hello World!`.
*&---------------------------------------------------*
*& Implementations                                   *
*&---------------------------------------------------*
START-OF-SELECTION.
  WRITE text.
```

Syntax check   Before we execute the program, let's check the syntactic correctness. To do this, select the **Check** function, for instance, from the context menu of the program name in the object list. You should see a message in the status line stating that no syntax errors were found. Put this to a test by inserting an error. For instance, type WRTE instead of WRITE in the last statement, and check the syntax again. The error should immediately display in the lower section of the ABAP Editor (see Figure 2.39). Use the **Correct errors** function to correct the program directly.

Program activation   The error-free program can now be activated selecting function **Activate**. Programs with syntax errors can be activated, but they cannot be executed. During the activation of an ABAP program, the ABAP compiler uses the error-free source code to generate a byte code that is stored in the database. During program execution, the byte code is loaded into the AS ABAP program memory, and interpreted by the ABAP runtime environment (virtual machine).

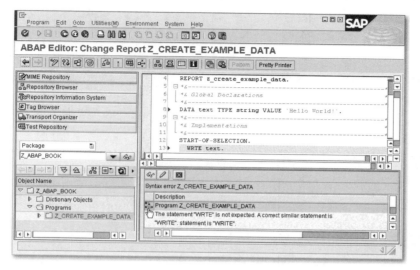

Figure 2.39 Syntax Check

After successful activation, an executable program is available to every dialog user of the ABAP-based SAP system using **System • Services • Reporting**. If you change and store the source code of the program without activating it, the active version is not affected. The new version is only executed after a new activation.

Program execution

You can also start program execution directly from the Object Navigator, selecting **Execute • Direct** in the context menu of the program name (or just hit F8). The expected "Hello World!" output appears in a special screen for list-like text output. The DATA statement declares a data object text of type string as a text string, and provides it with a start value. We generally call the results of the DATA statement data objects, because the statement can be used to declare more than simply elementary fields. The WRITE statement here can be seen as the ABAP equivalent to System.out.println(...) in Java, or to printf in C. Therefore, it can be used for simple test output, but should no longer be used in production. In fact, it is a statement from classical list processing (see Section 9.3), which has been replaced by new concepts.[9]

List output

---

9 The fact that the WRITE statement, as shown here, leads directly to an output with no further action to be taken, applies only to executable programs.

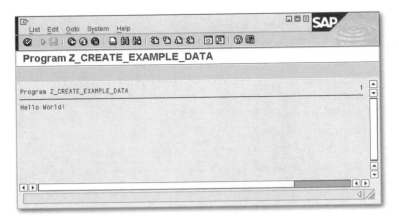

Figure 2.40 List Output

Standard
processing block If you select **Back**, **Exit**, or **Cancel** in the output, you will return to the Object Navigator. So the function of the WRITE statement is clear. But what about START-OF-SELECTION? As indicated in Section 2.5.3, the implementation part of an ABAP program always consists of processing blocks. The START-OF-SELECTION statement introduces a processing block of the same name, which plays the same role in executable programs as the main() method of a Java program. That is, when such a program is executed, the implementation of this processing block is automatically called. This is where we see the effect of the program type. Only when you run an executable program in the ABAP runtime environment is a process started, which handles the calling of the START-OF-SELECTION processing block. You will learn about another type of program execution in Section 2.8.5.

Message output As promised, we will now introduce another "Hello World!" program. Change the program from Listing 2.3 into the program shown in Listing 2.4, activate it, and execute it.

Listing 2.4 The Second "Hello World" Program

```
*&--------------------------------------------------------*
*& Report Z_CREATE_EXAMPLE_DATA                           *
*&--------------------------------------------------------*

REPORT z_create_example_data.

*&--------------------------------------------------------*
*& Global Declarations                                    *
*&--------------------------------------------------------*
DATA text TYPE string VALUE `Hello World!`.
```

```
*&--------------------------------------------------------*
*& Implementations                                        *
*&--------------------------------------------------------*
START-OF-SELECTION.
  MESSAGE text TYPE 'I'.
```

As a result, a dialog window greets the world (see Figure 2.41). This type of output is a so-called *informational message*. Instead of I, try using E or X for the type of message, and see what happens; but, don't do this without saving your work first! You can find out more about messages in Section 9.4.

Figure 2.41 Informational Message

2.5.5   Copying Programs

This concludes our "Hello World" detour. In the next section, we'll focus on our auxiliary program. If you like your "Hello World" program so much that you want to save it, you can copy it into another program first. To do this, select **Copy** from the context menu of the program name, and enter, for instance, „Z_HELLO_WORD" as the target program. A dialog window opens and prompts you for which partial objects in the program that you want to copy. Here you can see that a program is made up of much more than just its source code. For our minimal program, the default entry will suffice. If you click on **Copy** again, the usual prompt for the package and transport request will appear for the target program. Then the program is copied, and you can find the new program under the **Programs** node in the Repository Browser.

2.6   Implementing the Auxiliary Program

Now that you've got a gulp of some ABAP air, we can implement the auxiliary program. Based on this auxiliary program, you will get to know the following ABAP features:

- Simplification of the syntax using chained statements
- Declaration of data
- Assignment of values
- Access to databases
- Handling of exceptions
- Program testing using the ABAP Debugger

2.6.1 Source Code for the Auxiliary Program

Now let's turn our attention to the population of our database tables with sample data. To do this, we need the rather lengthy program shown in Listing 2.5. Create such a program and activate it.

Listing 2.5 Auxiliary Program to Populate the Database Tables

```
*&---------------------------------------------------------------*
*& Report   Z_CREATE_EXAMPLE_DATA                                *
*&---------------------------------------------------------------*

REPORT z_create_example_data.

*&---------------------------------------------------------------*
*& Global Declarations                                           *
*&---------------------------------------------------------------*
DATA: customer_wa   TYPE zcustomers,
      customer_tab  TYPE HASHED TABLE
                    OF zcustomers
                    WITH UNIQUE KEY id.

DATA: car_wa  TYPE zcars,
      car_tab TYPE HASHED TABLE
              OF zcars
              WITH UNIQUE KEY license_plate.

*&---------------------------------------------------------------*
*& Implementations                                               *
*&---------------------------------------------------------------*
START-OF-SELECTION.
* Fill internal customer table
  customer_wa-id   = '00000001'.
  customer_wa-name = 'Maximilien Vomact'.
  INSERT customer_wa INTO TABLE customer_tab.

  customer_wa-id   = '00000002'.
  customer_wa-name = 'Benjacomin Bozart'.
  INSERT customer_wa INTO TABLE customer_tab.
```

```
        customer_wa-id   = '00000003'.
        customer_wa-name = 'Johanna Gnade'.
        INSERT customer_wa INTO TABLE customer_tab.

        customer_wa-id   = '00000004'.
        customer_wa-name = 'Dolores Oh'.
        INSERT customer_wa INTO TABLE customer_tab.

        ...

* Update customer database table from internal table
    TRY.
        DELETE FROM zcustomers.
        INSERT zcustomers
              FROM TABLE customer_tab.
        IF sy-subrc = 0.
          MESSAGE 'Customer table updated'
                  TYPE 'I'.
        ENDIF.
      CATCH cx_sy_open_sql_db.
        MESSAGE 'Customer table could not be updated'
                TYPE 'I' DISPLAY LIKE 'E'.
    ENDTRY.
* Fill internal car table
    car_wa-license_plate  = '1234XX CA'.
    car_wa-category       = 'A'.
    INSERT car_wa INTO TABLE car_tab.

    car_wa-license_plate  = '5678YY NY'.
    car_wa-category       = 'A'.
    INSERT car_wa INTO TABLE car_tab.

    car_wa-license_plate  = '4321ZZ NV'.
    car_wa-category       = 'A'.
    INSERT car_wa INTO TABLE car_tab.

    car_wa-license_plate  = '5522HH NC'.
    car_wa-category       = 'B'.
    INSERT car_wa INTO TABLE car_tab.

    car_wa-license_plate  = '1717WW AZ'.
    car_wa-category       = 'C'.
    INSERT car_wa INTO TABLE car_tab.

    ...

* Update car database table from internal table
    TRY.
        DELETE FROM zcars.
        INSERT zcars
              FROM TABLE car_tab.
```

```
      IF sy-subrc = 0.
        MESSAGE 'Car table updated'
                TYPE 'I'.
      ENDIF.
    CATCH cx_sy_open_sql_db.
      MESSAGE 'Car table could not be updated'
              TYPE 'I' DISPLAY LIKE 'E'.
  ENDTRY.
```

The auxiliary program from Listing 2.5 already contains a few very important concepts of the ABAP programming language. If you are already interested in detailed information on the particular language elements, place your cursor in the ABAP Editor on an element and press ⌞F1⌝. This opens the ABAP keyword documentation for the corresponding language element (more on this in Section 2.10).

2.6.2 Chained Statements

Chained statements are a feature of the ABAP syntax that reduces the amount of typing needed and improves readability. A chained statement groups together statements that have an identical beginning. To form a chained statement, after the identical part of the statements, you insert a colon. Then the remaining parts of the statements are listed, separated by commas. The fixed part of a statement is not limited to a keyword, so that skillful use can result in very efficient formulations. In our auxiliary program, two pairs of DATA statements are combined into chained statements. You should never forget, however, that a chained statement actually represents multiple statements, and that the compiler will always break the chained statement down into its individual parts. So our program actually contains four DATA statements for the declaration of four data objects.

2.6.3 Data Declarations

You're already familiar with the data declaration using DATA from the "Hello World" programs in Section 2.5.4. While we only declared an elementary text string there, here we see some rather complex data objects, namely structures and internal tables.

In this regard, ABAP makes our lives pretty easy, since our DATA statements can refer directly to our database tables ZCUSTOMERS and ZCARS from Section 2.4.

The database objects `customer_wa` and `car_wa` are *structures* whose structure is culled from the definitions of the corresponding database tables in the ABAP Dictionary. A structure can be put into operand positions either wholly or by component (more on this in Section 5.1.4).

Structures

The database objects `customer_wa` and `car_wa` are referred to as *internal tables*, whose structure is culled from the definitions of the corresponding database tables in the ABAP Dictionary. An internal table is a dynamic data object that consists of an arbitrarily long sequence of rows of the same data type. In addition to the row type, an internal table is defined by its table type (in this case, `HASHED`) and a table key (here `id` or `license_plate`). An internal table can be accessed in its entirety or by rows. Our internal tables can be regarded as images of the database tables in the working memory (more on this in Section 5.1.5).

Internal tables

2.6.4 Assigning Values to Data Objects

In the implementation part, we write literal values for the components of the structures, and insert the contents of the populated structures into the corresponding internal tables using `INSERT`. You can see that structure components can be accessed using the structure name and component name separated by a dash (-). It is also apparent that the component names are identical to the names of the fields in the database tables from Section 2.4.

The use of literals shown here is of course only permitted in this type of auxiliary program. In real applications, you would not write this type of value to your database tables.

2.6.5 Database Accesses

One of ABAP's biggest strengths is its direct integration of SQL commands into the language. SQL, the Structured Query Language, is a largely standardized language for accessing relational databases. In ABAP, the Data Manipulation Language (DML) portion is mapped by a set of statements called *Open SQL* (more on this in Section 10.1.2).

Open SQL

Here, we use the Open SQL statements `DELETE` and `INSERT`, first to completely empty our database tables, then to populate them with the entire contents of the corresponding internal tables.

Here, too, we must note that this kind of careless use of Open SQL is really not a good idea. In real applications, you would need to consider all kinds of questions, like verification of permissions and data consistency.

2.6.6 Exception Handling

The auxiliary program also gives you a little insight into exception handling (more on this in Section 8.2):

- On the one hand, the return value sy-subrc is evaluated after INSERT. The predefined field sy-subrc (if you look closely, this is the component subrc of the structure sy) is set by many statements in order to indicate success or failure of the statement. Only the value 0 is generally considered a success.

- On the other hand, a TRY control structure is used to catch the predefined exception cx_sy_open_sql_db with a CATCH statement, if the exception should occur in one of the Open SQL statements.

You already know the MESSAGE statement, used here for exception handling, from Section 2.5.4.

2.6.7 Testing the Auxiliary Program using the ABAP Debugger

If you execute the auxiliary program directly using **Execute • Direct** from the context menu of the program name, and, if all goes well, you will see the two dialog windows output with MESSAGE indicating that the database tables have been updated (see Figure 2.42).

Figure 2.42 Success Message

Breakpoint   If you want to know more about how the program works, you can also execute it step by step in the ABAP Debugger. To do this, you can either select **Execute • Debugging** in the context menu of the program name, or you can set a breakpoint on a statement using **Set/Delete Breakpoint**.

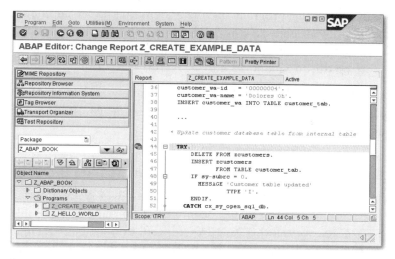

Figure 2.43 Setting a Breakpoint

If, as shown in Figure 2.43, you set a breakpoint on the first TRY   **New debugger**
statement and run the program normally, the program execution
will stop before the selected statement, and the ABAP Debugger will
start. Here we are using the new ABAP Debugger included in the SAP
NetWeaver 2004s ABAP Trial Version. The debugger opens in a new
window and controls the execution of the program (the program is
thus the *debuggee*; see Section 13.2.1). In the debugger window, you
can use different tools. Among other things, you can display the content of data objects like the table customer_tab (see Figure 2.44).

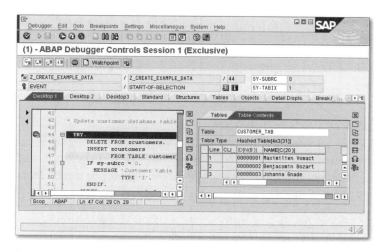

Figure 2.44 Internal Table in the (New) ABAP Debugger

You can debug the program in single steps ($\boxed{F5}$), set additional breakpoints by double-clicking in the first column of the editors, continue program execution until the next breakpoint ($\boxed{F8}$), and so on (more on this in Section 13.2.3).

Prior to Release 6.40 (SAP NetWeaver '04), there was only an ABAP Debugger that ran in the same window, not controlling the debugged program from outside.

2.6.8 Result of the Auxiliary Program in the Data Browser

To check whether the content shown in Figure 2.44 of the internal table customer_tab has actually been written to the database table ZCUSTOMERS, we call the Data Browser tool in the Object Navigator, as shown in Figure 2.45, for the database table. This assumes that the **Data Browser/Table View Maintenance** property is defined for the table, as shown in Figure 2.17.

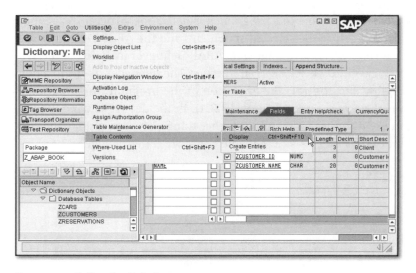

Figure 2.45 Calling the Data Browser

If the Data Browser can be called, the selection screen shown in Figure 2.46 displays. The Data Browser generates this input screen from the fields of the database table.

Since we only expect a few entries, we confirm the selection screen with **Execute** ($\boxed{F8}$) and are rewarded with a display of the content of our table (see Figure 2.47). Check the contents of ZCARS in the same way. By this time, you may have realized that the Data Browser generates a (temporary) ABAP program for each table, which reads the table contents using Open SQL and displays it as a list.

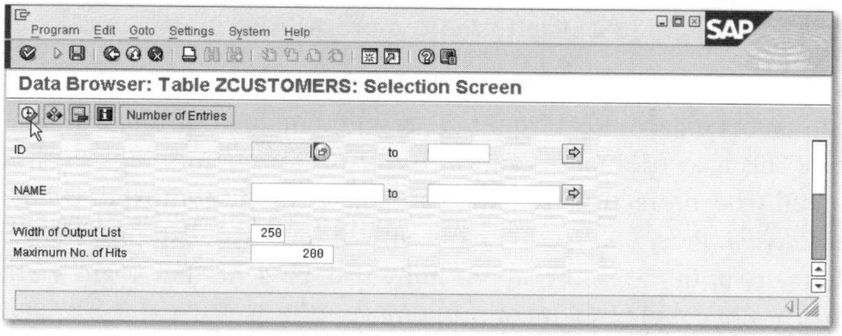

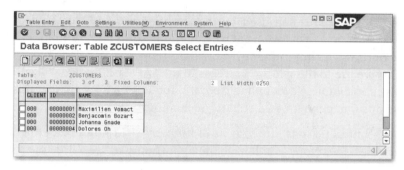

Figure 2.46 Selection Screen of the Data Browser

Figure 2.47 Table Contents in the Data Browser

2.7 User Dialog

Now we have done all the preparatory work. We have created database tables and populated them with data. We can therefore turn our attention to the project itself, which will reserve rental cars from the rental car table for customers from the customer table.

Such a reservation should be performed by a person, say a sales clerk. So our program needs a way of communicating with a person. In the last millennium, when the previous edition of this book was written, not a lot of thought needed to go into how this kind of user dialog would be structured. For user dialogs, the presentation layer of the earlier SAP Basis system provided only the SAP GUI, which, in turn, provided only a limited set of screens (dynpro screens, selection screens, lists: see Chapter 9). For the AS ABAP, which replaces the old SAP Basis, things look a little different. Besides the SAP GUI-supported user dialogs, the presentation layer now also provides web-based user dialogs, which are implemented for ABAP with Business Server Pages (BSPs) and Web Dynpro ABAP.

Decoupling Therefore, to be ready for any kind of user dialog, an application program must be decoupled from the presentation logic as much as possible. This is a striking difference from ABAP programming as it has generally been practiced to date, particularly in the context of *Online Transaction Processing* (OLTP) or with interactive list processing, where in both cases the application and presentation logic were intrinsically coupled within a program.

To decouple the presentation logic from the application logic, it is useful to encapsulate the presentation logic in suitable classes or programs, which are then used by the application logic. This kind of encapsulation is what we want to use for our sample application. For the purpose of simplification, we will limit the presentation components we use to the selection screens in the SAP GUI, but we will still strive for complete decoupling from the application logic, so that this remains independent of the dialog technology actually used.

For technical reasons, the screens of the SAP GUI cannot be defined in classes. Therefore, you'll have the opportunity to see a little of the predecessor technology of classes, the function groups, since these support this kind of screen. At the same time, we will tell you more about the following concepts:

► Function groups as ABAP programs
► Program organization using include programs
► Creating and testing function modules

2.7.1 Using a Function Group

Function modules *Function groups*, just like executable programs, are nothing more than ABAP programs of a particular type. Function groups are unique in that they are the only program type, which can contain what we call *function modules*. Function modules are procedures with public interfaces that can be called from other programs.

In the object-oriented world, a function group would be a class, and its function modules would be its public static methods. This is how we want to look at the function group that we'll now create. In the procedural programming model, which is still very common in ABAP applications as the predecessor of the object-oriented programming model, function modules are used as reusable global procedures, which are stored centrally in a function library (see Section 7.2.1).

To create a function group named Z_CAR_RENTAL_SCREENS, select **Create · Function group** from the context menu of our package in the Repository Browser, and fill in the dialog window that appears as shown in Figure 2.48. Save the function group.

Creating a function group

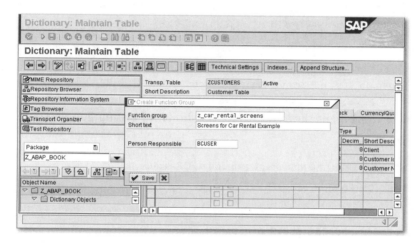

Figure 2.48 Creating a Function Group

You can then find the function group Z_CAR_RENTAL_SCREENS in the Repository Browser. Activate it there. You will also see that the ABAP Workbench has already created include programs for you under the appropriate nodes. Function groups are thus automatically organized by the include programs that we've already mentioned. Select the upper include program to edit it (see Figure 2.49).

2.7.2 Top Include of the Function Group

This upper include is the TOP include of the function group, which is provided for the global declaration part. In Figure 2.49, we can see that the introductory statement of a function group is FUNCTION-POOL, and that it is located in the TOP include in the case of a function group.

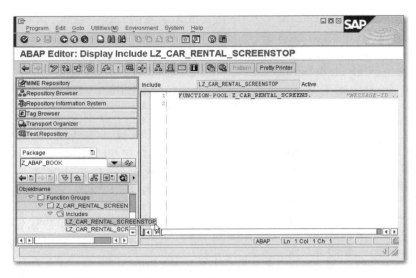

Figure 2.49 TOP Include of the Function Group

Now implement the TOP include as shown in Listing 2.6, and activate it.

Listing 2.6 Listing 2.6 Implementation of the TOP Include

```
FUNCTION-POOL z_car_rental_screens.

* Selection Screen for customer id
SELECTION-SCREEN BEGIN OF SCREEN 1100
                 AS WINDOW TITLE text-cid.
PARAMETERS id TYPE zcustomers-id.
SELECTION-SCREEN END OF SCREEN 1100.

* Selection Screen for reservation data
SELECTION-SCREEN BEGIN OF SCREEN 1200
                 AS WINDOW TITLE text-rsv.
PARAMETERS category TYPE zcars-category OBLIGATORY
                                        VALUE CHECK.
PARAMETERS day_from TYPE zreservations-date_from.
PARAMETERS day_to   TYPE zreservations-date_to.
SELECTION-SCREEN END OF SCREEN 1200.

* Input check for selection screen
AT SELECTION-SCREEN.
  CASE sy-dynnr.
    WHEN 1200.
      IF day_to < day_from.
        MESSAGE 'DAY_TO must not be before DAY_FROM'
```

```
          TYPE 'E'.
      ENDIF.
    ENDCASE.
```

In the TOP include, you can add declarations that are visible throughout the entire function group. In an object-oriented context, data objects declared here would be called private static attributes of the function group. The function modules in a function groups have access to these data objects.

Here, we define two so-called *selection screens* that can be used for entering customer and reservation data. These are special dynpros, which can be generated with ABAP statements like SELECTION-SCREEN and PARAMETERS, as shown in Listing 2.6 (more on this in Section 9.2). Our selection screens will be identified by dynpro numbers 1100 and 1200. Input fields are created with PARAMETERS. Note again the reference to the database tables in the ABAP Dictionary. Matching input fields are generated for fields in our own database tables. For more information, feel free to try F1 on the language elements.

Selection screen

In addition, we want to use the definition of the selection screens to introduce you to the concept of text elements in the ABAP Workbench. In the statements SELECTION-SCREEN BEGIN OF SCREEN, you can see the identifiers text-cid and text-rsv. However, we haven't defined these data objects in our function group. Instead, these identifiers refer to so-called *text symbols*, which can be used as character fields in a program. Text symbols are a component of the text elements of a program, which can be defined outside the actual source code. .As the texts of data elements in the ABAP Dictionary, text elements are linked to translation. During program execution, the text is always displayed in the login language. This automatically makes your program multilingual without the need for a translator to change the source code. You should therefore use text symbols wherever the text of the program will be displayed in the user interface. To keep our example as simple as possible, we will not follow this rule consistently in this book, except in the example shown here (more on this in Section 5.1.10).

Text elements

To manage the text symbols in a program, either select **Goto • Text elements** in the ABAP Editor, or double-click on the text-... identifier to navigate directly to the text element maintenance (see Figure 2.50). You can enter appropriate texts as shown here. In this case,

Text symbols

these are the titles of the selection screens. If you want, you can also switch to the **Selection texts** tab to create meaningful names for the input fields of the selection screens. The simplest solution would be to check the **Dictionary Reference** checkbox for every entry, to ensure that the texts we already created will be taken from the ABAP Dictionary.

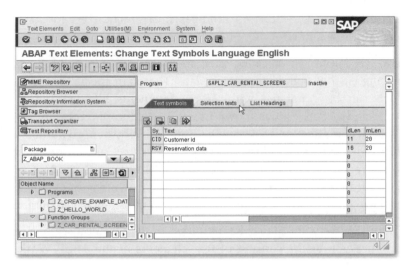

Figure 2.50 Text Element Maintenance

Selection screen processing

Save and activate the text symbols and return to the TOP include. At the end, you find a AT SELECTION-SCREEN statement. This statement introduces a processing block, which is called by the ABAP runtime environment if a user action (selection of the **Execute** function or F8 pressed) occurs on a selection screen of the current program (see Section 9.2.6). Here, we perform a plausibility check for reservation data entered in selection screen 1200. You should find it relatively easy to see the meaning of these statements. By implementing the processing block in the TOP include, of course, we are breaking the rule that only declarations should be placed in the TOP include. In fact, this type of processing block should be implemented in specially provided include programs. But in this case, we want to save you and ourselves the work for this simple sample application. Remember that the separation into include programs is only for organizational reasons. For the ABAP compiler, a function group, like any standalone ABAP program, is its own compilation unit in which all include programs are expanded.

2.7.3 Creating Function Modules

To complete the function group, it still needs an interface to other programs in the form of function modules. We want to create two function modules, so we start by selecting **Create • Function module** in the context menu of the function group in the Repository Browser.

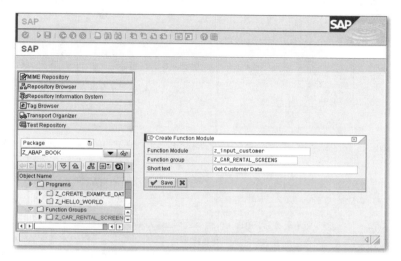

Figure 2.51 Creating a Function Module

By now, you should be quite familiar with the next dialog window. Fill it out as shown in Figure 2.51. After completing the usual organizational confirmations, the Function Builder tool appears, in which you must first define the interface for the function module. To do this, go to the **Export** tab and enter an output parameter as shown in Figure 2.52. Again, note the reference to the ID field of our database table ZCUSTOMERS.

Parameter interface

Next, we implement the first function module on the **Source code** tab, as shown in Figure 2.53. The FUNCTION and ENDFUNCTION statements, along with a listing of the parameter interface in comments, are already provided by the ABAP Workbench.

Source code

The source code is really self-explanatory. The selection screen 1100 is called, and after it is successfully completed (sy-subrc contains 0) the user input in selection screen parameter id is assigned to output parameter customer_id of the function module. The function module thus encapsulates the selection screen call. Now activate the function module.

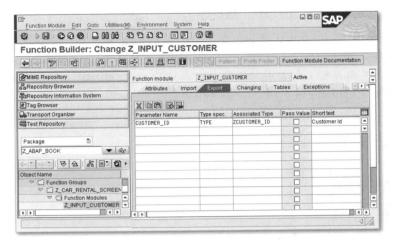

Figure 2.52 Interface of the First Function Module

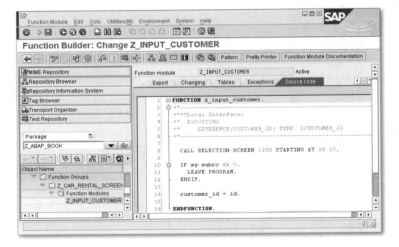

Figure 2.53 Implementation of the First Function Module

Main program

Note that the source code of a function module displayed by the Function Builder is nothing more than an include program, which is integrated into the function group. To better understand this relationship, select **Go to • Main program**, which will take you into the actual function group as an ABAP program whose actual name is SAPLZ_CAR_RENTAL_SCREENS and which contains only INCLUDE statements. Navigate through the include programs by double-clicking to find the code we've written so far. The Function Builder generally protects us from this kind of technical detail; however, if we wanted to create our own include program for selection screen processing, for instance, we would have to generate this code using forward navigation from the main program.

Lastly, repeat the steps to define a second function module with the properties shown in Figures 2.54 and 2.55, and activate it.

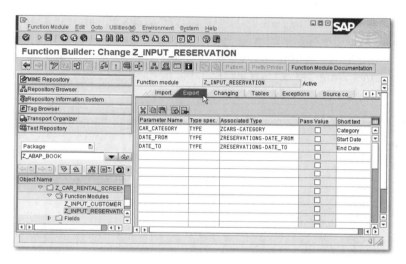

Figure 2.54 Interface for the Second Function Module

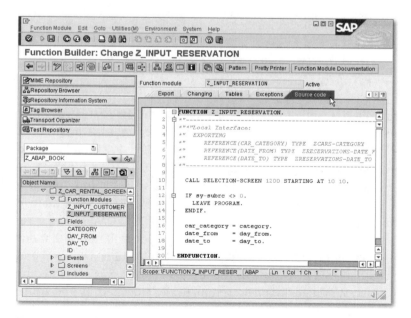

Figure 2.55 Implementation of the Second Function Module

2.7.4 Testing Function Modules

One of the more attractive characteristics of function modules is that they can be tested directly in the Function Builder. Simply select **Test • Test** from the context menu of a function module in the Repository Browser. In the following window, you can enter possible input parameters and start the test with F8. After that, the selection screen that we defined for Z_INPUT_CUSTOMERS will appear. If you then select the input help key F4 for the input window ID, the selection list shown in Figure 2.56 will magically appear containing the names from the ZCUSTOMERS table in the database.

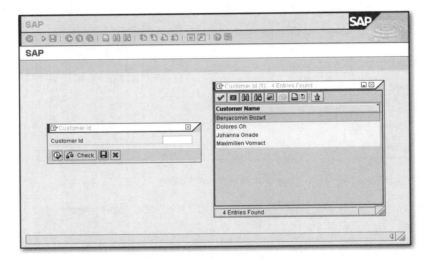

Figure 2.56 Selection Screen with Selection List

Search help   If you select a name from the selection list, the associated customer number from the database table will be placed into the input field. We didn't explicitly program this functionality. We simply linked the id parameter with the database field zcustomers-id via the TYPE specification (see Listing 2.6). But it is precisely this link that also results in the display of the search help window. Remember that we defined a search help for this field in the ZCUSTOMERS database table. If you now look at Figure 2.28 again, you will notice that our definition simply means that the content of NAME is displayed and the content from ID is copied. The associated logic was generated by the ABAP Workbench and is automatically executed by the ABAP runtime environment upon request.

If you use **Execute** (F8) to confirm the selection screen with a value for the ID field, the function module is executed, and the test environment shows you the value of the output parameter CUSTOMER_ID.

You can test the function module Z_INPUT_RESERVATION in the same way. The input help for the input field CATEGORY provides precisely those three values specified in Figure 2.32 as the value range for the domain. If you enter a different value here, the entry is rejected, as shown in Figure 2.57. This is due to the VALUE CHECK specification we made in Listing 2.6 after the definition of this parameter. The OBLIGATORY addition forces you to enter a value in the field.

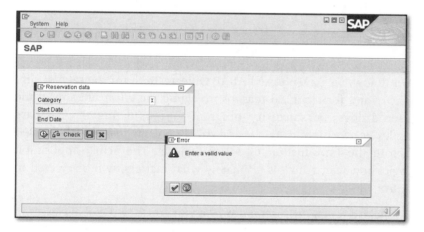

Figure 2.57 Value Check Against Domain

The input fields for reservation data provide an interactive calendar as an input help. If you enter a date for DAY_FROM here, which falls after DAY_TO, you will see the message in Figure 2.58. We programmed this message ourselves with the MESSAGE statement in Listing 2.6 after AT SELECTION-SCREEN.

This concludes the introduction of the user dialogs we need, and now we turn our attention to the actual application logic.

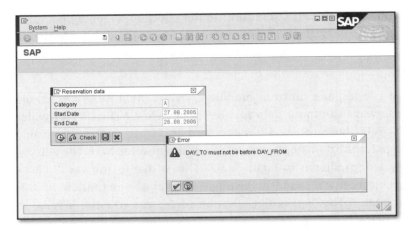

Figure 2.58 Self-Programmed Value Check

2.8 Application Logic

Until now, we haven't used ABAP Objects. Both for the sake of simplicity and for technical reasons involving the encapsulation of the user dialogs, our auxiliary program for populating the database tables was written using classical ABAP tools, which already existed before the introduction of ABAP Objects. The actual application logic, however, which is ultimately what matters, will be created in ABAP Objects.

To make a rental car reservation, we will create two global classes in the class library of our AS ABAP. In addition to the usual classes, we will also need two exception classes to trigger exceptions in the normal classes. Global classes can be used in other ABAP programs. We will demonstrate this by creating a local application class in a program whose `main` method will then be called to execute the application. In the final section of the introduction, you will encounter the following:

▶ The Class Builder

▶ Attributes and methods

▶ Constructors

▶ References and objects

▶ Transaction codes

▶ Reporting

2.8.1 Exception Classes

Exceptions and exception handling are topics that every application developer has to deal with (more on this in Section 8.2). Here, we simply want to touch on this broad subject.

An *exception class* is a special class, which is used as the basis for exceptions that can be handled. There are predefined exception classes for exceptions in the runtime environment, and self-defined exception classes for your own applications. In Listing 2.3, we already handled exceptions that are based on the predefined exception class CX_SY_OPEN_SQL_DB. Now we will create our own exception classes.

To create an exception class, select **Create · Class library · Class** from the context menu of our package in the Repository Browser, and fill in the dialog window that displays as shown in Figure 2.59.

Creating an exception class

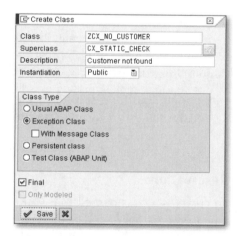

Figure 2.59 Creating an Exception Class

You can see that the first step in creating exception classes is the same as for usual classes. However, if you check **Exception Class**, the ABAP Workbench automatically sets CX_STATIC_CHECK as a superclass in the **Superclass** field. This is because exception classes must be subclasses of specially predefined superclasses. When you save the exception class, you will get your first glimpse of the Class Builder (see Figure 2.60).

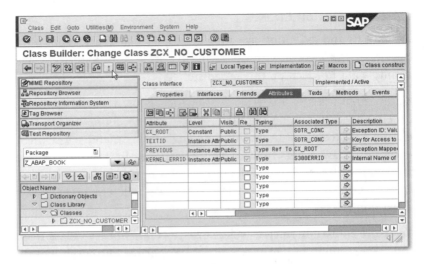

Figure 2.60 Class Builder for Exception Class

Class Builder For the time being, we don't want to do any more than simply acti-vate the exception class. Our exception class has no other significant properties than the fact that it exists with this name, which fully sat-isfies our requirements for the sample program.

Repeat the steps for creating an exception class for a second excep-tion class named ZCX_NO_CAR_AVAILABLE, with the description "No car available".

2.8.2 Creating a Class for Reservations

The first normal class we want to create is a class named ZCL_CAR_RESERVATIONS for the processing of reservation data. The class will serve as a template for a single object in which the rental car book-ings are stored and can be handled.

To create the class, proceed as you would with the exception classes, except that in the **Create Class** dialog, you should select **Usual ABAP Class** (see Figure 2.61). We leave the **Final** checkbox checked. This means that no subclasses may be derived from our class. Further-more, we select the **Private** item in the **Instantiation** field. This means that objects of this class may be generated only within the class itself.

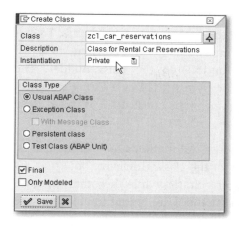

Figure 2.61 Creating the Reservation Class

After saving, you will find yourself back in the Class Builder. Unlike the exception class from Figure 2.60, in a normal class no components are predefined. The components of the class must be created manually in the corresponding tabs, like **Methods** and **Attributes**.

Class components

Declaring Methods

First, we declare the methods for the reservation class in the appropriate tab, as shown in Figure 2.62.

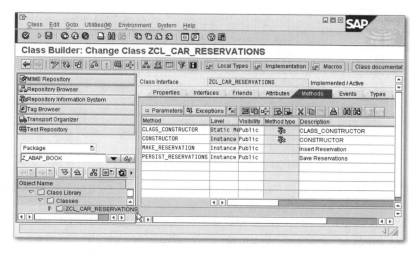

Figure 2.62 Methods of the Reservation Class

Constructor The first two methods CONSTRUCTOR and CLASS_CONSTRUCTOR have predefined names and are the constructors for the class. To create the constructors, you can simply click on the **Constructor** (F5) and **Class constructor** (F6) buttons in the Class Builder. The instance constructor is automatically executed every time an object of the class is generated, while the static constructor is called once before the first access to the class.

Enter the other methods as shown. All methods are **Public**, that is, they can be called by any user of the class. However, note that the static constructor has the property **Static**, while the other methods are **Instance Methods**. Instance methods are bound to objects of the class, while a static method is always available.

Defining interface parameters To define interface parameters for a method, place the cursor on the method and click on the **Parameters** button. Define the interface of the method MAKE_RESERVATION as shown in Figure 2.63. Our method has only input parameters, whose types are all determined by reference to our database tables ZCUSTOMERS, ZCARS, and ZRESERVATIONS.

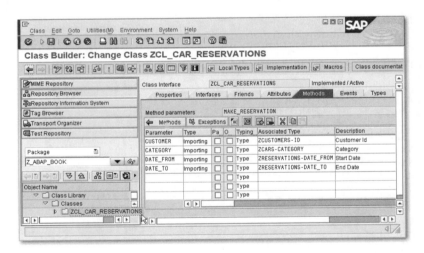

Figure 2.63 Parameters of the Reservation Method

The MAKE_RESERVATION method should be able to trigger one of the exceptions already defined. To do this, click on the **Exceptions** button and then enter the name of the exception class ZCX_NO_CAR_AVAILABLE (see Figure 2.64). It is important that you check the **Exception Classes** checkbox. Otherwise, the predecessor of the current technology will be used (see Section 8.2.2). The other methods need no interface parameters or exceptions.

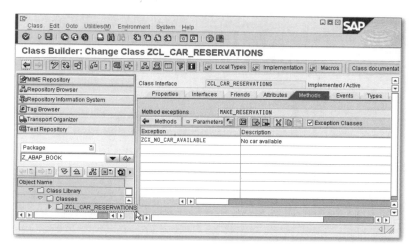

Figure 2.64 Exception for the Reservation Method

The methods in our reservation class should work with a memory representation of the database table ZRESERVATIONS, that is, with an internal table with a matching row structure. The data type for such an internal table can either be created in the ABAP Dictionary or locally in the program.[10] In our example, we will demonstrate the use of a local data type.

Internal table

Local Data Type

In the Class Builder, select the function **Goto · Class-local types · Local class definitions/types**, or click on the **Types** button, and in the ABAP Editor, which then appears, enter a TYPES statement as shown in Figure 2.65.

You should already know the syntax of the TYPES statement from the DATA statements in Listing 2.4. However, no data object is defined here in the form of an internal table, but rather only the template for a data object, a table type. Based on the experience you have from Section 2.7.2, you may already realize that we are editing an include

---

10 Note in this context that the definition of the database table in the ABAP Dictionary represents a structure to ABAP, but not an internal table.

program here, which constitutes the global declaration part in the main program of the global class.

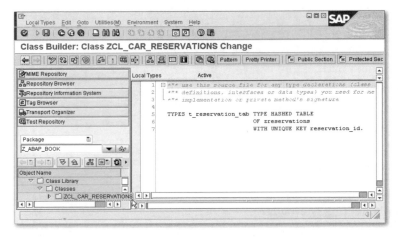

Figure 2.65 Local Type for a Global Class

Declaring Attributes

We'll create a public static attribute and a private instance attribute. An *attribute* is a data object declared within a class. A *static attribute* is always present. An *instance attribute* is always assigned to an object of a class and determines its state. A *private attribute* is only visible within its own class. Create the attributes in the corresponding tab, as shown in Figure 2.66.

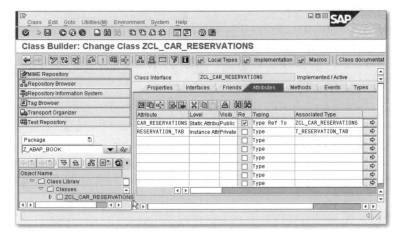

Figure 2.66 Attributes of the Reservation Class

The public static attribute CAR_RESERVATIONS was typed with **Type Ref To** and the **Reference type** ZCL_CAR_RESERVATIONS. This means that the attribute is a reference variable. Reference variables are essential to working with objects. This is because reference variables contain references that can point to objects. It is not possible to address objects in any other way than with reference variables. Our attribute can therefore point to objects in its own class. Furthermore, we selected **Read-Only** for the attribute, which means that it may be readable from outside the class, but cannot be changed.

Reference variable

The other attribute RESERVATION_TAB is simply a private internal table, whose row type corresponds to that of database table ZRESER-VATIONS.

Implementing Methods

After completion of all declarative activities, the external and internal components of the class are now defined. In principle, the class could now be activated, and its components addressed wherever they are visible.

Of course, at the moment, the implementation of the methods is still missing. In object-oriented programming, classes without complete implementation are not unusual as templates for fully implemented classes (in ABAP Objects this is done using abstract classes and interfaces; see Section 6.2.5).

To implement a method, select it as shown in Figure 2.62 with a double-click or the **Source code** function. Then the ABAP Editor will display with predefined statements METHOD and ENDMETHOD, between which you can insert the source code shown in the following listing.

We begin in Listing 2.7 with the static constructor, whose implementation consists of a single statement. CREATE OBJECT is used to create an object of class ZCL_CAR_RESERVATIONS. After this statement is executed successfully, the static attribute car_reservations contains a reference to the object. Since the static constructor is executed once before the class is addressed for the first time in a program, we are implementing the so-called *singleton pattern* here, in which there exists exactly one object per class. Object creations from outside are impossible, since that's how we defined the class (see Figure 2.61).

Static constructor

Listing 2.7 Implementation of the Static Constructor

```
METHOD class_constructor.
  CREATE OBJECT car_reservations.
ENDMETHOD.
```

Instance
constructor

Next, the instance constructor is implemented in Listing 2.8. This constructor is executed when the CREATE OBJECT statement runs, and performs object initialization. In our case, we supply the private instance attribute of the class, that is, the internal table reservation_tab, with the data of the ZRESERVATIONS database table. With SELECT, you can become familiar with the Open SQL statement for the reading of data from database tables.

Listing 2.8 Implementation of the Instance Constructor

```
METHOD constructor.
  SELECT *
         FROM zreservations
         INTO TABLE me->reservation_tab.
ENDMETHOD.
```

Reservation

In Listing 2.9, we implement the reservation of a rental car for a customer in the make_reservation method. The method contains the customer number, the rental car category desired, and the time period requested, as input parameters. DATA is used to declare local auxiliary variables. To determine whether a car of the desired category is available in the requested time period, rental cars of this category are read out of the database table in a SELECT loop until a reservation is possible. The SELECT statement terminated by an ENDSELECT statement represents an ABAP feature that is not available in standard SQL. In this loop, the availability is tested for every car read in. To do this, the reservation table is searched using a LOOP loop for rows in which the current car is already reserved in the requested time. If no such reservation is found, then sy-subrc is not equal to zero, and the new reservation can be inserted. After a successful reservation, the method is terminated with RETURN. If the SELECT loop is exited using ENDSELECT, the reservation could not be made, and we trigger the exception provided for that possibility.

Listing 2.9 Making a Reservation

```
METHOD make_reservation.
    DATA: license_plate    TYPE zcars-license_plate,
          reservation_wa   LIKE LINE OF reservation_tab,
          reservation_num  TYPE i,
          mess             TYPE string.
    reservation_num = lines( reservation_tab ).
    SELECT license_plate
           FROM zcars
           INTO (license_plate)
           WHERE category = category.
      LOOP AT reservation_tab
        TRANSPORTING NO FIELDS
        WHERE license_plate = license_plate
              AND NOT ( date_from > date_to OR
                        date_to   < date_from ).
      ENDLOOP.
      IF sy-subrc <> 0.
        reservation_wa-reservation_id  = reservation_num + 1.
        reservation_wa-customer_id     = customer.
        reservation_wa-license_plate   = license_plate.
        reservation_wa-date_from       = date_from.
        reservation_wa-date_to         = date_to.
        INSERT reservation_wa INTO TABLE reservation_tab.
        IF sy-subrc = 0.
          CONCATENATE license_plate ' reserved!' INTO mess.
          MESSAGE mess TYPE 'I'.
        ELSE.
          MESSAGE 'Internal error!' TYPE 'I' DISPLAY LIKE 'E'.
          LEAVE PROGRAM.
        ENDIF.
        RETURN.
      ENDIF.
    ENDSELECT.
    RAISE EXCEPTION TYPE zcx_no_car_available.
ENDMETHOD.
```

Finally, in Listing 2.10, we implement the method for persistent storage of the reservation table in the database, simply by deleting the prior content of the ZRESERVATIONS table and replacing it with the content of the internal table `reservation_tab`.

Persistent storage

119

Listing 2.10 Saving the Reservation Table

```
METHOD persist_reservations.
  DELETE FROM zreservations.
  INSERT zreservations
         FROM TABLE reservation_tab.
ENDMETHOD.
```

All in all, an object of our ZCL_CAR_RESERVATIONS class thus represents the content of the ZRESERVATIONS database table in the memory, and provides methods for its manipulation. Unlike a real application, in our simple example, we do not ensure data consistency (i. e., by setting of locks or by verifying permissions). We will address this in more detail in Sections 10.1.3 and 10.5.

2.8.3   Creating a Class for Customer Objects

The second normal class that we will create is a class for customer objects. Every object in such a class represents a customer from the ZCUSTOMERS database table, who can perform rental car bookings.

To create the class, we proceed as we did for the class for reservations, populating the **Create Class** dialog window with data as shown in Figure 2.67. In the **Instantiation** field, we select the **Public** item, indicating that every user of the class can generate corresponding objects.

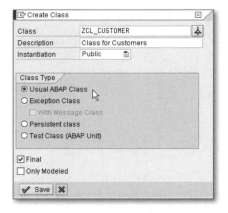

Figure 2.67 Creating the Customer Class

Class components   The components of the class must be created in the Class Builder again. This time, let's begin with the attributes.

Attributes

For the customer class, we need a private instance attribute, which we can create in the appropriate tab, as shown in Figure 2.68.

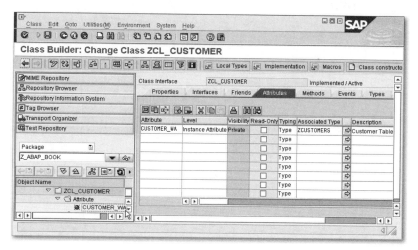

Figure 2.68 Attribute of the Customer Class

We declare our instance attribute with reference to the structure of the ZCUSTOMERS database table in the ABAP Dictionary, and thus map another relational database table to a class. Since this procedure is relatively common, the *ABAP Object Services* provide a predefined encapsulation for it (see Section 10.2).

Methods

On the **Methods** tab, create two methods for the customer class (see Figure 2.69). The first method, CONSTRUCTOR, is again the instance constructor of the class, which is automatically executed after the creation of an object of this class. Constructors have the same predefined names in all classes.

Instance
constructor

This time, you should also define an interface for the instance constructor. Place the cursor on the CONSTRUCTOR method, and click on the **Parameters** button to determine its interface parameters, as shown in Figure 2.70. An instance constructor can only have input parameters. We define such input parameters named id with reference to the ID field of the ZCUSTOMERS database table.

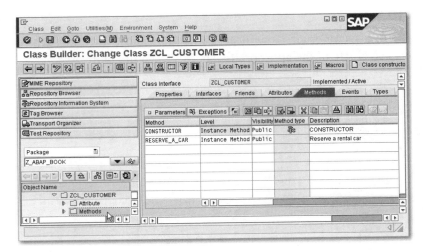

Figure 2.69 Methods of the Customer Class

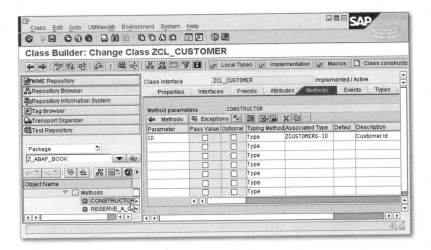

Figure 2.70 Parameters of the Instance Constructor

Exceptions

The instance constructor should be able to trigger one of the exceptions already defined. To do this, select the **Exceptions** button and then enter the name of the exception class ZCX_NO_CAR_AVAILA-BLE (see Figure 2.71). Don't forget that the **Exception Classes** checkbox must be checked.

Select the instance constructor by double-clicking on it or selecting the **Source code** function to implement it as shown in Listing 2.11.

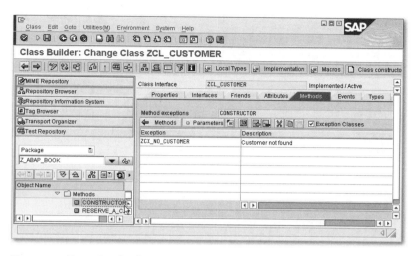

Figure 2.71 Exception for the Instance Constructor

Listing 2.11 Implementation of the Instance Constructor

```
METHOD constructor.
  SELECT SINGLE *
         FROM zcustomers
         INTO customer_wa
         WHERE id = id.
  IF sy-subrc <> 0.
    RAISE EXCEPTION TYPE zcx_no_customer.
  ENDIF.
ENDMETHOD.
```

For each object generated, the instance constructor reads the row identified by the content of the input parameter id from the ZCUS-TOMERS table using SELECT and assigns it to the private attribute customer_wa with the same type. If the row is not found, the return value sy-subrc is not equal to zero, and we use RAISE EXCEPTION to trigger the exception declared in the interface of the instance constructor.

The RESERVE_A_CAR method should make it possible for a customer object to reserve a rental car, and must therefore have the input parameters shown in Figure 2.72. You can see from the **Type Ref To** typing method that the method expects a reference to an object of the ZCL_CAR_RESERVATIONS reservation class.

Reservation method

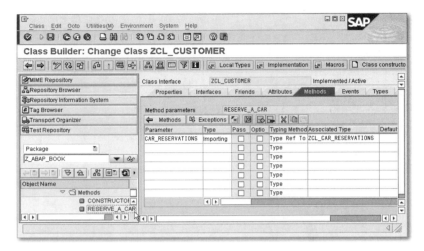

Figure 2.72 Parameters of the Reservation Method

As an exception, for the reservation method as well as for the corresponding method in the reservation class, the exception class ZCX_NO_CAR_AVAILABLE should be entered (see Figure 2.73).

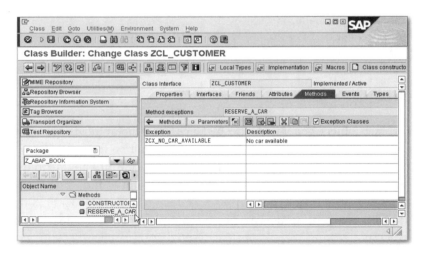

Figure 2.73 Exception for the Reservation Method

Implement the reservation method as shown in Listing 2.12. The implementation of the method consists of two calls. First, the CALL FUNCTION calls the function module Z_INPUT_RESERVATION that we created, and assigns its output parameters to local auxiliary variables. These are then passed along with the code me->customer_ wa-id to the make_reservation method of the object referenced by the input parameter car_reservations. It is not strictly necessary to use the me-> prefix, but it underlines the fact that a component of the current object is intended (me is the so-called *self-reference*). If the make_reservation method called triggers its ZCX_NO_CAR_AVAILABLE exception, this is automatically passed along out of reserve_a_car, since the same exception is also declared in that interface.

Listing 2.12 Implementation of the Reservation Method

```
METHOD reserve_a_car.
  DATA: category  TYPE zcars-category,
        date_from TYPE zreservations-date_from,
        date_to   TYPE zreservations-date_to.
  CALL FUNCTION 'Z_INPUT_RESERVATION'
    IMPORTING
      car_category = category
      date_from    = date_from
      date_to      = date_to.
  car_reservations->make_reservation(
                        customer  = me->customer_wa-id
                        category  = category
                        date_from = date_from
                        date_to   = date_to ).
ENDMETHOD.
```

This concludes the definition of both of our normal classes in the class library. Use the **Check** function to take another look at the consistency of the classes, and ensure that all components of the classes are activated.

Like the Function Builder (see Section 2.7.4), the Class Builder also provides a test environment for classes. For instance, you can select the **Test** function in the Repository Browser from the context menu of a class. Testing a class, however, is a little harder than simply testing function modules, particularly if the class, like ZCL_CAR_RESERVATIONS, can only be privately instantiated or if a method like RESERVE_A_CAR of the ZCL_CUSTOMER class is expecting an object reference as an input parameter. If you want, feel free to try out the tool. But we would rather program the use of the class.

Testing a class

2.8.4 Application Program

Now that we have created our classes as a service in the class library, we only need a user to conclude this example. This could, of course, be another global class in the class library, but we would prefer to demonstrate using local classes in programs at this point.

Local classes

All classes created using the Class Builder can be accessed from other ABAP programs. In addition, ABAP Objects allows you to create local classes in any ABAP programs that are valid only for the current program. Contrary to global classes, in the case of local classes you have to type the entire definition into the ABAP Editor—in fact this is not necessarily any slower.

Subroutine pool

In the course of this practical introduction, what you have seen as ABAP programs, in the sense of self-contained compilation units, are executable programs and function groups. The Class Builder creates a main program for each global class. The type of that main program is class pool, but the main programs operate in the background and are transparent to the user. For our local class, we choose a different type, called a *subroutine pool*. The advantage of using this type is that it has practically no properties. Executable programs, as you saw in Section 2.5.4, are implicitly controlled by the ABAP runtime environment. Function groups form a framework for associated function modules. In contrast, subroutine pools are in essentially just source code. Historically, subroutine pools are main programs for subprograms, which can be called from other programs (see Section 3.2.4). In ABAP Objects, the use of subprograms is obsolete. The program type subroutine pool, however, can still be used as a useful framework for local classes.

To create the subroutine pool, you should proceed in exactly the same way as you did when you created the auxiliary program in Section 2.5. Use the name "Z_RENTAL_CAR_RESERVATION". The only difference from creating an executable program is that you must select **Subroutine pool** instead of **Executable program** in the dialog window shown in Figure 2.36. Enter the source code from Listing 2.13 into the subroutine pool and activate it.

Listing 2.13 Local Class of a Subroutine Pool

```
*&---------------------------------------------------------------*
*& Subroutinen-Pool   Z_RENTAL_CAR_RESERVATION           *
*&---------------------------------------------------------------*

PROGRAM  z_rental_car_reservation.

---------------------------------------------------------------
* Class for car rentals
---------------------------------------------------------------

* Declarations
CLASS cl_car_rental DEFINITION.
  PUBLIC SECTION.
    CLASS-METHODS main.
ENDCLASS.

* Implementations
CLASS cl_car_rental IMPLEMENTATION.
  METHOD main.
    DATA: id           TYPE zcustomers-id,
          customer     TYPE REF TO zcl_customer,
          ans          TYPE c LENGTH 1,
          reservations TYPE REF TO
                       zcl_car_reservations.

    "Create a customer
    CALL FUNCTION 'Z_INPUT_CUSTOMER'
      IMPORTING
        customer_id = id.
    TRY.
        CREATE OBJECT customer EXPORTING id = id.
      CATCH zcx_no_customer.
        MESSAGE 'Unknown customer'
                TYPE 'I' DISPLAY LIKE 'E'.
        RETURN.
    ENDTRY.
    "Create object for reservations
    reservations =
      zcl_car_reservations=>car_reservations.
    DO.
      "Customer reserves a car
      TRY.
          customer->reserve_a_car( reservations ).
        CATCH zcx_no_car_available.
          MESSAGE 'No car available!'
```

```
        TYPE 'I' DISPLAY LIKE 'E'.
    ENDTRY.
    CALL FUNCTION 'POPUP_TO_CONFIRM'
      EXPORTING
        text_question        = 'Other reservations?'
        text_button_1        = 'Yes'
        text_button_2        = 'No'
        display_cancel_button = ' '
      IMPORTING
        answer               = ans.
    IF ans = '2'.
      EXIT.
    ENDIF.
  ENDDO.
  "Persist data on database
  reservations->persist_reservations( ).
  ENDMETHOD.
ENDCLASS.
```

The program in Listing 2.13 clearly shows the division mentioned in Section 2.5.3 into a declaration part and a procedural part.

Class definition The declaration part contains the declaration of a local class cl_car_rental. Everything you can do in the Class Builder by filling out screen templates can also be noted between the statements CLASS ... DEFINITION and ENDCLASS. After all, the Class Builder generates precisely this type of code in the background. Our local class contains exactly one public static method main with no interface parameteres, which is declared with the CLASS-METHODS statement.

Class implementation In the procedural part, every method of a local class must be implemented between CLASS ... IMPLEMENTATION and ENDCLASS. The statements METHOD and ENDMETHOD are already familiar to you from the global classes.

Customer object The main method is a user of our global classes. After querying a customer number using the prepared function module Z_INPUT_CUSTOMER, an attempt is made after TRY to use CREATE OBJECT to generate an object of the customer class from Section 2.8.3 for this customer, and the customer number is passed to the instance constructor of the customer class. If the customer number is unknown, the instance constructor triggers exception zcx_no_customer (see

Listing 2.11). This exception is handled after CATCH by a message and by leaving the method.

After this, the auxiliary variable reservations is assigned the static attribute car_reservations from the reservation class zcl_car_reservations from Section 2.8.2. The selector => is used to address a static component of a class. There is a rather complex behavior involved. The addressing of zcl_car_reservations results in the execution of the static constructor of the reservation class from Listing 2.7 before the assignment, which generates an object of the class, resulting in the execution of the instance constructor from Listing 2.8. After generating the object, the static attribute car_reservations holds a reference to the object, and this is assigned to reservations. Instead of using the auxiliary variable reservations, we could always work directly with zcl_car_reservations=>car_reservations in our program. The auxiliary variable makes the program easier to understand, though.

Reservation object

The DO statement opens a loop terminated with ENDDO, in which the customer object can perform multiple reservations.

DO loop

The statement after TRY calls the method reserve_a_car of the customer object, passing the reference to the reservation object in reservations. The selector -> is used here for the addressing of an instance component of an object to which the object reference variable in front (here, customer) is pointing. If the exception zcx_no_car_available occurs, it is handled with a message.

Method call

Then the function module POPUP_TO_CONFIRM predefined by the system is used to ask whether another reservation should be made for the customer, and the loop is then either continued, or terminated with EXIT.

Finally, the method persist_reservations of the reservation object is called before the main method finishes to write out the changes to the reservations to the database.

Now we still have to find a way to execute the main method.

2.8.5 Creating a Transaction Code

If you try to execute the activated subroutine pool like an executable program by means of **Test** (F8), you will quickly discover that it won't work. A subroutine pool has no predefined starting point, like START-OF-SELECTION for executable programs. Executable programs represent a real exception in this case among the other program types. For all other program types (and this is true in principle for executable programs as well), the magic word for program execution is *transaction*.

Transaction

The name "transaction," like the name "report" for an executable program, is historical in nature and the reason for its usage in this context is explained by the fact that a classical ABAP application program generally executed a business transaction on the database table. For us, a transaction simply means the execution of an ABAP program via a so-called *transaction code*. A transaction code, in turn, is simply an identifier that is associated with an entry point for an ABAP program. So all we need to do is to associate a transaction code with the main method of the subroutine pool.

To create a transaction code, select **Create · More … · Transaction** from the context menu of our package in the Repository Browser, and fill in the dialog window that appears as shown in Figure 2.74.

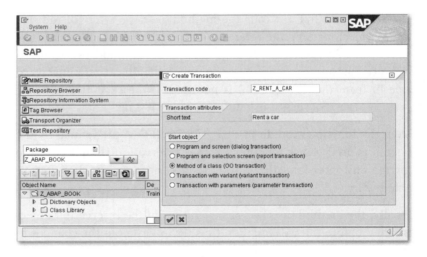

Figure 2.74 Creating a Transaction Code

OO transaction

You can see that there are different entry points in ABAP programs that can be associated with transaction codes, from which we select the **Method of a class**. In the next screen, you must maintain the properties of the so-called *OO transaction*, as shown in Figure 2.75.

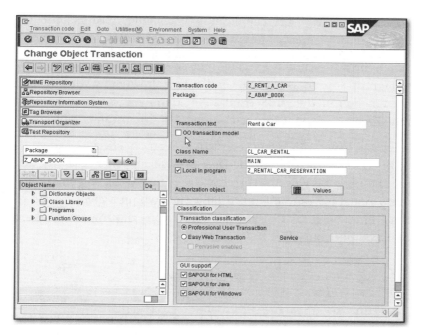

Figure 2.75 Properties of a Transaction

First, remove the check from **OO transaction model**. Otherwise, the transaction code can only be associated with a method from a global class, and at the same time is subject to transaction management in Object Services (see Section 10.2.4). Then you can fill in the input fields as shown in order to associate the transaction code with the method `main` of local class `cl_car_rental` in program `z_rental_car_reservation`, and save the OO transaction.

This concludes the creation of our sample application. In the Repository Browser of the Object Navigator, you should now see all the components of the application, hierarchically organized, and you can access them at will.

2.8.6 Executing the Transaction

Now you can call the `main` method via transaction code Z_RENT_A_CAR in AS ABAP. For testing, it should suffice to select **Execute** in the Object Navigator. But you can also insert the transaction code into your Favorites menu in SAP Easy Access, as mentioned at the end of Section 2.2.1, or you can simply type it into the input field of the standard toolbar. In a real application, you would, of course, provide it to your users as a function in a suitable interface.

When the transaction is executed, the selection screens of our function group appear, as expected and as you already saw while testing the function module in Section 2.7.4. Here, you can now perform rental car reservations for the customers in the customer table.

After you have made a few reservations, you can check the contents of the reservation table in the Data Browser in order to verify that the application is working correctly (see Figure 2.76). As you can see, every rental car can be booked only once within a given period of time. In the next section, you'll see how you can program this kind of list output yourself.

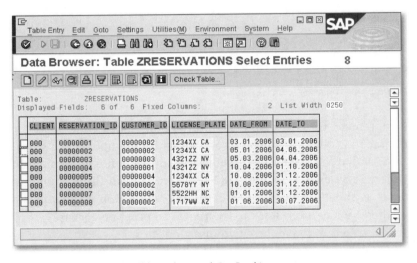

Figure 2.76 Reservation Table with Rental Car Bookings

Debugging mode If the functions of this sample application interest you in greater detail, we recommend running it in debugging mode. For instance, use **Set/delete breakpoint** to set a breakpoint on the assignment of the reference to the reservation object to auxiliary variable reserva-tions in the cl_car_rental class in the z_rental_car_reservation program. Execute the statement in a single step and watch the contents of the reference variable. Prior to creating the object, the debugger shows the content "{O:INITIAL}" as a sign that the reference variable isn't pointing anywhere. After the execution of CREATE OBJECT, though, "{O:nn*\CLASS=ZCL_CAR_RESERVATIONS}" is displayed, meaning that the reference variable now points to an object of this class (the number "nn" is an internal code that can take on different values). You can select the contents of the reference variable by double-clicking on it to display the contents of the attributes and so on (see Figure 2.77).

Figure 2.77 Application Program in the ABAP Debugger

2.8.7 Reporting

The sample application presented in the last few sections handled transactional tasks, that is, data is entered, processed, and stored. Transactional tasks are one of the pillars of business programming. The other is reporting, that is, searching, reading, and presenting stored data. ABAP provides everything you need for reporting. ABAP was originally an acronym for the German phrase "Allgemeiner Berichts-Aufbereitungs Prozessor," that is, "Generic Report Preparation Processor," so it's not accidental that the introductory statement for an executable program is REPORT and an executable program is started using **System • Services • Reporting**.

Prerequisites All you need for simple reporting is:

- Open SQL to read data from database tables
- Internal tables for temporary storage and processing of data in the program memory
- A viewer to present tables on the screen

To conclude our practical introduction, Listing 2.14 shows an executable program that works as a report. The report reads all the data from our reservation table into an internal table, and presents it in the *SAP List Viewer* (ALV). Figure 2.78 shows the list output of our report, which shows the same data as the data browser in Figure 2.76.

Listing 2.14 Report

```
REPORT z_show_reservations.

CLASS report_reservations DEFINITION.
  PUBLIC SECTION.
    CLASS-METHODS show_all.
ENDCLASS.
CLASS report_reservations IMPLEMENTATION.
  METHOD show_all.
    DATA: reservations TYPE TABLE OF zreservations,
          alv          TYPE REF TO cl_salv_table.
    SELECT *
           FROM zreservations
           INTO TABLE reservations
           ORDER BY date_from.
    TRY.
        cl_salv_table=>factory(
          IMPORTING r_salv_table = alv
          CHANGING t_table = reservations ).
        alv->display( ).
      CATCH cx_salv_msg.
        MESSAGE 'ALV display not possible' TYPE 'I'
                DISPLAY LIKE 'E'.
    ENDTRY.
  ENDMETHOD.
ENDCLASS.
START-OF-SELECTION.
  report_reservations=>show_all( ).
```

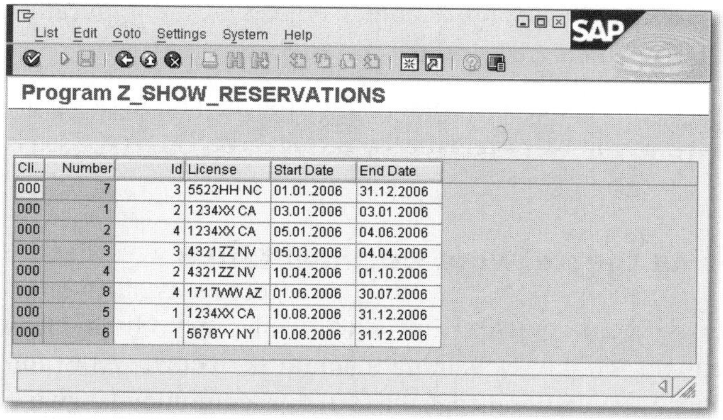

Cli...	Number	Id	License	Start Date	End Date
000	7	3	5522HH NC	01.01.2006	31.12.2006
000	1	2	1234XX CA	03.01.2006	03.01.2006
000	2	4	1234XX CA	05.01.2006	04.06.2006
000	3	3	4321ZZ NV	05.03.2006	04.04.2006
000	4	2	4321ZZ NV	10.04.2006	01.10.2006
000	8	4	1717WW AZ	01.06.2006	30.07.2006
000	5	1	1234XX CA	10.08.2006	31.12.2006
000	6	1	5678YY NY	10.08.2006	31.12.2006

Figure 2.78 List Output

2.9 Summary

If you've followed this practical introduction from beginning to end, you've already learned a few things about ABAP and you now have solid basic knowledge about the ABAP Workbench that will come in handy throughout this book:

- You can work with the tools in the ABAP Workbench, the navigation mechanisms, and the ABAP Debugger.
- You know what repository objects are and have an idea of how they are managed in packages.
- You know the role of ABAP programs in implementing applications in the layer between the persistence and the presentation layers.
- You can create and use database tables.
- You have gotten to know the definitions in the ABAP Dictionary as the connection between the components of an application.
- You know the syntax of ABAP.
- You know the general structure of ABAP programs.
- You know that ABAP programs can have different program types.
- You have already worked with global and local classes.
- You know how ABAP programs are executed.

You can use the result of this practical introduction as a starting point for extending the application on your own. For instance, you could create not just one, but many customer objects in the application program and have them make rental car reservations.

In the course of this book, the topics that we touched on in this practical introduction will be systematically introduced.

2.10 Using the Keyword Documentation

In the listings of our practical introduction, we have used many ABAP statements without explaining them in more detail. As is normal for a fourth Generation Language (4GL) programming language, the tokens of an ABAP statement are generally already meaningful enough to express their function. Control structures like IF ... ENDIF are already familiar to any developer anyway. We will systematically cover the important ABAP-specific concepts in the chapters that follow.

For detailed explanations of all the ABAP language elements introduced in this book, however, we refer you to the *The Official ABAP Reference* published by SAP PRESS, and the ABAP keyword documentation available online. This documentation is available to you in all phases of program development, and you can access it most easily by placing the cursor on an ABAP word in the ABAP Editor and pressing the [F1] key. Figure 2.79 shows the ABAP keyword documentation for the SELECT statement.

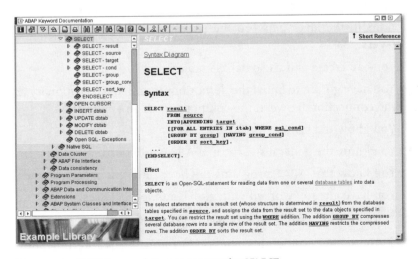

Figure 2.79 ABAP Keyword Documentation for SELECT

The ABAP keyword documentation was completely reworked in terms of content and form for Release 6.40, and represents a broad knowledge base for all aspects of the ABAP programming language. The new appearance is shown here. If you don't have access to an ABAP system at Release 6.40 or higher, we refer you again to *The Official ABAP Reference* and *The ABAP Quick Reference* from SAP PRESS.

The documents of the ABAP keyword documentation are organized in a tree structure, which reflects their topical relationships. Behind each entry node on a topic, there are documents introducing the topic.

Display

As you can see in Figure 2.79 for SELECT, complicated syntax diagrams are simplified by using pseudosyntax, making their function comprehensible at a glance. You can navigate from the simplified syntax diagram to the actual syntax for partial expressions. To display the complete syntax diagram, you can select **Short Reference** in the upper right-hand corner of the screen, where pseudosyntax is used only occasionally (see Figure 2.80). You can also click on **Syntax Diagram** to view graphical syntax diagrams.

Figure 2.80 Short Reference for SELECT

The ABAP keyword documentation offers you four different types of reference, which are denoted by different colors:

References

- ▶ References within documents or to other documents in the tree structure (blue)

- ▶ References to documents in the SAP Knowledge Warehouse (red)

- ▶ Calls of programs and transactions of the current AS ABAP in a different window (green)

- ▶ References to the ABAP glossary (gray)

Knowledge Warehouse
The Knowledge Warehouse, whose documents are also available through the SAP Help Portal (*http://help.sap.com*), contains introductory and advanced documentation on ABAP topics, like the description of associated tools. The ABAP keyword documentation, on the other hand, is part of the ABAP scope of delivery and is available in AS ABAP.

ABAP glossary
The ABAP glossary is an integral part of the ABAP keyword documentation, which explains the terms used in the documentation. In the glossary entries, reference is generally made to other glossary terms or to documents in the tree structure. A list of all glossary entries is also in the tree structure (see Figure 2.81).

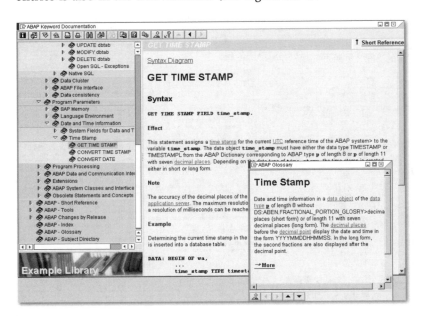

Figure 2.81 ABAP Glossary

Index search
To search for ABAP language elements or other ABAP terms, the ABAP keyword documentation provides an index search and a full-

text search. When using the ⌑F1⌑ help on a keyword, the index searches an index of all language elements based on an indexing of the documents, which can be viewed as a document in the tree structure. If you enter a term into the display window of the ABAP keyword documentation after selecting the function **Help on ...** in the ABAP Editor, after calling the ABAPHELP transaction, or after selecting **Index search**, the index search also searches a keyword list and the list of glossary entries. If no exact matching term can be found, a similarity search is performed. Figure 2.82 shows the list of hits in the index search if you search for "XML". As you can see, there are two XML additions for the CALL TRANSFORMATION statement, a keyword that refers to an overview article, and a glossary entry for XML.

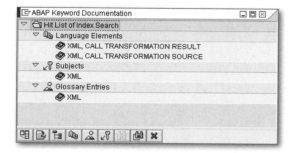

Figure 2.82 Hit List of the Index Search

Full-text search can be used as an alternative to index searching if you enter terms manually. Furthermore, the hit list of the index search can be switched to full-text search by clicking on the appropriate icon, and vice versa. After a full-text search, the positions found in the selected document are highlighted (see Figure 2.83).

Full-text search

Last but not least, we would like to mention that you can double-click on the **Example Library** picture to navigate from the display of the ABAP keyword documentation to a list of executable sample programs.[11]

Example library

---

11 In the next release of SAP NetWeaver, the display and use of the executable sample programs will be fully integrated into the ABAP keyword documentation and its index search.

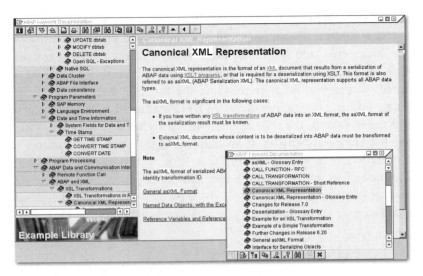

Figure 2.83 Full-Text Search

"Basic research = What I do, when I don't know what I'm doing."—Wernher von Braun

3 Basic Principles of ABAP

This chapter describes the role of ABAP within SAP NetWeaver and gives you an overview of the technical fundamentals and the organization of an ABAP program.

3.1 ABAP and SAP NetWeaver

This section describes the role of ABAP in SAP NetWeaver and introduces you to the Application Server ABAP (AS ABAP).

3.1.1 SAP NetWeaver

Not that long ago, the world of ABAP was relatively simple. There were SAP systems (generally R/3 systems) based on SAP Basis, which represented a runtime environment for ABAP programs.

Today, SAP's technology platform is called *SAP NetWeaver*, and the R/3 system has evolved into a complete product family currently known as *mySAP Business Suite*. With SAP NetWeaver, SAP is distributing its technology as a proprietary product for the first time. The former SAP Basis system (which was also named "SAP Web Application Server" in the interim) was not independently marketed, but was usually only delivered along with an R/3 system. Ultimately, an SAP Basis became equated with an R/3 system without any application programs. Conversely, an R/3 system was an SAP Basis system with application programs.

Technology platform

In SAP NetWeaver, there is a much stronger separation between technology and application. The goal of the SAP NetWeaver platform is to allow SAP customers to bring together their IT solutions, be they SAP or non-SAP solutions, in such a way that the user can see them as a single closed system. In short, SAP NetWeaver offers an entire group of so-called *usage types*. Important usage types include:

- Application Server (AS)
- Business Intelligence (BI)
- SAP NetWeaver Portal (EP)
- Mobile Infrastructure (MI)
- Process Integration (PI)

The users of SAP NetWeaver can decide which of the usage types they need, individually or in combination, for their requirements. You will find an introduction and case studies for this in the book *SAP NetWeaver Roadmap* by Steffen Karch and Loren Heilig (SAP PRESS 2005). The primary argument in favor of using such a technology platform is that SAP NetWeaver offers capabilities that can be linked together easily to apply to certain scenarios, such as "application development in ABAP." For example, at a demo jam session at the US SAP TechEd 2005 (in Boston), the application server's ABAP programming was used to perform a demonstration using a very common mobile device (Blackberry™). This corresponds to linking the usage type MI with AS.

3.1.2 The Application Server

The usage type Application Server (AS) is responsible for the persistent storing of data and its processing. For that reason, AS plays an integral role in SAP NetWeaver (see Figure 3.1). It offers programming interfaces that allow other components of SAP NetWeaver, such as the SAP NetWeaver Portal, to request data, have it edited, or store it, without these other components needing to directly access the actual data storage. The primary data storage of a NetWeaver AS is usually a central database.

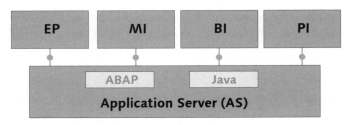

Figure 3.1 Central Role of the Application Server (AS)

The application server essentially offers two programming inter- ABAP and Java
faces, ABAP and Java. To put it more precisely, the "Application
Server" usage type in SAP NetWeaver comprises two usage types: the
Application Server ABAP (AS ABAP) and the Application Server Java
(AS Java). Both application servers work on different data (different
database schemes that can nevertheless be located in the same database) and are linked together by allowing mutual access through the
Java Connector (JCo, see Section 12.2.5). When you install an application server, you can opt for one of the two variants, or you can
decide to install both variants at the same time:

▶ The AS Java allows for application programming in Java based on
J2EE. You will find more information on this in the book *Java Pro-
gramming with the SAP Web Application Server* by Karl Kessler,
Peter Tillert, and Panayot Dobrikov (SAP PRESS 2005).

▶ The AS ABAP allows for application programming in ABAP, based
on ABAP Objects. The AS ABAP is what the current book is about.

3.1.3 The Application Server ABAP

The Application Server ABAP (AS ABAP) is the part of the application
server usage type in SAP NetWeaver with which applications can be
programmed in ABAP. It provides the ABAP runtime environment
that is a virtual machine for ABAP programs independent of the
hardware, operating system, and database system. The ABAP Workbench, with its integrated change and transport system (CTS), is used
to create applications. It is part of the scope of delivery. Currently,
most of the applications that SAP delivers are programmed in ABAP
and are executed on installations of AS ABAP.

Figure 3.2 shows a very simplified overview of the main Application
Server ABAP components.

AS ABAP can be used by people or by other software, including the
remaining components of SAP NetWeaver. People can access it using
user interfaces that are available in the form of web browsers or SAP
GUIs installed on desktop PCs. Other software components generally
access it through the network, for which two main protocols are
used: HTTP/HTTPS/SMTP for Internet connections and SAP's own
Remote Function Call (RFC) protocol for calling ABAP functionality
through any external clients. For connecting to the Internet, the AS

ABAP uses a so-called *Internet Communication Manager* (ICM). The RFC interface is responsible for RFC connections.

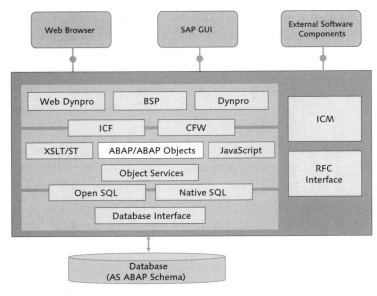

Figure 3.2 Application Server ABAP (AS ABAP)

If you have been using SAP technology for some time, you will quickly notice in Figure 3.2 that the components of the old SAP Basis you are already familiar with—namely SAP GUI, Dynpro, ABAP, Open SQL, Native SQL, the database interface, and RFC—still exist as they always have as part of AS ABAP, and that you can therefore also regard the AS ABAP as a compatible enhancement of SAP Basis for the requirements of SAP NetWeaver.

Layer architecture Although the term "client-server architecture" has actually been rendered obsolete in the context of SAP NetWeaver, most of the components of AS ABAP can be divided according to their tasks into three layers of a client-server system, which play an essential role, particularly, when the system is used with the user interfaces:[1]

▶ Presentation layer

▶ Application layer

▶ Persistence layer

---

1 Incidentally, this applies equally to the NetWeaver AS Java, into which many proven ABAP concepts were transferred.

Presentation Layer

The components of the presentation layer are responsible for everything to do with the presentation of data for users and the receiving of user entries. User interfaces for AS ABAP include commercial web browsers and SAP's SAP GUI (Graphical User Interface). When web browsers are used in application programs, HTML pages prepared in the presentation layer are accessed. Application programs access these HTML pages through the classes and interfaces of the Internet Connection Framework (ICF), which wrap the HTML pages. Presentation in a web browser is based on Web Dynpro ABAP and Business Server Pages (BSP):

Web browser vs. SAP GUI

▶ **Web Dynpro ABAP**

The term Web Dynpro stands for an MVC-based technology[2] for creating platform-independent web-based interfaces. There is a version for AS Java and a version for AS ABAP, both of which are based on exactly the same architecture and differ from each other only by the programming language used. Web Dynpro for ABAP is SAP's future standard UI technology for the development of web applications in the ABAP environment, because the MVC approach means that provision is made automatically for the decoupling of the presentation and application logic (see Section 9.5).

MVC

▶ **Business Server Pages (BSP)**

A Business Server Page, similar to a Java Server Page (JSP), is a user interface coded in HTML of an AS ABAP Internet application; some of its content is dynamic. Business Server Pages can incorporate server-side scripts written directly in ABAP (or JavaScript). When you compile a script written in ABAP, an ABAP objects class is generated in the application layer whose methods implement the functions of the script.

HTML plus dynamic content

Business Server Pages represent the predecessor technology of Web Dynpro ABAP. They are more fundamental than web dynpros in that the MVC approach is supported, but is not a prerequisite. Web applications that consist of more than one server page should therefore, if possible, be realized by web dynpros for

---

2 The Model View Controller (MVC) concept separates the different interests of a program. It consists of three components. The data model (model) describes the application, the presentation (view) describes the display, the program control (controller) describes the reaction to user actions.

which the MVC approach has already been appropriately implemented. For more information on Business Server Pages see the book *Web Programming in ABAP with the SAP Web Application Server* by Frédéric Heinemann and Christian Rau (2nd Edition, SAP PRESS 2005).

SAP GUI ▶ **Dynpro (Dynamic program)**
When you use the SAP GUI that is available in versions for MS Windows, Java and web browser, screens are displayed that are based on an SAP dialog interface. The presentation in the SAP GUI is based on the (classical) dynpro technology.

A dynpro defines a user interface of an ABAP program in a window of the SAP GUI. Each dynpro is a component of an ABAP program. The screen of a dynpro can contain a set of predefined screen elements or GUI controls. Access to the latter is wrapped by the classes of a Control Framework (CFW). In addition to the actual screen, a dynpro also contains a screen processing logic written in a separate programming language that calls so-called *dialog modules* in the corresponding ABAP program. In addition to general dynpros, which are created with a special editor, there are also special dynpros (for selection screens and lists) that are generated directly from ABAP statements.

Although the separation in the ABAP program (model), screen (view), and screen processing logic (controller) would, in theory, allow for the use of the MVC approach, this method is not supported by a framework and appropriate tools for dynpros. In particular, it is not required that presentation logic for dynpros coded in ABAP, for example, an input check, be separated from the actual application logic. In most dynpro-based applications, presentation logic and application logic are often tightly coupled in *a single* program, which makes such a program difficult to maintain, less robust, and almost impossible to reuse. For this reason, the user interfaces of new applications should be designed primarily with Web Dynpro ABAP, even if it is not initially intended to use the system via the Internet.

In the future, classical dynpros should be reserved for special applications whose presentation can remain restricted to the SAP GUI and which could only be implemented using web dynpro technology with great difficulty. One example is the ABAP Workbench, whose interface is based on dynpros and which does not necessarily need to be operative using a web browser. When you use classical dynpros, however, you must always ensure yourself that the presentation logic and application logic are kept separate.

Application Layer

The application layer is the software layer of AS ABAP in which application programs are executed. The application layer contains a kernel written primarily in C/C++ that serves as a platform for application programs, which is independent from hardware, operating system, and database. The kernel of AS ABAP provides processors (Virtual Machines) for the following programming languages:

Virtual Machines

▶ **ABAP with ABAP Objects**
ABAP (Advanced Business Application Programming), together with its integrated enhancement ABAP Objects, is the programming interface of SAP NetWeaver AS for business management applications. The corresponding ABAP processor accounts for the largest part of the AS ABAP kernel. ABAP programs are created with the ABAP Editor, which can be used either as an independent application, or as an add-on to other tools such as Object Navigator or Class Builder.

▶ **XSLT and ST**
XSLT (Extensible Stylesheet Language Transformation) allows XML formats to be converted into any other XML formats. Simple Transformation (ST) is an SAP-specific language used to transform ABAP data to XML and vice versa. The AS ABAP kernel contains SAP-specific XSLT processors and ST processors to execute XSLT and ST programs. XSLT and ST programs are edited with the Transformation Editor of the ABAP Workbench and can be called with the ABAP statement CALL TRANSFORMATION (see Section 12.5.3).

▶ **JavaScript**
A JavaScript (JS) Engine is also integrated into the kernel of the AS ABAP. JavaScript programs can be executed here. Variables of the script can be linked to data objects of an ABAP program. This engine was introduced to also allow JavaScript as a language for the server-side scripting in BSPs beside ABAP; however, there is no dedicated editor for JavaScript programs in the ABAP Workbench. In ABAP programs, the CL_JAVA_SCRIPT system class

offers an interface to the JavaScript Engine; however, use of this language on AS ABAP has only negligible significance and therefore will not be discussed any further in this book.

In the same way that AS ABAP plays a central role in SAP NetWeaver (see Figure 3.1), the ABAP programming language and the programs written in ABAP play an integral role in AS ABAP. An ABAP program generally receives entries from the presentation layer or from other software components, processes data from or saves data in the persistence layer, and transfers processed data to the presentation layer or to external clients. The corresponding data transfer can be performed either rather directly or through frameworks. Examples where there is a direct data transfer between application programs and the other layers include the use of classical dynpros in the presentation layer and database tables accessed via Open SQL. Additionally, frameworks can be used that, although they are entirely or partially also programmed in ABAP, disconnect the direct data access from the application program. Examples include the ICF and CFW frameworks between the application program and presentation layer and Object Services (consisting of a persistence, transaction, and query service; see Section 10.2) between the application program and the persistence layer.

Persistence Layer

The persistence layer is the AS ABAP software layer in which persistent data is held in a database. Each AS ABAP accesses a central database on which its entire dataset is stored. This means that not only the application types, but also all administrative data, Customizing settings, and ABAP source codes, for example, are contained here.

Database interface In principle, the central database can be accessed by ABAP programs through the database interface of AS ABAP. This interface makes AS ABAP independent from the database system that is actually used. The database interface is an interface to the database of an ABAP-based SAP system and is integrated into the ABAP runtime environment. The database interface is subdivided into an Open SQL interface and a native SQL interface:

▶ **Open SQL**
  Open SQL is the collective term for a subset of the Structured Query Language (SQL) realized by ABAP statements and includes

the Data Manipulation Language (DML) portion. The statements of Open SQL access the AS ABAP database through the Open SQL interface, irrespective of the platform. With Open SQL, you can read (SELECT) and change (INSERT, UPDATE, MODIFY, DELETE) data in database tables that are defined in the ABAP Dictionary. The Open SQL interface converts Open SQL statements into manufacturer-specific SQL and passes it onto the database system.

▶ **Native SQL**

Native SQL refers to statements that can be executed in ABAP programs between the EXEC SQL and ENDEXEC statements. Database-specific SQL statements and some SAP-specific statements are possible. The native SQL interface passes on the manufacturer-specific SQL statements, unchanged, to the database system.

Only the statements from Open SQL should be used in application programs. More information on this subject will be provided in Section 10.1.

Communication Components

We have already mentioned the communication components ICM and RFC interface. Those are positioned somewhat aside from the three layers:

▶ **ICM**

The Internet Communication Manager (ICM) is a process in the AS ABAP kernel that allows it to communicate directly with the Internet via HTTP/HTTPS/SMTP. The ICM allows connection to web-based presentation components such as Web Dynpro ABAP and BSP. In addition, it enables an AS ABAP to act both as a client and as a server for Web services (see Section 12.4). ABAP programs access the ICM through the classes and interfaces of the Internet Communication Framework (ICF) (see Section 12.3).

Communication with the Internet

▶ **RFC Interface**

This is the classical functional AS ABAP interface. A Remote Function Call (RFC) is an invocation of a function that is located in a different system than the one in which the calling program is running. Calls are possible between different AS ABAPs, or between an AS ABAP and an external system. On an AS ABAP, the functions are realized by function modules (see Section 7.2.1). In

Function call

external systems, specially programmed functions are called, instead of function modules, whose interface simulates a function module. You will find more on RFCs in Section 12.2.

3.1.4 The ABAP Runtime Environment

The Application Server ABAP described in the last section forms the environment of every ABAP program. Without an AS ABAP installation, no ABAP programming is possible. An ABAP program is therefore independent of the hardware and the actual operating system, but it cannot be executed without an AS ABAP. The infrastructure of the AS ABAP serves as a mediator for the communication between the ABAP applications and the users of the Application Server on the one hand, and the database system on the other hand.

We can therefore simplify the image from Figure 3.2 to that of Figure 3.3 by saying that each ABAP program is embedded in a runtime environment provided by AS ABAP.

Processes and processors

For an ABAP program, the ABAP runtime environment represents the highest controlling instance. Without it, no ABAP program would be able to run. This is because not only is it responsible for communication with the outside world, but also for the sequential processing of an ABAP program. For this, the runtime environment contains so-called *processors* that execute the ABAP programs. The execution of an ABAP program is always synonymous with a process in the ABAP runtime environment, which controls the ABAP program from its outside by calling certain units (so-called *processing blocks*, see Section 3.2.6), as we have indicated in Figure 3.3. The picture is thus of fundamental importance for the entire ABAP programming. There is a whole array of purpose-oriented processors. However most of these are primarily connected to procedural (event-oriented), non-object-oriented ABAP programming (see Chapter 7) and have greatly lost their significance for modern programming in ABAP Objects.

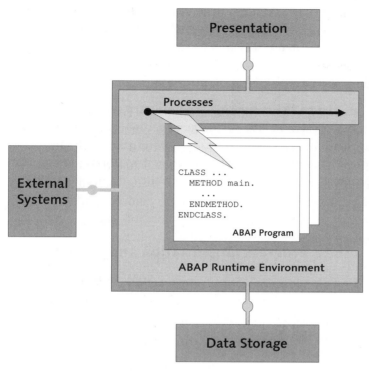

Figure 3.3 The ABAP Runtime Environment

3.1.5 The Text Environment

The text environment is an important part of the runtime environment of an ABAP program. It affects all of the operations that depend on the AS ABAP character set. The text environment consists of a language, a system code page, and a locale. By default, the text environment of an AS ABAP is determined by the logon language with which a user logs onto the AS ABAP.

The language affects, among other things, the data preparation for displays on the screen or when printing. Furthermore, it determines from which text pool the source code-independent texts of a program are read. These are headers, captions for input fields on screens, and the so-called *text symbols* (see Section 5.1.10).

Language

An AS ABAP is either a Unicode system or a non-Unicode system. The system code page of a Unicode system is UTF-16. A non-Unicode system is either a single code page system with a non-Unicode sys-

Unicode system

tem code page, such as ASCII, or an MDMP system (multi-display-, multi-processing system) with several non-Unicode system code pages. SAP recommends that an AS ABAP be set up only as a Unicode system. In a Unicode system, you must set the program attribute **Unicode Checks Active** (see Section 3.2.5) for each ABAP program.

Locale
The locale defines the language- and country-specific features of characters, for example, the sort sequence, conversion between capital and small letters, etc. In Unicode systems, the locale properties are defined in an operating-system-independent library; in non-Unicode systems, the locale is dependent on the current operating system.

3.2   ABAP Program Organization and Properties

This section presents the general organization of ABAP programs. We will describe the structure of ABAP programs, how ABAP programs are executed on AS ABAP, what program types there are, and what attributes they have.

3.2.1   ABAP Program Design

Each ABAP program that represents a compilation unit (these are all programs except for include programs, see Section 3.3.1) begins with a program introduction (such as REPORT, PROGRAM, or FUNCTION-POOL) as the first statement and then consists of a global declaration part and an implementation part. This separation is not expressed by syntactic limits. Instead, it should always be expressed by comments or a matching source code modularization through include programs.

Global Declaration Part

Declarations
The global declaration part follows directly after the program introduction. In the global declaration part of a program, declarative statements can be listed for:

- Data types (see Section 5.1.2)
- Object types (classes and interfaces, see Chapters 4 and 6)
- Data objects (variables and constants, see Section 5.1.1)
- Field symbols (see Section 11.1.1)

The definitions listed in the global declaration part of a program are visible in the implementation part of the program.[3] During programming with ABAP Objects, a global declaration part mainly contains the declarations of classes and interfaces. For reasons of encapsulation, all other declarations should be done only within classes. Data objects, in particular, are only declared as attributes of classes then. The declaration of data objects that are visible in the entire program is meanwhile only necessary in exceptional cases (interface work areas for classical dynpros, see Section 9.1.6).

Implementation Part

Under the global declaration part follows the implementation part, in which the functions of a program are implemented in processing blocks. Each operational statement, that is, essentially every non-declarative statement of a program, is part of a processing block. Processing blocks are indivisible syntactical units, and a processing block cannot contain any other processing block. The main processing blocks of ABAP Objects are the methods of the classes declared in the global declaration part. The methods of a class are syntactically bundled in the implementation part of the program. In addition to the implementations of methods, an implementation part can also contain additional processing blocks that support the procedural/event-oriented programming model (see Chapter 7). The sequence in which implementations are listed in the implementation part is irrelevant.

Processing blocks

An important differentiating characteristic for processing blocks is whether they can contain local data:

▶ Processing blocks with local data are called *procedures*. The procedures of ABAP Objects are methods. In addition, function modules also play a role (see Section 7.2.1). A third type of procedure is the *subroutine*, however, subroutines must be considered to be obsolete in the context of ABAP Objects (see Section 7.2.2). All procedures have interfaces that allow the passing of parameters and exception handling.

Procedures

---

3 More accurately, a declaration is visible in all of the statements that follow the declaration statements.

▶ In addition to procedures, ABAP also knows processing blocks without local data. These are known as *dialog modules* for processing classical dynpros (see Section 9.1.9) and *event blocks*, which handle events of processes in the ABAP runtime environment. For programming with ABAP Objects, dialog modules and event blocks act as points of entry into a program (see Section 3.2.2) from which methods are called; however, these processing blocks should no longer contain any functional coding.

The example in Listing 3.1 shows the general design of an ABAP program.

Listing 3.1 Local Class of a Subroutine Pool

```
REPORT z_program_layout.

**********************************************************
* Global Declarations
**********************************************************
INTERFACE intf.
  METHODS meth IMPORTING text TYPE csequence.
ENDINTERFACE.
CLASS cls DEFINITION.
  PUBLIC SECTION.
    INTERFACES intf.
ENDCLASS.
CLASS demo DEFINITION.
  PUBLIC SECTION.
    CLASS-METHODS main.
ENDCLASS.
**********************************************************
* Implementations
**********************************************************
CLASS cls IMPLEMENTATION.
  METHOD intf~meth.
    MESSAGE text TYPE 'I'.
  ENDMETHOD.
ENDCLASS.
CLASS demo IMPLEMENTATION.
  METHOD main.
    DATA oref TYPE REF TO intf.
    CREATE OBJECT oref TYPE cls.
    oref->meth( 'Hello ABAP!' ).
```

```
  ENDMETHOD.
ENDCLASS.
START-OF-SELECTION.
  demo=>main( ).
```

After the program introduction REPORT follows the global declaration part with the definition of an interface and two classes. The methods of the classes are implemented in the implementation part. In addition, the implementation part contains an event block START-OF-SELECTION, in which the static method main of the demo class is called. This method contains a local reference variable through which an object of the cls class is created and whose interface method meth is called, passing a value to the text parameter. This event block is the point of entry to the program. If you create and execute the program in the ABAP Editor (SE38) *as an executable program* (see Section 3.2.4), a process in the ABAP runtime environment triggers the corresponding event, whereupon the event block is called by the runtime environment. An ABAP program is therefore never run sequentially from top to bottom. Only the code within a processing block is executed sequentially.

3.2.2 ABAP Program Execution

From our discussion in Section 3.2.1, it is clear that executing an ABAP program must be synonymous with calling a processing block. Processing blocks can either be called from the ABAP runtime environment or from other processing blocks—the latter is also possible beyond the program boundaries. Each time a program is executed, at least one processing block is called by the runtime environment as a point of entry, which, in turn, can call additional processing blocks (in ABAP Objects these are methods) of the same program or in other programs (in ABAP Objects these are class pools and also function groups).[4] When you call the first processing block of a program, the entire program is loaded into the memory. When the last processing block of a program is terminated, control is returned to the calling program or the runtime environment.

Point of entry

---

4 Using the ABAP Debugger you can view a list of the calls of processing blocks that have been made up to that point and navigate into these at any point in a program.

Termination There are two ways to end the execution of a processing block. First, the execution is always complete when the last statement of the processing block has been executed. Secondly, you can explicitly exit a processing block using the statement

RETURN RETURN.

During each such termination, control is returned to the caller of the processing block, that is, either to the runtime environment or to the calling processing block. Besides these two proper terminations, a processing block can be terminated by an exception. Depending on whether or not it is possible to treat the error with the recourses of ABAP, the runtime environment either calls the exception handler or terminates the current program altogether (more on this in Section 8.2).

3.2.3 ABAP Program Calls

If you're using the AS ABAP via the SAP GUI, you have two options for starting ABAP programs:

▶ Calling executable programs
▶ Calling by using transaction codes

All other uses of ABAP programs are accomplished through interfaces (see Figure 3.2) and are based either on calling function modules via the RFC interface (see Section 12.2), or on calling methods of the ICF (see Section 12.3), where the procedures then act as points of entry.

In this context, we should point out once again that ABAP programs, like all development objects that can be edited in the ABAP Workbench, are repository objects (see Section 2.2.2), and after their activation are in principle visible for every user or every program of an AS ABAP. To restrict this general accessibility, the attributes of the corresponding package (see Section 2.3) can be set accordingly, or authorization checks (see Section 10.5) can be provided.

Calling Executable Programs

An executable program (see Section 3.2.4) can be executed directly in the ABAP Editor using the **Execute** function or using Transaction

SA38. When you call an executable program, a special process is started in the ABAP runtime environment that first triggers the event that calls the event block `START-OF-SELECTION` from which you can then branch into methods. Further events then follow, but they no longer have any significance for programming with ABAP Objects (see Section 7.1.1). An important property of executable programs is that they can also be started in background processing and not only as a dialog application.

To call an executable program from another program, that is, in ABAP Objects from a method, the statement

`SUBMIT ...`

SUBMIT

can be used. From a technical point of view, the accessibility through `SUBMIT` is the main characteristic of an executable program. From the user's perspective, executable programs are the only ABAP programs that can be started by entering their name; internally, however, all that happens is that the specified program is called through `SUBMIT`. In the `SUBMIT` statement, you can use the addition `AND RETURN` to specify whether the system returns to the caller after the called program is terminated.

You are already familiar with examples for executing executable programs with our "Hello World" programs in Section 2.5.4.

Calling via Transaction Codes

A transaction code is a development object that can be created in the ABAP Workbench (transaction maintenance SE93). A transaction code is a twenty-character identifier that is linked with a point of entry for a program, and a transaction is the execution of an ABAP program via a transaction code.[5] There are essentially two types of transactions:

Transaction

▶ **Dialog transactions**

In these transactions, the transaction code is linked with a dynpro of an ABAP program. When the transaction is called, the corre-

---

5 This definition of the term *transaction* for a program execution is based on its general definition in Online Transaction Processing (OLTP), where it stands for a user request. In the context of accesses to database tables, however, "transaction" stands for a status change in the database.

sponding program is loaded and the dynpro is called. The corresponding processor of the ABAP runtime environment is the dynpro processor. For more information, see Section 9.1.4.

▶ **OO transactions**

In these transactions, the transaction code is linked with a method of a local or global class. When the transaction is called, the corresponding program is loaded and the method is executed; with instance methods an object of the class is created. OO transactions can also be linked with the transaction service of the Object Services (see Section 10.2.4).

The most direct way to execute a transaction is to enter an "/n" or "/o" directly followed by a known transaction in the input field of the system function bar of a window of the SAP GUI. /n immediately terminates the current application, while /o opens a parallel main session (see Section 10.2.4) in a new window. The most popular method is of course to link your transaction codes to functions of the SAP GUI and to offer them to the user as menu entries or buttons.

To call a transaction from another program, that is, from a method, the statements

CALL
TRANSACTION

`CALL TRANSACTION ...`

and

LEAVE TO
TRANSACTION

`LEAVE TO TRANSACTION ...`

can be used. After `CALL TRANSACTION`, the system returns to the calling program, and it is irrevocably exited with `LEAVE TO TRANSACTION`. To be precise, with the `LEAVE TO TRANSACTION` statement, apart from the calling program, even all previous programs of a call sequence (see Section 3.4.4) with their data are deleted from the memory. Once the called program is terminated, the program execution returns to the point from which the first program of the call sequence was started.

You have already seen an example for executing an OO transaction in our practical introduction in Section 2.8.5, in which this form of program call is used to start the sample application.

3.2.4 ABAP Program Types

Unlike Java, where programs are simply containers for classes, there are different ABAP program types that play different roles on the AS ABAP. The reason for the multitude of program types is due to the historical development of the ABAP language. Prior to ABAP Objects, for different tasks there were also different specialized program types, which were supported by special processes of the ABAP runtime environment. The earlier program types were not discarded with ABAP Objects. Instead, it was possible to create local classes and interfaces in almost every program. In addition, two special program types were introduced for global classes and interfaces.

Specialization

The following list contains all of the ABAP program types, with the exception of include programs (see Section 3.3.1). We also provide recommendations for their use in ABAP Objects. A tabular overview of the most important attributes of all program types can be found in Appendix A.3.

- ▶ **Class Pools**

  A class pool is a container for exactly one global class that can be used in other programs. In addition to the global class, data types and local object types (classes and interfaces) can be declared in the declaration part of a class pool for use in the global class. A class pool is loaded into the memory by using the global class. For example, a public method of the global class can be called from another ABAP program, or it is linked with a transaction code. When you program with ABAP Objects, the class pool is automatically the most important program type, because all of your reusable code is programmed there. A class pool is created with the Class Builder of the ABAP Workbench, which means that it is generally not displayed as a single continuous source code. Similarly, one normally never gets to see the program introduction `CLASS-POOL`.

  Global class

- ▶ **Interface Pools**

  An interface pool is a container for exactly one global interface that can be included in the classes of other programs (class pools). You use an interface by implementing it in classes. For using such classes, you can create interface reference variables with reference to the interface Like class pools, you create interface pools in the Class Builder. The program introduction is `INTERFACE-POOL`.

  Global interface

Function modules ▸ **Function Groups**

Function groups (also known as function pools) are the only programs that can contain function modules. Function modules are procedures that are designed to be called from other programs. Function groups and their function modules are the procedural predecessors of global classes with public methods. Like executable programs and module pools, function groups can also contain dynpros as components, which is not possible in class pools. Function groups are therefore the first choice when programming with ABAP Objects, if you intend to work with classical dynpros (see Section 9.1.15). Function groups are also required for remote function calls. For other purposes, no new function groups and function modules should be created. Furthermore, no more functional coding should be created in function modules; instead, you should branch from there into methods. Of course, you can continue to call existing function groups that contain reusable function modules from methods. A function group is maintained with the Function Builder of the ABAP Workbench. The program introduction is FUNCTION-POOL.

Subroutines ▸ **Subroutine Pools**

As the name suggests, subroutine pools are containers for subroutines (see Section 7.2.2) that can be called by other programs. Since the use of subroutines—and in particular, calling them externally—is obsolete in programming with ABAP Objects, no more new subroutine pools should be created for this purpose. On the other hand, you can certainly create local classes in subroutine pools and connect their public methods to a transaction code (for example, see the practical introduction in Section 2.8.5). A subroutine pool that contains a class with a main method that is connected to a transaction code is very similar to a Java program. A subroutine pool is maintained directly with the ABAP Editor of the ABAP Workbench. The program introduction is PROGRAM.

Reporting ▸ **Executable Programs**

An executable program was originally designed for reporting, where database content is read and displayed under certain selection conditions according to the IPO principle (input, processing, output). Hence the program introduction with REPORT. Only executable programs can be called using their name, thereby starting a special process in the ABAP runtime environment (see Section

7.1.1). For the programming with ABAP Objects, executable programs should only be used if direct execution using the name is important. From a technical point of view, executable programs are currently only required for background processing. When using executable programs today, you should only handle the event START-OF-SELECTION of the reporting process and jump from the corresponding processing block directly to a method of a local class. An executable program is maintained directly in the ABAP Editor of the ABAP Workbench.

► **Module Pools**

Module pools were originally designed for the so-called dialog programming with dynpros. Like executable programs and function groups, a module pool can contain dynpros as components. In the classical dialog programming, a dynpro of a module pool is linked with a transaction code, which is called through a dialog transaction. The module pool acts as a container for the dialog modules called by the dynpro flow logic. Most of the handling of the dynpros, as well as the entire application logic of a dialog transaction, was programmed there. Module pools no longer play a role in programming with ABAP Objects. Instead, function groups should be used as carriers of dynpros. A module pool is directly maintained with the ABAP Editor of the ABAP Workbench. The program introduction is PROGRAM.

Dialog
programming

► **Type Groups**

Type groups are a predecessor technology for general type definitions in the ABAP Dictionary (see Section 5.1.7) and in global classes or interfaces (see Section 4.5). A type group only contains a declaration part with definitions of data types and constants that, unlike with the remaining program types, are also visible in other programs, if the type group is notified there through the TYPE-POOLS statement. No more new type groups should be created for the programming with ABAP Objects. Instead, types and constants can be published by global classes and interfaces. This has been possible, without any restrictions, since Release 6.40. Nevertheless, you can continue to use existing type groups. A type group is maintained with the ABAP Dictionary tool of the ABAP Workbench. The program introduction is TYPE-POOL.

Global data types

On a productive AS ABAP, you'll find all of these program types in all of their different forms, especially if it contains older application programs. But, for a new development with ABAP Objects, you should use only the recommended program types, as they are summarized here once again:

► You use class and interface pools for reusable code in global classes and interfaces.

► You now create function groups only where technically necessary, that is, as containers for dynpros and for RFC-enabled function modules.

► Subroutine pools can serve as Java-like programs in which you can call exactly one `main` method from outside.

► In principle, the same applies for executable programs as for subroutine pools. Albeit you can call them using `SUBMIT`, which is technically necessary for background processing.

► New module pools or type groups should no longer be created for programming with ABAP Objects.

Most of the program types are determined automatically by the corresponding tool. You can and should only choose the program type yourself for programs that are directly maintained in the ABAP Editor. This affects executable programs, module pools, and subroutine pools. In addition to the above program types, which represent independent compilation units, there are also so-called include programs, which are used for the source code modularization of another program (see Section 3.3.1).

The program type principally leaves the program design, which is outlined in Section 3.2.1, unchanged. Depending on the type, however, different program components may be permitted. For instance, the entire implementation part is absent in an interface pool or a type group.

3.2.5 Other Program Attributes

When you create a program, you can define additional attributes besides the program type, depending on the tool (ABAP Editor, Class Builder, Function Builder, etc.). Like the different program types, there are historical reasons as to why there are so many of these program attributes (see Figure 2.36 in Chapter 2). Generally, the predefined settings of the ABAP Workbench don't need to be changed here:

▶ **Unicode Checks Active**

This attribute should always be activated. It defines a program as a Unicode program in which stricter syntax rules apply and where certain statements reveal more easily understood semantics than in non-Unicode programs. There are:

▶ stricter static type checks

▶ a strict separation of byte- and character string processing

▶ a handling of structured data objects according to their layout

▶ no uncontrolled accesses to memory areas

Only Unicode programs can be executed in Unicode systems and generally produce the same results here as in non-Unicode systems.[6] In this book, we assume that the Unicode checks are always active. You can read up on the differences between Unicode programs and non-Unicode programs in the ABAP keyword documentation or *The Official ABAP Reference* book published by SAP PRESS.

▶ **Fixed-Point Arithmetic**

This attribute determines that for decimal numbers of the type p (packed numbers, see Section 5.1.3) the position of the decimal separator is taken into account in calculations. This attribute should be taken as a given. The option of deactivating this attribute only has historical reasons (which applies equally, in the same way, to the deactivation of the Unicode checks!).

▶ **Logical Database**

This attribute, which can only be set for executable programs, links such a program with a so-called logical database, which, in reality, is a collection of subroutines that are called in a certain sequence by the ABAP runtime environment to read hierarchical database tables. For programming with ABAP Objects, you should no longer use this option. Instead, you can also call logical databases from methods using a special function module called LDB_PROCESS. For more information, see Section 7.1.1.

Unicode program

Decimal separator

Hierarchical database tables

---

6 A Unicode system is a system in which all of the characters are coded in a single code page in a Unicode character representation. The system code page of an AS ABAP in a Unicode system is UTF-16 with a platform-dependent byte sequence. All ABAP programs of such an application server must be Unicode programs; however, Unicode programs can also be executed on non-Unicode application servers.

3.2.6   Processing Blocks

This section briefly discusses the possible processing blocks in the implementation part of an ABAP program. All processing blocks that can be used besides methods support the procedural/event-oriented programming model, and play a lesser role for programming with ABAP Objects. Nevertheless, like the obsolete program types, you will find all types of processing blocks in existing programs. The table in Appendix A.3 summarizes what processing blocks can appear in what program type. You will find more on the individual processing blocks in the corresponding chapters, which are referred to below.

Procedures

Procedures have a local data area and can have a parameter interface in which, aside from formal parameters, exceptions can also be declared.

ABAP Objects
▶ **Methods**

In the object-oriented ABAP programming, methods are the only relevant processing blocks (see Section 6.1). Each method is a component of a class. An object-oriented ABAP program is therefore built from methods that are organized in classes. But, this is only checked for class pools. In other programs still other processing blocks can appear. However, this should be kept to a minimum. Such processing blocks should not contain any functional code; rather, they should contain call methods.

External procedures
▶ **Function Modules**

These procedures are the predecessors of methods for external procedure calls in the procedural programming model (see Section 7.2.1). They can only be created in function groups, which can be considered as forerunners to global classes. Since many functions of an AS ABAP are still offered in function modules, they can continue to be called from methods. Furthermore, there are technical reasons (encapsulation of dynpros in function groups, RFC), which continue to make it necessary to create new function modules.

Internal procedures
▶ **Subroutines**

These procedures are the predecessors to methods for internal procedure calls in the procedural programming model. Subroutines are replaced entirely by methods and should no longer be used due to their conceptual flaws (see Section 7.2.2). You can create local classes for internal modularization in all program types that can contain operational code (see Section 4.3).

Dialog Modules and Event Blocks

Dialog modules and event blocks are processing blocks without a local data area and without a parameter interface. The absence of local data, formal parameters, and the possibility of forwarding exceptions represent the greatest weakness of these processing blocks. They can work only with global data from the declaration part of their ABAP program, which prevents any acceptable data encapsulation. Dialog modules and event blocks should therefore contain little or no operational code other than method calls.

▶ **Dialog Modules**

Dynpro coupling

Dialog modules can be implemented in ABAP programs that support their own dynpros (executable programs, function groups, module pools). They represent the functional interface between ABAP programs and dynpros and are called from the dynpro flow logic (see Section 9.1.9). Dialog modules are required for complex dynpros to be able to react to specific user entries. On the other hand, with simple dynpros, or if you're exclusively using GUI controls, dialog modules are rarely needed nowadays.

▶ **Event Blocks**

Event-orientation

Event blocks are a specialty of classic ABAP. Classical ABAP programs—and executable programs in particular (see Section 7.1.1)—are event-oriented. This means that when the program is executed, the corresponding process in the ABAP runtime environment triggers events that can be handled by event blocks in the ABAP program, but do not have to be.[7] Unlike all other processing blocks, event blocks are introduced by a single keyword, but are not explicitly completed by a keyword. Instead, they are completed by the next processing block or the end of the program. We recommend that you always flag the end of an event block in the

---

7 If an appropriate event block is implemented in the ABAP program for an event of the runtime environment, it is executed. Otherwise, the event has no effect. Conversely, event blocks are also not executed in an ABAP program whose event does not occur when the program is executed.

program with a comment line. ABAP Objects, on the other hand, has an explicit event concept where events are triggered by a statement in methods and are handled by special methods (see Section 6.5). The classical event blocks can be subdivided into:

▸ Event block for the *program constructor event*. This event block is initiated by LOAD-OF-PROGRAM. The corresponding event is triggered for a program at the exact moment it is loaded into the memory (internal session, see Section 3.4.5). You can use the statements within this processing block to initialize the (global) data of a program. This event block therefore resembles the constructor of a class. Because a function group can be thought of as being similar to a global class, with its function modules as public (static) methods, you can also easily use this event block there as a program constructor. However, if you follow our other recommendations, an implementation in other program types will not be necessary.

▸ Event blocks for *reporting events* that are triggered by the reporting processor of the ABAP runtime environment if an executable program is executed (see Section 7.1.1). Of these events, when you program with ABAP Objects, you should now only implement the START-OF-SELECTION, which was already mentioned several times, as a point of entry into an executable program. Note that the introduction of the corresponding event block with START-OF-SELECTION is optional. That means START-OF-SELECTION is the standard event in an executable program, and operational code without explicit assignment to a processing block is automatically assigned to the event block START-OF-SELECTION, if it appears at the start of the implementation part.[8] However, you should not use this option.

▸ Event blocks for *selection screen events* that are triggered by the selection screen processor of the ABAP runtime environment during selection screen processing (see Section 9.2.6). Selection screens are special dynpros, and event blocks for selection screen events are the event-controlled equivalent to dialog modules, for which the dynpro process logic is integrated into the ABAP runtime environment. Generally, the same applies to using these event blocks as for dialog modules.

---

8 On the other hand, unassigned code between complete processing blocks is considered to be dead code and is reported by the syntax check.

▶ Event blocks for *list events* that are triggered by the list proces-   List event
sor of the ABAP runtime environment during classical list
processing (see Section 9.3.5). Here we can again distinguish
between events of the list creation and interactive list events
when the list is displayed. For programming with ABAP
Objects, the creation and processing of classical lists is obsolete in most cases, apart from for private test purposes, so that
event blocks for list events scarcely still need to be implemented.

3.3   Source Code Organization

The source code of an ABAP program can be organized through
include programs or macros.

3.3.1   Include Programs

You can spread the source code of an ABAP program across several
include programs. Include programs are typically automatically generated by the ABAP Workbench when you create programs such as
class pools or function pools. However, you can also create include
programs directly in the ABAP Editor by specifying the corresponding program type.

An include program is ABAP source code that cannot be compiled   INCLUDE
separately. Instead, an include program is integrated into another
program with the following statement:

INCLUDE incl.

During the syntax check and the compiling of a program, the
INCLUDE statements contained are replaced by the source code of the
include programs. An include program can incorporate other include
programs, but not itself.

Include programs are the method of choice to split large ABAP programs into individual organizational units. Include programs make
large programs much easier to handle. In particular, include programs can also be transported individually, which allows, for example, individual methods or function modules to be processed independently of their class pool or their function group.

TOP include   The *TOP include* plays an important role here. It is designated for the global declaration part (see Section 3.2.1) of an ABAP program. The naming convention is that the name of a top include ends with "TOP". It can be created automatically when you create an ABAP program in the ABAP Workbench by simply selecting the corresponding checkbox (see Figure 2.35 in Chapter 2). When you organize a program using include programs, all statements of the global declaration part should be included by the top include. The reason is that the syntax check and compiler always include the top include if an include program of a program is checked or compiled, so that all declarations made there are always available.[9] However, for the same reason, a top include should not contain any operational code.

No multiple usage!   Although an include program can be included in various ABAP programs, include programs should never be used for the multiple usage of source code in several compilation units. In particular, we advise against the re-use of type definitions, data declarations, local classes or other processing blocks. Instead, you can use global classes or interfaces. The reason for this is that the inclusion of an include program in several programs dramatically restricts both their maintainability and that of the include program itself. Changes to such an include program can make the including programs syntactically incorrect. In particular, this is reason enough for not incorporating include programs that have not been created in the same system. Furthermore, an include program that is included in several programs is loaded several times into the program memory of the application server, if the programs are used in parallel. With large include programs in particular, this can lead to much more memory consumption than for one-off loading of individual reusable compilation units.

Although include programs are actually syntactically only limited in that they must contain complete ABAP statements, you should not distribute processing blocks across several include programs. For the minimum size of an include program, we recommend the declaration part of a local class (see Section 4.3.2) or a processing block (method). For the maximum size, we recommend the entire global

---

9 Otherwise, particularly self-defined include programs are generally checked individually, so that a useful syntax check is sometimes only possible on the entire ABAP program, which is built from the include programs.

declaration part of a program or the implementation part of a local class (see Section 4.3.2). The names of include programs should correspond to those that are proposed by the ABAP Workbench.

Listing 3.2 shows how include programs can be used to organize an ABAP program.

Listing 3.2 Use of Include Programs

Main program:

```
REPORT z_include_demo.

INCLUDE z_include_demo_top.
INCLUDE z_include_demo_impl.
INCLUDE z_include_demo_start.
```

Top-Include z_include_demo_top:

```
INCLUDE z_include_demo_decl1.

CLASS demo DEFINITION.
  PUBLIC SECTION.
    CLASS-METHODS main.
  ...
ENDCLASS.
```

Declaration include z_include_demo_decl1:

```
INCLUDE z_include_demo_decl2.

CLASS helper1 DEFINITION.
  PUBLIC SECTION.
    CLASS-METHODS meth1
      RETURNING VALUE(p1) TYPE string.
  ...
ENDCLASS.
```

Declaration include z_include_demo_decl2:

```
CLASS helper2 DEFINITION.
  PUBLIC SECTION.
    CLASS-METHODS meth2
      RETURNING VALUE(p2) TYPE string.
  ...
ENDCLASS.
```

Implementation in `z_include_demo_impl`:

```
CLASS demo IMPLEMENTATION.
  METHOD main.
    DATA text TYPE string.
    text = helper1=>meth1( ).
    MESSAGE text TYPE 'I'.
  ENDMETHOD.
ENDCLASS.
```

```
INCLUDE z_include_demo_impl1.
```

Implementation include `z_include_demo_impl1`:

```
CLASS helper1 IMPLEMENTATION.
  METHOD meth1.
    p1 = helper2=>meth2( ).
  ENDMETHOD.
  ...
ENDCLASS.
```

```
INCLUDE z_include_demo_impl2.
```

Implementation include `z_include_demo_impl2`:

```
CLASS helper2 IMPLEMENTATION.
  METHOD meth2.
    p2 = `Test`.
  ENDMETHOD.
  ...
ENDCLASS.
```

Implementation in `z_include_demo_start`:

```
START-OF-SELECTION.
  demo=>main( ).
```

After the include programs are resolved, `z_include_demo` is a program in which helper classes are each declared before the class in which they are required. Through the source code modularization, the demo class is the one that is most prominently visible in the program.

3.3.2 Macros

Macros that are defined between `DEFINE` and `END-OF-DEFINITION` can still appear in existing ABAP programs. Such macros are used in the same program instead of ABAP statements. We advise against using macros for the following reasons:

▶ Macros significantly impair the readability of a program.

▶ ABAP only offers the most basic macro support.

▶ Macros cannot be debugged.

For the source code organization, you should use include programs instead of macros. Procedures are preferable for the functional modularization.

3.4 Software and Memory Organization of AS ABAP

This section provides an introduction to the software and memory organization of an AS ABAP. The goal is to show you where ABAP programs are executed and what data they can access. We will also introduce terms that will be needed elsewhere.

3.4.1 AS ABAP as a System

In the world of ABAP, AS ABAP represents the most comprehensive unit. AS ABAP is the system in which an ABAP program runs. In the past, it also comprised the entire "SAP system." As we already mentioned, ABAP programs run in the AS ABAP application layer and can access its central database from there. Actually, the application layer is not a single unit, but is distributed across several parallel application servers to make it scalable.

Consequently, there is no common AS ABAP memory that can be accessed from each ABAP program.

3.4.2 Application Server

From a software point of view, the application layer of an AS ABAP is spread across at least one,[10] but usually several, application servers. If an AS ABAP has several application servers, they are usually

Message server

---

10 The most popular examples to illustrate this are probably the test versions of AS ABAP that can be installed on a laptop, or the earlier mini-basis systems, one of which is provided on the DVD that comes with the book.

also installed on several machines, whose operating systems don't have to be identical. It is also possible, however, for one or several application servers of one or several AS ABAPs to be installed on a single machine.[11] In addition to the application servers, there is also a message server in the application layer that is responsible for communication between the application servers.

Work process

Each application server provides a range of services for operating the AS ABAP. The services of an application server are implemented by so-called *work processes*, whose number and type are set when the AS ABAP is started. Work processes are software components that can execute an application. Each ABAP program is executed by an appropriate work process on an application server. There are different types of work processes for different applications: dialog, enqueue, background, spool, and update work processes.

If the application layer of an AS ABAP is spread across several application servers, generally not every application server makes that service available. Instead, it depends on the services of the application server where an ABAP program is actually executed. For instance, a program with user dialogs needs dialog services, which a program in the background processing does not need.

You should also note that each work process is logged on as a user to the database system for the entire runtime of an AS ABAP. During the AS ABAP runtime, a database logon cannot be passed on from one work process to another.

In summary, ABAP programs run on application servers that communicate with the presentation layer, the central database layer, and between each other via the message server. An ABAP program can only access memory that is administered by an application server (otherwise, it would not be possible to distribute application servers across different machines).

---

11 The term *application server* therefore appears in the ABAP world under three different guises: first, as part of the name "SAP NetWeaver Application Server ABAP"; secondly, as the software component "application server," onto which the application layer of an AS ABAP is distributed; and thirdly, the machines on which the application layer of an AS ABAP physically runs are often also simply referred to as "application servers."

Figure 3.4 shows where an ABAP program runs on an application server and what memory areas it can access here.

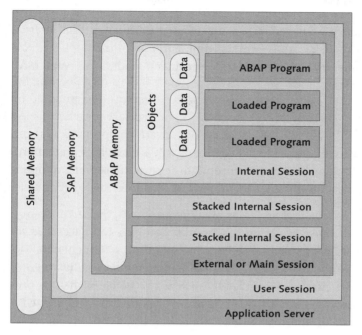

Figure 3.4 ABAP Program on an Application Server

The memory areas of an application server that can be accessed in an ABAP program are as follows:

Memory areas

▶ The Shared Memory of the application server

▶ The SAP Memory of a user session

▶ The ABAP Memory of a main session

▶ The roll area of an internal session

The shared memory is the memory area that is used by all parts of an application server together. The remaining memory areas are allocated as needed and are assigned to their contexts, which are explained in the next paragraphs.

Shared memory

Each application server has its own shared memory. The ABAP runtime environment uses the shared memory for programs, program data, and buffers (e. g., for the SAP buffering, see Section 10.1.4). ABAP programs can access shared objects (see Section 6.6) and data clusters (see Section 10.4) in the shared memory, where especially shared objects play an important role.

The memory areas of an application server are administered with SAP Memory Management. You can learn more about the internal workings of an AS ABAP and its administration in the book *SAP R/3 System Administration* by Sigrid Hagemann and Liane Will (SAP PRESS 2004).

3.4.3 User Session

If a dialog user or an external client (via RFC or ICF) logs on to an AS ABAP, it is connected to an appropriate application server and opens a user session on this AS.

SAP memory   Each user session is assigned its own memory area, the SAP memory, in which all ABAP programs of a user session have joint access to so-called SPA/GPA parameters. The corresponding statements are SET PARAMETER and GET PARAMETER. These parameters are only suited to saving short character-type fields, such as the name of the last programs called. The input fields of dynpros can be linked to SPA/GPA parameters and in order to prefill them before a dynpro is called.

3.4.4 Main Session

At least one main session or external mode is opened for each user session. In dialog processing, a user session can manage up to 16 (prior to SAP NetWeaver 2004s, six) main sessions, each of which is linked to a separate window. If you execute the function **Create New Session** in the SAP GUI, or enter a transaction code behind /o in the input window of the standard toolbar, you open a new main session in a new window. From an ABAP program, you can open a new main session via RFC (CALL FUNCTION STARTING NEW TASK, see Section 12.2.3).

ABAP memory   Each main session is assigned a separate memory area, known as the ABAP memory, in which data clusters (see Section 10.4) can be stored. The data in the ABAP memory is retained during a sequence of program calls within a call sequence.

Call sequence   A call sequence is formed if you can return from the called program to the calling program. This is always the case when you call an ABAP program with SUBMIT AND RETURN or CALL TRANSACTION. Only the programs of a call sequence have common access to data in the ABAP memory, and this is primarily for data transfer during program calls. When the first program of a call sequence is terminated, the corresponding ABAP memory is also released.

3.4.5 Internal Session

With each call (via SUBMIT or CALL TRANSACTION or LEAVE TO TRANSACTION) of an ABAP program in a main session, an *internal session* is opened. A memory area called a *roll area* is assigned to the internal session, in which the data and objects of an ABAP program are stored while it is executed. This is the actual memory of an ABAP program. With program calls, a maximum of nine internal sessions can be stacked as a call sequence in a main session. In a main session, only the internal session of the program that is just running exists in an active version. All memory content of previous programs is saved on the stack.

Calling programs

You can load additional programs (e. g., class pools, function groups) into the internal session of a program using external procedure calls (methods, function modules) or by using public components of global classes.[12] An internal session will exist for as long as its first program, the *main program*, is executed. The additionally loaded programs and their data also remain loaded until the end of the internal session.

Load programs

While the data declared in a program is only visible in that program, all programs of an internal session have joint access to anonymous data objects (see Section 11.1.2) and instances of classes created with CREATE. Within the internal session, references to objects can be copied from one program to procedures of another program. However, the programs of an internal session cannot access the objects of a previous internal session of a call sequence. Instead, you can create

Data and objects

---

12 From a conceptual point of view, it is sufficient to say that a "program is loaded with its data into an internal session." From a technical point of view, each internal session is divided into a Program Execution Area (PXA) and a roll area. The PXA is a further common memory area of the application server in which the unchangeable data (bytecodes) of the programs that are currently running there is stored. Only the roll area is individually reserved for an internal session and contains its changeable data.

shared objects in the shared memory of the application server (see Section 6.6) to access objects across all modes.

On 64-bit platforms, an internal session can theoretically require up to 4 TB of memory. On 32-bit platforms, the theoretical maximum limit is 4 GB. Generally, the effective maximum limit lies below the theoretical maximum limit, because ultimately, only the physically installed main memory is available, and this must be spread across all of the memory requirements.

"I invented the term Object-Oriented, and I can tell you I did not have C++ in mind."
—*Alan Curtis Kay*

4   Classes and Objects

This chapter describes the basic principles of object-oriented programming in ABAP. A brief introduction into object-oriented programming is followed by a description of classes and objects as a basis of ABAP Objects. Based on this overview of classes and objects, we will discuss the remaining ABAP language elements and advanced concepts of ABAP Objects in the following chapters.

4.1   Object Orientation

Because it would exceed the scope of this book, we cannot provide you with a comprehensive introduction into object-oriented programming; however, this does not mean that we won't use this opportunity to point out the advantages of using object-oriented programming over classical, procedural programming. If you're already experienced with object-oriented programming, this chapter should interest you because it describes how the concept of object-oriented programming has been implemented in ABAP Objects. If you don't have any experience with object-oriented programming, you will learn about its basic concepts on the basis of ABAP Objects in this chapter.

In the real world, we can identify a multitude of objects, all of which contain specific characteristics and functions. Let's take a car, for example: Its characteristics include an engaged gear, its speed, and so on. Moreover, it has functions such as starting the engine, accelerating, or applying the brakes. In object orientation (OO), we refer to the characteristics of an object as *attributes*, while its functions are referred to as *methods*. The concept of object orientation in the soft-

Real world objects

177

ware consists of transferring the view of real-world objects to software objects as well. For example, when working with a business software system, you will regularly encounter items that can be regarded as objects and thus have corresponding counterparts in the real world. Examples of such objects include customers, materials, invoices, and so on.

Software objects   The goal of object-oriented programming is to map such real-world objects including their attributes and methods to software objects as close to reality as possible. Program flows must be designed in such a way as they would occur in the real world. If that can be achieved, the dialog between the user and the developer is made easier to a large extent. In simple terms, the user can express requirements to a program in a language that he or she is familiar with, while the developer can implement these requirements in a more direct way than in the classical programming model.[1]

The object-oriented programming model encapsulates attributes and methods that pertain to a specific object and uses a defined interface to provide the user with access to these attributes and methods. The defined interface, in turn, hides the actual implementation details of the object. In an ideal scenario, the attributes of an object are only changed by the methods of the object and not directly by the user of the object. In this way, you can ensure that the object is constantly in a consistent state. Remember the example of the car. In order to change the speed of a car in the real world, you must either step on the accelerator or apply the brakes. With regard to a software object, this means that the respective methods must be called. A software object that represents a car should not allow you to simply change the value of its speed since this would not correspond to the real world.

An object-oriented programming language supports this concept by using the appropriate language elements. We refer to a programming language as being object-oriented if its language elements support the following characteristics:

---

1   The requirements of the user and the implementation by the programmer are separated by the phase of object-oriented modeling. The description of this phase would far exceed the focus of this book, which is why we would like to refer you to the wide range of literature available on this topic.

▶ **Abstraction**

This refers to the ability to reflect processes of the real world as being as lifelike as possible in the programming language. Such processes can be business or technical processes. The object-oriented programming model reflects (*models*) real-world problems in classes and maps them in objects during the execution of a program.

▶ **Encapsulation**

The details of the implementation are hidden behind well-defined and documented interfaces. These interfaces ensure that the abstract presentation of an object is used only in compliance with its specification.

▶ **Inheritance**

New abstractions, in other words classes, are derived from existing ones. Therefore, they inherit all attributes and methods of their superordinate classes and can extend and specialize those classes. For example, in our car example, we could specialize a general class "vehicle" by introducing subclasses like "automobile" or "truck." You can further specialize those subclasses, for instance, by deriving "semitrailer truck" or "dump truck" from "truck."

▶ **Polymorphism**

Different objects can present the same interface to the outside world. As a user, you merely need to know the interface and use it to access objects of different classes without knowing the details of those objects. In the real world, you can regard the basic control elements of a car as such an interface, for example. If you know these control elements, you can get in almost any car in the world and pull away without having to know the actual type of car you are currently driving.

If a programming language provides language elements that support those concepts, you can use it for object-oriented programming. ABAP Objects meets these requirements.

Note, however, that not every program that has been developed based on such a language is actually object-oriented. Object orientation is a program paradigm or concept designed to master the inherent complexity of a software. With regard to business software, it usually doesn't make much sense to model a single report that works

Complexity

somewhat independently of the remaining system as completely object-oriented. On the other hand, this doesn't mean that you should still use the ABAP language elements of the procedural, event-based programming model here.

Analysis and design

For large applications, the object-oriented concept requires a very profound planning phase. Today, several acknowledged methods for object-oriented analysis (OOA) and object-oriented design (OOD) exist that can be used to obtain clean and stable object models. Furthermore, there are predefined design patterns for a multitude of classical design problems. These patterns ensure stability, maintainability, and not least, the investment protection of the software.

But you will also see that using the language elements of ABAP Objects can bring some advantages, even if you don't remodel your entire application as object-oriented. You can, for instance, use the advanced concepts of data and function encapsulation provided by the classes also in small, self-contained programs.

4.2   Object-Oriented Programming in ABAP

Object-oriented programming is based on the encapsulation of data and its associated functionality in classes. The classes, in turn, are used to create instances (objects). ABAP Objects represents the part of the ABAP programming language that allows for object-oriented programming on the basis of classes. ABAP Objects was introduced with Release 4.6 of the former SAP Basis as an extension of the existing ABAP language. It was then extended with several new properties in later releases. In Release 6.10, Object Services were introduced to persistently store objects in the database; in Release 6.40, shared objects (i. e., objects in the shared memory of the application server) were added.

ABAP Objects

ABAP Objects basically consists of a set of ABAP statements that support the object-oriented programming of AS ABAP as follows:

- Definition of local and global classes
- Creation of objects from classes
- Specialization of classes via inheritance

► Independent interfaces that can be used in classes

► Event concept that is integrated into the language

For downward compatibility, ABAP Objects was introduced as an addition to the existing language. This means:

► For the implementation of methods, the same ABAP language is used as has already been used for the classical processing blocks, even though it has been adjusted in parts.

► You can extend existing, procedural code by object-oriented code. For example, you can create local classes or call methods of global classes in almost every program type (see Section 3.2.4).

► You can call existing reusable, procedural units (usually function modules) from methods.

The advantages of downward compatibility are that ABAP developers don't need to learn a completely new language and investments in existing code are protected. The disadvantage of downward compatibility is that ABAP is constantly being extended by new features, while outdated and obsolete language elements cannot really be eradicated, which negatively affects the entire appearance of the language. Due to the many different parallel concepts and programming models, ABAP often seems to be very complex and difficult to learn.

Downward compatibility

We therefore think that developers should limit themselves to using only one programming model in new developments or when reorganizing existing software. And of course, this model should be the object-oriented programming model that replaces all previous models and provides orthogonal and easy-to-learn concepts to solve problems.

In this context, you should note that the introduction of ABAP Objects at least made it possible to streamline the existing ABAP syntax to a certain extent. Because all programming code that had been implemented in classes needed to be recreated from scratch, specific syntax rules could be introduced without affecting the requirement of downward compatibility. In classes, you will note the following:

Syntax cleansing

► Many outdated and obsolete language constructs are forbidden, which are allowed outside of classes only for reasons of compatibility.

► Many additions must be explicitly specified, which are implicitly added outside of classes.

► You can easily identify and prevent an incorrect or potentially dangerous handling of data.

Therefore, in classes, a way of using the ABAP language is enforced that would be desirable outside of classes as well, but cannot be established due to compatibility reasons. This book generally presents only syntax that can also be used within classes.

4.3 Classes

Classes form the basis of every object-oriented programming language. A class is the pattern or template for an object, much like a data type is the template for a data object. A class is therefore also referred to as an object type in the ABAP type hierarchy; data types and object types are located in one and the same namespace (see Section 5.1.1).

Instances   To be able to use objects in a program, you must first define classes. You can create different objects on the basis of a class. All these objects have the same methods, whereas their attributes usually have different values. Let's return to our car example. The constructional drawings for the car represent a class. Based on these drawings, you can manufacture identical cars that provide the same functions, but whose attributes can have very different values. One car may currently be in fourth gear, while another one is in reverse gear. Although both cars are based on the same construction specification, they are completely independent of each other. The cars represent instances of the construction plan. Correspondingly, we refer to *objects* as *instances* of *classes.*[2]

4.3.1 Global and Local Classes

In ABAP Objects, we distinguish between global and local classes. Both of them are classes as defined up until now, that is, an object

---

[2] The available literature on object-oriented programming languages unfortunately confuses the terms "class" and "object" rather frequently, and often objects are referred to when classes are actually meant. Examples include terms such as "instances of objects" or "object instances."

doesn't tell you immediately (at first glance, that is) whether it is an instance of a global class or a local class.

The difference between global and local classes has to do with their visibility on AS ABAP:

▶ A global class is visible and can be used in every program of the same AS ABAP, provided that no limitation by the package of the class exists. The global classes of an AS ABAP form its class library.

▶ A local class is only visible in the program in which it is defined.

Local classes can be defined in any ABAP program, except type groups and interface pools, and they can be used only in those programs. Global classes can only be created in class pools using the Class Builder tool of the ABAP Workbench.

As we already mentioned, the use of local and global classes to create objects is completely identical except for their visibility. You can create objects of local classes only in the same ABAP program, whereas you can use any ABAP program to create objects of global classes. Correspondingly, you should define global classes whenever you need objects of the same type in different programs, whereas you should use local classes for objects that are only required in one program.

Furthermore, you can use local classes to modularize any program. This holds true particularly for class pools that can not only contain their global class, but also any number of local classes to be used in the global class. The subroutines provided in classic ABAP for internal modularization (see Section 7.2.2) are therefore replaced by the methods of local classes.

Modularization

With regard to their global and local visibility, classes also behave like data types (see Section 5.1.2) that are distinguished into global data types in the ABAP Dictionary and local data types in any program.

Note

4.3.2 Creating Classes

Classes are always declared in the declaration part of a program, and they are implemented in its implementation part (see Listing 3.1 in Chapter 3). This holds true for both local and global classes. With regard to local classes, you must enter the relevant statements for the

Class pool and ABAP Editor

required program in the ABAP Editor. For global classes, you must use the Class Builder. To define a global class, you must fill the relevant input templates of the Class Builder with data. The Class Builder then generates the corresponding statements in the class pool of the class. The only code that you must enter for global classes is the implementation of the methods. The Class Builder hides the class pool behind its user interface. However, those of you who prefer to use the keyboard instead of the mouse, can select **Goto • ... Section** in the Class Builder, which enables you to edit the code of a global class in the ABAP Editor.

The Class Builder contains a small testing environment that can be used to test the functionality of the methods of a global class. But in order to carry out extensive tests, you should use the ABAP Unit tool (see Section 13.3) that enables you to test any procedural units. You can release a global class for use by making the relevant entry in its properties in the Class Builder.

Declaration Part and Implementation Part

In terms of the syntax, each class definition always consists of a declaration part (in the declaration part of a program) and an implementation part (in the implementation part of the same program). The declaration part contains a description of all components of the class. The most important components are:

▶ Attributes

▶ Methods

▶ Events

You implement the methods of the class in the implementation part.

CLASS—
ENDCLASS

The statements to be used to define classes are CLASS and ENDCLASS. The basic structure of a class is as follows:

```
CLASS myclass DEFINITION.
  ...
ENDCLASS.

...

CLASS myclass IMPLEMENTATION.
  ...
ENDCLASS.
```

The upper two statements define the declaration part, while the lower two statements define the implementation part of a `myclass` class. As mentioned earlier, you can enter these statements in almost all ABAP programs to create local classes there.

With global classes, you usually wouldn't see this structure directly. Once you've created a global class (see Section 2.8.2), the Class Builder displays the empty class as shown in Figure 4.1,[3] and you can enter the components of the class.

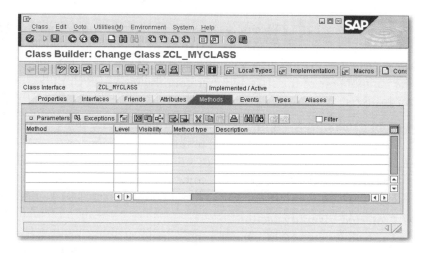

Figure 4.1 Empty Class in Class Builder (SE24)

As you can see, we selected an arbitrary name for the local class, while we preface a global class with "CL_" for SAP and "ZCL_" or "YCL_" in the customer namespace. Note that a local class in a program hides a global class of the same name. The hiding of global names by local names is a general rule in ABAP. Thus it is advisable to use different global names and local names to prevent global names from being inadvertently hidden by local names. For classes, the aforementioned convention has become standard in SAP pro-

Naming conventions

---

3 Instead of navigating through the Object Navigator (SE80) every time, you might also call the Class Builder directly via transaction SE24 to edit global classes. The Class Builder tool manages all components that are necessary for a class by itself. For other ABAP programs that can contain components such as dynpros, which, in turn, can be edited using different tools, or for large programs that consist of include programs, it is generally more convenient to have all components displayed in a hierarchy in the Object Navigator.

grams. In addition to the syntax rule stating that we want names to begin with a letter and to consist solely of letters, numbers, and underscores ("_"), we don't want to define anything else except that names should be as meaningful as possible within programs. Of course, you can create a naming convention that meets your requirements as much as possible. For example, it is quite common to use the prefix "lcl_" for local classes.

Visibility Sections

The components of a class are declared in the declaration part of the class. Each component must be assigned to one of the following three visibility sections. The visibility sections define the visibility of the components of the class and therefore the interfaces of the class for its users.

▶ **Public Visibility Section**
All components that are assigned to this section can be accessed by all external users, the methods of subclasses (inheritors), and by the methods of the class. These components represent the interface between the class and the external world.

▶ **Protected Visibility Section**
The components of this section can be accessed by the methods of the subclasses (inheritors) and the methods of the class. They represent the interface between the class and its subclasses, but are not part of the interface between the class and the outside world.

▶ **Private Visibility Section**
Components in this section can only be used within the methods of the class. They are not part of the interfaces of the class.

An external user of a class can see only its public components, whereas both the private and protected components represent the invisible, internal part of the class to the external user. This enables you to change the internal implementation of a class without having to invalidate its users.

PUBLIC,
PROTECTED,
PRIVATE

The syntax used to separate the declaration part of a class into the three visibility sections is as follows:

```
CLASS myclass DEFINITION.
  PUBLIC SECTION.
    ...
```

```
PROTECTED SECTION.
...
PRIVATE SECTION.
...
ENDCLASS.
```

In the Class Builder, you must select the assignment of a component to a visibility section separately for each component in that you choose the option **Public**, **Protected**, or **Private** for each component in the **Visibility** column (see Figure 4.1). However, if you prefer writing programming code to filling input fields, you can select **Goto •** **Public Section**, **Protected Section** or **Private Section** to enter the complete declaration part of a global class, in the same way as that of a local class in the ABAP Editor.[4]

The ability to define visibility sections is one of the aspects that makes object-oriented programming so much better than procedural programming. This option explicitly supports the principle of encapsulation, that is, of both data encapsulation and functional encapsulation.

Encapsulation

By assigning components to a visibility section, you can determine which components should be part of the interface and which components should be encapsulated. The interface of a class should be easily understandable and stable. Components that are needed only within a class (or its subclasses) should not be accessible from outside. The components that are visible to the outside world must be documented and comprehensible for the user. They should not put the object into an inconsistent status. In particular, you should avoid using changeable public attributes because they can be changed directly by the user. If you have to set an attribute directly to a specific value (i. e., the value does not result from a complex operation), we recommend using non-changeable attributes and associated methods that receive the value to be changed as parameters and then modifying the attribute within the object. A useful naming convention for such a method is set_attr, attr being the name of the attribute. If only methods are used to change attribute values, the state of an object—being determined by the values of its attributes— is completely encapsulated.

Interface

4 Once you have selected **Goto • Public Section**, you can even access the CLASS ... DEFINITION statement directly where you can edit the properties of the class.

Class vs. program Thus the class is the encapsulation unit of the object-oriented programming model. In the procedural programming model, on the other hand, the entire program represents the smallest possible unit of encapsulation, and the visibility of all program components is fixed. In comparison to classes, the data that is declared in the declaration part of a program represents the private components of the program, while the externally accessible processing blocks are its public methods. A counterpart to the protected components of a class does not exist. As already mentioned, it makes sense to compare a function group with its private data and public function modules to a class (see Section 7.2.1). Unfortunately, even subroutines that are primarily used for internal modularization can be called from any other program, which means they are part of a program's public interface. Therefore, only the object-oriented programming model allows you to explicitly publish data (but, as described above, this data should not be changeable) and to protect procedures from unwanted use (which is equally important for encapsulation).[5]

Procedures Procedures as such cannot be regarded as encapsulation units, because they only exist during the time in which they are executed and thus cannot map any continuous state. Although the local data of a procedure is only visible within the procedure, it can be used as temporary work areas only. This is the very core of the procedural programming model in which procedures work on data that is stored in a different location. This holds true for both methods within classes and function modules as well as subroutines within a program. Classes therefore introduce an encapsulation level beneath programs, which, in conjunction with explicit object creation (see Section 4.6), provides entirely new programming options that go far beyond the limits of the procedural concept.

Controlling the Instantiation

Instantiation In addition to the visibility of the components of a class, the type of instantiation of the class plays a major role with regard to its use. Out of the group of users to whom a class is visible, the type of instantiation defines those users who can also create objects of that class. As

---

5 Strictly speaking, ABAP programs do not even encapsulate their global data, because there are ways to access this data using specific dynamic statements which, however, we won't describe any further in this book.

is the case with the visibility sections of components, there are three types of instantiation:

- Public instantiation
- Protected instantiation
- Private instantiation

Only those classes that can be publicly instantiated allow any user to create objects. Classes with protected instantiation also allow the creation of objects in methods of subclasses. In classes with private instantiation, it is only the class itself that can create objects.

The syntax that controls the instantiation of a class is as follows:

```
CLASS myclass DEFINITION
              CREATE PUBLIC|PROTECTED|PRIVATE.
    ...
ENDCLASS.
```

If you don't specify any value, the class can be publicly instantiated by default. In the Class Builder, you can define the type of instantiation of a global class in the **Properties** tab of the class (see Figure 4.2).

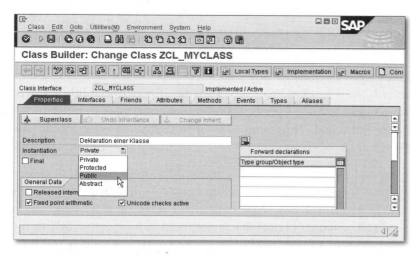

Figure 4.2 Instantiation of a Global Class

If a class cannot be instantiated by external users who are supposed to use objects of that class, the class must provide those users with access to its objects. A common way to do this is to provide a static (factory) method that creates an object of the class and returns a ref-

Factory method

189

erence to the object (see Section 4.6.5). With regard to encapsulation, it has some advantages if a class can create its objects by itself. If necessary, it can, for instance, check the parameters passed to the constructor (see Section 4.7) in order to ensure that only consistent objects are created.

Suspending the Encapsulation

Typically, classes are strictly separated into external (public) and internal (protected and private) components. An external user can only access the public components of a class. However, in some cases, classes must cooperate very closely so that they need to access the protected and private components of each other. To avoid having to reveal those components to all users simultaneously, you can use the concept of *friendship* between classes.

Friends A class can offer friendship to other classes (and interfaces). For this purpose, you can use the FRIENDS addition of the CLASS ... DEFINITION statement behind which all classes (and interfaces) are listed that are to be granted friendship. In the Class Builder, you must enter friends in the **Friends** tab. These friends are granted access to the protected and private components of the class that grants the friendship and can always create instances of this class, irrespective of the CREATE addition of the CLASS statement.

Granting a friendship is a one-sided process. A class that grants friendship is not automatically a friend of its friends. Inheritors of friends also become friends; however, the granting of friendship cannot be inherited. The friend of a superclass is not automatically the friend of its subclasses.

Containers and agents As in real life when establishing friendships, in the context of classes as well, the granting of friendship should be handled with care. A case in which it makes sense to grant a friendship is when a class is used as a container of data that is supposed to be accessed by specific other classes. Another possible scenario consists of storing the services of classes in specific service classes (agents). For this purpose, the service classes require access to the internal components of the class. For example, you can use those agents to manage objects of classes that cannot be instantiated publicly. In other words, the corresponding factory method is not provided by the class itself, but by an agent that is a friend of the class. This concept is used in Object Services (see Section 10.2). Furthermore, it is very useful to grant friendship to a test class of ABAP Unit (see Section 13.3) if the test class is supposed to test private methods.

4.4   Attributes and Methods

This section describes the most important components of a class: its attributes and methods. After that, we'll also examine data types as components of classes. Chapter 6 describes additional components.

All the components of a class lie within one namespace. The names of all components within one class must be different. A method cannot have the same name as an attribute. This is also true for components that are inherited from superclasses (see Section 6.2).

Namespace

In local classes, attributes and methods must be declared in one of the available visibility sections. In global classes, you must specify the visibility for each component (see, for example, Figure 4.3). In addition to the visibility, we must also have a look at another property of components in classes.

4.4.1   Instance Components and Static Components

Apart from the visibility, you must define for each component whether it is an instance component or a static component. The instance components of a class exist independently of each other for each instance of the class (in other words, for each object) and can only be addressed there. The static components of a class exist only once per class, that is, all objects of a class share the same static components. The static components are independent of objects and can be addressed via the name of the class. Whereas static components are always available, the lifecycle of instance components is linked to the lifecycle of objects. In particular, you can use the static components of a class without creating an instance of the class beforehand.

Basically, the syntax for declaring instance components and static components is the same where the keywords used to declare static components begins with CLASS-. In the Class Builder, you must select either **Instance** or **Static** in the **Level** column to indicate whether a component is a static or an instance component (see Figure 4.1).

191

In object-oriented programming, you will primarily use instance components as these are the components of objects. Static attributes can be useful if all objects of a class actually require access to shared data. If a class must be used that does not yet have any objects, static methods are needed, for example, as factory methods in order to create objects.

Classes and objects

Although you can create classes that contain only static components, we don't recommend that you do this too often, because you can only use this type of a class in a purely procedural context (i. e., so that work completely without using object orientation). Even if you're certain that you never want to use different objects of one class, it is always better to define a class that supports the singleton pattern (see Section 4.7.2) instead of using static components. The benefits of real object orientation are that you can control the lifecycle of an object and that in ABAP you cannot redefine static methods in subclasses.

4.4.2 Attributes

Data objects

Attributes are the data objects of a class. Their content defines the state of an object. You can define attributes of classes in the same way that you define all data objects that can be used in ABAP. In addition to the attributes of classes, there is also the program data that can be created in the declaration part of a program as well as the local working data of procedures. You can use all data types of the extensive ABAP type hierarchy for attributes, as well as for all data that can be declared in ABAP. Because of the scope and the importance of this topic, we will discuss data objects and data types in a separate section (see Section 5.1), whereas here we'll only describe what you need to do in order to create attributes.

DATA and CLASS-DATA

The syntax for the declaration of an instance attribute `attr` is:

```
DATA attr TYPE dtype [READ-ONLY].
```

The syntax for the declaration of a static attribute `attr` is:

```
CLASS-DATA attr TYPE dtype [READ-ONLY].
```

After the `TYPE` addition, you must specify or construct a `dtype` data type of the ABAP type hierarchy (more on this in Section 5.1). The `READ-ONLY` addition can only be specified in the public visibility section of a class. When you use this addition, a public attribute can be read externally, but can only be changed by methods of the class. Using this addition enables you to avoid having to provide a method (usually a `get_attr` method) for each read access to a private attribute. The direct access to an attribute is faster than a method call.

Listing 4.1 illustrates an example for the declaration part of a local class `static_vehicle` in which a private static attribute `speed` is declared.

Listing 4.1 Declaration of the Attribute of a Class

```
CLASS static_vehicle DEFINITION.
  PUBLIC SECTION.
    ...
  PRIVATE SECTION.
    CLASS-DATA speed TYPE i.
ENDCLASS.
```

In the Class Builder, you can simply enter the attributes and their properties in the **Attributes** tab (see Figure 4.3).

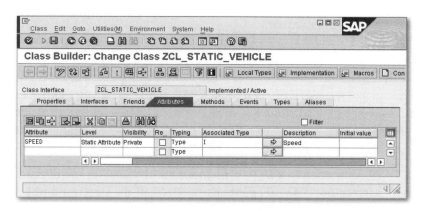

Figure 4.3 Static Attribute of a Global Class

Constants

The attributes declared with `DATA` and `CLASS-DATA` or with **Instance Attribute** or **Static Attribute** in the Class Builder are variables, that is, their values can be overwritten in the methods of their classes. In addition, you can declare constant attributes whose value is defined during the declaration and cannot be changed afterwards.

The syntax for the declaration of a constant `attr` is:

```
CONSTANTS attr TYPE dtype VALUE val.
```

The value `val` of the constant must be specified after the `VALUE` addition. In the Class Builder, you can create a constant by specifying **Constant** in the **Level** column of the **Attributes** tab and enter the value in the **Initial value** column (see Figure 4.3). You can also use the `VALUE` addition and the **Initial value** column for variable attributes to define an initial value.

Because the values of constants are defined independently from the instance of a class, they belong to the static attributes of a class and can be used in the same way.

4.4.3 Methods

The behavior of the objects of a class is implemented in its methods. Methods are the procedures of a class. In their role as procedures, methods are processing blocks with a parameter interface in which you can declare local data. Besides methods, ABAP contains function modules (see Section 7.2.1) and subroutines (see Section 7.2.2) as procedures, which are not part of a class.

As is the case with all components of classes, you must distinguish between instance methods and static methods. Instance methods can use all components of their own class, while static methods can access only static attributes and trigger static events. To call instance methods, you first have to create an object of the class. Static methods can be called independently of objects.

Like all components of a class, methods are declared in the declaration part. In addition, all methods declared in the declaration part must be implemented in the implementation part of the class, provided they are not abstract (see Section 6.2.5).

METHODS and CLASS-METHODS — The syntax for the declaration of an instance method `meth` is:

```
METHODS meth
    [IMPORTING iᵢ          TYPE type ...]
    {[EXPORTING eᵢ         TYPE type ...]
    [CHANGING  cᵢ          TYPE type ...]}
    |[RETURNING VALUE(r) TYPE type ...]
    [RASING    eᵢ]
```

Correspondingly, the syntax for the declaration of a static method `meth` is:

```
CLASS-METHODS meth
  ...
```

The additions shown here—IMPORTING, EXPORTING, CHANGING, RETURNING, and RAISING—define the parameter interface of the method in that they define the input, output, input/output parameters, or a return value. Furthermore, they define the exceptions that may leave the method. You must specify the type of each parameter using a TYPE addition. The syntax is exactly the same for static methods, but we have not listed it here. Section 6.1 contains details on method declaration, while Section 8.2 describes exceptions.

Parameter interface

Both instance methods and static methods are implemented in the implementation part of the class between the statements

METHOD— ENDMETHOD

```
METHOD meth.
  ...
ENDMETHOD.
```

The METHOD statement does not require any additions, because the properties of the method are defined during its declaration.

Listing 4.2 extends the local class from Listing 4.1 with two public static methods, `accelerate` and `show_speed`, and with an implementation part.

Listing 4.2 Declaration and Implementation of Methods

```
CLASS static_vehicle DEFINITION.
  PUBLIC SECTION.
    CLASS-METHODS: accelerate IMPORTING delta TYPE i,
                   show_speed.

  PRIVATE SECTION.
    CLASS-DATA speed TYPE i.
ENDCLASS.
CLASS static_vehicle IMPLEMENTATION.
  METHOD accelerate.
    speed = speed + delta.
  ENDMETHOD.
  METHOD show_speed.
    DATA output TYPE string.
    output = speed.
    MESSAGE output TYPE 'I'.
```

```
  ENDMETHOD.
ENDCLASS.
```

In the Class Builder, you must enter the methods and their properties in the **Methods** tab (see Figure 4.4).

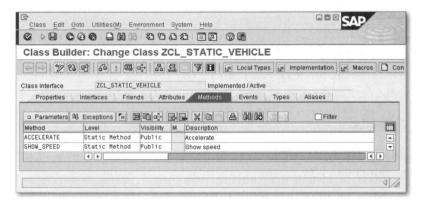

Figure 4.4 Static Methods of a Global Class

To define the parameter interface, you must select the **Parameters** function for each method and enter the interface parameters including their properties there (see Figure 4.5).

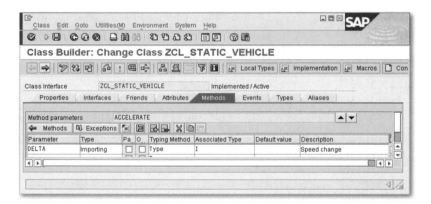

Figure 4.5 Interface Parameters in a Global Class

To implement a method, double-click on the method name or select the **Source code** function in the tab, and implement the method. The **Signature** function enables you to show and hide a display of the parameter interface (see Figure 4.6).

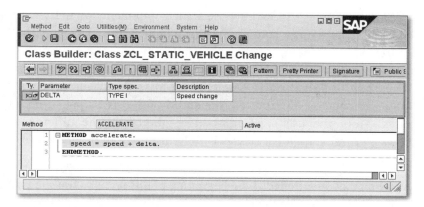

Figure 4.6 Method Implementation in a Global Class

4.4.4 Using Static Components

The class in Listing 4.2 contains only static components and can therefore be used directly. To use the local class, you could, for instance, write an executable program as the one shown in Listing 4.3.

Listing 4.3 Using a Local Class

```
REPORT z_drive_local_static_vehicle.

CLASS static_vehicle DEFINITION.
  ...
ENDCLASS.
CLASS static_vehicle IMPLEMENTATION.
  ...
ENDCLASS.
START-OF-SELECTION.
  static_vehicle=>accelerate( 100 ).
  static_vehicle=>accelerate( 200 ).
  static_vehicle=>show_speed( ).
```

To use the global class, Listing 4.4 will suffice.

Listing 4.4 Using a Global Class

```
REPORT z_drive_global_static_vehicle.

START-OF-SELECTION.
  zcl_static_vehicle=>accelerate( 100 ).
  zcl_static_vehicle=>accelerate( 200 ).
  zcl_static_vehicle=>show_speed( ).
```

Listings 4.3 and 4.4 show how the static components of a class are accessed. The syntax consists of the name of the class and the addressed component, which are separated by the class component selector =>. In this case, the accelerate method is called twice, while show_speed is called once. Numbers are passed to accelerate as input parameters. As expected, the speed of 300 is output in both cases. From the user's point of view, therefore, the difference between local and global classes is only in the location where they can be used.

As we already mentioned at the beginning of this section, you should avoid using a class like the one shown in Listing 4.2, which has only static components. The reason for not using such a class is illustrated by this very example. What's the use of the static_vehicle class for modeling vehicles if we cannot create any different vehicle objects from it? To do that, we must use instance attributes that can have different values in different objects. Listing 4.5 shows the conversion of the static_vehicle class to a vehicle class that can be used for real object orientation.

Listing 4.5 Class as a Template for Objects

```
REPORT z_vehicle.

CLASS vehicle DEFINITION.
  PUBLIC SECTION.
    METHODS: accelerate IMPORTING delta TYPE i,
             show_speed.
  PRIVATE SECTION.
    DATA speed TYPE i.
ENDCLASS.
CLASS vehicle IMPLEMENTATION.
  METHOD accelerate.
    speed = speed + delta.
  ENDMETHOD.
  METHOD show_speed.
    DATA output TYPE string.
    output = speed.
    MESSAGE output TYPE 'I'.
  ENDMETHOD.
ENDCLASS.
```

As you can see, only the keywords for the declaration of the components have changed. In the Class Builder, you can copy ZCL_STATIC_

VEHICLE to ZCL_VEHICLE and replace each **Static** component with **Instance** in the **Level** property.[6] The `vehicle` and ZCL_VEHICLE classes do not contain any static components and therefore can no longer be used directly. Instead, you can create objects.

4.4.5 Editor Mode of the Class Builder

In addition to editing components in tabs, the Class Builder also provides an editor mode that enables you to edit the visibility sections of a global class directly in the ABAP Editor. You can switch to this mode via **Goto • ... Section** or by clicking on the arrow buttons in the tabs for attributes or types (see Section 4.5).

Figure 4.7 uses the example of ZCL_VEHICLE to demonstrate what the public visibility section in the ABAP Editor looks like. As you can see, the Class Builder does nothing more than generate ABAP code. You should already be familiar with the `CREATE PUBLIC` addition in the `CLASS zcl_vehicle DEFINITION` statement from Section 4.3.2. The `PUBLIC` addition marks the `zcl_vehicle` class as the global class of the class pool and can only be set by the Class Builder.[7]

You can also use this view to edit the declarations of all visibility sections of a global class. In particular, you can fully utilize the complete syntax for type definitions here (see Section 5.1), which is not possible if you use the tabs. For example, if a `c` type attribute is to be created with a certain length and without a reference to a known type, you can enter this as follows in the ABAP Editor:

```
DATA text TYPE c LENGTH len.
```

In this case, the **Attributes** tab (see Figure 4.3) does not display any type, but you can use the arrow button to navigate to the declaration in the visibility section. However, this procedure is not recommended for attributes. Instead, you can declare independent data types in classes that you can then reference in attributes.

---

6 You can also generate a global class as a copy of a local class by selecting **Object Type • Import • Program-local classes** in the initial screen of the Class Builder (SE24).

7 The fact that input parameter `delta` is preceded by the `!` character represents a precaution of the Class Builder. The `!` character is an escape character that can be written directly in front of an identifier in order to distinguish the identifier from an ABAP word of the same name.

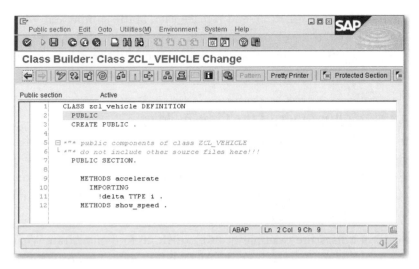

Figure 4.7 Public Section of a Global Class

4.5 Data Types as Components of Classes

In classes, data types occur usually as the properties of attributes. Those bound data types belong to the static properties of a class, and you can reference them in statements that contain a LIKE addition without having to create an object (see Section 5.1).

In addition, ABAP Objects allows you to declare any independent data types within any visibility section of local or global classes. Such types are also static components of a class and are available as instance-independent to class users.

TYPES   The syntax for the declaration of an independent data type mytype is similar to the DATA statement for attributes:

TYPES mytype **TYPE** dtype.

After the TYPE addition, you must specify or construct a dtype data type of the ABAP type hierarchy (more on this in Section 5.1.2). Users and, of course, all components of this class can refer to the self-defined type in statements that contain a TYPE addition.

In the Class Builder, you can enter independent types and their properties in the **Types** tab. Figure 4.8 shows the example of a class that we'll use in one of the later chapters in this book.

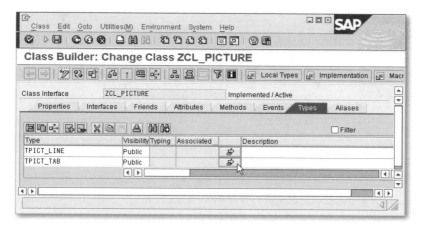

Figure 4.8 Self-Defined Types of a Global Class

As is the case with attributes, you can define the types either by referencing known types or by directly editing the corresponding visibility section. To do that, you must click on the associated arrow button or select **Goto • Public Section**. Contrary to attributes, types are commonly defined in this way. Except when defining reference types, we don't recommend that you declare an independent type by referring to an existing one; however, it may be necessary in certain situations, for example, because of a package check.

Figure 4.9 displays the declaration of the data types from Figure 4.8 in the public visibility section of the global class to which you can navigate by clicking on the arrow button. The type is used for a byte field of length 1022. Moreover, a table type is declared whose row type is defined by the preceding type. These types are required in the class. You should always use this type of declaration as part of the class instead of a global declaration in the ABAP Dictionary if the semantic type properties of a dictionary type are not needed (see Section 5.1.7).

Types that are declared in this way can be used behind a TYPE addition wherever the class is visible and usable, for example, in the following way:

```
DATA pict_line TYPE zcl_picture=>tpict_line,
     pict       TYPE zcl_picture=>tpict_tab.
```

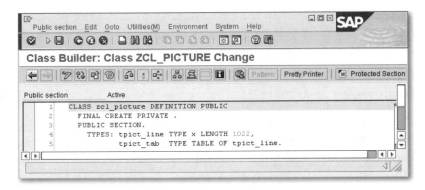

Figure 4.9 Declaration of Types in the ABAP Editor

4.6 Objects and Object References

The vehicle in Listing 4.5 and the ZCL_VEHICLE class in Figure 4.7 contain only instance components and therefore represent mere type definitions from which you can create objects via instantiation. What we still need in order to be able to use those classes are the objects, that is, the instances of the classes.

4.6.1 Creating and Referencing Objects

Object references
To create an object and then access it, you need object references in object reference variables. An object reference is nothing more than the address of an object in the memory. An object reference variable is a data object that can contain object references and therefore points to objects. An object reference variable is either initial or points to exactly one object. However, you should note that several reference variables can point to the same object. In addition to object reference variables, ABAP also contains data reference variables that can point to data objects, in other words, to the instances of data types (see Section 5.1.6).

The syntax for the declaration of object reference variables (to be more precise, at this point we are only dealing with class reference variables) is:

REF TO DATA oref TYPE REF TO myclass.

This declares an object reference variable, oref, that can point to objects of the myclass class. The REF TO addition allows you to refer to all classes that are visible at this stage. These are either the local classes of the same program, or all global classes (in the context of the limitations set by your package). To create an object of a class, you can use

```
CREATE OBJECT oref [TYPE myclass].
```

CREATE OBJECT,
object creation

This statement creates an object of the `myclass` class to which the object reference variable `oref` points after a successful instantiation. The `TYPE myclass` addition is optional. If it is not specified, the type of the object reference variable is automatically used. The explicit specification of the class from which an object is created becomes important if an object is to be created for a different class than the one that is specified for `oref` (polymorphism, see Section 6.4).

Listing 4.6 shows the creation of two objects of global class ZCL_VEHICLE that corresponds to the local class `vehicle` in Listing 4.5, and the call of its methods.

Listing 4.6 Vehicle Objects

```
REPORT z_drive_vehicles.

CLASS demo DEFINITION.
  PUBLIC SECTION.
    CLASS-METHODS main.
ENDCLASS.
CLASS demo IMPLEMENTATION.
  METHOD main.
    DATA: vehicle1 TYPE REF TO zcl_vehicle,
          vehicle2 TYPE REF TO zcl_vehicle.
    CREATE OBJECT: vehicle1,
                   vehicle2.
    vehicle1->accelerate( 100 ).
    vehicle1->show_speed( ).
    vehicle2->accelerate( 200 ).
    vehicle2->show_speed( ).
  ENDMETHOD.
ENDCLASS.
START-OF-SELECTION.
  demo=>main( ).
```

We use the static method `main` of the local class `demo` of an executable program as a framework. This method is called in the START-OF-

SELECTION event block. In the main class, we define two object reference variables, vehicle1 and vehicle2, of the zcl_vehicle type and apply the CREATE OBJECT statement to those two variables. If the local class vehicle from Listing 4.5 were defined in the same program, the reference variables could also be declared with a reference to this class.

Figure 4.10 shows a simplified illustration of the situation in the internal session of the ABAP program after the CREATE OBJECT statements have been executed. There are two objects of the ZCL_VEHI-CLE class to which the reference variables point. The objects can be used via the reference variables. Note that only the components of the public visibility section can be accessed from outside. This is symbolized by the outer shells in the figure that protect the interior of the objects.

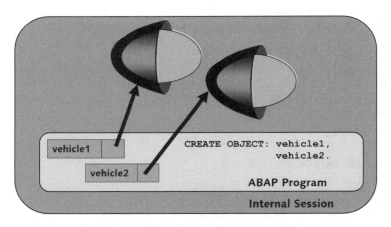

Figure 4.10 Reference Variables, Object References, and Objects

Object component selector

Listing 4.6 also shows how the instance components of objects are accessed. The syntax consists of an object reference variable that points to an object, and the addressed component, separated by the object component selector ->. Behind the object component selector, you can also specify static components of the class. In our case, the instance methods accelerate and show_speed are called once in each object. Numbers are passed to accelerate as input parameters. As expected, each object outputs the passed speed. The syntax of the method call consists simply of a method name followed by a pair of parentheses in which the parameter transfer takes place (see Section 6.1.2 for more information).

4.6.2 The Self-Reference "me"

An object reference variable provides access to all components of an object that are visible where the variable is used. As shown by the access to the instance attribute `speed` in the vehicle class methods, all components of the method's own class can be accessed within an instance method, even without using a reference variable. In addition, each instance method contains a predefined reference variable of the type of the current class. This variable is called `me`. It always contains a reference to its own object and cannot be overwritten in the method. This reference variable, or rather the reference it contains, is called self-reference. The self-reference can be used to address an object's own components. For example, the `speed` attribute can also be addressed via `me->speed`.

We recommend the consistent use of the complete specification with `me->` as it indicates within a method that a component of its own class is accessed instead of a local data object of the method or a global data object of the program.[8] In any case, you must specify `me` if an attribute of the class is hidden by a local data object of the same name or by an interface parameter. Lastly, you can, of course, also use `me` to assign or pass a reference to the method's own object to other reference variables or objects.

4.6.3 Assigning References

As with other variables, you can make assignments between reference variables (see Section 5.2.2). In Listing 4.7, we modified the program from Listing 4.6 in such a way that reference variable `vehicle2` is assigned the reference from `vehicle1` instead of creating its own object.

Listing 4.7 Assigning Reference Variables

```
REPORT z_drive_vehicle.

CLASS demo DEFINITION.
  PUBLIC SECTION.
    CLASS-METHODS main.
ENDCLASS.
```

---

8 For the same reason, you should also place the name of a class at the beginning when accessing a static component of that class. Ideally, the methods in Listing 4.2 should use `static_vehicle=>speed` instead of just `speed`.

```
CLASS demo IMPLEMENTATION.
  METHOD main.
    DATA: vehicle1 TYPE REF TO zcl_vehicle,
          vehicle2 TYPE REF TO zcl_vehicle.
    CREATE OBJECT vehicle1.
    vehicle2 = vehicle1.
    vehicle1->accelerate( 100 ).
    vehicle2->accelerate( 200 ).
    vehicle1->show_speed( ).
    vehicle2->show_speed( ).
  ENDMETHOD.
ENDCLASS.
START-OF-SELECTION.
  demo=>main( ).
```

Figure 4.10 shows a simplified illustration of this situation in the internal session of the ABAP program after the assignment has been made.

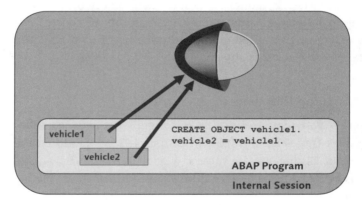

Figure 4.11 Assigning Reference Variables

Reference semantics After the assignment vehicle2 = vehicle1 has been made, two reference variables point to the same object. This means that, the content of the reference variable (i. e., the object reference) is copied and not the referenced object (reference semantics).[9] The original object remains unchanged and exists only once in the memory.

---

9 ABAP Objects does not support any statement that enables you to copy an object itself. If this is absolutely necessary, you can serialize an object and deserialize it into a different object (see Section 12.5.3).

You can equally use each reference variable that points to an object (strictly speaking, this holds true only if the reference variables are of the same type). In our example, both calls of `accelerate` accelerate the same vehicle and both outputs show the speed of 300.

Whereas it is usually not necessary to access an object with multiple reference variables within one context (procedure, class, or program), assignments between reference variables are always required if references to objects are to be passed to other methods or objects, or if the references are to be stored in a different way.

Section 6.4 contains more detailed information on assignments between reference variables and the associated rules.

4.6.4 Multiple Instantiation

In the example in Listing 4.6, we showed the creation of two objects of a class. Needless to say, the use of different reference variables shown there quickly reaches its limit if it becomes necessary to create more than just two or three objects of a class. Listing 4.8 shows you how to manage any number of objects for the same class.[10]

Listing 4.8 Multiple Instantiation

```
REPORT z_drive_many_vehicles.

CLASS demo DEFINITION.
  PUBLIC SECTION.
    CLASS-METHODS main.
ENDCLASS.
CLASS demo IMPLEMENTATION.
  METHOD main.
    DATA: vehicle     TYPE REF TO zcl_vehicle,
          vehicle_tab TYPE TABLE OF
                      REF TO zcl_vehicle,
          n           TYPE i VALUE 5,
          speed       TYPE i.
    DO n TIMES.
      CREATE OBJECT vehicle.
      speed = sy-index * 10.
      vehicle->accelerate( speed ).
```

---

10 In fact, you can even manage objects of different classes in this way. See Section 6.4 for more information on this topic.

```
          APPEND vehicle TO vehicle_tab.
        ENDDO.
        LOOP AT vehicle_tab INTO vehicle.
          vehicle->show_speed( ).
        ENDLOOP.
      ENDMETHOD.
    ENDCLASS.
    START-OF-SELECTION.
      demo=>main( ).
```

Internal table To collect the references to all objects created, we use TABLE OF to create an internal table vehicle_tab.[11] In a DO loop, we create vehicle objects, assign a speed to them, and then use APPEND to append them to the internal table. Figure 4.12 shows a simplified illustration of the situation in the internal session of the ABAP program after executing the loop.

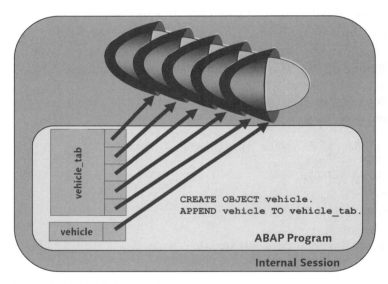

Figure 4.12 Multiple Instantiation

Each row of the internal table references an object, and the single reference variable vehicle points to the object that was created last. After that we use a LOOP to import the internal table row by row into vehicle again and output the speed for each object.

---

11 As the name suggests, internal tables are much more powerful than what is shown here. Section 5.5 provides more information on this topic.

The handling of several objects via an internal table shown here 4GL demonstrates the synthesis from the 4GL language ABAP and the object-oriented language elements of ABAP Objects. Other object-oriented languages such as Java do not provide any direct language elements that would solve the task shown here. To be able to manage any number of objects, those languages would have to use class-based solutions from libraries. To solve most of the important programming tasks, ABAP Objects can refer to powerful language constructs of the ABAP programming language. As demonstrated in this section, those language elements can and should be integrated smoothly and very efficiently in object-oriented programming.

4.6.5   Object Creation in a Factory Method

In Section 4.3.2, we introduced the control of class instantiation in the context of encapsulation. In Listing 4.9, we want to supply the respective example based on our simple vehicle example.

Listing 4.9 Factory Method

```
REPORT z_vehicle_factory.

CLASS vehicle DEFINITION CREATE PRIVATE.
  PUBLIC SECTION.
    CLASS-METHODS create RETURNING VALUE(ref)
                         TYPE REF TO vehicle.
    METHODS: accelerate  IMPORTING delta TYPE i,
             show_speed.
  PRIVATE SECTION.
    DATA speed TYPE i.
ENDCLASS.

CLASS demo DEFINITION.
  PUBLIC SECTION.
    CLASS-METHODS main.
ENDCLASS.

CLASS vehicle IMPLEMENTATION.
  METHOD create.
    CREATE OBJECT ref.
  ENDMETHOD.
  METHOD accelerate.
    me->speed = me->speed + delta.
  ENDMETHOD.
  METHOD show_speed.
    DATA output TYPE string.
```

209

```
      output = me->speed.
    MESSAGE output TYPE 'I'.
  ENDMETHOD.
ENDCLASS.
CLASS demo IMPLEMENTATION.
  METHOD main.
    DATA vehicle TYPE REF TO vehicle.
    vehicle = vehicle=>create( ).
    vehicle->accelerate( 100 ).
    vehicle->show_speed( ).
  ENDMETHOD.
ENDCLASS.
START-OF-SELECTION.
  demo=>main( ).
```

In contrast to the vehicle class from Listing 4.5, we declare vehicle in Listing 4.9 with the CREATE PRIVATE addition. The static method create creates a vehicle object; the return value ref that is defined using RETURNING is used directly as a reference variable here. In the main method of the demo class, the create method is functionally called in an assignment, which causes the local variable vehicle to be assigned the reference to the created object.

Agent   In Listing 4.10, we migrate the object creation into a special class, vehicle_agent, without removing the private instance creation. For that reason, vehicle_agent must be declared as a friend of vehicle.

Listing 4.10 Agent Class

```
REPORT z_vehicle_agent.

CLASS vehicle_agent DEFINITION DEFERRED.

CLASS vehicle DEFINITION CREATE PRIVATE
              FRIENDS vehicle_agent.
  PUBLIC SECTION.
    METHODS: accelerate IMPORTING delta TYPE i,
             show_speed.
  PRIVATE SECTION.
    DATA speed TYPE i.
ENDCLASS.

CLASS vehicle_agent DEFINITION.
  PUBLIC SECTION.
    CLASS-METHODS create RETURNING VALUE(ref)
```

```
                    TYPE REF TO vehicle.
ENDCLASS.
CLASS demo DEFINITION.
  PUBLIC SECTION.
    CLASS-METHODS main.
ENDCLASS.
CLASS vehicle IMPLEMENTATION.
  METHOD accelerate.
    me->speed = me->speed + delta.
  ENDMETHOD.
  METHOD show_speed.
    DATA output TYPE string.
    output = me->speed.
    MESSAGE output TYPE 'I'.
  ENDMETHOD.
ENDCLASS.
CLASS vehicle_agent IMPLEMENTATION.
  METHOD create.
    CREATE OBJECT ref.
  ENDMETHOD.
ENDCLASS.
CLASS demo IMPLEMENTATION.
  METHOD main.

    DATA vehicle TYPE REF TO vehicle.

    vehicle = vehicle_agent=>create( ).

    vehicle->accelerate( 100 ).
    vehicle->show_speed( ).

  ENDMETHOD.
ENDCLASS.
START-OF-SELECTION.
  demo=>main( ).
```

The example in Listing 4.10 also allows us to mention another special case that may sometimes become necessary when using local classes. If a local class is referred to within a class and the local class hasn't been declared yet, it must be made known using the CLASS DEFINITION DEFERRED statement. This is because, for performance reasons, the ABAP Compiler compiles a program in one single process. If you don't publish the local class, the FRIENDS addition would cause a syntax error due to an unknown class. If, in our example, we swapped the sequence of the declaration parts of vehicle and

CLASS DEFINITION DEFERRED

vehicle_agent, vehicle would have to be made known before vehicle_agent using the DEFERRED statement.

4.6.6 Garbage Collection

Objects occupy space in the main memory. If they are no longer needed, they can and should be deleted. The critical elements for the existence of an object are reference variables. As long as a reference variable points to an object, the object is necessary. What this means is that an object can be deleted when no more reference variable points to the object.

Garbage Collector The Garbage Collector of the ABAP runtime environment is responsible for the deletion of objects. The Garbage Collector deletes objects that are no longer referenced by reference variables. The Garbage Collector is called periodically by the ABAP runtime environment. It traces reference variables of deleted objects. This means, if an object that is no longer referenced contains attributes of the reference variable type, its references are traced by the Garbage Collector. If no reference variable points to the objects found in this process, those objects are deleted as well, as shown in Figure 4.13.

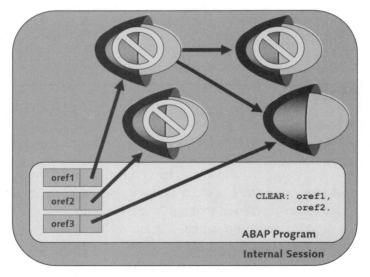

Figure 4.13 Garbage Collection

You can explicitly initialize references to objects using the CLEAR statement (see Section 5.2.3). If you initialize the two reference variables `oref1` and `oref2` shown in Figure 4.13, the only object that will be kept alive after the next call of the Garbage Collector is the object referenced by `oref3`.

In addition to the `CLEAR` statement, there are many other mechanisms that can cause references to objects to disappear. For example, when a reference is assigned, the original reference in the target variable is lost; or a reference variable is a local variable of a method that is deleted completely when the method ends.

On the other hand, you should note that many references to objects can exist—often unexpectedly—that keep the objects alive, although you might think you have initialized all reference variables. For example, the methods of an object can be registered as event handlers (see Section 6.5), or objects are managed or used by frameworks that cannot be accessed directly. To delete these kinds of references, event handlers must be deregistered and special methods of the frameworks must be called. Otherwise, memory leaks can occur, which may result in memory bottlenecks, particularly if many objects or large objects are used.

Memory leaks

Thus, when working with objects, you should always keep their memory in your mind. Always release unused objects for the Garbage Collector, and use the Memory Inspector tool to check if the garbage collection was successful (see Section 13.4).

4.7   Constructors

The status of an object is determined by the values of its attributes. In this context, the question arises as to which status an object has immediately after its creation. Such an initial status is defined by the initial values of the attributes. These initial values are either values that depend on the data type (see Section 5.1.3), or values that are specified explicitly: either with the `VALUE` addition or in the **Initial Value** column of the Class Builder.

Initialization

Very often, this static initialization of an object is not sufficient. Instead, the initial status of an object should be controlled during object creation. But if only those methods that were introduced up until now were available to you, you would have to declare methods for this task and call those methods immediately after each object creation. The latter is rather prone to errors, because users would not be forced to initialize an object appropriately.

To automate the initialization of objects, you can use constructors. A constructor is a special method that is executed automatically by the runtime environment. Constructors are used to put an object into a defined initial status. A constructor cannot be called like usual methods. As with all components of classes, we distinguish between instance constructors and static constructors.

4.7.1 Instance Constructor

The instance constructor is a predefined method of a class called con-structor. This method is automatically executed once, immediately after the creation of an object of the class. Thus, the instance constructor serves to initialize individual instances. If you want to use the constructor, you must declare and implement it like a usual method.

constructor   The syntax for the instance constructor of local classes is:

```
CLASS myclass DEFINITION
                CREATE PUBLIC|PROTECTED|PRIVATE.
  PUBLIC SECTION.
    METHODS constructor
            [IMPORTING iᵢ TYPE type ...]
            [RASING    eᵢ].
  ...
ENDCLASS.

CLASS myclass IMPLEMENTATION.
  METHOD constructor.
    ...
  ENDMETHOD.
ENDCLASS.
```

The easiest way to implement the instance constructor for global classes is to select the **Edit • Create Constructor** function in the Class Builder. The current release status still requires the instance constructor to be declared in the public visibility section of the class. However, the actual visibility is determined by where the class can be instantiated, which is defined using the CREATE addition of CLASS

DEFINITION. The permission to create an object is equivalent to a permission to execute the constructor.[12]

The parameter interface of an instance constructor is limited to input parameters, because the instance constructor is exclusively used to define an object status and is not supposed to provide any other behavior. To fill the input parameters of the instance constructor with values, the CREATE OBJECT statement contains an addition:

```
CREATE OBJECT oref EXPORTING iᵢ = aᵢ.
```

Each non-optional input parameter i must be linked to an actual parameter a via the = sign after EXPORTING (see also Section 6.1.2).

If an exception occurs in an instance constructor, the created object will be deleted immediately during the execution of the CREATE OBJECT statement, and the corresponding reference variable is set to its initial value. The exception can be handled, as described in Section 10.2.1.

The example in Listing 4.11 shows the use of the instance constructor in order to assign a color to vehicles of the vehicle class from Listing 4.5.

Listing 4.11 Instance Constructor

```
REPORT z_colored_vehicle.

CLASS demo DEFINITION.
  PUBLIC SECTION.
    CLASS-METHODS main.
ENDCLASS.

CLASS vehicle DEFINITION.
  PUBLIC SECTION.
    METHODS: constructor IMPORTING color TYPE string,
             accelerate  IMPORTING delta TYPE i,
             show_speed.
  PRIVATE SECTION.
    DATA: color TYPE string,
          speed TYPE i.
ENDCLASS.

CLASS vehicle IMPLEMENTATION.
  METHOD constructor.
```

---

12 In the next release of SAP NetWeaver, you can declare the constructor in the visibility section that matches the instantiatibility.

```
      me->color = color.
  ENDMETHOD.
  METHOD accelerate.
    me->speed = me->speed + delta.
  ENDMETHOD.
  METHOD show_speed.
    DATA output TYPE string.
    output = me->speed.
    CONCATENATE me->color `: ` output INTO output.
    MESSAGE output TYPE 'I'.
  ENDMETHOD.
ENDCLASS.
CLASS demo IMPLEMENTATION.
  METHOD main.
    DATA: red_vehicle   TYPE REF TO vehicle,
          blue_vehicle  TYPE REF TO vehicle,
          green_vehicle TYPE REF TO vehicle.

    CREATE OBJECT:
      red_vehicle   EXPORTING color = `Red`,
      blue_vehicle  EXPORTING color = `Blue`,
      green_vehicle EXPORTING color = `Green`.

    red_vehicle->accelerate( 100 ).
    blue_vehicle->accelerate( 200 ).
    green_vehicle->accelerate( 300 ).

    red_vehicle->show_speed( ).
    blue_vehicle->show_speed( ).
    green_vehicle->show_speed( ).
  ENDMETHOD.
ENDCLASS.
START-OF-SELECTION.
  demo=>main( ).
```

Three vehicles with different colors are created and accelerated in the main method of the demo class. The output shows the color and speed.

4.7.2 Static Constructor

The static constructor is a predefined method of a class called class_constructor. This method is automatically executed once for each class in a program before the class is accessed for the first time. Therefore, the static constructor is used to initialize the static attributes of a class. If you want to use the constructor, you must declare and implement it like a usual method.

The syntax for the static constructor of local classes is:

class_constructor

```
CLASS myclass DEFINITION.
  PUBLIC SECTION.
    CLASS-METHODS class_constructor.
  ...
ENDCLASS.

CLASS myclass IMPLEMENTATION.
  METHOD class_constructor.
    ...
  ENDMETHOD.
ENDCLASS.
```

The easiest way to implement the static constructor for global classes is to select the **Edit · Create Class Constructor** function in the Class Builder. The static constructor must always be declared in the public visibility section of the class. A static constructor does not have any parameter interface and cannot propagate any exceptions.

In Listing 4.12, the static constructor helps us to remove a minor flaw from Listing 4.10. In Listing 4.10, a `vehicle_agent` class is used as an agent, although from an object-oriented point of view, an agent should actually be an object of an agent class. However, because we still want exactly one instance to exist that functions as an agent for our vehicle class, we use the static constructor to apply the singleton principle.[13]

Singleton

Listing 4.12 Static Constructor

```
REPORT z_singleton_vehicle_agent.

CLASS vehicle_agent DEFINITION DEFERRED.
CLASS vehicle DEFINITION CREATE PRIVATE
  ...
ENDCLASS.
CLASS vehicle_agent DEFINITION CREATE PRIVATE.
  PUBLIC SECTION.
    CLASS-DATA agent TYPE REF TO vehicle_agent
                     READ-ONLY.
```

---

13 A singleton is an object-oriented design pattern. A class that is defined according to this pattern allows you to create exactly one object for each program.

```
        CLASS-METHODS class_constructor.
        METHODS create RETURNING VALUE(ref)
                    TYPE REF TO vehicle.
ENDCLASS.

CLASS demo DEFINITION.
  PUBLIC SECTION.
    CLASS-METHODS main.
ENDCLASS.

CLASS vehicle IMPLEMENTATION.
  ...
ENDCLASS.

CLASS vehicle_agent IMPLEMENTATION.
  METHOD class_constructor.
    CREATE OBJECT vehicle_agent=>agent.
  ENDMETHOD.
  METHOD create.
    CREATE OBJECT ref.
  ENDMETHOD.
ENDCLASS.

CLASS demo IMPLEMENTATION.
  METHOD main.
    DATA: agent   TYPE REF TO vehicle_agent,
          vehicle TYPE REF TO vehicle.
    agent   = vehicle_agent=>agent.
    vehicle = agent->create( ).

    ...

  ENDMETHOD.
ENDCLASS.

START-OF-SELECTION.
  demo=>main( ).
```

Listing 4.12 shows only the differences between the z_singleton_ vehicle_agent and z_vehicle_agent programs. In the vehicle_ agent class, the static components have been converted into instance components, while a CREATE PRIVATE addition, a static attribute agent, and the static constructor have been added.

In the main method of the demo class, the static attribute vehicle_ agent=>agent is assigned to a local reference variable agent. The static constructor is called when the vehicle_agent class is addressed for the first time. Then, exactly one object of the class is created and the reference is assigned to the static attribute vehicle_agent=>agent. If vehicle_agent=>agent is accessed again at a later stage, it will still contain the reference to the only existing object. The agent object can now be used to create a vehicle object.

We introduced the local reference variable agent here to emphasize its function. But even shorter than

```
agent   = vehicle_agent=>agent.
vehicle = agent->create( ).
```

would be the following statement, which has the same meaning:

```
vehicle = vehicle_agent=>agent->create( ).
```

This statement directly uses the static attribute of the agent class. The statement also demonstrates that operands can contain more than just one component selector.

4.7.3   Destructors

If an object contains a constructor method that is called every time the object is created, you might infer that there must be also a method that is called when the object is deleted by the garbage collection. In fact, many programming languages contain these kinds of methods that are referred to as destructors. For several reasons (performance, transaction concept, etc.), ABAP Objects does not provide any destructors for application development.

4.8   Local Declarations of a Class Pool

The main program of a global class is a class pool. Technically speaking, a class pool is a regular ABAP program that is structured according to Section 3.2.1. The Class Builder generates the declaration part of the global class in the global declaration part, while the implementation part is generated in the implementation part of the class pool. Correspondingly, there's nothing that speaks against carrying out additional declarations and implementations in the class pool, which can then be used in the global class. As shown in Figure 4.7, the global class has the PUBLIC identifier. In addition, you can create local types, classes, and interfaces in a class pool. However, local data and processing blocks other than methods are not permitted.

4.8.1 Local Types in Class Pools

To create a local type in a class pool, select **Goto • Class-local types • Local Class definitions/Types** in the Class Builder. This takes you to the ABAP Editor for an include program that is integrated in the global declaration part of the class pool. Here you can define program-local types using the TYPES statement, and you can integrate type groups using the TYPE-POOLS statement.

Local types that are defined in this way can be used within the class pool; however, the local types can be referenced only in the private visibility section of the global declaration part of the global class. The public and protected sections can also be used from other programs that therefore must have access to the types used in those sections.

We already introduced a local type for the global reservation class in Section 2.8.2 of our practical introduction (see Figure 2.65).

4.8.2 Local Classes in Class Pools

Local classes are declared in the same include program as local types. To create a local class in a class pool, you must also select **Goto • Class-local types • Local Class definitions/Types** in the Class Builder. To implement the local classes, select **Goto • Class-local Types • Local Class implementations**. This takes you to the ABAP Editor for an include program that is integrated in the implementation part of the class pool.

Modularization
You can use local classes to modularize a class pool beyond the methods of the global class. In the class pool, the local classes play the same roles as the local classes in other ABAP programs. They are not visible from outside. You can use the methods of the local classes to store reusable functions from the actual class. If you want to provide a local class with access to the protected and private components of the global class, you must declare it as a local friend of the class. To do that, you can use the following special statement:

LOCAL FRIENDS
```
CLASS global_class DEFINITION
                   LOCAL FRIENDS ... local_class ...
```

This statement does not have an associated ENDCLASS statement and can be contained in the include for the local class definitions.

The modularization of a global class through local classes of the class pool is a recommended procedure. The advantage of using this method instead of exclusively using private methods of the global class is that you can keep a clear overview of the global class and that you can keep the list of methods on the **Methods** tab in the Class Builder manageable. The use of local classes in a global class is, in particular, not limited to a purely functional modularization via static methods.[14] The local class can, of course, use all object-oriented concepts, from instantiation to inheritance to events.

4.9   Using ABAP Objects on the AS ABAP

You have now gotten to know classes and objects as a basis of object-oriented programming with ABAP Objects on the AS ABAP. Figure 4.14 shows what an ideal object-oriented ABAP world would look like.

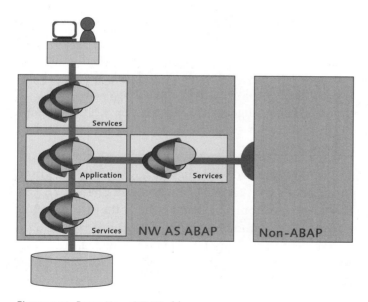

Figure 4.14 Brave New OO World

The entire application code would be written in ABAP Objects and encapsulated in application classes. The presentation and persistence

Object-oriented ABAP world

---

14 If, for instance, you wanted to modularize function groups internally in procedural ABAP, only subroutines were available as functional means.

layers as well as external systems would not be accessed in the application objects. Instead, the access to external layers would be encapsulated in specific service classes and would occur via proxy objects. This is already possible today for the presentation and persistence layers. Interfaces to external systems are partly wrapped in classes:

▶ Class-based frameworks exist between application classes and the presentation layer, such as the GUI CFW (Control Framework, see Section 9.1.17), DOI (Desktop Office Integration), BSP, and Web Dynpro (see Section 9.5).

▶ Between the application classes and the persistence layer, there are the class-based Object Services for handling persistent objects in the database.

▶ To establish the connection between application classes and the Internet, there are the interfaces and classes of the *Internet Connection Framework* (ICF) that wraps the access to the *Internet Communication Manager* (ICM).

Admittedly, no purely class-based layer currently exists between application classes and the programming interfaces of external systems. You still need to call remote-enabled function modules in application and service objects (see Section 12.2). We also mentioned that, for reasons of downward compatibility, ABAP Objects was added to the existing language. So, despite the existing options, the situation in application programs today can be illustrated as shown in Figure 4.15.

Real ABAP world   The real ABAP world is a mixed world in which ABAP Objects is used alongside and together with classical concepts (see Chapter 7). Frequently, classes are used only in places where the use of ABAP Objects is mandatory without revising the entire application, because the required functionality is no longer provided. An example is the usage of the GUI CFW with classical dynpros. Vice versa, applications can be programmed as object-oriented and still use the classical interfaces to the other layers.

As mentioned earlier, one of our goals in this book is to encourage you to program in ABAP Objects as often as possible, that is, you should try to approach the pure OO world shown in Figure 4.14.

For that purpose, it is not necessary to always carry out a complete object-oriented modeling process. Of course, this is necessary for large and complex projects, and there are examples of such projects in which ABAP Objects has proven its worth. However, if you're not a real "OO wizard," you don't need to become a slave to an academic OO paradigm.

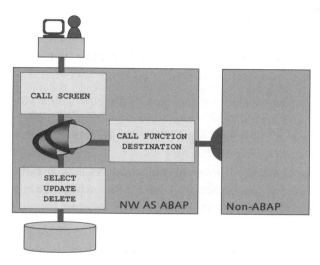

Figure 4.15 Real ABAP World

Use ABAP Objects with common sense and in accordance with your requirements. In particular, you can and should use all the helpful, tried and tested 4GL properties of ABAP such as internal tables and Open SQL in your method implementations. If you use ABAP Objects without an extensive OO design phase (i. e., free of UML), using a conservative approach to get started with object-oriented programming can prove to be a very wise decision. You should always begin such a defensive way of programming as restrictively as possible, since you can loosen the restrictions later on to reflect your requirements. The magic word in this context is "encapsulation." This means:

Defensive programming

▶ Keep the number of public components of a class as small as possible, in other words, keep the public interface small. Components that can be private should be private.

▶ If you use public attributes, declare them as READ-ONLY.

▶ Consider the private instantiation of classes.

▶ Declare classes as FINAL, that is, no subclasses can be derived (see Section 6.2.6).

By taking these rules into account, you will quickly be able to write applications in ABAP Objects that are much more robust and easier to maintain than if you used procedural ABAP.

4.10   Summary and Perspective

This introduction of classes and objects forms the basis for all further descriptions of ABAP and ABAP Objects.

In the following chapter, we'll introduce you to the basic ABAP language elements that are required for the implementation of applications in ABAP Objects. Although these language elements are not bound to ABAP Objects, nevertheless, we want to describe them in the context of object-oriented programming (i. e., we'll only carry out declarations in the declaration part of a class, whereas we'll implement functionality only in methods).

Chapter 6 contains a more detailed description of ABAP Objects in that it provides information on other concepts such as method interfaces and calls, inheritance, interfaces, and polymorphism. For many developers, these concepts represent the actual core of object-oriented programming. In that same chapter, we'll also discuss the event concept.

"The limits of my language are the limits of my world."
—Ludwig Wittgenstein, *Tractatus logico-philosophicus, 5.6.*

5 Basic ABAP Language Elements

The primary purpose of any program is the processing of data, irrespective of the programming language in which it is written. This premise holds true for object-oriented programming, as well as for the classic procedural type of programming. Therefore, every programming language requires declarative language elements that define the data of a class or of a program, and operational language elements that execute the operations with this data. These language elements form the basis of each function that a class or program can provide.

In ABAP Objects, you can declare data either as attributes in the different visibility sections of a class (see Section 4.3.2), or as local working data in methods. The operations to be carried out with this data are implemented in the methods. For historical reasons, ABAP contains additional contexts in which you can declare and process data. This book generally focuses on programming with ABAP Objects, the basic principles of which have been described in Chapter 4. Although if some short sample programs provided in Chapter 4 have not been implemented completely, you should always consider them as components of classes. Moreover, we assume that you use only Unicode programs (see Section 3.2.5), that is, the program property **Unicode checks active** is always set.

5.1 Data Types and Data Objects

5.1.1 Data Objects

The operational language elements of a method (or of another processing block) use data that is stored in the working memory of the program. Typically, the working memory is a part of the memory area of the program's internal session (see Section 3.2.5). In addition,

Data

you can directly access data that is shared by several programs via the shared objects memory (see Section 6.6). External data such as inputs on the user interface or data from the database must always be transported into the working memory of a program in order to be processed using ABAP statements. If you want to preserve the contents of a data object over the runtime period of a program (or its lifecycle in the shared memory), you must store the contents persistently before the program terminates (see Chapter 10).

Data object   A section of the working memory whose content can be addressed and interpreted by ABAP statements is referred to as a data object.[1] ABAP statements use data objects in that they are specified in operand positions. You can create data objects by using declarative statements or by using CREATE DATA during program execution. Data objects that have been created using declarative statements are assigned a name and can be addressed through this name. We will describe this property in greater detail in this section. Data objects created using CREATE DATA are not assigned a name and can be addressed only via reference variables, similar to class instances (see Section 10.1.2).

Declaring a data object   The most important statement for declaring a data object is DATA. Let's look at a simple DATA statement:

DATA

```
DATA text TYPE c LENGTH 20 VALUE 'Data Object'.
```

This statement creates a data object that can be accessed via the name text by the statements of the context in which the data object is visible. Its length consists of 20 characters and its initial content is 'Data Object'. The TYPE c addition ensures that the content is stored in the memory in a character-encoded way. The name and technical type properties of a data object are uniquely defined for its entire lifecycle.

Context of a data object   A data object that is created using a declarative statement is valid for the context that contains the statement. The following contexts are possible:

▶ **Methods**
Data declarations in methods and other procedures (function modules, subroutines, see Section 7.2) create local data that can be

---

1 An alternative name for data object could simply be *field*.

addressed via their names within their procedure and that exist during the execution of a procedure. The local data of a procedure cannot be accessed via their names from outside of the procedure.[2]

▶ **Classes**

Data declarations in the declaration part of classes[3] either create instance attributes or static attributes (see Section 4.4.2). Instance attributes can be addressed in all instance methods, while static attributes can be addressed in all methods via their names. The lifecycle of an instance attribute depends on the lifecycle of an object, while the lifecycle of a static attributes depends on the lifecycle of an internal session. The attributes of classes can be addressed via their names from outside the class, provided their visibility allows for that.

▶ **Programs**

Data declarations in the global declaration part of a program create program-global data objects that can be addressed anywhere in the program via their names. The lifecycle of a program-global data object is bound to the lifecycle of its program in the internal session. Program-local data cannot be addressed from outside of its program.[4]

The most specific context in which you can declare a data object is a procedure. Within a procedure, you cannot open a context that is more specific than the context of the procedure.[5] Although the ABAP syntax allows you to write `DATA` statements to any location within a procedure, the declared data objects are valid in the entire procedure. The place of declaration merely restricts the static visibility of the data object for subsequent statements. For this reason, you should list all declarative statements of a procedure at its beginning.

Local context

In addition to procedures, classic ABAP contains dialog modules and event blocks as additional processing blocks. These processing blocks do not have any local data context. Data declarations in such a

Dialog modules and event blocks

---

2 An access via data references is possible. Note, however, that such a reference becomes invalid at the end of the procedure.

3 This also includes attributes that are declared by integrating interfaces in a class.

4 Exceptions are the so-called interface work areas that are basically obsolete (`TABLES`, `COMMON PART`) and a few very specific dynamic addressings.

5 In particular, a `DATA` statement within a control structure such as `IF—ENDIF` does not open a context that is limited to the control structure.

processing block are assigned to the global declaration part of the program. If you still have to use those processing blocks—which is usually the case with classical dynpros and selection screens (see Chapter 9)—we strongly recommend that you do not use any declarative statements inside these processing blocks.

Program-global data

In the ABAP Objects world, data is generally encapsulated in classes. You should avoid using program-global data wherever possible.[6] The only reason why program-global data is still needed today is due to the data transport between dynpros and ABAP programs (see Section 9.1.10).

Hiding

Each of the three possible contexts for data objects has its own namespace. The local data objects of a procedure[7] can have the same names as the attributes of their class, and so on. A local data object that has the same name as a more global data object hides the more global data object in its context. To avoid hiding the attributes of a class, you can always address the attributes using an appropriate selector (->, =>). Because this is not possible for program-global data objects, you should adhere to a naming convention such as using the prefix g_.

Figure 5.1 shows an overview of the possible contexts of data objects.

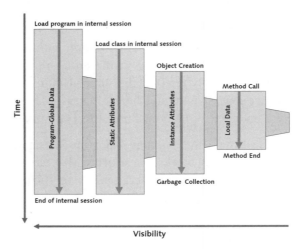

Figure 5.1 Contexts of Data Objects

---

6 Particularly because programs are not real encapsulation units.

7 In this context, they also include the interface parameters of the procedure.

5.1.2　Data Types

The DATA statement shown above contains the following addition:

```
... TYPE dtype ...
```

This addition is used in many ABAP statements to specify a data type. In our example, TYPE defines the data type of the data object. The data type determines how the data is stored in the memory, and it tells an ABAP statement how to handle the data. Data types reflect the fact that different types of data exist for different types of usage. For example, we distinguish between character-like data that is used to store and display textual contents, and numerical data that is used for numbers needed to carry out calculations.[8] Whereas for character-like data every character is individually encoded according to a specific code page such as Unicode, and the data objects can have different lengths, the entire value of numerical data is encoded platform-dependently and stored in an area whose length is predefined. The length of data objects that represent integers, for instance, is always 4 bytes.

ABAP Type Hierarchy

The primary task of ABAP programs consists of processing business data that is usually stored persistently in a database. To support this task, ABAP contains an extensive hierarchy of possible data types that are tailored for specific operations with business data. The range of data types contains elementary text fields as used in the preceding examples, a special numerical type that allows for business calculations, as well as complex, table-like types that enable a structured program-internal storage of data from database tables. Figure 5.2 displays the ABAP type hierarchy in its full splendor.

The left-hand side of the figure shows the hierarchy of all types that are possible in ABAP, as well as the objects that can have such a type. The right-hand side lists the generic data types that are assigned to individual nodes of the type hierarchy. (Section 5.1.9 provides more information on this topic.)

Types and objects

8　In addition, there is byte-like data that allows direct access to individual bytes.

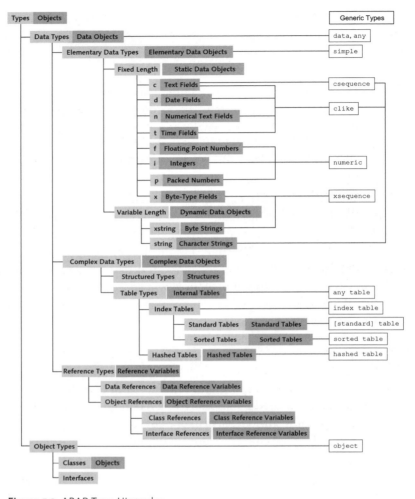

Figure 5.2 ABAP Type Hierarchy

Object types   Note that in addition to data types, the ABAP type hierarchy also contains object types as equal subnodes of a common generic term, "type".[9] This reflects the fact that a data object is nothing more than an instance of a data type, exactly as an object of ABAP Objects is an instance of a class. You already know the object type, class, from Chapter 4. A class describes an object completely. In Chapter 6, we'll introduce the object type, interface. An interface describes a partial aspect of an object and can be integrated by a class. Contrary to data

9 Data types and object types are also located in one single namespace. Consequently, a TYPE REF TO reference is always unique.

types, object types can describe both data and functionality; however, a class without methods also describes only a data object.

The possible data types are divided into three groups:

► **Elementary Data Types**

These data types are not made up of other types. An elementary data type is always specified by one out of 10 built-in ABAP types. There are eight built-in data types of fixed length: four character-like types for text fields (c), numerical text fields (n), date fields (d), and time fields (t). Three numerical types for integers (i), binary floating point numbers (f), and packed numbers (p). One byte-like type for byte fields (x). In addition, there are two built-in ABAP types of variable length: one character-like type for text strings (string) and one byte-like type for byte strings (xstring).

► **Complex Data Types**

These data types can be made up of any combination of other data types. They allow you to manage and work with semantically related datasets under a common name. There are no built-in complex data types. A complex data type must be constructed from existing types. There are structured types, that is, sequences of any other data types,[10] as well as table types. The latter consist of a sequence of any number of lines of the same line type. Each complex data type can be separated into individual elementary data types (i. e., built-in ABAP types) or reference types.

► **Reference Types**

Reference types describe data objects (reference variables) that contain references to other objects. There are types for data references (i. e., references to data objects), and for object references (i. e., references to instances of classes).

All elementary data types that can be used in ABAP are based on the 10 built-in ABAP types. But, except for data types such as i or d, for which all properties are already defined, you cannot use the built-in types directly. In fact, even for elementary data types, you must define additional properties such as the length or number of decimal places before you can use a type. You should always define complex data types and reference types yourself.

---

10 A structure is akin to a class without methods.

Defining Data Types

There are two ways to define data types in ABAP:

- ▸ As a property of a data object
- ▸ As an independent data type

Bound data type

Now, let's look at the DATA statement from Section 5.1.1. Based on the built-in ABAP type c, a text field of length 20 is created. At the same time, a bound data type of that property is created. In fact, you can create all types of the type hierarchy shown in Figure 5.2 as bound types; however, you cannot use the TYPE addition to reference such a type. Instead, you must use

LIKE

```
... LIKE dobj ...
```

You can use this addition in all ABAP statements that allow for the use of a TYPE addition. For example, you can create a second data object that has the same data type as text:

```
DATA second_text LIKE text VALUE 'Another Data Object'.
```

If this was the only way in which to define data types, we could only define data types in the contexts permitted for data objects, and consequently, we would have to create objects even for the purpose of defining types. However, this would consume a lot of memory. For this reason, ABAP provides independent data types as templates for data objects, similar to the classes that can be used as templates for objects.

Independent data type

The ABAP statement to be used to declare an independent data type is TYPES. The syntax is almost identical to the DATA statement.[11] The TYPES statement for an independent character-like data type t_text of length 20 would be as follows:

TYPES

```
TYPES t_text TYPE c LENGTH 20.
```

To declare a data object of this type, we again use the TYPE:

```
DATA text TYPE t_text VALUE 'Data Object'.
```

This means, you can use the TYPE addition to create new data types and to reference independent data types.

---

11 Of course, no data-object-specific additions can be used, such as VALUE that specifies an initial value.

The question now is where can we declare and use independent data types? In Section 4.3.2, we learned that we can use the Class Builder to declare classes globally in the class library and locally in ABAP programs. For data objects, we know the three contexts, procedure, class, and program from Section 5.1.1. Data types allow both options, that is, global and local. Independent data types can be defined as follows for usage in one or several programs:

▶ **Global Data Types**

Like classes of the class library, these data types can be used in all programs if permitted by the package check. There are three different ways to define global data types:

Global and local data types

▷ **ABAP Dictionary**

The ABAP Dictionary is a special storage for the declarations of data types that are visible in all repository objects. Data types in the ABAP Dictionary can contain semantic information to be used in user interfaces. Furthermore, the structures for the database tables of the AS ABAP are defined here. The data types of the ABAP Dictionary are not declared using the TYPES statement, but only using input templates of the ABAP Dictionary tool in the ABAP Workbench (**Dictionary Objects** node in the Object Navigator or Transaction SE11).

▷ **Global Classes and Interfaces**

As already indicated in Section 4.5, you can declare any type of the type hierarchy in the public declaration part of global classes (and global interfaces) using the TYPES statement. These types can be used by all users of a class (or interface), for example, to pass on data objects with a correct type to the interface parameters of methods of the class.

▷ **Type Groups**

Type groups represent the predecessor technology to public type declarations in global classes and interfaces. Type groups are special ABAP programs introduced with the TYPE-POOL statement. They must not contain anything more than the declaration of types using the TYPES statement (additionally, constants are also allowed). You can maintain a type group in an ABAP Editor that is integrated in the ABAP Dictionary tool. If a type group is published in the global declaration part of an ABAP program using the TYPE-POOLS statement, the program can use the types of the type group.

▶ **Program-local Data Types**
These data types can only be used in the context in which they were declared using the TYPES statement. You can declare program-local data types in the same contexts as the data objects of a program (see Section 5.1.1), and their visibility and lifecycle are the same as those of data objects.

  ▷ **Global Declaration Part**
  Data types declared here can be used in all subsequent declarations and in the implementation part.

  ▷ **Local Classes and Interfaces**
  Data types declared here can be used in the classes and interfaces themselves, as well as in the remaining parts of the program if permitted by their visibility.

  ▷ **Procedures**
  Data types declared here can only be used in the procedure.

Data types and data objects in the global declaration part of a program, as well as in procedures, are defined in separate namespaces. This means that a data object and a data type can have the same name, which, however, is not recommended. In the declaration part of a class and in an interface, all components are located in one single namespace anyway. As is the case with data objects, local data types hide global data types.

Usage

With so many different ways to declare data types, the question arises as to when you should use which option. For this purpose, we provide a few tips in the following section before we delve into the details of the individual data types.

Bound versus independent It is good programming style to create a self-defined data type only as an independent type. If you really want to adhere to this rule, you must also note that every use of a built-in ABAP type whose properties are not completely predefined in the runtime environment creates a new bound type in a DATA statement. The declaration of an independent data type increases the maintainability of a program for the following reasons:

▶ An independent data type usually has a semantic meaning.

▶ An independent data type can be created centrally and reused at different locations.

▶ A local declaration can be easily transferred to more central locations.

Of course, the general principle of defensive programming we introduced in Section 4.9 also involves data types. In other words, you should declare data types as locally as possible and as globally as necessary:

Local versus global

▶ Within methods or other procedures, independent types are usually required only for auxiliary variables whose data types are not covered by more global type of the same application.

▶ The declaration of global data types in the public visibility section of global classes and in interfaces completely replaces the creation of type groups and enables you to create global data types in the semantic environment in which they are needed. Existing type groups such as the system type group ABAP can still be used.

▶ You should carefully consider whether you want to create data types in classes/interfaces or in the ABAP Dictionary. Typically, the use of data types in classes or interfaces is also coupled to the use of those classes or interfaces. Apart from their package binding, the general data types provided can be used in a relatively unrestricted way. This can easily result in an overloading of the ABAP Dictionary with large quantities of data types that are actually designed only for specific purposes. For this reason, you should create types in the ABAP Dictionary only if it is an absolute requirement that they be located in the Dictionary. Examples of these types include those whose semantic properties are required for the definition of dynpro fields (see Section 9.1.6).

▶ Before creating a global type, you should check whether you can reuse an existing type; however, you should only reuse those data types that meet your requirements exactly. Never use a type with semantic properties just because of its technical properties. Alternatively, you must avoid creating global data types that have a purely technical meaning (i. e., you should always define the semantic meaning as well).

TYPE versus LIKE Lastly, you often have two options, that is, you can either use the TYPE addition to refer to an independent data type, or the LIKE addition to refer to a data object of the corresponding type:[12]

- Use the LIKE addition whenever your declaration is directly linked to a data object. Examples of this include auxiliary variables in procedures that must have the same type as interface parameters or their components. This keeps your program valid even if the data type of the data object changes.

- In all other cases, you should use the TYPE addition to directly reference appropriate independent data types.

5.1.3 Elementary Data Types and Data Objects

You can define elementary data types and data objects by using a direct TYPE reference to one of the 10 built-in ABAP types from Figure 5.2. There are eight built-in data types whose length must be statically defined and two data types, where the memory consumption of the corresponding data objects can change dynamically during program execution.

Built-In Data Types for Static Data Objects

Table 5.1 lists the eight built-in data types for elementary data objects of fixed length.

Type	Length	Standard Length	Initial Value	Explanation
i	4 bytes		0	Integer
p	1–16 bytes	8 bytes	0	Packed number
f	8 bytes		0	Binary floating point number
c	1–65535 characters	1 character	' ... '	Text field
n	1–65535 characters	1 character	'0...0'	Numeric text field

Table 5.1 Built-In ABAP Types for Static Data Objects

---

12 In older programs and outside of ABAP Objects, you may still encounter a LIKE reference to structures of the ABAP Dictionary. In this case, LIKE works like TYPE, but this feature should no longer be used.

Type	Length	Standard Length	Initial Value	Explanation
d	8 characters		'00000000'	Date field
t	6 characters		'000000'	Time field
x	1–65535 bytes	1 byte	'00 ... 00'	Byte field

Table 5.1 Built-In ABAP Types for Static Data Objects (cont.)

The "Length" column indicates the minimum and maximum number of bytes or characters that a data object can occupy. The fact that an interval is specified for the p, c, n, and x types means that these data types are incomplete or generic and require you to use the LENGTH addition after TYPE in order to provide additional information on their length; otherwise, you cannot use them to declare data types and data objects.[13] If you don't specify any length when declaring data types and data objects of those types, the runtime environment implicitly uses the standard length. The other types, i, f, d, and t, are not generic but complete. You don't need to specify any length when using them to declare a data type or data object. In fact, specifying a length in this instance is forbidden.

Generic type

Data types or data objects that are declared using one of those eight data types always have the length that is specified during their declaration. The utilized memory space is statically defined for these kinds of data objects, which is why they are referred to as static data objects. The initial value is the value that a static data object has at the beginning of its context if the VALUE addition is not used during its declaration.

Static data objects

We can subdivide the eight types into three numeric (i, p, f), four character-like[14] (c, n, d, t), and one byte-like type (x) . The numeric types can be used to carry out calculations; the character-like types are used to display content as text; and the hexadecimal type represents the non-encoded content of a byte.

---

13 Moreover, type p is generic with regard to the number of decimal places.

14 Concerning the character-like fields, the memory space actually occupied in terms of bytes depends on the code page that is used. Whereas an ASCII character occupies only one byte, a Unicode character can occupy up to four bytes.

Numeric type i

Type i is a data type for integers in the value range between -2^{31} and $+2^{31}-1$ (4-byte integer). It is often used for index or count variables.

Example:

```
DATA n TYPE i.
n = 5.
DO n TIMES.
  ...
ENDDO.
```

A data object n of type i defines the number of passes of a loop.

Numeric type p

Type p is a data type for packed numbers in the Binary Coded Decimals (BCD) format with a fixed number of decimal places (fixed point format). The number of decimal places is defined during the declaration of a data type or data object using the DECIMALS addition after TYPE. The default value is 0. The value range of the numbers depends on the length of the data object as well as on the number of decimal places. The maximum size of a number of type p is 16 bytes. It can consist of a maximum of 31 decimal digits and up to 14 decimal places. Numbers of type p should be used if you want to perform calculations to the exact decimal place; however, you should note that a calculation using data objects of type p takes more computing time than does a calculation using data objects of type i or f.[15] Type p is particularly useful for monetary amounts, dimensions, weights, and so on. However, if you don't set the program property, **Fixed point arithmetic**, data objects of this type are interpreted as integers.

Example:

```
DATA number TYPE p DECIMALS 2.
number = 3 / 4.
```

After this calculation, the data object number of type p has the value 0.75.

Numeric type f

Type f is a data type for binary floating point numbers. A binary floating point number consists of three components: the plus/minus sign, a 16-digit mantissa, and the exponent. The mantissa contains the digits of the number, while the exponent specifies the position of

---

15 The next release of SAP NetWeaver will provide two new data types, decfloat16 and decfloat34, for decimal floating point numbers. These data types will combine all the advantages of data types p and f.

the decimal point. The value range of a binary floating point number lies approximately between 1.8EE+308 and -2.2EE-308 for the negative range, and between +2.2EE-308 and +1.8EE+308 for the positive range, and it contains the number 0. Due to their internal structure that consists of dual fractions, binary floating point numbers cannot present all decimal numbers exactly. For that reason, you can use type f if large value ranges are needed and accuracy is not imperative.[16]

Example:

```
DATA result TYPE f.
result = sqrt( 2 ).
```

After the assignment, the data object result of type f has the following value: 1.4142135623730951E+00.

Type c is a data type that can be used for any character string of fixed length. You can generally use type c data objects for character-like content that doesn't have any other meaning and for which having a fixed length is critical, as is the case, for instance, when you couple objects to input and output fields of the user interface. ABAP contains many language elements for the processing of character strings (see Section 5.4).

Character-like type c

Example:

```
DATA text_line TYPE c LENGTH 72.
text_line = 'ABAP Programming is fun!'.
IF text_line IS NOT INITIAL.
  MESSAGE text_line TYPE 'I'.
ENDIF.
```

The text_line data object of type c is assigned a character string in a literal, which is then output as a message. A logical expression checks whether the data object is filled.

Type n is a special case of type c for numeric characters, but not a numeric data type. This type can only contain numbers, but these numbers cannot be directly used to carry out calculations. Typical areas of use are bank routing numbers, ZIP codes, P.O. box numbers,

Character-like type n

---

16 The introduction of decimal floating point numbers in the next release of SAP NetWeaver will resolve this issue, and the use of data type f will become obsolete.

and so on. You can also use this data type to couple objects to input and output fields of the user interface that may only contain numbers.

Example:

```
DATA postal_code TYPE n LENGTH 5.
postal_code = '69189'.
```

The postal_code data object of type n contains only numbers.

Character-like type d

Type d is a data type for date information in the format, YYYYMMDD (YYYY indicates the year, MM the month, and DD the day). If you use a date field in the positions of operands where a numerical value is expected, the date is regarded as a number that corresponds to the number of days that have passed since 00010101. Other operations utilize the character-like nature. You can also use this data type to couple objects to input and output fields of the user interface that may only contain valid date information.

Example:

```
DATA date TYPE d.
date = sy-datum.
date = date + 2.
```

The date data object of type d is assigned the current date in the sy-datum system field. After the calculation, it is assigned the date of the day after tomorrow.

Character-like type t

Type t is a data type for time information in the format, HHMMSS (HH being the hour, MM the minute, and SS the second). If you use a time field in the positions of operands where a numerical value is expected, the time is regarded as a number that corresponds to the number of seconds that have passed since midnight (000000). Other operations utilize the character-like nature. You can also use this data type to couple objects to input and output fields of the user interface that may only contain valid time information.

Example:

```
DATA time TYPE t.
time = sy-uzeit.
time = time + 3600.
time+2(4) = '0000'.
```

The `time` data object of type `t` is assigned the current time in the `sy-uzeit` system field. Then one hour is added before the last four digits are overwritten with zero characters via a subfield access. The data object now contains the next clock hour.

Type `x` is a data type used for storing byte strings of fixed length. Type `x` data objects can generally be used for byte-like content where the fixed length is important. Although most ABAP applications are business applications that don't need to deal with byte strings very often, ABAP also contains many language elements for processing byte strings.

Byte-like type x

Example:

```
DATA hex TYPE x LENGTH 3.
hex = 'F72AB3'.
```

The `hex` data object of type `x` is assigned a character-like literal whose characters represent the hexadecimal presentation of values of six half-bytes. After the assignment, the byte string contains three bytes in the memory that have the following decimal values: 247, 42, and 179.

Built-In Data Types for Dynamic Data Objects

ABAP contains two built-in data types, `string` and `xstring`, for elementary data objects of variable length. In contrast to static data objects, the length and the memory requirement of dynamic data objects are not fixed during the declaration. Instead, the length can change, depending on the content during program execution. We generally refer to those data objects as dynamic data objects. Therefore, the strings described here are dynamic data objects. In addition to strings, internal tables (see Section 5.1.5) are also dynamic data objects.

Dynamic data objects

Type `string` is a data type that can be used for any character string of variable length (text strings). Type `string` data objects should be generally used for character-like content where fixed length is not important.

Character-like type string

Example:

```
DATA text_string TYPE string.
text_string = 'ABAP Programming is fun!'.
```

The text_string data object of type string is assigned the same character string as in the above example for type c. Whereas the type c data object had a fixed length of 72, the length of the text string is dynamically set to 24 and can be changed at any time by other assignments.

Byte-like type xstring

Type xstring is a data type that can be used for any byte string of variable length (byte strings). Type xstring data objects should be generally used for byte-like content where fixed length is not important.

Example:

```
DATA x_string TYPE xstring.
x_string = 'FF'.
```

The x_string data object of type xstring is assigned the hexadecimal presentation of a byte value. Therefore, the length of the byte string is dynamically set to one byte and can be changed at any time by other assignments.

Deep data type

Internally, dynamic data objects are managed via references. A reference of fixed length is attached to the memory address of a string and points to the actual dynamic data object. This kind of data type is referred to as a deep data type, which has some important implications for the use of those types (see Section 5.1.8).

Declaring Elementary Data Types and Data Objects

The variants of the TYPES and DATA statements for defining elementary data types or data objects are as follows:

TYPES, DATA

```
TYPES dtype TYPE abap_type [LENGTH len] [DECIMALS dec].
DATA  dobj  TYPE abap_type [LENGTH len] [DECIMALS dec]
            [VALUE val] [READ-ONLY].
```

Except for two additions that can only be specified when declaring data objects, the syntax of both statements is identical. The statements define a data type, dtype, or a data object, dobj, respectively. After the TYPE addition, one of the 10 built-in ABAP types, abap_type, is specified here.

LENGTH

The LENGTH addition must be used for the incomplete types, p, c, n, and x, to specify a length. If no length is specified, which in the case of types is only possible outside of classes, the runtime environment adds the standard length from Table 5.1 in both statements.[17] Alternatively, you can use the following syntax for the length output; however, this is no longer recommended.

```
TYPES dtype(len) TYPE abap_type ...
DATA  dobj(len)  TYPE abap_type ...
```

The DECIMALS dec addition is used to define the number of decimal places for packed numbers of type p. If no decimal places are specified—which in the case of TYPES is only possible outside of classes—the runtime environment adds the value 0 in both statements.

DECIMALS

You can use the VALUE val addition to define an initial value for data objects. This value is then used instead of the standard value from Table 5.1. The initial value is typically specified as a literal (see Section 5.1.10).

VALUE

The READ-ONLY addition can be used to declare an attribute in the public visibility section of a class in such a way that its contents cannot be changed from outside of the class (see Section 4.4.2).

READ-ONLY

Listing 5.1 shows a simple example of elementary data types and data objects. All operands of a calculation refer to the same local data type. The accuracy of the calculation is defined by this data type. You can change the accuracy by modifying the type in a central location of the method.

Listing 5.1 Elementary Data Types and Data Objects

```
REPORT z_elementary_types_and_objects.

...
  METHOD main.
    TYPES calc_type TYPE p LENGTH 8 DECIMALS 2.
    DATA: number_1  TYPE calc_type VALUE 3,
          number_2  TYPE calc_type VALUE 4,
          result    TYPE calc_type,
          output    TYPE string.
    result = number_1 / number_2.
    output = result.
```

---

17 Likewise, the runtime environment will set the type to c if no type is specified. Again, for TYPES, this abbreviated form is only permitted outside of classes and even there, it shouldn't be used any longer.

```
        MESSAGE output TYPE 'I'.
      ENDMETHOD.
  ...
```

5.1.4 Structured Data Types and Data Objects

Structured data types belong to the complex data types; they are not elementary, but consist of a sequence of other data types. The data object of a structured data type is also referred to as a *structure*. The units that make up a structured type or a structure are its components. You can access an entire structure or the individual components.

Declaring Structures

The variants of the TYPES and DATA statements for defining structured data types or data objects are as follows:

BEGIN OF, END OF
```
TYPES|DATA: BEGIN OF structure,
              k1 TYPE|LIKE ...,
              k2 TYPE|LIKE ...,
              ...
              kn TYPE|LIKE ...,
            END OF structure.
```

Note that the colon and the commas indicate that we are dealing with several TYPES and DATA statements here. The statements with the BEGIN OF structure and END OF structure additions define the beginning and end of a structure called structure. All statements that lie in-between declare the components of the structure. The components of a structure can be of any data type, that is, they can be elementary data types, a structure, an internal table, or a reference type.

Substructure
A component that is structured itself is referred to as a substructure. A structure that contains substructures is called a *nested structure*.[18] To create substructures, you can nest statements using BEGIN OF and END OF, or you can declare a component that references a structured type.

---

18 We can only refer to a structure as a deep structure if it contains at least one deep component such as an elementary field of type string, a reference variable, or a table.

Using Structure Components

To use a single structure component `comp` in an operand position, you must append the component's name to the name of the structure via a hyphen (-):[19]

```
... structure-comp ...
```

Structure component selector

In ABAP, we therefore refer to the hyphen as the *structure component selector*. For nested structures, you must concatenate the structure names to access internal components.

Let's look at the address in Listing 5.2 as an example of a structure. The address consists of the following components: name, street, and city.

Listing 5.2 Structured Data Types and Data Objects

```
REPORT z_structured_data.

CLASS demo DEFINITION.
  PUBLIC SECTION.
    TYPES: BEGIN OF t_street,
             name TYPE c LENGTH 40,
             no   TYPE c LENGTH 4,
           END OF t_street.
    CLASS-METHODS main.
  PRIVATE SECTION.
    CLASS-DATA: BEGIN OF address,
                  name   TYPE c LENGTH 30,
                  street TYPE t_street,
                  BEGIN OF city,
                    zipcode TYPE n LENGTH 5,
                    name    TYPE c LENGTH 40,
                  END OF city,
                  country TYPE c LENGTH 3 VALUE 'SOL',
                END OF address.
ENDCLASS.

CLASS demo IMPLEMENTATION.
  METHOD main.
    address-name         = 'Luke Skywalker'.
    address-street-name  = 'Milky Way'.
    address-street-no    = '123d'.
    address-city-zipcode = '64283'.
```

---

19 If a data reference variable points to a structure, you can also use the object component selector: `dref->comp`.

```
          address-city-name      = 'Tatooine'.
     ENDMETHOD.
  ENDCLASS.
  START-OF-SELECTION.
    demo=>main( ).
```

For the street, we created a separate structured type t_street with the components, name and no. For the address, we declare a structure address as a data object,[20] and we declare the street component with type t_street. The city component is also further divided into the two components zipcode and name. You can see how the individual components are addressed in the assignments. Although the name indicator occurs three times, each component can be uniquely addressed by its structure name.

Integrating Structure Components

Nested structures contain a hierarchy of structure components that is reflected in the concatenation of the names. If you want to integrate the components of a structure into another structure and ensure that the components of the resulting structure are all located at the same level, you can use the INCLUDE statement:

INCLUDE
```
     TYPES|DATA BEGIN OF struc1.
        . . .
        INCLUDE TYPE|STRUCTURE struc2 AS name
             [RENAMING WITH SUFFIX suffix].
        . . .
     TYPES|DATA END OF struc1.
```

You must use the variant with TYPE for data types, while the variant with STRUCTURE must be used for data objects. The INCLUDE statement is not an addition to the TYPES or DATA statements. Instead, it interrupts the chained statement that must be restarted afterwards.

The components of the struc2 structure are transferred as components into the struc1 structure. They can either be addressed commonly under the name name, or individually by their component names. If naming conflicts with existing components occur, you can use the RENAMING addition to append a suffix ending to the compo-

---

20 As you can see, everything we discussed for DATA also holds true for CLASS-DATA, for the declaration of static attributes.

nent names. In this way, you can integrate a structure several times into another structure. Listing 5.3 shows an example:

Listing 5.3 Integrating Structure Components

```
REPORT z_include_structure.

CLASS demo DEFINITION.
  PUBLIC SECTION.
    CLASS-METHODS main.
  PRIVATE SECTION.
    CLASS-DATA: BEGIN OF street,
                  name TYPE c LENGTH 40,
                  noff TYPE c LENGTH 4,
                END OF street.
    CLASS-DATA: BEGIN OF city,
                  zipcode TYPE n LENGTH 5,
                  name TYPE c LENGTH 40,
                END OF city.
    CLASS-DATA: BEGIN OF address,
                  name TYPE c LENGTH 30.
                  INCLUDE STRUCTURE street AS str
                    RENAMING WITH SUFFIX _str.
                  INCLUDE STRUCTURE city AS cty
                    RENAMING WITH SUFFIX _cty.
    CLASS-DATA: END OF address.
ENDCLASS.
CLASS demo IMPLEMENTATION.
  METHOD main.
    address-name        = 'Han Solo'.
    address-name_str    = 'Crab Nebula'.
    address-no_str      = '18'.
    address-zipcode_cty = '69121'.
    address-name_cty    = 'Dark Star'.
  ENDMETHOD.
ENDCLASS.
START-OF-SELECTION.
  demo=>main( ).
```

The components of the address structure are all located at the same level. Naming conflicts between the name components are avoided by the use of different endings. You can use this type of structure definition, for example, to avoid complex nested structures with long name chains. However, there are also places in which all the components of a structure have to be located at one level, for example, when you declare structures for database tables in the ABAP Dictionary.

5.1.5 Table Types and Internal Tables

In addition to structures, table types represent the second complex data type of the ABAP type hierarchy. The data objects of table types are internal tables. Similar to strings, internal tables are dynamic data objects, that is, the data type defines all properties statically with the exception of the memory consumption. An internal table consists of a dynamic sequence of lines of the same data type. The table type describes the line type, the table category, and a table key. Like strings, internal tables are internally managed by references. In that sense, internal tables are also deep data types.

Declaring Internal Tables

The variants of the TYPES and DATA statements to define table types and internal tables are as follows:

TABLE OF
```
TYPES|DATA itab TYPE|LIKE STANDARD|SORTED|HASHED TABLE
                OF dtype|dobj
                WITH [NON-]UNIQUE KEY comp ...
```

Table category
You can use STANDARD TABLE, SORTED TABLE, or HASHED TABLE to define the table category that determines the type of storage and access. We distinguish between standard tables, sorted tables, and hashed tables (more on this in Section 5.5.1).

Line type
The line type can be any data type that is visible at this location. The line type is addressed using TYPE ... dtype or LIKE ... dobj. An internal table can contain any number of lines of the specified line type.[21] Thus, the line type is fixed during declaration, but not the number of lines. ABAP contains a specific set of statements to populate and read internal tables. We'll discuss these statements in Section 5.5.2.

Because you can use any line type, internal tables can include elementary types, reference types, structures, and even other internal tables. This results in countless designing options for very complex data layouts, particularly when using structures as line types whose components, as you know, can also have any data types.

---

21 The maximum number of lines depends on different conditions (see Section 5.1.8).

An internal table has a unique or non-unique table key that can be defined by listing its components. Table key

The traditional line type of an internal table that corresponds to the familiar picture of a table containing rows and columns is a structure that consists of purely elementary components. Such an internal table is ideally suited to include several rows of a database table dbtab and can, for instance, be defined as follows: Flat line type

```
TYPES|DATA itab TYPE HASHED TABLE
                OF dbtab
                WITH UNIQUE KEY col1 col2 ...
```

This statement creates a table type or an internal table as a hashed table whose line type has the same structure as a database table dbtab from the ABAP Dictionary. The WITH UNIQUE KEY addition allows you to specify columns of the database table as unique keys, which avoids the existence of duplicate lines. The Open SQL statements of ABAP have specific additions that read data from database tables into such internal tables and vice versa (see Section 10.1.2).

5.1.6 Reference Types and Reference Variables

Reference types are data types for data objects that can contain a reference to other data objects or to instances of classes. Those data objects are referred to as *reference variables*. Depending on the type of object that is referenced, we speak of *data reference variables* or *object reference variables* that can either contain data references or object references. If a reference variable contains a reference to an object, we also say that it *points to the object*, and the reference variable can be referred to as a *pointer*.

Declaring Reference Types and Reference Variables

The variants of the TYPES and DATA statements to define reference types and reference variables are as follows:

```
TYPES|DATA ref TYPE|LIKE REF TO data|dtype|dobj.
TYPES|DATA ref TYPE REF TO class|interface.
```
REF TO

The first statement creates a reference type or a reference variable respectively for a data reference. The type specification defines the static type of a reference variable. After TYPE, you can specify the Data reference built-in generic `data` type (see Section 5.1.9) or any non-generic type. After `LIKE`, you can specify a data object that is visible at this location whose type will be used. The static type determines the object to which a reference variable can point. A data reference variable that is typed using `data` can point to any data object. A data reference variable that is typed using a complete type can point only to data objects of the corresponding type; however, it does also allow access to its components and direct dereferencing. For more information, see Section 11.1.2.

Object reference

The second statement creates a reference type or a reference variable respectively for an object reference. You should already be familiar with object reference variables as a basis for handling objects in ABAP Objects (see Section 4.6). The static type of an object reference variable can be a class or an interface. Chapter 6 contains a detailed description of possible static types and the handling of object reference variables.

Using reference variables

You can provide a reference variable with a reference via a `CREATE` statement, an assignment, and—in the case of data references—by using a special `GET REFERENCE` statement. If a reference variable contains a reference, you can use the object component selector (`->`) to access the components of the data object or object that the reference variable points to:

Object component selector

```
... ref->comp ...
```

In the case of completely typed data reference variables, you can use the dereferencing operator (`->*`) to access the entire data object that is referenced.

Dereferencing

```
... ref->* ...
```

For assignments between reference variables, reference semantics are used in which pointers are switched from object to object. This technique is different from the usual value semantics in which the actual working data is copied.

5.1.7 Data Types in the ABAP Dictionary

In the previous sections, we introduced the `TYPES` and `DATA` statements that are closely related to each other. You can use both statements to create new data types or to reference existing data types. As we already indicated in Section 5.1, these statements enable you to declare data types and data objects in the contexts of an ABAP program (procedures, local classes/interfaces, and program-global declaration part).

Furthermore, you can use TYPES to declare data types in cross-program contexts, namely in the public visibility section of global classes and interfaces (see Section 4.5) as well as in type groups. Cross-program data types are necessary if you want to use data that must be made available to all programs of a package, or if you want to transfer data between programs.

Global data types

In addition to the global data types that can be declared using the TYPES statement, the ABAP Dictionary functions as a central global storage for type descriptions that can be accessed by all repository objects, provided this is permitted by the package check. Global data types are stored in the ABAP Dictionary similar to the way global classes are stored in the class library. The ABAP Dictionary tool for global data types is the counterpart to the Class Builder for global classes.[22] However, whereas the Class Builder only generates ABAP source code in a class pool, the ABAP Dictionary tool does not generate any TYPES statements. Instead, the type definitions are created directly in the repository where they play a specific role for all three layers of an AS ABAP (see Figure 5.3).

ABAP Dictionary

Regarding ABAP programs, the data types of the ABAP Dictionary play the same role as the global types that are declared using the TYPES statement in classes and interfaces: They can be used after TYPE additions. The specific characteristic of types in the ABAP Dictionary is that you can also use them to define input and output fields in dynpro screens (see Section 9.1.6) as well as to declare the table structure of database tables (see Section 10.1.1):

Dynpro fields and database tables

▸ Data types of the ABAP Dictiory enable a type-specific transfer of values between dynpros and ABAP programs, and they even provide input checks and input helps in the user interface. For this reason, you can assign semantic information such as descriptive texts, help texts, or value tables to the data types of the ABAP Dictionary.

---

22 Global classes and global data types of the ABAP Dictionary are located in one namespace!

► ABAP programs are primarily used for accessing the database tables of the AS ABAP. These database tables are also defined in the ABAP Dictionary. When doing so, first a structured type is created in the ABAP Dictionary. Based on this structured type a physical database table is generated in the database system then. To use data from database tables, you must declare data objects in an ABAP program that directly reference the type of the database table in the ABAP Dictionary. Even if a database table is modified at a later stage, the ABAP programs that reference this type are updated automatically.

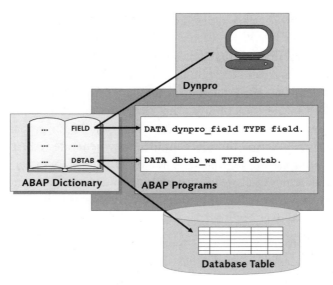

Figure 5.3 Central Role of the ABAP Dictionary on the AS ABAP

The two aforementioned aspects are the main reasons for a continued use of data types in the ABAP Dictionary even today. On the other hand, we recommend using global types in the corresponding classes and interfaces for the transfer of data between ABAP programs, that is, for the typing of interface parameters (see Section 6.1.1). Each data type in the ABAP Dictionary that is not required for technical purposes only adds to the overloading of the Dictionary with types that—on top of all this—are located in a common, system-wide namespace.

Separation of concerns Although it is technically feasible as well as convenient to use the same type for both the dynpro fields and the database tables, this is no longer recommended.[23] Because of the separation of concerns (see Section 9.1.15), you should create different types for dynpro fields and for database tables, as shown in Figure 5.3, and use these types in different ABAP programs. As you will see in Section 9.1.15, it is advisable to use a function group to encapsulate the presentation logic for the upper ABAP program of Figure 5.3, whereas the application logic of the lower ABAP program of Figure 5.3 should ideally be programmed in methods of its global class or local classes.

Creating Data Types in the ABAP Dictionary

In the ABAP Dictionary, you can generally create the same types of the type hierarchy shown in Figure 5.2 as you can using the TYPES statement. As with the Class Builder, here, too, you make a definition by entering values into screen templates. In the ABAP Dictionary, however, you cannot navigate to a maintenance in the ABAP Editor. All non-elementary types are created on the basis of built-in data types.

The ABAP Dictionary contains many more built-in types than the ABAP programming language, and these types also have different names. The difference between the data types is based on the fact that the built-in data types of the ABAP Dictionary must be compatible with the external data types of the database tables supported by the AS ABAP. If, in an ABAP program, you reference a data type from the ABAP Dictionary, the elementary components of that data type are converted into the built-in data types of the ABAP programming language. Table 5.2 provides an overview of all built-in data types of the ABAP Dictionary and their counterparts in ABAP programs.

Built-in data types of the ABAP Dictionary

Dictionary Type	Description	ABAP Type
ACCP	Posting period	n
CHAR	Character	c
CLNT	Client	c
CUKY	Currency key for currency field	c
CURR	Currency field	P

Table 5.2 Built-In Types of the ABAP Dictionary

---

23 This used to be the common procedure in classic ABAP.

Dictionary Type	Description	ABAP Type
DATS	Date	d
DEC	Calculation/amount field	p
FLTP	Binary floating point number	f
INT1	1-byte integer	b
INT2	2-byte integer	s
INT4	4-byte integer	i
LANG	Language	c
LCHR	Long character string	c
LRAW	Long byte string	x
NUMC	Numeric text	n
PREC	Accuracy of a quantity field	s
QUAN	Quantity field	p
RAW	Byte string	x
RAWSTRING	Variable byte string	xstring
STRING	Variable character string	string
TIMS	Time	t
UNIT	Unit of a quantity field	c

Table 5.2 Built-In Types of the ABAP Dictionary (cont.)

You cannot directly reference the built-in data types of the ABAP Dictionary in an ABAP program. Instead you must reference types of the ABAP Dictionary that are created on the basis of those data types. Note that we didn't include the ABAP types b and s for the Dictionary types INT1 and INT2 in Table 5.1. The reason is that the types b and s cannot be directly specified in ABAP. However, they are internally assigned to all data types and data objects that reference either of the two Dictionary types, INT1 and INT2. The ABAP types b and s behave like type i, but their value ranges are more limited: 0 to 255 or -2^{15} and $+2^{15}-1$, respectively

ABAP Dictionary tool

You can call the ABAP Dictionary tool directly in the Object Navigator, as shown in Figure 5.4. Transaction SE11 also enables you to directly enter the Dictionary.

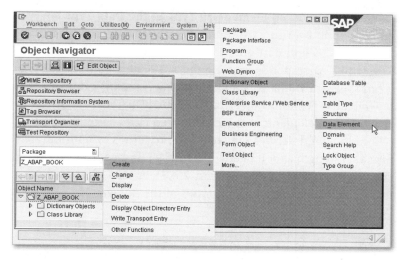

Figure 5.4 Calling the ABAP Dictionary

You can define elementary data types and reference types as well as structured data types or table types by selecting the items, **Data Element**, **Structure**, and **Table Type**. The **Database Table** and **View** items enable you to define structures in order to create or access database tables (see Section 10.1.1).

The elementary data types of the Dictionary are defined as *data elements* (see Figure 5.5 which has been taken from Section 2.4.2).

Data elements

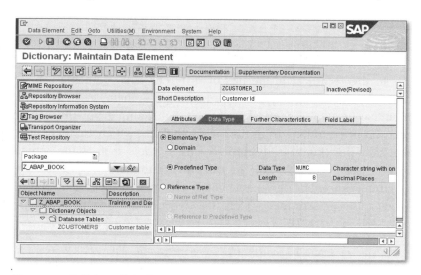

Figure 5.5 Defining a Data Element

Once you have selected **Elementary Type** in the **Data Type** tab, you have two options: You can either directly specify a built-in type including its technical properties such as the length or decimal places, which corresponds to using the TYPES statement in ABAP, or you can specify a **Domain**. Similar to a data element, a domain is an independent repository object in the ABAP Dictionary that can be used by all data elements that are permitted to do so by the package check. A domain describes the technical properties of built-in types, such as their length and, if needed, the decimal places (see Figure 5.6 which has been taken from Section 2.4.3). A data element with a domain adopts the technical properties of the domain.

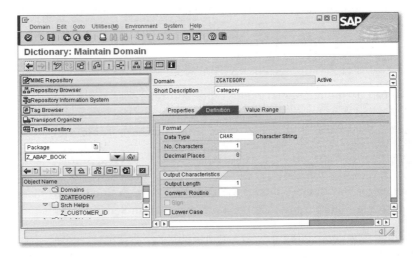

Figure 5.6 Defining a Domain

Semantics While the technical properties of different data elements can be defined for reuse purposes within a single domain, each data element has its own semantical properties. For example, you must enter texts of different lengths in the **Field Label** tab, which are then automatically positioned in dynpro screens by tools such as the Screen Painter (see Section 9.1.5). The **Documentation** and **Supplementary Documentation** buttons enable you to create texts that are displayed when a user presses the [F1] key in a screen of the data element type (see Section 9.1.13).[24]

---

24 All these texts are linked to the translation mechanism of the ABAP Workbench. If you have set up your AS ABAP as a translation system, the texts will be automatically forwarded to the translation worklist of your translators.

Every ABAP program can use the data elements of the ABAP Dictionary for the declaration of its own data types, data objects, or other typings once the data elements have been activated. Because of their semantical properties, data elements are particularly well suited for the creation of Dictionary types that are used in dynpros. The semantical properties are not needed for database tables.

Reference types are also defined as data elements in the ABAP Dictionary. To do this, you must select **Reference Type** in Figure 5.5. In the **Name of Ref. Type** field, you can either specify **DATA** for generic data reference types, or a global class or global interface from the class library for object reference types. Alternatively, you can create a completely typed data reference type by selecting **Reference to Predefined Type**.

Reference types

In the ABAP Dictionary, structured types are referred to as *structures*. Structures are composed of any combination of other data types of the ABAP Dictionary. Thus their components can be data elements, other structures, table types, database tables, or views. The input screen for the components of structures is similar to the one that is used for database tables except that it doesn't provide any database-specific input options such as **Search Help** or **Technical Settings**. Figure 5.7 shows the definition of the SYST structure whose components are the data types of the ABAP system fields (see Section 5.1.10).

Structures

Instead of a data element, you can also directly specify a built-in Dictionary type from Table 5.2 for a structure component (or a field of a database table) when you select **Predefined Type**. Such a structure component lacks the semantical properties of a data element, and therefore it should be used internally rather than in user interfaces. Usually a field of a database table does not require any texts that are displayed in user interfaces. If, for reusability purposes, you create a data element for internal structures or database tables, you must define texts, but also you should ensure that the data element is documented for internal use only. A good example in this context is the predefined structure SYST from Figure 5.7, which is a purely technical structure whose components must not appear in any user interface. The structure and data elements are documented correspondingly.

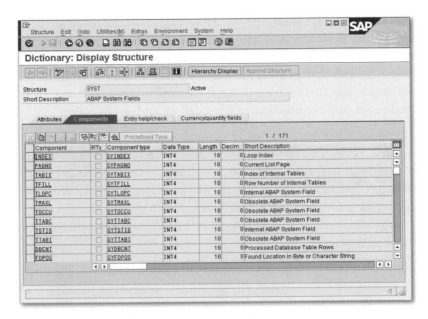

Figure 5.7 Definition of a Structure

INCLUDE To include the components of existing structures into new structures at the highest hierarchy level, you can select **Edit • Include • Insert** when creating a structure. This function provides the same options as the INCLUDE statement in ABAP programs (see Section 5.1.4) in order to create structures with a single hierarchy level from other structures. Structures that are defined in this way are particularly interesting as templates for database tables, because you cannot use any nested structures.[25]

Table types Like table types that have been declared using the TYPES statement, the table types of the ABAP Dictionary describe the properties of an internal table in the ABAP program. You should therefore never mistake table types for database tables! Figure 5.8 displays the existing table type SPFLI_TAB. The **Line Type** tab shows that the line type is created with a reference to the structure of database table SPFLI. As an alternative, you could also use an elementary line type that is

---

25 From a technological point of view, APPEND structures are related to INCLUDE structures, but they are semantically different. APPEND structures enable you to append components to existing structures or database tables in customer systems. However, these enhancement techniques are not discussed in the current edition of this book.

defined like a data element. The table category (**Initialization and Access**) and table key (**Key**) are defined in the other tabs.

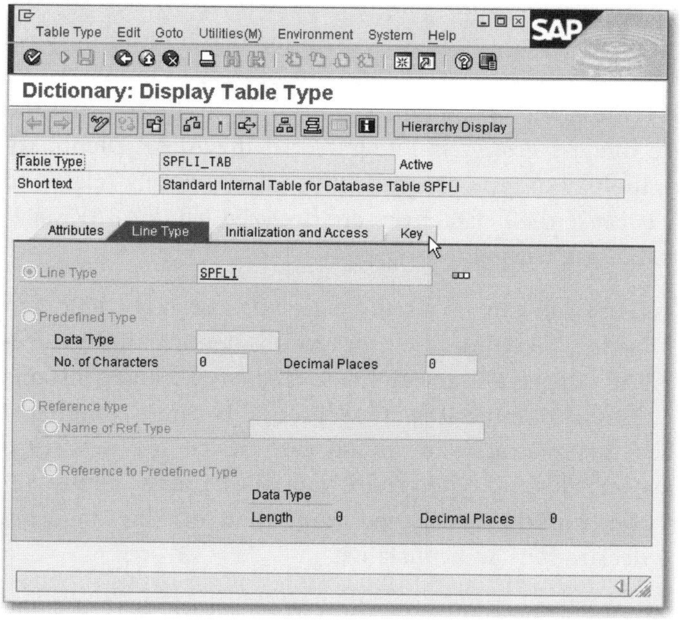

Figure 5.8 Table Type in the ABAP Dictionary

The following coding section shows the typical use of such a table type, namely, the declaration of an internal table to store data from a database table:

```
DATA itab TYPE spfli_tab.

SELECT *
       FROM spfli
       INTO TABLE itab.
```

Using Type Groups

To conclude our description of data types in the ABAP Dictionary, we want to briefly mention type groups. Figure 5.4 shows type groups as part of the Dictionary objects. There are historical reasons for that. Prior to Release 4.5, only flat structures including database tables could be defined as data types in the ABAP Dictionary. ABAP programs did not allow any direct reference to individual data elements unless you referred to the components of structures or data-

259

base tables. Therefore, to be able to store any kind of data types across different programs, type groups were used.

TYPE-POOL Type groups are specific ABAP programs that are introduced by the TYPE-POOL statement and can only contain the declarations of types and constants. The data types and constants of a type group must be prefixed with the name of the type group. Despite the fact that the maintenance of type groups is integrated in the ABAP Dictionary tool, the technology of type groups is much more closely related to class pools, because their data types are declared using ABAP statements, as is the case with object types.

Since Release 4.5, you can create any data type as a real Dictionary type, which made type groups more or less obsolete. With the introduction of ABAP Objects and the ability to create types and constants in global classes and interfaces, type groups became completely obsolete. For this reason, you should not create any new type groups; however, existing type groups can still be used. Figure 5.9 shows a section from the ABAP type group that contains language-related type declarations and constants.

The following coding section shows how you can use the types and constants of the ABAP type group that are displayed in Figure 5.9. The abap_bool type replaces the Boolean data type for truth values, which currently is not yet built-in into the language (see Section 5.2.5).

```
TYPE-POOLS abap.

DATA flag TYPE abap_bool.
...
IF flag = abap_true.
  ...
ELSEIF flag = abap_false.
  ...
ELSE.
  flag = abap_undefined.
ENDIF.
```

In ABAP Objects, type pools are replaced by language-related classes and interfaces that can also be used for storing such types and constants. For example, the class CL_ABAP_CHAR_UTILITIES contains constants for processing character strings.

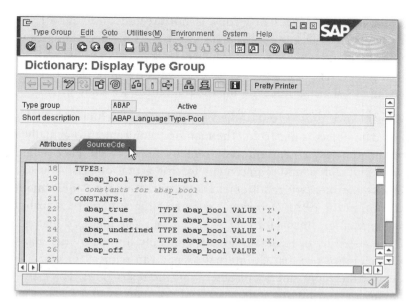

Figure 5.9 ABAP Type Group

5.1.8 Flat and Deep Data Types

We already mentioned that strings and internal tables belong to the deep data types. Because the descriptions "flat" and "deep" for data types are often misunderstood, we thought it might be helpful to briefly summarize their meaning at this point.

All data types in which the content of their data objects represents actual working data are referred to as *flat* data types. Thus all elementary data types of fixed length are flat. All data types in which the content of their data objects are references that point to working data in different locations of the memory are referred to as *deep* data types. Accordingly, reference types that are provided for an explicit handling of references are deep. But also the data types for the dynamic data objects—strings and internal tables—are implicitly managed by references and are therefore deep as well.

In assignments between deep data objects, you must distinguish between *reference semantics* and *value semantics*. For assignments between reference variables, reference semantics applies: Only the references are copied, but not the referenced objects. For assignments between dynamic data objects, value semantics applies: The referenced object is copied and a new reference is created. Here you

Reference semantics vs. value semantics

should note that the actual copy is not created until one of the involved data objects is accessed via write access the next time (copy-on-write semantics). For performance reasons, a so-called *sharing* takes place prior to a write access even with dynamic data objects. During this sharing process, only the references are copied.

Memory requirement

Contrary to the other data objects, the memory requirement of a deep data object is not fixed. The memory requirement is actually a combination of a constant requirement for the reference (eight bytes) and a dynamic requirement for the actual objects. You can identify the memory requirement using the **Memory Requirement** function in the ABAP Debugger, or by creating a memory snapshot for the Memory Inspector (see Section 13.4). The memory that can be requested by deep data objects is generally limited by the maximum memory size that an internal session can request for working data. Furthermore, there are other, specific restrictions. For example, strings and internal tables can only contain as many places or lines as can be addressed with a four-byte integer ($+2^{31}$-1). The size of strings and hashed tables is further restricted by the biggest memory block that can be requested at a time (2 GB maximum).

Flat and deep structures

Finally, we want to describe the meaning of *flat* and *deep structures*. A structure is referred to as a *flat* structure if it contains only flat types as components, that is, elementary data types of fixed length. Nesting doesn't play a role in this context. Even a nested structure is flat unless a substructure contains a deep component. On the other hand, we refer to a structure that contains a deep component in any of its nesting levels as a *deep* structure (see Figure 5.10). Naturally, deep structures cannot be accessed in the same way as flat structures (e. g., via subfield access, see Section 5.4.3).

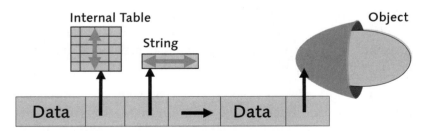

Figure 5.10 Deep Structure

5.1.9 Generic Data Types

The previous sections described the details of all data types of the type hierarchy displayed in Figure 5.2 that can be used to declare data objects using the DATA statement. Those types describe the technical properties of a data object either completely or they must be complemented with the missing values when using them in the TYPES or DATA statements, as is the case with the built-in ABAP types, c, n, p, and x when used to define new data types or to declare data objects. This section describes the generic data types that are displayed on the right-hand side in Figure 5.2.

You can use data types not only to declare data types and data objects, but also for typings. Typings are specifications of data types after a TYPE addition (or of data objects after LIKE) in the definitions of interface parameters for procedures (see Section 6.1.1) or in the definition of field symbols (see Section 11.1.2). The actual data type of interface parameters (formal parameters) and of field symbols is determined during the assignment of a data object at program runtime. A typing makes sure that only specific data objects can be assigned, and it defines in which operand positions you can use a formal parameter or a field symbol. If a completely known data type is specified in a typing, which, for instance, was created using the TYPES statement or in the ABAP Dictionary, you can only use data objects of this very type as actual parameters for passing data to procedures or for assignments to field symbols.[26]

Typings

However, it is often the case that interface parameters and field symbols should be typed generically. This means that the data type determined during runtime is only partially checked or not checked at all. This enables dynamic programming in which, for example, you can use procedures that work with different types of actual parameters. But at least a partial typing is often necessary to ensure a modicum of type security. Section 6.1.1 contains a comprehensive example, which illustrates how you must type a formal parameter so that it can be used as an internal table in a method.

Generic typing

A set of predefined generic ABAP types is available for these kinds of typings, which—with the exception of c, n, p, and x—can only be

Generic ABAP types

---

26 In a typing using the LIKE statement, the type that is adopted from an existing data object is always completely known.

used exclusively for typings. Table 5.3 lists the predefined generic types in the first column, while the second column describes the types they comprise. You can assign a data object with a type from the second column to a formal parameter or field symbol that is typed with a generic type from the first column.

Generic Type	Types Comprised
any, data	All data types[27]
any table	All table types (table-like types)
c, n, p, x	The corresponding built-in types with generic lengths (and generic decimal places)
clike	c, d, n, t, string and flat structures containing purely character-like components (character-like types)
csequence	c and string (text-like types)
hashed table	Hashed tables
index table	Standard tables and sorted tables (index tables)
numeric	i (b, s), p, and f (numeric types)
simple	c, d, f, i (b, s), n, p, t, string, x, xstring and flat structures containing purely character-like components (elementary types)
standard table, table	Standard tables
sorted table	Sorted tables
xsequence	x and xstring (byte-like types)

Table 5.3 Predefined Generic Data Types in ABAP

In the right-hand column next to clike and simple, you can see that a flat structure with purely character-like components can be regarded as a single character-like elementary field. You will encounter this characteristic once more when dealing with the conversion rules (see Section 5.2.2).

Generic internal tables

Besides the predefined generic types listed in Table 5.3, ABAP does not contain any other generic types, with one exception: If a table type is defined using the TYPES statement or if it is defined in the ABAP Dictionary without specifying a key, this table type is also a

---

27 In the current release, the any type has the same effect as data, but this type may be extended to object types.

generic type that can be used only in typings.[28] The generic table types listed in Table 5.3 indicate that the specified table category is used for typing, whereas line type and table key are not fixed. Section 5.5.1 contains more details on generic table types.

At this point, the mere list of generic types that can be used in ABAP should suffice. Section 6.1.1 provides more information on how these types are used in the context of their primary field of application—the typing of interface parameters.

5.1.10 Further Details in Data Objects

The previous sections provided a detailed introduction to the ABAP type concept. You have learned how to use the TYPES and DATA statements in order to define data types and data objects. The syntax of both statements is very similar because you can also create a new data type when declaring data objects. That data type, however, is then only available as a property of the object. Whereas you can define data types in the ABAP Dictionary even without using the TYPES statement, the data types of data objects are generally bound to declarations in ABAP programs, which can be globally visible only if they are public attributes of global classes or interfaces.

The following sections provide additional important information about data objects. In particular, we would like to introduce some other types of data objects that can occur in ABAP besides the variables described so far.[29] We'll start with the data objects that bear a name.

Named Data Objects

All data objects that we have declared using the DATA statement up to this point have a name by which they can be addressed in the program. These data objects are referred to as *named* data objects. Moreover, you can assign values to data objects declared using the DATA statement during program execution. For this reason, we classify all

Variables

---

28 If no key is specified during the declaration of a data object, a default value is added.

29 We will introduce other specific data objects such as selection screen parameters (see Section 9.2) or table work areas (see Section 9.1.10) as they are needed in the respective chapters.

data objects that are declared using the DATA statement as variables. You can read and change the contents of variables in a program. Variables are undoubtedly the most frequently used data objects in ABAP programs; therefore, DATA is the most important declaration statement. The variable attributes of classes are also declared using DATA or CLASS-DATA respectively.

Constants Constants are named data objects whose value cannot be changed during the entire runtime of an ABAP program. Constants are declared using the CONSTANTS statement, not the DATA statement. The syntax of the CONSTANTS statement is the same as that of the DATA statement, the only difference being that the use of the VALUE addition is mandatory in the CONSTANTS statement and that you cannot use the READ-ONLY addition in the declaration part of classes:

CONSTANTS **CONSTANTS** const ... **VALUE** val|{IS INITIAL}.

The VALUE addition is used to define the value of the constant that cannot be changed at runtime. Any attempt to assign a new value to the const constant in the program results in syntax or runtime errors. You can declare structured constants like variables with the BEGIN OF and END OF additions. Note that in this case, the individual components must have a VALUE addition.

For val, you can either specify a literal (see Section 5.1.10) or another constant that is visible and can be used in this place. You can use IS INITIAL to set a constant to its type-specific initial value.[30] Because there are no literals available for reference types and internal tables, you can define those constants only with their initial values, that is, a constant internal table is always empty, and a constant reference never points to an object.

You can increase the readability of an application by declaring constants with meaningful names for frequently recurring values. In particular, you should avoid using "magic numbers" (numeric literals in operational statements). You should always use constants when you know upfront that a data object should be accessed as read only. A commonly used example of constants is the following:

```
CONSTANTS pi TYPE f VALUE '3.14159265359'.
DATA: radius TYPE p DECIMALS 2,
```

---

30 The IS INITIAL addition can also be used with DATA, but that's not necessary.

```
   area     TYPE p DECIMALS 2.
...
area = pi * radius ** 2.
```

Before coming to the literals, we would once again like to draw your attention to the text symbols that we already described in the introduction. Text symbols are special, named data objects that are not defined using declaration statements, but instead as part of the text elements of a program via the text element maintenance of the ABAP Workbench (see Figure 5.11 which has been taken from Section 2.7.2). You can enter any kind of text behind three-figure identifiers. These identifiers can consist of letters and numbers.

Text symbol

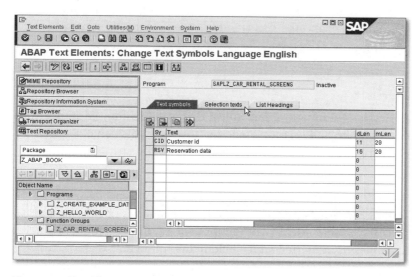

Figure 5.11 Text Element Maintenance

You can use a text symbol in an ABAP program under the name text-### like a constant data object, ### being the three-figure identifier. When a text symbol is used, it has data type c and the length specified in the **mLen** column. The content is derived from the current text pool of the program.[31] You can also link a text symbol to a text field literal by using the syntax, '...' (###) (see below). The text symbol replaces the literal during program execution if it exists in

---

31 The text pool contains the text elements of the program. Several text pools can be defined in different languages for a program. When a program is loaded in an internal session, the text elements of the text pool of the logon language are read by default.

the currently loaded text pool. In contrast, when using text-### , the text symbol is treated like an empty one-figure text field if it does not exist in the text pool.

Like all text elements of an ABAP program, text symbols are linked to the translation.[32] Consequently, you can use text symbols in all places where you want to display texts from the program on the user interface, without having to bother about the logon language of a specific user. The runtime environment automatically uses the text in the logon language and therefore enables your program to be executable in multiple languages, without requiring a translator translate the source code. For example, the following line shows the output of a text symbol that is linked to a literal. The abbreviation of the text symbol is msg, and the text is output as an information message:

```
MESSAGE 'I am a message'(msg) TYPE 'I'.
```

Literals

A literal is an unnamed data object that is defined in the source code of a program and is completely determined by its value. Possible literals are numeric literals, text field literals, and string literals.

Numeric literals

A numeric literal is a literal that is defined by a sequence of digits with optional plus/minus signs. If the value ranges between $-2^{31}+1$ and $2^{31}-1$, the data type is i; otherwise, it is p (without decimal places). Numeric literals with more than 31 digits are not supported. Examples of numeric literals include the following:

```
... 1234567890 ...
... -987654321 ...
```

However, you cannot use numeric literals to represent numbers with decimal places or numbers in a scientific notation, because a decimal point outside of text literals is always regarded as the end of a statement. To represent non-integers or floating point numbers with mantissa and exponent, you must use character-like literals that are then converted from a text-type type into a numeric type according to the associated conversion rules (see Section 5.2.2).

---

32 The maximum length, mLen, of a text symbol should be selected in such a way that sufficient space is available for the translation. For example, the German word "Feld" consists of 5 letters in English: "field".

```
DATA: float TYPE f,
      pack  TYPE p DECIMALS 1.
float = '-765E-04'.
pack  = '-8473.67'.
```

After the assignments, the `float` and `pack` fields display the values -7.6499999999999999E-02 and -8473.7 respectively in the Debugger. As you can see, the binary floating point number is internally treated less exactly than the literal value,[33] while the packed number is rounded to its decimal places.

A text field literal is an alphanumeric character string enclosed by single quotes (') whose maximum length is limited to 255 characters. Every text field literal has the built-in data type `c`, and its length is defined by the number of characters. Examples of text field literals include the following:

Text field literals

```
'SAP AG' or 'Walldorf'.
```

The minimum length of a text field literal is one character. The specification of '' is equal to ' '. To combine several text field literals into one text field literal—for example, to increase the readability in the ABAP Editor—you can use the literal operator &:

```
cfield = 'This ' &
         'is only ' &
         'one text field literal'.
```

If, on the other hand, you extend a single text field literal across several editor lines—which, however, is only permitted outside of classes—all places between the two single quotes are interpreted as significant characters.

To display a single quote within a text field literal, you must specify two single quotes in a row so that it is not interpreted as the end of the text literal.

```
MESSAGE 'Welcome to Bob''s Bar!' TYPE 'I'.
```

String literals represent the counterpart of data type `string` to text field literals of data type `c`. Instead of single quotes ('), single back quotes (`) are used to enclose string literals:

String literals

```
`String Literal`.
```

---

33 This problem will no longer exist with the decimal floating point numbers that will be available as of the next release of SAP NetWeaver.

The empty string literal `` ` ` `` represents a string of length 0. To display a back quote within a string literal, you must specify two back quotes in a row. Single quotes, on the other hand, can be represented directly in string literals. The same holds true for back quotes in text literals. Thus the following string literal shows a recommended alternative to the above expression:

```
MESSAGE `Welcome to Bob's Bar!` TYPE 'I'.
```

An important difference between text field literals and string literals is that in many operand positions in text field literals no closing spaces are considered, as is the case with all data objects of type c. In string literals, closing spaces are always significant. For this reason, you should generally not define text field literals using closing spaces.

Using literals   A typical way to use literals is to place them after the VALUE addition in the DATA or CONSTANTS statements. When doing so, you should note that only three out of the 10 possible elementary ABAP types[34] are covered by literals of the same type. You must therefore always try to use one of the three types of literals that is most appropriate, and it must be possible to convert the contents into the desired type (see Section 5.2.2). The following lines represent two different literals as equivalent replacements for a literal of type x.

```
CONSTANTS hex1 TYPE x LENGTH 1 VALUE 'FF'.
CONSTANTS hex2 TYPE x LENGTH 1 VALUE 255.
```

However, you should be very economic when using literals in operational statements. Instead of using numeric literals, it usually makes more sense to use numeric constants. And instead of character-like literals, you should use text symbols in most cases. The extended syntax check (see Section 13.1.2) informs you about text field literals that are not linked to a text symbol. You may use character-like literals only in cases that involve technical content, which is not supposed to be displayed in the user interface. In those cases, you can use a pseudo-comment to hide the message of the extended program check, as shown in the following program line:

```
APPEND '<html>' TO html. "#EC NOTEXT
```

---

34 As of the next release of SAP NetWeaver, there will even be 12 possible elementary types due to the new decfloat types.

Anonymous Data Objects

In addition to the named data objects and literals, a third type of unnamed data object exists, which is referred to as an *anonymous data object*. Anonymous data objects are neither declared like named data objects nor are they defined in the source code like literals. Instead, they are created during the runtime of a program by using the following statement:

```
CREATE DATA dref TYPE type.
```

CREATE DATA

This statement is the direct counterpart to the object creation using CREATE OBJECT. The data object created is an instance of the data type specified using type and is referenced using a data reference variable dref. Section 11.1.2 provides more detailed information on anonymous data objects.

Predefined Data Objects

ABAP contains a small set of predefined data objects that can be accessed in any ABAP program without having to declare them. These include a constant, space, of type c and length 1, which contains a space character, and the self-reference me that points to the current object in every instance method.

The most commonly used predefined data objects are probably the *system fields*. System fields are filled by the runtime environment depending on the context, that is, their values at runtime vary depending on the context. You can use them to query the system status in a program. Although system fields are variables,[35] you should only access them in read-only mode; otherwise, important information for the continued program execution might be lost.[36] The few exceptions in which system fields could also be overwritten in ABAP programs, in order to control the system behavior, have meanwhile become obsolete.

System fields

With the exception of sy-repid, the names and data types of all system fields are defined as components of the structured data type

---

35 With the exception of sy-repid, which is really a constant.
36 A rather secure method to have a program respond in an undefined way or to crash it totally is to use the statement CLEAR sy that initializes all system fields of the sy structure.

SYST in the ABAP Dictionary. In every ABAP program, the runtime environment creates a structure called `sy` from this data type and fills the individual components during program execution. Thus you can address the individual system fields using `sy-comp` in ABAP programs. Listing 5.4 shows a simple example.

Listing 5.4 System Fields

```
REPORT z_system_fields.

CLASS demo DEFINITION.
  PUBLIC SECTION.
    CLASS-METHODS main.
ENDCLASS.
CLASS demo IMPLEMENTATION.
  METHOD main.
    DATA: output TYPE string,
          date   TYPE c LENGTH 10,
          time   TYPE c LENGTH 8.
    WRITE sy-datum TO date.
    WRITE sy-uzeit TO time.
    CONCATENATE `Hello user `        sy-uname
                ` today's date is ` date
                ` and the time is ` time
                ` o'clock.` INTO output.
    MESSAGE output TYPE 'I'.
  ENDMETHOD.
ENDCLASS.
START-OF-SELECTION.
  demo=>main( ).
```

sy-subrc One of the most important system fields is `sy-subrc`—the so-called *return value* or *return code*. Many ABAP statements set `sy-subrc` to 0 if they are executed successfully; otherwise, they set it to a value unequal to 0. It is advisable to check the content of `sy-subrc` after each statement that sets the return code before the processing continues.

There are specific system fields for many statements, such as `sy-index` for loops or `sy-tabix` for internal tables. For each statement, the ABAP keyword documentation describes which system fields are affected. On the other hand, the `sy` structure also contains many components that are either provided only for internal use or no longer supplied at all. Appendix A.2 contains a list of system fields that can be used in application programs.

5.2 Operations and Expressions

In Section 5.1, we provided comprehensive details on data types and data objects in ABAP programs. In this section, we address the basic operations you can carry out on data objects, as well as the specifics you must be aware of. We also discussed the ways in which the possible operations on a data object depend on its data type.

5.2.1 Assignments

Assignments represent the core of data processing, because they determine how to move the data into the data objects. Consequently, the name of the associated ABAP statement is MOVE. This statement has the same function as the assignment operator =, which appears a little more modern. To assign the content of a source field to a target variable, you can use the following statements:

```
MOVE source TO destination.
```

MOVE, =

or

```
destination = source.
```

The effects of both statements are absolutely identical. In both cases, a variable data object destination is assigned the content of the data object source. Of course, source can either be variable or a data object whose value must not be changed in the position of the statement, such as a constant or a READ-ONLY attribute. Regarding the combination of operands, we must basically distinguish between three cases that determine the execution of the value assignment:

1. The source and destination data objects are compatible. This means their data types match in all technical properties. During the copy process,[37] the content of source is transferred byte by byte into the target field destination. In elementary data types, the technical properties consist of the built-in ABAP type, the length, and the number of decimal places. In structured types, the technical properties are defined by the composition of substructures and elementary data types. The component names don't play any particular role. The technical properties of table types are the table category, the line type, and the table key.

Compatible

---

37 The copy process can also be delayed when copy-on-write (sharing) comes into play.

Convertible   2. The `source` and `destination` data objects are not compatible but convertible. This means that a conversion rule between the data types is defined in ABAP. In this case, the content of `source` is first converted according to this rule before it is transferred into the target field `destination`. Here you should note that a conversion requires a substantial amount of extra computing time that shouldn't be neglected, particularly when large quantities of data are to be processed. We'll introduce the conversion rules in the next section (Section 5.2.2).

Incompatible and   3. If the data objects are neither compatible nor convertible, no
inconvertible   assignment is possible. If this status is already detected during the syntax check, a syntax error occurs; otherwise, an exception will be raised.

5.2.2 Type Conversions

The above assignment rules indicate that an assignment without type conversion can only be carried out between compatible data objects whose technical properties match in every respect. In all other cases, either a type conversion needs to be done for the assignment, or the assignment is not feasible. Among other things, this means that a conversion even takes place for an assignment between two data objects of type `c` if the lengths of the two data objects differ.

Operand positions   Type conversions are not limited to pure assignments, however, as they can also occur in the operand positions of other statements. Most operand positions of statements are assigned an operand type. For example, you can only use numeric types for an arithmetic operation, while a character-like type is necessary to obtain a character-like output of a value. However, ABAP does allow you to use data objects in statements even if the data types of those objects are actually not suited for the operations in question. To make this possible, the runtime environment also carries out a type conversion into the operand type according to the respective conversion rule prior to the actual use. Thus, if a character-like data object contains a textual representation of a number, you can still carry out calculations with it because the representation is converted into a real numeric value before the calculation begins. Again, you should note this incurs additional runtime costs, which is why you should always try to use the most appropriate types.

In ABAP, the rules for type conversions are designed in such a way   **Conversion rules**
that the largest possible number of data types can be converted into
each other without any error. Of course, the basic rule that says the
content of a source field must represent a reasonable value for the
data type of the target variable must always be fulfilled. If it can be
statically determined that a type conversion doesn't make any sense,
the data types are inconvertible. For example, it's pointless to allow
conversions between data types d and t or between elementary
fields and internal tables.

The following sections briefly describe the most important conversion rules. Here, we distinguish between conversion rules for

- Elementary data types
- Structures
- Internal tables
- Reference variables

Assignments Between Elementary Data Types

There are 10 built-in elementary data types.[38] ABAP contains conversion rules between all those types with the exception of types d (date
field) and t (time field), between which a conversion doesn't make
sense. The following sections provide a brief overview of the most
important basic rules. You can find a detailed list of all individual
rules in *The Official ABAP Reference* book (SAP PRESS 2004).

- **Text-type to text-type**
  During the conversion between text-type data objects of data
  types c and string, the characters are transferred as left-aligned. If
  necessary, target fields of type c are filled with space characters on
  the right-hand side, or the right-hand side is truncated. For target
  fields of the string type, the transferred characters determine the
  length. Here you should note that closing spaces are transferred
  for source fields of the string type, not for those of type c.[39]

---

38 Here, we summarize types b and s (see Section 5.1.7) under i; however, note
    that the value ranges are different.
39 This holds true for all fields of data type c (hence also for text field literals), par-
    ticularly if the source field contains nothing more than space characters. Prior to
    the introduction of string literals in Release 6.10, a popular strategy was to find
    the most convenient way to fill strings with only space characters.

- **Text-type to numeric**
  During the conversion of text-type data objects to numeric data objects of data types i, p, and f, the content of the source field must represent a number in an appropriate notation (mathematical, commercial, or scientific). The value of the number is converted into the internal representation of the target field.

- **Text-type to byte-like**
  During the conversion of text-type data objects to byte-like data objects of data types x and xstring, the content of the source field must contain values in hexadecimal notation. Each character of the source field determines the contents of a half-byte of the target field.

- **Numeric to numeric**
  During the conversion between numeric data objects, the value of the source field is converted into the internal representation of the target field. If necessary, the value can be rounded commercially.

- **Numeric to text-type**
  During the conversion of numeric data objects to text-type data objects, the value of the source field is represented in the target field as a character string, either in commercial or in scientific notation, depending on the data type. In a commercial notation, the plus/minus sign is placed after the number, while the scientific notation consists of a mantissa and an exponent.[40] If the target field is not long enough, the value is either rounded or truncated.

- **Numeric to byte-like**
  During the conversion of numeric to byte-like data objects, the value of the source field is first converted to i. Then, its internal representation is transferred without further conversion.

- **Byte-like to byte-like**
  During the conversion between byte-like data objects, the bytes are transferred as left-aligned. If necessary, target fields of type x are filled with hexadecimal 0 on the right-hand side, or the right-hand side is truncated. For target fields of the xstring type, the transferred bytes determine the length.

---

40 The new decfloat data types that come with the next release of SAP NetWeaver will also generate the mathematical notation in which the plus/minus sign prefaces the number.

▶ **Byte-like to text-type**

During the conversion of byte-like data objects to text-type data objects, the values of the bytes of the source field are represented in hexadecimal notation in the target field.

▶ **Byte-like to numeric**

During the conversion of byte-like data objects to numeric data objects, the final four bytes of the source field are interpreted as an internal representation of a data object of type i; this number is converted into the data types of the target fields.

In addition to the above rules, there are specific rules for the conversion of the special types, n, d, and t for numeric texts, date, and time. Depending on their counterpart, these types are interpreted either as character-like or numeric. The numeric value of a numeric text is, of course, the number that is represented by its digits; the numeric value of a date is the number of days that have passed since 01.01.0001; and the numeric value of a time is the number of seconds that have passed since midnight.

Special conversions using n, d, t

```
DATA: numc TYPE n LENGTH 8 VALUE '20060627',
      date TYPE d,
      num1 TYPE i,
      num2 TYPE i.
date = numc.
num1 = numc.
num2 = date.
```

The num1 field is assigned the value 20060627 because the content of numc is regarded as a number. The num2 field receives the value 732490, that is, the number of days that have passed between 06/27/2006 and 01/01/0001.

In addition to those straightforward rules, the principle that says nearly every elementary type should be convertible into any other elementary type without raising an exception—if possible—sometimes results in rather peculiar rules. Let's look at the following example that illustrates the effects of the rule for converting text-type data objects into numeric texts, which may appear somewhat surprising:

```
DATA: strg TYPE string,
      numc TYPE n LENGTH 4.

strg = `5 + 8`.
numc = strg.
```

At first glance, you would probably expect a representation of the value 13 as the result in numc. However, the actual result is 0058, because according to the documented conversion rule, the characters of the source field that represent numbers are placed as right-aligned in the target field, while the left-hand side of the target field is filled with 0. Characters of the source field that do not represent numbers are ignored. You can see that you should use some of the type conversions with utmost caution, particularly when the special types, n, d, and t, are involved. For this reason, we would once again like to refer you to *The Official ABAP Reference* book and the ABAP keyword documentation that contains an exact overview of all rules.

Conversion errors The existence of a conversion rule does not always guarantee that an assignment can actually be made. As you can see in the above example, ABAP lets a lot pass, but fortunately not everything. Usually, the content of the source field must meet the requirements of the target field and, of course, must not exceed the value range of the target field; otherwise, a treatable exception will be raised.[41] Listing 5.5 demonstrates this for the conversion of a text-type data object into the different numeric types.

Listing 5.5 Conversion of Texts into Numeric Values

```
REPORT z_type_conversions.

SELECTION-SCREEN BEGIN OF SCREEN 100.
PARAMETERS number TYPE c LENGTH 30.
SELECTION-SCREEN END OF SCREEN 100.

CLASS demo DEFINITION.
  PUBLIC SECTION.
    CLASS-METHODS main.
  PRIVATE SECTION.
    CLASS-METHODS convert
      CHANGING target TYPE numeric.
ENDCLASS.

CLASS demo IMPLEMENTATION.
  METHOD main.
    DATA: i_target TYPE i,
          p_target TYPE p LENGTH 8 DECIMALS 2,
          f_target TYPE f.
```

---

41 Unfortunately, the assignment of text fields to date fields of type d or to time fields of type t doesn't raise an exception if invalid formats are generated in those types.

```
    DO.
      CALL SELECTION-SCREEN 100.
      IF sy-subrc <> 0.
        EXIT.
      ENDIF.
      convert( CHANGING target = i_target ).
      convert( CHANGING target = p_target ).
      convert( CHANGING target = f_target ).
    ENDDO.
  ENDMETHOD.
  METHOD convert.
    DATA:  msg TYPE c LENGTH 50,
           typ TYPE c LENGTH 1.
    DESCRIBE FIELD target TYPE typ.
    TRY.
        target = number.
        WRITE target TO msg LEFT-JUSTIFIED.
        CONCATENATE `Type ` typ `: ` msg INTO msg.
      CATCH cx_sy_conversion_error.
        CONCATENATE `Input not convertible to ` typ
          INTO msg.
    ENDTRY.
    MESSAGE msg TYPE 'I'.
  ENDMETHOD.
ENDCLASS.

START-OF-SELECTION.
  demo=>main( ).
```

You can use the program from Listing 5.5 to test the respective conversion rules. If you enter a text that cannot be interpreted as a number, the conversion fails. If you enter plain numbers such as "-123.55", every conversion will work. However, if you enter the value "+123.55e+3" into the input field, you will see that conversions to i and p are impossible, while the assignment to type f provides a result. Thus, i and p do not allow for scientific notation.

Assignments with Structures

Assignments that involve structures would most probably lead you to expect that the assignment of a structure to another structure is only possible if the two structures are compatible. But here as well, ABAP is very flexible as it also allows other combinations. The strict compatibility is only required for deep structures (see Section 5.1.8) as a prerequisite for the assignment.

Deep structures

279

Flat structures Flat structures allow for assignments between incompatible structures and even between flat structures and elementary fields. Prior to the introduction of Unicode, this was achieved—horribile dictu!—by just considering the involved structures as one single field of type c. We leave it up to you to deduce the consequences![42]

Fortunately, the technical requirements of Unicode that come with Release 6.10 have put an end to this very insecure procedure. In Unicode programs—and we only use such programs—the so-called *Unicode fragment view* of the flat structures involved determines whether an assignment can be made. This is a reasonable compromise between the requirement of full compatibility and the old procedure, because it allows you to convert many non-Unicode programs that have been programmed in a clean and proper manner into Unicode programs with very little modification needed.

Unicode fragment view The Unicode fragment view decomposes a structure into byte-like and character-like areas, numeric components, and deep components, as well as in alignment gaps.[43] Regarding the fragments of nested structures, the elementary components of the lowest nesting level are considered.

Conversion rules The conversion rules between flat incompatible structures state the following:

- Flat structures whose Unicode fragment views are identical can be assigned without prior conversion.
- Flat structues of different lengths whose initial sections have the same Unicode fragment view across the length of the shorter structure can be assigned without conversion in the length of the shorter structure. Surplus components are either truncated or they are filled with type-specific initial values.

The rules for conversions between flat structures and elementary fields are basically the following:

---

42 Just think of space paddings, or imagine that potential alignment gaps between individual components are not taken into account.

43 Alignment gaps are bytes that are inserted in front of components, which contain alignment requirements within a structure so that the required alignment can be attained. Components with alignment requirements must begin at addresses that can be divided by a specific number. For example, it must be possible to divide the address of a binary floating point number by 8.

▸ If a structure is purely character-like, it is treated like a data object of type c during the conversion.

▸ If the structure is not completely character-like, the elementary field must be of type c, and the structure must begin with a character-like fragment that is at least as long as the elementary field. The assignment occurs exclusively between this fragment and the elementary field.

With the exception of one special case, no other conversion rules exist, which means that no assignments are possible for other combinations. For more details on this topic, we refer you once more to *The Official ABAP Reference* book and the ABAP keyword documentation. The following code section shows a common example of two structures with identical Unicode fragment views that can be assigned to each other without any problem:

```
DATA: BEGIN OF struc1,
        idx1  TYPE i,
        year  TYPE n LENGTH 4,
        month TYPE n LENGTH 2,
        day   TYPE n LENGTH 2,
      END OF struc1.

DATA: BEGIN OF struc2,
        idx2 TYPE i,
        date TYPE d,
      END OF struc2.
...
struc1 = struc2.
...
struc2 = struc1.
```

Assignments Between Internal Tables

Internal tables can only be assigned to internal tables. The assignment of an internal table depends only on the line type, not on the table category or table key. Internal tables can be assigned to each other if their line types are compatible or convertible. The assignment of individual lines of the source table to the lines of the target table is based on the same semantics as the assignment between individual data objects of the respective line types.

Assignments between internal tables can trigger runtime errors even in the case of compatible line types if duplicate entries would be created in a target table that has a unique table key. The assignment of large tables can also lead to memory bottlenecks that result in program terminations.

Sharing You should note that as of Release 6.10 the so-called sharing is always applied to strings in assignments of internal tables whose line types do not contain any tables themselves. To save memory, the actual copy process does not take place until a change is made to one of the tables involved (copy-on-write semantics). In this way, you may be able to avoid or delay a memory bottleneck.

Assignments Between Reference Variables

The content of a reference variable can only be assigned to another reference variable; data references can only be assigned to data reference variables; and object references can only be assigned to object reference variables. A conversion is not necessary for the assignment. For an assignment to take place, the static type of the target reference variable must be more general than or equal to the dynamic type of the source reference variable. The static and dynamic types are defined as follows:

Static type
- ▶ The static type is defined during the declaration of a reference variable (see Section 5.1.6).

Dynamic type
- ▶ The dynamic type is not fixed but determined during the runtime of a program. It is the data type of the data object or the class of the object to which a reference variable points.

If the assignment is successful, the target reference variable points to the same object as the source reference variable, that is, the target reference variable adopts the dynamic type of the source reference variable. Section 6.4 describes this topic in more detail for object reference variables. See Section 11.1.2 for data reference variables.

5.2.3 Special Assignments

In addition to the general type of assignment using MOVE or the assignment operator =, ABAP provides several special types of assignments.

Assigning Structures by Components

The assignment rules for structures described in Section 5.2.2 refer to a structure as a whole. The source and target structures are considered as units during an assignment; however, in some cases, you may want to assign only individual components of a structure to the components of another structure. You could use several MOVE statements to do that, but ABAP provides a special statement for this:

```
MOVE-CORRESPONDING source_struc TO destination_struc.
```

MOVE-
CORRESPONDING

This statement identifies all components that have the same name in both structures and assigns them individually according to the respective assignment rules without affecting other components. Nested structures are completely dissolved in this process. The following code section contains an example in which the components of a structure are assigned to the components of two other structures that have the same names.

```
DATA: BEGIN OF name,
        title        TYPE c LENGTH 3,
        first_name   TYPE string,
        second_name  TYPE string,
      END OF name.

DATA: BEGIN OF location,
        street       TYPE string,
        street_no    TYPE c LENGTH 4,
        city         TYPE string,
        zip_code     TYPE n LENGTH 5,
        country      TYPE string,
      END OF location.
DATA BEGIN OF address.
INCLUDE STRUCTURE name.
INCLUDE STRUCTURE location.
DATA END OF address.
...
MOVE-CORRESPONDING address TO: name,
                               location.
```

Although this statement may be useful in many situations, it has one big disadvantage, namely, that it is based on the names of structure components. But what's in a name, you may ask. This question is especially justified for the names of structure components, which do not constitute a type. It is therefore imperative that you adhere to self-defined naming conventions in order to use this statement so that it makes sense.

When working with structure components, an often used alternative is to access the structures via field symbols that can be linked in many ways to structures or their components by using the ASSIGN statement (see Section 11.1.1).

Formatted Assignment

The internal representation of data in data objects is usually not suited for a direct output of the values to the user. In particular, this holds true for numeric data in data objects of numeric data types whose code cannot be used for a direct presentation. Prior to displaying the contents of those data objects, they must be converted into character-like data that can be output so that the user understands them. ABAP contains an assignment statement—WRITE TO—that explicitly carries out this task.

WRITE TO
    WRITE source **TO** destination **format_options**.

This statement formats the content of an elementary data object source and assigns it to a flat character-like data object, destination.

If no format_options additions are specified, formatting is carried out according to type-dependent predefined rules that can also depend on user-specific values or regional settings (see *The Official ABAP Reference* book). The following code section creates character-like representations of packed numbers with different decimal separators by explicitly setting specific countries.

```
DATA: text    TYPE c LENGTH 20,
      number TYPE p DECIMALS 2 VALUE '123.45'.

SET COUNTRY 'DE'.
WRITE number TO text.
MESSAGE text TYPE 'I'.

SET COUNTRY 'US'.
WRITE number TO text.
MESSAGE text TYPE 'I'.
```

You can extend the predefined formatting rules by using a set of additions called format_options that either complement or replace the formatting rules. Examples include JUSTIFIED additions to define the alignment or DECIMALS and EXPONENT additions for the formatting of numbers. In addition, ABAP provides general formatting templates and specific date templates. The following code section contains two examples. You can find more details in the keyword documentation.

```
DATA: text   TYPE c LENGTH 50,
      number TYPE f VALUE '123.45'.

WRITE number TO text EXPONENT -10 RIGHT-JUSTIFIED.
MESSAGE text TYPE 'I'.
WRITE sy-datum TO text DD/MM/YY.
MESSAGE text TYPE 'I'.
```

Lastly, we should mention that data types in the ABAP Dictionary can even be linked with specific function modules, the so-called *conversion routines* that are responsible for formatting content for output and for converting input into internal formats. These routines are automatically executed when you use the WRITE TO statement, and they also can be overwritten.

Conversion routines

Setting Variables to Their Initial Value

To conclude the section on assignments, we want to briefly describe the statement that enables you to reset variables to their type-specific initial value:

```
CLEAR dobj.
```

CLEAR

The CLEAR has the following effect on data objects of different data types:

▶ **Elementary data objects**
Depending on the data type, the content of elementary data objects is reset to the initial value listed in Table 5.1.

▶ **Structures**
The elementary components are initialized in accordance with their data type.

▶ **Internal tables**
All lines of the internal table are deleted.

▶ **Reference variables**
Assignment of the so-called null reference that points to no object.

5.2.4 Calculations

Calculation expression

In ABAP, calculations are generally carried out in *calculation expressions*. A calculation expression is either an arithmetic expression or a bit expression. This book only describes arithmetic expressions. In addition to arithmetic expressions, a separate self-explanatory statement exists for each of the four basic arithmetic operations: ADD, SUBTRACT, MULTIPLY, and DIVIDE. We won't elaborate on these statements any further.

Arithmetic Expressions

Arithmetic operators

An arithmetic expression formulates a calculation whose result is a numeric value. In an arithmetic expression, numeric operands are linked to each other via arithmetic operators. The operands can be preceded by plus/minus signs and may contain explicit parentheses. Table 5.4 provides a list of possible operators.

Operator	Calculation
+	Adds the operands
-	Subtracts the right-hand operand from the left-hand operand
*	Multiplies the operands
/	Divides the left-hand operand by the right-hand operand
DIV	Integer segment resulting from the division of the left-hand operand by the right-hand operand
MOD	Integer remainder resulting from the division of the left-hand operand by the right-hand operand
**	Exponentiation of the left-hand with the right-hand operand

Table 5.4 Arithmetic Operators

If no parentheses are used, the usual priority rules apply. In the event of a division by 0, an exception is raised that can be caught (see Section 8.2). However, if the numerator is also 0, ABAP has the peculiar feature of not raising an exception for a division by 0 and instead setting the result to 0 without any further notification.[44]

---

44 The exception is handled by ABAP itself, so to speak.

The operands of an arithmetic expression can be numeric data objects or built-in functions. By numeric data objects, we, of course, refer to all data objects that have one of the three numeric types, i, f, and p. In addition, numeric data objects also include byte-like and character-like data objects whose content can be interpreted as numeric on the basis of the conversion rules (see Section 5.2.2).

Numeric data objects

Built-In Functions

Built-in functions are predefined functions with a numeric return value. In the current SAP NetWeaver 2004s Release, you can use these functions only as operands of calculation expressions. You can specify a built-in function func using the following syntax:

```
... func( arg ) ...
```

This syntax corresponds to calling a functional method using one input parameter (see Section 6.2.2).[45] If a functional method has the same name, it hides a built-in function.

The built-in functions can be divided into mathematical functions and description functions. The mathematical functions can be further subdivided into numeric functions for numeric arguments of any kind and floating point functions whose argument and return value consist of a floating point number:

▶ The built-in numeric functions are abs, sign, ceil, floor, trunc, and frac for determining the absolute value, plus/minus sign, etc.

▶ The built-in floating point functions are the usual cos, sin, tan, acos, asin atan, sinh, cosh, tanh, exp, log, log10, and sqrt.

The numeric functions are overloaded in the sense that the data type of the argument determines the data type of the return value.

The description functions return properties of their argument. For example, charlen determines the length of a character in terms of bytes, strlen defines the number of characters of a data object, and lines determines the number of lines in an internal table.

---

45 Thus, functional methods provide a way to extend the built-in functions by self-defined functions.

The COMPUTE Statement

The current Release (SAP NetWeaver 2004s) allows calculation expressions to occur only on the right-hand side of a COMPUTE statement. For example, you can specify an arithmetic expression in a program as follows:

COMPUTE `COMPUTE result = ( ( exp( x ) - exp( -1 * x ) ) / 2 ).`

For those expressions, you should note that in the ABAP syntax each operand, each operator, and each parenthesis represents a separate word that must be separated by at least one space character from the adjacent words.

The specification of the COMPUTE statement is optional, that is, you can also write the above expression in the following way:

`result = ( ( exp( x ) - exp( -1 * x ) ) / 2 ).`

However, please do not confuse this expression with the assignment described in Section 5.2.1. The existence of an arithmetic expression on the right-hand side of an equals sign (=), which can simply be caused by using a plus/minus sign (+/–) in front of the operand, always means that a COMPUTE statement is used instead of a simple assignment.

Calculation type   The essential difference between an assignment and a calculation using the COMPUTE statement is that a calculation has a calculation type, which is also influenced by the target field. The calculation type corresponds to one of the three numeric data types, i, p, or f, and is determined by the operand with the largest value range prior to the calculation. The value range of data type f is larger than that of data type p, which, in turn, is larger than that of data type i.[46] The operands of the entire arithmetic expression and the result field, result, are considered in this process. If functions are used as operands, it is either the arguments of the functions or the functions themselves that determine the data type. Prior to executing the calculation, all operands of the arithmetic expression are converted into the calculation type, which, in turn, determines the calculation method and calculation accuracy:

---

46 Exception: If operator ** is used, the calculation type is always f, regardless of the operands.

▶ Calculations using calculation type i are carried out on the basis of an integer arithmetic; if necessary, each intermediate result is commercially rounded to an integer.

▶ Calculations using calculation type p are carried out based on a decimal floating point arithmetic with a precision of 31 decimal places;[47] if necessary, surplus decimal places of each intermediate result are commercially rounded. The decimal separator is only taken into account during the calculation if the **Fixed point arithmetic** checkbox is checked in the program properties (see Section 3.3.5).

▶ Calculations using calculation type f are carried out based on the standardized binary floating point arithmetic of the respective platform. All intermediate results are binary floating point numbers and can therefore be correspondingly inaccurate.

The final result of a calculation appears internally first in the calculation type and is then converted into the result type, if necessary. However, you should always note that too many conversions have a negative effect on the computing speed. If possible, ensure that you always declare all operands and the result field using the same numeric data type.

The procedure for determining the calculation type and the execution of the calculations, including the commercial rounding of intermediate results, distinguishes ABAP from most other programming languages and demonstrates that especially the calculations using type p are provided primarily for use in business applications.

Outlook on the Next Release of SAP NetWeaver

In the current SAP NetWeaver 2004s Release, calculations are still closely linked to the COMPUTE statement, that is, you can use arithmetic expressions only on the right-hand side of a COMPUTE statement. In the next release of SAP NetWeaver, the usability of arithmetic expressions and functions will be substantially extended. Operand positions in which you can then use those expressions include the following:

---

47 In case of an overflow, the precision is set internally to 63 decimal places.

▸ Operands of logical expressions (see Section 5.2.5)

▸ Actual parameters for input parameters of functions[48]

▸ Many numeric operand positions such as index specifications when accessing internal tables

In addition, the introduction of the new `decfloat` types in the next release of SAP NetWeaver will, of course, affect calculations and their calculation types.

Date and Time Calculations

The conversion of the operands of an arithmetic expression into the calculation type together with the respective conversion rules (see Section 5.2.2) allows for direct date and time calculations. Listing 5.6 shows an example of date calculation.

Listing 5.6 Date Calculation

```
REPORT z_last_day_of_last_month.

CLASS demo DEFINITION.
  PUBLIC SECTION.
    CLASS-METHODS main.
ENDCLASS.
CLASS demo IMPLEMENTATION.
  METHOD main.
    DATA: date TYPE d,
          result_txt TYPE c LENGTH 50.
    date       = sy-datum.
    date+6(2) = '01'.
    date       = date - 1.
    WRITE date TO result_txt.
    CONCATENATE `Last day of last month: `
                result_txt INTO result_txt.
    MESSAGE result_txt TYPE 'I'.
  ENDMETHOD.
ENDCLASS.
START-OF-SELECTION.
  demo=>main( ).
```

The date of the current day is set to the first day of the current month by assigning the system field `sy-datum` and by accessing a subfield

---

48 This enables the nesting of method calls.

(see Section 5.4.3).[49] If you deduct one day here, you will obtain the last day of the previous month.

To correctly calculate with dates and times, of course, requires that a date or time exists in a valid format in a source field. You can check the valid contents of date and time fields as follows: If the content of a date or time field is invalid, the runtime environment sets the result of the conversion into a numeric value to 0. Because a conversion is also carried out in logical expressions with different operand types (see the following Section 5.2.2), it is often possible to query the validity in a single expression:

Validity

```
DATA: date TYPE d.

date = '20000231'.

IF date = 0.
    ...         "Error
ELSE.
    ...         "OK
ENDIF.
```

The logical expression is true because date contains an invalid value and is set to 0 for the comparison. Strictly speaking, the logical expression is also true for the valid date of 01.01.0001. While this date would rarely occur in application programs, the time check does pose a problem because the valid time 00:00:00 may very well occur. In this case, you can use auxiliary fields:

```
DATA time TYPE t.

DATA: test1 TYPE i,
      test2 TYPE t.

time = 'ABCXYZ'.

test1 = time.
test2 = test1.

IF time <> test2.
    ...         "Error
ELSE.
    ...         "OK
ENDIF.
```

---

49 Here the character-like nature of the date field is utilized.

The content of `test2` does not correspond to the content of `time` because `time` is set to 0 when it is assigned to `test1`.

Timestamp If you want to mark data uniquely, you often need more precise values for the date and time than those you can obtain using the system fields, `sy-datum` and `sy-uzeit`. For this purpose, you can use *timestamps*. In an ABAP program, you can place a current timestamp in a `time_stamp` field using the

GET TIME STAMP `GET TIME STAMP FIELD` time_stamp.

statement. The timestamp is always globally unique because it is stored in UTC time (Coordinated Universal Time), irrespective of the local time zone. Timestamps can be requested in short and long form. The short form contains the current date including the time. In the long form, there are seven decimal places reserved for fractions of seconds that allow an accuracy of up to 100 nanoseconds[50]. The data type of the target field `time_stamp` determines which form is requested. You can declare this target field with a reference to the data elements, TIMESTAMP and TIMESTAMPL, of the ABAP Dictionary. There are other statements available to handle stamps, such as `CONVERT TIME STAMP` or `CONVERT DATE` that convert the timestamp into a date and time of a specific time zone and vice versa, taking into account daylight saving time.

5.2.5 Logical Expressions

A logical expression either returns the value "true" or "false" as a result. Because ABAP does not contain a Boolean data type to adopt these values[51], you cannot use logical expressions on the right-hand side of assignments. Instead, you can use logical expressions to formulate conditions in control structures (see Section 5.3) or other statements such as `CHECK` (see Section 5.3.2) or `ASSERT` (see Section 8.3).

---

50 Depending on the hardware of the application server, however, the maximum precision cannot always be reached.

51 Frequently, the missing Boolean data type is replaced with data objects of type `c` and length 1. If the data object contains an "X", it is interpreted as "true". The "false" value, on the other hand, is represented by a space character. The predefined ABAP type group contains the `abap_bool` type and the constants `abap_true` and `abap_false` for this purpose (see Section 5.1.7).

Comparisons

In the majority of logical expressions, the contents of two operands are compared with each other by using a relational operator.

```
... operand1 operator operand2 ...
```

You can use data objects, built-in functions, and functional methods as operands.[52] Table 5.5 provides an overview of relational operators that are available in ABAP to carry out comparisons between all data types. In addition to the usual symbols, you can also use abbreviations such as LE instead of <=. However, this is not recommended.

Relational Operator	Description
=, EQ	equal to
<>, NE	not equal to
<, LT	less than
<=, LE	less than or equal to
>, GT	greater than
>=, GE	greater than or equal to

Table 5.5 Relational Operators

When using the operators from Table 5.5, the data types of the two operands must either be compatible or convertible, similar to assignments.

Comparing compatible elementary data objects

No conversion is carried out during a comparison of compatible elementary operands. Numeric fields (type i, f, p) are compared with each other with regard to their numeric values. Character-like fields are generally compared with each other from left to right. The first different character from the left determines which operand is bigger. In this process, operands of type c and string are compared lexicographically and by differentiating between uppercase and lowercase letters, while operands of type n are compared on the basis of the represented numeric values. If the operands have type d or t and contain a valid date or time specification, the later date or time is greater than the earlier one. Correspondingly, byte-like fields (type x and xstring) are compared on the basis of their byte values.

---

52 As of the next release of SAP NetWeaver, you will also be able to specify calculation expressions as operands.

Comparing incompatible elementary data objects Operands may have different technical properties in logical expressions; however, it must be possible to convert them into each other, as is the case with assignments. The conversion rules for logical expressions enhance the rules for type conversions for assignments from Section 5.2.2. You can find the exact rules in *The Official ABAP Reference* book. We only describe the most important properties in this section.

Let's look at operands that have the same data types but different lengths. In this case, the shorter operand is converted to the length of the longer one prior to the comparison. The following rule is particularly important here:

Text fields of type c are filled with space characters on the right.[53] For this reason, the following expression is "true":

```
'abc ' = 'abc'
```

As a matter of fact, "abc " and "abc " are compared with each other. However, you must use caution regarding strings! If there is a string on the right-hand side that contains "abc ", the comparison is false because a different conversion takes place here (see Rule 4 below).

For operands of different data types, the same conversions are carried out as for assignments, but according to a fixed hierarchy.

1. If one of the operands has a numeric data type (i, f, p), a numeric comparison takes place. The comparison type is determined like the calculation type of an arithmetic expression (see Section 5.2.4) and converted correspondingly.

2. If one of the operands is a date field of type d or a time field of type t and the other operand is a numeric field, the system converts date or time field into the numeric type. If the other operand is character-like, the date and time fields are also regarded as being character-like.

3. If one of the operands has data type n and the other has data type c, string, x or xstring, the contents of both operands are converted to data type p.

4. If one of the operands is a text field of type c and the other operand is a text string of type string, the text field is converted into

---

53 Correspondingly, numeric texts of type n are filled with 0 on the left-hand side.

a string; note that closing spaces will be lost in this process. Correspondingly, the same rule applies to x and xstring.

5. If one of the operands has a byte-like type and the other operand has a character-like type c or string, the content of an operand of type x is converted to c, while the content of an operand of type xstring is converted to string.

As with assignments, ABAP also tries to link different data types with each other in the most optimal way in comparisons. To save runtime costs for unnecessary conversions, and particularly to prevent unwanted surprises, we recommend that you use compatible operands, that is, operands that can be combined in a comparison in a way that makes sense, without producing unexpected results.

Of course, you can also compare reference variables with each other in ABAP. Two reference variables are equal when they point to the same object. Otherwise, they are different. A size comparison for reference variables is defined internally and always provides the same results in the same context. It can make sense to use a size comparison for sorted arrays of references, such as in internal tables, in order to find specific references.

Comparing reference variables

In the same way in which you can make assignments between structures, you can also compare structures with other structures or with elementary fields.

Comparison between structures

Compatible structures are decomposed into their individual components, which are then compared with each other. Two compatible structures are identical if all their components are identical. Regarding different structures, the first component that is different determines which of the structures is bigger or smaller.

Incompatible structures can be compared with each other if they are flat and if their Unicode fragment views (see Section 5.2.2) are identical in the length of the shorter structure. Before the comparison can be carried out, the shorter structure is filled up to the length of the longer structure in a type-specific way, and the comparison is based on the Unicode fragment view.

Structures can be compared with elementary fields if they contain only character-like flat components, or if their Unicode fragment is character-like and flat and its length matches at least the length of the elementary field, which, in turn, must be of type c. In this case,

ABAP handles the entire structure or the first Unicode fragment as an operand of type c.

Comparing
internal tables

Internal tables can also be compared with each other. A prerequisite for comparing internal tables is that its line types can be compared. The first criterion for a comparison between internal tables is the number of lines. The more lines an internal table contains, the bigger it is. If two internal tables contain the same number of lines, they are compared with each other line by line and component by component. If the components of the table lines are nested internal tables, they are compared with each other recursively. If the internal tables are unequal, the first unequal line pair determines the result of the comparison.

Other relational
operators

In addition to the general relational operators from Table 5.5, ABAP also contains specific relational operators for certain data types:

▶ The operators CO, CN, CA, NA, CS, NS, CP, and NP determine whether a character string contains certain characters, strings, or patterns. The logical expression 'ABAP Objects' CS 'ABAP' is, for instance, true.

▶ The operators BYTE-CO, BYTE-CN, BYTE-CA, BYTE-NA, BYTE-CS, and BYTE-NS represent the counterparts of the above character string operators for byte strings.

Logical Expressions with Predicates

Apart from logical expressions with relational operators, you can also use logical expressions with predicates, which provide information about an operand:

BETWEEN

▶ BETWEEN
Checks the affiliation with an interval

```
... operand1 BETWEEN operand2 AND operand3 ...
```

IN seltab

▶ IN seltab
Evaluates the conditions in a selection table (see Section 9.2.4)

```
... operand IN seltab ...
```

IS INITIAL

▶ IS INITIAL
Checks the initial value

```
... operand IS INITIAL ...
```

▶ **IS BOUND**

Checks whether a reference variable points to an object

`... ref IS BOUND ...`

IS BOUND

▶ **IS ASSIGNED**

Checks whether a field symbol is assigned a data object (see Section 11.1.1)

`... <fs> IS ASSIGNED ...`

IS ASSIGNED

▶ **IS SUPPLIED**

Checks whether an actual parameter is bound to a formal parameter of a procedure (see Section 6.2.2)

`... parameter IS SUPPLIED ...`

IS SUPPLIED

Using the last three expressions, in particular, can be important for the correct execution of dynamic programs (see Chapter 11) and to avoid possible exceptions.

Linking and Negating Logical Expressions

To combine several logical expressions into a single one, you must use the Boolean operators, AND or OR.[54]

AND, OR

▶ Expressions linked using AND are true if all logical expressions involved are true.

▶ Expressions linked using OR are true if it least one of the logical expressions involved is true.

You can negate the result of a logical expression by using the Boolean operator NOT as a prefix. NOT has priority over AND, while AND has priority over OR.

NOT

You can, however, place logical expressions in parentheses to change the priorities. As in arithmetic expressions, ABAP interprets each parenthesis as a single word. For this reason, each parenthesis must be preceded and followed by at least one space character.

Parentheses

ABAP processes logical expressions from the left to the right. If the system detects that one of the partial expressions is fulfilled or not fulfilled, no other comparisons or checks are carried out for this par-

---

54 As of the next release of SAP NetWeaver, the Boolean operator EQUIV will be added for an equivalence link.

tial expression. Therefore, you can increase the processing speed by arranging logical expressions in such a way that comparisons that often return a "false" result are placed at the beginning of an AND sequence, while complex comparisons such as the search for character strings are located at the end of a link.

5.3 Control Structures

Control structures decompose a processing block (usually a method) into statement blocks and control the program flow within the processing block. Possible control structures are *sequences*, *conditional branches*, and *conditional* and *unconditional loops*. Whereas sequences are trivial, branches and loops must be defined using *control statements*. In this respect, the concepts of ABAP are similar to those of other programming languages. Control structures must be self-contained within their processing block, but they can be nested, that is, a statement block within a control structure can contain self-contained control structures.

5.3.1 Conditional Branches

To execute statements only under certain conditions in ABAP, you can use the control structures IF ... ENDIF or CASE ... ENDCASE.

General Branches

To execute not more than one statement block on the basis of any logical expression, you can use the IF control structure:

IF, ELSEIF, ELSE, ENDIF

```
IF log_exp1.
   statement_block1
ELSEIF log_exp2.
   statement_block2
...
ELSE.
   statement_blockn
ENDIF.
```

The logical expressions log_exp are checked from top to bottom, starting with the IF statement. The statement block that is located after the first true logical expression is executed. If none of the logical expressions is true, the statement block after the ELSE statement is executed. If the ELSE statement is not specified, it may result in no processing block being executed. However, we recommend that you always close an IF control structure with an ELSE statement. Listing 5.7 shows an example of a nested IF control structure.

Listing 5.7 IF Control Structure

```
REPORT z_branching.

CLASS demo DEFINITION.
  PUBLIC SECTION.
    CLASS-METHODS main.
ENDCLASS.
CLASS demo IMPLEMENTATION.
  METHOD main.
    DATA result_txt TYPE string.
    IF sy-saprl < '45A'.
      CONCATENATE 'ABAP Release ' sy-saprl
                  ' is not object-oriented'
                  INTO result_txt RESPECTING BLANKS.
    ELSE.
      IF sy-saprl < '46A'.
        CONCATENATE 'ABAP Release ' sy-saprl
                    ' is partly object-oriented'
                    INTO result_txt RESPECTING BLANKS.
      ELSE.
        CONCATENATE 'ABAP Release ' sy-saprl
                    ' is fully object-oriented'
                    INTO result_txt RESPECTING BLANKS.
      ENDIF.
    ENDIF.
    MESSAGE result_txt TYPE 'I'.
  ENDMETHOD.
ENDCLASS.
START-OF-SELECTION.
  demo=>main( ).
```

Case Distinctions

A special type of the IF control structure is available for simple case distinctions:

```
CASE dobj.
  WHEN operand1 [OR operand2 [OR operand3 ...]].
```

CASE, WHEN, ENDCASE

```
       statement_block1
  WHEN ...
     statement_block2
  ...
  WHEN OTHERS.
     statement_blockn
ENDCASE.
```

The system checks from top to bottom, starting with the first WHEN statement, whether the contents of the operand operand agree with the contents of one of the operands, operand1, operand2, ..., and processes the statement block following the first agreement. If no agreement is found, the statement block after the WHEN OTHERS statement is executed. If the WHEN OTHERS statement is not specified, it may result in no processing block being executed. However, we recommend that you always close a CASE control structure with a WHEN OTHERS statement. Listing 5.8 shows an example of a case distinction that evaluates a subfield (see Section 5.4.3) of the sy-datum system field.

Listing 5.8 CASE Control Structure

```
REPORT z_case.

CLASS demo DEFINITION.
  PUBLIC SECTION.
    CLASS-METHODS main.
ENDCLASS.
CLASS demo IMPLEMENTATION.
  METHOD main.
    CASE sy-datum+4(2).
      WHEN '12' OR '01' OR '02'.
        MESSAGE 'Winter' TYPE 'I'.
      WHEN '03' OR '04' OR '05'.
        MESSAGE 'Spring' TYPE 'I'.
      WHEN '06' OR '07' OR '08'.
        MESSAGE 'Summer' TYPE 'I'.
      WHEN '09' OR '10' OR '11'.
        MESSAGE 'Autumn' TYPE 'I'.
      WHEN OTHERS.
        MESSAGE 'Illegal Date' TYPE 'I'
          DISPLAY LIKE 'E'.
    ENDCASE.
  ENDMETHOD.
ENDCLASS.
```

```
START-OF-SELECTION.
  demo=>main( ).
```

After this brief description of program branches, we would now like to turn our attention to loops.

5.3.2 Loops

Loops enable you to execute a statement block several times. We distinguish between conditional and unconditional loops. This section describes the basic loops. In addition, other loop statements are available, for example, for loops at internal tables (see Section 5.5.2) or for reading rows from database tables (see Section 10.1.2).

Unconditional Loops

ABAP contains the DO control structure for unconditional loops:

```
DO [n TIMES].
  statement_block
ENDDO.
```

DO, ENDDO

The statement block in the loop is repeatedly executed until the number of passes defined by n TIMES has been reached, or until the loop is left using a statement such as EXIT (see below). During a loop pass, the sy-index system field contains the number of loop passes that have occurred up to this point including the current pass. If, in a nested loop, you want to access the index of an outer loop from within an inner loop, you must use an auxiliary variable. Listing 5.10 contains an example of this.

Conditional Loops

ABAP contains the WHILE control structure for conditional loops:

```
WHILE log_exp.
  statement_block
ENDWHILE.
```

WHILE,
ENDWHILE

The statement block in the loop is repeatedly executed as long as the logical expression log_exp is true, or until the loop is left using a statement such as EXIT (see below). Here as well, sy-index is set to the current loop index in each pass. Listing 5.9 shows a simple example of using a WHILE loop.

Listing 5.9 WHILE Loops

```
REPORT z_while.

CLASS demo DEFINITION.
  PUBLIC SECTION.
    CLASS-METHODS main.
ENDCLASS.
CLASS demo IMPLEMENTATION.
  METHOD main.
    DATA text TYPE string VALUE `One Two Three`.
    WHILE sy-subrc = 0.
      REPLACE ` ` IN text WITH `-`.
    ENDWHILE.
    MESSAGE text TYPE 'I'.
  ENDMETHOD.
ENDCLASS.
START-OF-SELECTION.
  demo=>main( ).
```

The loop simulates the function of the statement:

```
REPLACE ALL OCCURRENCES OF ` ` IN text WITH `-`.
```

Of course, in a real application you would have to use the ALL OCCUR-RENCES addition of the REPLACE statement instead of the less efficient WHILE loop for the simple case that no further action is to take place in the loop.

Leaving Loops Early

You can also leave the statement block of a loop in a way that is controlled by the program. For this purpose, ABAP contains several different termination statements that can be used in all loops possible in ABAP:

CONTINUE ▶ The CONTINUE statement terminates the current loop pass without any condition. The remaining statements of the statement block are skipped and the next loop pass is executed.

CHECK ▶ The CHECK log_exp statement terminates the current loop pass with a condition. If the result of the logical expression log_exp is false, CHECK works in the same way as CONTINUE.

EXIT ▶ The EXIT statement terminates the entire current loop without any condition. The current loop pass terminates immediately and the program flow continues after the closing statement of the loop (here: ENDDO or ENDWHILE).

The CONTINUE statement is permitted only in loops. You should also use CHECK and EXIT only in loops. If CHECK or EXIT are located outside of a loop, the entire current processing block is left. For a program-driven leaving of processing blocks, you should use the RETURN statement instead whose effect is always the same, particularly within loops.

RETURN

Finally, Listing 5.10 shows a brief example that employs the CHECK statement in a DO loop in order to output only the even values of the loop index.

Listing 5.10 CHECK within a DO Loop

```
REPORT z_check.

CLASS demo DEFINITION.
  PUBLIC SECTION.
    CLASS-METHODS main.
ENDCLASS.
CLASS demo IMPLEMENTATION.
  METHOD main.
    DATA: is_zero TYPE i,
          n_index TYPE n.
    DO 5 TIMES.
      is_zero = sy-index MOD 2.
      CHECK is_zero = 0.
      n_index = sy-index.
      MESSAGE n_index TYPE 'I'.
    ENDDO.
  ENDMETHOD.
ENDCLASS.

START-OF-SELECTION.
  demo=>main( ).
```

5.4   Processing Character and Byte Strings

The contents of all character-like data objects of types c, d, n, t, and string are referred to as character strings. On the other hand, the contents of byte-like data objects of type x or xstring are referred to as byte strings.

ABAP contains a range of operations and comparisons that are specifically provided for the processing of character and byte strings. The statements for both processing types are very similar to each other and are usually based on the same keywords. And yet, the processing of character and byte strings is strictly separated. Each of the ABAP statements that can be used for both character and byte string processing has the optional addition

IN CHARACTER
MODE, IN BYTE
MODE `... IN CHARACTER|BYTE MODE ...`

You use this addition to define which type of processing you want to be executed. If you do not specify this addition, a character string processing is carried out. Note that you can apply character string processing only to character-like data objects, and byte string processing only to byte-like data objects. In the strictest sense, this only holds true in classes and Unicode programs, which, in this instance, is okay because this book handles only those programs.[55] Character-like data objects in particular include flat structures with purely character-like components.

The following sections describe some statements and the associated operations for processing character and byte strings. Here, we primarily describe character string processing. You can directly transfer the functions of most statements from character string to byte string processing. When doing so, you must simply note that instead of the individual characters of a character-like operand, the bytes of a byte-like operand are processed.

Closing spaces In character string processing, you should note that closing spaces are usually ignored[56] in type c operands (and other flat character-like data objects) and always considered in strings.

---

55 The strict distinction between character string and byte string processing was forced by the introduction of Unicode in Release 6.10, because in a Unicode system a character is usually no longer represented by only one byte. Due to this strict distinction, it was possible to remove implicit behavior from the language.

56 You can find details on the exact behavior of each operand in *The Official ABAP Reference* book.

5.4.1 Operations with Character Strings

The statements described in the following sections are used to execute operations with character strings and can also be used for byte string processing.

```
CONCATENATE dobj1 dobj2 ... INTO result
  [SEPARATED BY sep] [RESPECTING BLANKS].
```

CONCATENATE

This statement concatenates the contents of individual data objects. You can insert separators and consider closing spaces. Instead of individual data objects, you can also concatenate the lines of internal tables.

```
SPLIT dobj AT sep INTO result1 result2 ... .
```

SPLIT

This statement splits a data object at the position of specific separators into individual data objects. The lines of internal tables can also be used as target objects.

```
SHIFT dobj [BY num PLACES] [LEFT|RIGHT].
```

SHIFT

This statement shifts the characters of a data object by a specific number of places to the left or right.

Other statements that can be used exclusively for character string processing include the following:

▶ CONDENSE for the deletion of space characters

▶ CONVERT TEXT for the creation of a format that can be sorted

▶ OVERLAY for overlaying two character strings

▶ TRANSLATE for the transformation of characters

To demonstrate the statements for character string processing, Listing 5.11 shows the admittedly rather cumbersome implementation of the deletion of the first two words of a text string via the detour of an internal table. The next section introduces language elements that are more appropriate for this purpose.

Listing 5.11 Character String Processing

```
REPORT z_string_processing.

CLASS demo DEFINITION.
  PUBLIC SECTION.
    CLASS-METHODS main.
ENDCLASS.
```

```
CLASS demo IMPLEMENTATION.
  METHOD main.
    DATA: text       TYPE string,
          text_tab TYPE TABLE OF string.
    text = `ABAP and ABAP Objects`.
    MESSAGE text TYPE 'I'.
    SPLIT text AT ` ` INTO TABLE text_tab.
    DELETE text_tab FROM 1 TO 2.
    CONCATENATE LINES OF text_tab
      INTO text SEPARATED BY ` `.
    MESSAGE text TYPE 'I'.
  ENDMETHOD.
ENDCLASS.
START-OF-SELECTION.
  demo=>main( ).
```

5.4.2   Find and Replace

This section describes two very important statements that are used for character string processing: FIND and REPLACE.[57]

To run searches in character strings, you can use

FIND
```
FIND {FIRST OCCURRENCE}|{ALL OCCURRENCES}
     OF {SUBSTRING sub_string}|{REGEX regex} IN dobj
     [{RESPECTING|IGNORING} CASE]
     ...
```

To make replacements in character strings, you can use

REPLACE
```
REPLACE {FIRST OCCURRENCE}|{ALL OCCURRENCES}
        OF {SUBSTRING sub_string}|{REGEX regex} IN dobj
        WITH new
        [{RESPECTING|IGNORING} CASE]
        ...
```

The basic variants of the FIND and REPLACE statements shown here are very similar to each other. Whereas FIND merely searches for the first occurrence or all occurrences of a substring or pattern in dobj and reports the result, REPLACE additionally replaces the location(s) found with the contents of new.

---

57 Both statements contain variants to carry out FIND and REPLACE runs in character-like internal tables.

After a successful run, both statements set the `sy-subrc` system field to 0 and contain other additions that can be used to return the number, position, and length of the locations found either in individual fields, a structure, or in an internal table. The `SECTION OF` addition also enables you to limit the search area in `dobj`. Another variant of the `REPLACE` statement allows you to carry out position-based replacements instead of pattern-based replacements. During a position-based replacement, an area specified by an offset and a length is replaced in `dobj`.

The most important characteristic of those statements is that you can use `SUBSTRING` to find a substring and `REGEX` to search for a regular expression.

Finding Substrings

The search for a substring is comparably simple. If you specify `SUBSTRING` in `dobj`, the `FIND` and `REPLACE` statements search for the exact character string as it is specified in `substring`.[58] Listing 5.12 shows a simple example.

Listing 5.12 Finding and Replacing Substrings

```
REPORT z_find_replace_substring.

CLASS demo DEFINITION.
  PUBLIC SECTION.
    CLASS-METHODS main.
ENDCLASS.

CLASS demo IMPLEMENTATION.
  METHOD main.
  DATA text TYPE string.
  text = 'Programming SAP Web AS with ABAP'.
  FIND FIRST OCCURRENCE
    OF SUBSTRING 'web as' IN text
    IGNORING CASE.
    IF sy-subrc = 0.
      REPLACE ALL OCCURRENCES
        OF SUBSTRING 'Web AS' IN text
        WITH 'NetWeaver'
        RESPECTING CASE.
      REPLACE ALL OCCURRENCES
```

---

58 You can also omit the `SUBSTRING` addition.

```
          OF SUBSTRING 'ABAP' IN text
          WITH 'ABAP Objects'
          RESPECTING CASE.
      ENDIF.
      IF sy-subrc = 0.
        MESSAGE text TYPE 'I'.
      ENDIF.
    ENDMETHOD.
ENDCLASS.
START-OF-SELECTION.
  demo=>main( ).
```

Search with Regular Expressions

The search with regular expressions is much more powerful but also more complex than the search for exact substrings. A regular expression is a pattern made up of literals and special characters that describes a set of strings according to an international standard. You can use regular expressions via libraries in many programming languages, such as C or Java. After the REGEX addition of the FIND and REPLACE statements, ABAP supports the direct specification of extended regular expressions according to POSIX standard 1003.2.[59] Additionally, the classes CL_ABAP_REGEX and CL_ABAP_MATCHER enable the object-oriented handling of regular expressions.

POSIX standard   Regular expressions enable you to define complex patterns, each of which describes not only one character string but a set of character strings. You can, for instance, use those patterns to do the following:

▶ Find all character substrings within a character string that match a specific pattern

▶ Replace all character substrings within a character string that match a specific pattern

▶ Check whether a character string matches a specific schema, for example, for an email address or a credit card number

The find and replace processes are supported by specific find and replace patterns that allow for, among other things, the use of special characters in the replacement text that refer to the respective found locations.

---

59   For this purpose, the ABAP kernel implements the Boost Regex Library. Copyright (c) 1998–2004, Dr. John Maddock.

A detailed description of the capabilities of regular expressions or a comprehensive introduction to this topic would exceed the scope of this book. For that reason, we'll provide you with an overview of some of the important special characters for regular expressions in Table 5.6, followed by some brief examples of their use in ABAP. For more detailed information, see the ABAP keyword documentation and the wide range of literature on regular expressions.

Special Character	Description	Example	Describes	Does not describe
.	Any character	.	a, 9, Ä, #, .	aa, space character
r*	No repetition or any number of repetitions of r	ab*	a, ab, abb, abbb	b, aba
r+	One or any number of repetitions of r	ab+	ab, abb, abbb	a, b, aba
r{m,n}	m to n repetitions of r	a{2,4}	aa, aaa, aaaa	a, aaaaa, aba
r{m}	Exactly m repetitions of r	a{3}	aaa	a, aa, aaaa, bbb
r?	r is optional	ab?a	aa, aba	abba, aca
r|s	r or s	a+|b+	a, b, aa, bb, aaa	ab, aabb
( )	Subgroups	a(b|c)a	aba, aca	aa, abca
\	Escape character	\.	.	a, 9, Ä, #

Table 5.6 Important Special Characters in Regular Expressions

You should note that in regular expressions the special characters, * and +, always define repetitions of previous regular expressions and that they don't represent the usual wildcard characters.

Listing 5.13 Search with Regular Expressions · · · · · · · · · · · · · · · · · · **FIND REGEX**

```
REPORT z_find_regex.

CLASS demo DEFINITION.
  PUBLIC SECTION.
    CLASS-METHODS main.
ENDCLASS.
```

```
CLASS demo IMPLEMENTATION.
  METHOD main.
    DATA: text        TYPE string,
          regx        TYPE string VALUE `(.AT)|(\<.at\>)`,
          result_tab TYPE match_result_tab.
    text = `Cathy's cat with the hat sat on Matt's mat.`.
    FIND FIRST OCCURRENCE OF REGEX regx IN text
      IGNORING CASE RESULTS result_tab.
    FIND FIRST OCCURRENCE OF REGEX regx IN text
      RESPECTING CASE RESULTS result_tab.
    FIND ALL OCCURRENCES OF REGEX regx IN text
      IGNORING CASE RESULTS result_tab.
    FIND ALL OCCURRENCES OF REGEX regx IN text
      RESPECTING CASE RESULTS result_tab.
  ENDMETHOD.
ENDCLASS.
START-OF-SELECTION.
  demo=>main( ).
```

In Listing 5.13, a character string called text is searched four times for substrings that match the regular expression regx. The special characters of the regular expression have the following meaning:

▶ The parentheses () define two subgroups that are linked as alternative expressions via |.

▶ The period . represents any individual character.

▶ \< and \> stand for the beginning and end of words.

The remaining AT and at characters are literals. Thus the regular expression describes a string of three characters, the first character being an individual character of any type, while the two other characters are "AT"; alternatively, it describes a word that consists of three characters, the first one being any individual character, while the other two characters are "at". The offsets and lengths of the found locations are returned in internal table result_tab. When executing the program in the debugger, you will find the following:

▶ In the first search run, the program finds the string "Cat" of "Cathy". This location matches the expression ".AT" but not "\<.at\>".

▶ In the second search run, the program finds the string "cat", which matches the expression "\<.at\>", but not ".AT".

▶ In the third search run, the program finds all substrings that consist of three characters and end with "at": "Cat", "cat", "hat", "sat", "Mat", and "mat". All these locations match the expression ".AT"; however, only the words "cat", "hat", "sat", and "mat" match "\<.at\>".

▶ In the fourth search run, which also takes uppercase and lowercase spelling into account, the program finds the words "cat", "hat", "sat", and "mat". They all match the expression "\<.at\>"; however, none of the found locations matches ".AT".

Starting with the next release of SAP NetWeaver, you will find an elaborate version of this example as DEMO_REGEX in AS ABAP. This version will enable you to enter any text and regular expression, and it will highlight the locations detected in a specific color.

Listing 5.14 shows how you can replace texts in HTML files by using a regular expression without destroying the tags. For this purpose, the character string to be replaced is combined with a regular expression regx in repl.

Listing 5.14 Replacement with Regular Expressions

REPLACE REGEX

```
REPORT z_replace_regex.

CLASS demo DEFINITION.
  PUBLIC SECTION.
    CLASS-METHODS main.
ENDCLASS.
CLASS demo IMPLEMENTATION.
  METHOD main.
    DATA: html TYPE string,
          repl TYPE string,
          regx TYPE string.
    html = `<title>This is the <i>Title</i></title>`.
    repl = `i`.
    CONCATENATE repl '(?![^<>]*>)' INTO regx.
    REPLACE ALL OCCURRENCES OF REGEX regx IN html
      WITH `<b>$0</b>`.
    MESSAGE html TYPE 'I'.
  ENDMETHOD.
ENDCLASS.
START-OF-SELECTION.
  demo=>main( ).
```

The special characters of the regular expression have the following meaning:

- `(?! )` defines a negated look-ahead condition.
- `[^ ]` defines a negated value set of single characters (here: the literals `<` and `>`).
- `*` defines a concatenation of any length of the preceding single character, including no character.

Consequently, the regular expression is appropriate for all occurrences of the contents of `repl` that do not close with `>`. The `REPLACE` statement makes use of the fact that the content of the found location can be specified as `$0` in the replacement text if a regular expression is used. The result of the replacement looks as follows:

```
<title>Th<b>i</b>s <b>i</b>s the <i>T<b>i</b>tle</i></title>
```

All "i" characters have been replaced by "i" except for those located within tags.[60]

CL_ABAP_REGEX, CL_ABAP_ MATCHER

Finally, Listing 5.15 shows us how to use the class CL_ABAP_ MATCHER to verify the format of an email address that has been entered. A selection screen is repeatedly called in a `DO` loop until the address entered matches the regular expression that is represented by an object of the class CL_ABAP_REGEX in this case. The special character `\w` represents any alphanumeric character including underscore; all other characters have been described in Table 5.6. This should make it easy for you to interpret the regular expression.

Listing 5.15 Comparison Using a Regular Expression

```
REPORT z_match_regex.

SELECTION-SCREEN BEGIN OF SCREEN 100 AS WINDOW.
PARAMETERS email TYPE c LENGTH 30 LOWER CASE.
SELECTION-SCREEN END OF SCREEN 100.

CLASS demo DEFINITION.
  PUBLIC SECTION.
    CLASS-METHODS main.
ENDCLASS.
```

---

60 By the way, the color highlights of the found locations in the full text search in the ABAP keyword documentation displayed in Figure 2.83 are based on this regular expression.

```
CLASS demo IMPLEMENTATION.
  METHOD main.
    DATA: regex   TYPE REF TO cl_abap_regex,
          matcher TYPE REF TO cl_abap_matcher.
    CREATE OBJECT regex
      EXPORTING pattern = `\w+(\.\w+)*@(\w+\.)+(\w{2,4})`
                ignore_case = 'X' .
    DO.
      CALL SELECTION-SCREEN 100 STARTING AT 10 10.
      IF sy-subrc <> 0.
        EXIT.
      ENDIF.
      matcher = regex->create_matcher( text = email ).
      IF matcher->match( ) IS INITIAL.
        MESSAGE 'Wrong Format' TYPE 'S' DISPLAY LIKE 'E'.
      ELSE.
        MESSAGE 'Format OK' TYPE 'S'.
        EXIT.
      ENDIF.
    ENDDO.
  ENDMETHOD.
ENDCLASS.
START-OF-SELECTION.
  demo=>main( ).
```

The simple examples shown demonstrate how powerful regular expressions can be. Just imagine having to program the tasks described in this book using traditional means. Still, when using regular expressions, you should be mindful of the fact that due to their wide range of capabilities they can easily become very complex. Although it may prove rather tempting to solve every task with a single regular expression, it is often preferable to distribute complex operations to several regular expressions and to use those expressions together with other suitable operations for character strings. This enhances the readability and maintainability of a program.

5.4.3   Subfield Access

For character and byte string processing, in particular, ABAP provides a notation that allows access to subareas of a character-like or byte-like operand. This notation is the offset/length specification:

```
... dobj[+off][(len)] ...
```

Offset/length
specification

The segment of the data object `dobj` with the offset specified in `off` and the length in characters or bytes specified in `len` is used. When an offset is specified without a length, the remaining subfield is addressed; if a length is specified without an offset, the first `len` characters are addressed. In read positions, a subfield access is possible for all character-like and byte-like data objects. In write positions, no subfield access to strings is possible. Subfield accesses are even permitted for structures, as long as those structures consist only of flat character-like components, or at least contain such a start segment and access is limited to that segment.

Listing 5.16 shows a simple example of a subfield access. A `date` field is composed of subfields of the system field `sy-datum` and other formatting characters.

Listing 5.16 Subfield Access

```
REPORT z_offset_length.

CLASS demo DEFINITION.
  PUBLIC SECTION.
    CLASS-METHODS main.
ENDCLASS.

CLASS demo IMPLEMENTATION.
  METHOD main.
    DATA date TYPE string.
    CONCATENATE `Year: `    sy-datum(4)
                `, Month: ` sy-datum+4(2)
                `, Day: `   sy-datum+6(2)
            INTO date.
    MESSAGE date TYPE 'I'.
  ENDMETHOD.
ENDCLASS.

START-OF-SELECTION.
  demo=>main( ).
```

You can also solve this task in a more elegant way by using a regular expression:

```
date = sy-datum.
REPLACE REGEX '(\d{4})(\d{2})(\d{2})' IN date
        WITH 'Year: $1 Month: $2 Day: $3'.
```

Exceptions If you try to address a memory area outside of a data object, a syntax error or an exception is triggered. Particularly for the dynamic specification of offset and length and when accessing strings, you should ensure that the addressed subfield is located within the memory boundaries of the data object prior to the access; functions such as `strlen` can be very helpful here.

5.4.4 Functions for Character String Processing

Most of the built-in description functions mentioned in Section 5.2.4 are provided for character string processing. The most important function is

```
... strlen( arg ) ...
```
strlen

This function returns the number of characters of the argument, excluding the closing spaces in data objects of fixed length, whereas the closing spaces are included in the count for data objects of type `string`. The counterpart of `strlen` for byte strings is `xstrlen`. Another useful character function is `charlen` that helps you to determine the length of a character in terms of bytes.

Listing 5.17 shows an example of using `strlen` to carry out a dynamic subfield access. The input field `input` is decomposed[61] over the length of its significant characters into the lines of an internal table and then reassembled. Of course, we could also obtain the final result more easily by using a replace run with a regular expression.

Listing 5.17 Using strlen

```
REPORT z_strlen.

PARAMETERS input TYPE c LENGTH 30 LOWER CASE.
CLASS demo DEFINITION.
  PUBLIC SECTION.
    CLASS-METHODS main.
ENDCLASS.
CLASS demo IMPLEMENTATION.
  METHOD main.
    DATA: len    TYPE i,
          itab   TYPE TABLE OF string,
          idx    TYPE sy-index,
          result TYPE string.
    len = strlen( input ).
```

---

61 This decomposition would not be possible using the `SPLIT` statement because you wouldn't be able to specify an appropriate separator.

```
      DO len TIMES.
        idx = sy-index - 1.
        APPEND input+idx(1) TO itab.
      ENDDO.
      CONCATENATE LINES OF itab INTO result SEPARATED BY '+'.
      MESSAGE result TYPE 'I'.
    ENDMETHOD.
ENDCLASS.
START-OF-SELECTION.
  demo=>main( ).
```

In addition to the built-in functions, the global class CL_ABAP_STRING_UTILITIES, among others for instance, also provides methods that enable you to process character strings, such as the assignment of text fields to strings, without truncating the closing spaces.

5.4.5 Relational Operators for Character String Processing

In Section 5.2.5, we already described the relational operators CO, CN, CA, NA, CS, NS, CP, and NP for character string processing. For more details regarding their functionality, see *The Official ABAP Reference* book.

These operators provide a subset of the functions that can actually be covered by using regular expressions in FIND or with CL_ABAP_MATCHER as well. The benefit of using the relational operators is that you can use them directly in all places where you have to make a decision with logical expressions, which is not (yet) possible if you use regular expressions. Listing 5.18 contains a real-life example.

Listing 5.18 Character String Comparison

```
REPORT z_string_operator.

PARAMETERS subject TYPE abdocusubjects-text.

CLASS demo DEFINITION.
  PUBLIC SECTION.
    CLASS-METHODS main.
  PRIVATE SECTION.
    TYPES: BEGIN OF subject_line,
             text   TYPE abdocusubjects-text,
             object TYPE abdocusubjects-object,
           END OF subject_line.
    CLASS-DATA: subject_list TYPE TABLE OF subject_line,
```

```
              langu          TYPE sy-langu.
    CLASS-METHODS: get_subject_list,
                   display_subject_list,
                   handle_double_click
                       FOR EVENT double_click ...
ENDCLASS.
CLASS demo IMPLEMENTATION.
  METHOD main.
    get_subject_list( ).
    CONCATENATE '*' subject '*' INTO subject.
    DELETE subject_list WHERE text NP subject.
    display_subject_list( ).
  ENDMETHOD.
  ...
ENDCLASS.
START-OF-SELECTION.
  demo=>main( ).
```

An internal table called `subject_list` contains a list of ABAP subjects in the `text` column, and the associated documents of the ABAP keyword documentation in the `object` column. The table is filled in a `get_subject_list` method from database table ABDOCUSUBJECTS. The problem to be solved now is to create a hit list that matches the user input in the `subject` parameter. For this purpose, a pattern is created from the input, and the relational operator `NP` (No Pattern) is used to remove all lines from the internal table that do not match the pattern; the "*" characters are used as wildcard characters to represent any character string. It can hardly be easier![62]

If, for example, the term "file" is entered, a hit list is passed to the `display_subject_list` method. The output of this method is shown in Figure 5.12. If the user selects a line, the associated document from the ABAP keyword documentation is called in the `handle_double_click` method. The implementation of those methods follows exactly the example of Listing 9.51 in Section 9.3.7.

---

62 If you want to preserve the internal table, the hit list would instead have to be extracted line by line into another table using the `CP` (Covers Pattern) operator (`LOOP` statement, see Section 5.5.2).

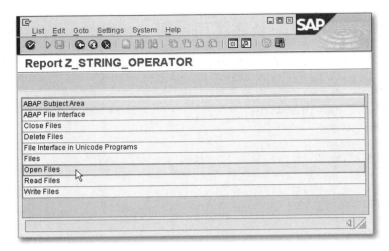

Figure 5.12 Hit List Resulting from a Character String Comparison

5.5 Internal Tables

Internal tables are data objects of the most powerful data type available in ABAP. They allow you to store a variable amount of data of a fixed structure in the memory and enable you to efficiently use this data. The name "internal table" dates back to a time when the line type of an internal table was exclusively limited to flat structures and internal tables were mainly used to store tabular data in the memory. In fact, the line type can be any type of the ABAP type hierarchy for quite some time now (see Figure 5.2).

Internal tables are implicitly managed by the runtime environment. ABAP contains a set of special, highly optimized statements that you can use when working with internal tables. This kind of handling complex dynamic data objects with a few simple statements makes internal tables one of the most powerful language elements in ABAP. In fact, there is hardly any application program that doesn't need an internal table.[63] The following sections describe the essential attributes of internal tables, as well as the statements you need when working with internal tables.

---

63 On the other hand, ABAP doesn't contain any arrays as they are commonly used in other programming languages and whose memory requirement is fixed during program execution.

5.5.1   Attributes of Internal Tables

In Section 5.1.5, we already described the declaration of internal tables. You learned that internal tables contain three essential attributes:

- Line type
- Table category
- Table key

Line Type

The main characteristic of internal tables is that any number[64] of lines of any line type can be stored in the memory and the actual amount is only determined at program runtime. The bandwidth of internal tables ranges from arrays of elementary fields over classical database-like tables, that are very well suited for storing data from database tables, to very complex dynamic data objects whose lines or line components can themselves consist of internal tables. Reference variables in internal tables allow you to manage large quantities of objects.

Listing 5.19 shows the declaration of an internal table using the most simple line type possible: a standard table `array` whose line type is an elementary data type `i` and whose key consists of the entire line. The example also shows two typical applications that are used to fill and process an internal table: `APPEND` and `LOOP AT`.

Listing 5.19 List of Numbers in an Internal Table

```
REPORT z_simple_internal_table.

CLASS demo DEFINITION.
  PUBLIC SECTION.
    CLASS-METHODS main.
ENDCLASS.
CLASS demo IMPLEMENTATION.
  METHOD main.
    DATA: array  TYPE STANDARD TABLE
                 OF i WITH KEY table_line,
          numtxt TYPE n LENGTH 10.
```

---

64 "Any number" means that the number is limited only by the capacity limits described in Section 5.1.8.

```
     DO 5 TIMES.
       APPEND sy-index TO array.
     ENDDO.
     LOOP AT array INTO numtxt.
       MESSAGE numtxt TYPE 'I'.
     ENDLOOP.
   ENDMETHOD.
ENDCLASS.
START-OF-SELECTION.
  demo=>main( ).
```

Table Category

There are three categories of internal tables:

▶ **Standard tables**

The lines standard tables which are declared using the STANDARD TABLE addition are managed by an internal table index. When a standard table is filled, new lines are either appended at the end of the table or inserted in a specific position. If lines are inserted in or deleted from standard tables, the index is reorganized, not the remaining lines of the table.

▶ **Sorted tables**

Sorted tables which are declared using the SORTED TABLE addition, are managed via a table index, as is the case with standard tables. In contrast to standard tables, however, the entries are always sorted in ascending order according to the table key, which enables an optimized key access in addition to the index access.

▶ **Hashed tables**

In hashed tables, which are declared using the HASHED TABLE addition, the sequence of entries is not managed by an internal table index but by a hash algorithm. The position of an entry is directly calculated from the unique key value using a *hash function*. Hashed tables are optimized for key access, but they (currently) don't allow any index access.

Therefore, the table category determines the way an internal table is internally managed and the way in which it is accessed within the ABAP program. The table category does not affect an access to the entire internal table, as it occurs for instance in assignments and comparisons. It does, however, affect the specific statements for processing internal tables. In this context, a clear technical distinction must be made:

▶ **Access to table lines via a table index**

Presently, only standard tables and sorted tables contain a table index that numbers the lines from 1 to the existing number of lines. Those tables are referred to as *index tables* and they are the only types of tables where an index access is possible. Once an index table has been accessed, the system field `sy-tabix` is always filled with the index of the line that is addressed. As of the next release of SAP NetWeaver, internal tables can contain additional sorted secondary indexes, which will then enable an index access to hashed tables as well.

▶ **Access to table lines via the table key**

This type of access is possible with all table categories; however, key access is not optimized for standard tables. Here, a linear search across all lines is carried out. As of the next release of SAP NetWeaver, you can create additional secondary table keys for internal tables that will allow for an optimized key access to standard tables as well.

The index access is always the fastest way to access an internal table, provided, of course, that the index is known. For this reason, an index access is often preceded by a key access in order to define a starting point.

The decision regarding which table category you want depends on the type of operations that you want to use to access the table and also, how often you want to access the table in your program:

▶ In ABAP, standard tables represent the counterpart of dynamic arrays of any type. The standard scenario for the use of a standard table is that it is filled once by appending lines, and then it is sorted before it is processed sequentially in a loop. The starting point for the sequential processing must first be searched using a key specification that is geared towards the sorting.[65] However, if key accesses represent the main types of operations, you should try to avoid using large standard tables of more than 100 lines because of the linear search processes.

---

[65] In this case, you can use the `BINARY` addition of the `READ` statement to carry out a binary search.

- ▶ Sorted tables are useful if both a fast key access and an index access are necessary and if the lines should already be sorted during the filling of the table. During a key access, a binary search is performed, which results in a logarithmic dependency of the performance on the number of lines.

- ▶ Hashed tables are always useful if the key access represents the central type of operation. The access costs are constant and don't depend on the number of lines. Because the table key of hashed tables must be unique, you must use sorted tables if non-unique keys are requested.

Runtime measurement

Figure 5.13 substantiates the aforementioned recommendations in that it displays a sample measurement of the average runtime for key accesses to the different table categories based on the number of lines in a logarithmic presentation. For each of the three table categories, the key access times for all lines were measured and an average value was established based on those measurements. From approximately 50 lines onwards, the shapes of the graphs follow the predicted manner, and with a total of 10,000 lines, the key access to standard tables is two orders of magnitudes slower than the access to sorted tables and hashed tables! The associated program, Z_MEASURE_KEY_ACCESS, is included in the Z_ABAP_BOOK package.

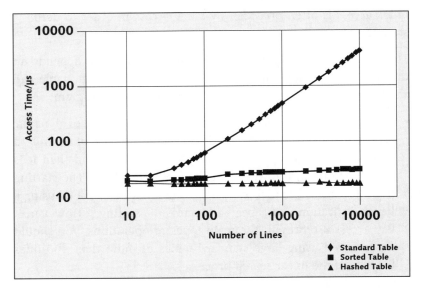

Figure 5.13 Runtime Measurement for Key Accesses to Internal Tables

Table Key

For all table categories, you can specify one of the following key definitions during the declaration:[66]

▶ For a structured line type, the key can be created from components comp of the line type where the sequence is important:

`[NON-]UNIQUE KEY comp1 ... compn.`

The sequence in which the components are specified is taken into account during the evaluation of the key.

▶ You can specify the pseudo-component table_line for any line type, but particularly for non-structured ones, which turns the entire line into a key:

`[NON-]UNIQUE KEY table_line.`

▶ In addition, you can also specify a standard key. In structured tables, the standard key consists of all components that don't have a numeric data type (i, f, p) and are not tables themselves. If the line type is elementary, the standard key is equal to table_line:

`[NON-]UNIQUE DEFAULT KEY.`

table_line

Typically, you should not use the standard key for structured line types; however, for standard tables, it is important to keep the standard key in mind. If the key specification is omitted in the declaration of a corresponding data object, the table key is implicitly set to the standard key.

Standard key

The UNIQUE and NON-UNIQUE additions are used to define whether the key is unique or non-unique. If it is unique, a line with a specific content in the key fields may occur only once in the internal table. Whereas standard tables may contain only non-unique keys and hashed tables may contain only unique keys, sorted tables can be defined with both key types.

UNIQUE, NON-UNIQUE

Once again, you should note that standard tables always have a key, but that the key access to those tables is executed only via a linear search; whereas, sorted tables are accessed using a binary search and the hash algorithm is used for hashed tables. For this reason, sorted tables and hashed tables are also often referred to as key tables.

---

66 As of the next release of SAP NetWeaver, this will be the primary table key that can be complemented with secondary table keys.

Short Forms for Standard Tables and Generic Table Types

The syntax used for the declaration of internal tables using TYPES and DATA contains some peculiarities that may lead to some confusion, which makes it worthwhile to take a closer look at *The Official ABAP Reference* book. The following is a short form:

TYPE TABLE OF   `DATA itab TYPE TABLE OF dtype.`

During compilation, this DATA statement is automatically complemented to become

```
DATA itab TYPE STANDARD TABLE OF dtype
          WITH NON-UNIQUE DEFAULT KEY.
```

Data objects must always be completely specified. Although the syntax allows incomplete specifications such as the omitting of specific details (table category or key), those details are always added implicitly. The following is also a short form:

`TYPES itab TYPE TABLE OF dtype.`

However, this short form is only complemented in the following way:

`TYPES itab TYPE STANDARD TABLE OF dtype.`

You can omit the key specification completely or in part (no specification of uniqueness) for the TYPES statement. Such a statement declares a generic data type (see Section 5.1.9) that can be used only to type formal parameters (see Section 6.1.1) or field symbols, but not to declare data objects.[67]

Currently, the declaration of internal tables represents the only way to create generic types using the TYPES statement. Apart from omitting the key specification, TYPES also enables you to specify one of the two generic table types, ANY TABLE and INDEX TABLE from Table 5.3, instead of using one of the three table categories:

ANY TABLE,   `TYPES itab TYPE ANY|INDEX TABLE OF dtype ...`
INDEX TABLE

---

67 The fact that a table type without a key specification is generic is often overlooked when it is used for typing purposes. However, you should note that this fact can easily cause a procedure to behave differently.

These table types have a fixed line type; however, the table category is generic. With these types, you can specify the table key without a specification of uniqueness only.

For field symbols or interface parameters that are typed using ANY TABLE, you can program only those access types that are permitted for all table categories. In particular, you cannot use index accesses because these are not permitted for hashed tables. On the other hand, you can program index accesses for field symbols and interface parameters of the generic type INDEX TABLE as the actual type can only be a standard table or a sorted table.

Initial Memory Requirement

As we already mentioned, internal tables are managed internally, and their internals don't require your attention, as long as there are no memory bottlenecks. However, if you look at the ABAP keyword documentation, the following addition to the declaration of internal tables might catch your eye:

```
... INITIAL SIZE n.
```

INITIAL SIZE

What does this addition mean? Internal tables are stored in individual blocks in the memory. The above addition enables you to influence the size of the first block by specifying the initially required number of table lines, n. If you do not specify this initial size, the runtime environment automatically allocates an appropriate memory area. In both cases, further memory is allocated if the current block is no longer sufficient. We recommend that you specify an initial memory requirement only when the number of entries in the table is already known and you want to set the initial main memory requirement as precisely as possible. This can be particularly important for internal tables that are themselves components of tables and contain only a few lines.

Example of Internal Tables

We will conclude this section on the characteristics of internal tables with an example of the definition of internal tables, as shown in Listing 5.20. The example shows the definition of two internal tables, t_address_tab and company_tab, where t_address_tab is nested in company_tab. For this purpose, t_address_tab is defined as a table type. The `addresses` component of the `company` structure is declared using this type. The data type of `company` is used as a line type for the `company_tab` and `company_sorted_tab` tables.

Listing 5.20 Definition of Internal Tables

```
REPORT z_internal_tables.

CLASS demo DEFINITION.
  PUBLIC SECTION.
    CLASS-METHODS main.
  PRIVATE SECTION.
    TYPES:
      BEGIN OF t_address,
        street TYPE c LENGTH 20,
        city   TYPE c LENGTH 20,
      END OF t_address,
      t_address_tab TYPE STANDARD TABLE
                    OF t_address
                    WITH NON-UNIQUE KEY city.
    CLASS-DATA:
      BEGIN OF company,
        name      TYPE c LENGTH 20,
        addresses TYPE t_address_tab,
      END OF company,
      company_tab LIKE HASHED TABLE
                  OF   company
                  WITH UNIQUE KEY name,
      company_sorted_tab LIKE SORTED TABLE
                         OF   company
                         WITH UNIQUE KEY name.
ENDCLASS.
```

5.5.2 Working with Internal Tables

When working with internal tables, we must distinguish between the access to single lines and the access to the entire table. Let's begin with the access to single lines. As we already described in the previous section, we must further distinguish between key accesses and index accesses in this context. As you know, although the index access is generally the fastest way to access a line in an internal table because a direct reference exists internally, it is often not the optimal type of access, especially when working with data from database tables. With index accesses, the program must know the assignment between the index and the contents of the table line, whereas during the key access the contents of the table line themselves are evaluated. For this reason, the key access is more appropriate for many applications, but also slower.

In this section, we will only describe the most important static forms of statements for internal tables. For information on the many other options available, please refer to *The Official ABAP Reference* book. The section will conclude with an example that uses some of the statements introduced here. For each successful access to lines of internal tables, the system field sy-subrc is filled with the value 0; otherwise, it is assigned a value unequal to 0. During index accesses, sy-tabix is filled with the line number of the line being processed with regard to the table index.

sy-tabix

Inserting Table Lines

To fill an internal table with lines, you must use the INSERT statement. For index accesses, the basic structure of the syntax is as follows:

```
INSERT line INTO itab INDEX idx.
```

INSERT

This statement inserts the data object line before the line that contains the index idx into the internal table itab. After that, the new line is assigned the index idx, and the index of the subsequent lines is increased by one.

The syntax for key accesses is as follows:[68]

INDEX/TABLE

```
INSERT line INTO TABLE itab.
```

This statement inserts the data object line into the internal table itab in the following way:

▶ For standard tables, line is simply appended to the internal table as the last line. This means that in the case of standard tables, INSERT actually does not work as in the case of a real key access,

---

68 In most statements for the processing of internal tables, index accesses and key accesses differ in such a way that the former contain the INDEX addition, while the latter contain the TABLE addition. Nevertheless, the statements for index accesses and key accesses are often very similar. Therefore, you must program very accurately to avoid causing a program behavior that doesn't meet your expectations.

but in exactly the same way as the APPEND statement described below.

► In sorted tables, line is inserted into the sort sequence of the internal table according to its key values.

► For hashed tables, line is inserted into the internal table by the hash management according to its key values.

The data type of line must be compatible with the line type of the internal table. The following statements enable you to declare those data types:

LINE OF   TYPES|DATA line {TYPE|LIKE} **LINE OF** itab.

You can also insert several lines from a different table with a compatible line type into an internal table by replacing the line statement in the above INSERT statements with the following expression:

LINES OF   ... **LINES OF** jtab [**FROM** idx1] [**TO** idx2] ...

This option allows you to insert the lines of table jtab one by one into itab in compliance with the rules that apply to inserting a single line. If jtab is an index table, you can use the FROM and TO additions to insert only parts of the table.

Inserting Aggregated Table Lines

If you use INSERT to insert a line into an internal table with a unique key whose key values already exist, sy-subrc is set to 4, and the line is not inserted. This is a common way to avoid having duplicate entries in internal tables. In addition, ABAP provides a specific statement that also enables you to create tables without duplicate entries:

COLLECT   **COLLECT** line **INTO** itab.

If the table does not yet contain a line with an identical key, COLLECT works in the same way as a key access via INSERT. If you try to use the COLLECT statement to insert a line whose key values already exist in the table, the values of the numeric non-key-fields of data object line are added to the corresponding fields of the table line. Therefore, you can use the COLLECT statement specifically for totaling numeric values that belong to unique keys. In all other cases, you should use the INSERT statement.

You should use the COLLECT statement primarily for hashed tables. In contrast, its use for standard tables is error-prone and obsolete.

Appending Table Lines

A special notation exists to append either one or several lines to standard tables:

APPEND line **TO** itab.

APPEND

or

APPEND LINES OF jtab [**FROM** idx1] [**TO** idx2] **TO** itab.

The APPEND statement appends each of the specified lines as the last line to the internal table. This statement provides an expedient way to fill standard tables with lines. Because you don't need to find an insertion point and the table key of standard tables is never unique, you don't need to search the table for existing entries. The APPEND statement can also be used for sorted tables, but this requires that the lines to be appended must match the sorting.

Reading Table Lines

To read the contents of individual lines from an internal table, you can use the READ statement. The syntax for index accesses is as follows:

READ TABLE itab INDEX idx
       {INTO wa}|{ASSIGNING <fs>}|{REFERENCE INTO dref}.

READ TABLE

This statement copies the contents of the line with index idx to a work area, wa, assigns the line to the field symbol <fs>, or sets the data reference in the reference variable dref to this line.

The syntax for key accesses is as follows:

READ TABLE itab FROM key ...

or

READ TABLE itab
       WITH TABLE KEY comp1 = f1 ... compn = fn ...

TABLE KEY

In the first case, key is a data object that is compatible with the line type of the internal table and whose key components must be supplied with values before the READ statement. Then the first line of the internal table is read whose key values match those specified in key. In the second case, you must specify a value f for each component comp of the table key.

There is also a variant of the READ statement available that allows the specification of a free key:

WITH KEY

```
READ TABLE itab
            WITH KEY comp1 = f1 ... compn = fn ...
```

If you don't use the TABLE addition before KEY, you can use any component comp of the internal table as search keys. For unstructured line types, you can specify the pseudo-component table_line for both the table key and the free key.

INTO,
ASSIGNING,
REFERENCE INTO

Now, let's examine how the result of the READ statement is determined. Here you have the following three options:

- ▸ If you specify INTO wa, the contents of the line that has been found are transported to data object wa. The data type of the data object must therefore be compatible with the line type of the internal table and should be declared as such. The READ statement also provides an addition for this output variant, TRANSPORTING. This addition enables you to select the components that you actually want to transport into the data object.

- ▸ If you specify ASSIGNING <fs>, no values will be transported. Instead, the field symbol <fs> is bound to the table line in the memory after the statement. In turn, the table line can be evaluated or modified using <fs>.

- ▸ If you specify REFERENCE INTO dref, no values will be transported either. Instead, the data reference variable dref points to the table line in the memory after the statement. The table line can be evaluated or modified using dref->....

Figure 5.14 summarizes the three options. Whereas field symbols and data reference variables allow direct access to the line that has been found, a work area wa represents a completely independent data object whose contents can nevertheless be used to change table lines, as we will see shortly.

However, only if you really want to modify the work area wa without affecting the internal table do you need to specify INTO wa. For pure read-only access or to change the contents of the internal table, the ASSIGNING <fs> and REFERENCE INTO dref additions are the much better choice, particularly with regard to system performance. By the way, you can also use those two additions with the INSERT, COLLECT, APPEND, and MODIFY statements, which enables you to access the line that has been edited last. Chapter 11 contains more information on field symbols and data references.

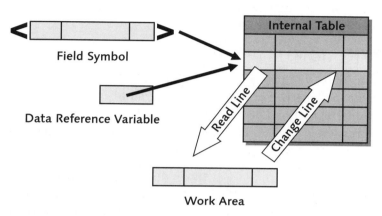

Figure 5.14 Accessing Internal Tables

Sequential Processing of Internal Tables

In addition to reading a single line using the READ statement, you can also read several individual lines from an internal table by using a specific loop:

```
LOOP AT itab                                                        LOOP
     {INTO wa}|{ASSIGNING <fs>}|{REFERENCE INTO dref}.
   ...
ENDLOOP.
```

The LOOP statement reads lines from internal table itab sequentially. The line that has been read is available in the statement block of the loop either in a work area or via a field symbol or data reference variable, as is the case after a READ statement.

The sequence in which the table lines are read depends on the table category. Standard tables and sorted tables are read based on their ascending table index. The lines of hashed tables are read either in the sequence in which they were inserted into the table or in the sort sequence if they were sorted with the SORT statement.

sy-tabix

In index tables, the system field `sy-tabix` is filled with the index of the current line in each loop pass. Once the loop has been completely processed, `sy-tabix` is assigned the value that it had prior to entering the loop. In index tables, you can use the additions

FROM, TO

```
... FROM idx1 TO idx2.
```

to limit the number of lines to be processed, which can have a positive effect on the runtime. To restrict the number of lines for any kind of table, you can use the

WHERE

```
... WHERE log_exp.
```

addition. Here, you may specify a logical expression after WHERE in which the first operand of each comparison must be a component of the internal table. The statement processes all lines for which the logical expression is "true".[69] If a component has a reference type, you can even specify components of the objects referenced by line contents on the left-hand side by using the object component selector `->`.

Control level processing

You can also carry out a so-called *control level processing* in the statement block between the LOOP and ENDLOOP statements. A control level is a coherent set of lines of an internal table whose contents are identical in a start segment of the lines. Control levels are created by a corresponding sorting of the internal table. To evaluate the control levels, you can use the control statements AT and ENDAT:

AT NEW, AT END OF

```
LOOP AT itab ...
  ...
  AT NEW comp.
    ...
  ENDAT.
  ...
  AT END OF comp.
    ...
  ENDAT.
  ...
ENDLOOP.
```

These control structures further divide the LOOP loop into several statement blocks that are triggered by control level changes. With control level processing, you can avoid querying line contents using

---

69 As of the next release of SAP NetWeaver, you will also be able to specify the WHERE condition dynamically.

logical expressions. A common use of control level processing is the formatting of data for an aggregated presentation in lists. Listing 9.31 contains an example of control level processing.

Modifying Table Lines

To modify the contents of a line in an internal table, you would usually access the line directly using a field symbol or a data reference variable that is linked with a line after a READ statement or in a LOOP loop. There is also a statement is available to assign the contents of a work area to a line. The syntax for index accesses is as follows:

```
MODIFY itab FROM line INDEX idx.
```

MODIFY

This statement assigns the contents of data object line to the table line with the index idx. The syntax for key accesses is as follows:

```
MODIFY TABLE itab FROM line.
```

In this case, a search run is carried out in the internal table itab to find the first line whose key values match the values of the corresponding components in line. The line is then overwritten with the contents of line. This means you must declare the data object line in accordance with the line type, fill its key fields with search values, and populate all other components with the values to be modified prior to executing the statement.

Similar to the LOOP statement, the MODIFY statement also provides a WHERE addition that allows you to specify a logical expression to modify several lines of an internal table in compliance with a condition:

```
MODIFY itab FROM line
        TRANSPORTING comp1 ... compn
        WHERE log_exp.
```

WHERE

In this case, you must use the TRANSPORTING addition to specify which components of the data object line you want to assign to the corresponding line components. You cannot specify any components of the table key after TRANSPORTING for sorted tables or hashed tables. Optionally, the TRANSPORTING addition can also be used for the other variants of the MODIFY statement.

Deleting Table Lines

To delete a line of an internal table, you can use the `DELETE` statement. The syntax for index accesses is as follows:

DELETE

```
DELETE itab INDEX idx.
```

This statement deletes the table line with index `idx`. The syntax for key accesses is as follows:

```
DELETE TABLE itab FROM key.
```

or

```
DELETE TABLE itab
    WITH TABLE KEY comp1 = f1 ... compn = fn.
```

These two variants work in the same way as they do with the `READ` statement. In the first case, `key` must again be a data object that is compatible with the line type of the internal table, and the first line that is found whose key values match those specified in `key` is deleted. In the second case, you must enter the key values by specifying a value `f` for each component `comp` of the table key.

To delete several lines of an internal table using one statement, you can use the `DELETE` statement in the following way for index tables:

```
DELETE itab [FROM idx1] [TO idx2].
```

All lines with indexes between `idx1` and `idx2` are deleted.[70] You can use the following variant for all table categories:

WHERE

```
DELETE itab WHERE log_exp.
```

The `WHERE` addition, which is analogous to the `LOOP` statement, allows you to specify a logical expression to delete several lines of an internal table in compliance with a logical condition. Listing 5.18 contains an example in which the character-like contents of a column are evaluated.

---

70 This statement can also lead to a typical situation whereby errors are introduced when working with internal tables. If the `TABLE` addition is not specified after `DELETE`, the system interprets the operand after `FROM` as an index entry; whereas when the `TABLE` addition exists, the system regards the operand as a work area for the key access. So ensure that you use the right syntax.

Sorting Internal Tables

To sort an internal table by the contents of its key fields, you can use the following statement:

`SORT itab [ASCENDING|DESCENDING].`   SORT

You can use the `ASCENDING` and `DESCENDING` additions to define whether you want to sort the table in ascending or descending order, ascending being the default setting. Of course, it only makes sense to use the `SORT` statement for standard tables and hashed tables since sorted tables are always sorted by the table key in ascending order. Hashed tables are typically sorted before they are processed in a `LOOP` loop, because their lines are only available in sorted order within such a loop. The sorting of a standard table, on the other hand, also affects index accesses because the sorting changes the assignment of the index to the table lines.

If you want to sort a table independently of the table key, you can use the `SORT` statement with the `BY` addition:

`SORT itab BY ... comp [ASCENDING|DESCENDING] ...`   SORT BY

Here you can either specify components `comp` of the internal table in the desired sort order or you specify the pseudo-component `table_line`. For each component, which you want to sort the table by, you can individually define whether you want to sort in ascending or descending order. If the component has a reference type, you can even use the object component selector `->` to sort the table by all visible components of the referenced objects.

When sorting a table, you should note that, by default, numeric and   AS TEXT
byte-like components are sorted by their value, while character-like components are sorted by their binary presentation (code page). To obtain a textual sorting of the character-like components, you must use the `AS TEXT` addition.

Operations with the Entire Table

As we already mentioned, you can address the complex data objects in ABAP in their entirety, provided the operation makes sense. Of course, this also holds true for internal tables, which is why we want to briefly summarize some of these operations in the following paragraphs:

▶ **Assigning internal tables**
As shown in Section 5.2.2, you can assign an internal table to another internal table if the line types of both tables are compatible or convertible. Regarding the general possibility of those assignments, the table category and key do not play any role. However, as with all assignments, the contents must fulfill all requirements. For example, an exception would be raised if a hashed table with non-unique key values was created due to an assignment.

CLEAR, FREE ▶ **Initializing internal tables**
You can intialize internal tables like other data objects using the CLEAR statement. Resetting an internal table to its initial value means that all lines are deleted. Alternatively, you can also use the FREE statement that releases the entire reserved memory, whereas the memory continues to be reserved for the table if you use CLEAR.

▶ **Comparing internal tables**
As we mentioned in Section 5.2.5, you can even compare internal tables with each other in logical expressions. When doing so, the numbers of lines are compared first followed by a comparison of the lines themselves.

▶ **Passing data with internal tables**
Internal tables can, of course, be passed on to interface parameters when procedures are called. Furthermore, internal tables often act as a means of storing or reading data. In particular, all Open SQL statements contain variants that allow you to directly exchange data from database tables with internal tables (see Section 10.1.2).

Both during assignments, as well as during passing internal tables as actual parameters by value to formal parameters, the sharing process with its copy-on-write semantics is used for performance reasons, as described in Section 5.1.8.

Example of Using Internal Tables
Listing 5.21 shows the implementation of the demo class from Listing 5.20, which uses the internal tables declared in that listing as well.

Listing 5.21 Working with Internal Tables

```
REPORT z_internal_tables.

...

CLASS demo IMPLEMENTATION.
  METHOD main.
    DATA: address TYPE t_address,
          idx     TYPE sy-tabix,
          output  TYPE c LENGTH 80,
          text    TYPE REF TO zcl_text.
    FIELD-SYMBOLS <fs> LIKE company.
* Prepare text output
    text = zcl_text=>get_handle( ).
* Filling Internal Tables
    company-name    = 'Racing Bikes Inc.'.
    address-street = 'Fifth Avenue'.
    address-city   = 'New York'.
    APPEND address TO company-addresses.
    address-street = 'Second Street'.
    address-city   = 'Boston'.
    APPEND address TO company-addresses.
    INSERT company INTO TABLE company_tab.
    CLEAR company.
    company-name    = 'Chocolatiers Suisse'.
    address-street = 'Avenue des Forets'.
    address-city   = 'Geneve'.
    APPEND address TO company-addresses.
    address-street = 'Kleine Bachgasse'.
    address-city   = 'Basel'.
    APPEND address TO company-addresses.
    address-street = 'Piazza di Lago'.
    address-city   = 'Lugano'.
    APPEND address TO company-addresses.
    INSERT company INTO TABLE company_tab.
* Reading Internal Tables
    READ TABLE company_tab
        WITH TABLE KEY name = 'Racing Bikes Inc.'
        ASSIGNING <fs>.
    WRITE <fs>-name TO output.
    text->add_line( output ).
    LOOP AT <fs>-addresses INTO address.
      CLEAR output.
      WRITE: sy-tabix       TO output+4(4),
             address-street TO output+8(20),
             address-city   TO output+28(20).
```

```
        text->add_line( output ).
      ENDLOOP.
      text->add_line( space ).
* Modifying Internal Tables
      address-street = 'Rue des Montagnes'.
      address-city   = 'Geneve'.
      READ TABLE company_tab
          WITH TABLE KEY name = 'Chocolatiers Suisse'
          INTO company.
      READ TABLE company-addresses TRANSPORTING NO FIELDS
              WITH TABLE KEY city = address-city.
      idx = sy-tabix.
      MODIFY company-addresses FROM address INDEX idx.
      MODIFY TABLE company_tab FROM company.
* Moving and sorting Internal Tables
      company_sorted_tab = company_tab.
      LOOP AT company_sorted_tab INTO company.
        WRITE company-name TO output.
        text->add_line( output ).
        SORT company-addresses.
        LOOP AT company-addresses INTO address.
        CLEAR output.
          WRITE: sy-tabix        TO output+4(4),
                 address-street  TO output+8(20),
                 address-city    TO output+28(20).
          text->add_line( output ).
        ENDLOOP.
      ENDLOOP.
* text output
      text->display( ).
  ENDMETHOD.
ENDCLASS.
START-OF-SELECTION.
  demo=>main( ).
```

First we fill the internal tables with some lines. Because the company-addresses component is a standard table, we use APPEND to append the address structure line by line. However, for the hashed table company_tab, we must insert company using the INSERT statement.

Then we use READ to assign a line from company_tab to the field symbol <fs> and process its table-type component addresses in a loop. The contents of the lines are assigned to the address structure. Because addresses is an index table, we can evaluate sy-tabix.

To modify the contents of the `street` component in a line of the internal table `addresses`, we determine the index of the requested line using a `READ` statement and use this index in the `MODIFY` statement. Then we use the key access of the `MODIFY` statement so that the modification will take effect in the corresponding line of the external hashed table.

Lastly, we assign the hashed table to a sorted table of the same line type. This ensures that the entries are automatically sorted by the table key `name`. The entries of the internal standard table, on the other hand, are sorted using the `SORT` command.

To output some of the results, we use the wrapping of the text edit control shown in Appendix A.6. The output of the program is displayed as shown in Figure 5.15.

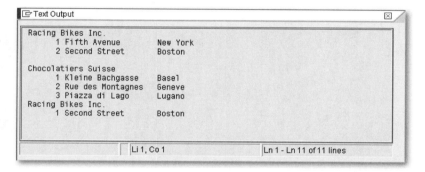

Figure 5.15 Sample Program for Internal Tables

A physician, a civil engineer, and a computer scientist were arguing about what was the oldest profession in the world. The physician remarked, "Well, in the Bible, it says that God created Eve from a rib taken out of Adam. This clearly required surgery, and so I can rightly claim that mine is the oldest profession in the world." The civil engineer interrupted and said, "But even earlier in the book of Genesis, it states that God created the order of the heavens and the earth from out of the chaos. This was the first and certainly the most spectacular application of civil engineering. Therefore, fair doctor, you are wrong; mine is the oldest profession in the world." The computer scientist leaned back in her chair, smiled, and then said confidently, "Ah, but who do you think created the chaos?"
—Grady Booch, Object-Oriented Analysis and Design with Applications

6 Advanced Concepts in ABAP Objects

The above quotation is from a book entitled *Object-Oriented Analysis and Design with Applications* by Grady Booch (Addison-Wesley 1995), where it is used to introduce a chapter discussing "the inherent complexity of software." One advantage of the object-oriented approach is its ability to handle complexity. In Chapter 4, you were introduced to classes and objects as a basis for object orientation, and to attributes and methods as underlying components of these classes and objects. We can sum up what you have already learned as follows:

▶ Objects constitute the key concept in object-oriented programming. An object is a self-contained unit whose status is determined by the values of its attributes, whose behavior is determined by its methods, and whose identity is defined by its address in the memory. An object is accessed by reference variables,

Basic principles

which refer to this address. An object in a program that performs a certain task should reflect a real object of the task 1:1 as far as possible. With objects, a clear distinction can be made between the public interface and the private and protected components, which are not externally visible. One object can interact with another by accessing its attributes directly in a method, calling methods, or triggering an event (see Section 6.5.2).

▶ Classes consist of source code containing the definition of possible objects. An object is always an instance of a class, which is addressed by at least one reference variable. All components and properties of its objects are declared in a class. The basis for encapsulation in ABAP Objects is always the class, rather than the object.[1] Classes are either global for all programs or local in a single program. They can be specialized by inheritance (see Section 6.2), and can incorporate standalone interfaces as a public interface (see Section 6.3).

▶ Attributes describe the status of an object. Technically speaking, attributes (instance attributes) are the local variables of an object, which cannot normally be changed directly from the outside. A class may also contain static attributes, which are jointly used by all objects of the class. Static attributes may be variables or constants.

▶ Methods allow objects to perform operations. A method (instance method) always works in a specific object. In other words, it reads and changes the status of this object, and interacts with other objects by calling their methods or by triggering events. A method has a parameter interface (see Section 6.1.1), and can pass on exceptions (see Section 8.2). A class may also contain static methods, which only access static attributes, and can only trigger static events.

You may have already realized how powerful these components of ABAP Objects can be when used to program application programs; however, there is more to ABAP Objects than just these basic elements. In this chapter, you'll become familiar with additional concepts that are essential for advanced object-oriented design.

---

1 The private components of an object of a class are visible to another object of the same class.

▶ **Method Interfaces and Method Calls**
Chapter 4 introduced methods in their fundamental role as the operational components of classes. Section 6.1.1 examines the parameter interface of methods in more detail, and focuses in particular on the various options with method calls.

▶ **Specialization by Inheritance**
ABAP Objects supports simple inheritance, whereby a class can be declared as the direct subclass of exactly one superclass. All classes of ABAP Objects are part of an inheritance hierarchy tree originating in one common superclass. In addition to its own components, a subclass also contains the components of its superclass. The implementation of superclass methods can be overwritten in subclasses. The concept of inheritance is discussed in Section 6.2.

▶ **Standalone Interfaces**
The public visibility section of a class is its external interface. ABAP Objects allows you to create standalone interfaces, which can be used by classes as part of their interface, or even as their complete interface. Objects belonging to various classes that use the same interface can be handled by outside users in the same way. An standalone interface may also comprise several other interfaces. The interface concept is described in Section 6.3.

▶ **Object Reference Variables and Polymorphism**
Objects in a program can only be accessed by object references in object reference variables. The type of the object reference variables determines exactly what a program can do with an object. There are both class reference variables and interface reference variables. The latter enable exclusive access to the interface components of a class. The concepts of inheritance and independent interfaces allow you to assign object references between reference variables of different types according to certain rules. This opens up the possibilities of polymorphism, whereby the same reference variable can be used to access objects belonging to different classes with different behavior. This is discussed in Section 6.4.

▶ **Events and Event Handling**
A method of an object is normally executed after a direct call. In this case, the calling object and the called object are closely coupled. Events are used to decouple the caller from the called method. In ABAP Objects, events, like attributes and methods, are component type of classes. An object can trigger an event in a

method, and methods of other objects can handle this event. This corresponds to an indirect method call because the calling method does not need to know anything about the possible event handlers. The event concept is described in Section 6.5.

▶ **Shared Objects**
Objects as instances of classes exist in the memory area of a program, and are deleted at the latest when the program is exited. As a result, cross-program access to objects is not generally possible. However, ABAP Objects enables cross-program access with shared objects, which are objects in the shared memory of an application server. The concept of shared objects is discussed in Section 6.6.

The basic concepts of ABAP Objects, which were introduced in Chapter 4 (i.e., classes with attributes and methods, objects, and object references), are used in almost all object-oriented programming languages. The advanced concepts introduced in this chapter comprise, on the one hand, a selection of tried and tested advanced techniques adopted by ABAP Objects based on the standards of well-known object-oriented programming languages like Java or C++, and, on the other hand, specialized techniques that are unique to ABAP Objects. When this language was designed, special care was taken to ensure that the focus on business applications was not lost.

ASAP principle
Certain concepts of object-oriented programming, such as multiple inheritance, which is used in C++, for example, would have served only to increase the complexity of the language, without offering any additional benefits for SAP applications. In accordance with the ASAP principle, of "As Simple As Possible," ABAP Objects was made as easy to understand as possible, and only well-established object-oriented concepts were used. Following the example of Java, the interface concept was introduced in place of multiple inheritance. The correct application of inheritance and interfaces represents the crowning achievement of object-oriented programming, and provides a range of options for managing complexity.[2]

The range of options for defining a parameter interface for methods is, in contrast, specific to ABAP. Similarly, the concept of fully inte-

---

2 However, we do not wish to conceal the fact that the incorrect use of concepts like inheritance may cause major problems. Meticulous object-oriented modeling is essential, particularly when advanced concepts of object orientation are used to manage complex applications.

grating events into the language scope of ABAP Objects as independent components of classes is not a feature of all object-oriented programming languages.

6.1 Method Interfaces and Method Calls

We have defined and called methods on many occasions in the previous chapters. The next two sections discuss the finer points of methods in ABAP Objects.

6.1.1 Parameter Interfaces of Methods

The parameter interface of a method is defined by the additions to the METHODS and CLASS-METHODS statements when the method is declared, or by the selection of **Parameters** in the Class Builder. No further details of the parameter interface are required in the implementation section between METHOD and ENDMETHOD. However, you can display the interface during implementation of global classes.

The parameter interface of a method comprises formal parameters and exceptions. The declaration of exceptions is discussed in Section 8.2. Formal parameters are keyword parameters, to which an actual parameter can or must be assigned when the method is called. Within a method, formal parameters can be used via their names in operand positions. The possible usage kinds depend on the parameter properties. The following properties can be defined for a formal parameter:

Formal parameters

- The parameter type
- Kind of parameter passing
- Parameter typing
- Supply type of the parameter

In principle, a parameter interface can contain any number of parameters; however, a small number is recommended. An ideal parameter interface contains only a small number of input parameters or none at all, and a return value.

At this point, we should point out that methods in ABAP Objects cannot be overloaded. In other words, you cannot use the same method

No overloading

names with different parameter interfaces, even when you redefine methods in subclasses.

Parameter Type

You can define the following parameters:

▶ **Input Parameters**
Input parameters are specified after the IMPORTING addition to the METHODS or CLASS-METHODS statement, or are declared by selecting **Importing** in the **Type** column on the **Parameters** tab page in the Class Builder. When a method is called, the value of the assigned actual parameter is assigned to the input parameter. Input parameters for which pass by reference is defined cannot be overwritten in the method. Input parameters for which pass by value is defined are not passed to the actual parameter when the procedure is exited.

▶ **Output Parameters**
Output parameters are specified after the EXPORTING addition to the METHODS or CLASS-METHODS statement, or are declared by selecting **Exporting** in the **Type** column on the **Parameters** tab page in the Class Builder. When a method is called, the value of the assigned actual parameter is not assigned to an output parameter for which pass by value is defined. Output parameters can be overwritten in the method. If the procedure is exited without errors using ENDMETHOD or RETURN, the output parameter is passed to the actual parameter.

▶ **Input/Output Parameters**
Input/output parameters are specified after the CHANGING addition to the METHODS or CLASS-METHODS statement, or are declared by selecting **Changing** in the **Type** column on the **Parameters** tab page in the Class Builder. When a method is called, the value of the assigned actual parameter is assigned to the input/output parameter, and, if the method is exited without errors using END-METHOD or RETURN, the input/output parameter is passed to the actual parameter. Input/output parameters can be overwritten in the method.

Functional method

▶ **Return Value**
A method can have only one return value, for which pass by value must be declared. This return value can be declared after the

RETURNING addition to the METHODS or CLASS-METHODS statement, or by selecting **Returning** in the **Type** column on the **Parameters tab page** in the Class Builder. A return value is handled in the same way that an output parameter is handled in the method; however, a method with a return value is a functional method, which, in addition to the return value, can have only input parameters. A functional method can be used in operand positions. The return value is then used in these positions.[3]

When you declare a parameter, you must always select the type that matches the behavior of that parameter exactly. A parameter that is received but not changed by the method is an input parameter. A parameter that is output but is not received is an output parameter or a return value. A parameter that is received, changed, and output is an input/output parameter.

This may appear to be stating the obvious, but, as you will see, parameters do not have to behave in accordance with their type.

Kind of Parameter Passing

You can define the way a formal parameter is passed either as pass by reference or as pass by value for each individual parameter, with the exception of the return value, for which pass by value is set by default.

The syntax for pass by reference is shown below using the example of an input parameter ipara:

METHODS meth IMPORTING ipara ...   REFERENCE

Equally, you can also use:

METHODS meth IMPORTING REFERENCE(ipara) ...

The syntax for pass by value is shown below using the example of the return value return:

METHODS meth RETURNING VALUE(return) ...   VALUE

---

3   Functional methods (as opposed to function modules) are the natural extension of integrated functions (see Section 5.2.4) by self-defined functions in the same way as self-defined data types extend the built-in ABAP types.

In the Class Builder, you define the kind of parameter passing by selecting the **Pass by value** check box on the **Parameters** tab page or leaving this blank. Therefore, pass by reference is the standard transfer type, which is used unless a different type is specified, both in the syntax and in the Class Builder. What is the difference between these transfer types?

- **Pass by Reference**
  With pass by reference, a reference to the actual parameter is passed to the method for each formal parameter for which an actual parameter is specified when you call the method, regardless of the parameter type. The method thus uses the actual parameter itself, and changes to formal parameters have a direct effect on the actual parameter.

- **Pass by Value**
  With pass by value, a local data object is created as a copy of the actual parameter for each formal parameter when the method is called. In the case of input parameters and input/output parameters, the value of the actual parameter is assigned to this data object. The value of the formal parameter is only assigned to output parameters, input/output parameters, and return values if the method is exited without errors using ENDMETHOD or RETURN.

Parameter type and kind of passing   The kind of parameter passing is a technical property, which defines the behavior of a formal parameter. Only with pass by value does the actual behavior always correspond to the behavior defined by the parameter type. The following points apply to pass by reference:

- Output parameters are not necessarily initial at the start of the method (output parameters behave like input/output parameters).

- Changes to output parameters and input/output parameters are effective, even if the method terminates with an exception.

- Input parameters that are passed by reference cannot be explicitly changed in the method. Their values may change, however, if they are linked to global actual parameters and if these parameters are changed during the method is executed.

Therefore, a method should always be programmed in such a way that the behavior of its parameters corresponds to the semantics defined by the parameter type:

▶ Do not execute read access to an output parameter that is passed by reference because its initial value is not defined.

▶ If you add lines to an internal table or extend a string that is defined as an output parameter that is passed by reference, you must initialize the parameter before the first access.

▶ Give due consideration to the value you set for output parameters or input/output parameters that are passed by reference before an exception is triggered to ensure that a calling program can execute adequate exception handling.

A number of precautionary methods are thus required for pass by reference, which do not apply to pass by value. So why is pass by reference even necessary? The answer is performance.

Pass by reference and pass by value

In ABAP, pass by reference always performs better than pass by value, because no data object has to be created when a procedure is called, and no data transport takes place. For performance reasons, pass by reference is usually preferable to pass by value, unless explicit or implicit write access to an input parameter is required, or you want to ensure that an output parameter or an input/output parameter is only returned if the procedure is completed without any errors. If possible, these cases should be limited to the transfer of parameters smaller than approximately 100 bytes.[4]

Performance as against robustness

The example in Listing 6.1 is of a small and probably unexpected situation, which may occur if pass by reference is used without due consideration.

Listing 6.1 Transfer Type of Formal Parameters

```
REPORT z_parameter_passing.

CLASS demo DEFINITION CREATE PRIVATE.
  PUBLIC SECTION.
    CLASS-METHODS main.
  PRIVATE SECTION.
    METHODS: meth1 IMPORTING value(idx)     TYPE i,
             meth2 IMPORTING reference(idx) TYPE i.
```

---

4 With strings and internal tables, the disadvantage in terms of performance of pass by value compared with pass by reference can even be compensated for by the integrated Copy-on-Write semantics (the concept of sharing, see Section 5.1.7). This is the case for input parameters in particular, provided that they are not changed.

```
      DATA msg TYPE string.
ENDCLASS.
CLASS demo IMPLEMENTATION.
  METHOD main.
    DATA oref TYPE REF TO demo.
    CREATE OBJECT oref.
    DO 2 TIMES.
      oref->meth1( sy-index ).
      oref->meth2( sy-index ).
    ENDDO.
  ENDMETHOD.
  METHOD meth1.
    DO 3 TIMES.
      msg = idx.
      CONCATENATE `meth1: ` msg INTO msg.
      MESSAGE msg TYPE 'I'.
    ENDDO.
  ENDMETHOD.
  METHOD meth2.
    DO 3 TIMES.
      msg = idx.
      CONCATENATE `meth2: ` msg INTO msg.
      MESSAGE msg TYPE 'I'.
    ENDDO.
  ENDMETHOD.
ENDCLASS.
START-OF-SELECTION.
  demo=>main( ).
```

In the main method, two methods are called with an identical implementation in a DO loop. The first method, meth1, outputs the content of sy-index , which is passed by value, three times as expected, in other words, "1", "1", "1" during the first call, and "2", "2", "2" during the second call. The second method, meth2, outputs "1", "2", "3" during both calls. The DO loop in meth1 and meth2 sets the global system field sy-index and thus also the formal parameter idx (passed by reference) in meth2.

The method with pass by value is therefore more robust. However, this example also shows that global parameters like system fields—changes to which are not subject to the direct control of a method—should not be simply passed to methods in this way from the calling program. The expected result is also returned by meth2 if a local auxiliary variable is implemented in main, to which sy-index is assigned and which is then passed to meth2.

Typing

You must type each formal parameter of a method. Typing simply means that you assign a type to a formal parameter. As with data declaration, the syntax used for this purpose is a TYPE or LIKE addition, which you must specify after each formal parameter, for example:

```
METHODS meth EXPORTING opara TYPE dtype ...
```

With local classes, any visible type can be specified here. In the Class Builder, fill the **Typing (Type, Type Ref To** or **Like)** and **Reference type** columns accordingly on the **Parameters** tab page in order to specify the type,. Since the type you specify must also be accessible to all users of the method, you can only specify built-in ABAP types, global types from the ABAP Dictionary, or types from the public visibility section of a global class for public methods. With protected methods, additional types from the protected visibility section of the class can also be used, while types from the private visibility section and local types from the class pool can be used for private method types only.

The main difference between typing and data declaration is that a formal parameter is assigned its actual data type only when it is linked to an actual parameter when a method is called. All technical properties of the actual parameter are then passed to the formal parameter.

In order for an actual parameter to be passed, its data type must match the typing of the formal parameter. To be more precise, its technical type properties must be compatible with the data type used for the typing. The technical properties of an elementary type are the built-in ABAP type (c, d, f, i, n, p, t, string, x, xstring), the length (for c, n, p, x), and the number of decimal places (for p). The technical property of a structured type is its structure, based on substructures and elementary components (the component names are irrelevant). The technical properties of an internal table are the table type (STANDARD, HASHED, SORTED), line type, and table key.

Checking typing

351

Generic typing

The typing of a formal parameter may be complete or generic. For complete typing, use TYPE to refer to a complete data type, or LIKE to refer to a data object. For generic typing, you can use the built-in generic types (any, any table, c, clike, csequence, data, hashed table, index table, n, numeric, object, simple, sorted table, standard table, table, x, xsequence—see Section 5.1.9). Internal table types are also generic if the table key is not fully defined.

Formal parameters that have complete typing can always be regarded as local data objects of this type, with all type properties known inside the method. Generic types differ in terms of static and dynamic access. The type properties used for typing are only used for static access. With dynamic access,[5] the type properties of the assigned actual parameter are used. These properties may differ from the typing in terms of the non-technical properties, such as component names.

Operand position

In addition to checking the data type of an assigned actual parameter, the typing defines how the formal parameter can be used as an operand of statements in the method. With one exception, formal parameters can be used in all operand positions that are not excluded by the typing. For example, a generic formal parameter with the typing any can be assigned to any formal parameter that has the same typing. In that case, an exception occurs at runtime if types for which no conversion rules exist (see Section 5.2.2) are assigned. Internal tables constitute the exception to this rule. In this case, table accesses are only permitted to formal parameters that have a corresponding typing.

The example provided in Listing 6.2 shows various typings and their effects on how formal parameters are used in the methods.

Listing 6.2 Typing of Formal Parameters

```
REPORT z_parameter_typing.

CLASS demo DEFINITION.
  PUBLIC SECTION.
    METHODS: meth1 IMPORTING ipar TYPE any,
             meth2 IMPORTING ipar TYPE any table,
             meth3 IMPORTING ipar TYPE index table.
ENDCLASS.
```

---

5 With dynamic access to a component during an operation on an internal table, for example.

```
CLASS demo IMPLEMENTATION.
  METHOD meth1.
    DATA num TYPE string.
    num = ipar.
    "READ TABLE ipar INDEX 1
    "               TRANSPORTING NO FIELDS.
    "READ TABLE ipar WITH KEY table_line = '...'
    "               TRANSPORTING NO FIELDS.
  ENDMETHOD.
  METHOD meth2.
    DATA num TYPE string.
    "num = ipar.
    "READ TABLE ipar INDEX 1
    "               TRANSPORTING NO FIELDS.
    READ TABLE ipar WITH KEY table_line = '...'
                    TRANSPORTING NO FIELDS.
  ENDMETHOD.
  METHOD meth3.
    DATA num TYPE string.
    "num = ipar.
    READ TABLE ipar WITH KEY table_line = '...'
                    TRANSPORTING NO FIELDS.
    READ TABLE ipar INDEX 1
                    TRANSPORTING NO FIELDS.
  ENDMETHOD.
ENDCLASS.
```

Three conceivable uses of the input parameter are specified in the methods, while the statements that result in syntax errors for the respective typing are commented out:

▶ The `ipar` input parameter of the `meth1` method is typed as completely generic. It can be assigned to the `num` local variables; however, no read operations can be executed for internal tables. When the method is called, any data objects can be passed to the formal parameter. But, if an internal table is passed, an exception occurs during the assignment to `num`.

▶ The `ipar` input parameter of the `meth2` method is typed with an internal table that is generic in terms of table type, line type, and table key. It cannot be assigned to the `num` local variable. Only key access can be executed for internal tables because only these accesses are permitted for all table types. When the method is called, any internal tables can be passed to the formal parameter.

▶ The `ipar` input parameter of the `meth3` method is typed with an index table that is generic in terms of line type and table key. It cannot be assigned to the `num` local variable. However, all accesses can be executed for internal tables because key and index accesses are possible for index tables. When the method is called, only index tables (and no hash tables) can be passed to the formal parameter.

Formal parameters should be as appropriately typed as possible. The typing must comply with both the implementation requirements and the expectations of the calling program. If you want or need to use a generic type, you should always be as specific as possible. Use generic types like `csequence`, `numeric`, `simple`, and `xsequence` instead of `any`. For example, `csequence` is usually an appropriate typing for text processing. The typings `standard table`, `sorted table`, `index table`, or `hashed table` are similarly preferable to `any table`.

Generic or complete The more generic the typing you use, the more careful you must be when using the formal parameter in the implementation to avoid exceptions. Accordingly, you should avoid assigning formal parameters with a typing that is completely generic if you do not want to first check the type at runtime (see Section 11.2) or handle possible exceptions (see Section 8.2).

Unless generic typing is required, you should always use complete typing. Only formal parameters with complete typing always behave in the same way and can be tested locally. You must be particularly careful to ensure that you don't use generic typing by mistake when you actually intend to use complete typing. This frequently occurs with internal tables with a generic key.

Supply Type

For every formal parameter that awaits a value—input parameters and input/output parameters—by standard, an actual parameter must be specified when the method is called. The assignment of actual parameters to output parameters and return values is always optional.

For input parameters and input/output parameters, this rule can be avoided by declaring the parameter as optional. The syntax is shown below, using the example of an input/output parameter:

METHODS meth **CHANGING** cpara **TYPE** dtype **OPTIONAL** ...   OPTIONAL

or

METHODS meth **CHANGING** cpara **TYPE** dtype **DEFAULT** dobj ...   DEFAULT

No actual parameters have to be specified when the method is called for a formal parameter that is declared as optional. An optional formal parameter for which no actual parameter is specified is initialized in accordance with its type. With the addition DEFAULT, the value and type of an appropriately specified replacement parameter dobj are copied.

In the Class Builder, you can make a formal parameter optional by selecting the **Optional** column, or by entering a value in the **Default value** column.

We recommend that you make all formal parameters optional, with the exception of those for which a different entry is actually required each time the method is called. Otherwise, you force your callers to specify unnecessary actual parameters, for which type-specific auxiliary variables often have to be created.

Ensure that the predefined initialization of optional parameters is sufficient or, if you must initialize such a parameter explicitly, for example, in dependence of other parameters. With the special predicate

... IS SUPPLIED ...

you can even use a logical expression to react differently in the method, depending on whether an actual parameter is assigned to an optional parameter.

6.1.2   Method Calls

This section discusses the options for calling methods statically. A dynamic method call is also possible (see Section 11.4). When a method is called, actual parameters must be passed to all non-optional formal parameters (in other words, all input parameters and input/output parameters that are not defined as optional). Actual parameters can be connected to optional formal parameters. The actual parameters must match the typing of the formal parameters.

The following sections describe static method with increasing complexity of the method interface.

Static Method Calls

The simplest method has no interface parameters. Accordingly, the method call is also simple. The statement is as follows:

No parameters

```
meth( ).
```

With `meth`, you specify the method as it can be addressed as a component of a class or an object in the current location, that is, directly with its name `meth` in a method of the same class, or with `oref->meth` or `class=>meth` everywhere the method is visible.

If the method has one non-optional input parameter, the statement is as follows:

One input parameter

```
meth( dobj ).
```

The `dobj` data object is passed to the input parameter as an actual parameter. If the method has several non-optional input parameters, the statement is as follows:

Several input parameters

```
meth( i1 = dobj1 i2 = dobj2 ... ).
```

A data object is explicitly assigned to each input parameter. If actual parameters are to be assigned to any formal parameters, the syntax is as follows:

Any parameter

```
meth( EXPORTING i1 = dobj1 i2 = dobj2 ...
      IMPORTING o1 = dobj1 o2 = dobj2 ...
      CHANGING  c1 = dobj1 c2 = dobj2 ... ).
```

With `EXPORTING`, you supply the input parameters defined with `IMPORTING`. With `IMPORTING`, you receive values from output parameters defined with `EXPORTING`. With `CHANGING`, you assign the actual parameters to the input/output parameters defined with `CHANGING`. The equal sign is not an assignment operator in this case. Instead, its function is to bind actual parameters to formal parameters. This syntax includes the previous short forms and can be used instead.

Finally, you can add a `CALL METHOD` to all of the previous syntax forms, for example:

CALL METHOD

```
CALL METHOD meth( i1 = dobj1 i2 = dobj2 ... ).
```

However, this specification is merely unnecessary syntactical noise and can be omitted (as of Release 6.10).[6]

Functional Method Call

You may notice that we haven't mentioned the RETURNING parameter of a functional method[7] in our discussion of method calls. This is because functional methods are intended to be used in operand positions. Nevertheless, there is also a separate statement for calling a functional method:

```
meth( EXPORTING i1 = dobj1 i2 = dobj2 ...
      RECEIVING r  = dobj ).
```

RETURNING parameter

Here, RECEIVING receives the return value in dobj; however, this statement is seldom if ever used in practice. The functional equivalent for the above call is as follows:

```
dobj = meth( i1 = dobj1 i2 = dobj2 ... ).
```

The call of the functional method can be specified in an operand position, which, in this case, is the source field of an assignment, without specifying RECEIVING. When the statement is executed, the method is called and the return value is used as an operand. In the example shown above, it is assigned to dobj. The actual parameters are assigned to input parameters using the three syntax forms described above for no input parameters, one input parameter, or several input parameters.

```
... meth( ) ...
... meth( dobj ) ...
... meth( i1 = dobj1 i2 = dobj2 ... ) ...
```

Functional methods can be used in the same places as built-in functions (see Section 5.2.4). A functional method called with meth(a) hides an built-in function with the same name:

▸ As the source field of an assignment

▸ As an operand in an arithmetic expression

▸ As an operand in a logical expression

---

6 The CALL METHOD language element is only required for the dynamic method calls still.

7 Remember that a function method can have any number of input parameters and only one return value that is passed by value.

▶ As an operand in the `CASE` statement

▶ As an operand in the `WHEN` statement

▶ As an operand in the `WHERE` condition for internal tables

If a functional method called in an operand position sends a class-based exception, this can be handled within a `TRY` control structure.[8] As of the next release of SAP NetWeaver, you will be able to use functional methods as well as built-in functions and complete arithmetic expressions in almost all operand positions where it is useful to do so. You will be able to use them, in particular, as actual parameters for input parameters of methods, which will allow you to nest method calls.

In Listing 6.3, we have implemented two functional methods `get_area` and `get_volume`, to calculate the circular area and volume of a cylinder in a class called `cylinder`.

Listing 6.3 Functional Methods

```
REPORT z_functional_method.

SELECTION-SCREEN BEGIN OF SCREEN 100.
PARAMETERS: p_radius TYPE i,
            p_height TYPE i.
SELECTION-SCREEN END OF SCREEN 100.
CLASS demo DEFINITION.
  PUBLIC SECTION.
    CLASS-METHODS main.
ENDCLASS.
CLASS cylinder DEFINITION.
  PUBLIC SECTION.
    METHODS: constructor IMPORTING i_radius TYPE numeric
                                   i_height TYPE numeric,
             get_area    RETURNING value(r_area)   TYPE f,
             get_volume  RETURNING value(r_volume) TYPE f.
  PRIVATE SECTION.
    CONSTANTS pi TYPE f VALUE '3.14159265'.
    DATA: radius TYPE f,
          height TYPE f.
ENDCLASS.
CLASS cylinder IMPLEMENTATION.
  METHOD constructor.
```

---

8 Classical exceptions cannot be handled in this case.

```
    me->radius = i_radius.
    me->height = i_height.
  ENDMETHOD.
  METHOD get_area.
    r_area = pi * me->radius ** 2.
  ENDMETHOD.
  METHOD get_volume.
    r_volume = me->get_area( ) * me->height.
  ENDMETHOD.
ENDCLASS.
CLASS demo IMPLEMENTATION.
  METHOD main.
    DATA: oref   TYPE REF TO cylinder,
          volume TYPE string.
    CALL SELECTION-SCREEN 100 STARTING AT 10 10.
    IF sy-subrc = 0.
      CREATE OBJECT oref EXPORTING i_radius = p_radius
                                   i_height = p_height.
      volume = oref->get_volume( ).
      CONCATENATE `Volume: ` volume INTO volume.
      MESSAGE volume TYPE 'I'.
    ENDIF.
  ENDMETHOD.
ENDCLASS.
START-OF-SELECTION.
  demo=>main( ).
```

The `main` method of the `demo` class uses a function call to `get_volume` on the right side of an assignment, and assigns the result to the `volume` string. The `get_volume` method calls `get_area` in an arithmetic expression. The calculation type of this expression is `f`.

6.2   Inheritance

In object orientation, inheritance refers to the specialization of classes by deriving subclasses from superclasses.

6.2.1   Basic Principles

Classes provide a construction plan for objects. Suppose you create two classes called "Car" and "Truck". You want to implement methods for both classes, which control the objects or return information about their location and speed. Even at this stage, you can foresee that some parts of the classes will have to be written twice. The inheritance mechanism of an object-oriented programming language provides options that help you to reuse the same or similar parts of a class, and to create a hierarchy of classes.

Superclasses and subclasses

If we examine the two classes (i.e., "Car" and "Truck") in more detail, it becomes clear that both classes comprise types of vehicles. If you want to create a third class called "Dump truck" it will comprise a specific type of truck. To create a hierarchy relationship between these classes, classes can be derived from each other using inheritance. In our example, "Car" and "Truck" are derived from the "Vehicle" class, while "Dump truck" are derived from the "Truck" class. Derived or more specific classes are referred to as *subclasses*, while more general classes are called *superclasses*.

Simple inheritance

The concept of simple inheritance is implemented in ABAP Objects. According to this concept, each class can have several subclasses but only one superclass.[9] In simple inheritance, inheritance relationships are represented by an inheritance tree. Every class in an object-oriented programming language in which simple inheritance is implemented has a unique position as a node in an inheritance tree. This also applies to all the classes we have dealt with up to now, although we have not yet spoken of them in terms of inheritance. For each class, a unique path can be traced back through their superclasses in the inheritance tree until you reach exactly one root node. This root node is the superclass of all classes in the inheritance tree.

Root class

Figure 6.1 illustrates this relationship. The root node of the inheritance tree in ABAP Objects is the predefined, empty, and abstract class object.

Derivation

Inheritance simply means that a subclass inherits all components (attributes, methods, events, etc.) of its superclass and can use them like its own components. In each subclass, new elements can be added or methods can be redefined in order to specialize, without this having any impact on the superclass. Elements can only be added in subclasses. It would go against the inheritance concept to remove elements in a subclass.

---

9 Other programming languages, such as C++, allow a class to be derived from several classes. This mechanism, which is referred to as *multiple inheritance*, is not implemented in ABAP Objects.

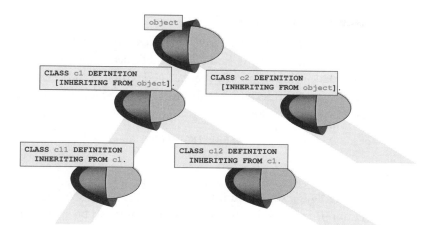

Figure 6.1 Inheritance Tree in ABAP Objects

In accordance with this concept, the direct subclasses of the empty `object` root class do not inherit any components from its superclass. Instead, they can add new components. This situation applies to all our sample classes up to now. All classes in ABAP Objects that do not explicitly inherit from another class are implicit direct subclasses of `object`.

Implicit subclasses

When subclasses of explicitly defined classes are created, these inherit the components of their superclasses and can add new components. Classes become increasingly specialized the further away you move from the root in the inheritance tree. As you move towards the root node, on the other hand, the classes become more generalized.

Specialization/ generalization

If you look at a class that is located near the bottom of the inheritance tree, you will notice that the inherited components of the class originate in all classes along the path between this class and the root class, which is the superclass of all classes. In other words, the definition of a subclass is composed of the definitions of all of its superclasses right up to `object`. The relationship between a subclass and its superclasses should always be expressed as "is a"; for example, "a cargo plane is a plane is a means of transportation is an object." If this is fulfilled, subclasses can always be handled the same way as superclasses (see polymorphism in Section 6.4).

Composition

6.2.2 Creating Subclasses

A superclass has no knowledge of any subclasses it may have. Only a subclass is aware that it is the heir of another class. Therefore, an inheritance relationship can only be defined when a subclass is declared. The syntax for deriving a subclass (`subclass`) from a superclass (`superclass`) is as follows:

INHERITING
FROM

```
CLASS subclass DEFINITION INHERITING FROM superclass.
  ...
ENDCLASS.
```

It therefore involves a simple addition to the `CLASS DEFINITION` statement. Any non-final class that is visible at this point can be specified for `superclass`. To create a subclass in the Class Builder, select **Superclass** on the **Properties** tab page. Then enter any non-final, global class as a superclass in the **Inherits from** field. The **Undo inheritance** and **Change inheritance** options allow you to change the inheritance relationship (see Figure 6.2).

Figure 6.2 Inheritance in the Class Builder

To display the components in a subclass that were inherited from the superclass, select the menu option **Utilities • Settings**, and select the **Display Inherited Components Also** option.

For each class that does not have an explicit `INHERITING FROM` addition, the system implicitly adds the `INHERITING FROM object` addition, which means that any class without an `INHERITING` addition is automatically a direct subclass of the `object` root class.

Listing 6.4 shows the implementation of our example based on vehicles. In this implementation, two classes (`car` and `truck`) are derived from the `vehicle` class.

Listing 6.4 Simple Example of Inheritance

```
REPORT z_inheritance.

CLASS demo DEFINITION.
  PUBLIC SECTION.
```

```abap
        CLASS-METHODS main.
ENDCLASS.

CLASS vehicle DEFINITION.
  PUBLIC SECTION.
    METHODS: accelerate IMPORTING delta TYPE i,
             show_speed.
  PROTECTED SECTION.
    DATA speed TYPE i.
ENDCLASS.

CLASS car DEFINITION INHERITING FROM vehicle.
ENDCLASS.

CLASS truck DEFINITION INHERITING FROM vehicle.
  PUBLIC SECTION.
    METHODS: load IMPORTING freight TYPE string,
             unload.
  PROTECTED SECTION.
    DATA freight TYPE string.
ENDCLASS.

CLASS vehicle IMPLEMENTATION.
  METHOD accelerate.
    me->speed = me->speed + delta.
  ENDMETHOD.
  METHOD show_speed.
    DATA output TYPE string.
    output = me->speed.
    MESSAGE output TYPE 'I'.
  ENDMETHOD.
ENDCLASS.

CLASS truck IMPLEMENTATION.
  METHOD load.
    me->freight = freight.
  ENDMETHOD.
  METHOD unload.
    CLEAR me->freight.
  ENDMETHOD.
ENDCLASS.

CLASS demo IMPLEMENTATION.
  METHOD main.
    DATA: car_ref   TYPE REF TO car,
          truck_ref TYPE REF TO truck.
    CREATE OBJECT: car_ref,
                   truck_ref.
    car_ref->accelerate( 130 ).
    car_ref->show_speed( ).
```

```
      truck_ref->load( `Beer` ).
      truck_ref->accelerate( 110 ).
      truck_ref->show_speed( ).
      truck_ref->unload( ).
   ENDMETHOD.
ENDCLASS.

START-OF-SELECTION.
   demo=>main( ).
```

The vehicle class contains a protected attribute (speed) and two public methods (accelerate and show_speed). Note that we have explicitly specified that vehicle inherits from object. Normally, we do not specify the INHERITING addition for such classes. The car and truck classes are both derived from vehicle. Therefore, they inherit the attribute and methods of the vehicle class. Since speed is declared in the PROTECTED SECTION, it is also visible in the subclasses. The truck class is specialized with an additional attribute for freight and additional methods for loading and unloading (load and unload). In this example, the car class receives no additional components. This means that its objects are the same as those of the vehicle class. Since no methods have been added, car does not require an implementation part.

In the main method of the demo class, we use the reference variables car_ref und truck_ref to generate one object each for the two subclasses and call their methods. The accelerate and show_speed methods can be used in both subclasses; however, the load and unload methods can be used only in truck.

6.2.3 Visibility Sections and Namespaces in Inheritance

There are three different visibility sections in a class, in which the components of the class are declared (see Section 4.3.2). A subclass inherits all components of its superclasses without changing their visibility. For that reason, only the public and protected components of its superclasses are visible in a subclass. In contrast, the private components are contained in the subclass but are invisible.[10] The visibility sections of a subclass therefore contain the following components:

---

10 Note, however, that the methods inherited from the superclass use the private attributes of the superclass, unless these inherited methods are redefined in the subclass.

▶ **PUBLIC**

The public visibility section of a subclass contains all public components of all superclasses, plus its own additional public components. These components can be accessed externally using component selectors.

▶ **PROTECTED**

The protected visibility section of a subclass contains all protected components of all superclasses, plus its own additional protected components. These components cannot be accessed externally using component selectors. From an external point of view, "protected" is the same as "private."

▶ **PRIVATE**

The private visibility section of a subclass contains only the subclass's own private components. These components can only be accessed in the method implementations of the subclass.

Since all visible components in a class must have unique names, all public and protected components of all classes along an inheritance path in the inheritance tree belong to the same namespace and have unique names. Private components, which are only visible within a class and cannot be used in subclasses, must only have unique names within their own class.

Namespace

The implications of this are as follows: A superclass is not aware of any subclasses it may have. If you create a non-final class in a class library and release it for use, you can never know, as a developer, which subclasses your class will eventually have other than those you define yourself. If you then subsequently add new components to the public or protected section of your class, and any of its subclasses happen to have a component of its own with the same name, this becomes syntactically incorrect. Therefore, it is only secure to add private components. In global classes, not only the external interface but also the interface with any possible subclasses must remain stable.

Therefore, to limit the subclasses of a class to at least the same package, non-final classes should preferably be organized in packages for which the **Package Check as Server** property is activated (see Section 2.3.3).

6.2.4 Method Redefinition

A subclass inherits all public and protected methods additionally to its own components.[11] When a method is called in the subclass, it is executed in the same way it was implemented in the superclass, and even uses the private components of the superclass. However, since the main purpose of inheritance is to specialize classes, the behavior of the method of a superclass may be too general for the more specific purpose of the subclass. In some cases, the implementation of superclass must be enhanced in the subclass, while in other instances, the implementation must be completely changed. However, the semantics of the method must remain stable for the external user, because all this user ever sees is the constant interface (including the documentation) and not the implementation itself.

New implementation

Instance methods can be redefined in subclasses to specialize the behavior of subclass objects. Static methods cannot be redefined. Redefining a method means creating a new implementation of the method in a subclass without changing the interface.[12] The method is still declared in the superclass. Previous implementations of the method in preceding superclasses remain unchanged. When a method is redefined in a subclass, an additional implementation is created, which hides the previous implementation when the subclass and further subclasses are used.

Access

Every reference that refers to an object of the subclass uses the redefined method. This is always the case, regardless of the type of the reference variables (for more details, see Section 6.4). This applies in particular to the self reference me. Therefore, if a superclass method (meth1) contains the call of a method (meth2) belonging to the same class, which is redefined in a subclass, the call of the meth1 method in an instance of the superclass results in the execution of the original method (meth2), while the call of the meth1 method in an instance of the subclass results in the execution of the redefined method (meth2).

---

11 The private methods are also inherited in principle, but are not visible in the subclass.

12 Some other object-oriented programming languages permit the overloading of functions or methods. This means that a separate, changed parameter interface can be defined for an overwritten or redefined method. ABAP Objects does not currently support this mechanism.

Like the methods belonging to the subclass, a redefined method accesses the private attributes of the subclass.

The syntax for redefining an instance method in a subclass is as follows:

REDEFINITION

```
METHODS meth REDEFINITION.
```

This statement must be specified in the declaration part of the subclass in the same visibility section as the actual declaration of the method in the superclass. The definition of the interface is not repeated.

In the Class Builder, you redefine an inherited method by displaying it on the **Methods** tab. To do so, you must use the **Settings** function of the Class Builder to select the **Display Inherited Components Also** entry. Then, you must highlight the method and select the **Redefine** function (see Figure 6.3).

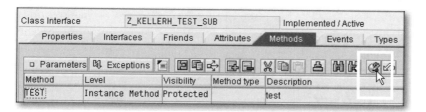

Figure 6.3 Redefinition of an Inherited Method

A new implementation must be created for each redefined method in the redefining subclass. In global classes, the Class Builder does this as part of the **Redefine** process, and you can navigate to the implementation in the same way as with normal methods. In local classes, you must enter the implementation yourself in the implementation part as for normal methods.

Implementation

In the implementation of a redefined method, you can use the pseudo reference super-> to access the original method of the direct superclass. This overrides the hiding of the redefined method. You must always use this pseudo reference if you want to first copy the functionality of the superclass and then enhance it.

Pseudo reference

We can now apply method redefinition to our example from Listing 6.4. Listing 6.5 shows how this differs from Listing 6.4.

Listing 6.5 Method Redefinition

```
REPORT z_method_redefinition.

...

CLASS car DEFINITION INHERITING FROM vehicle.
  PUBLIC SECTION.
    METHODS show_speed REDEFINITION.
ENDCLASS.
CLASS truck DEFINITION INHERITING FROM vehicle.
  PUBLIC SECTION.
    METHODS: accelerate REDEFINITION,
             show_speed REDEFINITION,
             load IMPORTING freight TYPE string,
             unload.
  PROTECTED SECTION.
    DATA freight TYPE string.
  PRIVATE SECTION.
    CONSTANTS max_speed TYPE i VALUE '80'.
ENDCLASS.

...

CLASS car IMPLEMENTATION.
  METHOD show_speed.
    DATA output TYPE string.
    output = me->speed.
    CONCATENATE `Car, speed: ` output INTO output.
    MESSAGE output TYPE 'I'.
  ENDMETHOD.
ENDCLASS.
CLASS truck IMPLEMENTATION.
  METHOD accelerate.
    super->accelerate( delta ).
    IF me->speed > truck=>max_speed.
      me->speed = truck=>max_speed.
    ENDIF.
  ENDMETHOD.
  METHOD show_speed.
    DATA output TYPE string.
    output = me->speed.
    CONCATENATE `Truck with `
                me->freight
                `, speed: `
                output
      INTO output.
```

```
    MESSAGE output TYPE 'I'.
  ENDMETHOD.
  ...
ENDCLASS.
CLASS demo IMPLEMENTATION.
  METHOD main.
    DATA: car_ref    TYPE REF TO car,
          truck_ref TYPE REF TO truck.
    CREATE OBJECT: car_ref,
                   truck_ref.
    car_ref->accelerate( 130 ).
    car_ref->show_speed( ).
    truck_ref->load( `Beer` ).
    truck_ref->accelerate( 110 ).
    truck_ref->show_speed( ).
    truck_ref->unload( ).
  ENDMETHOD.
ENDCLASS.

START-OF-SELECTION.
  demo=>main( ).
```

We specialize the accelerate method in the truck class and the
show_speed method in both subclasses:

▶ In the truck class, we introduced a maximum speed max_speed
that cannot be exceeded in accelerate. In the new implementation, the speed is therefore set by calling super->accelerate via
the previous implementation, and then checked and adapted, if
necessary.

▶ The show_speed method is extended by specific outputs in both
subclasses. The previous implementation is not used for this purpose.

All redefined methods keep their original semantics in spite of the
new implementation. You will notice that this requires some programming discipline because we can also implement the methods in
a completely different way (for more information, see Section 6.4.3).
A test tool that might help you check the stability of applications is
ABAP Unit (see Section 13.3).

6.2.5 Abstract Classes and Methods

If you want to use a class just as a template for subclasses and don't need any objects of this class, you can define the class as an abstract class. The syntax for defining an abstract class is:

ABSTRACT

```
CLASS class DEFINITION ABSTRACT.
  ...
ENDCLASS.
```

To create an abstract class in the Class Builder, select **Abstract** in the **Instantiation** input field on the **Properties** tab (see Figure 6.4).

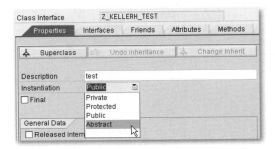

Figure 6.4 Abstract Global Class

Objects cannot be created from an abstract class using CREATE OBJECT. Instead, abstract classes are used as a template for subclasses. From an abstract class, actual subclasses can be derived from which objects can then be created.

Single instance methods can be identified as abstract as well. The syntax is:

```
METHODS meth ABSTRACT.
```

In the Class Builder, you can identify a method as **Abstract** in its Detail view (see Figure 6.5).

Implementation

An abstract method cannot be implemented in its own class, but only in a concrete subclass. Therefore, abstract methods can only be created in abstract classes. Otherwise, it would be possible to create an object with an addressable method but without its implementation. To implement an abstract method in a subclass, you use the method definition mechanism discussed in Section 6.2.4. The only difference to a real redefinition is that you cannot use the super-> pseudo reference in the method.

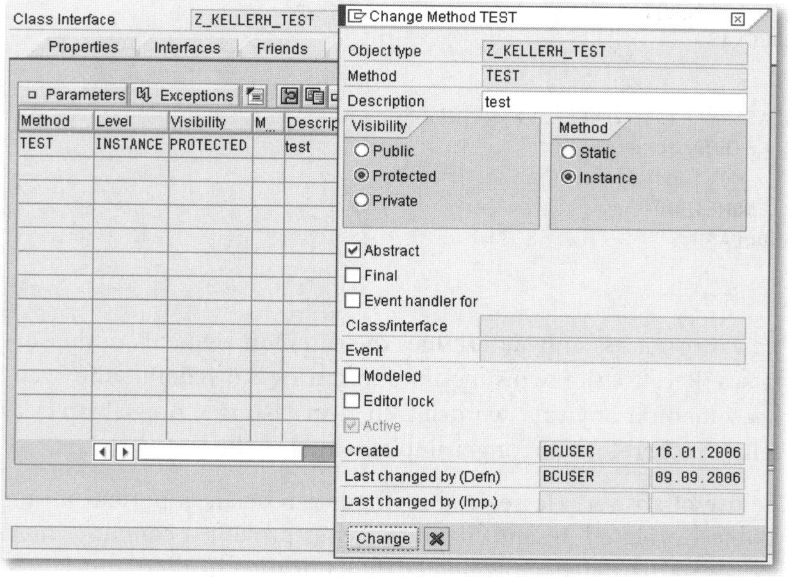

Figure 6.5 Abstract Method

In an abstract class, both concrete and abstract methods can be declared. Concrete methods are declared and implemented as usual. With the exception of instance constructers, concrete methods can even call abstract methods, because names and interfaces are completely known. The behavior of the abstract method, however, is defined during the implementation in a subclass and can therefore vary in different subclasses.

In our example in Listing 6.5, the `vehicle` superclass is rather rudimentary and is not used for creating any objects. To prevent this also syntactically, the class can be defined as abstract, as shown in Listing 6.6. Listing 6.6 only demonstrates the differences in comparison with Listing 6.5.

Listing 6.6 Abstract Class and Method

```
REPORT z_abstract_class.

...

CLASS vehicle DEFINITION ABSTRACT.
  PUBLIC SECTION.
    METHODS: accelerate IMPORTING delta TYPE i,
             show_speed ABSTRACT.
  PROTECTED SECTION.
```

```
    DATA speed TYPE i.
ENDCLASS.

...

CLASS vehicle IMPLEMENTATION.
  METHOD accelerate.
    me->speed = me->speed + delta.
  ENDMETHOD.
ENDCLASS.

...
```

The vehicle class only determines the common elements of the sub-classes. Because the two subclasses in Listing 6.5 redefine the show_speed method anyway, we declared it in Listing 6.6 as abstract as well. It is therefore no longer implemented in the vehicle class.

Design The use of abstract classes and methods can be an important means of object-oriented design. Abstract classes provide a common interface and a partially implemented functionality to their subclasses, but cannot perform any relevant operations on their attributes themselves. In a payroll system, for example, you can imagine a class that already implements many tasks like bank transfers, but only includes the actual payroll function in an abstract manner. It is then the task of various subclasses to perform the correct payroll calculation for different work contracts.

Interfaces Because ABAP Objects does not support multiple inheritance, the usage of abstraction via abstract classes is always restricted to the subclasses of a specific node of the inheritance tree. Interfaces are another means of solving similar tasks, irrespective of the position in the inheritance hierarchy. They are discussed in Section 6.3.

6.2.6 Final Classes and Methods

Just as abstract classes and methods require a definition of subclasses in order to work with the classes, there can be adverse situations where you want to protect a whole class or a single method from uncontrolled specialization. For this purpose, you can declare a class or an instance method as final. This can make sense particularly if you want to make changes to a class at a later stage without causing any subclasses to become syntactically or semantically incorrect (see the namespace of components in inheritance in Section 6.2.3). If you follow the defensive procedure for programming the AS ABAP using

ABAP Objects, which was introduced in Section 4.9, the declaration of final classes is always recommended.

The syntax for defining a final class is:

```
CLASS class DEFINITION FINAL.
...
ENDCLASS.
```

FINAL

In the Class Builder, you create a final class by selecting the **Final** checkbox on the **Properties** tab (see Figure 6.4). You cannot derive any more subclasses from a final class. A final class therefore terminates a path of the inheritance hierarchy. All instance methods of a final class are automatically final.

In a non-final class, individual instance methods can be declared as final. The syntax is:

```
METHODS meth FINAL.
```

In the Class Builder, you can identify an instance method as **Final** in its **Detail view** (see Figure 6.5). A final method cannot be redefined in subclasses. A final method cannot be abstract at the same time. A class can be final and abstract at the same time, but only its static components are usable in this case. Although you can declare instance components in such a class, it is not recommended.

6.2.7 Static Attributes in Inheritance

To use a static component of a class, instances of the class are not required. If instances exist, they share the static components. How does inheritance affect static components, and static attributes in particular?

Like all components, a static attribute exists exactly once within a path of the inheritance tree. A subclass can access the contents of the public and protected static attributes of all superclasses. Alternatively, a superclass shares its public and protected static attributes with all subclasses. In inheritance, a static attribute is therefore not assigned to a single class, but to a path of the inheritance tree. It can be accessed from outside via the class component selector (=>) using all class names involved, or from inside in all affected classes where a static attribute is visible. Changes to the value are visible in all relevant classes. Listing 6.7 shows a simple example.

Inheritance tree

Listing 6.7 Static Attributes in Inheritance

```
REPORT z_static_attributes.

CLASS demo DEFINITION.
  PUBLIC SECTION.
    CLASS-METHODS main.
ENDCLASS.
CLASS c1 DEFINITION.
  PUBLIC SECTION.
    CLASS-DATA a1 TYPE string.
ENDCLASS.
CLASS c2 DEFINITION INHERITING FROM c1.
  ...
ENDCLASS.
CLASS demo IMPLEMENTATION.
  METHOD main.
    c2=>a1 = 'ABAP Objects'.
    MESSAGE c1=>a1 TYPE 'I'.
  ENDMETHOD.
ENDCLASS.
START-OF-SELECTION.
  demo=>main( ).
```

Static constructor When addressing a static attribute belonging to a path of an inheritance tree, you always address the class in which the attribute is declared, irrespective of the class name used in the class component selector. This is important for calling the static constructor (see Section 6.2.8). A static constructor is executed when a class is addressed for the first time. If a static attribute is addressed via the class name of a subclass but declared in a superclass, only the static constructor of the superclass is executed.

Static methods Static methods cannot be redefined in ABAP Objects, because static components should occur exactly once (i. e., not more or less) in a path so that they can be shared by all subclasses.

6.2.8 Constructors in Inheritance

Constructors are used for initializing the attributes of a class (see Section 4.7). While instance constructors can set the instance attributes of every single object during the instancing process, the static constructors are responsible for the static attributes of the class before the class is first accessed. Because a subclass inherits all attributes of its superclasses in inheritance, this automatically begs the question "How can the constructors ensure that the inherited attributes are initialized as well when the subclass is used?"

Instance Constructors

Every class has a predefined instance constructor named `constructor`. Instance constructors thus deviate from the rule that there are only unique component names along a path of the inheritance tree. Consequently, the instance constructors of the individual classes of an inheritance tree must be completely independent of one another. To avoid naming conflicts, the following rules apply:

▶ Instance constructors of superclasses cannot be redefined in subclasses.

▶ Instance constructors cannot be explicitly called via the `constructor( )` statement.

After an object has been created with the CREATE OBJECT command, the instance constructor is automatically invoked. Because a subclass contains all superclass attributes that are visible to it, the contents of which can be set by instance constructors of these classes, the instance constructor of a subclass must ensure that the instance constructors of all superclasses are executed as well.[13] For this purpose, the instance constructor of every subclass must contain a call

super->constructor

```
super->constructor( ... ).
```

of the instance constructor of the direct superclass, even if the constructor is not explicitly declared. The only exceptions to this rule are the direct subclasses of the root node, `object`. The `super->constructor( ... )` statement is the only exception from the rule that constructors cannot be explicitly called.

In superclasses in which the instance constructor is not explicitly declared and implemented, the implicitly existing implementation of the instance constructor is run. It automatically ensures that the instance constructor of the next higher superclass is called.

Before an instance constructor is run, you must supply its non-optional input parameters. These are searched for as follows:

Input parameters

---

13 In particular, the private attributes of superclasses can only be initialized in the superclasses' own constructors.

▶ **Provision in** CREATE OBJECT
Starting with the class of the created object, the first explicitly defined instance constructor is searched for in the corresponding path of the inheritance tree. This is the instance constructor of the class itself, or the first explicitly defined instance constructor of a superclass.

▶ **Provision in** super->constructor(...)
Starting with the direct superclass, the first explicitly defined instance constructor is searched for in the corresponding path of the inheritance tree.

In CREATE OBJECT or in super->constructor(...), respectively, the interface of the first explicitly defined instance constructor is provided with values like a normal method:

▶ If there are no input parameters, no parameters are transferred.

▶ Optional input parameters can be provided with values.

▶ Non-optional input parameters must be provided with values.

If there is no explicitly defined instance constructor in the path of the inheritance tree up to the object root class, no parameters will be transferred.

Inheritance tree   For both CREATE OBJECT and super->constructor(...), the first explicit instance constructor must therefore be regarded and, if one exists, its interface must be provided with a value. When working with subclasses, you therefore need to know the entire path very well because when creating a subclass object that resides at the lower end of the inheritance tree, a situation can occur whereby parameters must be transferred to the constructor of a superclass positioned much closer to the root node.

The instance constructor of a subclass is split into two parts by the super->constructor(...) call required by the syntax. In the statements before the call, the constructor behaves like a static method. Before the call, it does not have access to the instance attributes of its class, that is, instance attributes cannot be addressed until after the call.

3-phase model   The execution of a subclass instance constructor can therefore be divided into three phases that are presented in the comment lines of Listing 6.8.

Listing 6.8 Three-Phase Model of an Instance Constructor

```
METHOD constructor.
  " Phase 1: Access to static attributes only
  ...
  " Phase 2: Execution of super class constructor(s)
  CALL METHOD super->constructor EXPORTING ...
  " Phase 3: Access to instance attributes only
  ...
ENDMETHOD.
```

In the individual phases, the instance constructor can execute the following tasks:

▶ **Phase 1**
Here you can prepare the call of the superclass instance constructor, for example, you can determine the actual parameters for its interface.

▶ **Phase 2**
In this phase, the instance constructor of the superclass is executed, which is again divided into three phases, if implemented.

▶ **Phase 3**
The attributes of all superclasses are now correctly initialized. Using these values, the necessary initializations for the own instance attributes can be performed.

Therefore, during the instantiation of a subclass, a nested call of the instance constructors from the subclass to the superclasses takes place, where the instance attributes of the highest superclass can be addressed only as of the deepest nesting level. When returning to the constructors of the subclasses underneath, their instance attributes can also be addressed successively.

The methods of subclasses are not visible in constructors. If an instance constructor calls an instance method of the same class via the implicit self-reference me, the method is called in the way in which it is implemented in the class of the instance constructor, and not the possibly redefined method of the subclass to be instantiated. This is an exception to the rule that whenever instance methods are called, the implementation is called in the class of the instance to which the reference is pointing.

Self-reference

Listing 6.9 shows the behavior of instance constructors in inheritance using a simple example.

Listing 6.9 Instance Constructors in Inheritance

```
REPORT z_constructor_inheritance.

CLASS demo DEFINITION.
  PUBLIC SECTION.
    CLASS-METHODS main.
ENDCLASS.

CLASS vessel DEFINITION.
  PUBLIC SECTION.
    METHODS constructor IMPORTING i_name TYPE string.
  PROTECTED SECTION.
    DATA name TYPE string.
ENDCLASS.

CLASS ship DEFINITION INHERITING FROM vessel.
  ...
ENDCLASS.

CLASS motorship DEFINITION INHERITING FROM ship.
  PUBLIC SECTION.
    METHODS constructor IMPORTING i_name      TYPE string
                                  i_fuelamount TYPE i.
  PRIVATE SECTION.
    DATA fuelamount TYPE i.
ENDCLASS.

CLASS vessel IMPLEMENTATION.
  METHOD constructor.
    name = i_name.
  ENDMETHOD.
ENDCLASS.

CLASS motorship IMPLEMENTATION.
  METHOD constructor.
    super->constructor( i_name ).
    fuelamount = i_fuelamount.
  ENDMETHOD.
ENDCLASS.

CLASS demo IMPLEMENTATION.
  METHOD main.
    DATA: o_vessel    TYPE REF TO vessel,
          o_ship      TYPE REF TO ship,
          o_motorship TYPE REF TO motorship.
  CREATE OBJECT:
    o_vessel    EXPORTING i_name      = 'Vincent',
    o_ship      EXPORTING i_name      = 'Mia',
    o_motorship EXPORTING i_name      = 'Jules'
                          i_fuelamount = 12000.
```

```
  ENDMETHOD.
ENDCLASS.
START-OF-SELECTION.
  demo=>main( ).
```

This example shows three consecutive classes of the inheritance hierarchy. The `vessel` class has an instance constructor with an input parameter. From `vessel`, we derive the `ship` class that does not explicitly declare and implement the instance constructor. From `ship`, we derive `motorship`. This class again has an explicit instance constructor with two input parameters. We create an object from every class and provide the parameter interface of the constructors with actual parameters. The constructors are called as follows:

▶ The object created using `o_vessel` is initialized at `CREATE OBJECT` in the explicit instance constructor of `vessel`, where an attribute is set using the passed actual parameter.

▶ The object created using `o_ship` is also initialized at `CREATE OBJECT` via the instance constructor of `vessel`, because it is called by the implicit instance constructor of `ship`. Its parameter interface needs to be provided with actual parameters.

▶ The object created using `o_motorship` is initialized in the explicit instance constructor of `motorship`. In this constructor, the instance constructor of the direct superclass must be called via `super->constructor`. The implicit instance constructor of `ship` calls the explicit instance constructor of `vessel`. Its parameter interface needs to be provided with actual parameters.

You can best understand the behavior of the program if you run it line by line in the ABAP Debugger.

Static Constructors

Every class has a static constructor named `class_constructor`. With regard to the namespace along an inheritance tree, the same rules that apply to the instance constructor also apply to the static constructor.

When a subclass is addressed for the first time in a program, its static constructor is run. Before that, however, the preceding static constructors of the entire inheritance tree must have been run. Because

Call

a static constructor should be called only once during the execution of a program, when a subclass is addressed for the first time, the next higher superclass is searched whose static constructor has not yet run. Then this static constructor is executed first, followed by the constructors of all subclasses up to and including the addressed subclass. In contrast to instance constructors, a static constructor does not have to explicitly call the static constructor of its superclass. Instead, the runtime environment automatically ensures that the static constructors are called in the correct order. In a subclass, you can always assume that the static attributes of the superclasses have been correctly initialized.

6.2.9 Instantiation in Inheritance

A subclass includes the object descriptions of all superclasses. The instantiation of a subclass therefore means the instantiation of all superclasses in a single object, where the initialization of the superclass attributes is ensured by calling the superclass constructors, as described in Section 4.3.2.

The additions CREATE PUBLIC|PROTECTED|PRIVATE of the CLASS statement or the corresponding Class Builder settings, respectively, control for each class who can create an instance of the class or call its instance constructor (see Section 4.3.2). In inheritance, this results in three scenarios whose behavior is defined in ABAP Objects as follows:

▶ **Superclass with Public Instantiation**
The instance constructor of the superclass is publicly visible. If the instantiatiability of a subclass is not explicitly specified, it inherits the public instantiation of the superclass. The instantiatiability of a subclass can be explicitly specified in one of the three ways. A subclass can control the visibility of its own instance constructor independently of the superclass.

▶ **Superclass with Protected Instantiation**
The instance constructor of the superclass is visible in subclasses. If the instantiatiability of a subclass is not explicitly specified it inherits the protected instantiation of the superclass. The instantiatiability of a subclass can be explicitly specified in one of the three ways. A subclass can control the visibility of its own instance constructor independently of the superclass and can thus also

publish the protected instance constructor of the superclass in the specified section.

▶ **Superclass with Private Instantiation**
The instance constructor of the superclass is visible only in the superclass. There are two different scenarios here:

▶ The subclass is not a friend of the superclass.
Because only the superclass itself can call its instance constructor, the subclass cannot be instantiated. Therefore, the subclass has an implicit addition, CREATE NONE. The instantiatiability of the subclass cannot be explicitly specified because this would mean a publication of the superclass constructor in the specified section.

▶ The subclass is a friend of the superclass.
If the instantiatiability of the subclass has not been explicitly specified, it inherits the private instantiation of the superclass. The instantiatiability of a subclass can be explicitly specified in one of the three ways. As a friend, a subclass can publish the private constructor of the superclass in the specified section.

If a superclass with private instantiation has been defined in a path of the inheritance tree, no subclass can be instantiated by external users, and a subclass cannot even instantiate itself because it does not have access to the instance constructor of the superclass! The obvious thing to do would be to make a class defined for private instantiation a final class in order to prevent subclasses from being derived.

Private superclass

Exceptions from this rule only exist if a privately instantiatable superclass offers its friendship to its subclasses. This is not often the case, though, because a superclass usually does not know its subclasses. However, a superclass can offer its friendship to an interface as well, which can then be implemented by its subclasses (see Section 6.3.3). As always, when offering friendship, you should proceed very carefully in this case as well, for example, by restricting the usage of the friendly interface to the current package.

6.3 Standalone Interfaces

In ABAP Objects, interfaces of classes can be defined independently from a class as standalone interfaces.

6.3.1 Basic Principles

Point of contact
The only part of a class that is relevant to an external user is its public interface that is made up of the components of its public visibility section. All other components are irrelevant to the user. This aspect becomes clear particularly when using abstract methods in abstract classes (see Section 6.2.5). Basically, such classes are used to define nothing but interfaces that can only be used with objects of subclasses.

No multiple inheritance
Because ABAP Objects does not support multiple inheritance, the usage of abstract classes for defining interfaces is restricted to their subclasses. However, it is also desirable to be able to define generally valid interfaces that can equally be used in several classes.

Decoupling
Such generally valid interfaces can be provided via standalone interfaces. Standalone interfaces are independently definable interfaces without implementation that can be integrated and implemented in classes. Standalone interfaces are used to achieve a looser coupling between a class and a user, because they provide an additional access layer (protocol). Two scenarios are possible:

▶ A class entirely or partially provides its public interface to the user via one or several standalone interfaces and thus decouples the user from the actual class definition. Every standalone interface describes an independent aspect of the class and only provides this aspect and nothing else to a user. This can positively affect the maintainability of a class.

▶ A user has an exact idea of how an object should be used and defines an standalone interface containing all wanted components. Every class that is to fulfill this task integrates this interface and provides the functionality.

BAdI
A very nice application example of this decoupling is given by the enhancebility of delivered ABAP application programs in customer systems using Business Add-Ins (BAdIs). BAdIs are based on standalone interfaces that are declared in the original system. The actual functionality of a BAdI is provided only in follow-up systems by implementing the standalone interface in classes.[14]

---

14 The comprehensive topic of enhancing and modifying ABAP applications of AS ABAP will not yet be discussed in this edition.

Because standalone interfaces are just interfaces without implementation, you cannot create any objects from them—similar to abstract classes. Instead, they are integrated and implemented in classes. If a class implements a standalone interface, it can be addressed via this interface. There are specific interface reference variables for this purpose. These can point to objects of all classes that contain the respective standalone interface. Because any classes can integrate the same interface, their objects can be addressed via the same interface reference variable.

Interface reference variables

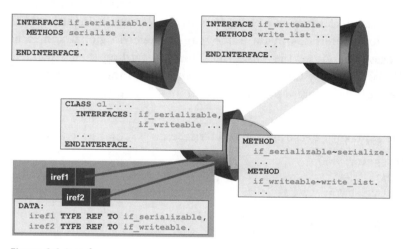

Figure 6.6 Interfaces

Figure 6.6 illustrates the role of interfaces in a graphical way. In our representation of objects with a core that is separated from the external user by a shell, standalone interfaces can be imagined as empty shells that can be used by classes instead of their own shells or as parts of their own shells.[15] For example, if a class wants to provide services like outputting its attributes in a list or serialization, it can implement the corresponding standalone interfaces. Users who are only interested in these different aspects of objects access these via interface reference variables. In the following sections, we will discuss the language elements shown in Figure 6.6 in detail.

---

15 Compared to Figure 6.1, you can clearly see that the integration of standalone interfaces in classes can also be regarded as a multiple inheritance of interfaces to classes. Because standalone interfaces don't have their own method implementations, there are no conceptual problems like those that occur in multiple inheritance of classes.

6.3.2 Creating Interfaces

With regard to their declaration, interfaces in ABAP Objects play the same role as classes. Just like classes, interfaces are object types that reside in the namespace of all types. While a class describes all aspects of a class, an interface only describes a partial aspect. As mentioned above, standalone interfaces can be regarded as special abstract classes without implementation that can be used in multiple classes.

Accordingly, the declaration of a standalone interface hardly varies from the declaration of a class. As with classes, we distinguish global and local interfaces in the same way that we do global and local classes. Therefore, the same rules apply regarding their usability. Global interfaces can be used in any program if the package assignment of the program permits it. Local interfaces can only be used in the same program.

INTERFACE—
ENDINTERFACE

The syntax for declaring a local interface is:

```
INTERFACE intf.
    DATA ...
    CLASS-DATA ...
    METHODS ...
    CLASS-METHODS ...
    ...
ENDINTERFACE.
```

Basically, the declaration of an interface corresponds to the declaration part of a class, where instead of CLASS—ENDCLASS, you simply use INTERFACE—ENDINTERFACE. Interfaces can contain exactly the same components as classes. Unlike classes, however, interfaces don't need to be divided into different visibility sections because interface components are always integrated in the public visibility section of classes.

To create a global interface, use the Class Builder just as you would for global classes. In the Object Navigator, select **Create • Class Library • Interface**. In Transaction SE24, after selecting **Create**, select the **Interface** object type instead of **Class**.[16]

---

16 If you observe the naming convention IF_... bzw. ZIF_..., an interface is created automatically.

Figure 6.7 shows the Class Builder for a global interface ZIF_DRIVE_ **Class Builder**
OBJECT. You see the familiar user interface that you know from
working with classes. When creating components, you need to specify the same input as you do for classes, except for the assignment to
a visibility section. In the shown example, we created the same
methods ACCELERATE and SHOW_SPEED as in ZCL_VEHICLE presented in Figure 4.7 in Chapter 4. The shown interface can therefore
serve as an interface to objects that can be driven.

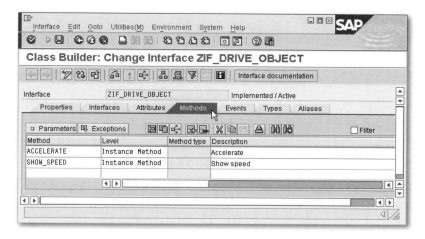

Figure 6.7 Global Interface

The Class Builder generates the corresponding ABAP statements in a
program of the interface pool type, the source code of which can also
be edited directly via **Goto • Interface Section** (see Figure 6.8). As in
class pools, the addition PUBLIC identifies the interface as a global
interface that can be used in all programs. Apart from the declaration
of the global interface, an interface pool cannot contain any local
type declarations except for the publication of type groups.[17]

The essential difference between interfaces and classes is that there is **Abstraction**
no implementation part for an interface. Therefore, it is not necessary to add DEFINITION to INTERFACE. The methods of an interface are
all abstract. They are fully declared, including their parameter interface, but not implemented in the interface. Like the subclasses that

---

17 In interface pools, declarations like these would not be of any use. They are possible in class pools, but can only be used in the private section of the global class.
This section does not exist for interfaces.

implement the abstract methods of their abstract superclasses, all classes that want to use an interface must implement its methods.[18]

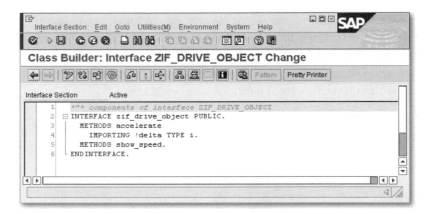

Figure 6.8 Source Code of an Interface Pool

6.3.3 Implementing Interfaces in Classes

Every class can implement one or more interfaces. The essential requirement for implementing an interface is that the interface is known to the implementing class. Therefore, it must be declared globally in the class library or locally in the same program. Additionally, the usage of the interface must be permitted by the package assignment.

INTERFACES The syntax for implementing interfaces is:

```
CLASS class DEFINITION.
  PUBLIC SECTION.
    INTERFACES: intf1, intf2 ...
    ...
  ...
ENDCLASS.
```

Interfaces are therefore integrated using the INTERFACES statement in the public visibility section of a class. Only global interfaces can be integrated in the public visibility section of a global class. You can do this on the **Interfaces** tab of Class Builder.

---

18 Strictly speaking, however, this similarity applies only to instance methods. In interfaces, you can also define static methods without implementation. This is not possible in abstract classes because static methods cannot be redefined.

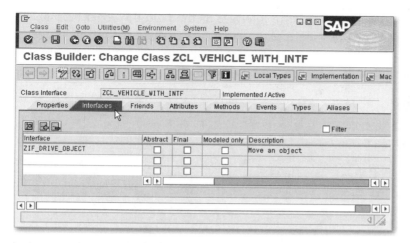

Figure 6.9 Integrating the Interface

In Figure 6.9, we copied the ZCL_VEHICLE class shown in Figure 4.7 to a new class ZCL_VEHICLE_WITH_INTF, deleted its method, and specified the interface ZIF_DRIVE_OBJECT shown in Figure 6.7. In the **Abstract** and **Final** columns, you can specify that all methods of the interface should be either abstract or final in the class. In the INTERFACES statement, this is expressed by the optional addition ALL METHODS ABSTRACT|FINAL.

Implementing an interface extends the public interface of the class by the interface components. Every comp component of an implemented intf interface becomes a full component of the class and is identified within the class via the name

intf~comp

```
... intf~comp ...
```

Interface components are inherited to subclasses like class-specific public components. A class can have its own component of the same name like an interface component, or various implemented interfaces can contain components of the same name. All reside in one namespace and are distinguished in the class by different intf~ prefixes. The tilde sign (~) is the interface component selector.

Figure 6.10 shows how the methods of the interface ZIF_DRIVE_OBJECT are presented in ZCL_VEHICLE_WITH_INTF. In the detailed view (see Figure 6.5), you can specify for every single method if it is to be abstract or final. The INTERFACES statement has the optional additions for this purpose, ABSTRACT METHODS and FINAL METHODS.

Otherwise, however, an interface method can no longer be changed in a class. The same applies to interface attributes. The only property that can be changed when integrating it in a class is the initial value (addition DATA VALUES to INTERFACES).

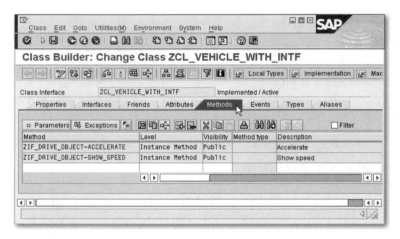

Figure 6.10 Interface Methods

A class must implement all concrete (non-abstract) methods of all integrated interfaces in its implementation part. In the Class Builder, this is achieved via the usual procedure, by selecting **Code** for every interface method. In the ZCL_VEHICLE_WITH_INTF class, we basically used the method implementations of ZCL_VEHICLE (see Listing 6.10).

Listing 6.10 Implementation of Interface Methods

```
CLASS zcl_vehicle_with_intf IMPLEMENTATION.
  METHOD zif_drive_object~accelerate.
    speed = speed + delta.
  ENDMETHOD.
  METHOD zif_drive_object~show_speed.
    DATA output TYPE string.
    output = speed.
    CONCATENATE `Vehicle speed: ` output INTO output.
    MESSAGE output TYPE 'I'.
  ENDMETHOD.
ENDCLASS.
```

If a class does not declare its own components in its public visibility section, but only integrates standalone interfaces, the entire public interface of the class is defined via standalone interfaces; and standalone interfaces and its public interface are indeed the same for this class. This applies to our sample class ZCL_VEHICLE_WITH_INTF. The interface to the outside world that had so far been built of the class's own components is now completely outsourced to the ZIF_DRIVE_OBJECT interface.

Listing 6.11 summarizes what we have just described using the example of a local interface. The public interface of the vehicle class from Listing 4.5 is outsourced to a local standalone interface; however, the local vehicle class could just as easily implement the global interface ZIF_DRIVE_OBJECT instead of a local interface drive_object.

Listing 6.11 Declaration and Implementation of a Local Interface

```
REPORT z_vehicle_with_intf.

INTERFACE drive_object.
  METHODS: accelerate IMPORTING delta TYPE i,
           show_speed.
ENDINTERFACE.
CLASS vehicle DEFINITION.
  PUBLIC SECTION.
    INTERFACES drive_object.
  PRIVATE SECTION.
    DATA speed TYPE i.
ENDCLASS.
CLASS vehicle IMPLEMENTATION.
  METHOD drive_object~accelerate.
    speed = speed + delta.
  ENDMETHOD.
  METHOD drive_object~show_speed.
    DATA output TYPE string.
    CONCATENATE `Vehicle speed: ` output INTO output.
    output = speed.
    MESSAGE output TYPE 'I'.
  ENDMETHOD.
ENDCLASS.
```

6.3.4 Access to Interfaces of Objects

Objects are always accessed via object reference variables. Until now, we worked with object reference variables that were declared with a reference to a class:

Class reference
variable

```
DATA cref TYPE REF TO class.
```

By using these reference variables, you can address all those compo-nents of an object's `class` class that are visible at the current posi-tion. This kind of object reference variable is therefore referred to as a class *reference variable*.

As you saw in the previous section, the interface components of an interface implemented in a class are handled as full components. You might therefore be tempted to address the interface components of an object as follows:

```
... cref->intf~comp ...
```

In point of fact, this works. You can try this with our ZCL_VEHICLE_WITH_INTF class; however, this kind of access is not recommended. The external user of a class should be able to access its components without having to worry about the technical composition of the interface. Standalone interfaces and the class-specific components both define different sets of components. They should be used directly, but not in mixed forms as shown above. In short, the inter-face component selector should only be used within classes (and interfaces, see Section 6.3.6).

To access the interface components of objects, ABAP Objects includes interface reference variables. These are object reference var-iables that are declared with a reference to an interface:

Interface reference
variables

```
DATA ref TYPE REF TO intf.
```

An interface reference variable can point to the objects of all classes implementing the `intf` interface. Using such a reference variable, all components of the interface of an object can be addressed directly via

```
... iref->comp ...
```

In contrast to `cref->intf~comp`, the interface reference variable `iref->comp` expresses that components of a class are accessed that are hierarchically on the same level but reside in a different part of the interface. An interface reference variable enables you to address those components of an object that were added to the object's class via the implementation of the `intf` interface that was used to declare the class. Other components—class-specific components or compo-nents of other interfaces—cannot be addressed via an interface refer-ence variable (not even dynamically, see Sections 11.1.1 and 11.4.1).

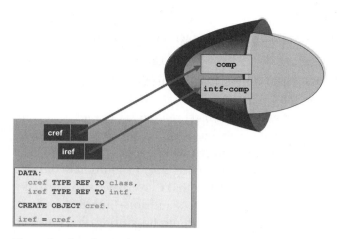

Figure 6.11 Interface Reference Variables

Figure 6.11 shows how class and interface reference variables point to the same object, where the interface reference variable only knows its own interface components, and the class reference variable should only be used to address the non-interface components of the class.

The code in Figure 6.11 already shows how interface reference variables can point to objects. You can simply assign a class reference variable pointing to an object to an interface reference variable. Usually, this is an up cast (see Section 6.4.2 for more information). **Up Cast**

This can be accomplished even more comfortably if you're only interested in the interface components of a class. For example, you are naturally only interested in the interface components of a class if the entire public interface of a class is defined via an standalone interface. In these situations, creating the objects of the class via an interface reference variable will suffice:

```
CREATE OBJECT iref TYPE class EXPORTING ...
```
CREATE OBJECT

Via the TYPE addition, you specify the class of the object to be created and provide the instance constructor with EXPORTING, if necessary. However, you don't need a class reference variable to create the object. The only prerequisite is that the class class (or one of its superclasses) contain the intf interface.

A user of object reference variables usually works with objects without having to deal with the details of their implementation. In con- **User view** trast to the work with class reference variables, a user of an interface reference variable normally doesn't even need to know from which class the object it is working with originates.

The example shown in Listing 6.12 demonstrates the usage of interface reference variables. The methods `main` and `output` of the `demo` class exclusively work with such object reference variables that were all created with a reference to our sample interface ZIF_DRIVE_OBJECT. For this purpose, an internal table type is declared in `demo` the line type of which is such a reference type. In addition to our global sample class CL_VEHICLE_WITH_INTF, we have also created a local class `electron` that contains the standalone interface as well, but specifically implements the methods by storing the speed in units of the speed of light (c=300.000).

From each of the two classes, an object is created and accelerated, and the object reference is appended to an internal table. Then this table is transferred to the `output` method where the `show_speed` interface method is executed line by line.

Listing 6.12 Standalone Interface Reference Variables

```
REPORT z_drive_many_objects.

CLASS demo DEFINITION.
  PUBLIC SECTION.
    CLASS-METHODS main.
  PRIVATE SECTION.
    TYPES iref_tab_type TYPE TABLE OF
                             REF TO zif_drive_object.
    CLASS-METHODS output IMPORTING iref_tab
                         TYPE iref_tab_type.
ENDCLASS.

CLASS electron DEFINITION.
  PUBLIC SECTION.
    INTERFACES zif_drive_object.
  PRIVATE SECTION.
    CONSTANTS c TYPE i VALUE 300000.
    DATA speed_over_c TYPE p DECIMALS 3.
ENDCLASS.

CLASS electron IMPLEMENTATION.
  METHOD zif_drive_object~accelerate.
    me->speed_over_c = me->speed_over_c + delta / c.
  ENDMETHOD.
  METHOD zif_drive_object~show_speed.
```

```abap
      DATA output TYPE string.
      output = me->speed_over_c.
      CONCATENATE `Electron speed/c: ` output INTO output.
      MESSAGE output TYPE 'I'.
    ENDMETHOD.
ENDCLASS.
CLASS demo IMPLEMENTATION.
  METHOD main.
    DATA: iref_tab TYPE iref_tab_type,
          iref     LIKE LINE OF iref_tab.
    CREATE OBJECT iref TYPE zcl_vehicle_with_intf.
    iref->accelerate( 100 ).
    APPEND iref TO iref_tab.
    CREATE OBJECT iref TYPE electron.
    iref->accelerate( 250000 ).
    APPEND iref TO iref_tab.
    demo=>output( iref_tab ).
  ENDMETHOD.
  METHOD output.
    DATA iref LIKE LINE OF iref_tab.
    LOOP AT iref_tab INTO iref.
      iref->show_speed( ).
    ENDLOOP.
  ENDMETHOD.
ENDCLASS.
START-OF-SELECTION.
  demo=>main( ).
```

Although the example is similar to the one shown in Listing 4.8, it has a completely new quality. As before, the internal table is a collection of pointers to objects. Because these pointers are interface reference objects, however, the classes and thus the behavior of the objects managed by an internal table can vary.

You should pay special attention to the output method. This method is an example of the user mentioned above who works with objects without knowing their classes. The output method receives a table with reference variables and knows that it can call a show_speed method there. The actual implementation is irrelevant to it. This matches the concept of polymorphism that is illustrated in Figure 6.14 exactly and will be further discussed in the corresponding section. For the moment, it will suffice just to note that syntactically identical method calls in a loop lead to different output.

6.3.5 Access to Static Interface Components

Because interfaces can contain the same components as classes, static components are possible as well. You cannot access the static components of an interface using the name of the interface and the class component selector. The only exceptions are constants declared via CONSTANTS:

```
... intf=>const ...
```

The static components belong to the static components of every implementing class. This means that static attributes have different values depending on the class and that static methods can be differently implemented in every class. To access the static components of interfaces, independently of the instance, you would have to use the name of an implementing class and the interface component selector:

```
... class=>intf~comp ...
```

Alias names However, this should be the exception for the reasons mentioned in Section 6.3.4. Instead, implementing classes should declare aliases (see Section 6.3.7) for the static components of interfaces and therefore make them addressable via the class name like their own static components. Naturally, you can always use interface reference variables for accessing static components after you created objects from the implementing classes.

6.3.6 Composing Interfaces

In Figure 6.9, it is apparent that the Class Builder provides the **Interfaces** tab as well for an interface as it does for a class. Accordingly, the INTERFACES statement cannot only be used in classes but also in the declaration of an interface:

```
INTERFACE intf1.
  INTERFACES: intf2, intf3, ...
  ...
ENDINTERFACE.
```

Component interface This mechanism allows you to compose several interfaces into one interface. The composition of interfaces can be useful when modeling complex applications.

The set of components of an interface `intf1` that integrates additional interfaces (i. e., `intf2`, `intf3`, ...) are composed of its own components and the components of the integrated interfaces. The components all reside on the same level. An interface containing at least one other interface is called composite or nested interface. An interface integrated in another interface is called a component interface. A component interface can be composed itself. Let's now look at the nesting of interfaces shown in Listing 6.13.

Listing 6.13 Composite Interfaces

```
INTERFACE intf1.
   ...
ENDINTERFACE.

INTERFACE intf2.
   INTERFACES: intf1 ...
   ...
ENDINTERFACE.

INTERFACE intf3.
   INTERFACES: intf1, intf2 ...
   ...
ENDINTERFACE.
```

The composite interface `intf3` has a component `intf2` that is composed itself. Although it seems like the nesting of several interfaces caused a component hierarchy, this is not the case. All component interfaces of a composite interface are on the same level. A nesting of names like `intf3~intf2~intf1` is not possible.

In the example above, the component interface `intf1` of the composite interface `intf2` becomes a component interface of `intf3`. A composite interface contains each component interface exactly once. Although `intf1` is integrated in `intf3` both directly as a component interface of `intf3` and indirectly via `intf2`, it only occurs once. In `intf3`, it can only be addressed under the name `intf1`, even if it was not integrated directly.

If a composite interface is implemented in a class, all interface components of the interface behave as if their interface had been implemented only once. The interface components of the individual component interfaces extend the public interface of the class by its original name. Because every interface is included exactly once in a composite interface, naming conflicts cannot occur. The way an

Implementation

implemented interface is composed is irrelevant when it is implemented in a class. Next, let's look at the example shown in Listing 6.14:

Listing 6.14 Implementation of Composite Interfaces

```
INTERFACE intf1.
  METHODS meth.
ENDINTERFACE.

INTERFACE intf2.
  INTERFACES intf1.
  METHODS meth.
ENDINTERFACE.

INTERFACE intf3.
  INTERFACES intf1.
  METHODS meth.
ENDINTERFACE.

INTERFACE intf4.
  INTERFACES: intf2, intf3.
ENDINTERFACE.

CLASS class DEFINITION.
  PUBLIC SECTION.
    INTERFACES intf4.
ENDCLASS.

CLASS class IMPLEMENTATION.
  METHOD intf1~meth. ... ENDMETHOD.
  METHOD intf2~meth. ... ENDMETHOD.
  METHOD intf3~meth. ... ENDMETHOD.
ENDCLASS.
```

A method meth of the same name is declared in three individual interfaces and thus implemented in three different ways using the interface component selector. The composition of the interfaces does not play any role. The intf1~meth method is implemented only once, although it occurs in two interfaces, intf2 and intf3. The name intf4 does not show up in the implementation part of the class at all.

If you list one or more of the other interfaces—intf1, intf2, or intf3—in addition to intf4 in the declaration part of the class mentioned above, the components and the implementation part of the class do not change at all, because the compiler always ensures for a class as well as in composite interfaces that every component exists only once.

If the class of an object implements a composite interface, the object is accessed in the same way as if the class implemented every interface individually. This means that interface components should be accessed using interface reference variables of the type of the appropriate component interface. This can always be achieved using the corresponding assignments to interface reference variables (up casts, see Section 6.4.2). The interface component selector should not be used for this purpose; however, it can be used in a composite interface to make the components of component interfaces as accessible as native components via aliasing.

Access

6.3.7 Alias Names for Interface Components

The complete name of a component that is added via an interface to a class or another interface is `intf~comp`. For this name, you can define an alias name at the level at which the interface is integrated using the `INTERFACES` statement:

`ALIASES` name `FOR` intf~comp.

ALIASES

Alias names can be assigned when interfaces are implemented in the declaration part of a class or when interfaces are composed in the declaration of an interface. In the Class Builder, you can enter alias names for classes and for interfaces in the **Aliases** tab (see Figure 6.12).

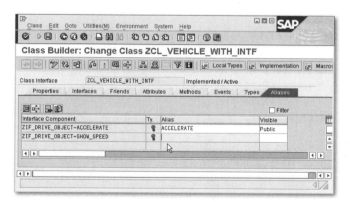

Figure 6.12 Alias Names

Alias Names in Classes

In classes, alias names belong to the namespace of the components of a class and must be assigned to a visibility section just like the other components. The visibility of an alias name from outside the class depends on its visibility section and not on the visibility section of the assigned interface component.

In Listing 6.15, we modify the example of Listing 6.12 by using alias names. For this purpose, in the local class electron, we declare an alias name accelerate for the zif_drive_object~accelerate interface method as we did for ZCL_VEHICLE_WITH_INTF (see Figure 6.12). Listing 6.15 shows only the differences between it and Listing 6.12.

Listing 6.15 Alias Names in Classes

```
REPORT z_drive_via_aliases.

...

CLASS electron DEFINITION.
  PUBLIC SECTION.
    INTERFACES zif_drive_object.
    ALIASES accelerate FOR zif_drive_object~accelerate.
  PRIVATE SECTION.
    ...
ENDCLASS.
CLASS electron IMPLEMENTATION.
  METHOD accelerate.
    me->speed_over_c = me->speed_over_c + delta / c.
  ENDMETHOD.
  ...
ENDCLASS.
CLASS demo IMPLEMENTATION.
  METHOD main.
    DATA: vehicle  TYPE REF TO zcl_vehicle_with_intf,
          electron TYPE REF TO electron,
          iref_tab TYPE iref_tab_type.
    CREATE OBJECT vehicle.
    vehicle->accelerate( 100 ).
    APPEND vehicle TO iref_tab.
    CREATE OBJECT electron.
    electron->accelerate( 250000 ).
    APPEND electron TO iref_tab.
    demo=>output( iref_tab ).
  ENDMETHOD.
  ...
ENDCLASS.
START-OF-SELECTION.
  demo=>main( ).
```

The interface method can now be implemented in the class via its alias name and called by a user like a direct method of the class. Here, we change the `main` method in which the classes for the object creation must be known, anyway so that the objects are created via class reference variables. Because of the alias name, the class reference variables can be used to call the interface method `accelerate` without using the interface component selector. Nothing is changed in the `output` method, which does not need to know the classes.

Using alias names, a class can publish its interface components as class-specific components, so to speak. In particular, alias names can be used in classes to further on address class-specific components that are outsourced to standalone interfaces in the course of a development cycle using their old name. Then, the users of the class don't need to be adapted to the new names.

In our sample class ZCL_VEHICLE_WITH_INTF, we converted the methods from ZCL_VEHICLE to interface methods. Just imagine if we had made this change directly in ZCL_VEHICLE! All users would have become syntactically incorrect. By introducing alias names simultaneously, however, the class would have remained addressable.

Alias Names in Composite Interfaces

Because names cannot be concatenated in composite interfaces, alias names provide the only means of addressing those components that would otherwise not be available in the composite interface. Let's look at the example shown in Listing 6.16.

Listing 6.16 Alias Names in Interfaces

```
INTERFACE intf1.
  METHODS meth1.
ENDINTERFACE.

INTERFACE intf2.
  INTERFACES intf1.
  ALIASES meth1 FOR intf1~meth1.
ENDINTERFACE.
INTERFACE intf3.
  INTERFACES intf2.
  ALIASES meth1 FOR intf2~meth1.
ENDINTERFACE.
```

The intf3 interface can use the alias name meth1 in intf2 to address the meth1 component of the intf1 interface in its own ALIASES statement. Without alias names in intf2, this would not be possible because the name intf2~intf1~m1 is not permitted. Now the user of intf3 can access the component meth1 in intf1 without having to know anything about the composition of the interface:

```
DATA i_ref TYPE REF TO intf3.
...
i_ref->meth1( ... ).
```

Without alias names in intf3, the access would look as follows:

```
i_ref->intf1~meth1( ... ).
```

The user would have to know that intf3 is composed of intf2, which is composed of intf1. For global interfaces, in particular, the user should not have to look at the composition of an interface in the Class Builder before he can use a method of the interface. Of course, it is not necessary that the alias names always match the original names.

6.3.8 Interfaces and Inheritance

To conclude the description of interfaces, we will discuss the relationship of standalone interfaces to inheritance and compare both concepts in a summary.

The concepts of standalone interfaces and inheritance are independent of each other and totally compatible. Any number of interfaces can be implemented in the classes of an inheritance tree, but every interface can be implemented only once per inheritance tree path. Thus, every interface component has a unique name intf~comp throughout the inheritance tree and is contained in all subclasses of the class implementing the interface. After their implementation, interface methods are full components of a class and can be redefined in subclasses. Although interface methods cannot be identified as abstract or final in the interface declaration, every class can specify these settings when implementing the interface.

Coupling   The usage of inheritance always makes sense when different classes have a generalization/specialization relationship. For example, if we regard two classes "cargo plane" and "passenger plane", both classes contain components that can be declared in a common "plane" superclass. The big advantage of inheritance is that the subclasses take on and reuse all properties already programmed in the superclass. At the same time, this causes a very tight coupling between superclasses and subclasses. A subclass strongly depends on its superclass, because it often largely consists of the superclass components. A subclass must know its superclass exactly. This became particularly clear, for example, in the discussion of instance constructors in inheritance (see Section 6.2.8). Every change to non-private components of a superclass changes all of its subclasses. Conversely, subclasses can also affect the design of superclasses due to specific requests. If you use inheritance for defining classes, you should ideally have access to all classes involved because only all of the classes in a path of the inheritance tree make a reasonable whole. On the other hand, it is dangerous to just link to some superclass by defining a subclass if the superclass does not belong to the same package, or was explicitly shared as a superclass in the package interface.[19]

The implementation of interfaces is always recommended when interfaces or protocols are to be described without having to use a specific type of implementation. An additional layer is introduced between user and class that decouples the user from an explicit class and therefore makes it much more independent. Interfaces allow the user to handle the most different classes, which don't need to be related to each other. In object-oriented modeling, interfaces provide an abstraction that is independent of classes. Irrespective of the actual implementation, the services required by a user can be described. Additionally, interfaces also implement an aspect of multiple inheritance, because several interfaces can be implemented in a class. If a programming language permits a real multiple inheritance, this multiple inheritance is usually used in the sense of interfaces as well. This means that only abstract classes with exclusively abstract methods are suitable as different superclasses of a single subclass. Otherwise, the question would arise regarding which method implementation is actually used in a subclass if it is already implemented

Decoupling

---

19 A complete package concept that allows you to predefine and check such specifications in the package interface will only be implemented in the next SAP NetWeaver release.

in several superclasses.[20] As with superclasses in inheritance, you should note that for interfaces as well later changes to an interface might make all classes implementing the interface syntactically incorrect.

6.4   Object References and Polymorphism

Object references are the linchpin when dealing with objects. They are used for creating and addressing objects. As the contents of object reference variables, they can be assigned to other variables or passed to procedures.

Object reference variables are divided into class reference variables and interface reference variables. When using interface reference variables, we already observed that the type of a reference variable does not have to match the type of the referenced object. In this section, we will have a closer look at this fact and at the resulting polymorphic behavior of method calls.

6.4.1   Static and Dynamic Type

In this section, we define two important terms for reference variables, that is, their static *type* and dynamic type.

Static type | The static type of a reference variable `oref` is the type that is specified after

```
... oref TYPE REF TO class|intf ...
```

in the declaration. As with all data objects, the static type is fixed during the entire runtime of a program. For object reference variables, the object types `class` for class reference variables and `intf` for interface reference variables are possible as static types.[21]

---

20 This is the "diamond" problem of multiple inheritance. A method that is declared in a superclass is redefined in two subclasses, which, in turn, make up the superclass of another subclass. Which implementation is used in this subclass? For interfaces, this problem does not occur, because in the implementation of composite interfaces every interface method exists only once.

21 Accordingly, data types are possible as static types for data reference variables that can point to data objects (see Section 11.1.2).

The dynamic type of a reference variable is the class of the object to which the reference variable is currently pointing. The dynamic type is not fixed during runtime. A reference variable `oref` usually receives its dynamic type via assignments, parameter transfers, or via

```
CREATE OBJECT oref TYPE class.
```

Figure 6.13 illustrates the relationship of the static type and the dynamic type.

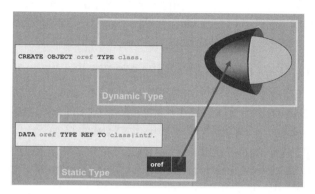

Figure 6.13 Static Type and Dynamic Type

The static type and the dynamic type don't need to be the same. The sameness of static and dynamic type as it exists, for example, after the statement

```
CREATE OBJECT oref.
```

is actually a special case. The dynamic type determines the actual behavior of an object. The static type, on the other hand, determines the user view of an object. A client that is, an ABAP program or a procedure, works with object reference variables and usually only knows their static type.[22] Via an object reference variable, those components of an object can be accessed using the object component selector (->) that are declared in the static type (class, interface) and visible to the user.[23] The static type thus determines the dynamic

---

22 You can check the dynamic type of a reference variable in the ABAP Debugger at any time by looking at its value. There the name of the class of the current object is displayed. In the program, the methods of the RTTI (see Section 11.2.1) can be used to determine the dynamic type of a reference variable.

23 Strictly speaking, this only applies to the static access. For information about the dynamic access, see Sections 11.1.1 and 11.4.1.

type in that all components of the static type must exist in the dynamic type. This is ensured by the "golden rule of reference variables":

Golden rule *The static type is always more general or equal to the dynamic type.*

The syntax check and the ABAP runtime environment ensure that this rule is never broken. The static type can never be more specific than the dynamic type. This means that all components that can be addressed via a reference variable definitely exist in the referenced object. Therefore, a user does not necessarily need to know the actual dynamic type of the object with which it is working.

The actual meaning of the golden rule for the two possible types of reference variables in ABAP Objects is:

▶ For a class reference variable, the static type is a class. The dynamic type can be the same class or one of its subclasses.

▶ With an interface reference variable, the static type is an interface. The dynamic type can be any class implementing the interface, particularly even a subclass of such a class.

Different static and dynamic types are therefore possible not only for interface reference variables (see Section 6.3.4), but also for class reference variables because superclass reference variables can point to subclass objects. For an interface reference variable, the static type is always different from the dynamic type and thus always more general than the latter.

Interface inheritance Because every subclass inherits all components of its superclasses in the same visibility section, public and protected interfaces of a subclass are always also composed of the public or protected interfaces of their superclasses. Alternatively, from the point of view of the superclass, its public and protected interface remains unchanged in every one of its subclasses, regardless of how deep you go in the inheritance tree. Therefore, every user that can access objects of superclasses can access the objects of their subclasses in the same way. The corresponding part of the interface is completely identical. The inheritance of constant interfaces again illustrates the similarity between superclasses and standalone interfaces.

The position of the static type in the inheritance tree defines the view of the user on an object in the sense that the set of statically addressable components of an object is more restricted the closer to the node the static type resides. Reference variables of the static type of the `object` root class can point to the objects of all classes in ABAP Objects, but don't know any components.

An interface reference variable can point to the objects of all classes implementing the corresponding interface. It is immaterial if the interface is implemented directly or as a component interface of a composite interface. Additionally, it doesn't matter if the interface is implemented in the class itself or in one of its superclasses. In all of these cases, it is ensured that the interface components are available in the public interface of the referenced object.

6.4.2 Assignments Between Reference Variables

After an assignment between reference variables, both reference variables point to the same object. The target variable takes on the dynamic type of the source variable. The golden rule thus restricts the assignability of reference variables in that the static type of the target variable must be the same or more general than the dynamic type of the source variable. Two cases can be distinguished:

- ▶ The golden rule can be verified statically during the syntax check.
- ▶ The golden rule can only be checked dynamically, that is, at runtime.

The compliance with the golden rule is statically ensured if the static type of the target variable is more general or equal to the static type of the source variable, because the dynamic type of the source variable can never be more general than its static type. Because only static types play a role in this context, the validity of such an assignment can already be verified in the syntax check. The following applies to the possible combinations:

Static checking

- ▶ For assignments between two class reference variables, the class of the target variable must be the same class or a superclass of the source variable.
- ▶ For assignments between two interface reference variables, the interface of the target variable must be the same interface or component interface of the source variable.

405

▶ For assignments of class reference variables to interface reference variables, the class of the source variable or one of its superclasses must implement the interface of the target variable.

▶ For assignments of interface reference variables to class reference variables, the only class possible for the target variable is the `object` root class.

Up Cast This kind of assignment is referred to as up cast, because you only assign more specific reference variables to equal or more general ones and thus can only move upwards in the inheritance tree. An alternative expression is widening cast, because the target variable can take on more dynamic types in comparison to the source variable.

Like an assignment between non-reference variables, an up cast assignment can be performed using the equal sign (=) or the `MOVE ...` `TO` statement. A passing of reference variables to formal parameters of procedures and the class specification after `TYPE` in `CREATE OBJECT` are only possible in the case of an up cast. In code lines, this looks as follows:

Inheritance
```
DATA: o_super TYPE REF TO superclass,
      o_sub   TYPE REF TO subclass.
...
CREATE OBJECT o_sub.
o_super = o_sub.
```

If `subclass` is a subclass of `superclass`, the reference to the object of the subclass in `o_sub` can be assigned to the `o_super` reference variable. You can even spare the intermediate assignment step. Using the `TYPE` addition of the `CREATE OBJECT` statement known from Section 6.3.4, it is even easier:

```
DATA o_super TYPE REF TO superclass.
...
CREATE OBJECT o_super TYPE subclass.
```

This statement creates an object of the `subclass` class to which the `o_super` reference variable is pointing.[24] You therefore can create

---

24 If the `superclass` class is abstract and does not contain any of its own implementations, the class reference variable `o_super` plays almost the same role as an interface reference variable, with the exception that only objects of its own subclasses can be referenced (no multiple inheritance).

objects of all subclasses of a superclass superclass without having to create reference variables for the subclasses.

If o_super is a reference variable of the static type of the object root class, it can be assigned references to all kinds of objects. These reference variables can serve as general containers for objects, but do not permit a static access to their components. The dynamic access is shown as "Dynamic Access" and "Dynamic Invoke" in Chapter 11.

The up cast for interface reference variables was already discussed in Section 6.3.4. The assignment of a class reference variable to an interface reference variable or the usage of an interface reference variable in CREATE OBJECT is the prerequisite for accessing an object via an interface reference variable. Also for the composite interfaces discussed in Section 6.3.6, the up cast—here the assignment of specific to general interface reference variables—is the recommended way of accessing the components of a component interface via interface reference variables. Listing 6.17 shows a schematic example.

Interfaces

Listing 6.17 Up Cast for Interface References

```
REPORT z_interface_up_cast.

INTERFACE i1.
  METHODS meth.
ENDINTERFACE.
INTERFACE i2.
  INTERFACES i1.
  METHODS meth.
ENDINTERFACE.
CLASS c1 DEFINITION.
  PUBLIC SECTION.
    INTERFACES i2.
ENDCLASS.
CLASS demo DEFINITION.
  PUBLIC SECTION.
    CLASS-METHODS main.
ENDCLASS.
CLASS demo IMPLEMENTATION.
  METHOD main.
    DATA: iref1 TYPE REF TO i1,
          iref2 TYPE REF TO i2.
    CREATE OBJECT iref2 TYPE c1.
    iref1 = iref2.
```

```
      CALL METHOD iref1->meth.
      CALL METHOD iref2->meth.
   ENDMETHOD.
ENDCLASS.
CLASS c1 IMPLEMENTATION.
   METHOD i1~meth.
      MESSAGE 'Method of interface i1' TYPE 'I'.
   ENDMETHOD.
   METHOD i2~meth.
      MESSAGE 'Method of interface i2' TYPE 'I'.
   ENDMETHOD.
ENDCLASS.
START-OF-SELECTION.
   demo=>main( ).
```

An interface i2 that is composed of an interface i1 and its own method meth is implemented in a class c1. The class implements the methods of both interfaces. In the main method, we use the interface reference variable iref2 to create an object of the class c1 (up cast). The assignment of iref2 to iref1 is another up cast from i2 to i1. A reverse assignment would not be possible, because i1 is included in i2 and not vice versa. Via the interface reference variables, the methods of the respective interfaces are called.

Generic type

Assignments of interface reference variables to class reference variables are not possible because the dynamic type of the source variable can be any class implementing the interface, and it cannot be statically verified if the class of the target variable is indeed more general or equal. The only exception is the root class object that does not have any components. It therefore plays the same role for object references as the completely generic data type data does for data objects.

Dynamic checking

In most cases, the up cast is totally sufficient for most implementations, and it is common practice that the user accesses objects via the interface of a superclass or of an standalone interface. We will further investigate this when we discuss the polymorphism; however, there may be times when you want to change back from a less detailed view to a more detailed view. In such a case, the compliance with the golden rule is not statically granted. If the static type of the target variable is more specific than the static type of the source variable, the assignability can only be checked at runtime. This includes, for example, all assignments of superclass reference variables to sub-class reference variables, or of interface reference variables to class reference variables.[25]

This kind of assignment is called down cast because a more general reference variable is assigned to a more specific reference variable and you thus move downward in the inheritance tree. The alternative expression is narrowing cast, because the target variable can only adopt less dynamic types in comparison to the source variable.

Down cast

An assignment that falls into the down cast category cannot be performed using the equal sign (=) or the MOVE ... TO statement. For example, the syntax check issues an error message for the following assignment:

```
DATA: o_ref1 TYPE REF TO object.
      o_ref2 TYPE REF TO class.
...
o_ref2 = o_ref1.
```

At runtime, the reference variable o_ref1 can contain references to the objects of all classes, and it is not possible to statically verify if o_ref1 actually points to an object of the class class or one of its subclasses. This check can only be performed at runtime immediately before executing the assignment. To explicitly instruct ABAP to skip the static check, the casting operator

```
oref2 ?= oref1.
```

?=

or the equal statement

```
MOVE oref1 ?TO oref2.
```

?TO

can be used. The question mark explicitly shifts the checking of the golden rule from the syntax check to the program runtime. The following lines do not cause any syntax error:

```
DATA: o_ref1 TYPE REF TO object.
      o_ref2 TYPE REF TO class.
...
o_ref2 ?= o_ref1.
```

---

25 The only exception is the assignment of interface reference variables to class reference variables of the static type object, because this is always the most general type.

The assignment is only executed if the golden rule is then fulfilled for the target variable; otherwise, the exception CX_SY_MOVE_CAST_ERROR is caused, which can be handled in a TRY control structure. The object referenced by the source variable must therefore contain all components that can be used via the target variable. For parameter passing and object creations, a down cast is not possible.

Inheritance

Listing 6.18 shows an example of up cast and down cast in inheritance. The example is based on the method redefinition in Listing 6.5, and Listing 6.18 only shows the differences to Listing 6.5.

Listing 6.18 Down Cast in Inheritance

```
REPORT z_inheritance_down_cast.

CLASS vehicle DEFINITION DEFERRED.
CLASS demo DEFINITION.
  PUBLIC SECTION.
    CLASS-METHODS: main,
                   use_vehicle IMPORTING vref
                               TYPE REF TO vehicle.
ENDCLASS.

...

CLASS demo IMPLEMENTATION.
  METHOD main.
    DATA: vref1 TYPE REF TO vehicle,
          vref2 TYPE REF TO vehicle.
    CREATE OBJECT: vref1 TYPE car,
                   vref2 TYPE truck.
    demo=>use_vehicle( vref1 ).
    demo=>use_vehicle( vref2 ).
  ENDMETHOD.
  METHOD use_vehicle.
    DATA truck_ref TYPE REF TO truck.
    TRY.
        truck_ref ?= vref.
        truck_ref->load( `Beer` ).
      CATCH cx_sy_move_cast_error.
    ENDTRY.
    vref->accelerate( 130 ).
    vref->show_speed( ).
  ENDMETHOD.
ENDCLASS.
START-OF-SELECTION.
  demo=>main( ).
```

In contrast to Listing 6.5, the `main` method of the `demo` class in Listing 6.18 creates superclass reference variables of the type `vehicle` (up cast) and passes the handling of vehicles on to a method named `use_vehicle`. In `vref`, this method expects a reference of the static type `vehicle` and can thus handle all vehicle subclasses (up cast). However, to be able to access the specific properties of a subclass, here `truck`, the superclass reference must be assigned to the corresponding subclass reference (down cast). Only if the down cast is successful, the `load` subclass method is executed. The other methods are already declared in the superclass and can be called via `vref`. Depending on the passed object, the behavior of `accelerate` and `show_speed` is different (polymorphic, see Section 6.4.3).

Listing 6.19 shows an example of the down cast when using interfaces. The example is based on Listing 6.12, and Listing 6.19 only shows the differences to Listing 6.12.

Interfaces

Listing 6.19 Down Cast with Interfaces

```
REPORT z_interface_down_cast.

CLASS demo DEFINITION.
  ...
  PRIVATE SECTION.
    ...
    CLASS-METHODS: output   IMPORTING iref_tab
                            TYPE iref_tab_type,
                 serialize IMPORTING iref
                            TYPE REF TO
                              zif_drive_object.
ENDCLASS.
CLASS electron DEFINITION.
  PUBLIC SECTION.
    INTERFACES: zif_drive_object,
              if_serializable_object.
  PRIVATE SECTION.
    ...
ENDCLASS.
...
CLASS demo IMPLEMENTATION.
  ...
  METHOD output.
    DATA iref LIKE LINE OF iref_tab.
    LOOP AT iref_tab INTO iref.
```

```
      iref->show_speed( ).
      serialize( iref ).
  ENDLOOP.
ENDMETHOD.
METHOD serialize.
  DATA: sref TYPE REF TO if_serializable_object,
        xml_string TYPE xstring.
  TRY.
      sref ?= iref.
      CALL TRANSFORMATION id
                          SOURCE object = sref
                          RESULT XML xml_string.
  CATCH cx_sy_move_cast_error.
      RETURN.
  ENDTRY.
  CALL FUNCTION 'DISPLAY_XML_STRING'
      EXPORTING xml_string = xml_string.
  ENDMETHOD.
ENDCLASS.
START-OF-SELECTION.
  demo=>main( ).
```

Another global interface, IF_SERIALIZABLE_OBJECT, is integrated in the `electron` class. This interface is delivered by SAP. The attributes of objects containing the interface can be serialized to XML via an XSL transformation that is called using the `CALL TRANSFORMA-TION` statement (see Section 12.5.3). For this purpose, the `demo` class contains an additional `serialize` method that is called in the `output` method in every loop pass.

The `serialize` method is passed an interface reference variable of the static type ZIF_DRIVE_OBJECT. Before the serialization takes place, it is checked if the referenced object is serializable. This happens using the down cast, which, in our example, is successful for the `electron` object but not for the object of ZCL_VEHICLE_WITH_INTF. The result of the serialization is displayed in an HTML Browser Control by a function module existing in AS ABAP.[26]

---

26 Admittedly, the usage of the non-released function module is an example of how this should not be done. In the Function Builder (SE37), we simply entered "*display*xml*", pressed [F4], and selected a promising name from the hit list. Actually, we should have continued to look for a released module or copied the found module to our package. For our simple example, however, it's legitimate to use the non-released function module.

The two interfaces ZIF_DRIVE_OBJECT and IF_SERIALIZABLE_ OBJECT are completely independent of each other and can be integrated in any classes. The first interface enables the "driving" of objects; the second interface is for serializing them. A class like `elec-tron` can integrate both interfaces if it wants to provide both services. Using our down cast from `iref` to `sref`, we switch the user view to the object. Both reference variables point to the same object, but each address a different aspect.

Standalone interfaces

6.4.3 Polymorphism

With the static and dynamic types of object reference variables, as well as the golden rule and its influence on assignments introduced in the previous sections, we are now well prepared for Polymorphism (Greek for many shapes). Polymorphism is frequently regarded as one of the most important concepts of object orientation.

We know that general reference variables can point to specialized objects and that the user normally only knows the type of the reference variable. This is illustrated in Figure 6.14.

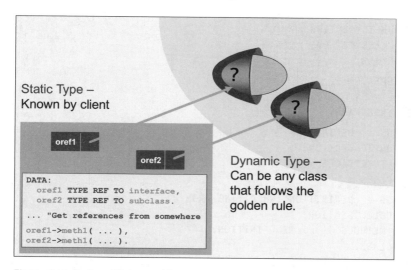

Figure 6.14 Basics of Polymorphism

The difference between static and dynamic type opens up a programming dimension that exists only in object orientation and that does not have any equivalent in procedural programming. Via reference variables, the user statically calls the methods of objects, the dynamic type of which determines the implementation of a method that is actually executed. It is always the most specific method implementation that is found and executed.

Polymorphism can be used for addressing differently implemented methods that belong to different objects of different classes via the same identifier and the same interface. Therefore, it is not the objects that behave in a polymorphic way, but the reference variables that can take on different dynamic types.

In inheritance, the behavior of a method defined in a superclass can vary in every subclass due to redefinition. When standalone interfaces are used, every interface method is specifically implemented in every implementing class. If standalone interfaces and inheritance are implemented at the same time, you can combine both kinds of polymorphism. Listing 6.20 summarizes the variants of polymorphism.

Listing 6.20 Polymorphism

```
REPORT z_polymorphism.

CLASS demo DEFINITION.
  PUBLIC SECTION.
    CLASS-METHODS main.
ENDCLASS.

INTERFACE i1.
  METHODS m1.
ENDINTERFACE.

CLASS c1 DEFINITION.
  PUBLIC SECTION.
    INTERFACES i1.
ENDCLASS.

CLASS c2 DEFINITION INHERITING FROM c1.
  PUBLIC SECTION.
    METHODS i1~m1 REDEFINITION.
ENDCLASS.

CLASS c3 DEFINITION.
  PUBLIC SECTION.
  INTERFACES i1.
ENDCLASS.

CLASS user DEFINITION.
  PUBLIC SECTION.
```

```
        CLASS-METHODS meth IMPORTING ref TYPE REF TO i1.
ENDCLASS.

CLASS c1 IMPLEMENTATION.
  METHOD i1~m1.
    MESSAGE 'I do this, ...' TYPE 'I'.
  ENDMETHOD.
ENDCLASS.

CLASS c2 IMPLEMENTATION.
  METHOD i1~m1.
    MESSAGE '... and I do that, ...' TYPE 'I'.
  ENDMETHOD.
ENDCLASS.

CLASS c3 IMPLEMENTATION.
  METHOD i1~m1.
    MESSAGE '... and I do nothing!' TYPE 'I'.
  ENDMETHOD.
ENDCLASS.

CLASS user IMPLEMENTATION.
  METHOD meth.
    ref->m1( ).
  ENDMETHOD.
ENDCLASS.

CLASS demo IMPLEMENTATION.
  METHOD main.
    DATA iref TYPE REF TO i1.
    CREATE OBJECT iref TYPE c1.
    user=>meth( iref ).
    CREATE OBJECT iref TYPE c2.
    user=>meth( iref ).
    CREATE OBJECT iref TYPE c3.
    user=>meth( iref ).
  ENDMETHOD.
ENDCLASS.

START-OF-SELECTION.
  demo=>main( ).
```

A `meth` method in a `user` class apparently always does the same thing, but produces three different results. There are two different implementations of the interface method `m1` as well as a redefinition of this method in a subclass.

Naturally the question arises regarding whether it makes sense to have different implementations of one and the same method.

Although the interface of a superclass method in inheritance or of an standalone interface method is stable, you are not restricted regarding the syntax when implementing the source code, that is, you can program the method in whichever way you like. Because a user normally knows only the static type of the reference variable but not the dynamic one, a method that shows a completely unpredictable behavior with every call is simply not usable. In that case, polymorphism would be more harmful than helpful.

Semantic rules   A user must be able to anticipate the behavior of a method that is documented in the method declaration in a superclass or an interface. In other words:

> *Subclasses must be usable via the interfaces taken on by the superclasses or standalone interfaces in a way that the user does not notice any difference.*[27]

Technically, a user must be able to use a static type independently of the dynamic type. This leads to strict semantic rules of how a redefined method or an interface method may be implemented in a class:

▶ The redefinition of a method in a subclass must obtain the semantics of the previous implementation. In this context, it is helpful to call it via the pseudo reference `super`. The redefinition may solely be used for specialization. The other inherited components (attributes and events) may only be used in the sense that was intended in the superclass.

▶ In its method implementations, every class implementing an standalone interface must follow exactly the semantics of the method as it is declared in the interface. Naturally, the details of the implementation vary from class to class. The result must always correspond to the interface documentation, though.

A class implementing methods must always fulfill its contract with a user, so to speak, the terms of which are imposed on it by the interface and the documentation of the method. The latter can originate from superclasses or interfaces, but are valid in every class. The interface of a class is a description (protocol layer) from which the user

---

27 In object orientation, this rule is known as the *Liskov Substitution Principle* (LSP), (according to Barbara Liskov: *Data Automation and Hierarchy*. SIGPLAN Notices 23; May 1988).

may expect a specific behavior. Every class implementing a method is obliged to do so in a way that fulfills the expectations.

Only the observance of these rules makes polymorphism a significant advantage of object orientation. Only then is it immaterial to the user with which class the user is actually working because it can rely entirely on the statically known interface. In inheritance, the rules can be easily observed by ensuring that—when you create the subclasses—they (i. e., the subclasses) have an "is a" relationship to the superclass.

Therefore, the benefit of polymorphism is that a user can handle different classes via uniform interfaces. The implementation details are irrelevant as long as the results are correct.

Benefits

If you want to provide polymorphic objects, you should use this concept in moderation. Inheritance, in particular, is one of the most powerful properties of an object-oriented programming language; however, it can also be relatively delicate so that you should never disregard the possibility of creating polymorphism via standalone interfaces. Inheritance is always necessary whenever reusable methods are to be provided in superclasses. In the context of proactive programming, paths of the inheritance tree should always be as short as possible and, preferably, be terminated with final classes.

As a summarizing example of polymorphism, we will now look at a rudimentary implementation of classes for different kinds of bank accounts. We begin in Listing 6.21 with a global interface[28] that describes the account number and methods for pay-in, withdrawal, and transfer as the main properties of a bank account.

Interface

Listing 6.21 Interface for Bank Accounts

```
INTERFACE zif_account PUBLIC.
  DATA id TYPE zaccounts-id READ-ONLY.
  METHODS deposit
    IMPORTING
      amount TYPE zaccounts-amount.
  METHODS withdraw
    IMPORTING
      amount TYPE zaccounts-amount
```

---

28 The interface and the following global classes have been created in the Class Builder, but we only show the code here.

```
      RAISING
        zcx_negative_amount.
  METHODS transfer
    IMPORTING
      amount TYPE zaccounts-amount
      target TYPE REF TO zif_account
    RAISING
      zcx_negative_amount.
ENDINTERFACE.
```

Abstract class

The abstract global class shown in Listing 6.22 integrates the interface and already implements the methods. The instance constructor of the class reads the required data from the database.

Listing 6.22 Abstract Class for Bank Accounts

```
CLASS zcl_account DEFINITION PUBLIC ABSTRACT
                                CREATE PUBLIC.
  PUBLIC SECTION.
    INTERFACES zif_account.
    ALIASES id FOR zif_account~id.
    METHODS constructor
      IMPORTING id TYPE zaccounts-id.
  PROTECTED SECTION.
    DATA amount TYPE zaccounts-amount.
ENDCLASS.

CLASS zcl_account IMPLEMENTATION.
  METHOD constructor.
    SELECT SINGLE amount
           FROM zaccounts
           INTO (amount)
           WHERE id = id.
    me->zif_account~id = id.
  ENDMETHOD.
  METHOD zif_account~deposit.
    me->amount = me->amount + amount.
  ENDMETHOD.
  METHOD zif_account~withdraw.
    me->amount = me->amount - amount.
  ENDMETHOD.
  METHOD zif_account~transfer.
    me->zif_account~withdraw( amount ).
    target->deposit( amount ).
  ENDMETHOD.
ENDCLASS.
```

The concrete global class shown in Listing 6.23 inherits from the abstract class and specializes it as a checking account. The specialization is that when the account is overdrawn, an event (see Section 6.5) is triggered, which, in turn, triggers some sort of handling of the debit interest.

Concrete subclass with event

Listing 6.23 Concrete Class for Current Accounts

```
CLASS zcl_checking_account DEFINITION PUBLIC
       INHERITING FROM zcl_account FINAL
       CREATE PUBLIC.
  PUBLIC SECTION.
    EVENTS overdraw
      EXPORTING
        value(id)     TYPE zaccounts-id
        value(amount) TYPE zaccounts-amount.
    METHODS zif_account~withdraw REDEFINITION.
ENDCLASS.

CLASS zcl_checking_account IMPLEMENTATION.
  METHOD zif_account~withdraw.
    super->zif_account~withdraw( amount ).
    IF me->amount < 0.
      RAISE EVENT overdraw
        EXPORTING id = me->zif_account~id
                  amount = me->amount.
    ENDIF.
  ENDMETHOD.
ENDCLASS.
```

The concrete global class shown in Listing 6.24 inherits from the abstract class and specializes it as a savings account. The specialization is that when the account is overdrawn, an exception is thrown (see Section 8.2) that must be handled when the method is called.

Concrete subclass with exception

Listing 6.24 Concrete Class for Saving Accounts

```
CLASS zcl_savings_account DEFINITION PUBLIC
  INHERITING FROM zcl_account FINAL
  CREATE PUBLIC.
  PUBLIC SECTION.
    METHODS zif_account~withdraw REDEFINITION.
ENDCLASS.

CLASS zcl_savings_account IMPLEMENTATION.
  METHOD zif_account~withdraw.
    IF me->amount > amount.
```

```
        super->zif_account~withdraw( amount ).
    ELSE.
      RAISE EXCEPTION TYPE zcx_negative_amount.
    ENDIF.
  ENDMETHOD.
ENDCLASS.
```

Application program

The program shown in Listing 6.25 works with bank accounts in a very general way. The access to bank accounts is exclusively done via interface reference variables. Because the interface methods WITH-DRAW and TRANSFER declare an exception in their interface, it must be handled accordingly (see Section 8.2.1). For potential account overdrafts, an event handler is registered (see Section 6.5.4). Except for the object creation, the actual account type is irrelevant. The usage is independent of the account type and relies on the appropriate implementation of the addressed objects.

Listing 6.25 Usage of the Bank Accounts

```
REPORT z_banking.

CLASS demo DEFINITION.
  PUBLIC SECTION.
    CLASS-METHODS: main,
                   withdraw
                     IMPORTING
                       account TYPE REF TO zif_account
                       amount  TYPE zaccounts-amount,
                   transfer
                     IMPORTING
                       source TYPE REF TO zif_account
                       target TYPE REF TO zif_account
                       amount TYPE zaccounts-amount.
ENDCLASS.
CLASS demo IMPLEMENTATION.
  METHOD main.
    DATA: account1 TYPE REF TO zif_account,
          account2 TYPE REF TO zif_account,
          acc_hndl TYPE REF TO zcl_account_management.
    CREATE OBJECT: account1 TYPE zcl_checking_account
                     EXPORTING id = '00000815',
                   account2 TYPE zcl_savings_account
                     EXPORTING id = '00004711',
                   acc_hndl.
```

```
    SET HANDLER
      acc_hndl->handle_debit_balance FOR ALL INSTANCES.
    demo=>withdraw( account = account1
                    amount  = 100 ).
    demo=>transfer( source = account1
                    target = account2
                    amount = 500 ).
    demo=>withdraw( account = account2
                    amount  = 1000 ).
    demo=>transfer( source = account2
                    target = account1
                    amount = 1000 ).
  ENDMETHOD.
  METHOD withdraw.
    DATA text TYPE string.
    TRY.
        account->withdraw( amount ).
      CATCH zcx_negative_amount.
        text = account->id.
        CONCATENATE `Withdrawal not possible from `
                    text
                    INTO text.
        MESSAGE text TYPE 'I'.
    ENDTRY.
  ENDMETHOD.
  METHOD transfer.
    DATA text TYPE string.
    TRY.
        source->transfer( amount = amount
                          target = target ).
      CATCH zcx_negative_amount.
        text = source->id.
        CONCATENATE `Transfer not possible from `
                    text
                    INTO text.
        MESSAGE text TYPE 'I'.
    ENDTRY.
  ENDMETHOD.
ENDCLASS.
START-OF-SELECTION.
  demo=>main( ).
```

Without polymorphism, a uniform handling of different account types would not be feasible. You would have to use different reference variables for every account type, which would be very awkward, particularly when transferring references to procedures or when storing references in internal tables. Additionally, new account types can be added without invalidating the users. Without polymorphism, existing user code would have to be adapted to new account types if these account types were to be used in addition to the existing ones. The prerequisite for meaningful results is that every new subclass will implement the methods of the superclass in a semantically correct way.

Benefits

The big advantage of polymorphism is that you can write generic programs that behave consistently towards new requests. You can do without control structures like CASE—ENDCASE or IF—ELSE—ENDIF to steer the dynamic types of reference variables apart, which considerably increases the maintainability of programs (Caseless Programming). At least on the user side, the source codes are structured in a more straightforward way and are therefore easier to read.

6.5   Events and Event Handling

Up to now, we got to know attributes and methods of classes as components of classes. Attributes describe the state of an object; methods access attributes and change the state of the class. These two types are the minimal range of components that an object-oriented language must provide. With events, ABAP Objects provides a third kind of component that is not included in every object-oriented language. Basically, events enable the objects of a class or a class itself to publish changes to its state. Other objects and classes can then react to this change of state.

Example

We'll use an example to describe how events work. Aboard an aircraft there are passengers, the cabin crew, and the pilots. The pilots and the passengers can press a button that calls a flight attendant. As soon as the event "call button pressed" occurs, the flight attendant determines who pressed the button and performs an appropriate action. Therefore, we are dealing with three classes (passenger, pilot, and cabin crew). The instances of the passenger and pilot classes are able to trigger events in which the instances of the class cabin crew take interest in the event and react accordingly by executing an appropriate method. Why do we introduce events instead of simply having the pilots and passengers call a method in the instances of the cabin crew? There are two reasons:

▶ When we press the call button, we don't know which flight attendant, i. e., which instance of the cabin crew, is going to react. In other words, the trigger of an event does not know the handler.

▶ The cabin crew (or a completely different instance) can decide whether the event is even acknowledged. For example, the call button is ignored during take-off and landing. Therefore, the trigger of an event does not even know if the event will have any effect.

Both events cannot be implemented using normal method calls. To call a method, the addressee must be known and a called method must always react. Triggering events, however, is an indirect method call.

Therefore the benefit of the event concept is that it can establish a loose coupling between objects or classes. This is also referred to as the Publish-and-Subscribe mechanism. An object or a class can trigger an event, and another object or a class can be interested in the event. Triggering classes or objects don't know who will be interested in the event and what the handler will do with it. In ABAP Objects, the Publish-and-Subscribe mechanism takes place on two levels, i. e., statically at the time of declaration and during the program execution.

Publish and Subscribe

The Publish-and-Subscribe mechanism is implemented in ABAP Objects as follows:

▶ **Events**
A class can contain events as instance or static components. Every method can trigger the events of its class.

▶ **Event handler**
An event handler is a method of another class or the same class that can handle an event, that is, that can be indirectly called by the event. The role of a method as an event handler is statically specified during its declaration.

▶ **Registration of handlers**
The handling of an event by a proper event handler can be explicitly turned on and off. Without an appropriate registration, no handling takes place.

Figure 6.15 summarizes this in a graphic and introduces the corresponding syntax.

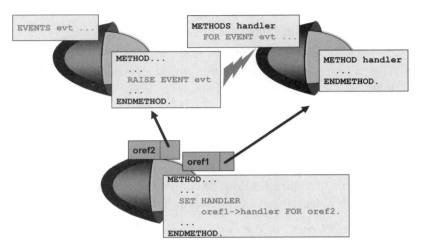

Figure 6.15 Event Triggers and Handlers

In a class, different events can be declared for which event handlers can be created in different classes. Alternatively, a class can implement event handlers for the events of different classes.

6.5.1 Declaring Events

The declaration of an event is the static publishing in the Publish-and-Subscribe mechanism. Like all components of a class, events are declared in one of the three visibility sections of the class or in an interface. An event that is defined in the protected section of a class, for example, can only be handled by objects of the subclasses or its own class. As with attributes and methods, we distinguish instance events and static events. The syntax for declaring an instance event is:

EVENTS   `EVENTS` evt `[EXPORTING ... VALUE(`e_i`) TYPE` type `...]`

Accordingly, a static event is declared as follows:

CLASS-EVENTS   `CLASS-EVENTS` evt `[EXPORTING ... VALUE(`e_i`) TYPE` type `...]`

Instance events can only be triggered in instance methods. Static events can be triggered in instance and static methods.

An event has an optional parameter interface that may exclusively contain output parameters that are passed by value. This interface enables the transfer of actual parameters to the formal parameters of event handlers when events are triggered. The parameter interface of an event handler is determined by the parameter interface of the event.

In addition to the output parameters that you define with EXPORTING, each instance event also has an implicit output parameter named sender. This output parameter has the type of an object reference variable. After the event has been triggered using the RAISE EVENT statement, sender points to the triggering object.

sender

In global classes, events are declared on the **Events** tab of Class Builder. Figure 6.16 shows the declaration of the instance event OVERDRAW that was already presented as code in Listing 6.23.

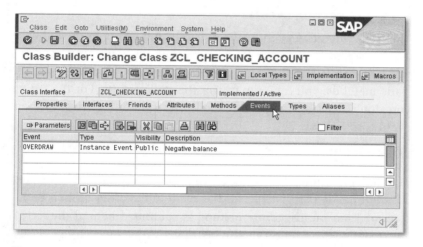

Figure 6.16 Event in the Class Builder

The parameter interface is declared as for methods (see Figure 6.17), where the type of the parameter does not have to be specified.

Parameter interface

In Figure 6.17, you see that parameters of events can be defined as optional in the **Optional** column, just like the input parameters of methods. When triggering an event, optional event parameters do not necessarily have to be provided with values.

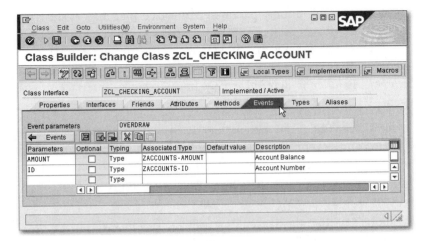

Figure 6.17 Parameter Interface of Events

6.5.2 Triggering Events

The triggering of an event is the dynamic publishing in the Publish-and-Subscribe mechanism. In instance methods, you can trigger the instance events and the static events of the corresponding class; in static methods, you can only trigger the static events. For the latter, you don't need any object creation. The syntax for triggering an event is as follows:

RAISE EVENT

```
RAISE EVENT evt EXPORTING ... eᵢ = aᵢ ...
```

This statement interrupts the execution of the method and executes all event handlers registered for the event in the order of their registration. Then the triggering method is continued behind the RAISE EVENT statement. Events can also be triggered during event handling. Using the EXPORTING addition, actual parameters must be attached to all non-optional exporting parameters of the event. By doing so, the input parameters of the event handlers are provided with values.

The definition and the triggering of events are illustrated using the example described above. In Listings 6.26 and 6.27, we define two global classes, ZCL_PILOT and ZCL_PASSENGER, that can trigger the event for pressing a call button.

Listing 6.26 Class for Pilots

```
CLASS zcl_pilot DEFINITION PUBLIC
  FINAL CREATE PUBLIC.
```

```
  PUBLIC SECTION.
    EVENTS call_button_pressed.
    METHODS call_flight_attendant.
ENDCLASS.

CLASS zcl_pilot IMPLEMENTATION.
  METHOD call_flight_attendant.
    RAISE EVENT call_button_pressed.
  ENDMETHOD.
ENDCLASS.
```

Listing 6.27 Class for Passengers

```
CLASS zcl_passenger DEFINITION PUBLIC
  FINAL CREATE PUBLIC.
  PUBLIC SECTION.
    DATA class TYPE string READ-ONLY.
    EVENTS call_button_pressed
      EXPORTING value(seat_number) TYPE i.
    METHODS constructor
      IMPORTING seat_number TYPE i.
               class       TYPE string.
    METHODS call_flight_attendant.
  PRIVATE SECTION.
    DATA seat_number TYPE i.
ENDCLASS.

CLASS zcl_passenger IMPLEMENTATION.
  METHOD constructor.
    me->seat_number = seat_number.
    me->class       = class.
  ENDMETHOD.
  METHOD call_flight_attendant.
    RAISE EVENT call_button_pressed
      EXPORTING seat_number = me->seat_number.
  ENDMETHOD.
ENDCLASS.
```

In both classes, we declare an event call_button_pressed for the case that the call button was pressed. Both classes have a method that triggers the event with RAISE EVENT. In the passenger class, the event has a parameter that must be used when the event is triggered to indicate the seat number from which the call was made. The seat number and class of every passenger are set via the instance constructor.

6.5.3   Event Handlers

The declaration of an event handler is the static subscription in the Publish-and-Subscribe mechanism. Every class can contain event handlers for the events of other classes or their own class. Event handlers are methods that are specifically identified as such. The corresponding syntax is:

FOR EVENT

```
[CLASS-]METHODS handler FOR EVENT evt OF class|intf
                IMPORTING ... eᵢ ... [sender].
```

The addition FOR EVENT makes a method an event handler and assigns it to exactly one event of a class class or an intf interface. The class or interface specified for the event handler determines which objects or classes can trigger the execution of the event handler. In an instance event, an event handler can be triggered by all objects, the classes of which are equal to or more specific than class, or that implement the intf interface directly or via a superclass. For a static event, the same applies to the class.

Inheritance

Using the example of inheritance, Figure 6.18 shows the classes that can trigger an event handler. Although all classes of the inheritance tree shown in the figure contain the event evt, only classes below or equal to cl_trigger can trigger the shown handler.

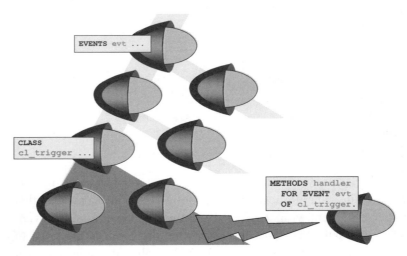

Figure 6.18 Events in Inheritance

The parameter interface of an event handler may exclusively contain input parameters that were defined with the same names as output parameters when the event was declared. An event handler does not need to take all parameters. With the exception of the implicit parameter `sender`, the input parameters are not typed by the event handler but take over the typing of the output parameters of the event. This enables the loose coupling between trigger and handler. The trigger is independent of potential handlers, because an event handler may not expect any other parameters except those that can be sent by the event.

In addition to the parameters explicitly declared for the event, event handlers for instance events can also import the implicit parameter `sender`. In the event handler, the static type of this input parameter is set to the `class` class or the `intf` interface specified behind `EVENT evt OF`. If the event handler is called by an instance event, `sender` passes on a reference to the triggering object. If an event handler imports `sender`, it can access the triggering object using this parameter.

sender

Global event handlers are defined in the Class Builder in the **Detail View** of methods (see Figure 6.19). Under **Parameters**, only parameters of the event, including the predefined `sender` parameter, can be entered.

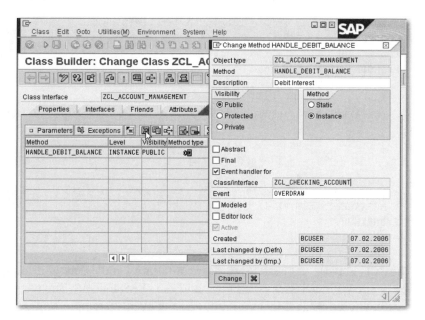

Figure 6.19 Global Event Handler

We will now extend our example from Section 6.5.2 by the global event handler shown in Listing 6.28.

Listing 6.28 Event Handler

```
CLASS zcl_flight_attendant DEFINITION PUBLIC
  FINAL CREATE PUBLIC.
  PUBLIC SECTION.
    METHODS constructor
      IMPORTING title TYPE string.
    METHODS help_the_pilot
      FOR EVENT call_button_pressed OF zcl_pilot.
    METHODS help_a_passenger
      FOR EVENT call_button_pressed OF zcl_passenger
      IMPORTING seat_number sender.
  PRIVATE SECTION.
    DATA title TYPE string.
ENDCLASS.

CLASS zcl_flight_attendant IMPLEMENTATION.
  METHOD constructor.
    me->title = title.
  ENDMETHOD.
  METHOD help_the_pilot.
    DATA text TYPE string.
    CONCATENATE me->title ` helps pilot` INTO text.
    MESSAGE text TYPE 'I'.
  ENDMETHOD.
  METHOD help_a_passenger.
    DATA text TYPE string.
    text = seat_number.
    CONCATENATE me->title
                ` helps `
                sender->class
                ` passenger on seat `
                text
                INTO text.
    MESSAGE text TYPE 'I'.
  ENDMETHOD.
ENDCLASS.
```

The ZCL_FLIGHT_ATTENDANT class contains a handler method for the events of the classes ZCL_PILOT and ZCL_PASSENGER. The handler method `help_a_passenger` imports the event parameters `seat_number` and `sender`.

6.5.4 Registering Event Handlers

The registration of an event handler is the dynamic subscription in the Publish-and-Subscribe mechanism. For an event handler to react to a triggered event, it must be registered accordingly at runtime. Only the registration couples event handlers to triggers. This coupling can be dissolved at any time. In our aircraft example, the coupling would be established after the take-off phase and dissolved before landing.

The syntax for registering event handlers for instance events is:

```
SET HANDLER handler1 handler2 ... FOR oref|{ALL INSTANCES}
                        [ACTIVATION act].
```

SET HANDLER

This statement registers the event handlers `handler1`, `handler2`, ... for corresponding instance events of the object to which the `oref` reference variable provided after `FOR` is pointing. The event handlers are specified like the methods of a static method call (see Section 6.1.2). The static type of `oref` is restricted by the specified event handler. It must be more specific or equal to the `class` classes and implement all `intf` interfaces that were used when declaring the individual event handlers. When `oref` is specified, event handlers are registered for the events of exactly one object.

FOR OREF

Alternatively, using `ALL INSTANCES`, event handlers can be registered for all objects, the instance events of which they can handle. This registration also applies to all objects that are not created until after the `SET HANDLER` statement. In static events, the addition `FOR` is omitted completely, and the registration is performed for all classes and interfaces that can be handled by the specified handler. This means that in one statement, either only instance events or only static events can be registered.

FOR ALL INSTANCES

The optional addition `ACTIVATION` determines if the specified handlers are to be registered ("X") or deregistered (" "), where registration is the default setting. Technically, the `SET HANDLER` statement manages entries in invisible system tables. Every registration is equal to a line in a system table assigned to the potential triggers (individual object, all instances, all classes or interfaces). When an event is triggered via `RAISE EVENT`, the event handlers of the corresponding system table are called. The registration of an instance method as an event handler sets a reference from a system table to the appropriate

System tables

object. With respect to the Garbage Collector, this reference acts like a reference in a reference variable, that is, objects registered as handlers are not deleted as long as they are registered. If the Garbage Collector deletes a single triggering object, the entire corresponding system table is also deleted, thereby canceling all of its registrations.

Generating objects

In Listing 6.29, we can now conclude our aircraft example by creating objects of the classes created so far for pilots, passengers, and flight attendants, registering the event handlers and triggering the events.

Listing 6.29 Using Events

```
REPORT z_events.

CLASS demo DEFINITION.
  PUBLIC SECTION.
    CLASS-METHODS main.
ENDCLASS.

CLASS demo IMPLEMENTATION.
  METHOD main.
    DATA:
      pilot      TYPE REF TO zcl_pilot,
      passenger1 TYPE REF TO zcl_passenger,
      passenger2 TYPE REF TO zcl_passenger,
      purser     TYPE REF TO zcl_flight_attendant,
      stewardess TYPE REF TO zcl_flight_attendant.

    CREATE OBJECT:
      pilot,
      passenger1 EXPORTING seat_number = 11
                           class       = `Business Class`,
      passenger2 EXPORTING seat_number = 333
                           class       = `Economy Class`,
      purser     EXPORTING title = `Purser`,
      stewardess EXPORTING title = `Stewardess`.

    SET HANDLER:
      purser->help_the_pilot       FOR pilot,
      stewardess->help_a_passenger FOR ALL INSTANCES.

    pilot->call_flight_attendant( ).
    passenger1->call_flight_attendant( ).
    passenger2->call_flight_attendant( ).

  ENDMETHOD.
ENDCLASS.

START-OF-SELECTION.
  demo=>main( ).
```

We create a pilot, two passengers, and two objects of the ZCL_FLIGHT_ATTENDANT class, a purser, and a stewardess. The purser reacts to the pilot event with the event handler `help_the_pilot`, and the stewardess reacts to all passenger events with the `help_a_passenger` method. Although purser and stewardess are instances of the same class, they are coupled to different triggers. Comprehend this program by executing it line by line in the ABAP Debugger!

6.6 Shared Objects

In Section 4.4.5, we introduced the creation of objects without further discussing the memory area in which they reside and where they can be accessed. The objects we dealt with so far reside in the internal session of an ABAP program (see Section 3.4.5). This means that objects can be accessed only within an internal session:

Internal session

- On the one hand, the program that created an object can always access it.

- On the other hand, references to objects can be passed on to loaded programs via external procedure calls (methods, function modules, etc.).

However, it is not possible to access the objects of upstream programs of a call sequence (see Section 3.4.4), or of completely independent programs. Therefore, references cannot be passed on to called programs.

It is a common scenario that at the beginning of an application, an object reads a large amount of data from the database into an attribute—normally an internal table—and remains in memory throughout the entire application. The application accesses the object and works with the data that has been processed. If several parallel applications work with the same data and if these applications are long running, a large part of the memory is unnecessarily used for the same kind of data. It therefore makes sense to store shared and stable data in a common memory area for all programs.

Scenario

If we recall the presentation of an ABAP program on the application server in Chapter 3 (see Figure 6.20), we find that only the shared memory of the application server is suitable for storing objects that can be accessed in a cross-mode way. The ABAP Memory is only

Shared memory

available within a call sequence, and the SAP Memory is user-specific. However, all ABAP programs of an application server can access the Shared Memory.

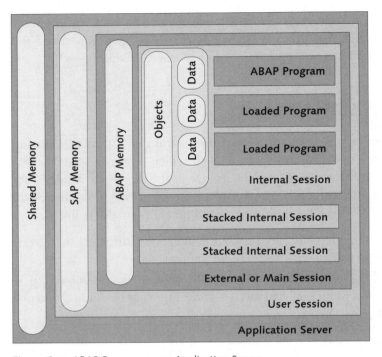

Figure 6.20 ABAP Program on an Application Server

For frequent database accesses, AS ABAP includes an implicit mechanism called SAP buffering, where the raw data from the database is already buffered in the Shared Memory (see Section 10.1.4). For the explicit and object-oriented access to the Shared Memory, shared objects have recently (SAP NetWeaver 2004) been introduced.

Shared Objects Memory

The Shared Memory contains an area called Shared Objects Memory where objects can be stored as shared objects. This includes both instances of classes and anonymous data objects (see Section 11.1.2). In this section, we will only discuss instances of classes.

Because all programs of an application server can access shared objects, it is apparent that the storage of and access to shared objects cannot be achieved without a certain degree of management effort. The following sections introduce the programming interface for shared objects.

6.6.1 Basics—Areas and Co.

The management of and the access to the Shared Objects Memory are performed via areas. The Shared Objects Memory is divided into area instances that can exist in different versions. The actual Shared Objects are stored in the area instance versions. In the most elementary case (without versioning), an area instance consists of a single area instance version.

Area instance

An area is a repository object that describes the technical properties of area instances. The term "area" in this context should not be confused with a memory area in the Shared Objects Memory, which applies only to area instances. Instead, an area defines the properties of area instances, similar to a class that specifies the properties of its objects. There can be several area instances of an area. In simple terms, an area is just a collection of settings that describe the properties of area instances, like versioning, lifetime, and so forth.

Area

For every area, a global area class of the same name is generated. However, this is not a template for area instances but for area handles. An area handle is an object of an area class whose methods can be used by ABAP programs to access the area instances of the relevant area and thus the shared objects stored therein. Area classes provide the only possible means of access from ABAP programs to the Shared Objects Memory. The corresponding methods set and respect the corresponding locks.

Area class and area handle

To be able to store objects as shared objects in area instances, their classes must be identified as Shared Memory-enabled. The syntax is:

```
CLASS class DEFINITION ... SHARED MEMORY ENABLED.
```

In global classes, the **Shared Memory-enabled** property can be selected in the Class Builder.

SHARED MEMORY-ENABLED

During its definition, every area must be assigned a global Shared Memory-enabled class as an area root class. An area instance where shared objects are stored must contain at least one instance of the area root class as a root object. The root object can contain working data itself and reference other shared objects (instances of Shared Memory-enabled classes or data objects) of the area instance. An area handle has an attribute named ROOT that can be used to address the root object.

Area root class

6.6.2 Accessing Shared Objects

Figure 6.21 illustrates the access to shared objects. The access is achieved via an area handle, that is, by means of an object of an area class. The shared objects are stored in an area instance version in the Shared Memory. The properties of area handle and area instance are specified by the corresponding area in the ABAP Workbench (see Section 6.6.3).

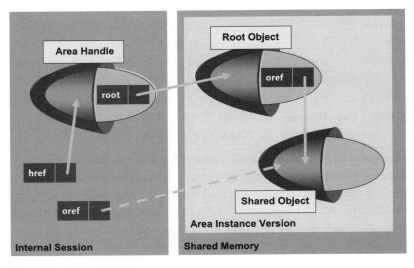

Figure 6.21 Shared Objects

References The initial access from an internal session to the shared objects of an area instance is always achieved via the area handle ROOT reference variable pointing to the root object. This object can reference more shared objects and also refer to external objects. Figure 6.21 shows an area instance version with two shared objects, the root object and another object. From an internal session, a reference to a shared object can only be used as long as this session is connected to the area instance via an area handle, because this handle provides the required lock of the area instance. The oref reference shown in this figure should therefore be resolved for security reasons before the access via the area handle is terminated. The same applies to references from shared objects to objects of the internal session.[29]

---

29 An exception occurs if you try to use a shared object, the area instance version of which is not connected.

While an area instance version is attached to an internal session via an area handle, it can be regarded as its extension. Any references between the memory areas are admissible, and depending on the lock, read or write accesses can be used. Area instance versions to which no area handles are attached are ideally self-contained, that is, there should only be references within an area instance version.

The static attributes of a Shared Memory-enabled class are not treated differently from those of a normal class. This means that they are created in the internal session of a program when the class is loaded therein. If different programs access the same shared objects, the static attributes of the corresponding classes exist in the programs several times and independently of each other.

Static attributes

6.6.3 Creating an Area

To create areas, the ABAP Workbench includes the **Area Management** tool (transaction SHMA). The creation of an area generates the area class of the same name. Therefore, the area name should follow the naming conventions for global classes. Every area class inherits from the predefined class CL_SHM_AREA, which, in turn, inherits from CL_ABAP_MEMORY_AREA. Every area handle therefore contains a set of predefined methods and attributes that are the same for all areas.

When an area is created, the area properties are set. These are divided into basic properties, fixed and dynamic area properties, and runtime settings. Basic properties are involved in the generation of the area class. Although fixed and dynamic area properties are not involved in the generation, they are regarded as a part of the development object. Runtime settings can be changed at runtime, which is not considered to be a change to the development object.

The following list displays important area properties. For more information, refer to the system's online help.

Area properties

- ▶ **Basic properties**
  In addition to the area name, the area root class must be specified as a basic property. More basic properties are whether an area is client-dependent (see Section 10.14), whether an area can be built automatically via an area constructor class, and whether an area is

transactional, that is, if changes are coupled to database commits (see Section 10.1.3).

▶ **Fixed and dynamic properties**
The difference between fixed and dynamic properties is whether or not existing area instances need to be invalidated when the developer makes a change. The fixed area properties determine the context of an area and whether versioning takes place. The context of an area specifies the visibility and the lifetime of an area instance. In addition to the application server as the most general context, user session, main session, and ABAP Memory (call sequence) are possible contexts as well (see Figure 6.20). Versioning determines if there can be just one or several area instance versions for an area instance. The dynamic area properties are the specification of a potential area constructor class and the kind of displacement when running out of memory.

▶ **Runtime settings**
The runtime-dependent area settings determine in which situations an area is built via the potential area constructor class, how large an area (all area instances) or a single area instance version can get, the maximum number of versions allowed, and whether there is a restriction on the lifetime of the area instances.

As an example, we would like to introduce a very simple area that can be used in applications working with the flight data model. For the area, we create the global Shared Memory-enabled class shown in Listing 6.30 to use it as the area root class.

Listing 6.30 Area Root Class

```
CLASS zcl_flight_list DEFINITION PUBLIC
  FINAL CREATE PUBLIC SHARED MEMORY ENABLED.
  PUBLIC SECTION.
    DATA flight_list TYPE spfli_tab READ-ONLY.
    METHODS set_flight_list
      RAISING zcx_no_flights.
ENDCLASS.

CLASS zcl_flight_list IMPLEMENTATION
  METHOD set_flight_list.
    SELECT *
           FROM spfli
           INTO TABLE flight_list.
    IF sy-subrc <> 0.
```

```
      RAISE EXCEPTION TYPE zcx_no_flights.
    ENDIF.
  ENDMETHOD.
ENDCLASS.
```

As a public attribute, the global class ZCL_FLIGHT_LIST contains an internal table `flight_list` of the existing type SPFLI_TAB from the ABAP Dictionary, which is filled by a `set_flight_list` method. This table contains the unchangeable data that is to be accessed from different programs. Figure 6.22 shows the properties of the ZCL_FLIGHTS area in transaction SHMA.

Figure 6.22 Creating an Area

Barring two exceptions, the standard values were accepted. We turned off versioning and restricted the lifetime after the last access to five minutes. We turned off versioning because we are not planning to change the data in the area instance at program runtime. The restriction of the lifetime prevents space in the shared memory from being consumed without actually being used by a program.

6.6.4 Locking

The access to shared objects is controlled via locks. The locking concept of shared objects is similar to that of a file system. This means that there are exclusive locks for creating or changing shared objects in area instances, and read locks for accessing shared objects:

▶ **Read lock**
If a read lock is set on an area in a program, the current area instance version can be read. Within an internal session, there can be a maximum of one read lock for an area instance. Across several sessions, there can be several read locks on an area instance version.

▶ **Write lock**
If a write lock is set for an area in a program, a new area instance version can be created and can be populated with data.

▶ **Update lock**
If an update lock is set for an area in a program, the data of the current area instance version can be changed for areas without versioning. For areas with versioning, a new area instance version is created that can then be changed.

A change lock (write or update lock) locks an area instance version exclusively. Only previous versions can be read-accessed in parallel. On an application server, there can be a maximum of one change lock on an area instance. Without versioning, a change lock can only be set if there is currently no read lock. With versioning, a change lock can be set on an area instance even if there are read locks.

Setting locks The locks are set when an internal session is attached to an area instance via an area handle (see the following section). A lock therefore always refers to all shared objects of an area instance. Basically, this locking concept supports two application scenarios for shared objects:

Shared buffer ▶ **Usage as a shared buffer**
A shared buffer contains a large amount of data that is changed rarely (once a week up to once a day). The amount of data can be very large. In general, the data of a shared buffer is provided once by a single program, and many users read-access the shared buffer simultaneously. A typical area of application for a shared buffer is the storage of a catalog or other stable lists.

▶ **Usage as an exclusive buffer**

Exclusive buffer

An exclusive buffer contains data that is write- or read-accessed by only one user across transaction boundaries. The data can be created by the same user or another user. A typical field of application for an exclusive buffer is the storage of a shopping cart that is first populated by the customer and later read by the salesperson.

Other scenarios, for example, free shared memory programming with many change accesses of parallel users, are not supported by the current locks.

6.6.5 Working with Shared Objects

The Shared Objects Memory is accessed via the methods and attributes of the area handle that are partly inherited from the superclasses CL_SHM_AREA and CL_ABAP_MEMORY_AREA and partly generated when an area is created. To work with area instances, the current internal session must be attached to them via an area handle. This is achieved using the following static methods of the area class:

▶ **ATTACH_FOR_READ**

Attaching an area handle

This method attaches an area handle to the current area instance version of an existing area instance and sets a read lock. Until the attachment is removed, it is possible to read-access the attached area instance version in the program.

▶ **ATTACH_FOR_WRITE**

This method creates a new area instance version, attaches the area handle to it, and sets a write lock. By specifying a name, several area instances of an area can be created, each with its own versioning. Until the attachment is removed, it is possible to change-access the new area instance version in the program. Without versioning, the new area instance version replaces a potential earlier area instance version. With versioning, a new empty area instance version is created.

▶ **ATTACH_FOR_UPDATE**

This method attaches an area handle to an existing area instance and sets an update lock. Until the attachment is dissolved, it is possible to change-access the attached area instance version in the program. Without versioning, the area handle is attached to the current area instance version. With versioning, the new area instance version is created as a copy of the previous version.

If such a method is not successful because there are no area instances yet that could be read- or change-accessed, or an existing lock denies access, an exception is thrown that is defined as a subclass of CX_SHM_ATTACH_ERROR.

Dissolving the connection In the case of success, all methods return a reference to an area handle that holds one of the three possible locks on the attached area instance version. To solve the attachment of an area handle to an area instance version and to simultaneously cancel the corresponding lock, you have the following options:

▶ An area handle attached to an area instance version via a read lock can be detached from the area instance using the DETACH instance method. This also removes the read lock. Additionally, a read lock is automatically removed at the end of an internal session.

▶ An area handle attached to an area instance version via a change lock must be explicitly detached from the area instance via the instance methods DETACH_COMMIT or DETACH_ROLLBACK. This removes the change lock with or without committing the changes.

When disconnecting, the area instance should be completed, that is, no reference may point from the internal session to a shared object and vice versa. An area handle that is not attached to an area instance version is inactive and cannot be used.

Creating shared objects While there is a change lock for an area instance version, shared objects can be created from Shared Memory-enabled classes. For this purpose, there is a specific variant of CREATE OBJECT:

AREA HANDLE `CREATE OBJECT` oref **AREA HANDLE** `area_handle ...`

Following the addition AREA HANDLE, you must specify a reference variable of the static type of an area class that points to an area handle, which is attached to an area instance version via a change lock.

The addition AREA HANDLE also exists for the CREATE DATA statement for creating anonymous data objects, which is described in Section 11.1.2.

Setting root objects If a change lock is detached using DETACH_COMMIT, an instance of the area root class must be set as the root object of the area instance version. For this purpose, the SET_ROOT instance method of the area handle must be called while the change lock is set. The root object is the only shared object that can be addressed directly after attaching an area handle to an area instance version. For that reason, the area handle contains a ROOT instance attribute of the static type of the area root class. In the simplest case, an area instance version contains only one object of the area root class, which is then set as the root object.

The methods presented above for setting and removing locks on area instances are actually usable everywhere within an application; however, we recommend that you encapsulate the entire access to the shared memory in specific classes and that you let an application program work only with these classes. An application program remains more readable, secure, and maintainable if it does not have to deal with the entire mechanism of locking and accessing shared objects. Ideally, two classes manage the accessing of shared objects:

Usage note

▶ A loader creates and changes area instances.

▶ A broker takes care of the read access to area instances and can also contain the necessary authorization checks (see Section 10.5.2).

In the following sample program, we merged loader and broker into a single class. Listing 6.31 shows the code of the global class ZCL_FLIGHT_LIST_HANDLER that encapsulates the access to shared objects in the ZCL_FLIGHTS area shown in Figure 6.22.

Listing 6.31 Access to Shared Objects

```
CLASS zcl_flight_list_handler DEFINITION PUBLIC
  FINAL CREATE PRIVATE.
  PUBLIC SECTION.
    CLASS-DATA flight_list_handler
      TYPE REF TO zcl_flight_list_handler.
    CLASS-METHODS class_constructor.
    METHODS get_flight_list
      RETURNING
        value(flights) TYPE REF TO spfli_tab
      RAISING
        zcx_no_flights.
  PRIVATE SECTION.
    DATA area_handle TYPE REF TO zcl_flights.
    METHODS create_flight_list
      RAISING
```

```abap
          cx_shm_attach_error
          zcx_no_flights.
ENDCLASS.

CLASS zcl_flight_list_handler IMPLEMENTATION.
  METHOD class_constructor.
    CREATE OBJECT flight_list_handler.
  ENDMETHOD.
  METHOD get_flight_list.
    DATA flight_list TYPE REF TO zcl_flight_list.
    IF area_handle IS INITIAL.
      TRY.
            area_handle = zcl_flights=>attach_for_read( ).
        CATCH cx_shm_attach_error.
          TRY.
              me->create_flight_list( ).
              area_handle = zcl_flights=>attach_for_read( ).
            CATCH cx_shm_attach_error.
              CREATE OBJECT flight_list.
              flight_list->set_flight_list( ).
          ENDTRY.
      ENDTRY.
    ENDIF.
    IF area_handle IS NOT INITIAL.
      GET REFERENCE OF
        area_handle->root->flight_list INTO flights.
    ELSEIF flight_list IS NOT INITIAL.
      GET REFERENCE OF
        flight_list->flight_list INTO flights.
    ELSE.
      RAISE EXCEPTION TYPE zcx_no_flights.
    ENDIF.
  ENDMETHOD.
  METHOD create_flight_list.
    DATA: area_handle TYPE REF TO zcl_flights,
          flight_list TYPE REF TO zcl_flight_list,
          exc_ref     TYPE REF TO zcx_no_flights.
    area_handle = zcl_flights=>attach_for_write( ).
    CREATE OBJECT flight_list AREA HANDLE area_handle.
    area_handle->set_root( flight_list ).
    TRY.
        flight_list->set_flight_list( ).
      CATCH zcx_no_flights INTO exc_ref.
        area_handle->detach_rollback( ).
```

```
        RAISE EXCEPTION exc_ref.
      ENDTRY.
    area_handle->detach_commit( ).
  ENDMETHOD.
ENDCLASS.
```

The class is structured in such a way that, in an internal session, there can only be one instance of it that is created in the static constructor (Singleton). The GET_FLIGHT_LIST method serves as a broker. It tries to set a read lock on an area instance. Because there can be only one read lock on an area instance within an internal session, it is always first queried whether there already is an area handle.[30] In case of a failure, the CREATE_FLIGHT_LIST method is called that acts as a loader. It tries to set a write lock and to build an area instance with a root object. Potential exceptions are propagated to the calling method. Note that a DETACH_ROLLBACK is executed before a potential exception ZCX_NO_FLIGHTS is forwarded from SET_FLIGHT_LIST to the caller. Without explicitly removing the change lock, there would be a program crash at the end of the current internal session at the latest.

Read and write lock

If the area built has been successful, GET_FLIGHT_LIST tries to set another read lock. If no area instance could be built, GET_FLIGHT_LIST creates—as an emergency measure – an object of the ZCL_FLIGHT_LIST class in the current internal session and populates the internal table FLIGHT_LIST. Lastly, the return value of the method is assigned a data reference to the flight list, either in the root object of the shared object or in the local object.

Note that the write lock in CREATE_FLIGHT_LIST is explicitly closed, while a read lock in GET_FLIGHT_LIST remains until the end of the internal session. In areas without versioning, the latter is possible only if no change accesses are expected after an area has been built.

The code in Listing 6.32 finally shows an application program that works with the data from the shared object in the ZCL_FLIGHTS area.

---

30 Alternatively, the CX_SHM_READ_LOCK_ACTIVE exception could have been handled, which would have been less performant.

Listing 6.32 Usage of Shared Objects

```abap
REPORT z_shared_objects.

CLASS demo DEFINITION.
  PUBLIC SECTION.
    CLASS-METHODS main.
  PRIVATE SECTION.
    CLASS-METHODS display
      IMPORTING value(table) TYPE any table.
ENDCLASS.

CLASS demo IMPLEMENTATION.
  METHOD main.
    DATA: flight_list_handler
            TYPE REF TO zcl_flight_list_handler,
          flight_list TYPE REF TO spfli_tab.
    flight_list_handler =
      zcl_flight_list_handler=>flight_list_handler.
    TRY.
        flight_list =
          flight_list_handler->get_flight_list( ).
      CATCH zcx_no_flights.
        MESSAGE 'No flight list available' TYPE 'I'
                DISPLAY LIKE 'E'.
        RETURN.
    ENDTRY.
    demo=>display( flight_list->* ).
  ENDMETHOD.
  METHOD display.
    DATA alv TYPE REF TO cl_salv_table.
    TRY.
        cl_salv_table=>factory(
          IMPORTING r_salv_table = alv
          CHANGING  t_table      = table ).
        alv->display( ).
      CATCH cx_salv_msg.
        MESSAGE 'ALV display not possible' TYPE 'I'
                DISPLAY LIKE 'E'.
    ENDTRY.
  ENDMETHOD.
ENDCLASS.

START-OF-SELECTION.
  demo=>main( ).
```

In the main method, an object of our ZCL_FLIGHT_LIST_HANDLER class is created, and then a reference to the flight list is read. If the flight list was accessed successfully, it is output in the `display` method using the ALV (SAP List Viewer). In the application program, whether the data resides in the shared memory or, in the case of failure, in a local object of the ZCL_FLIGHT_LIST class, is irrelevant. If no data can be read from the database, an appropriate message is returned.

6.6.6 Managing Shared Objects

The shared memory is a valuable resource. Profile parameters specify how large the areas of the shared memory can become for different requests like programs, program data, implicit buffers, and the Shared Objects Memory. In SAP Memory Management (Transaction ST02), the current memory consumption can be viewed.

In contrast to most other requests to the shared memory, the programming with shared objects introduced in this section is performed explicitly. While the other requests are made implicitly, and the ABAP runtime environment automatically ensures an optimum usage of the shared memory, a developer has great freedom when using shared objects, and must therefore ensure also that all unused memory is released.

To support developers and system administration in managing shared objects, there is a specific monitor for the Shared Objects Memory. It can be called via Transaction SHMM or from Transaction SHMA. The monitor shows the properties of current area instances and also enables change actions. Some of the functions of the Shared Objects Monitor include:

Shared Objects Monitor

- Displaying all area instances, their versions, and the current locks
- Displaying the contents of area instance versions
- Displaying the memory consumption
- Changing the state of area instance versions (from active to obsolete)
- Deleting area instances

The Shared Objects Monitor thus enables you to observe the usage of the Shared Objects Memory, to influence it, if necessary, and to draw conclusions regarding its usage. For example, if an application stores shared objects over longer periods without setting any read locks, this is a questionable usage of the shared memory, and you should at least consider a restriction of the lifetime of the area instance versions.

If our sample program from Listing 6.32 is run twice in parallel within five minutes (the display of the list remains on the screen), the display of the Shared Objects Monitor looks as shown in Figure 6.23. There is an area instance version of our area ZCL_FLIGHTS that takes up approximately 8 MB and has two read locks. The other areas are used by the ABAP runtime environment. If you select an area, more detailed information is displayed, for example, who is holding the locks. Because the lifetime in our area is restricted, the area instance version disappears five minutes after the last read lock has been removed. Go ahead. Try it.

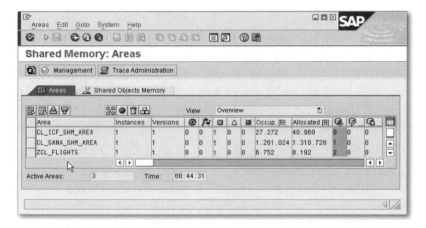

Figure 6.23 Shared Objects Monitor

"Your father's light-saber. This is the weapon of a Jedi knight. Not as clumsy or as random as a blaster. An elegant weapon from a more civilized time."
—*Obi-Wan Kenobi to Luke Skywalker*

7 Classic ABAP—Events and Procedures

ABAP is a language that has continuously evolved. All versions, including those being released today, include innovations that tailor the language to meet the needs of modern business application programming. One innovation was the introduction of ABAP Objects that opens the wide world of object-oriented programming to ABAP developers. Another similar innovation was the introduction of Unicode programs to enable AS ABAP to handle Unicode. Given this history, you can see that there was an ABAP that existed before ABAP Objects. This version of ABAP continues to exist. We call it classic ABAP.

Changes and innovations are introduced to ABAP in accordance with the principle of strict downward compatibility. This is good for you and your investment in existing programs, but it's bad for the aesthetics with regard to orthogonality and the scope of ABAP. New designs coexist with old ones. And that situation applies overall— from the entire programming model to individual statements or supplements added to statements. As a developer, you can choose from a supply of varying and possibly confusing options to reach your goal. We can only heartily recommend that you use the latest options as much as possible.

Downward compatibility

In general, use only new statements and additions rather than the old ones that were replaced by the new statements. For example, when searching in a character string, it would appear that you could choose between the SEARCH and FIND statements; however, the SEARCH statement is supported only for reasons of downward com-

Obsolete statements

patibility. Of course, you'll still find SEARCH in lots of existing programs. When you write new programs or revise existing ones, you should use only the far preferable FIND statement. That's why this book does not use any obsolete statements.[1]

Programming models As we indicated in Section 4.9, it's not that easy to separate the world into new and old (i. e., good and bad) with regard to the programming models to be used. ABAP Objects supports the object-oriented programming model. The programming model of the classic ABAP is event-oriented and procedural. The following sections will describe the difference.

When ABAP Objects was introduced, SAP had already cultivated a long history with ABAP. Classic ABAP had been used to program the entire primary SAP product at the time—SAP R/3. That made it impossible to consider a big-bang approach that would introduce ABAP Objects and simultaneously replace the earlier versions of ABAP. But it was also impossible to introduce ABAP Objects as a completely independent product, because doing so would mean that it could not be used in existing programs and that developers would have to learn a completely new language.

ABAP Objects enhances ABAP Therefore, ABAP Objects exists alongside the traditional concepts, and it is ensured that either ABAP Objects or classic ABAP can call each other's statements. ABAP Objects enhances earlier versions of ABAP, but it does not replace them. On its own, ABAP Objects cannot handle certain tasks such as remote calls (see Section 12.2), the use of traditional dynpros (see Section 9.1), or direct program execution (see Section 3.2.2). For this very reason, we recommend that you work with ABAP Objects as much as possible and use the classic concepts only when technically necessary, or when you must access existing functionality that is still programmed in classic ABAP.

This chapter introduces you to the programming concepts of classic ABAP. They are still used in many existing application programs, and you will have to use them to some extent even in new developments.

---

1 Of course, obsolete statements are still described as part of the scope of the language in The Official ABAP Reference (SAP PRESS 2004) and the ABAP keyword documentation.

7.1   Event-Oriented Program Execution

As noted in Section 3.1.4, processes of the ABAP runtime environment are the driving force of ABAP program execution. ABAP programs are containers for executable processing blocks. At least one of the processing blocks must be called by a process of the ABAP runtime environment to execute a program. For the methods of ABAP Objects, you can use the object-oriented (OO) transactions introduced in Section 3.2.3. This section describes classic program execution in more detail. It focuses primarily on the execution of executable programs and dialog transactions.

7.1.1   Executable Programs

Executable programs can be started directly via their names. Examples of starting a completed program include the use of Transaction SA38 (path: **System • Services • Reporting**) or selecting the **Execute** function when editing the program in the ABAP Workbench. Technically speaking, the only thing that occurs here is the execution of the

`SUBMIT ...`   SUBMIT

statement for the executable program. The execution of the `SUBMIT` statement starts a predefined process in the runtime environment, a process that triggers a defined series of events. An executable program (and only an executable program) can contain event handlers in the form of event blocks for precisely these events. An event block is executed when it exists for one of the triggered events. In other cases, the event has no effect.

Another property of executable programs that is important even today is that the `SUBMIT` statement enables you to execute them in the background. You can place executable programs into background jobs either during a start via interfaces like Transaction SA38 or by using menu path **System • Services • Jobs • Job Definition**. The system services **Job Definition** and **Job Overview** (Transactions SM36 and SM37) provide a complete environment to manage, schedule, and analyze background jobs. Of course, you can also handle everything through your own programs by adding `VIA JOB` to the `SUBMIT` statement, but this approach would require the assistance of a couple `JOB_...` function modules of function group BTCH. Section 9.2.9 pro-

Background processing

vides an example for this and of how you can use SUBMIT to transfer parameters to called programs.

Events The events of the ABAP runtime environment and the associated event blocks behave just like the events and event-handlers of ABAP Objects (see Section 6.5), but should not be confused with them. The events of the ABAP runtime environment are predefined; they are triggered implicitly and are not handled by methods. A dynamic registration or deregistration is impossible.

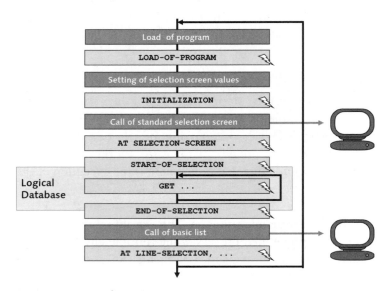

Figure 7.1 Events After SUBMIT

Figure 7.1 illustrates the actions executed in the ABAP runtime environment after SUBMIT and the events triggered by the execution.

1. The program is loaded in its own internal session.

2. After loading the program, the event for the program constructor, LOAD-OF-PROGRAM, is triggered, as occurs for all ABAP programs.

3. When a standard selection screen (see Section 9.2.8) is declared for the program, implicit start values are set for its fields.

4. The INITIALIZATION event is triggered. In executable programs, this event plays a role similar to that of the program constructor.

Selection screen 5. When a standard selection screen has been declared for the program, it is automatically processed. During processing of the

selection screen, selection screen events—AT SELECTION-SCREEN
. . . (see Section 9.2.6)—are triggered, one of them prior to the
display of the selection screen. In background processing, the
processing of the selection screen is hidden, and values must be
transferred to it when the program is called.

6. The next event is the START-OF-SELECTION event. This book generally uses this event as the only starting point for executable
programs.

7. When the program's properties are linked to a logical database, a
series of GET events follows. The properties and the sequence of
the events depend on the logical database. A logical database is a
special ABAP program that contains the definiton of a standard
selection screen and a series of subroutines that encapsulate reading data from database tables. During the execution of an executable program with a logical database, the ABAP runtime environment calls the subroutines of the logical database in a sequence,
which is derived from the hierarchical structure defined for the
logical database. When a subroutine reads a row of a database
table, table, it uses the PUT table statement to trigger the GET
table event of the runtime environment. The GET table event
can be handled in a corresponding event block of the executable
program. The data transfer is carried out within a common data
area.

Logical database

8. When the logical database has ended its data selection, the runtime environment triggers the END-OF-SELECTION event. The data
that has been read can be analyzed entirely in the corresponding
event block. Without a connection to a logical database, END-OF-
SELECTION is triggered immediately after START-OF-SELECTION,
and handling is unnecessary.

9. At the conclusion of an executable program, the ABAP runtime
environment automatically calls the display of the basic list that
might have been written to the list buffer during execution of the
program (see Section 9.3.2). User actions on the list cause list
events. Leaving the list terminates the program, thereby ending
its internal session. In background processing, the list is not displayed. It must be transmitted to the SAP spool system as a print
list.

List

10. If a standard selection screen is displayed in Step 5, the program is automatically restarted by reloading it into a new internal session. This loop can be ended only when the user stops the processing of the selection screen, or the program is left early using a statement such as LEAVE PROGRAM.

Reporting

With the option to enter selection parameters on a selection screen, the follow-up data processing that is completely aligned with the use of a logical database and the output of the data to a list, the predefined flow of an executable program after SUBMIT supports the classical tasks of reporting according to the IPO (input—processing—output) principle. For that reason, we also call the process of the runtime environment that generates this flow the *reporting process*; the related events—INITIALIZATION, START-OF-SELECTION, GET, and END-OF-SELECTION—are referred to as *reporting events*. We'd like to remind you that the sequence, in which the corresponding event blocks are implemented, in the implementation part of an executable program, does not influence the program flow.

An executable program is therefore a highly specialized tool that is controlled by an extremely implicit process of the runtime environment. Because the processing of screens and data within the same program and in event blocks that do not even support local data is promoted, particularly good support for the indispensable separation of concerns (see Chapter 9) is not present.

Due to the fact that we recommend encapsulating the processing of selection screens (like dynpros in general, see Section 9.1.15) in function modules and consider displaying classic lists in productive programs as obsolete, we no longer need those parts of the reporting processes.

LDB_PROCESS

The use of logical databases is basically a very good idea, because these databases already support the separation of concerns in that the task of reading the data is separated from processing the data. You can create logical databases in the Logical Database Builder (Transaction SE36) of the ABAP Workbench. You will also find additional documentation there. Unfortunately, SAP has not yet offered an object-oriented solution for logical databases that is based on the event concept of ABAP Objects. We suggest that you don't use logical databases with a connection to executable programs because of their strongly implicit behavior and the lack of an explicit parameter interface. You can use existing logical databases independently of executable programs with function module LDB_PROCESS.

Of all the actions and events discussed in this chapter up until now, only START-OF-SELECTION remains as the one event in modern ABAP programming with ABAP Objects for which we want to implement an event block as a starting point in an executable program. As shown in all the examples in this book, this event block should not really contain anything other than the call of a main method. As already shown in Section 2.8.7, ABAP Objects can handle the reporting tasks of reading, formatting, and outputting data just as well.

START-OF-SELECTION

For the sake of completeness—and because you will unfortunately encounter it repeatedly in existing executable programs—we want to remind you (see Section 3.5.3) that START-OF-SELECTION is the standard event of an executable program. The programs in Listings 7.1 and 7.2 are completely identical in terms of function. When you debug the program in Listing 7.1, you will also see in the call hierarchy that the MESSAGE statement is executed after the START-OF-SELECTION event.

Standard event

Listing 7.1 Implicit START-OF-SELECTION

```
REPORT z_start_of_selection_1.

MESSAGE 'I am START-OF-SELECTION' TYPE 'I'.
```

Listing 7.2 Explicit START-OF-SELECTION

```
REPORT z_start_of_selection_1.

START-OF-SELECTION.
  MESSAGE 'I am START-OF-SELECTION' TYPE 'I'.
```

The program in Listing 7.3, however, does not contain a START-OF-SELECTION event block and has no effect after SUBMIT. It can be started only with an OO transaction.

Listing 7.3 No START-OF-SELECTION

```
REPORT z_start_of_selection_3.

CLASS demo DEFINITION.
  PUBLIC SECTION.
    CLASS-METHODS main.
ENDCLASS.
```

```
CLASS demo IMPLEMENTATION.
  METHOD main .
    MESSAGE 'I am method main' TYPE 'I'.
  ENDMETHOD.
ENDCLASS.
```

A statement written after an explicit processing block in the implementation part without an explicit assignment to a processing block cannot be reached and leads to a syntax error. Listing 7.4 shows a program with such an error.

Listing 7.4 Unreachable Statement

```
REPORT z_start_of_selection_4.

CLASS demo DEFINITION.
  PUBLIC SECTION.
    CLASS-METHODS main.
ENDCLASS.
CLASS demo IMPLEMENTATION.
  METHOD main .
    MESSAGE 'I am method main' TYPE 'I'.
  ENDMETHOD.
ENDCLASS.
demo=>main( ). "Syntax error
```

If the demo=>main( ) statement in Listing 7.4 came between the declaration and the implementation of the demo class, it would once again implicitly be part of the START-OF-SELECTION event block. Because the use of implicit behavior is prone to error and makes the program difficult to read, we recommend that you always specify START-OF-SELECTION explicitly, as shown in Listing 7.5. The sequence of the processing blocks within the implementation part is ultimately a matter of taste. But it should not be detrimental to readability and it should follow a recognizable pattern (top-down or bottom-up)—especially in large programs.

Listing 7.5 Explicit START-OF-SELECTION

```
REPORT z_start_of_selection_5.

CLASS demo DEFINITION.
  PUBLIC SECTION.
    CLASS-METHODS main.
ENDCLASS.
```

```
START-OF-SELECTION.
  demo=>main( ).
CLASS demo IMPLEMENTATION.
  METHOD main .
    MESSAGE 'I am method main' TYPE 'I'.
  ENDMETHOD.
ENDCLASS.
```

7.1.2   Dialog Transactions

Along with the execution of executable programs, calling dialog transactions represents the second pillar of program execution in classic ABAP. With the exception of OO transactions, all other transactions are also special dialog transactions, namely, parameter transactions and variant transactions. Just as executable programs have traditionally been intended for reporting, program execution via dialog transactions was intended for *dialog programming*, which was primarily used with module pool programs to access and change database tables.[2]

A dialog transaction links a transaction code with the dynpro of an ABAP program. Although all types of programs that can contain dynpros (module pools, executable programs, and function groups) can be used, dialog transactions most often use module pools that can only be called using transaction codes.

Module pool

The execution of a dialog transaction is therefore closely linked to classical dynpros, dynpro sequences, and the interaction of both with ABAP programs. See Section 9.1.4 for more detailed information. The following section introduces only the aspect of program execution.

Dynpros and more

As is the case with other transactions, a dialog transaction is called via its transaction code that is usually linked to a user interface element. The call from a program is carried out using CALL TRANSACTION or LEAVE TO TRANSACTION (see Sections 3.2.2 and 3.2.3). Figure 7.2 illustrates the events and actions of the ABAP runtime environment after the call of a dialog transaction.

---

2 The boundaries here are fluid. While there are indeed classical "dialog programs" that are used only to read data, an executable program can also change data, particularly when changes should be carried out in the background.

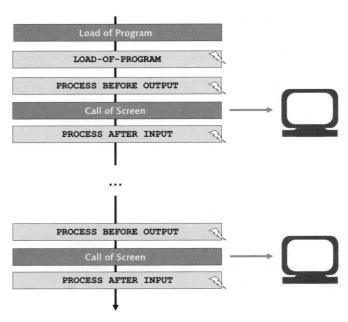

Figure 7.2 Events After the Call of a Dialog Transaction

Dynpro flow logic

After the call of a dialog transaction, the corresponding program is loaded into a separate internal session and the LOAD-OF-PROGRAM event is triggered. After LOAD-OF-PROGRAM, the initial dynpro of the dialog transaction is called. The *dynpro process* is the corresponding process of the ABAP runtime environment. The dynpro process triggers dynpro events like PROCESS BEFORE OUTPUT (PBO) and PROCESS AFTER INPUT (PAI). They are handled in the dynpro flow logic of the related dynpro rather than in the ABAP program.

PBO and PAI

Dynpros form dynpro sequences (see Section 9.1.4). The dynpro process processes all the dynpros of the dynpro sequence that starts with the initial dynpro of the dialog transaction. The following occurs for each dynpro:

1. Dynpro event PBO is triggered.

2. The screen layout of the dynpro is displayed.

3. Dynpro event PAI is triggered for every user action on the screen.[3]

---

3 In addition to the general PAI (process after input), special events—POH (process on help request) and POV (process on value request)—are triggered when the user selects F1 and F4.

You can call dialog modules of the ABAP program in the event blocks of the dynpro flow logic. They prepare the screen layout during PBO and analyze user entries during PAI. The procedure is repeated until the program is terminated with a statement like LEAVE PROGRAM or when the last dynpro of the dynpro sequence is reached.

As is also the case with traditional reporting, classic dialog programming does not support the separation of concerns concept particularly well. That's why in many classic dialog programs, implementation of the actual application coding uses dialog modules that don't support any local data and are actually intended only to handle dynpros. We therefore suggest the encapsulation of dynpros in function groups (see Section 9.1.15) instead of using dialog transactions.

7.1.3 Comparison Between Different Types of Classic Program Execution

Both types of classic program execution treated above are controlled by processes of the ABAP runtime environment via events. The reporting process handles executable programs, while the dynpro process handles dialog transactions. The reporting process can be started only via SUBMIT. The dynpro process, however, can be started either with dialog transactions or with the CALL SCREEN statement at any location in a program that contains dynpros. A dynpro process can therefore be embedded in a reporting process. Additionally, the ABAP runtime environment also includes a *selection screen process* and a *list process*. You can embed these processes in the reporting and dynpro processes by calling a selection screen or list processing. Selection screen and list processes also trigger events that can be handled in the ABAP program.

The essential difference between the execution of executable programs and that of dialog transactions is that the reporting process triggers a series of special events in a predefined sequence. Dialog transactions, on the other hand, process a sequence of dynpros that you can program in any way you want; the dynpro process triggers the same dynpro events for every dynpro.

Historically speaking, executable programs and dialog programs (dialog transactions with module pools) are specialized types of programs that were intended for different tasks:

Reports and
transactions

▶ Executable programs were reports designed for read-access to databases.

▶ Dialog programs used to handle transactions in a business sense; they executed accesses to database tables that changed their data.

Although very few technical limitations existed, mixed forms almost never occurred. For example, dynpro sequences were called only rarely in executable programs, and the use of selection screens and lists was limited to executable programs.

Classical program
execution today

Within the context of ABAP Objects, both types of specialized program execution have lost a great deal of importance, and the separation into different task areas hardly plays a role at all.

▶ Whenever possible, dialog transactions and module pools should no longer be used. You can use an OO transaction instead of a dialog transaction. When you use classical dynpros, you should encapsulate them into function groups and call them via function modules. The use of dialog modules in these kinds of function groups should be exclusively limited to handling dynpros. The dialog modules should not contain any application functionality.

▶ Executable programs can be used where programs should be executed via program names or where a SUBMIT statement is required technically—as is the case with background processing, for example. In executable programs, only the standard event, START-OF-SELECTION, should be implemented as the starting point and not contain anything other than a method call.

7.2   Procedural Modularization

The basic difference between classic ABAP and ABAP Objects is that classic ABAP has no classes and no explicit instantiation of objects. That means no option for object-oriented modularization, no way to encapsulate data in classes and objects, and no methods to work with this data.

Modularization

In classic ABAP, modularization is limited to functional modularization using procedures. Of course, procedures can contain local data, but they are unsuitable for data encapsulation, the reason being that the local data of a procedure is available only to this procedure and only during its execution. Consequently, this data is purely temporary working data.

The only level of real data encapsulation available in classic ABAP is the ABAP program itself. The global data of a program is visible only in the program and can be changed in its processing blocks. In this view, a program plays the same role in terms of its global data that a class plays in terms of its attributes. But that exhausts the similarity between classes and programs.

Data encapsulation

There is no explicit instantiation of ABAP programs or, in particular, multiple instantiation. The instantiation of a program occurs implicitly when it is loaded into an internal session via a program call or an external procedure call. One program instance is created per internal session and is then used for all subsequent accesses. Additionally, there is no explicit lifetime control. Once a program has been loaded, it exists along with its data until the internal session is terminated.

Instantiation

The lack of an option for explicit instantiation limits classic ABAP to procedural modularization. The feature permits making reusable functionality available in procedures. The procedures of classic ABAP are function modules for external modularization and subroutines for internal modularization. When you call such a procedure, you transfer input data to the parameter interface and collect the results there after execution of the procedure. The auxiliary variables you declare within a procedure are unnecessary outside of the procedure.

Procedural programming

A classical procedure cannot work with the encapsulated data of its own class, as is the case with a method. Instead, the data to be processed at each call must be transferred to a procedure, or the procedure must access globally available data. Please note that the other processing blocks of classic ABAP (event blocks and dialog modules) don't even have a parameter interface or support local data. In classic ABAP, outsourcing functionality in procedures was the approach recommended to improve the legibility and maintainability of programs and to provide a way to reuse functionality.

Data encapsulation and data transfer

7.2.1 Function Modules

Function modules are the predecessors of public methods of global classes. In general, public methods should replace function modules. But function modules have great importance in classic ABAP. In clas-

461

sic ABAP, they are by far the most frequently used procedures to make reusable functionality available across programs. Even today, some tasks can use only function modules rather than methods, such as *remote function calls* (see Section 12.2) or *update tasks* (see Section 10.1.3).

Function Builder

Function modules are procedures specifically intended for an external call from other ABAP programs. You can create function modules only in an ABAP program of the function group type. To create function groups and function modules, you must use the Function Builder of the ABAP Workbench. A function module in a function group is very similar to a static method in a global class. And the Function Builder is similar to the Class Builder. But while a method of a global class can be used only with knowledge of a class or an interface, each function module is its own repository object that can be directly used in all ABAP programs with its name—as long as it is allowed by the package check. That's why the name of each function module must be unique within AS ABAP.

Side effects

Although function modules are their own repository objects that often give an impression of being completely independent, you must always consider their role as a procedure of an ABAP program, both during development and use. During development of a function module, the syntactical correctness of the entire function group is assumed. When you use a function module that accesses the global data of a function group, it can influence the behavior of other function modules within the same group.

Function group

As with all ABAP programs, a function group can contain a global declaration part and, in addition to function modules, it can contain all processing blocks except event blocks for reporting events. Dynpros and selection screens are also an option.[4] When you call a function module, the entire function group with all its components is loaded in the internal session of the calling program. It remains there until the internal session is shut down, which is why you must plan how to organize your function modules into groups very carefully. Create different function modules in a common group only when they also use common components of the group, such as global data or dynpros, so that they are not unnecessarily loaded into the mem-

---

4 Function groups are the means of choice for encapsulating classical dynpros and selection screens.

ory. For the same reason, you should never mix frequently used function modules with rarely used function modules in one function group. Furthermore, function groups that are called frequently in a program should not be distributed across several different function groups so that only a few additional programs must be loaded. To monitor the use of a function group, you can use the test tool, Coverage Analyzer (see Section 13.1.3).

When you use the global data of a function group in the function modules of that function group, you must always note that this data remains in the function group that was loaded, even after you leave a function module. A function module of the same function group that is called later finds the data in exactly the same condition in which the previous function module left it.[5] You can take advantage of this feature by loading several internal tables into a function group once, and then using different function modules to access the table.[6] The LOAD-OF-PROGRAM event is well suited for the initialization of that kind of global data; however, you must also note that global data might be used for various purposes in different function modules. Therefore, make sure that a function module does not use incorrect values when you call it.

Global data

A function group must already exist when you create a function module. As noted in the practical introduction in Section 2.7.1, you create a new function group in the Object Navigator. For the examples in this chapter, we have created a new function group named Z_FLIGHT_LIST (see Figure 7.3).

Creating a function group

With the exception of class pools, it's worth investing time to determine how they are composed from include programs (see Section 3.3.1). To do this, you can click on the **Main program** button in the display of the function group in Figure 7.3. The button displays the function group in the ABAP Editor (see Figure 7.4).

Main program

---

5 In object-oriented terminology, a function group loaded in an internal session is an object with global data as private attributes. The function modules work with the attributes as public methods.

6 If the data is to be used without change and in several programs, storage in shared objects should, of course, be preferred (see Section 6.6).

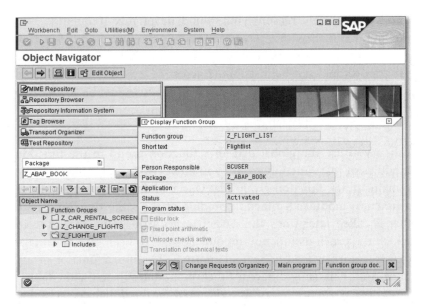

Figure 7.3 Function Group

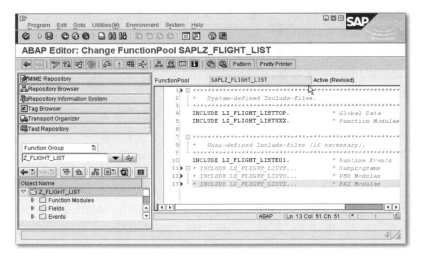

Figure 7.4 Function Group as Main Program

Naming
convention

You can see that the actual program name of a function group consists of the prefix "SAPL" and the name we have selected. You need this name whenever you want to address the entire function group. A function group is made up exclusively of include programs. According to the naming convention defined in the Function

Builder, the name of each include program consists of the prefix "L," the name of the function group, and a specific ending.

The first include program is the TOP include (see Section 3.3.1). It contains the global declaration part of the function group. Directly beneath are include programs that contain the function modules of the function group. The Function Builder generates these include programs. The includes for function modules must not be changed. In the lines in Figure 7.4 that have been commented out, you can remove the comment character if needed and use forward navigation to generate and integrate additional include programs to implement other processing blocks. The following illustrates the naming convention, which is prescribed by the Function Builder: the two periods (..) stand for a two-digit number.[7]

Include programs

▶ Ending "P..": Implementation of methods of local classes

▶ Ending "O..": Implementation of PBO modules

▶ Ending "I..": Implementation of PAI modules

▶ Ending "E..": Implementation of event blocks

▶ Ending "F..": Implementation of local subroutines

Additionally, include programs with a "D.." ending are foreseen for the declaration parts of local classes and can be integrated in the TOP include.[8]

In our sample function group, we have created an include program with an "E.." ending for the LOAD-OF-PROGRAM event. Listings 7.6 and 7.7 show the source code of the TOP include and of the include for the event blocks.

Listing 7.6 TOP Include of a Function Group

TOP include

```
*&---------------------------------------------------*
*&  Include           LZ_FLIGHT_LISTTOP
*&---------------------------------------------------*

FUNCTION-POOL z_flight_list.
```

---

7 Note that these include programs are intended for use in a single function group. We suggest the same for all include programs (see Section 3.3.1).

8 As of the next SAP NetWeaver release, all the include programs listed here will be defaulted as comments (a direct result of this book, given that the book and the Function Builder stem from the same corridor at SAP in Walldorf, Germany).

```
DATA: BEGIN OF g_buffer_line,
        carrid      TYPE spfli-carrid,
        flight_list TYPE spfli_tab,
      END OF g_buffer_line,
      g_buffer LIKE HASHED TABLE
               OF g_buffer_line
               WITH UNIQUE KEY carrid.
```

Listing 7.7 Constructor of a Function Group

```
*&---------------------------------------------------------------*
*&  Include           LZ_FLIGHT_LISTE01
*&---------------------------------------------------------------*

LOAD-OF-PROGRAM.
  g_buffer_line-carrid = 'LH'.
  SELECT *
         FROM spfli
         INTO TABLE g_buffer_line-flight_list
         WHERE carrid = g_buffer_line-carrid.
  INSERT g_buffer_line INTO TABLE g_buffer.
```

The FUNCTION-POOL statement that introduces the program is predefined and must not be removed. You can declare the global data of
the function group beneath it that can be accessed by all function
modules. As a demonstration, we declared an internal table that contains two components: a key field and an additional internal table of
type SPFLI_TAB from the ABAP Dictionary. We will use this table as
a local program buffer for data from a database table. In the LOAD-OF-
PROGRAM event block, we implement a program constructor that populates the internal table with start values.

Function modules You can create methods in any programs, but not local function modules. For that reason, you cannot directly enter the syntax to declare
a function module. Instead, you must always use the interface of the
Function Builder. As is the case when you create the methods of a
global class, the implementation is the only item that must be
entered in the ABAP Editor.[9]

---

9 Unlike the situation with global classes in class pools, the syntax for declaration
   of a function module cannot be displayed. The visible include programs contain
   only the implementation, while the interface is inserted as a comment.

To create function modules in an existing function group, use the **Function Builder**
Object Navigator as described in the practical introduction in Section
2.7.3. As an alternative, you can call the Function Builder independently as Transaction SE37. The disadvantage here is that you will not
have an overview of all the components of the function group. If you
use Transaction SE37 by itself, you might easily get the impression
that function modules are isolated development objects of AS ABAP.
It's true that function modules can be thought of and used in that
manner, but you should never forget their role as procedures of
function groups with all the related consequences.

The interface of the Function Builder contains tabs for the individual
elements of a function module (see Figure 7.5).

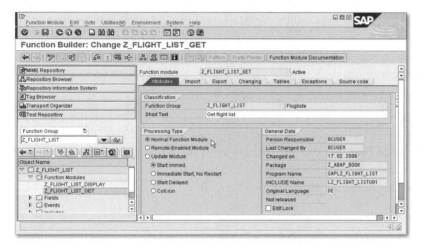

Figure 7.5 Attributes of a Function Module

You use the **Attributes** tab to set some important attributes of the **Attributes**
module. The **Processing Type** is particularly important. For example,
if you want to use the RFC interface (see Section 12.2) to access a
function module, you must identify the module as a **Remote-Enabled
Module**. Also note the **Update Module** process type, which is
described in greater detail in Section 10.1.3.

The definition of a parameter interface basically corresponds to that **Parameter
of a public method of a global class. There are three tabs for the fol- interface**
lowing types of parameters:

- ▶ Input parameters (**Import**)
- ▶ Output parameters (**Export**)
- ▶ Input-/Output parameters (**Changing**)

What applies to methods (see Section 6.1.1) also applies to these parameters. Note that a function module cannot have a return value. Instead, you can use the **Tables** tab to create special table parameters to transfer internal tables. This type of parameter is obsolete and should no longer be used.[10] Instead, you can type the other types of parameters as internal tables.

Typing   As is the case with the public methods of global classes, you can specify only built-in ABAP types, global types from the ABAP Dictionary, or types from the public visibility section of a global class during typing. As is the case with methods, you can select pass by reference or pass by value as the transfer type. Formal parameters can be optional, and the link to actual parameters can be checked in the function module using IS SUPPLIED.

Figure 7.6 shows the definition of an input parameter and Figure 7.7 shows the definition of an output parameter for function module Z_FLIGHT_LIST_GET of our function group Z_FLIGHT_LIST. The typing of both parameters is done with the data types of the ABAP Dictionary. The explanatory short texts are transferred from the ABAP Dictionary, but they can be changed.

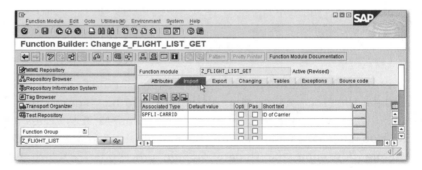

Figure 7.6 Input Parameter of a Function Module

---

10 Technically speaking, table parameters are CHANGING parameters passed by reference. They are typed as internal standard tables with a header line.

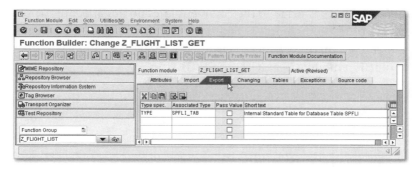

Figure 7.7 Output Parameter of a Function Module

In the **Exceptions** tab, you can enter the exceptions that can be trig- Exceptions
gered by a function module. As is the case with methods, we recommend using class-based exceptions. Because of the large number of
existing function modules that were created before the introduction
of class-based exceptions, you will still find the definition of classical
exceptions in the interfaces of many function modules (see Section
8.2.2). Figure 7.8 shows the declaration of class-based exception
ZCX_NO_FLIGHTS in the interface for Z_FLIGHT_LIST_GET, which
we have already used in the example for shared objects in Section
6.6.3.

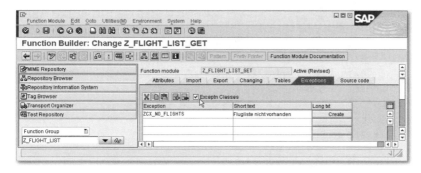

Figure 7.8 Exceptions of a Function Module

You can implement a function module in the **Source code** tab of the Implementation
ABAP editor. The procedure is the same as for the implementation of
methods. The only difference is that FUNCTION–ENDFUNCTION defines
the processing block rather than METHOD–ENDMETHOD. The declaration
of the parameter interface is displayed as a comment beneath FUNC-
TION, with a syntax that corresponds to the syntax of METHODS state-

ments.[11] Changes made to the comment lines do not affect the actual interface. The comment is regenerated each time one of the parameters defined there is changed. Listing 7.8 shows the implementation of function module Z_FLIGHT_LIST_GET.

FUNCTION –
ENDFUNCTION

Listing 7.8 Implementation of a Function Module

```
FUNCTION z_flight_list_get.
*"----------------------------------------------------------
*"*"Local interface:
*"  IMPORTING
*"     REFERENCE(CARRID) TYPE  SPFLI-CARRID
*"  EXPORTING
*"     REFERENCE(FLIGHT_LIST) TYPE  SPFLI_TAB
*"  RAISING
*"     ZCX_NO_FLIGHTS
*"----------------------------------------------------------
  DATA buffer_line LIKE LINE OF g_buffer.
  READ TABLE g_buffer
             WITH TABLE KEY carrid = carrid
             INTO buffer_line.
  IF sy-subrc = 0.
    flight_list = buffer_line-flight_list.
  ELSE.
    SELECT *
           FROM  spfli
           INTO  TABLE flight_list
           WHERE carrid = carrid.
    IF sy-subrc <> 0.
      RAISE EXCEPTION TYPE zcx_no_flights.
    ENDIF.
    buffer_line-carrid      = carrid.
    buffer_line-flight_list = flight_list.
    INSERT buffer_line INTO TABLE g_buffer.
  ENDIF.
ENDFUNCTION.
```

The function module attempts to read a flight list for the airline contained in input parameter CARRID from the internal table created in the global declaration part of the function group and to transfer the list to output parameter FLIGHT_LIST. If the list is not yet present, it

---

11 Here we can finally see the syntax of the declaration of the function module, which is otherwise hidden behind the interface. The related include program is restricted. It is considered during compilation, but not displayed.

is read from the database and inserted into the internal table.[12] If no data is found, exception ZCX_NO_FLIGHTS is triggered.

Listing 7.9 shows the implementation of an additional function module of our function group. It is simply a copy of the implementation of the `display` method from Listing 6.32.

Listing 7.9 Implementation of an Additional Function Module

```
FUNCTION z_flight_list_display.
*"----------------------------------------------------------
*"*"Local interface:
*"  IMPORTING
*"     VALUE(FLIGHT_LIST) TYPE  SPFLI_TAB
*"----------------------------------------------------------
  DATA alv TYPE REF TO cl_salv_table.
  TRY.
      cl_salv_table=>factory(
        IMPORTING r_salv_table = alv
        CHANGING  t_table      = flight_list ).
      alv->display( ).
    CATCH cx_salv_msg.
      MESSAGE 'ALV display not possible' TYPE 'I'
              DISPLAY LIKE 'E'.
  ENDTRY.
ENDFUNCTION.
```

Once all elements have been completed, a function module must be activated (as is the case with almost all repository objects). It can then be called in all the programs permitted by the package check.[13]

You can test function modules individually in the Function Builder. We have already shown the procedure in the practical introduction in Section 2.7.4. Because the task of a function module is mainly to enable the reuse of functionality, these kinds of individual tests are generally simpler than testing methods in the Class Builder. You can select **Function Module • Release** to release a completed and tested function module for use. Usually, you cannot change the interface of a function module once it has been released.

Testing and releasing function modules

---

12 This treatment of local program buffering is intended only to demonstrate access to the global data of a function group. It is in no way comparable to the options for shared objected introduced in Section 6.6.

13 Individual activation of a function module generally assumes an active function group. Activation of the entire function group activates all the function modules.

The syntax for calling a function module is as follows:

```
CALL FUNCTION func EXPORTING i1 = dobj1 i2 = dobj2 ...
                   IMPORTING o1 = dobj1 o2 = dobj2 ...
                   CHANGING  c1 = dobj2 c2 = dobj2 ...
                   TABLES    t1 = itab1 t2 = itab2 ...
```

You can use func to specify any function module of AS ABAP permitted by the package check.[14] Because each function module is unique, you don't have to specify the function group. Unlike the situation with a method call, a function module is not specified directly, but exclusively as the content of a character-like data object. Accordingly, it is always dynamic. But, because this chapter describes the static transfer of actual parameters, the real dynamic specification of the function module in a variable is unnecessary. With the static form illustrated here, the function module is therefore generally specified as a text field literal:

```
CALL FUNCTION '...' ...
```

When you insert the call of a function module with the **Sample** function of the ABAP Editor, the ABAP Workbench does exactly the same thing. Just try it out. Chapter 11 describes true dynamic calls.

Actual parameters   The static assignment of actual parameters to the formal parameters of the function module is completely identical to the call of methods with any parameters (see Section 6.1.2). Unlike the situation with a method call, the correctness of the syntax is checked only during an extended program check (see Section 13.1.2) rather than in a syntax check. That's why we strongly recommend using extended program checks. If a function module has non-optional table parameters, you must specify internal tables as actual parameters for these parameters after TABLES.

Exception handling   When class-based exceptions are declared in the parameter interface of the function module, they are handled with CATCH statements (see Section 8.2.1). As noted above, because many function modules with classical exceptions still exist, you must handle primarily these exceptions when you use CALL FUNCTION. A dedicated EXCEPTIONS

---

14 You can also call function modules locally within their function group. But, because the primary purpose of function modules is to be called externally, you can use methods of local classes for internal modularization (subroutines were used for that in the past).

addition is available for this purpose. It sets `sy-subrc` to a return value when a non-class exception is raised in the function module. For more detailed information, see Section 8.2.2.

Listing 7.10 shows the call of both function modules of function group Z_FLIGHT_LIST in the `main` method of a program.

Listing 7.10 Calling Function Modules

```
REPORT z_call_function.

SELECTION-SCREEN BEGIN OF SCREEN 100.
PARAMETERS p_carrid TYPE spfli-carrid.
SELECTION-SCREEN END OF SCREEN 100.

CLASS demo DEFINITION.
  PUBLIC SECTION.
    CLASS-METHODS main.
  PRIVATE SECTION.
    CLASS-DATA flights TYPE spfli_tab.
ENDCLASS.

CLASS demo IMPLEMENTATION.
  METHOD main .
    DO.
      CALL SELECTION-SCREEN 100
        STARTING AT 10 10.
      IF sy-subrc = 0.
        TRY.
            CALL FUNCTION 'Z_FLIGHT_LIST_GET'
              EXPORTING carrid      = p_carrid
              IMPORTING flight_list = flights.
            CALL FUNCTION 'Z_FLIGHT_LIST_DISPLAY'
              EXPORTING flight_list = flights.
          CATCH zcx_no_flights.
            MESSAGE 'No flights' TYPE 'I'
            DISPLAY LIKE 'E'.
        ENDTRY.
      ELSE.
        RETURN.
      ENDIF.
    ENDDO.
  ENDMETHOD.
ENDCLASS.

START-OF-SELECTION.
  demo=>main( ).
```

On a selection screen, an ID for an airline can be entered. The function modules Z_FLIGHT_LIST_GET and Z_FLIGHT_LIST_DISPLAY are called for this ID. Use the ABAP Debugger to observe how our small buffering of flight lists in a function group works.

7.2.2 Subroutines

Subroutines represent the predecessor technology of methods of local classes. Meanwhile, methods should replace subroutines completely. Subroutines used to serve the internal functional modularization of classical ABAP programs. You can no longer create any subroutines in class pools.

Unlike the situation with global classes and function modules, the ABAP Workbench does not provide any tools to create subroutines, because no external interface is needed. Instead, subroutines are written directly into the source code of a program, just like the methods of local classes. But unlike methods and function modules, subroutines are not split into declaration and implementation. A subroutine is both defined and implemented in the implementation part of a program. The syntax is:

FORM—
ENDFORM

```
FORM subr
  [USING      uᵢ          TYPE type ...]
  [CHANGING   cᵢ          TYPE type ...]
  [RASING     eᵢ].
  ...
ENDFORM.
```

The FORM statement defines a subroutine, subr, and its parameter interface. The subroutine is implemented between FORM and ENDFORM.

Parameter interface

The parameter interface differs somewhat from methods and function modules. Subroutines use the USING addition instead of IMPORTING, and there are no EXPORTING or RETURNING additions. You can type the parameters of subroutines just as you do with local methods. For subroutines, typing is not required, but we recommend it. If you do not specify a type, a formal parameter is set implicitly to the generic type, any.

Kind of parameter passing

By default, the kind of parameter passing is pass by reference and, like methods, can be set individually for each parameter with VALUE(...)as a pass by value. You cannot define the formal parameters of a subroutine as optional. You can declare class-based exceptions using RAISING, which means that you can propagate them from subroutines.

In terms of the parameter type, USING parameters behave like input parameters, and CHANGING parameters behave like input-/output parameters of methods (see Section 6.1.1), with one exception: USING parameters with pass by reference behave like CHANGING parameters. No syntax error occurs when they are overwritten in the subroutine. We strongly recommend that you handle USING parameters passed by reference just like true input parameters, that is, do not overwrite them.

Parameter type

As with function modules, you can still declare obsolete table parameters in the interface of a subroutine by using the TABLES addition, which must occur before USING. This kind of table parameter always has a header line of the same name, so that the subroutine then contains two formal parameters of the same name.[15]

Table parameters

The syntax for an internal call of a subroutine is:[16]

```
PERFORM subr
   USING    ... dobj1 dobj2 ...
   CHANGING ... dobj1 dobj2 ... .
```

PERFORM

You can directly specify every subroutine of the same program with subr. Dynamic variations of this statement also exist, but this book does not address them. Compared with the call of methods and function modules, note the missing assignment of the actual parameters to the formal parameters with the = operator. Only the sequence in which the actual parameters are specified matters here.

In PERFORM, for each formal parameter of the subroutine, a properly typed actual parameter must be specified in the same position as after FORM. The first actual parameter is transferred to the first formal parameter of the subroutine, and so on. The USING and CHANGING

---

15 In ABAP objects, a header line is a forbidden, obsolete work area of an internal table. Its type is the line type and it has the same name as the internal table. If you use an internal table with a header line in an operand position, in most cases, the header line is addressed and not the table body. To force access to the body of the table, you can enter square brackets [ ] after the identifier. This book does not address header lines any further.

16 Greetings from Cobol!

additions in the PERFORM statement play a subordinate, or describing role. The formal parameters of subroutines are pure positional parameters, not keyword parameters.

External subroutine call
Although subroutines in classic ABAP were generally intended for the internal functional modularization of an ABAP program, the PERFORM statement also contains a variant for the external call of a subroutine (subr) in another program (prog):

```
PERFORM subr IN PROGRAM prog ... .
```

Similar to the call of function modules, the external program is loaded into the internal session of the caller if it was not already present. At the same time, the system creates so-called *program groups* that define the program whose components are accessed by an externally called subroutine. This assignment can depend on the sequence of calls. This concept poses some difficulties that we cannot cover in detail in this book. We can only refer you to the ABAP keyword documentation and *The Official ABAP Reference* book. But even in classic ABAP, this concept already led to recommendations against external subroutine calls.

From the point of view of visibility, each subroutine of an ABAP program is automatically part of the public interface of the program because of the above statement. For example, in addition to its official function modules, each function group also implicitly offers its subroutines and does so even though no explicit and stable interface exists for them. Therefore, a calling program could, for instance, change the data of a function group without its control by calling internal help routines instead of the function modules. Only the new, operational package concept that will be introduced in the next release will prohibit such an access.

Subroutine pool
Although an external call of the subroutines of any program is actually a danger, with subroutine pools, classic ABAP provided even a program type that was especially intended for subroutines that could be called externally. With subroutine pools, it is at least apparent that their subroutines are intended for external calls. Still, that does not solve the conceptual problems of the lack of a public parameter interface and the organization into program groups.

There are enough good reasons to avoid creating and using subroutines these days:

▶ Compared with the parameter interface of methods, the parameter interface has definite weaknesses: positional parameters, a lack of a real import parameter in the case of pass by reference, no optional parameters, and only optional typing.

▶ The external call of the subroutine creates program groups in the internal session that are unnecessary for the external call of methods or function modules.

▶ Each subroutine implicitly belongs to the public interface of its program, which is generally undesirable.

You should use only the methods of local classes for internal modularization, because they provide an advanced parameter interface and prevent other programs from accessing it. Nowadays, the program type subroutine pool can and should be used only as a container for local classes where a method is linked to a transaction code (see the example in Section 2.8.4).

Methods instead of subroutines

The only reason for the continued existence of subroutines and the external call of subroutines, besides the usual justification of downward compatibility, is the GENERATE SUBROUTINE POOL statement of generic programming (see Section 11.5.1), for which no real object-oriented counterpart like GENERATE CLASS-POOL yet exists.

For the sake of completeness, but not for the sake of imitation, Listing 7.11 shows an example of the definition and internal use of subroutines. The example has the same effect as the call of function modules given in listing 7.10.

Listing 7.11 Subroutines

```
REPORT z_subroutines.

PARAMETERS p_carrid TYPE spfli-carrid.
DATA flights TYPE TABLE OF spfli.
START-OF-SELECTION.
  TRY.
    PERFORM flight_list_get
      USING    p_carrid
      CHANGING flights.
    PERFORM flight_list_display
      USING    flights.
  CATCH zcx_no_flights.
    MESSAGE 'No flights' TYPE 'I'
```

```
        DISPLAY LIKE 'E'.
    ENDTRY.
FORM flight_list_get
  USING     carrid       TYPE spfli-carrid
  CHANGING flight_list LIKE flights
  RAISING   zcx_no_flights.
  SELECT *
        FROM   spfli
        INTO   TABLE flight_list
        WHERE carrid = carrid.
  IF sy-subrc <> 0.
    RAISE EXCEPTION TYPE zcx_no_flights.
  ENDIF.
ENDFORM.
FORM flight_list_display
  USING flight_list LIKE flights.
  DATA alv TYPE REF TO cl_salv_table.
  TRY.
      cl_salv_table=>factory(
        IMPORTING r_salv_table = alv
        CHANGING  t_table      = flight_list ).
      alv->display( ).
    CATCH cx_salv_msg.
      MESSAGE 'ALV display not possible' TYPE 'I'
              DISPLAY LIKE 'E'.
  ENDTRY.
ENDFORM.
```

We see the implementation of subroutine `flight_list_display` here for the third time. We have already seen the identical coding in a function module in Listing 7.9 and in a method in Listing 6.32. That shows that an implementation is independent of the type of procedure. But it also shows that ABAP offers three concepts for the same purpose. For better legibility and maintenance of ABAP programs, we recommend limiting yourself to one concept, which would of course mean using methods instead of subroutines in this case.

> *"A man who commits a mistake and doesn't correct it is committing another mistake."*
> — Confucius

8 Error Handling

8.1 Robust Programs

One of the key quality criteria for software is the robustness of a program. If an error or problem occurs, the program should be able to deal with the situation appropriately and not crash. It should therefore behave deterministically. This chapter shows you how to make your ABAP programs robust.

8.1.1 Defensive Programming

Defensive programming is just one of the many names given to different programming techniques that aim to reduce errors and problems in a program. The goal of defensive programming is to avoid runtime and other errors in a program by considering possible errors right from the start, thereby preventing them before they occur. If you're considering passing on your procedures to other developers, adhering to these defensive programming techniques is especially important.

Since the technique is a general software development technique and not an ABAP-specific technique, we only want to address this topic briefly here. The following list therefore covers a few typical defensive programming scenarios as examples. These examples illustrate some very simple approaches that can make programs more robust (see also Section 4.9 on defensive programming with ABAP objects):

Defensive programming approaches

- ▶ **Validity Check for Parameters and Input Fields**
  This check executes a semantic verification in addition to the formal check, i. e., it checks the plausibility of the input data.

- ▶ **Definition and Clean Handling of Optional Parameters**
  Optional parameters and their default settings are frequent

sources of error in procedures. They can produce constellations that are legitimate in terms of form, but that make no sense from a content viewpoint.

▶ **Upfront Type Check**
The main tasks of a program include explicit and implicit type conversions. During dynamic programming, in particular, situations may arise in which the data object type does not permit an operation that should be applied to the data object.

▶ **Full Coverage for** `IF ... ENDIF` **and** `CASE ... ENDCASE`
These statements should be fully programmed, even if it seems obvious that certain cases cannot occur. Therefore, an `ELSE` or `WHEN OTHERS` branch should always exist.

You can add to this list as required; however, the message of each point in this list is always the same. In defensive programming, every little piece of code must be checked to determine whether anything could go wrong.

This methodology does not totally prevent errors from occurring. Even if programmers are extremely careful when creating a program, they cannot predict with certainty all of the undesirable situations that may arise during the runtime of a program. These situations are referred to as *exception situations*.

8.1.2 Exception Situations

Exception situations can have very different causes. Coding may actually be implemented incorrectly, or a called procedure (or software component) may be used incorrectly, if the wrong parameter is transferred, for example. Another frequent cause of exception situations is the interaction between a program and external resources, such as user entries, the file system, or the memory.

In all of these situations, a program should behave as robustly as possible. This doesn't just mean that a program shouldn't crash; it means ensuring that the exception situation is dealt with sensibly. The user of a software component should also be able to recognize that an exception situation has occurred and then be able to determine why it has occurred. If a software component cannot handle an exception situation, the exception should be forwarded to the caller to be handled.

A good exception concept must take into account all of these requirements. In this chapter, we will familiarize you with the exception concept for ABAP objects. You'll see that there is a wide range of options available to support you in creating robust software.

8.2   Exception Handling

Exception situations can be detected by either the program or the runtime environment. When the ABAP program or the runtime environment detects an exception situation, it triggers an exception.

Exceptions are either *treatable* or *untreatable*. Unhandled exceptions—all untreatable exceptions and all treatable exceptions that were not caught in the program—cause a runtime error. This means that the program terminates with a short dump (see Section 8.2.5). Treatable exceptions are predefined in the system, or can be self-defined. Nowadays (since Release 6.10), class-based exceptions should be used in ABAP. The exception handling prior to this release is known as *classic exception handling*, which we will look at briefly in Section 8.2.2. Whenever we use the term "exception handling" in the following sections, we will always be referring to class-based exception handling.

Treatable versus untreatable

8.2.1   Class-Based Exception Handling
Exception Classes

If an exception situation occurs in a program, an exception object (i.e., an instance of a predefined or self-defined exception class) is generated. This describes the error situation in detail with special information. Every exception class is derived directly or indirectly from the CX_ROOT superclass. In addition to the CX_ROOT class, there are three other abstract exception classes for structuring possible exceptions. Figure 8.1 shows all four classes and their relationships in the inheritance tree. The derivation of an exception class from one of these three classes determines whether an exception has to be declared explicitly in the interface of a procedure, when it is being propagated from it, and how the declaration is checked.

Superclasses   The key characteristics of the four classes are as follows:

▶ **CX_ROOT**
This is the superclass from which every exception class is directly or indirectly derived.

▶ **CX_STATIC_CHECK**
Exceptions from this category must be handled within procedures or declared as part of the interface. This is checked by both the compiler and the runtime environment.

▶ **CX_DYNAMIC_CHECK**
Here too, exceptions that leave a procedure must be declared in the interface. However, the check is performed at runtime only.

▶ **CX_NO_CHECK**
Neither the compiler nor the runtime environment checks whether an exception that leaves the context of a procedure has also been declared in the interface.

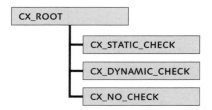

Figure 8.1 Superclasses for Exception Classes

Advantages   This exception class approach offers a range of advantages:

▶ Additional information that describes the exception context in detail can be stored in the exception objects. The error-handling program component therefore no longer needs to have precise knowledge about the error situation.

▶ The object-oriented exception handling concept also provides developers with the inheritance mechanism. This enables existing exception classes to be reused easily. New attributes can be utilized to document specific exception cases in more detail, for example.

▶ The inheritance concept enables similar exception cases to be grouped together easily. Normally, a superclass groups together all exception situations that are described by classes derived from this superclass.

We will look at the meaning of the abstract exception classes in more detail below.

Raising Exceptions

Exceptions can be raised in two ways: By the ABAP runtime environment, or explicitly in the code to display a specific exception situation.

The arithmetic statement x = 1 / 0, for example, causes an exception of the CX_SY_ZERODIVIDE class to be raised by the runtime environment. If the exception is not caught and handled, a runtime error occurs with the short dump displayed in Figure 8.2.

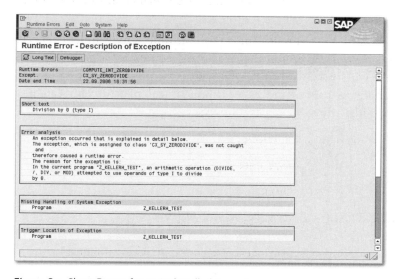

Figure 8.2 Short Dump for an Unhandled Exception

With the RAISE EXCEPTION statement, however, exceptions can be raised explicitly from the program code.

The statement

RAISE EXCEPTION TYPE cx_sy_zerodivide.   **RAISE EXCEPTION**

has the same effect as an unallowed division by zero. In both cases, an exception object is generated when the exception is raised. Its attributes contain information about the error situation.[1]

---

1 For performance reasons, the exception object is in fact only created if it is also used via the INTO addition in exception handling.

There is also a second method of raising an exception from the ABAP code in which no new exception object is generated. Instead, an existing object is used. In this case, the syntax is

```
RAISE EXCEPTION oref.
```

where `oref` is an existing exception object.

Catching and Handling Exceptions

Handlers If an exception occurs, the program flow is interrupted, an exception object is generated, and a handler is searched for this exception.[2] The exception is forwarded to the previous caller in the call hierarchy until a suitable handler is found. If no handler is found in the entire call hierarchy, the program terminates with a runtime error, and a short dump is generated, describing the unhandled exception. But how are exceptions actually caught, and what is a *handler*?

A handler is part of the `TRY–ENDTRY` control structure for catching exceptions. The syntax is as follows:

TRY, CATCH, CLEANUP
```
TRY.
  [try_block]
  [CATCH cx_class1 cx_class2 ... [INTO oref].
   [catch_block]]
  ...
  [CATCH cx_class3 cx_class4 ... [INTO oref].
   [catch_block]]
  ...
  [CLEANUP [INTO oref].
   [cleanup_block]]
ENDTRY.
```

The individual elements of the control structure have the following functions:

► The coding in the `TRY` block `try_block` defines a protected area whose exceptions can be handled in the subsequent `CATCH` blocks. If no exception occurs in the `TRY` block and its end is reached, processing continues after `ENDTRY`. If an exception occurs in the `TRY` block, the system looks for an exception handler in the same or in an outer `TRY–ENDTRY` control structure.

---

2 The basic principle of class-based exception handling in ABAP therefore involves changing the control flow of the program.

- The actual exception handlers consist of one or more optional CATCH blocks catch_block. These contain the program logic that is executed if the related exception occurs in the TRY block of the same TRY—ENDTRY control structure.

A CATCH block handles the exceptions from exception classes cx_class1 cx_class2 ..., which are specified after the CATCH statement, along with the exceptions from their respective subclasses. If the INTO addition is specified, a reference to the exception object is stored in oref, where oref must be an object reference variable whose static type must be more general or equal to the most general of the specified exception classes. oref can be used to access the attributes and methods of the exception object. This is important to gain relevant information about the exception that has occurred. When the end of a CATCH block is reached, processing continues after ENDTRY.[3]

The sequence of the handlers—or CATCH blocks—is very important. More specific exception classes must always be listed before more general exception classes. This ensures that the exception is always processed by the most specialized handler. If the exception classes are not specified in the correct sequence, a syntax error occurs.

Handler sequence

The CATCH block is not protected. Therefore, if errors are to be caught within the handler code, a separate, nested TRY—ENDTRY control structure must be used.

Catching errors in the handler

- A CLEANUP block is used to give the program or specific objects a consistent status again since the control flow of the program is generally changed when an exception occurs. You can find more information about this below in the section *Cleanup Tasks in Exception Handling*.

Look at the example in Listing 8.1 for catching and handling exceptions.

---

3 As of the next SAP NetWeaver release, class-based exceptions will be able to be raised in a way that allows them to be resumable. This will enable the program execution to be resumed after the statement that raised the exception during the handling of a resumable exception.

Listing 8.1 Handling Exceptions

```
REPORT z_exception_handling.

CLASS lcl_demo DEFINITION.
  PUBLIC SECTION.
    CLASS-METHODS
      main IMPORTING operand TYPE i.
ENDCLASS.
CLASS lcl_demo IMPLEMENTATION.
  METHOD main.
    DATA: x TYPE i,
          oError TYPE REF TO cx_root,
          txtError TYPE string.
    TRY.
      x = 1 / operand.
      x = SQRT( operand ).
      x = operand ** operand.

      CATCH cx_sy_zerodivide INTO oError.
        txtError = oError->get_longtext( ).
        MESSAGE txtError TYPE 'I' DISPLAY LIKE 'E'.

      CATCH cx_sy_arg_out_of_domain INTO oError.
        txtError = oError->get_longtext( ).
        MESSAGE txtError TYPE 'I' DISPLAY LIKE 'E'.

      CATCH cx_root INTO oError.
        txtError = oError->get_longtext( ).
        MESSAGE txtError TYPE 'I' DISPLAY LIKE 'E'.
    ENDTRY.
  ENDMETHOD.
ENDCLASS.

START-OF-SELECTION.
  lcl_demo=>main( operand = 0 ).
  lcl_demo=>main( operand = -1 ).
  lcl_demo=>main( operand = 1000000 ).
```

The example implemented in Listing 8.1 should execute three different arithmetic operations. The arithmetic operations (division, square root calculation, and potentialization) can trigger different error situations, depending on the value of the parameter transferred in operand. When the main method is called, the following error situations occur:

If the value 0 is transferred, the first arithmetic operation is division by zero. This is processed by the first handler for the cx_sy_zerodivide exception class. If the value -1 is transferred, the handler for the `cx_sy_arg_out_of_domain` exception class is executed, because the square root of a negative value cannot be calculated. In both cases, we provided the exact required exception classes in the handlers,.

The third handler that processes the `cx_root` exception class catches all exceptions for which no suitable handler could be found previously. This is the case with the third arithmetic operation because the permitted value range of the integer data type is exceeded. The `cx_sy_arithmetic_overflow` exception is created, which we did not exactly predict; however, because `cx_root` is the root of all exception classes in the class hierarchy, it can catch all the exceptions of its subclasses.

In each of the handlers, the relevant error message is output, supplying information about the precise reason for the error.

In this example, we could have grouped the individual exception classes directly, one after another in one single CATCH statement because we are executing the same coding in all cases.

Propagating Exceptions in a Call Hierarchy

The example in Listing 8.1 illustrates how exceptions can be caught and handled. We will find far more complex structures in productive software components. As a rule, procedures call other procedures, creating a corresponding call hierarchy. If an exception is not handled in a procedure, the system attempts to propagate it to the caller of the procedure.

The example in Figure 8.3 shows what the call hierarchy for displaying a website might look like. The following flow is executed:

Call hierarchy

1. The `show` method is called in a TRY block.

2. The `show` method, in turn, calls the `retrieve` method in a TRY block.

3. Within the `retrieve` method, RAISE EXCEPTION is used to raise the `cx_page_not_found` exception. Because the exception does not occur within a TRY block in the `retrieve` method, the next TRY block is searched for within the call hierarchy—in other words, the TRY block within the `show` method.

4. Here, a check is performed to see if a suitable handler exists for the `cx_page_not_found` exception. Since this is not the case, the exception is passed upwards again in the call hierarchy.

5. Here, a suitable handler is found for the exception.

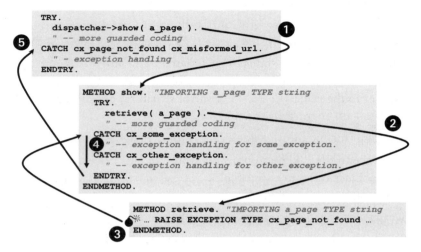

Figure 8.3 Propagating Exceptions

The general procedure for finding the correct handler for an exception is shown in Figure 8.4.

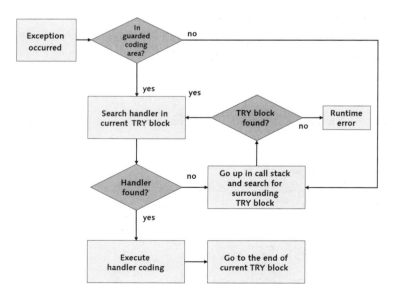

Figure 8.4 Identifying the Correct Exception Handler

Cleanup Tasks in Exception Handling

If an exception occurs and is caught and handled by a handler, the normal control flow of the program is changed, and a procedure is generally left early. This means that a program or certain objects may come into an inconsistent status, or that resources have not been released yet.

The CLEANUP block in the TRY–ENDTRY control structure is used to re-establish a consistent status. The statements in this block are executed if an exception occurs in a TRY block that is not caught by a handler in the same TRY–ENDTRY control structure, but in a surrounding TRY–ENDTRY control structure.

CLEANUP

If the INTO oref addition is specified after the CLEANUP keyword, a reference to the exception object is stored in oref, where oref must be an object reference variable of the cx_root type. The exception object can be accessed via oref.

After the CLEANUP block has been executed, the CLEANUP blocks for the surrounding TRY control structures are executed until the corresponding handler code has been executed. Figure 8.5 shows an example of the control flow process when the CLEANUP block is executed.

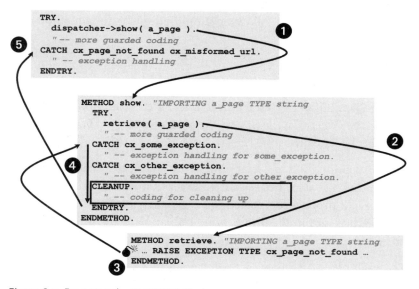

Figure 8.5 Executing the CLEANUP Block

This example is structured similarly to the example in Figure 8.3. The only difference is that the CLEANUP block is executed in step four here, in which no suitable handler has been found for the exception yet.

Leaving the CLEANUP block A CLEANUP block must be left in the normal way—in other words, executed through to the end—because the handler code has to be executed before the normal control flow of the program can proceed. Statements, such as RETURN or LEAVE TO, which would cause the CLEANUP block to be left early, result in a runtime error. In addition, exceptions that occur within a CLEANUP block must also be caught and handled there. Otherwise, a non-catchable runtime error would occur here too.

Declaring Exceptions in Procedure Interfaces

As mentioned in the previous section, the system attempts to propagate an exception, which is not handled in a procedure, to the caller of the procedure. In the parameter interface of a procedure, the exceptions that can be propagated from the procedure must be declared. This tells the caller which exceptions can be expected from the procedure.

RAISING To declare an exception in the interface of a procedure, the RAISING addition is used, as the following simplified syntax for a method declaration shows:

```
METHODS meth ...
            RAISING excl exc2 ....
```

In the Class Builder or Function Builder, the declaration is made by listing the exception classes in the **Exceptions** tab. The **Exception Classes** checkbox must be selected.

If an exception class is declared in an interface, this declaration also applies to all of its subclasses. If an exception is not declared, it cannot leave a procedure. Instead, an interface violation results if it is not handled within the procedure. A violation of the interface raises an exception from the predefined class CX_SY_NO_HANDLER.

The example in Listing 8.2 shows the effects of an exception declaration in an interface.

Listing 8.2 Declaring Exceptions

```
REPORT z_exception_declaration.

CLASS lcl_demo DEFINITION.
  PUBLIC SECTION.
    CLASS-METHODS:
      main.
  PRIVATE SECTION.
    CLASS-METHODS:
      calc IMPORTING operand TYPE i
           RAISING cx_sy_zerodivide.
ENDCLASS.

CLASS lcl_demo IMPLEMENTATION.
  METHOD calc.
    DATA: x TYPE i.
    x = 1 / operand.
    x = SQRT( operand ).
  ENDMETHOD.

  METHOD main.
    DATA: oError TYPE REF TO cx_root,
          txtError TYPE string.
    TRY.
      calc( operand = 0 ).
      CATCH cx_sy_zerodivide INTO oError.
        txtError = oError->get_longtext( ).
        MESSAGE txtError TYPE 'I' DISPLAY LIKE 'E'.
    ENDTRY.

    TRY.
      calc( operand = -1 ).
      CATCH cx_sy_arg_out_of_domain INTO oError.
        txtError = oError->get_longtext( ).
        MESSAGE txtError TYPE 'I' DISPLAY LIKE 'E'.

      CATCH cx_sy_no_handler INTO oError.
        txtError = oError->get_longtext( ).
        MESSAGE txtError TYPE 'I' DISPLAY LIKE 'E'.
    ENDTRY.
  ENDMETHOD.
ENDCLASS.

START-OF-SELECTION.
    lcl_demo=>main( ).
```

Within the main method, the calc method is called twice with different parameters. In the first case, the cx_sy_zerodivide exception is raised by transferring 0. This exception is declared in the interface of the `calc` method. Because the exception is not handled locally in the `calc` method, it is propagated to the caller, in other words, to the `main` method.

The second time `calc` is called, the value -1 is transferred. This generates the `cx_sy_arg_out_of_domain` exception when attempting to determine the square root. This exception is not declared in the interface and is not handled locally in the `calc` method. It is therefore not propagated and cannot be identified by the exception handler in the `main` method. The `cx_sy_no_handler` exception handler prevents the interface violation from causing a runtime error, but which indicates that the procedure was not implemented cleanly.

Exception categories

The example shows the effects of the violation of the procedure interface in which the exception was declared. The abstract superclasses for all exception classes CX_STATIC_CHECK, CX_DYNAMIC_CHECK, and CX_NO_CHECK, which were mentioned above, come into play here because the response to the interface violation does not have to be the same for all exception classes. All exceptions are derived from the superclasses and subdivided into these three categories. These categories determine whether an explicit declaration must be made and how this is checked:

▶ **CX_STATIC_CHECK**
Generally, exceptions that occur in a procedure must either be handled there or be declared in the procedure interface to tell the caller which exceptions are to be expected. If an exception class is derived from the CX_STATIC_CHECK class, a check is made statically at compile time. This checks whether all the exceptions that were raised in the procedure using RAISE EXCEPTION or that were declared in the interfaces of called procedures are either handled with CATCH or declared explicitly in the interface. If this is not the case, the syntax check issues a warning.

▶ **CX_DYNAMIC_CHECK**
If the program logic can exclude potential error situations, the related exceptions don't have to be handled or declared in the interface. This is the case, for example, if you know that an explicit query is made before a division to determine whether the denominator does not equal 0. In this case, the caller of a procedure should not have to implement an exception handling. For subclasses from the CX_DYNAMIC_CHECK exception class, therefore,

not every potential exception has to be handled or declared, just those exceptions whose occurrence cannot be excluded.

▶ **CX_NO_CHECK**

Exceptions that can occur at virtually any time should be derived from the CX_NO_CHECK exception class. These exceptions are always declared implicitly in the interface of each procedure.

Suppose you had to catch or declare all the exceptions that can occur with resource bottlenecks. If you followed the handling or declaration requirement consistently, these exceptions would have to be specified in nearly every interface, which would totally overload the code and render it unmanageable.

The caller of a procedure must therefore always consider that the procedure also propagates exceptions from the CX_NO_CHECK category, as well as the explicitly declared exceptions.

Table 8.1 shows in which cases which exception classes are to be used as a basis. This is particularly important when defining your own exceptions—an aspect that we will discuss in more detail in the following section.

Selecting the exception class

Exception Characteristic	Chosen Exception Class
The programmer must be forced to consider the exception situation.	CX_STATIC_CHECK
The programmer can prevent the exception from occurring with an additional security query (e. g., checking the denominator for 0 in the division).	CX_DYNAMIC_CHECK
The exception is a resource problem or another external factor. The exception can occur anytime and anywhere.	CX_NO_CHECK

Table 8.1 Selecting the Correct Exception Class

Defining Exception Classes

You can also define your own local or global exception classes, in addition to the predefined exception classes whose exceptions are raised by the runtime environment if an exception situation occurs, or which you can raise yourself. All exception classes are subclasses of one of the abstract exception classes described in the previous section: CX_STATIC_CHECK, CX_DYNAMIC_CHECK, or CX_NO_CHECK. No specific class can be directly derived from CX_ROOT.

Naming convention

For global exception classes, the following naming convention applies: The class names must start with the prefix CX_ or with the prefix ZCX_, YCX_, or /customer_namespace/CX_ in customer systems.

Attributes

Every exception class inherits the following attributes from CX_ROOT:

▸ **TEXTID**
This attribute is used to define different exception texts for a specific exception class. The attribute is generally set by the constructor, and influences the result of the GET_TEXT method.

▸ **PREVIOUS**
The PREVIOUS attribute is of the CX_ROOT reference type, and can contain a reference to a previous exception. The attribute is particularly useful, because it enables exceptions to be chained. This means that you can track the path of an exception right back to its origin, for example.

Methods

Every exception class also inherits the following methods from CX_ROOT:

▸ **GET_TEXT and GET_LONGTEXT**
These methods return the exception text or the long text of the exception text as a character string of the string type. We will look at the definition of exception texts in more detail in the next section.

▸ **GET_SOURCE_POSITION**
This method returns the program name of the main program, the name of any include program concerned, and the line number of the raising point.

You can also define any other attributes and methods you require, of course, in addition to the inherited attributes and methods. These enable additional information about an exception situation to be stored in the exception object.

Local exception classes

As mentioned previously, local exception classes can be defined in addition to global classes. Just like the global classes, these are derived from one of the three abstract exception classes or from an exception class of your choice. Since exceptions are usually more of a general component in a development project and are used in many different places in a program, however, you should consider when it really makes sense to use a local exception class.

This may be the case, for example, during the development phase for prototyping, or when implementing a specific software layer[4] if an exception can only appear in this particular layer of the program and be handled there accordingly.

Defining Exception Texts

As we have already seen, exception objects must be able to provide some information about an exception situation. This includes descriptive information texts that can also be used in error messages, for example.

Figure 8.6 shows the output from Listing 8.1. The output contains the long text for the exception object that is created if a user attempts to calculate the square root of a negative value.

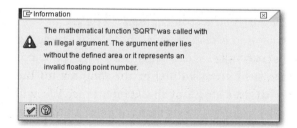

Figure 8.6 Exception Text for the cx_sy_arg_out_of_domain Exception

Exception situations can often be very similar, and the descriptive texts may vary only slightly in these cases. The exception text in Figure 8.6 could also apply to other functions to which a non-permitted argument has been transferred, for example. This is why exception texts can be parameterized. In this example, the name of the function with the non-permitted argument is defined as a parameter in the text.

Parameterization

---

4   As a rule, you can assume that larger software systems are built in multiple layers. For example, there may be layers that work very closely with the hardware or operating system, such as in order to communicate with the database, an application layer executes the actual business logic, and another layer is responsible for user interaction and output.

There are two ways of defining exception texts. These differ in terms of the flexibility of the parameterization and the cases where they are used:

▸ **Exception Texts in the Online Text Repository (OTR)**
This type of text can be defined with any number of placeholders. Each placeholder is represented by the name of an attribute from the exception class, which is enclosed by & characters. If the exception occurs, the placeholders are replaced by the content of the attributes. The texts are stored in the OTR, can contain a maximum of 255 characters, and are used primarily in system programs where the text must not be sent to the program user.

▸ **Messages as Exception Texts**
This type of exception text can be used if the exception class implements the interface IF_T100_MESSAGE. In this case, the short texts for messages from Database Table T100 (see Section 9.4.1) are used as exception texts. The text is identified by the message class[5] and the message number. Attributes from the exception class can be assigned to placeholders &1 to &4 or & in the message. If the exception occurs, the placeholders are replaced by the content of the attributes. These texts can contain a maximum of 72 characters, and can be sent to the program user during exception handling with the MESSAGE oref statement.

We will use two short examples to illustrate the use of exception texts. In the first example, we will define our own exception class, to which we will assign two alternative OTR texts.

Example: using OTR texts

First, we create the exception class in the Class Builder with the name ZCX_EXCEPTION_DEMO. In the **Texts** tab, we can find the exception texts. Each exception text consists of an ID and the actual exception text, whereby an exception ID is created with the name of the exception class in the standard setup. If the exception is raised later with RAISE EXCEPTION, the text that is connected to this exception ID is used as the exception text.

In Figure 8.7 you can see that we have also created another exception ID with the name ZCX_EXCEPTION_TEXT_02. In addition, we have

---

5 Please note that this is not a class in the sense of object orientation. This is simply a description for a group of multiple message texts that are collected under a common name: the "message class."

assigned a relevant text to the two exception IDs, containing a place-holder &TOKEN& to parameterize the output.

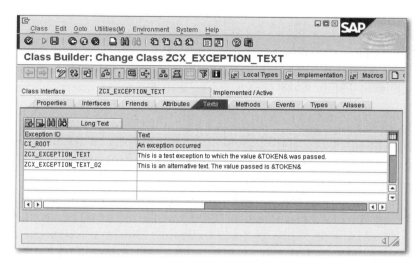

Figure 8.7 Defining Exception Texts

To ensure that the placeholder can also be given the required value later when the exception object is created, another attribute of the string type must be created with the same name as the placeholder, which, in this case, is TOKEN.

For each exception text, the Class Builder creates a static constant in the exception class, which has the same name as the exception text. This can be transferred to the TEXTID parameter of the constructor to determine the exception text when the exception is raised. If the parameter is not transferred, a predefined exception text is used. This has the same name as the exception class.

If we wanted to use the exception ID ZCX_EXCEPTION_TEXT_02 in our current example, and transfer the value "42", for example, the exception would be raised as follows:

```
DATA oref TYPE REF TO zcx_exception_text.
DATA txt  TYPE string.

TRY.
    RAISE EXCEPTION TYPE zcx_exception_text
      EXPORTING
        textid = zcx_exception_text=>zcx_exception_text_02
        token  = '42'.
```

```
    CATCH zcx_exception_text INTO oref.
      txt = oref->get_text( ).
      ...
ENDTRY.
```

Example:
using message
texts

Exception texts that are based on message classes are basically used in a similar way. However, the IF_T100_MESSAGE interface must be implemented in the exception class in this case.

Create a new exception class ZCX_EXCEPTION_TEXT_T100, and select the **With Message Class** checkbox when creating the exception class in the Class Builder (see Figure 8.8). In this case, the interface is included in the class definition automatically, and the Class Builder is prepared to use messages as exception texts.

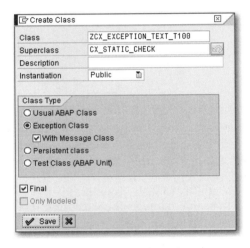

Figure 8.8 Exception Class with the IF_T100_MESSAGE Interface

In the **Attributes** tab, the attributes of the string type can now be defined that will serve as placeholders for the parameters of the exception texts. In our example, we want to create two placeholders with the names TOKEN1 and TOKEN2. Afterwards, go to the **Texts** tab. A standard exception ID with the name of the exception class has already been created here as well.

Exception ID

Unlike for the OTR texts, an exception ID consists of a message class, the message number, and an assignment of attributes from the class to a maximum of four placeholders. If you place the cursor in the line with the corresponding exception ID, and click on the **Message Text**

498

button, the system displays an input template where you can enter this information (see Figure 8.9).[6]

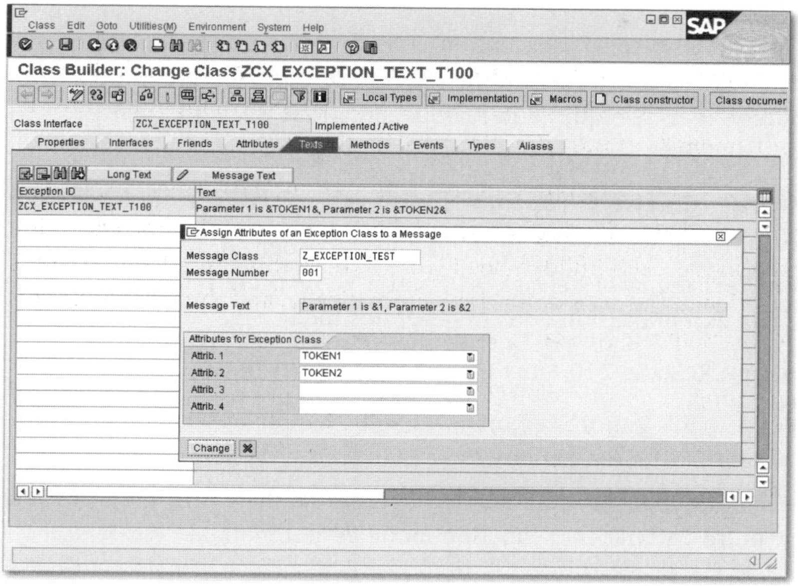

Figure 8.9 Using Messages as Exception Texts

Those exception texts are used as shown in the last example. If no TEXTID is specified when the exception object is created, the standard exception ID is used. To fill the placeholders for the exception texts with the required values, the corresponding attributes—in our example, TOKEN1 and TOKEN2—must be given the necessary values when the exception object is created. During the handling process, the text is output directly as a message with a variant of the MESSAGE statement, designed specifically for this purpose (see Section 9.4.2).

```
DATA oref TYPE REF TO zcx_exception_text_t100.

TRY.
    RAISE EXCEPTION TYPE zcx_exception_text_t100
      EXPORTING
        token1 = '42'
        token2 = 'the meaning of life'.
```

---

6 We have created our own message class Z_EXCEPTION_TEST for our example (see Section 9.4.1).

```
CATCH zcx_exception_text_t100 INTO oref.
  MESSAGE oref TYPE 'I'.
ENDTRY.
```

Exception texts in local exception classes

You can also specify exception texts for local exception classes. We will not go into this procedure in more detail here because this is rarely, if ever, required in real-life situations.

8.2.2 Classic Exception Handling

The class-based exception handling described in Section 8.2.1 has only existed as of Release 6.10 and it is the preferred means of handling exception situations in programs today.

Before Release 6.10, only the following types of exceptions existed:

► Catchable runtime errors that can be handled with the CATCH SYSTEM-EXCEPTIONS statement

► Self-defined, non-class-based exceptions that were only possible in the interfaces of function modules and methods

For reasons of downward compatibility, these older concepts can still be used to handle exceptions in ABAP. You may also come across concepts of classic exception handling when revising older programs so we would like to present these in brief in this section.

We would like to point out once again, however, that these concepts are no longer to be used for new programs, and that the class-based concept should now be the only concept used to handle exceptions.

Catchable Runtime Errors

If runtime errors are caused by situations that can be handled in a meaningful way in the program, they are *catchable*. Catchable runtime errors are grouped into *exception groups* that allow similar errors to be handled together.

You can handle catchable runtime errors with the following statement:

CATCH SYSTEM-EXCEPTIONS

```
CATCH SYSTEM-EXCEPTIONS excl = rcl ... excn = rcn.
  ...
ENDCATCH.
```

The exc expressions describe either a catchable runtime error or the name of an exception group. The rc expressions are numeric literals. If one of the specified runtime errors occurs in the statement block between CATCH and ENDCATCH, the program does not terminate, but moves directly to ENDCATCH instead. After ENDCATCH, the numeric value rc assigned to the runtime error is available as a return value in the sy-subrc system field. In the keyword documentation for CATCH, you can find a listing of all catchable runtime errors, their assignment to exception groups, and their assignment to keywords.

The CATCH and ENDCATCH statements define control structures that can be nested as deeply as you require, as do IF and ENDIF. However, CATCH SYSTEM-EXCEPTIONS can only be used to catch runtime errors from the current call level and not from called procedures.

Since Release 6.10, a predefined exception class CX_SY_... has been assigned to each catchable runtime error. This enables catchable runtime errors to be caught with a TRY control structure, fully replacing the catching process. The following two sections of coding handle the same exception. The method with the TRY control structure is the recommended procedure.

```
CATCH SYSTEM-EXCEPTIONS compute_float_zerodivide = 4.
  x = 1 / 0.
ENDCATCH.
IF sy-subrc = 4.
  MESSAGE 'Division by zero'
    TYPE 'I' DISPLAY LIKE 'E'.
ENDIF.

TRY.
    x = 1 / 0.
  CATCH cx_sy_zerodivide.
    MESSAGE 'Division by zero'
      TYPE 'I' DISPLAY LIKE 'E'.
ENDTRY.
```

It is not allowed to use the two constructs together in one processing block. This avoids mixing the old and new concepts (see also Section 8.2.4).

Self-Defined, Non-Class-Based Exceptions

Self-defined, non-class-based exceptions can be defined in the interfaces of function modules and methods.[7]

EXCEPTIONS For local class methods, the definition is carried out by assigning a name for the exception after the EXCEPTIONS addition of the [CLASS-] METHODS statement. For methods of global classes or function modules, the definition is carried out by assigning a name for the exception in the Class Builder or Function Builder in the **Exceptions** tab where that the **Exception Classes** checkbox is not selected here.

In a method or a function module that has non-class-based exceptions defined in its interface, these can be raised with the following statement:

RAISE exc RAISE exc.

Raising an exception terminates the procedure. The RAISE EXCEPTION statement for raising class-based exceptions must not be used in the same procedure, and no class-based exceptions can be declared in the interface with RAISING.

Please note that this type of exception should no longer be used in this way. In Section 8.2.4, we look briefly at the ideal way to convert the classic exception handling concept into the class-based concept.

EXCEPTIONS Self-defined, non-class-based exceptions are rendered treatable using the EXCEPTIONS addition of the CALL METHOD and CALL FUNCTION statements. This is achieved by assigning numeric values to the exceptions, which are moved to the sy-subrc system field when the exception occurs; however, the actual handling is carried out after the call by evaluating sy-subrc. If an exception that is raised in the procedure has not been assigned a numeric value, a runtime error occurs.

Methods and function modules that were created before Release 6.10, in particular, can still contain these exceptions, and must be handled accordingly when they are called. The following coding section shows an example of this:

---

7 The exceptions that can be defined in the interfaces of methods and function modules are, however, not real exceptions because the control flow does not change. They only cause the processing of the procedure to terminate early, and the sy-subrc return value to be set.

```
CALL FUNCTION 'DP_CREATE_URL'
    EXPORTING
        type                    = ...
        subtype                 = ...
    TABLES
        data                    = ...
    CHANGING
        url                     = ...
    EXCEPTIONS
        dp_invalid_parameter    = 1
        dp_error_put_table      = 2
        dp_error_general        = 3
        others                  = 4.
IF sy-subrc <> 0.
    ...
ENDIF.
```

When calling a function module, we assign values to its exceptions. If one of these exceptions occurs, the processing of the function module terminates, and the corresponding value is written in the sy-subrc field.

8.2.3 Messages in Exception Handling

Messages are texts that can be displayed via the MESSAGE statement. Messages are designed for error dialogs during dynpro processing, and are described in Section 9.4 accordingly. In this section, we just want to look at the special role messages play in an exception handling context.

In the last section, we raised self-defined, non-class-based exceptions with the RAISE statement. For this statement, we cannot provide an exception with text information. The only semantic of an exception is its name. If a corresponding error message is to be output during handling, the handler must supply the required text.

The MESSAGE statement for sending messages offers a RAISING addition as a substitute. This does not send any messages, but raises classic exceptions to which a message text is assigned instead. Listing 8.3 illustrates this with an example.

MESSAGE RAISING

503

Listing 8.3 Example for MESSAGE...RAISING

```abap
REPORT z_message_raising.

CLASS lcl_demo DEFINITION.
  PUBLIC SECTION.
    CLASS-METHODS
      divide IMPORTING numerator TYPE i
                       denominator  TYPE i
             EXPORTING result TYPE i
             EXCEPTIONS divide_zero.
ENDCLASS.
CLASS lcl_demo IMPLEMENTATION.
  METHOD divide.
    IF denominator = 0.
      MESSAGE 'Division by 0'
        TYPE 'A' RAISING divide_zero.
    ELSE.
      result = numerator / denominator.
    ENDIF.
  ENDMETHOD.
ENDCLASS.
START-OF-SELECTION.
  DATA l_result TYPE i.
  lcl_demo=>divide( EXPORTING  numerator = 1
                               denominator  = 0
                    IMPORTING  result = l_result
                    EXCEPTIONS divide_zero = 4 ).
  IF sy-subrc = 4.
    MESSAGE sy-msgv1 TYPE 'I' DISPLAY LIKE 'E'.
  ENDIF.
  lcl_demo=>divide( EXPORTING  numerator = 1
                               denominator  = 0
                    IMPORTING  result = l_result ).
```

For demonstration purposes, we have defined a classic exception divide_zero for the divide method in Listing 8.3. We raise this with the MESSAGE statement and the RAISING addition instead of with RAISE. We call the divide method twice with the denominator 0 so that the exception is raised each time.

The exception is handled during the first call. In this case, the system behaves as it does when the RAISE statement is used. The second time the method is called, the exception is not handled. In this case, the message is processed according to the specified message type (in this case, type "A", see Section 9.4.3), and the program terminates.[8]

In both cases, additional information about the exception is stored in the related system fields (see Appendix A.2[9]). We can find the required exception text in the sy-msgv1 system field, for example. In the example in Listing 8.3, we defined our own text by specifying a character string for the MESSAGE statement. Of course, the options described in Section 9.4.2 also exist for specifying messages from Table T100 or via object reference variables whose dynamic type implements the IF_T100_MESSAGE interface.

Messages can thus be used as forerunners of exception objects with texts. They can always be used if you want to supply additional error information in a procedure that is already using self-defined, non-class-based exceptions, and where the interface of the procedure must remain stable. In this case, you can replace the RAISE statement with MESSAGE ... RAISING. In programs that use this type of procedure, however, you should always map to the new class-based exceptions if possible, as described in the following section.

8.2.4 Combining Class-Based Exception Handling and Earlier Concepts

As mentioned previously, the procedures for classic exception handling that are described in Section 8.2.2 should no longer be used; however, for reasons of downward compatibility, these concepts still exist. You will also encounter these concepts in many older programs, therefore, we want to show you how to connect the old and new worlds while utilizing the benefits of the class-based exception concept.

Self-Defined, Non-Class-Based Exceptions

As you have seen in the previous sections, classic exceptions that can be defined by the EXCEPTIONS clause in methods or function modules are a completely different concept from those that can be defined by the RAISING clause.

---

8 We recommend that you use only message types that terminate the program if the exception is not handled. In this case, the system behaves as it does for RAISE.

9 In this case, the information was defined during the processing of the MESSAGE statement and was not provided by the runtime environment.

The two concepts cannot be mixed. You cannot use both clauses syntactically at the same time in the signature of a procedure. You are also not allowed to use the RAISE EXCEPTION statement within procedures that define classic exceptions with EXCEPTIONS. And vice versa, you are not allowed to use the RAISE or MESSAGE ... RAISING statements in procedures that define class-based exceptions in the interface with RAISING.

Do not mix the concepts!

You must therefore distinguish strictly between the two concepts, and, as a developer, you must opt for one of the concepts, whereby only class-based exceptions should still be used.

Of course, you may call another procedure during a procedure, which still uses the incorrect exception concept. Example: you call a function module that uses classic exceptions within a method where you are using class-based exceptions.

Catching classic exceptions

In this case, the classic exceptions must be caught, and a new, corresponding class-based exception raised, as shown in the following section of coding for a fictitious function module call:

Listing 8.4 Mapping Classic to Class-Based Exceptions

```
CLASS lcl_demo DEFINITION.
  PUBLIC SECTION.
    CLASS-METHODS divide RAISING cx_sy_zerodivide.
ENDCLASS.

CLASS lcl_demo IMPLEMENTATION.
  METHOD divide.
   CALL FUNCTION 'Z_DIVIDE' EXCEPTIONS zerodivide = 1.
   IF sy-subrc = 1.
     RAISE EXCEPTION TYPE cx_sy_zerodivide.
   ENDIF.
  ENDMETHOD.
ENDCLASS.
START-OF-SELECTION.
  TRY.
     lcl_demo=>divide( ).
   CATCH cx_sy_zerodivide.
     ...
  ENDTRY.
```

It is also possible for a procedure to be called, which calls a class-based exception, in a procedure containing classic exceptions. In this case, this class-based exception is caught by a TRY—ENDTRY control structure, and converted into a classic exception using RAISE.

Catchable Runtime Errors

As of Release 6.10, every catchable runtime error has an exception class assigned to it.[10] It can either be handled as a catchable runtime error or as a class-based exception, with the latter being recommended. Figure 8.10 shows, for example, that the exception group ARITHMETIC_ERRORS has been assigned to the CX_SY_ARITHMETIC_ERROR exception class. The two runtime errors—COMPUTE_INT_TIMES_OVERFLOW and COMPUTE_FLOAT_TIMES_OVERFLOW—have also been mapped to the CX_SY_ARITHMETIC_OVERFLOW exception class, for example.

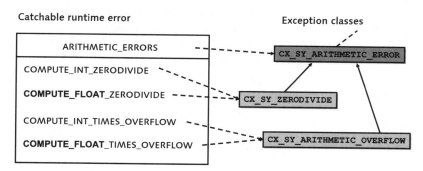

Figure 8.10 Mapping Catchable Runtime Errors to Exception Classes

SAP does not create new catchable runtime errors any more and existing runtime errors that are to be made treatable are no longer converted into catchable runtime errors, but are assigned exception classes instead.

As for the self-defined classic and class-based exceptions, the two concepts for catchable runtime errors must not be mixed either. The CATCH SYSTEM-EXCEPTIONS statement and a TRY-ENDTRY control structure must not be used simultaneously within a procedure, for example.

---

10 Please note, however, that not all predefined class-based exceptions have been assigned to a catchable runtime error.

This does not have any disadvantages in principle, however, because the assigned class-based exception is always created at the same time that a catchable runtime error, which could be caught using CATCH SYSTEM-EXCEPTIONS, is raised.

8.2.5 Runtime Errors

In the previous sections, we described how you can respond to an exception situation so that the program can continue instead of having to terminate. Unfortunately, this is not always possible. We will therefore take a brief look at runtime errors.

Runtime errors are caused by circumstances that do not permit the ABAP program to continue in any case. When ABAP programs are executed, there are two situations in which runtime errors can occur:

▶ A treatable exception is not handled.

▶ An untreatable exception occurs.

Every runtime error is identified by a name and assigned to a specific error situation.

Short dump

After a program has terminated with a runtime error, the system outputs a short dump that contains the name of the runtime error, the related exception class, contents of data objects, active calls, control structures, and so on, and that provides the option of navigating to the ABAP Debugger. In the standard setup, short dumps are stored in the system for 14 days and managed using Transaction ST22.

The **Keep** function in Transaction ST22 can be used to store short dumps without a time limit. If problems occur with an ABAP program that you cannot solve yourself, you can send the relevant extracts of the short dump to SAP. Short dumps are the problem-solving basis for both the hotline and remote consulting.

8.3 Assertions

Everything OK?

An *assertion* is the confirmation that a specific status of the data objects in a program actually exists. Assertions are typically used to ensure or check a consistent status at specific points in the program flow. An assertion therefore generally expresses an assumption that must apply in order for the program to continue to be executed.

8.3.1 Advantages of Assertions

Using assertions can help you to find more errors in programs and to improve the quality of a program.

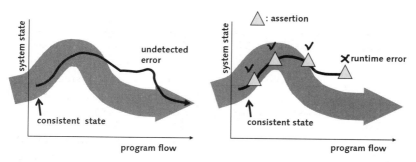

Figure 8.11 Using Assertions to Detect Hidden Errors

Figure 8.11 depicts two program flows. The broad gray arrow represents the range in which the data objects have a consistent status during the program flow. The diagram on the left shows that the data objects had an inconsistent status during a certain part of the program flow. Unfortunately, this inconsistent status has not led to an identifiable error situation—incorrect values could have been written to the database, for example. The effects of this error have not been captured by an error message or resulted in a program termination.

The diagram on the right, however, shows that the assumptions that were made are repeatedly checked at different points of the program flow, and that the program terminates if one of the assumptions does not apply. This termination indicates an earlier program error since this situation should not normally occur.

8.3.2 Using Assertions

The simplified syntax for the ASSERT statement is:

`ASSERT [ [ID group] CONDITION ] log_exp.`   **ASSERT**

An assertion is either always active, or its behavior can be controlled externally.[11] An assertion that is always active is expressed by just the logical expression `log_exp` after the ASSERT statement.

If the result of the check is true, the program flow continues as normal. If the result is false, the program terminates with the non-catchable runtime error ASSERTION_FAILED, in the case of an assertion that is always active.

If the ID group addition is specified, an assertion is defined that can be activated externally by linking it to a so-called *checkpoint group*. The behavior of the assertion can be managed externally by changing the checkpoint group with Transaction SAAB. The following settings are possible:

▶ **Inactive**
The assertion is inactive. In this case, the statement does not have any impact on the program flow.

▶ **Log**
If an incorrect result is delivered, an entry is written in a special log, which can also be evaluated in Transaction SAAB. The program execution then continues with the statement following ASSERT.

▶ **Break/Log or Break/Abort**
If an incorrect result is delivered, the program branches to the ABAP Debugger. In dialog processing, the ASSERT statement behaves like the BREAK-POINT statement. In background processing, the alternative setting is used, in other words, **Log** or **Abort**.

▶ **Abort**
This option generates the same behavior as an assertion that is always active. An untreatable exception is raised, and the program terminates with the ASSERTION_FAILED runtime error.

At this point, we should mention that the ability of the assertions to write to a log must not be used to log just any statuses of the program flow. A separate statement—LOG-POINT—is designed for this purpose.[12]

---

11 Assertions can be activated or deactivated so that time-consuming checks do not affect the speed of any productive programs unnecessarily. If you detect undesirable behavior when executing a productive program, you can activate the assertions and determine where the problem could lie (if implemented correctly).

12 When the program reaches an active log point, an entry is created in the same log, which is also used by the ASSERT statement, and the program execution continues with the statement following LOG-POINT. This log can also be evaluated using Transaction SAAB. You can find more information about this in the ABAP documentation.

Although both assertions and exceptions should support programmers in creating high-quality programs, exceptions focus more on the quality criterion "robustness." A program should still be able to run, even if it is faced with meaningless user entries or specific external influences, such as missing access rights for files.

Assertions versus exceptions

Assertions, on the other hand, target the quality criterion "correctness." In this case, the focus is on implementing a program so that it corresponds exactly to its specification. As a rule, the interaction between a software component (such as a method) and a user is regulated. On the one hand, a specific prerequisite is expected for the method so that it can be executed correctly. On the other hand, the user expects a specific result after the method has been executed.

This principle, which is also known as "design by contract" in software development, can be implemented using assertions. For that reason, ASSERT is used at the start of a method to check the precondition according to which the method may actually be executed. At the end of the method, a post-condition is checked, which states whether the method has functioned correctly.

Design by contract

"It is only shallow people who do not judge by appearances. The true mystery of the world is the visible, not the invisible."
—Oscar Wilde, The Picture of Dorian Gray

9   GUI Programming with ABAP

Every programming language needs a way for programs to interact with users. One way for programs to interact with users is via graphical user interfaces (GUI), which involve output devices like screens and input devices such as the mouse and keyboard. You can use this type of user interface with the Application Server ABAP (AS ABAP).

ABAP is the programming interface of AS ABAP. You can use ABAP to read data from the central AS database, edit it, and change it (see Figure 9.1). The secure, robust processing of critical enterprise data is the main task of ABAP and is also its greatest strength. It would certainly be understandable if ABAP were to be used only for those tasks. Referring to the architecture of AS ABAP that we already discussed in Chapter 3, that would mean that we could be limited primarily to interfaces like Remote Function Call (RFC) and Internet Communication Manager (ICM), and that there would be no direct access by users to the AS ABAP. ABAP would then have no need to provide user interfaces.

A programming language without any specific user interface is not unusual. For instance, SQL,[1] the programming interface for relational databases, works well without one. Then there are today's hot topics: Enterprise Service-Oriented Architecture (Enterprise SOA) and Enterprise Service Infrastructure (ESI). In this type of scenario, an AS ABAP is one service provider among many, offering its functionality through Web services (see Section 12.4) or similar protocols. In this world, users work with browser-based portals, for instance, without knowing the origin of a requested service.

ESA/ESI

---

1 Structured Query Language, a largely standardized language for accessing relational databases.

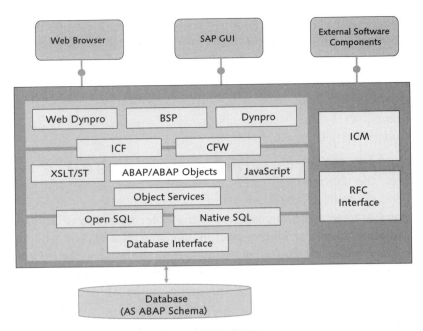

Figure 9.1 The Application Server ABAP (AS ABAP)

As Figure 9.1 clearly shows, however, and as experienced SAP users will probably attest, ABAP does indeed provide direct user interfaces for access to AS ABAP—both ABAP-specific, based on the SAP GUI, and browser-based. Even if data processing is the actual strength of ABAP, the direct integration of user interfaces, and especially the simple programming of those interfaces, have contributed a great deal to the success of the language and SAP applications based on it, like the R/3 system.

Separation of Concerns Other than in a classical R/3 system, in an IT world that continues to move in the direction of service orientation, however, you must be especially vigilant when considering how to provide a user interface in an application. The basic underlying concept that must be used for applications in general—and for user interfaces in particular—is "separation of concerns," a concept that originated with Edsger W. Dijkstra. According to the separation of concerns concept, the needs of an application must be identified and the software components distributed accordingly. For data processing, the general rule follows that a layer may never produce data that it consumes. If we apply this concept to the processing of user interfaces, it follows that those software components that present data should never be permitted to create that data by themselves, but instead should accept it from services.

One approach to separation of concerns for the programming of user interfaces, which consists of three components, is Model-View-Controller (MVC). A data model describes the application, the presentation (view) is responsible for display, and the program control (controller) handles reactions to user actions.

MVC

In this chapter, we first want to look at the different versions of dynpros, the classical user interfaces of the SAP GUI. In classical dynpros, the MVC approach is not directly supported. However, in Section 9.1.15 we will show you how using dynpros with ABAP Objects can automatically result in a separation of concerns. Then, we'll look at the new Web Dynpros, which are displayed in the browser and represent an SAP-specific implementation of the MVC approach. We won't cover Business Server Pages (BSP), the ABAP counterpart of Java Server Pages (JSP), in this book. Instead, we refer you to the book *Web Programming in ABAP with the SAP Web Application Server* by Frédéric Heinemann and Christian Rau (2nd Edition, SAP PRESS 2005). You will see how ABAP functionality can be provided in general for external access in Chapter 12.

9.1 General Dynpros

Dynpro stands for *Dynamic Program*. Dynpros are the classical user interfaces of an ABAP-based SAP system. Despite the increasing importance of Enterprise SOA and browser-based interfaces, there are still many SAP applications based on dynpros. A dynpro consists of the screen itself, the dynpro flow logic, and dynpro fields. A dynpro is always a component of a function group, an executable program, or a module pool. General dynpros are created using the Screen Painter tool. There are also special dynpros (selection screens and list dynpros), which are implicitly built by the runtime environment.

9.1.1 Screen

The screen is the part of a dynpro, which is visible and functional for the user. The screen of a general dynpro is defined with the Layout Editor of the Screen Painter, where its screen elements are defined.

SAP GUI   The presentation of a screen occurs as a part of a window in the SAP
GUI. The SAP GUI is a relatively independent software component of
the presentation layer of an AS ABAP. SAP GUI is usually installed on
the PC of each individual user in the version for MS Windows and
less often as a Java GUI. There is also a purely HTML-based version
of SAP GUI, which requires only a browser, but is somewhat less
powerful.

Windows   Like any GUI, the user interfaces of the SAP GUI are implemented on
the screen using windows. An SAP GUI window consists of different
bars (title bar, menu bar, standard toolbar, application toolbar, status
bar, and sometimes scroll bars) and the *screen* of a dynpro as its most
important component. Figure 9.2 shows the screen of the DEMO_
DYNPRO program in a window of the SAP GUI. The screen contains
all significant screen elements. Above the screen are the menu bar,
the standard toolbar with some predefined icons, and the application
toolbar with a demo pushbutton. At the lower edge of the screen is
the status bar, which can display short messages and system information.

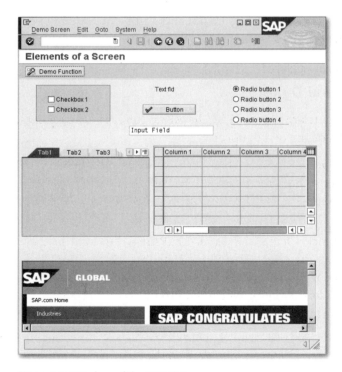

Figure 9.2 Window of the SAP GUI

9.1.2 Dynpro Flow Logic

Dynpro flow logic is the procedural part of a dynpro, and is written in a special programming language similar to ABAP. You may be surprised to learn that dynpro flow logic is not implemented in the presentation layer of the AS ABAP, but rather in the application layer or the ABAP runtime environment, just like an ABAP program. The dynpro flow logic of a general dynpro is defined using the source code editor of the Screen Painter.

Unlike an ABAP program, dynpro flow logic has no declaration part. The data objects of a dynpro, the dynpro fields, are therefore not declared in the source code of the dynpro flow logic. Like the implementation part of an ABAP program, this is subdivided into processing blocks. The only processing blocks allowed are the four event blocks shown in Listing 9.1:

Listing 9.1 Structure of the Dynpro Flow Logic

```
PROCESS BEFORE OUTPUT.
  ...
PROCESS AFTER INPUT.
  ...
PROCESS ON HELP-REQUEST.
  ...
PROCESS ON VALUE-REQUEST.
  ...
```

The related events are triggered by the ABAP runtime environment during the processing of a dynpro:

▶ The event block PROCESS BEFORE OUTPUT (PBO) is executed directly before sending the screen output. PBO is triggered at the point where a dynpro is called. The PBO processing prepares the screen output.

PBO

▶ The event block PROCESS AFTER INPUT (PAI) is executed by each user action on the screen that is associated with a function code. The purpose of PAI is to process user input. After the conclusion of the processing, either the next dynpro of a dynpro sequence is called, or dynpro processing is terminated.

PAI

▶ The event blocks PROCESS ON HELP REQUEST (POH) and PROCESS ON VALUE REQUEST (POV) are executed when the user selects field help [F1] or input help [F4] for a screen element. Self-defined help rou-

POH and POV

tines can be called at this point. After the processing terminates, processing of the current dynpro resumes.

You must specify the event block PROCESS BEFORE OUTPUT and it must come before PROCESS AFTER INPUT. The specification of PROCESS ON HELP-REQUEST or PROCESS ON VALUE-REQUEST assumes the presence of PROCESS AFTER INPUT.

Within these event blocks, a small selection of statements can be used that:

- call dialog modules of the ABAP program
- control data transport to the ABAP program
- handle error messages
- execute loops through screen tables
- integrate subscreens

9.1.3 Dynpros and ABAP programs

A dynpro is a component of an ABAP program, which is identified by a unique dynpro number. Every dynpro of a program can be called during the program's execution. A dynpro can also be called from outside the program (dialog transaction; see Section 7.1.2). This involves loading the program in its own internal session. Figure 9.3 shows a diagram of the interplay between a dynpro and its ABAP program.

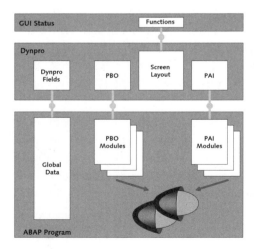

Figure 9.3 Dynpro and ABAP Program

During the processing of a dynpro, the dynpro controls the ABAP program because the dynpro flow logic calls the program's dialog modules. The dialog modules prepare output data and evaluate user input. Ideally, they do this by calling methods in classes or objects from ABAP Objects. To view an extension of this figure for use with classes, see Figure 9.20.

Dynpros have no parameter interface. Instead, there is a connection between the dynpro fields and the global data of the ABAP program. For every dynpro field, there must be a global data object of the same name in the ABAP program. After PBO processing and before the screen output is sent, the content of these global data objects in the ABAP program is transported into the dynpro fields of the same name. After a user performs an action on the screen, the contents of the dynpro fields are transported into the global data objects of the ABAP program that have the same name before or during PAI processing.

Data transport

An ABAP program can include multiple dynpros. From the dynpro point of view, multiple dynpros share the data declarations and dialog modules of their ABAP program. Historically, dynpros are actually older than ABAP programs. Before the development of the ABAP language, dynpros accessed application logic programmed directly in machine code.

Figure 9.3 also shows a so-called *GUI status*. A GUI status is another component of an ABAP program, which plays a role with dynpros. It defines the menu bar, standard toolbar, and application toolbar of the window, along with the function key assignments during the display of screen output of a dynpro. The GUI status is generally set during PBO processing, and determines most of the interactive functions, which a user can execute during display of the dynpro.

GUI status

9.1.4 Dynpro Sequences and Dynpro Calls

A dynpro is always part of a so-called *dynpro sequence*. A dynpro sequence is a sequence of dynpros that results because each dynpro has a so-called *next dynpro*. The next dynpro is either taken from the static definition of a dynpro, or it can be set dynamically in the ABAP program. The screens of a dynpro sequence are displayed in the same window.

Next dynpro

The first dynpro of a dynpro sequence is the *initial dynpro*. A dynpro sequence is terminated when an attempt is made to call the next dynpro with screen number 0. Different dynpro sequences can be nested within one another by calling a different dynpro sequence of the same program, or another ABAP program from within a dynpro sequence. New windows can be opened in the process. The simplest dynpro sequence consists of a single dynpro.

So, a call to a dynpro always starts a dynpro sequence. You can call dynpros from outside your ABAP program through a dialog transaction, or within your ABAP program with the CALL SCREEN statement. Figure 9.4 shows a diagram of the possible dynpro calls.

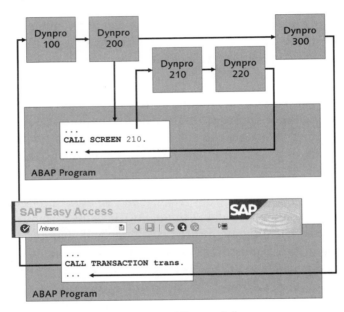

Figure 9.4 Dynpro Sequences and Dynpro Calls

Dialog transaction A dialog transaction is a transaction in which the transaction code is associated with a dynpro in an ABAP program. You create a dialog transaction just like an OO transaction in the Object Navigator (see Section 2.8.5), but selecting the type **Dialog transaction**. Figure 9.5 shows the properties of a dialog transaction. You can see that this associates the transaction code DEMO_TRANSACTION with dynpro 100 of the ABAP program SAPMDEMO_TRANSACTION (a module pool). The dynpro specified in a dialog transaction is the initial dynpro of the transaction.

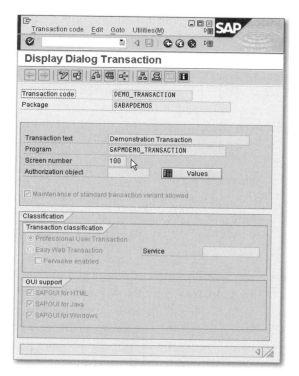

Figure 9.5 Dialog Transaction

A call to a dialog translation, like any transaction, can either occur in an ABAP program with the familiar statements CALL TRANSACTION or LEAVE TO TRANSACTION, or it can be called directly from the user interface of the SAP GUI, as indicated in Figure 9.5, by entering the transaction code into the input field in the standard toolbar. During the call to the transaction, the ABAP program of the dynpro is loaded in a separate internal session, and PBO processing of the initial dynpro is started. A call to a dialog transaction introduces the flow of a classical dialog program described in Section 7.1.2.

In Figure 9.5, dynpro 100 of an ABAP program is called using a dialog transaction. When the processing of a dynpro terminates because the end of PAI processing is reached, the next dynpro is called automatically. This means that at the end of PAI processing of one dynpro, the PBO processing of the next dynpro always starts. In Figure 9.5, dynpros 200 and 300 are the next dynpros of dynpro 100. In the ABAP program, the system field sy-dynnr always gives you the number of the currently active dynpro.

Calling the next dynpro
sy-dynnr

For every dynpro, a static next dynpro is specified in the Screen Painter. This static specification can be dynamically overwritten during dynpro processing in the ABAP program using the following statement:

SET SCREEN

SET SCREEN dynnr.

Then, at the end of the current dynpro processing, the dynpro with dynpro number dynnr will be called instead of the static next dynpro. Any dynpro in the same program can be specified as the next dynpro. In particular, a dynpro can have itself as the next dynpro, leading to repeated calls to the same dynpro. Since the next dynpro can be set dynamically, the flow of a dynpro sequence need not be statically determined, but can depend on factors like user actions or field contents.

Next dynpro 0

Dynpro number 0 plays a special role. There is no dynpro in a program with the screen number 0. Instead, you use this number to terminate a dynpro sequence. If you specify dynpro number 0 as the static next dynpro or in the SET SCREEN statement, at the end of processing for the current dynpro, execution returns to the spot just after the location where the first dynpro in the dynpro sequence was called. If the first dynpro was the initial dynpro of a transaction, for instance, the running ABAP program is ended and you're returned to the point just after the call to the transaction. The shortest dynpro sequence is a single dynpro, which is called by dialog transaction or using the CALL SCREEN statement, and then branches directly to the next dynpro 0.

CALL SCREEN

In every processing block of an ABAP program containing dynpros, you can use the statement

CALL SCREEN

CALL SCREEN dynnr.

to call an arbitrary dynpro of the program. The dynpro called is then the first dynpro of a new dynpro sequence. If, in a dynpro sequence called using CALL SCREEN, the next dynpro 0 is reached, the dynpro sequence is terminated and program execution resumes after the CALL SCREEN statement.

If the CALL SCREEN statement is executed during a dynpro sequence, that is, during PBO or PAI processing of a different dynpro, the dynpro sequence called is embedded into the running dynpro sequence. The current dynpro sequence is interrupted and a new one starts. Up to fifty dynpro sequences can be stacked onto a dynpro sequence that is started with a dialog transaction. In Figure 9.5, a dynpro sequence with initial dynpro 210 and next dynpro 220 is embedded into the dynpro processing of dynpro 200.

Nesting

You should stack up no more than forty dynpro sequences, since the runtime environment can also embed additional dynpro sequences, for instance, for help and error dialogs. An embedded dynpro sequence works with the global data of the ABAP program like any other dynpro. For that reason, during execution of a dynpro sequence, you should be careful not to overwrite fields, like the OK field (see Section 9.1.6), which are required by the dynpros of the current sequence.

A modal dialog box is a special type of a dynpro embedded with CALL SCREEN. You must create this kind of dynpro as a **Modal dialog box** in Screen Painter, which can then be called using the ABAP statement

Modal dialog box

```
CALL SCREEN dynnr
    STARTING AT x1 y1
    ENDING   AT x2 y2.
```

STARTING AT, ENDING AT

While the dialog box is displayed, the previous window remains visible, but is inactive. The options STARTING AT and ENDING AT can be used to determine the start position and end position of the dialog box relative to the previous window. For a modal dialog box, a next dynpro of 0 is recommended; otherwise, all dynpros of the dynpro sequence will be displayed in the dialog box. Up to nine modal dialog boxes can be stacked on top of a normal window.

Exiting Dynpros

If you take no action, a dynpro exits when it reaches the end of its PAI processing. You can also control the exiting of a dynpro with program code, by executing one of the following statements

```
LEAVE SCREEN.
```

LEAVE [TO] SCREEN

or

```
LEAVE TO SCREEN dynnr.
```

in the ABAP program.[2] The LEAVE SCREEN statement exits the current dynpro and goes directly to its next dynpro. The latter is either the static next dynpro from the Screen Painter, or one set using SET SCREEN. The LEAVE TO SCREEN statement is nothing more than an abbreviated form of the two statements:

```
SET SCREEN dynnr.
LEAVE SCREEN.
```

You should note that LEAVE SCREEN and LEAVE TO SCREEN don't exit the entire dynpro sequence; they simply go to another dynpro in the same sequence, unless that next dynpro has the number 0.

Classical dialog processing

As you saw in Chapter 7, calls to dynpro sequences through dialog transactions are a mainstay of classical ABAP. Dynpro sequences were the basis of every dialog-oriented application, which took different paths through screens based on user input. In a classical SAP system, like an R/3 system, in which the user dialogs were performed exclusively through the SAP GUI, dynpros were the driving component of the entire system. As soon as you logged into the SAP system, you were working with dynpros. Every screen you saw belonged to a dynpro. You entered your data in dynpros, and dynpros displayed the output data of the ABAP programs on the screen. Even today, when you log into an AS ABAP using SAP Logon, this is generally still the case. Most screen prints in this book show nothing more than screens from dynpros of the AS ABAP in SAP NetWeaver 2004s. By selecting **System • Status**, you can always locate the current dynpro and its ABAP program by reading the entries in fields **Screen number** and **Program (screen)**.

9.1.5 Creating Dynpros

Screen Painter

The tool used to create a dynpro is the Screen Painter. You create a dynpro for an ABAP program in the Object Navigator; for example, by selecting **Create • Screen** in the context menu of a program for which this is possible (function group, executable program, or module pool). Then, you are prompted to enter the dynpro number, which uniquely identifies the dynpro in the program. You can enter any four-digit number, except for 1000, which is reserved for the

---

2 Of course, statements also exit the current dynpro and all current dynpro sequences if they force the entire ABAP program to exit, like LEAVE PROGRAM.

standard selection screen of an executable program (see Section 9.2.8). From hereon, the dynpro can be edited in the Screen Painter. Editing has three main parts:

▶ Properties

▶ Layout

▶ Flow logic

Properties

The attributes (properties) of a dynpro, like those of ABAP programs, influence its execution in the ABAP runtime environment. You set the attributes of a dynpro on the corresponding **Attributes** tab of the Screen Painter. Figure 9.6 shows the attributes of dynpro 100 of the program DEMO_DYNPRO.

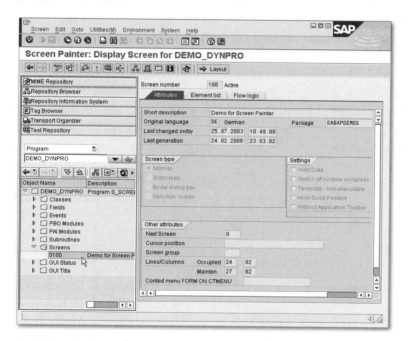

Figure 9.6 Dynpro Properties

The chief dynpro attributes are:

Dynpro attributes

▶ **Screen Type**
The dynpro type determines whether the screen of the dynpro occupies a whole GUI window (**Normal**) or should be displayed in

a new window (**Modal dialog box**). A dynpro of type **Subscreen** can be displayed in a special area of the screen of a different dynpro.

▶ **Next Screen**
This is where the static next dynpro (see Section 9.1.4) of the dynpro is specified, which can be dynamically overwritten in the ABAP program with the SET SCREEN statement.

▶ **Rows/Columns**
This is where you specify the size of the dynpro screen that you can edit in the Layout Editor.

Layout

The actual screen of a dynpro is edited with the Layout Editor of the Screen Painter, which you call with the **Layout** button. The Layout Editor enables you to arrange screen elements on the screen. Figure 9.7 shows the Layout Editor for dynpro 100 of the DEMO_DYNPRO program.

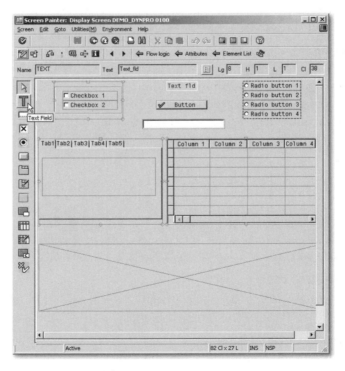

Figure 9.7 Layout Editor

You can select all the screen elements on the left side of the Layout Editor and place them on the screen area. There are screen elements that are used only to display content and those that allow user action. The most important screen elements are:

▶ **Text Fields and Frames**
Pure display elements whose content cannot be changed by the user or the ABAP program.

Screen elements

▶ **Input/Output Fields**
Fields used to display data from the ABAP program or allow the input of data by the user. They are associated with dynpro fields (see Section 9.1.6).

▶ **Buttons**
Areas on the screen that can be selected and that trigger the PAI event of the dynpro flow logic. A button is associated with a function code that is transmitted to the ABAP program.

▶ **Checkboxes**
Special input/output fields in which the user can check or uncheck to enter the value "X" or " ". Checkboxes, like buttons, can be associated with function codes.

▶ **Radio Buttons**
Special input/output fields that are grouped together using **Edit • Grouping • Radio button group • Define**. The user can always select just a single field in a group, which causes all the other fields to be automatically deselected. Radio buttons, like pushbuttons, can be associated with function codes.

▶ **Subscreens**
Areas on the screen in which the screens of different dynpros can be embedded.

▶ **Tab Strips**
Tabs on the screen which, when selected, can switch between different subscreens.

▶ **Table Controls**
Areas on the screen in which tabular input/output fields can be displayed.

▶ **Custom Controls**
Areas on the screen in which GUI controls can be displayed. GUI controls are standalone software components from the SAP GUI,

which can communicate with the ABAP program through the Control Framework (CFW) (see Section 9.1.17). The lowest rectangle in Figure 9.7 is such an area. In the DEMO_DYNPRO program, a browser control is shown (see Figure 9.3).

Attributes For each screen element, attributes (properties) like the appearance can be defined. You edit the properties of a screen element in the Layout Editor by double-clicking on the element. Figure 9.8 shows the properties of the button from dynpro 100 in the DEMO_DYN-PRO program. Instead of editing each element individually, you can also select the **Element list** tab of the Screen Painter, in which all screen elements and their attributes are listed.

Figure 9.8 Attributes of a Screen Element

Modification The attributes of a screen element defined in the Screen Painter can be modified in the ABAP program. For example, to make an input field named INPUT required and switch to a bright display, you can execute the following loop during PBO processing:

```
LOOP AT SCREEN.
  IF screen-name = 'INPUT'.
    screen-required   = '1'.
    screen-intensified = '1'.
    MODIFY SCREEN.
  ENDIF.
ENDLOOP.
```

Here, a loop is executed for each screen element in the current dynpro. Within the loop, the properties of the screen element are available in a predefined working area `screen` and can be modified using the special statement `MODIFY SCREEN`.[3]

Flow Logic

The dynpro flow logic is implemented in the **Flow logic** tab in the Screen Painter. The programming language of the dynpro flow logic consists of a few keywords and has a syntax similar to that of ABAP, but it should not be confused with ABAP.[4] Figure 9.9 shows the dynpro flow logic of dynpro 100 in the DEMO_DYNPRO program.

Figure 9.9 Dynpro Flow Logic

---

3 The `LOOP AT SCREEN` statement is similar to the `LOOP AT` statement for a loop over an internal table with a header line.

4 In the dynpro flow logic, like in ABAP, statement chains can be formed using colons and commas.

Event blocks

In the example shown, the event blocks PROCESS BEFORE OUTPUT and PROCESS AFTER INPUT are implemented for PBO and PAI processing. Statements that can be used in event blocks of dynpro flow logic are:

► MODULE to call ABAP dialog modules

► FIELD for control of data transport of dynpro fields to the ABAP program, and error handling

► CHAIN and ENDCHAIN to group module calls into processing chains

► LOOP and ENDLOOP for the execution of loops over table controls

► CALL SUBSCREEN for integration of a subscreen dynpro

You will learn more about the individual statements in the following sections.

Testing and checking dynpros

By selecting **Screen • Test** in the Screen Painter or in the context menu of a dynpro in the Object Navigator, you can test the screen of a dynpro without executing a separate ABAP program. In this test screen, functions like automatic field and input help (see Sections 9.1.13 and 9.1.14) can already be verified. You can use **Screen • Check** to check syntax, consistency, and layout. No checks should result in messages.

9.1.6 Dynpro Fields

Contrary to ABAP, in dynpro flow logic, there are no explicit data declarations. With the exception of the so-called *OK field* (see below), which is implicitly generated when a dynpro is created, dynpro fields are created during the definition of screen elements in the Layout Editor and are assigned to them. The data types of dynpro fields are determined either by reference to the ABAP Dictionary or by reference to global data objects of the ABAP program. The data type of a dynpro field is always described by an external data type of the ABAP Dictionary.

All screen elements, which can accept user input, are associated with dynpro fields. The Screen Painter provides a handy option with the F6 key, which involves assigning the properties of global data of the (activated) ABAP program or, of type definitions in the ABAP Dictionary and their texts, to the input/output fields of a dynpro (see Figure 9.10).

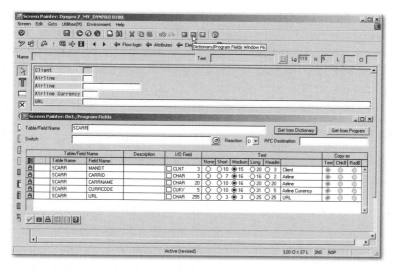

Figure 9.10 Transfer of Field Properties into the Dynpro

After PBO processing and before sending the screen, there is an automatic data transport of global data objects from the associated ABAP program into dynpro fields of the same name. After a user action on the screen and before or during PAI processing, there is a data transport in the reverse direction. **Data transport**

For this reason, you must assign unique names to all changeable screen elements. At the same time, the corresponding data objects must be declared in the ABAP program. The technical properties of the dynpro fields, like length and data type, should match the data types of the associated data objects in the ABAP program.

Purely display elements like text fields or frames are not associated with dynpro fields, and don't necessarily require unique field names. When creating screen elements to which a text field is automatically assigned—like checkboxes or radio buttons—text fields and screen elements have the same names.

The data types of the ABAP Dictionary play an integral role in the creation of dynpros. You can store semantic information in the ABAP Dictionary for every data type, in the form of descriptive texts, field help, and input help. If, as shown in Figure 9.10, you take over components with flat structure from the ABAP Dictionary, the dynpro uses this information. Subsequent changes to the data type automatically cause the dynpro fields to be updated. **ABAP Dictionary**

Interface
working area

There is one detail that you should remember. If dynpro fields are defined in the ABAP Dictionary with reference to flat structures, the global data objects of the same name in the ABAP program must have been declared as *interface working areas* using the TABLES statement. Otherwise, the data objects of the ABAP program are not associated with the dynpro fields, and their content is inaccessible.

TABLES

```
TABLES struct.
```

This statement, allowed only in the global declaration part of a program, declares a so-called *table work area* struct with the data type struct of the same name from the ABAP Dictionary. Regarding the data type of the data object struct, the statement is equivalent to:

```
DATA struct TYPE struct.
```

The declaration with DATA and a TYPE reference to the data type in the Dictionary, however, will not suffice for the association with the dynpro fields of the same name. This is the only place in which the statement TABLES is still needed today. In earlier releases, TABLES had additional meanings, which are now all obsolete.[5]

Conversely, a field defined with TYPE and DATA can only be associated with a dynpro field, which is declared without a reference to the ABAP Dictionary. However, some of the semantic information mentioned is lost in that case.

No database
tables!

Since the definition of database tables in the ABAP Dictionary corresponds to the type definition for flat structures, it is technically possible, and in many older programs also common, to create dynpro fields with reference to database tables and to include a corresponding TABLES dbtab statement in the ABAP program.[6] We strongly discourage you from using this practice. Database tables are provided for the persistent storage of data, not as elements of user interfaces. Under the premise of the "separation of concerns," user interfaces

---

5 From a technical standpoint, an interface working area is a data object, which is declared with the same name in different (ABAP) programs, and that is accessed by all these programs in common. Dynpro fields with dictionary references are stored in the dynpro as interface working areas and must therefore be declared as such in the ABAP program.

6 Hence the name "table working area." Table working areas were in fact once the only possible working areas in Open SQL statements (see Section 10.1.2). This usage has been obsolete since Release 4.0.

and application logic should be cleanly separated from one another. Therefore, we recommend creating structures in the ABAP Dictionary precisely tuned to the requirements of dynpros, which include all desired input and output fields for one or more dynpros of a program or package, along with the associated semantic information.

In addition to the dynpro fields assigned to screen elements, every dynpro contains a twenty-character *OK field*, which is not displayed directly on the dynpro. The OK field is always the last entry in the **Element list** tab of the Screen Painter. It is used in user actions like the clicking of a button to transfer the associated function code to the ABAP program. To activate the OK field, you must assign it a name in the element list. It has become a de facto standard to assign the same name on every dynpro—"OK_CODE"—to the OK field (see Figure 9.11).

OK field

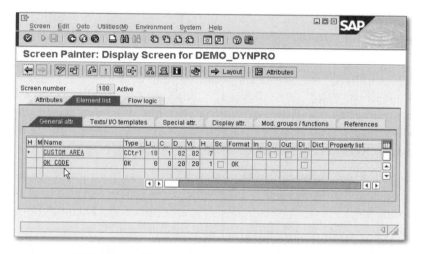

Figure 9.11 OK field in the Element List

To evaluate the OK field, you need a data object of the same name in the ABAP program, whose type can be determined by referring to the global type sy-ucomm:

```
DATA ok_code TYPE sy-ucomm.
```

So when the pushbutton BUTTON of dynpro 100 is clicked in the sample program DEMO_DYNPRO (see Figure 9.8), the value of the function code, that is, "PRESS", is written to the ok_code field of the ABAP program.

9.1.7 Function Codes and Functions

PAI A *function code* is a string of 1 to 20 characters, which can be assigned to certain control elements of the SAP GUI interface. When such a control element is selected, the dynpro event PAI is triggered and the function code is passed to the ABAP program in the system field sy-ucomm or the OK field of the dynpro. A function code can be assigned to screen elements and the functions of a GUI status. The selection of a control element with a function code triggers the event PAI, whereupon PAI processing is executed, while the screen of the current dynpro remains displayed and the system shows the user the familiar hourglass pointer.

Screen elements with function code
The following screen elements can be associated with a function code:

▶ Pushbuttons

▶ Checkboxes

▶ Radio buttons

While buttons without function codes don't make much sense, the association of checkboxes and radio buttons with function codes is not essential, and can be decided on a case-by-case basis. Input fields are generally not associated with a function code, and editing in them therefore does not trigger PAI processing, unless you use dropdown list boxes (see Section 9.1.14).

Bars As you know, a window in the SAP GUI, besides the screen of a dynpro, also contains various bars on which user actions can also be performed:

▶ Menu bar with different pulldown menus

▶ Standard toolbar with predefined buttons with icons, as well as a command field for direct input of certain functions

▶ Application toolbar with freely definable buttons

Figure 9.12 shows the bars (i. e., menu bar, toolbars, etc.) in the window of an SAP GUI again, which includes the title bar as well.

The functions of a window in the SAP GUI should primarily be made accessible through these tool bars. The association of function codes with screen elements should be reserved only for the most important functions, since a screen with too many buttons quickly becomes unusable.

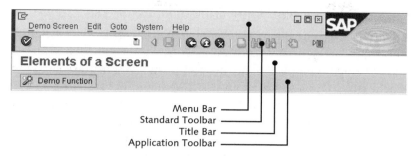

Figure 9.12 Bars in the SAP GUI

To manage bars and their functions, the so-called *GUI status* is used, which we already introduced in Figure 9.3. A GUI status, like a dynpro, is a standalone component of the ABAP program and is managed using the Menu Painter tool in the ABAP Workbench. A GUI status manages functions and provides them to the user of a dynpro. We differentiate different types of GUI status for different purposes:

GUI status

▶ Dialog status with menu bar, standard toolbar, and application toolbar for normal dynpros

▶ Special status for modal dialog box with only one application toolbar

▶ Special status for context menus that can be activated by using the right mouse button

All these status types can be defined at the same time in the same ABAP program, and they all work together with the same functions of the program. In the following, we initially limit our presentation to the dialog status.

You define the interactive functions provided in the bars of a window in the Menu Painter. You open the Menu Painter, for instance, by selecting **Create · GUI Status** in the context menu of a program in the Object Navigator.

Menu Painter

In the Menu Painter, you define the functions by entering function codes and function texts, and by associating them with the bars of the GUI status. You can use the same functions, consisting of function code and function text, multiple times within one GUI status.

Functions

Besides the bars, the function key assignments on the keyboard are also among the interactive elements of a GUI status. You can assign

Function keys

535

the function keys, like Enter or F5, to function codes as well. A function, which should be used on the application or standard toolbar, in fact, is required to be associated with a function key. The icons of the standard toolbar are already assigned to fixed function keys like F3 or Ctrl+S, and a corresponding function text like "Back" or "Save" is suggested. You can also assign icons to the functions in the application toolbar. The function keys F1, F4, and F10 cannot be assigned a function code. These functions are handled by the runtime environment. F1 and F4 call field and input help, while F10 positions the cursor in the menu bar. The function key F2 is always associated with the double click functionality of the mouse. This key can be assigned a function code. The associated function can then be called either with the F2 key or by double-clicking on a screen element.

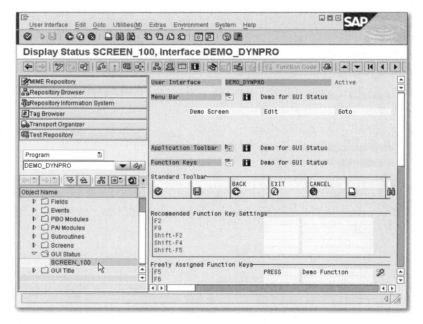

Figure 9.13 Menu Painter

Figure 9.13 shows the Menu Painter for the GUI status SCREEN_100 of the DEMO_DYNPRO program. Here, the function code PRESS, which was already used for the button of dynpro 100 (see Figure 9.8), is assigned to the F5 key. After double-clicking PRESS, this function is assigned to an icon. By opening the menu bar and the application toolbar, you can enter PRESS there as well. Three more new function codes, BACK, EXIT, and CANCEL, were defined by the entries in the standard toolbar and also entered in suitable menus in the menu bar, whereby the associated interface elements are activated. You can use the function **Extras · Adjust template** to include predefined functions as standard. This entry creates functions with suitable function texts in the correct places according to the SAP Style Guide.

The number of functions you can assign to the application or standard toolbar is limited by the number of function keys available. Therefore, you should assign the most common functions to the function keys and those bars, while less important functions are only located in the menus of the menu bar. There you can place any number of functions and define submenus.

It is worth noting that function key assignment, application toolbar, and menu bar, along with the GUI status, are all relatively independent components of the ABAP program. These components are composed to a GUI status in the Menu Painter. In Figure 9.13, each of these components initially has the name of the GUI status, but this can be overwritten at any time. You can therefore define sets of reusable assignments in a program, which offer the functions of the program in different ways, and you can also combine the functions of the program into different GUI status structures.

In the Menu Painter or in the context menu, **Interface · Check** enables you to verify the syntax, consistency, and layout of a GUI status. No checks should result in messages.

Checking the GUI status

The GUI statuses of a program are always activated together to form the interface of the program. This interface provides the user with a set of functions associated internally with function codes. The **Go to · Object lists · Function list** function in the Menu Painter gives you an overview of all functions in the ABAP program.

Activating the GUI status

Any arbitrary GUI status in the program can be set for the screen of a dynpro. It is important to reuse individual interface components in the same positions, since this promotes the usability of an application. To set a GUI status for display of a screen in a dynpro, that is, to provide its functions in the bars of the window, use the following statement during PBO processing:

Setting the GUI status

SET PF-STATUS   SET PF-STATUS status.

This statement specifies the GUI status for all subsequent dynpros in a program until the next SET PF-STATUS statement sets a different dialog status. In a transaction with one or only a few dynpros, you can often manage with a single GUI status, since you can use the EXCLUDING clause of the SET PF-STATUS statement to show or hide the functions of the GUI status for individual dynpros.

The title in the title bar is best specified at the same time as SET PF-STATUS using the following statement.

SET TITLEBAR   SET TITLEBAR title.

The GUI title is also an interface component of the program. To create a title, select **Create • GUI title** in the context menu of a program, for instance in the Object Navigator. Alternatively, of course, you can always use the forward navigation in the ABAP Workbench, which is activated when you double-click on title. A GUI title can only be activated together with the GUI status of a program.

PAI   In a window where a GUI status is set, its functions are available to the user on the same basis as the functions of screen elements with function codes. The selection of a function in the GUI status, with the exception of the aforementioned function keys [F1], [F4], and [F10], trigger the event PAI exactly like selecting such a screen element. So be sure that you use the same function codes for functions you want to use in both the GUI status and on the screen, so that they can be evaluated unambiguously in the ABAP program.

Evaluating the function code   The transport of a function code to the ABAP program is done using the OK field already introduced in Section 9.1.6. Once a user triggers the event PAI by selecting a function with a non-empty function code (e.g., the [Enter] key has a empty function code by default in the Menu Painter), both the predefined system field sy-ucomm and the OK field of the dynpro are filled with the associated function code. The value can be evaluated during PAI processing in the data objects of the ABAP program that have the same name.

OK field vs. sy-ucomm   When processing general dynpros, in an ABAP program, you should always use the OK field instead of the system field sy-ucomm, because this system field sy-ucomm allows read-access only. However, for the following reason, we recommend initializing the OK field before exiting the current dynpro. At PBO time, the contents of the OK field in the ABAP program are written to the OK field of the same name of the next dynpro, which means that it may be inadvertently prepopulated with an unwanted value. To prevent this situation from occurring, you should save the function code to an auxiliary variable at the start of PAI processing and initialize the OK field immediately. Then the contents of the auxiliary variable can be evaluated as shown in Listing 9.2. The listing shows the PAI module of the DEMO_DYNPRO program.

Listing 9.2 Evaluation of Function Codes in a PAI Module

```
MODULE user_command_0100 INPUT.
  save_ok = ok_code.
  CLEAR ok_code.
  CASE save_ok.
    WHEN 'BACK'.
      LEAVE TO SCREEN ...
    WHEN 'EXIT'.
      LEAVE PROGRAM.
    WHEN 'CANCEL'.
      LEAVE SCREEN.
    WHEN 'PRESS'.
      CALL METHOD screen_100=>handle_push_button.
  ENDCASE.
ENDMODULE.
```

9.1.8 Context Menus

A context menu is a menu bar that appears when a user right clicks on a screen. On the screens of the SAP GUI, a menu, which contains all functions assigned to function keys in the current GUI status, appears by default. For the DEMO_DYNPRO sample program, the standard context menu is displayed as shown in Figure 9.14.

Standard context menu

On the screens of dynpros, input/output fields, text fields, table controls, areas in frames and subscreens (see Section 9.1.16) can be associated with self-defined context menus. To do this, you must enter a value into the ON_CTMENU_ field (see Figure 9.8) in the attributes of the corresponding screen element, and define a subroutine of the same name (see Section 7.2.2) in the ABAP program as a callback routine. This subroutine must have a USING parameter of reference type cl_ctmenu. CL_CTMENU is a global class in the class library whose objects implement context menus.

Self-defined context menus

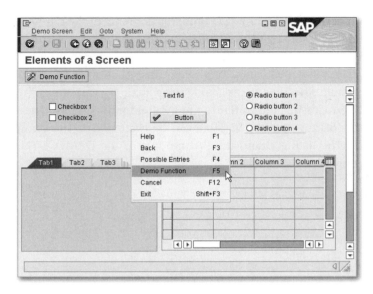

Figure 9.14 Standard Context Menu of the SAP GUI

For the input field INPUT of dynpro 100 in the DEMO_DYNPRO program, if the ON_CTMENU_ field has the value "INPUT", the subroutine shown in Listing 9.3 will be called when the user clicks on the input field with the right mouse button.

Callback routine

Listing 9.3 Callback Routine for Context Menu

```
* Callback routine for context menu
FORM on_ctmenu_input USING l_menu TYPE REF TO cl_ctmenu.
  CALL METHOD l_menu->add_function
                    EXPORTING fcode = 'PRESS'
                              text  = text-020.
ENDFORM.
```

The subroutine receives a reference to a context menu object from the runtime environment. In the subroutine, the menu entries of the context menu are defined. In Listing 9.3, the ADD_FUNCTION method adds a single function, which has the same function code as the pushbutton on the dynpro and the application toolbar. The ADD_FUNCTION method also has a parameter that allows it to set the function type.

The selection of the menu entry in Figure 9.15 triggers the event PAI, and the function code can be evaluated as usual during PAI processing in the OK field or in sy-ucomm.

540

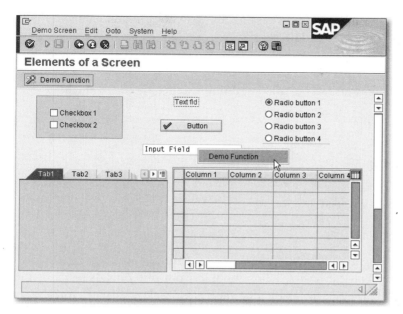

Figure 9.15 Self-Defined Context Menu

The CL_CTMENU class has other methods, which allow you to load (LOAD_GUI_STATUS) predefined menus defined with the Menu Painter in the current GUI status, or to add other context menu objects to a context menu on the same level (ADD_MENU) or as submenus (ADD_SUBMENU). Additional methods allow for the insertion of separators, the activation and deactivation of functions, and the positioning of the cursor on a function.

Predefined context menus

9.1.9 Dialog Modules

The significant tasks of the dynpro flow logic are to call dialog modules of the ABAP program and to control data transport between the dynpro and the ABAP program. In this section, we'll look at dialog modules first and then turn our attention to data transport.

A dialog module is the entry point for a dynpro into the ABAP program. During the processing of dynpro events (PBO, PAI, POH, POV), the dynpro flow logic calls suitable dialog modules in the program, which, in turn, call the appropriate processing in the program that ideally happens in methods of classes or objects.

Dialog modules are processing blocks without parameter interfaces and without local data area,[7] which are defined in the ABAP program between the MODULE and ENDMODULE statements. Dialog modules that can be called for PBO must have the OUTPUT qualifier, and dialog modules that can be called at PAI must have the INPUT qualifier:

MODULE—
ENDMODULE

```
* PBO Module
MODULE pbo_mod OUTPUT
  ...
ENDMODULE.

* PAI Module
MODULE pai_mod INPUT
  ...
ENDMODULE.
```

A dialog module is not bound to a certain dynpro of the ABAP program. You can call a dialog module from different dynpros of the ABAP program. By evaluating the system field sy-dynnr, you always know which dynpro has called the dialog module. Dialog modules can be defined in any ABAP program that supports dynpros (i. e., in function groups, executable programs, and module pools).

Module pools

In classical ABAP programming (see Section 7.1.2), one of the primary roles of module pools was to contain dynpros and to provide them with a collection of suitable dialog modules. The processing logic was often implemented directly in the dialog modules, which had the disadvantage that only global data could be used and that different concerns (dialog programming and application programming) were combined in a single functional unit. For that reason, we recommend that you think of dialog modules as pure entry points into an ABAP program, and that you use them only to call procedures, that ideally are implemented as methods. As an alternative to module pools, function groups are available to separate dynpro processing from application programs (see Section 9.1.15).

The statement in dynpro flow logic to call a dialog module is:

MODULE

```
MODULE mod.
```

This statement should not be confused with the ABAP statement of the same name for the definition of dialog modules. At PBO time,

---

7 Data declarations in dialog modules are added to the ABAP program's global data declarations and should therefore not be done.

you can use `MODULE` to call any dialog module defined with the `OUTPUT` addition. During PAI, POH, and POV, you can call any dialog module defined with the `INPUT` addition.

The dialog modules called at PBO time execute the PBO processing in the ABAP program, in which the display of the screen is prepared. The dialog modules called at PAI time execute the PAI processing in the ABAP program, in which the user input is evaluated and processed. The PAI processing of the current dynpro and the PBO processing of the next dynpro are performed in a work process on an application server of AS ABAP and are collectively called a *dialog step*. During a dialog step, a user sees the hourglass icon. The presentation server is active during the time a screen is ready for input, that is, until a user action triggers the event PAI. During this time, an application is not using a work process.

Dialog step

9.1.10 Data Transport

Data transport between the dynpro and the ABAP program can occur automatically or under program control. Automatic data transport is shown in Figure 9.16. Here, it is again apparent that data transport between dynpro and ABAP program occurs within an application server.

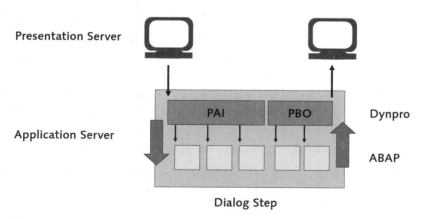

Presentation Server

Application Server

PAI   PBO   Dynpro

ABAP

Dialog Step

Figure 9.16 Automatic Data Transport

The automatic data transport from the dynpro to the ABAP program takes place at the beginning of a dialog step, that is, during the event PAI. The automatic data transport from the ABAP program to the

Automatic Data Transport

dynpro takes place at the end of a dialog step, that is, directly before the new screen is sent. By default, all data is transported between dynpro fields and the global ABAP fields of the application server that have the same name.

Program-control-led Data Transport During PAI processing, you can control the time when data transport from the dynpro to the ABAP program takes place by using the following statement in the PAI event block in the dynpro flow logic:

FIELD `FIELD dynp_field.`

This causes data transport of the given dynpro field `dynp_field` to occur at the moment when the `FIELD` statement is executed, rather than at the start of PAI processing. Therefore, only those fields that don't appear in a `FIELD` statement are transported at the start of PAI processing. This allows you to control the data transport precisely before calling individual dialog modules. Before data transport, the old values are still available in the ABAP variables. The control of data transport is important for conditional module calls and input check.

9.1.11 Conditional Module Calls

The combination of the `FIELD` statement and the `MODULE` statement allows the call of PAI modules to be dependent on conditions.

To call a module `mod` only when a dynpro field `dynp_field` is not empty, use:

ON INPUT `FIELD dynp_field MODULE mod ON INPUT.`

To call a module `mod` only when the value of a dynpro field `dynpro_field` has changed since PBO time,[8] use:

ON REQUEST `FIELD dynp_field MODULE mod ON REQUEST.`

The value of a dynpro field is generally changed by user input, but it can also be overwritten by the transfer of default values.

To link conditions with multiple dynpro fields and to subject multiple module calls to a single condition, you can combine dynpro fields and module calls into statement chains defined between `CHAIN` and `ENDCHAIN`:

---

8 This includes overwriting with the same value.

```
CHAIN.                                                              CHAIN—
  FIELD: dynp_field1, dynp_field2,...                              ENDCHAIN
  MODULE mod1 ON {CHAIN-INPUT|CHAIN-REQUEST}.
  FIELD: dynp_field3, dynp_field4,...
  MODULE mod2 ON {CHAIN-INPUT|CHAIN-REQUEST}.
  ...
ENDCHAIN.
```

The ON CHAIN-INPUT and ON CHAIN-REQUEST clauses work like the ON   CHAIN-INPUT,
INPUT and ON REQUEST for individual dynpro fields. A dialog module   CHAIN-REQUEST
is called when at least one of the fields previously listed in a FIELD
statement fulfills the processing chain of the condition. The function
of the FIELD statement for control of data transport is also completely retained in a processing chain.

9.1.12 Input Check

As a rule, it is necessary to check user input on screens for correctness and consistency before starting with the actual data processing
like database accesses. The runtime environment supports this with a
series of automatic input checks, but you can also program your own
checks.

Automatic Input Checks

The automatic input checks are executed during the event PAI before
data transport to the ABAP program and before calling dialog modules. If the automatic input check finds an error, it is displayed in the
status bar of the screen and the corresponding fields remain ready
for input. The user must correct the input, which triggers the PAI
again. The actual PAI processing is only started when the automatic
input check no longer finds an error.

The system executes the automatic input checks in the following
order:

1. **Required Inputs**
   Input fields can be marked as required in the Screen Painter. The
   user must fill in every required field before the actual PAI processing can start.

2. **Input Format and Value Range**
   The input fields on screens are templates that expect character

input in a format appropriate for their type, which can depend on predefined settings. An input field of type NUMC, for example, may only contain digits. A valid date of type DATS can, for example, contain a 10-character string with the format DD.MM.YYYY or with the format YYYY/MM/DD, whereby all characters except for the separator must be digits and the characters for DD and MM must be less than or equal to 31 and 12 respectively.

3. **ABAP Dictionary**
   If input fields were defined by taking them over from the ABAP Dictionary, and the referred field in the dictionary is associated with a check table through a foreign key relation, then the user may only enter values that exist as foreign keys in the check table. So there is an automatic database access executed here that you don't need to program. If the data type of the transferred field is based on a domain and the domain has fixed values, the user can enter only those values (see also Section 2.4.6).

The runtime environment supports the user to enter correct values with automatic input help (see Section 9.1.14).

Therefore, the automatically verified input must have been recognized as error-free before any module can be called. The user must fill in all required fields, and all checks against value lists and check tables must have been successful. If, for some reason, a user wants to cancel processing, it might happen that extensive and (for the user) unnecessary input must be completed before the screen can be exited.

Exit command To allow the user to leave a screen without checks, you need function codes of type "E". This type of function code can be entered in the properties of screen elements on the screen (see Figure 9.8) in the **FctTyp** field, or by double-clicking on a function in the Menu Painter under **Functional Type** (see Figure 9.17).

Frequently, all functions that can be used to leave the screen are assigned this function type. In Figure 9.13, these would be BACK, EXIT, and CANCEL.

Functions with function type "E" don't start normal PAI processing, but instead jump immediately to the following module call in the dynpro flow logic:

AT EXIT-
COMMAND

```
MODULE mod AT EXIT-COMMAND.
```

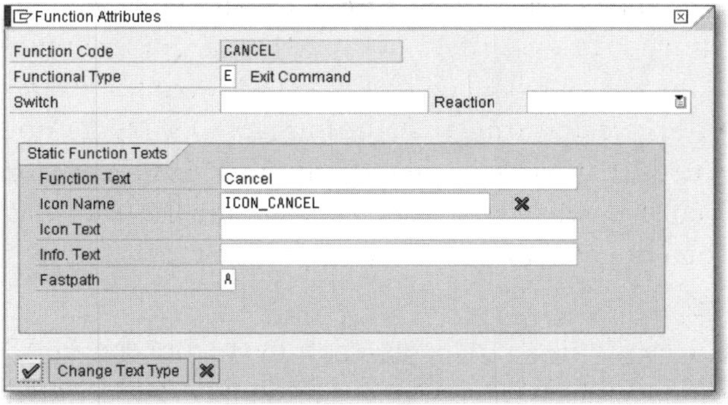

Figure 9.17 Function Type

Here, only the OK field is transported. Only if no MODULE statement has the addition AT EXIT-COMMAND will normal PAI processing be executed. Conversely, a normal untyped function code does not result in the execution of this statement.

In the PAI module called, you can use a suitable LEAVE statement to ensure that the entire program, a call chain, or only the current dynpro is exited. If you don't exit the dynpro in this module, normal PAI processing starts after it is finished, including automatic input check and the call to the normal PAI modules.

Self-Defined Input Checks

For input checks that are not automatically executed, you must use the FIELD statement to transport specific fields to be checked to suitably programmed dialog modules, and output an appropriate error dialog in case of errors. To do this, use the FIELD and CHAIN statements you already know from Sections 9.1.10 and 9.1.11.

To check a single field, use:

```
FIELD dynp_field MODULE mod.                                    FIELD
```

If you output a warning or error message in the mod dialog module, that is, you use the MESSAGE statement with the type "W" or "E" (see Section 9.4.3), the corresponding input field on the current dynpro is the only one prepared for input again, and the user can repeat the entry. Then PAI processing continues after the automatic checks, directly at the FIELD statement. The previous modules are therefore not called again.

To check multiple fields, use a statement chain:

CHAIN
```
CHAIN.
  FIELD: dynp_field1, dynp_field2,...
  MODULE mod1.
  FIELD: dynp_field3, dynp_field4,...
  MODULE mod2.
  ...
ENDCHAIN.
```

If you output a warning or an error message in one of the dialog modules in a statement chain, the input fields of all the fields listed in the statement chain are prepared for input again. Then PAI processing continues after the automatic checks, directly at the CHAIN statement.

If the same field appears in multiple FIELD or CHAIN statements, the PAI processing resumes at the first FIELD or CHAIN containing one of the fields listed in the FIELD or CHAIN where the error occurred and which were changed by the user the last time the screen was displayed.

9.1.13 Field Help

As you know, you can position the cursor on any input field on any screen in the SAP GUI and then press the [F1] or [F4] keys to get field help (direct help) or input help (value list) for the screen element. In this section, we'll show you the basis of field help, and in the next section we'll cover input help.

The field or [F1] help ranges from the display of fixed texts to calls to complete help applications such as when calling ABAP keyword documentation from Figure 2.79. The predefined texts are usually defined in the ABAP Dictionary, but any documentation components can be called.

Data Element Documentation

If input fields are defined by transfer from the ABAP Dictionary, the so-called data element documentation is automatically displayed when the user presses the [F1] key. The data element documentation is a text that can be specified in the ABAP Dictionary for every data element using **Go to • Documentation**. If the specified documentation of a data element doesn't match your application, you can also use **Go to • Additional documentation** to extend it with a program and dynpro-specific additional data element documentation.[9]

To display additional data element documentation, you must create the following event block in the dynpro flow logic for the Process On Help Request (POH) event:

Additional documentation

```
PROCESS ON HELP-REQUEST.
  FIELD dynp_field WITH num.
```

PROCESS ON HELP-REQUEST

Here, num is the number of the dynpro-specific additional data element documentation.

If the help texts from the ABAP Dictionary are not sufficient, you can call your own dialog modules for the POH event, and program any help functions there:

Self-defined field help

```
PROCESS ON HELP-REQUEST.
  FIELD dynp_field MODULE mod.
```

For the POH event, dialog modules can only be called in combination with the FIELD statement. The execution of the mod module takes place outside of normal PAI processing and is triggered when the user selects F1 for the given dynpro field. The FIELD statement during POH does not perform data transport of the dynpro field dynpfield.

In the dialog module called, you must ensure that a suitable help is displayed. To do this, for instance, you might use function modules like HELP_OBJECT_SHOW to display arbitrary texts written in SAP-script, or use suitable functional modules like IWB_HTML_HELP_BROWSER_CALL to access the SAP Knowledge Warehouse (SAP KW). You can also use GUI controls on dialog boxes to display your own HTML documents or to refer to the Internet.

9.1.14 Input Help

One of the great strengths of the classical screens in the SAP GUI is the extensive input help or F4 help for input fields, which always corresponds to the current data contents of the database. This is

---

9 This is unnecessary if you use special dictionary types that are defined for use on dynpros only, as we recommend.

largely due to the definition of search helps in the ABAP Dictionary, via which the desired database tables can be accessed with no special programming effort, and complete selection lists can be presented. In exceptional cases, however, you can also program your own input help in dialog modules.

Automatic Input Help

The ABAP Dictionary offers an entire hierarchy of automatic input help. If input fields are defined by transfer from the ABAP Dictionary, the corresponding input help is automatically displayed when the user presses the [F4] key. The following components of the ABAP Dictionary play a role in this process:

▶ **Fixed Values**
You can limit the value range for data elements when defining domains by giving fixed values (see Section 2.4.6), which also play a role for input help.

▶ **Check Tables**
Relations between relational database are formed in the ABAP Dictionary using foreign keys. A dependent table is called a *foreign key table*, and a referred table is a *check table* (see also Figure 2.34). For fields in the foreign key table, the key fields in the check table or the search help associated with the check table can be used as input help.

▶ **Search Help**
A search help is a standalone repository object that you can create with the Dictionary tool (SE11) of the ABAP Workbench. A search help is the primary means for implementing input help on fields in screens. In the ABAP Dictionary, search help can be associated with components of structures, data elements, and check tables. You can also associate screen help directly with dynpro fields in the Screen Painter.

Figure 9.18 shows the definition of a search help in the ABAP Dictionary. This search help defines which data in the hit list is read from the ZCUSTOMERS table (**Data retrieval**), that the values found are displayed immediately in a selection list without previous filtration (**Dialog behavior**), and that the NAME field is shown but the ID is returned (**Parameters**). To adapt a predefined search help to your needs more closely, you can also use the **Search help**

exit field to specify a self-defined function module with a special interface, which is then called at specific times during the execution of the search help.

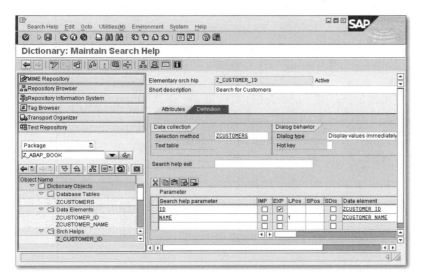

Figure 9.18 Creating Search Help

In the following list, the available automatic input helps are displayed with increasing priority. That means the input help with a lower number only applies if it is not overridden by the definition of an input help with a higher number. By *field* we mean a component of a structured data type in the ABAP Dictionary.

1. If no other input help is defined for dynpro fields of data type DATS and TIMS, an interactive calendar or clock aid is displayed.

2. If neither a check table nor a search help is defined for a field, the data element of the field is not associated with a search help, and the domain of the input field has fixed values, the fixed values are displayed as an input help.

3. If there is no check table for a field and it doesn't have its own search help, but the data element itself is associated with a search help, that particular search help is displayed.

4. If a check table without a text table and without its own search help is defined for a field and the field doesn't have its own search help, the content of the key fields in the check table are displayed as the input help.

551

5. If there is a so-called *text table* defined for the check table of a field, then, in addition to the key entries, the associated text from the text table will be shown in the input help in the login language of the user.

6. If the check table has its own search help, the search help is displayed with the values from the check table, thus enabling value transport of multiple parameters.

7. If a search help is directly associated with the field in the ABAP Dictionary, this search help is shown as the input help.

8. If a search help is bound directly to a dynpro field in the Screen Painter, this overrides all other mechanisms of the ABAP Dictionary.

If a search help is directly linked with fields in the ABAP Dictionary or dynpro fields, you must ensure that the search help provides only those values that also exist in the check table, so that there is no resulting error in the automatic input check.

Self-Defined Input Help

If the options for input help in the ABAP Dictionary, including search help texts, don't suffice, you can call your own dialog module in the Process on Value Request (POV) event and create a completely standalone input help.

PROCESS ON
VALUE-REQUEST

```
PROCESS ON VALUE-REQUEST.
  FIELD dynp_field MODULE mod.
```

As for the POH event, you can also only call dialog modules for POV in connection with the `FIELD` statement. The execution of the `mod` module takes place outside normal PAI processing and is triggered when the user selects F4 for the `dynp_field` field. For POV, too, there is no automatic data transport from the dynpro to the ABAP program, and the `FIELD` statement does not perform the transport of `dynp_field`. Conversely, after termination of the module or modules called, the PBO event is not triggered, and no data is automatically transported from the ABAP program to the dynpro.

Own value lists   In the `mod` dialog module, you can define your own value list, generally using database accesses, and provide it to the user for selection in arbitrary form, preferably in dialog boxes. The SAP List Viewer (ALV) is available for displaying the selection list.

In this case, you must handle the data transport between the dynpro and the ABAP program yourself. If your input help depends on values already entered, you will need to read these values at the start of POV processing, and you must transport the values selected by the user into the corresponding dynpro fields at the end of the POV processing. The function modules DYNP_VALUES_READ and DYNP_VALUES_UPDATE are available for this purpose.

However, you can also use what are partly functions of the search help mechanism of the ABAP runtime environment in the mod dialog module. The function group SDHI contains function modules prefixed with "F4IF," which are suitable for self-defined input help. The F4IF_INT_TABLE_VALUE_REQUEST function module is particularly useful. This function module shows a value list that is prepared in the form of an internal table on the screen and returns the user's selection into the corresponding dynpro fields.

Dropdown List Boxes

A dropdown list box is a special form of single-column value list that can be associated with an input field instead of the input help key F4 . When an input field is associated with a dropdown list box, the input can only be selected from that list. The actual value to be entered is assigned to each entry in a dropdown list box. The value shown is not used for the dynpro field, but that assigned value. A dropdown list box is a good choice for fairly small value lists, and when no values are allowed other than those in the list.

To attach a dropdown list box to an input field, you must set its **Dropdown** property in the Screen Painter to **List box**. Then you can determine the width of the list box with the **visLength** field and assign a function code to the input field.

A list box can be up to 80 characters wide, containing text fields associated with keys up to 40 characters in length. If the user selects a text field, the content of the text field is shown in the input field on the screen, and the content of the key is written to the actual dynpro field. The content and length of the screen field and dynpro field may thus not be identical in this case. If the input field has a function code, the PAI event is triggered afterwards. If you make no other changes to the properties of the input field, the dropdown list box is associated

Automatic input help

with the hierarchy of automatic input help listed above, and the first display column of the input help is shown in the text field.

Self-defined input help

The automatic input help can be overridden for dropdown list boxes as well. The program Z_DROP_DOWN_LIST_BOX is an example. There, the dropdown list box of an input field is filled in during POV processing. The dynpro flow logic contains the event block used to generate a value list (see Listing 9.4):

Listing 9.4 Generating a Value List for Input Help

```
PROCESS ON VALUE-REQUEST.
  FIELD sdyn_conn-carrid MODULE create_dropdown_box.
```

Listing 9.5 shows the corresponding ABAP code. In the create_ dropdown_box module, the value_help method of the local class dynpro_utilities is called. This uses the function module F4IF_ INT_TABLE_VALUE_REQUEST mentioned earlier to create the value list using an internal table, which is populated with values from the SCARR database table for this purpose.

Listing 9.5 Generating a Value List for Input Help

```
CLASS dynpro_utilities DEFINITION.
  PUBLIC SECTION.
    CLASS-METHODS value_help.
ENDCLASS.

CLASS dynpro_utilities IMPLEMENTATION.
  METHOD value_help.
    TYPES: BEGIN OF carrid_line,
             carrid   TYPE spfli-carrid,
             carrname TYPE scarr-carrname,
           END OF carrid_line.
    DATA carrid_list TYPE STANDARD TABLE OF carrid_line.
    SELECT carrid carrname
             FROM scarr
             INTO CORRESPONDING FIELDS
                  OF TABLE carrid_list.
    CALL FUNCTION 'F4IF_INT_TABLE_VALUE_REQUEST'
        EXPORTING
             retfield     = 'CARRID'
             value_org    = 'S'
        TABLES
             value_tab    = carrid_list
        EXCEPTIONS
```

```
              parameter_error = 1
              no_values_found = 2
              OTHERS          = 3.
    IF sy-subrc <> 0.
      ...
    ENDIF.
  ENDMETHOD.
ENDCLASS.

...

MODULE create_dropdown_box INPUT.
  dynpro_utilities=>value_help( ).
ENDMODULE.
```

Figure 9.19 shows how the contents of the `itab_carrid-carrname`
column are presented in the list box. When selecting an entry, however, the contents of the `itab_carrid-carrid` column are placed into
the dynpro field `sdyn_conn-carrid`.

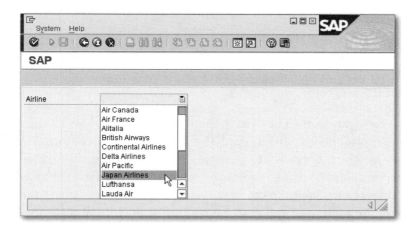

Figure 9.19 Dropdown List Box

9.1.15 Dynpros and Classes

So far, we've learned the following relevant facts about dynpros:

▶ Dynpros display screens in the SAP GUI.

▶ Dynpros form dynpro sequences, which can be called from dialog
transactions or from ABAP programs.

▶ Dynpros have an event-based flow logic that calls dialog modules
in ABAP programs.

▸ Data transport between dynpros and the ABAP program takes place through program-global data.

▸ Dynpros provide advanced options for input check.

In the following sections, we'll look at additional features, such as the use of special controls. At this point, however, let's examine how we can apply what we've learned about dynpros to the classes of ABAP Objects.

No dynpros in classes Unfortunately, the conceptual fit between dynpros and classes is essentially nonexistent. For an object-oriented access to user interfaces, you would expect the interface to be wrapped in classes whose objects could then be manipulated in the program and to whose events the program could react. For classical dynpros, however, there is no such wrapper. Class pools support neither dynpros nor dialog modules, for the following reasons:

▸ In class pools there are no global data declarations, so no data transport is possible from and to dynpros.

▸ Class pools only support methods as processing blocks.

Dialog modules, as indicated in Figure 9.3, may be able to work with local classes and their objects, but a global class cannot work with dynpros.

How can dynpros then be used in the world of ABAP Objects if they aren't even supported in class pools? If we look at the three program types in which dynpros are possible—function groups, executable programs, and module pools—the answer is relatively simple. Because a function group can be viewed as a global class, where the data in the global declaration part is equivalent to the private components and the function modules are equivalent to the public components, it is a suitable means for the wrapping of one or more dynpros in an application.

Function group In Figure 9.20, the ABAP program in Figure 9.3 is broken down into two layers. Between the application logic that is implemented in classes and the presentation that is displayed by dynpros, a layer implemented with function groups is inserted, which contains all the ABAP parts of the application that involve presentation logic. In such a function group, the global data and dialog modules required for dynpro processing are encapsulated with respect to the application.

An application can gain access to the user interface only by calling one or more function modules.

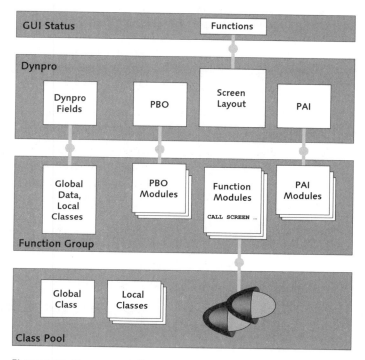

Figure 9.20 Dynpros and Classes

The consequent use of ABAP Objects therefore leads to the "separation of concerns" concept, whereby the application logic is automatically separated from the presentation logic. This makes an application more independent from the user interface then applications in which application logic and presentation logic are combined within a program (generally a module pool.) This makes programs less prone to error, easier to maintain, and simpler to convert to other GUI technologies.

Separation
of Concerns

Sample Application

To transfer the schema from Figure 9.20 to actual application cases, there will surely be some modeling effort involved. In the confines of this book, we will limit ourselves to a simple example, which demonstrates the basic functionality of dynpros, but which will certainly leave room for improvement from a modeling standpoint.

Our example will allow the user to change the airplane type of a flight connection interactively. The sample application is started using the transaction code Z_CHANGE_PLANETYPE. After calling this transaction, the screen of a dynpro appears to select a flight connection, as shown in Figure 9.21.[10]

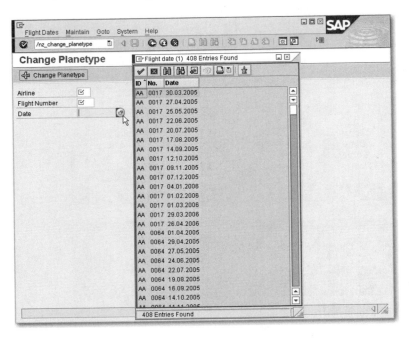

Figure 9.21 Dynpro for Selection of an Air Connection

All three input fields are required. The dynpro performs input checks and offers a number of input helps. A button allows the user to change the airplane type of the selected flight. If the user selects this function, the screen of another dynpro appears (see Figure 9.22).

Some information on the selected flight is displayed here. The user can enter a different airplane type and save it to the database. There is also an input help offered, and different entry checks are performed. If the user wants to save an airplane type whose number of seats will not accommodate the passengers already booked, an appropriate error message appears in the status bar, and the new type is not saved (see Figure 9.23). A successful save is confirmed.

---

10 If you remember the last edition of this book, you'll surely remember this example. The functionality hasn't actually changed, but the implementation has.

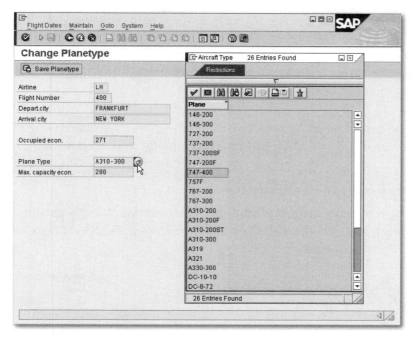

Figure 9.22 Dynpro to Change the Airplane Type

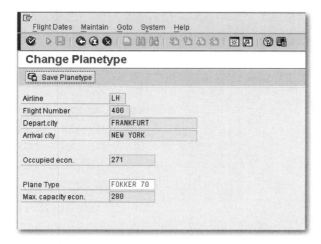

Figure 9.23 Error Message on a Dynpro

If the user wants to leave the screen with **Back** or **Exit** after entering a new airplane type without saving it, a modal dialog box appears with a prompt asking the user to confirm his or her intentions (see Figure 9.24).

Figure 9.24 Confirmation Prompt

The **Cancel** function, however, allows the user to quit processing of dynpros 100 and 200 at any time and without confirmation.

Organization of the Application

OO Transaction   The transaction used to start is an OO transaction. It is assigned the class START of the global class ZCL_CHANGE_PLANETYPE in its properties (see Figure 9.25).[11]

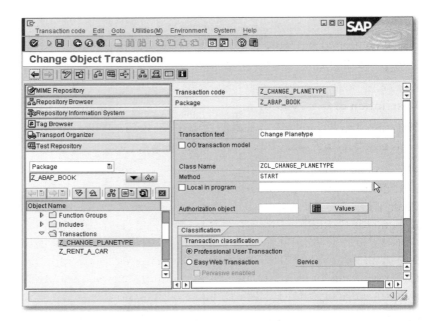

Figure 9.25 OO Transaction

The implementation of the START method is predictably simple and shown in Listing 9.6.

---

11 In the last edition, we still used a dialog transaction for this purpose, since in Release 4.6 there were no OO transactions at that time.

Listing 9.6 Implementation of the Start Method

```
METHOD start.
  CALL FUNCTION 'Z_CHANGE_PLANETYPE'.
ENDMETHOD.
```

The function module called Z_CHANGE_PLANETYPE belongs to the function group Z_CHANGE_FLIGHTS, and its implementation is also simple. It calls dynpro 100 of its function group (see Listing 9.7). This call starts a dynpro sequence whose flow results from the user actions on the dynpros.

Listing 9.7 Implementation of the Entry Function Module

```
FUNCTION z_change_planetype.
  CALL SCREEN 100.
ENDFUNCTION.
```

These simple steps have already completed the separation of concerns mentioned in Figure 9.20. A class-based application uses dynpros encapsulated in a function group.

Description of the Dynpros

The function group Z_CHANGE_FLIGHTS contains two dynpros with numbers 100 and 200.

The static next dynpro of dynpro 100 is dynpro 100 itself. If no other next dynpro is set in the program, it calls itself again. The three entry fields were created in the Layout Editor by simply taking over the three fields CARRID, CONNID, FLDATE from the structure DEMO_ CONN from the ABAP Dictionary, and in the properties (see Figure 9.8) of all three input fields, we went to the **Program** tab, looked for the **Entry** field, and set the value **required**. In the element list of the dynpro, we assigned the OK field the name "OK_CODE".

Dynpro 100

The DEMO_CONN structure is provided in the ABAP Dictionary especially for dynpros of the flight data model. It groups together fields used often in dynpros from the individual database tables, supplies suitable input help and input checks, and contains a mark column for table controls (see Section 9.1.16).

Listing 9.8 shows the dynpro flow logic from dynpro 100.

Listing 9.8 Dynpro Flow Logic from Dynpro 100

```
PROCESS BEFORE OUTPUT.
  MODULE set_status.

PROCESS AFTER INPUT.
  MODULE cancel AT EXIT-COMMAND.
  FIELD demo_conn-fldate MODULE user_command_100.
```

At PBO time, we call a dialog module `set_status`. At PAI time, we call two dialog modules, of which `cancel` is only called for function codes of type "E" and `user_command_100` is only called for normal function codes. The `FIELD` statement is used to execute a self-defined input check for `demo_conn-fldate`.

Dynpro 200   The static next dynpro of dynpro 200 is 200 itself. If no other dynpro is set in the program, it calls itself again. In the Layout Editor, we have taken the fields CARRID, CONNID, CITYFROM, CITYTO, SEATSOCC, PLANETYPE, and SEATSMAX from the DEMO_CONN structure in the ABAP Dictionary. For all fields except PLANETYPE, we have deactivated the **Input field** checkbox on the **Program** tab in the properties, so that these fields are used only for output. In the element list of the dynpro, we again assigned the OK field the name "OK_CODE".

Listing 9.9 shows the dynpro flow logic from dynpro 200.

Listing 9.9 Dynpro Flow Logic from Dynpro 200

```
PROCESS BEFORE OUTPUT.
  MODULE set_status.
PROCESS AFTER INPUT.
  MODULE cancel AT EXIT-COMMAND.
  CHAIN.
    FIELD demo_conn-planetype.
    MODULE: get_seatsmax_200 ON CHAIN-REQUEST,
            user_command_200.
  ENDCHAIN.
```

Dynpro 200 calls the same dialog modules `set_status` and `cancel` as dynpro 100. In a PAI processing chain, the dialog modules `get_seatsmax_200` and `user_command_200` are associated with the dynpro field `demo_conn-planetype`. The dialog module `get_seatsmax_200` should adapt the maximum available number of seats after every change to the airplane type. The dialog module `user_command_200` is called for all normal function codes. The association of the chain with `demo_conn-planetype` makes a self-defined input check possible for this field.

Description of the GUI Status

In our function group, we have created a GUI title SCREEN_100_200 (**Change airplane type**) and a GUI status SCREEN_100_200, both provided for common use by dynpros 100 and 200. The GUI status is a dialog status with which we manage the functions listed in Table 9.1.

Function Text	Function Code	Function Key	Application Toolbar	Standard Toolbar	Menu Bar
Back	BACK	F3		X	Go to
Quit	EXIT	Shift + F3		X	Flight data
Cancel	CANCEL	F12		X	Edit
Change airplane type	CHANGE	F5	X		Flight data
Save airplane type	UPDATE	F6	X		Flight data

Table 9.1 Functions in the GUI Status SCREEN_100_200

Table 9.1 should be read in such a way that, for instance, in the Menu Painter we have assigned the function code CHANGE to function key F5, a button in the application toolbar, and a menu entry in the **Flight data** menu. We have prepared the menu bars in the Menu Painter by selecting **Adjust template** and named the first menu **Flight data**.

For the **Cancel** function, we have selected function type "E"; all other functions have normal function codes. For individual functions, we have also created additional properties like tooltips and icons, which we won't describe here in any detail.

Description of the Function Group

The function group Z_CHANGE_FLIGHTS contains the entire ABAP code required for screen processing of our example application. It is, as usual, built of the include programs specified by the Function Builder (see Section 7.2.1), with the addition of the include programs for dialog modules and for the implementation of local classes (see Listing 9.10).

Listing 9.10 Include Programs of the Function Group

```
*********************************************************
*     System-defined Include-files.                  *
*********************************************************

INCLUDE lz_change_flightstop. " Global Data
INCLUDE lz_change_flightsuxx. " Function Modules
*********************************************************
*     User-defined Include-files (if necessary).     *
*********************************************************

INCLUDE lz_change_flightso01.   " PBO Modules
INCLUDE lz_change_flightsi01.   " PAI Modules
INCLUDE lz_change_flightsp01.   " Class Implementations
```

TOP include   Listing 9.11 shows the TOP include of the function group. The global data declarations are limited to the data objects needed for the processing of the dynpros. Since all input and output fields of the dynpros were taken from the DEMO_CONN structure from the ABAP Dictionary, an interface work area must be declared for these dynpro fields in the ABAP program using TABLES. In addition, we need only two more data objects for the handling of the OK field. We also declare a local auxiliary class confirm for the save prompt in dynpro 200.

Listing 9.11 TOP Include of the Function Group

```
FUNCTION-POOL z_change_flights.

TABLES demo_conn.
DATA: ok_code TYPE sy-ucomm,
      save_ok TYPE sy-ucomm.
CLASS confirm DEFINITION.
  PUBLIC SECTION.
    CLASS-METHODS popup RETURNING VALUE(rc)
                        TYPE syst-subrc.
ENDCLASS.
```

Listing 9.12 shows the include program for the single PBO module of
the function group.

Listing 9.12 Include Program for PBO Module

```
*&---------------------------------------------------*
*&  Include           LZ_CHANGE_FLIGHTSO01
*&---------------------------------------------------*
MODULE set_status OUTPUT.
  SET TITLEBAR  'TITLE_100_200'.
  CASE sy-dynnr.
    WHEN 100.
      SET PF-STATUS 'SCREEN_100_200' EXCLUDING 'UPDATE'.
    WHEN 200.
      SET PF-STATUS 'SCREEN_100_200' EXCLUDING 'CHANGE'.
  ENDCASE.
ENDMODULE.
```

Both dynpros in the function group share the PBO module set_status, in which the GUI title and GUI status are set. The dynpros are distinguished using the sy-dynnr system field. If we had created a separate dialog module for each dynpro, differentiation using sy-dynnr would not be necessary.[12]

Dynpro 100 and 200 use the same GUI status, but the EXCLUDING clause of the SET PF-STATUS statement is used to exclude different function codes. If you open the **Flight Dates** menu on dynpro 100 or 200, the functions **Change Planetype** and **Save Planetype** are both visible, but alternately inactive. Moreover, no button appears for the currently excluded function (see Figure 9.26).

Listing 9.13 shows the include for the two PAI modules of the program. Here is where the actual dynpro processing takes place.

Listing 9.13 Include Program for PAI Module

```
*&---------------------------------------------------*
*&  Include           LZ_CHANGE_FLIGHTSI01
*&---------------------------------------------------*
MODULE cancel INPUT.
  CASE sy-dynnr.
    WHEN 100.
```

---

12 For simplicity's sake, we implement the coding in the modules themselves. It would be better to call methods of a local class here.

```
            LEAVE TO SCREEN 0.
        WHEN 200.
            LEAVE TO SCREEN 100.
    ENDCASE.
ENDMODULE.
MODULE user_command_100 INPUT.
  save_ok = ok_code.
  CLEAR ok_code.
  CASE save_ok.
    WHEN 'CHANGE'.
      TRY.
          zcl_change_planetype=>get_flight(
            CHANGING conn_data = demo_conn ).
          SET SCREEN 200.
        CATCH zcx_no_flight.
          MESSAGE text-nof TYPE 'E'.
      ENDTRY.
    WHEN 'BACK' OR 'EXIT'.
      LEAVE TO SCREEN 0.
    WHEN OTHERS.
      LEAVE TO SCREEN 100.
  ENDCASE.
ENDMODULE.

MODULE get_seatsmax_200 INPUT.
  zcl_change_planetype=>get_seatsmax(
    CHANGING conn_data = demo_conn ).
ENDMODULE.

MODULE user_command_200 INPUT.
  save_ok = ok_code.
  CLEAR ok_code.
  CASE save_ok.
    WHEN 'UPDATE'.
      IF zcl_change_planetype=>check_seats(
          conn_data = demo_conn ) <> 0.
        MESSAGE text-nop TYPE 'E'.
      ENDIF.
      IF zcl_change_planetype=>update_planetype(
          conn_data = demo_conn ) = 0.
        MESSAGE text-chd TYPE 'I'.
      ELSE.
        MESSAGE text-nch TYPE 'I' DISPLAY LIKE 'E'.
      ENDIF.
      SET SCREEN 200.
    WHEN 'BACK' OR 'EXIT'.
      IF zcl_change_planetype=>compare_planetype(
```

```
            demo_conn-planetype ) = 4.
      IF confirm=>popup( ) = 2.
        LEAVE TO SCREEN 200.
      ENDIF.
    ENDIF.
    IF save_ok = 'BACK'.
      SET SCREEN 100.
    ELSEIF save_ok = 'EXIT'.
      SET SCREEN 0.
    ENDIF.
  WHEN OTHERS.
    LEAVE TO SCREEN 200.
  ENDCASE.
ENDMODULE.
```

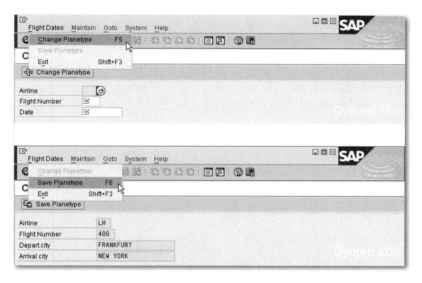

Figure 9.26 Excluded Functions in the GUI Status

The PAI module `cancel` is called when the user selects the **Cancel**   Cancel
function on dynpro 100 or 200, since this has the function type "E".
For dynpro 100, we jump to the dynamic next dynpro 0, thus ending
the dynpro sequence. For dynpro 200, we jump to the dynamic next
dynpro 100; from the user's point of view, we return to the first
screen.

The PAI module `user_command_100` is called by all normal functions   user_command_100
on dynpro 100. In this dialog module, we save the function code of
the `ok_code` field into `save_ok`, initialize `ok_code`, and identify the

selected function in a CASE structure.[13] For function code CHANGE, we call the static method GET_FLIGHT of the global class ZCL_CHANGE_PLANETYPE. The actual functionality of the application is implemented in the methods of the global class. After a successful execution of the GET_FLIGHT method, we set dynpro 200 as the dynamic next dynpro. For function codes BACK and EXIT, the dynpro sequence is ended directly.

If the GET_FLIGHT method cannot return a value, it triggers the exception ZCX_NO_FLIGHT, at which point the MESSAGE statement is used to output a text symbol[14] as an error message of type "E" (see Section 9.4.2). This stops PAI processing immediately, and the screen of dynpro 100 is shown again with the **Flight Date** field ready for input. This is our self-defined input check, which is implemented by combining the FIELD statement in the dynpro flow logic with the MESSAGE statement in the ABAP program.

get_seatsmax_200

The PAI module get_seatsmax_200 is executed by dynpro 200 every time the value of the demo_conn-planetype dynpro field is changed, and calls the GET_SEATSMAX method of the global class ZCL_CHANGE_PLANETYPE to adjust the value of the maximum available seats.

user_command_200

The PAI module user_command_200 is called by all normal functions on dynpro 200, where first the ok_code field is handled again. Depending on the function, we then call static methods of the global class ZCL_CHANGE_PLANETYPE or the program-local class confirm. For every function, after execution and evaluation of the corresponding methods, a suitable dynamic next dynpro is determined, defining the process of the dynpro sequence. The method CHECK_SEATS is used for another self-defined input check. If it returns a nonzero value, an error message is sent again and the display reverts to dynpro 200.

Local classes

Listing 9.14 shows the include program for the implementation of the local help class confirm in the function group.

---

13 Without the initialization of ok_code in the dialog modules, the program would not actually function as shown, particularly since the selection of $\boxed{\text{Enter}}$ would still be working on the previous function codes.

14 The direct use of a text symbol in a message may not be the recommended approach, but it works well in this example.

Listing 9.14 Implementation of the Local Auxiliary Class

```
*&--------------------------------------------------------*
*&  Include            LZ_CHANGE_FLIGHTSP01
*&--------------------------------------------------------*
CLASS confirm IMPLEMENTATION.
  METHOD popup.
    DATA ans TYPE c LENGTH 1.
    CALL FUNCTION 'POPUP_TO_CONFIRM'
      EXPORTING
        titlebar             = text-sec
        text_question        = text-que
        text_button_1        = text-yes
        icon_button_1        = 'ICON_CHECKED'
        text_button_2        = text-non
        icon_button_2        = 'ICON_FLIGHT'
        default_button       = '2'
        display_cancel_button = ' '
      IMPORTING
        answer               = ans.
    rc = ans.
  ENDMETHOD.
ENDCLASS.
```

The functional method popup encapsulates the call to the predefined function module POPUP_TO_CONFIRM[15] for the execution of the save prompt from Figure 9.24, simplifying its use in dialog module user_command_200 significantly. To determine the names of the icons, we've used the program SHOWICON.

Description of the Application Class

The global class ZCL_CHANGE_PLANETYPE contains the entire ABAP code needed for the data processing of our sample application. For the sake of simplification, we work only with static methods. For more advanced applications, you should consider object generation[16] and using events declared in classes.

---

15 Such functions can be found in the Reuse Library (call using **Environment •
   Reuse Library** in the Object Navigator) when the **Program objects** tab is
   selected for the **Standard dialogs** node.
16 In the start method, an object of the class would then be created and the reference passed to the function group. All other methods would be instance methods.

Listing 9.15 shows the entire ABAP code of the global class, which is composed of the code parts generated by Class Builder. You should already be familiar with the start method from Listing 9.6.

Listing 9.15 Global Application Class

```
CLASS zcl_change_planetype DEFINITION PUBLIC
     FINAL CREATE PUBLIC.
  PUBLIC SECTION.
    CLASS-METHODS start.
    CLASS-METHODS get_flight
      CHANGING conn_data TYPE demo_conn
      RAISING  zcx_no_flight.
    CLASS-METHODS get_seatsmax
      CHANGING conn_data TYPE demo_conn.
    CLASS-METHODS check_seats
      IMPORTING conn_data TYPE demo_conn
      RETURNING value(rc) TYPE syst-subrc.
    CLASS-METHODS update_planetype
      IMPORTING conn_data TYPE demo_conn
      RETURNING value(rc) TYPE syst-subrc.
    CLASS-METHODS compare_planetype
      IMPORTING planetype TYPE demo_conn-planetype
      RETURNING value(rc) TYPE syst-subrc.
  PRIVATE SECTION.
    CLASS-DATA planetype TYPE demo_conn-planetype.
ENDCLASS.

CLASS zcl_change_planetype IMPLEMENTATION.

  METHOD start.
    CALL FUNCTION 'Z_CHANGE_PLANETYPE'.
  ENDMETHOD.

  METHOD get_flight.
    SELECT SINGLE p~cityfrom p~cityto
                  f~seatsmax f~seatsocc f~planetype
           FROM ( spfli AS p
                  INNER JOIN sflight AS f
                    ON   p~carrid = f~carrid
                    AND  p~connid = f~connid )
           INTO CORRESPONDING FIELDS OF conn_data
           WHERE p~carrid = conn_data-carrid AND
                 p~connid = conn_data-connid AND
                 f~fldate = conn_data-fldate.
    IF sy-subrc <> 0.
      RAISE EXCEPTION TYPE zcx_no_flight.
    ENDIF.
```

```
        planetype = conn_data-planetype.
    ENDMETHOD.
    METHOD get_seatsmax.
        SELECT SINGLE seatsmax
               FROM    saplane
               INTO    conn_data-seatsmax
               WHERE   planetype = conn_data-planetype.
    ENDMETHOD.
    METHOD check_seats.
        IF conn_data-seatsmax < conn_data-seatsocc.
          rc = 4.
        ELSE.
          rc = 0.
        ENDIF.
    ENDMETHOD.
    METHOD update_planetype.
        UPDATE sflight
               SET planetype = conn_data-planetype
                   seatsmax  = conn_data-seatsmax
               WHERE carrid = conn_data-carrid AND
                     connid = conn_data-connid AND
                     fldate = conn_data-fldate.
        IF sy-subrc = 0.
       planetype = conn_data-planetype.
        ENDIF.
        rc = sy-subrc.
    ENDMETHOD.
    METHOD compare_planetype.
        IF zcl_change_planetype=>planetype <> planetype.
          rc = 4.
        ELSE.
          rc = 0.
        ENDIF.
    ENDMETHOD.
ENDCLASS.
```

The get_flight method, depending on the components passed from   **get_flight**
the demo_conn structure, reads the components required for dynpro
200 from the database tables SPFLI and SFLIGHT using an INNER
JOIN. If no data is found, the class-based exception ZCX_NO_FLIGHT
defined for this purpose is raised. The airplane type read is saved to
a private static attribute of the class for a later comparison.

get_seatsmax

The `get_seatsmax` method, depending on the `planetype` component of the `demo_conn` structure, reads the current value of the `seatsmax` component from the SAPLAN table.

check_seats

The `check_seats` method compares the maximum seat assignment for the current airplane type with the current seating of the flight and returns a corresponding return value.

update_planetype

The `update_planetype` method saves the new airplane type, including the new maximum number of seats, to the SLFIGHT database table. For this purpose, the Open SQL statement `UPDATE` is executed for the appropriate database row.[17] The return value `sy-subrc` from the `UPDATE` statement is returned as the return value from the method.

compare_
planetype

The `compare_planetype` method compares the specified airplane type with the private attribute of the class and returns a corresponding return value.

Return values

Note that we use an exception in only one of our methods, instead of writing the return value as in the other methods, which can be evaluated by the caller. Exceptions should be raised only where there is a real error. The failure of a database operation due to erroneous user input does not fall into this category.

Description of the Input Checks and Input Help

In our example, we implemented only two input checks and handled errors ourselves using `MESSAGE` statements. Other erroneous input from the user, like an invalid format for dates, or nonexistent airplane types, are automatically recognized by the dynpros. Moreover, all valid values are available in automatic input help.

Automatic checks
and help

These automatic checks and input help are determined for the DEMO_CONN in the ABAP Dictionary. An examination of these structures with the ABAP Dictionary tool (SE11) results in the following connections:

▶ For the CARRID component, the database table SCARR is given as a check table. Automatic input check thus checks the user input in

---

17 The use shown here of the `UPDATE` statement is only suitable for this little example program with test data. You find more about how to use Open SQL statements that change database contents in Section 10.1.3.

the **Airline** field against the contents of SCARR. The input help here is also implemented using the check table.

▶ For the CONNID component, the database table SPFLI is given as a check table. Here, the automatic input check checks the user input in the **Airline** and **Flight Number** fields against the contents of SPFLI.

There is a search help named SDYN_CONN_CONNID assigned to the component CONNID. This search help reads matching values from the SPFLI table and presents them as input help. If the user has entered a value for the **Airline** field, all associated flight numbers are read in and shown as a single-column list. If the user hasn't entered a value for the **Airline** field, all existing pairs of airlines and flight numbers are shown as a two-column list.

▶ For the FLDATE component, no check table has been specified. The automatic input check here only verifies the format of the user input in the **Flight Date** field. The user can enter a date here for which no flight exists in the SFLIGHT table. Therefore, we have used the FIELD and MESSAGE statements to program our own input check.

There is, however, a search help named SDYN_CONN_FLDATE bound to the FLDATE component. This search help, depending on earlier user entries, reads suitable values from the SFLIGHT table and presents them in one, two, or three columns.

▶ For the PLANETYPE component, the database table SAPLANE is given as a check table. Automatic input check thus also checks the user input in the **Plane Type** field against the contents of SAPLANE. The input help here is also based on the check table.

9.1.16 Dynpro Controls

A control is a software component of the ABAP runtime environment for the handling of complex screen elements. There are two types of dynpro controls that can be selected as a screen element in the Screen Painter:

▶ The *table control* is a screen element for the display and editing of tabular data.

▶ The *tabstrip control* is a screen element built of multiple tabstrip pages, and is displayed as an register.

The table control and tabstrip control are platform-independent controls, which are handled directly with dynpro and ABAP statements. They must be declared in the ABAP program with the CONTROLS statement. The creation of dynpro controls is supported by wizards in the Screen Painter. There are also platform-dependent GUI controls, which can be accessed in ABAP through the classes of the Control Framework (see Section 9.1.17).

Table Controls

Table controls display screen elements in tabular form and in a special frame on the screen. The screen elements used most often in table controls are input and output fields; however, text fields, checkboxes, and radio buttons can also be displayed in table controls. Figure 9.27 shows a table control with input fields.

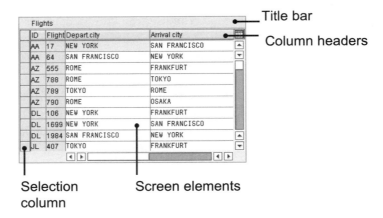

Figure 9.27 Table Control

Table control wizard

When creating a table control, fields must be assigned to it in the Layout Editor, suitable statements placed in the dynpro flow logic, and the processing of the table control must be implemented in the ABAP program. The Screen Painter supports this process with a table control wizard, which defines the table control in the Layout Editor and generates the processing of the table control in the dynpro flow logic and the ABAP program.

As an example, we will prepare the function group Z_TABLE_CONTROL shown in Listing 9.16. The listing shows the function group where the include programs are expanded.

Listing 9.16 Function Group for Table Control

```
FUNCTION-POOL z_table_control.

DATA conn_tab TYPE TABLE OF demo_conn.
DATA wa        TYPE demo_conn.

FUNCTION z_show_table_control.
*"----------------------------------------------------------
*"*"Local interface:
*"  IMPORTING
*"     REFERENCE(FLIGHT_LIST) TYPE  SPFLI_TAB
*"----------------------------------------------------------
  DATA: flight LIKE LINE OF flight_list,
        conn   LIKE LINE OF conn_tab.
  LOOP AT flight_list INTO flight.
    MOVE-CORRESPONDING flight TO conn.
    APPEND conn TO conn_tab.
  ENDLOOP.
  CALL SCREEN 100.
ENDFUNCTION.

*&---------------------------------------------------------*
*&  Include           LZ_TABLE_CONTROLO01
*&---------------------------------------------------------*
MODULE status_0100 OUTPUT.
  SET PF-STATUS 'SCREEN_100'.
  SET TITLEBAR  'TITLE_100'.
ENDMODULE.

*&---------------------------------------------------------*
*&  Include           LZ_TABLE_CONTROLI01
*&---------------------------------------------------------*
MODULE leave_program INPUT.
  LEAVE TO SCREEN 0.
ENDMODULE.

*&---------------------------------------------------------*
*&  Include           LZ_TABLE_CONTROLF01
*&---------------------------------------------------------*
```

The table control displays the data in the program-global internal table conn_tab, which we populate in the function module Z_SHOW_TABLE_CONTROL. For the internal table, we use the structured data type DEMO_CONN from the ABAP Dictionary, since this already has a MARK component of type CHAR and length 1, which can serve as a selection column in the table control. The include program LZ_TABLE_CONTROLF01 remains empty for the time being. In the GUI status SCREEN_100, the buttons provided in the standard toolbar to exit the dynpro have function type "E". Dynpro 100 is created with the next dynpro 100 and the dynpro flow logic shown in Listing 9.17.

Listing 9.17 Dynpro Flow Logic for Table Control

```
PROCESS BEFORE OUTPUT.
  MODULE status_0100.

PROCESS AFTER INPUT.
  MODULE leave_program AT EXIT-COMMAND.
```

Table control wizard

In the Layout Editor for dynpro 100, the table control wizard can be selected from the bar on the left side (*see* insert in Figure 9.28). Then, after drawing an area for the table control, the table control wizard appears, as shown in Figure 9.28. Follow the instructions and finish every step by clicking on the **Continue** button.

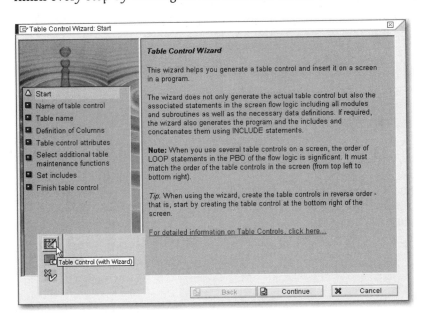

Figure 9.28 Table Control Wizard

1. **Name of table control**: Enter a name for the table control, like FLIGHTS.

2. **Table name**: Name CONN_TAB as the internal program table and WA as the table working area.

3. **Definition of columns**: Select the desired columns for the table control from the table, like CARRID, CONNID, CITYFROM, CITYTO, but not MARK.

4. **Table control attributes**: Specify the properties of the table control by selecting **Input**, for instance. Select **With selection column** and enter MARK as the **Selection column field**.

5. **Select additional table maintenance functions**: For instance, check the **Scroll** entry.

6. **Set includes**: Select the include programs in which the Table Control Wizard should create its code. The wizard suggests the suitable include programs in our function group, and the suggestion can be accepted without changes.

7. **Finish table control**: Confirm completion.

After the Table Control Wizard terminates, you see the table control generated, and four scroll buttons under it, in the Layout Editor of the Screen Painter (see Figure 9.29). Now activate the dynpro and the function group.

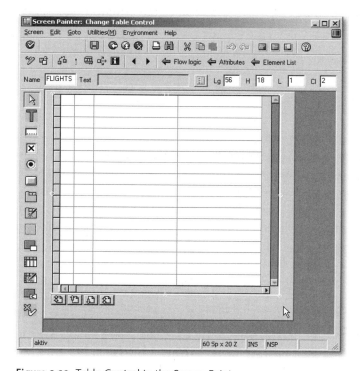

Figure 9.29 Table Control in the Screen Painter

Dynpro Flow Logic

Now look at the dynpro flow logic shown in Listing 9.18 for dynpro 100.

Listing 9.18 Dynpro Flow Logic with Table Control

```
PROCESS BEFORE OUTPUT.
  MODULE flights_change_tc_attr.
  LOOP AT   conn_tab
      INTO wa
      WITH CONTROL flights
      CURSOR flights-current_line.
    MODULE flights_get_lines.
  ENDLOOP.
  MODULE status_0100.

PROCESS AFTER INPUT.
  LOOP AT conn_tab.
    CHAIN.
      FIELD wa-carrid.
      FIELD wa-connid.
      FIELD wa-cityfrom.
      FIELD wa-cityto.
      MODULE flights_modify ON CHAIN-REQUEST.
    ENDCHAIN.
    FIELD wa-mark
      MODULE flights_mark ON REQUEST.
  ENDLOOP.
  MODULE flights_user_command.
  MODULE leave_program AT EXIT-COMMAND.
```

Steploop

The Table Control Wizard created one LOOP each for the PBO and PAI. Within these loops, the flow logic keywords FIELD, MODULE, and CHAIN are used. These loops are characteristic for the so-called *steploop technique*, in which groups of screen elements are repeatedly displayed and processed. Table controls encapsulate the steploop technique and completely replace its independent use. Except in absolutely exceptional cases, you shouldn't expect to find any LOOP statements in dynpro flow logic today without a connection to a table control. The syntax of the LOOP statement in dynpro flow logic is:

LOOP WITH
CONTROL

LOOP AT itab [INTO wa WITH CONTROL ctrl] [CURSOR cur].

This statement assigns the table control ctrl an internal table itab in the ABAP program and specifies a parallel loop execution over the table control lines shown on the screen and the internal table itab.

During each pass through the loop, the contents of the table control are transported between fields of the ABAP program and that of the table control that have the same name.

The clauses INTO and WITH CONTROL are only necessary during PBO and are not allowed during PAI. The dialog modules, which can be called during each pass through the loop, can be used during PBO to populate the table control and during PAI to update the internal table with user input. During a pass through the loop, the system field sy-stepl contains the current line in the table control, counting from the top line displayed, and sy-loopc contains the current number of table control lines on the screen. The CURSOR clause can be used during PBO to control which line in the internal table should appear first on the screen display, whereby cur must be a data object of the ABAP program with type i.

Next, let's look at the changes to the function group. In the TOP include, the wizard included the lines shown in Listing 9.19.

Listing 9.19 Declarations for a Table Control

```
CONTROLS flights TYPE TABLEVIEW USING SCREEN 0100.

DATA g_flights_lines LIKE sy-loopc.
DATA ok_code        LIKE sy-ucomm.
```

The most notable thing here is the CONTROLS statement. Every table control on a dynpro must be registered in the ABAP program using this statement and the clause TYPE TABLEVIEW. At the same time, this statement declares a deep structure with the same name as the control. The data type of this structure is cxtab_control from type group CXTAB. In the components of the structure, all properties of the table control are available for evaluation and modification. For instance, the component current_line contains the current line of the table control in the LOOP, which is calculated from the components top_line and sy-stepl. The cxtab_control structure is deep, since the cols component is an internal table of type cxtab_columns. Each column of the table control corresponds to a line in the internal table cols, whose individual components describe the column properties. You can modify the properties of the individual columns by modifying the corresponding components at runtime.

CONTROLS

Scrolling
The dialog modules and subroutines generated by the Table Control Wizard implement different services for the table control, like scrolling. The user interface of a table control automatically offers scroll bars. If program-controlled scrolling should also be offered, for instance, in reaction to functions in the GUI status, this can be implemented in the ABAP program using components of the `cxtab_control` structure, simply by assigning a value to the `top_line` component. For pagewise scrolling, the number of lines to be scrolled can be taken from the system field `sy-loopc` during the loop execution, containing the number of lines currently displayed. In its subroutine `compute_scrolling_in_tc`, our generated programming uses the existing system function module SCROLLING_IN_TABLE to scroll within the internal table.

To display the table control, we finally create the executable program shown in Listing 9.20.

Listing 9.20 Call to a Table Control

```
REPORT z_table_control.

CLASS demo DEFINITION.
  PUBLIC SECTION.
    CLASS-METHODS main.
ENDCLASS.
CLASS demo IMPLEMENTATION.
  METHOD main.
    DATA spfli_tab TYPE TABLE OF spfli.
    SELECT *
           FROM spfli
           INTO CORRESPONDING FIELDS
                OF TABLE spfli_tab.
    CALL FUNCTION 'Z_SHOW_TABLE_CONTROL'
      EXPORTING flight_list = spfli_tab.
  ENDMETHOD.
ENDCLASS.

START-OF-SELECTION.
  demo=>main( ).
```

The program calls our function module Z_SHOW_TABLE_CONTROL and passes it the data to be displayed. It is displayed in the table control in a way similar to Figure 9.27. So the Table Control Wizard helps you to create an error-free table control.

The Table Control Wizard specifies the most important properties of a table control. The table control created and its processing can, of course, be adapted afterwards to meet your requirements in the Screen Painter and in the ABAP program. For instance, properties, like the determination of a title or the specification of resizing capabilities, can, of course, be modified in the Layout Editor. For more details, please refer to the online documentation.

To conclude this section, we would like to point out that the `LOOP` statement of the dynpro flow logic in the PBO can appear in two different variants:

LOOP variants

- ▶ **LOOP AT** itab **WITH CONTROL** contrl.
- ▶ **LOOP WITH CONTROL** contrl.

Loops can be executed either with or without reference to an internal table. The Table Control Wizard created a loop with reference to an internal table. Without reference to an internal table, the dialog modules called within the loop must provide the table control with data. As an example for both variants, you can find the executable programs DEMO_DYNPRO_TABCONT_LOOP and DEMO_DYNPRO _TABCONT_LOOP_AT in AS ABAP.

Tabstrip Controls

Tabstrip controls implement tabs that are based on subscreen technology. Tabstrips can be a good way of simplifying complex sequences of individual screens. For instance, many tools in the ABAP Workbench, like the Class Builder or the Function Builder, offer their functionality in a single screen subdivided into tabstrip pages.

A subscreen is a screen in a subscreen dynpro and can be integrated into the subscreen areas of other screens. Subscreen areas are created using the Layout Editor. Subscreen dynpros are defined by selecting the **Subscreen** field in the dynpro properties (see Figure 9.6). To integrate a subscreen dynpro `dynnr` into the subscreen area `area` of a dynpro, the following statement can be used in the dynpro flow logic in the `PROCESS BEFORE OUTPUT` event block:

Subscreens

`CALL SUBSCREEN` area `INCLUDING` dynnr.

CALL SUBSCREEN

The statement simultaneously calls the PBO flow logic of the sub-screen dynpro at this point. In the PROCESS AFTER INPUT event block, the following statement can be used:

CALL SUBSCREEN area.

This calls the PAI flow logic of the subscreen dynpro integrated into area at this point.

Subscreens and buttons

One of the apparent ways of how subscreens can be used in applications is to link their appearance to buttons in the dynpro. Figure 9.30 illustrates this with dynpro 100 of the program DEMO_DYNPRO_SUBSCREEN present on the AS ABAP.

Figure 9.30 Subscreens

Tabstrip controls encapsulate this exact behavior. They offer the user an appropriate interface as tabs and free the developer from having to define individual elements. Since individual tabstrip pages are implemented by general subscreen dynpros, arbitrary screen elements like table controls or GUI controls can be displayed on them.

Creating tabstrip controls

To create a tabstrip control, you must do the following:

1. **Define a tabstrip area and its tabs in the Layout Editor.**
   Tabs are created simply by creating buttons with text and function codes in the top line of the tabstrip area, which are then automatically displayed as tabs.

2. **Assign subscreen areas to the tabs.**
   Each tab can be assigned its own subscreen area, or all tabs can use a common subscreen area, in which different subscreen dynpros

are integrated according to the user's selection. In the first option, the function code of each tab must be assigned the function type "P". Then scrolling between the tabstrip pages in the SAP GUI occurs without initiating PAI. In the second option, the function type is not changed. For each selection, PAI is triggered and scrolling is performed on the application server.

3. **Integrate subscreen dynpros into each subscreen area in the flow logic.**
   Depending on the scrolling method selected in Step 2, either one or more CALL SUBSCREEN statements must be used during PBO and PAI. You must define a subscreen dynpro for each tab. When scrolling in the SAP GUI, you can statically assign a subscreen dynpro to each subscreen area. When scrolling on the application server, you have to dynamically assign a subscreen dynpro to the individual screen areas. To do this, specify the dynpro number as a variable, which is supplied in the ABAP program.

4. **Enable processing in the ABAP program.**
   Each tabstrip control must be registered in the global declaration part as follows:

   ```
   CONTROLS ctrl TYPE TABSTRIP.
   ```
   CONTROLS

   With the TYPE TABSTRIP clause, this statement generates a structure named ctrl, from which you only need the activetab component. When scrolling on the application server, during PBO you must assign this component the function code of the tab whose page should be displayed. At the same time, you must assign the dynpro number of the associated subscreen dynpro to the global variable used in the CALL SUBSCREEN statement in the flow logic. When scrolling in the SAP GUI, you can take the function code of the tab of the currently displayed page from this component during PAI.

As for table controls, the Screen Painter also has a wizard for tabstrip controls. This wizard creates a tabstrip control in which scrolling is done either on the application server or on the presentation server. In five steps, tabs are created and assigned function codes, a subscreen dynpro is defined for each tab, the CALL SUBSCREEN statement is built into the flow logic, and scrolling is implemented in the ABAP program. As a demonstration, we've prepared a function group Z_ TABSTRIP_CONTROL, which looks exactly like the one for table con-

Tabstrip Control Wizard

trols from Listing 9.16, except that the TOP include has no declarations, the new function module Z_SHOW_TABSTRIP_CONTROL has no input parameters and contains only one statement CALL SCREEN 100, and we don't need an include program for subroutines. In the Layout Editor for dynpro 100, we call the Tabstrip Control Wizard, draw an area, and do the following in the wizard:

1. Select **Tabstrip name: TABSTRIP** and **Scrolling on the application server**.

2. Enter three tabs with the titles **Register 1**, **Register 2**, and **Register 3**.

3. Accept the suggested dynpro numbers 101, 102, and 103 for the **Subscreens** and acceptance of the suggested **Function codes** TABSTRIP_FC1, etc.

4. Accept the suggested include programs for the function group.

5. Select **Complete**.

The Layout Editor shows the tabstrip control generated (Figure 9.31).

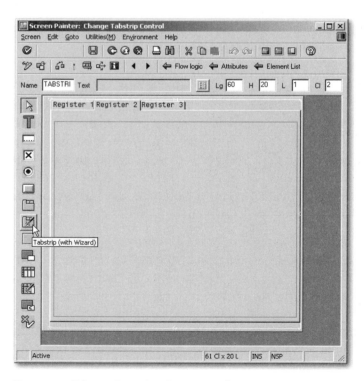

Figure 9.31 Tabstrip Control in the Layout Editor

In the dynpro flow logic, the wizard inserts the lines shown in Listing 9.21, the CALL SUBSCREEN statement being of particular importance.

Listing 9.21 Dynpro Flow Logic for Tabstrip Control

```
PROCESS BEFORE OUTPUT.
  MODULE tabstrip_active_tab_set.
  CALL SUBSCREEN tabstrip_sca
    INCLUDING g_tabstrip-prog g_tabstrip-subscreen.
  MODULE status_0100.

PROCESS AFTER INPUT.
  CALL SUBSCREEN tabstrip_sca.
  MODULE tabstrip_active_tab_get.
  MODULE leave_program AT EXIT-COMMAND.
```

In the TOP include of the function group, the declarations shown in Listing 9.22 were inserted. Besides the CONTROLS statement, a few data objects were also created to handle the tabstrip control.

Declarations

Listing 9.22 Declarations for the Tabstrip Control

```
CONSTANTS: BEGIN OF c_tabstrip,
             tab1 LIKE sy-ucomm VALUE 'TABSTRIP_FC1',
             tab2 LIKE sy-ucomm VALUE 'TABSTRIP_FC2',
             tab3 LIKE sy-ucomm VALUE 'TABSTRIP_FC3',
           END OF c_tabstrip.

CONTROLS tabstrip TYPE TABSTRIP.

DATA: BEGIN OF g_tabstrip,
        subscreen   LIKE sy-dynnr,
        prog        LIKE sy-repid
                    VALUE 'SAPLZ_TABSTRIP_CONTROL',
        pressed_tab LIKE sy-ucomm VALUE c_tabstrip-tab1,
      END OF g_tabstrip.

DATA ok_code LIKE sy-ucomm.
```

Listing 9.23 then shows the PBO and PAI modules added, which implement the scrolling described above on the application server by assigning the dynpro number for the subscreen dynpro.

PBO and PAI modules

Listing 9.23 Dialog Modules for the Tabstrip Control

```
MODULE tabstrip_active_tab_set OUTPUT.
  tabstrip-activetab = g_tabstrip-pressed_tab.
  CASE g_tabstrip-pressed_tab.
```

```
        WHEN c_tabstrip-tab1.
          g_tabstrip-subscreen = '0101'.
        WHEN c_tabstrip-tab2.
          g_tabstrip-subscreen = '0102'.
        WHEN c_tabstrip-tab3.
          g_tabstrip-subscreen = '0103'.
        WHEN OTHERS.
      ENDCASE.
  ENDMODULE.

MODULE tabstrip_active_tab_get INPUT.
    ok_code = sy-ucomm.
    CASE ok_code.
      WHEN c_tabstrip-tab1.
        g_tabstrip-pressed_tab = c_tabstrip-tab1.
      WHEN c_tabstrip-tab2.
        g_tabstrip-pressed_tab = c_tabstrip-tab2.
      WHEN c_tabstrip-tab3.
        g_tabstrip-pressed_tab = c_tabstrip-tab3.
      WHEN OTHERS.
    ENDCASE.
ENDMODULE.
```

The function module Z_SHOW_TABSTRIP_CONTROL can then be called directly via **Test/Execute** in the Object Navigator or in a program (e. g., Z_TABSTRIP_CONTROL), and displays the screen of dynpro 100 as shown in Figure 9.32.

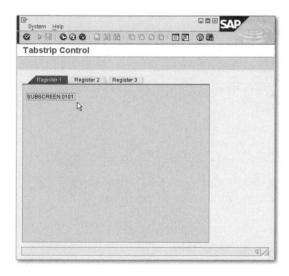

Figure 9.32 Tabstrip Control

The wizard has generated three subscreen dynpros with the numbers 101 through 103. These can now be edited in the Screen Painter and arbitrary screen elements added corresponding to the requirements of the program.

9.1.17 GUI Controls

GUI controls are independent software components of the presentation server that are installed with the SAP GUI. Examples of GUI controls are the Picture Control, the Browser Control, and the Tree Control. You can use GUI controls on dynpros in parallel with, or instead of, conventional screen elements. Figure 9.33 shows the screen of a dynpro with different GUI controls. The screen is divided into three areas in which the upper left shows a picture in a Picture Control, at the lower left a tree structure in a Tree Control, and on the right a web page in a Browser Control. At the top of the screen, an amodal dialog box shows an ALV Grid Control. The example program in this section shows the creation of this screen.

Figure 9.33 Dynpro with GUI Controls

The functionality contained in GUI controls, like scrolling in texts or lists, takes place on the presentation server, thereby relieving the application server of the load for these actions. On the other hand,

Data transfer

587

GUI controls often work with large quantities of data, which can lead to frequent data transfers between the ABAP program and the GUI control, thereby increasing network load. For that reason, when using GUI controls, you should always ensure that most of the work can be performed on the front end and that synchronization with the back end is kept to a minimum.

The Control Framework

Access to GUI controls is done using the so-called *Control Framework* (CFW). The CFW is implemented by a hierarchy of global classes whose names start with the prefix CL_GUI_. The common superclass is CL_GUI_OBJECT. The classes of the CFW encapsulate GUI controls and the screen containers for these controls. Figure 9.34 shows the class hierarchy and the functionality of the CFW.

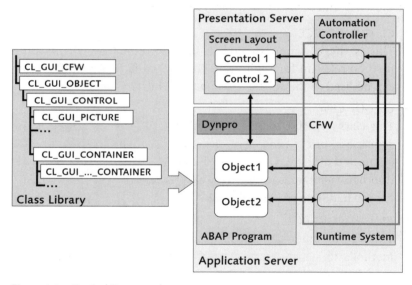

Figure 9.34 Control Framework

Automation controller

Contrary to other screen elements of a dynpro, GUI controls are software objects with their own interfaces, which are not connected to the usual data stream between application server and presentation server. Instead, the communication between the ABAP program and controls is handled by the CFW, which includes components in both the runtime environment on the application server and in an Automation Controller on the presentation server.

An important feature of the CFW is that for every GUI control delivered, there is a global class in the Class Library, and that when working with GUI control, for each control object on the screen there is a
proxy object of the corresponding class in the internal session of an
ABAP program. In the ABAP program, you work exclusively with the
proxy objects. The CFW passes the method calls to the actual GUI
control objects and informs the object of the ABAP program about
user actions on the GUI control by triggering events.

To work with a GUI control, you must create an object of the corresponding class, call its methods, and react to its events. Because all
classes in the CFW are part of a common inheritance hierarchy, the
interfaces for the individual control classes are standardized to a
large degree.

In the following section, we'll show you the most important classes
of the CFW and some of their most important components:

▶ **CL_GUI_OBJECT**
This is the common superclass for all control classes. Its only
method relevant for application programming is IS_VALID, which
can be used in the subclasses to query the status of a control.

▶ **CL_GUI_CFW**
This class, which is on the same hierarchy level as the preceding
superclass, offers some service methods of the CFW that are not
connected directly with a control, like FLUSH for the synchronization between application and presentation servers, or DISPATCH
for the handling of control events.

▶ **CL_GUI_CONTROL**
This is the superclass of the actual control classes. It contains
methods to set and read general control properties that can be
used in any subclass, like SET_VISIBLE to set visibility, or SET_
FOCUS to set the screen focus on a control.

Control Objects

The proxy objects (control objects) are generated from the subclasses
of CL_GUI_CONTROL. Here, we further distinguish between *application controls* and *container controls*. Application controls are the actual
GUI controls. Container controls are subclasses of the class CL_GUI_
CONTAINER and provide a uniform interface to bind the application

controls to particular areas of the screen in a dynpro. You must assign each application control to a container control.

Container controls

Every container control object in the ABAP program is a proxy for a screen area into which you can integrate other controls. The classes for container controls are:

▸ **CL_GUI_CUSTOM_CONTAINER**
The screen areas of custom containers are created as custom controls with the Layout Editor. Custom controls are simply rectangular areas on the screen of a dynpro that are assigned a name. When creating an object of the CL_GUI_CUSTOM_CONTAINER class, you must pass the name of such an area to the input parameter CONTAINER_NAME of the constructor.

▸ **CL_GUI_DOCKING_CONTAINER**
The screen areas of docking containers are attached to the screen edges of dynpros and are created when objects of class CL_GUI_DOCKING_CONTAINER are created. You need to use the SIDE input parameter of the constructor to determine which of the four sides the docking container should be attached to. To hang a docking container on the left edge, for instance, you must pass the constant DOCKING_CONTAINER=>DOCK_AT_LEFT.

▸ **CL_GUI_SPLITTER_CONTAINER**
The screen areas of splitter containers are sections of existing screen areas and are generated when objects of class CL_GUI_SPLITTER_CONTAINER are created. You need to use the PARENT input parameter of the constructor to pass a reference to an existing container object. You can then subdivide its area vertically and horizontally into a maximum of 16 x 16 new areas. You can use the GET_CONTAINER method to obtain references to each individual area.

▸ **CL_GUI_DIALOGBOX_CONTAINER**
The screen areas of dialog box containers are independent amodal dialog boxes that are created when objects of class CL_GUI_DIALOGBOX_CONTAINER are created. The PARENT parameter of the constructor can be used to pass a reference to a container control to which the dialog box is then attached. The dialog box then always stays in the foreground. If you pass the constant CL_GUI_CONTAINER=>DESKTOP to PARENT, the dialog box is treated like an independent window of the entire screen.

Figure 9.35 shows an overview of the possible container controls in an arrangement that corresponds to the example in Figure 9.33.

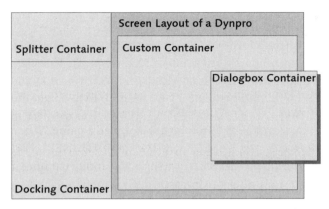

Figure 9.35 Container Controls

For the use of a GUI control in a screen area, you create the corresponding proxy object in the ABAP program. For each creation of an object for an application control with CREATE OBJECT, you need to use the PARENT input parameter of the constructor to pass a reference to a container object or an area in a splitter container. This assigns the control to the appropriate screen area. Application controls

The Control Framework classes of the most important application controls are:

▶ **CL_GUI_TOOLBAR**
The toolbar control allows you to create an application toolbar, which is independent of the GUI status. This class has methods like ADD_BUTTON for the definition of buttons with icons, texts, and function codes. Events like FUNCTION_SELECTED enable the ABAP program to react to function selections by the user. You can use the toolbar control to provide custom user interfaces for individual screen areas or dialog boxes. The application toolbar in the display of the ABAP keyword documentation (e.g., see Figure 2.79) is an example of the use of the toolbar control.

▶ **CL_GUI_PICTURE**
The Picture Control allows you to display arbitrary pictures in BMP, JPEG, or GIF formats on the screen. This class has a method LOAD_PICTURE_FROM_URL to load an image, and some methods to define image properties. Events like PICTURE_DBLCLICK

enable the ABAP program to react to user actions on the control. The airplane image in Figure 9.33 is an example of the use of Picture Controls.

▶ **CL_GUI_HTML_VIEWER**
The Browser Control allows you to display a browser for HTML pages and XML documents, for example, on the screen. This class has a SHOW_URL method to display data specified by a URL, and a LOAD_DATA method to generate a URL for an HTML document in an internal table. An event SAPEVENT allows you to react to specially formatted links (*<A HREF=SAPEVENT:"fcode">text</A>*) in the HTML document and then to evaluate the function code fcode. The display of the ABAP keyword documentation (see Figure 2.79) is an example of the display of HTML documents for which all links are evaluated in the associated ABAP program.

▶ **CL_GUI_TEXTEDIT**
The Textedit Control allows you to integrate a simple text editor into a screen with the usual functions—selection, searching, or replacing. The class has a method GET_TEXT_AS_STREAM to display the contents of an internal table in the text editor, and methods like HIGHLIGHT_LINES or FIND_AND_REPLACE to edit the text under program control. Events like DBLCLICK can be evaluated in the ABAP program beforehand. Before the introduction of the new ABAP Front-End Editor with SAP NetWeaver 2004s, the ABAP Editor was based on the Textedit Control.

▶ **CL_GUI_SIMPLE_TREE**
The Tree Control, for which there exists the simple tree and other variants with multicolumn trees or list trees, enables you to display hierarchical relationships in tree structures. This class has a method ADD_NODES to build the tree from a specially structured internal table, and methods like EXPAND_NODE or GET_SELECTED_NODE to use the tree. The hierarchical data must be provided in the ABAP program in an internal table with reference to a specific structured data type from the ABAP Dictionary. The data type of the internal table must first include the components of the predefined global structure TREEV_NODE. The components of TREEV_NODE, like NODE_KEY, RELATKEY, and RELATSHIP, define the relationships between the tree nodes. The possible values of these fields are constants of the CL_GUI_SIMPLE_TREE class like RELAT_LAST_CHILD. Events like NODE_

DOUBLE_CLICK or SELECTION_CHANGED enable the ABAP program to react to user actions in the tree display. The expanding and hiding of subnodes, however, takes place on the presentation server. Examples for usages of the tree control are the SAP Easy Access Menu and the Object Navigator, as well as hit lists and display of the ABAP keyword documentation.

▶ **CL_GUI_ALV_GRID**

The ALV Grid Control allows you to display lists and tabular data in the SAP List Viewer (ALV) on the screen and also to print them. It replaces classical screen lists (see Section 9.3.2). A user interface can be integrated into the display in the form of an application toolbar. The class has a SET_TABLE_FOR_FIRST_DISPLAY method, which is used to format the list output and pass data to the control. Two internal tables play a significant role: the actual list data, which is passed to the IT_OUTTAB parameter, and a field catalog of table type `LVC_T_FCAT`, which is passed to the IT_FIELD-CATALOGUE parameter. The field catalog contains a description of the properties of the data. The preparation of list output and any print lists is done on the basis of this field catalog. If you want to show list lines whose structure corresponds to a data type in the ABAP Dictionary, however, you don't need to create your own field catalog; just passing the name of the data type will suffice. Events like DOUBLE_CLICK or HOTSPOT_CLICK enable the ABAP program to react to user actions in the tree display. To display hierarchical lists, there is a special class CL_GUI_ALV_TREE.

Some application controls, like the Picture Control or the Tree Control, also allow you to implement a drag-and-drop functionality or provide context menus using special events. For examples of context menus in a tree structure, see the tree display of the Object Navigator.

For some controls, there are encapsulations (see below), which make working with the controls much easier. This is especially true for the ALV controls, which should no longer be used directly in new programs. **Note**

Controls and Dynpros

An application control cannot be created in isolation on the presentation server. It is always connected to a dynpro through a container control. This integrates the control processing into the dynpro processing of the ABAP runtime environment.

A container control is either bound to a section of a dynpro (custom container) or to an entire dynpro (docking and dialog box container). Splitter containers are indirectly bound to their dynpro through the parent container.

Popup level

In addition, every container control belongs by default to the *popup level* during which it was created. The popup level is the hierarchical level of a modal dialog box generated with the command CALL SCREEN ... STARTING AT. Up to nine dialog boxes can be stacked on top of a normal window. When creating the first custom, docking, or dialog box container in a popup level, an implicit container control is created for it, which is passed to the explicitly created control as its PARENT. References to these implicit container controls are available in the static attributes SCREEN0 through SCREEN9 of the CL_GUI_CONTAINER class, where SCREEN0 points to the container of the lowest normal window.

Visibility

The assignment to popup levels controls the visibility of GUI controls. Application controls are visible only when their container control is visible, and container controls are visible only on their own popup level. A control assigned to the dynpro in popup level 0 is therefore not visible when the same dynpro is called again as a modal dialog box. For technical reasons, the assignment to a popup level cannot be changed. However, you can use the LINK method of the CL_GUI_CONTAINER class to assign an application control to a different container control within a popup level.

Control Processing

The architecture of the Control Framework shown in Figure 9.34 has some differences when working with control objects in comparison with conventional screen elements, but also in comparison with other objects in ABAP Objects.

Control methods

To work with the controls of a dynpro, you use the methods of the control objects in the ABAP program. Generally, you will work with the methods of the application controls. However, sometimes methods of the container controls are required. In either case, a method call is not executed immediately on the presentation server. For performance reasons, it is first stored in an automation queue on the application server.

To keep network load low, the CFW sends the stored method calls and the associated parameters to the presentation server only when a synchronization point is reached. There, they are executed in order. This improves performance with often-used parameters, which can be large internal tables. There are automatic synchronization points, like the end of PBO processing. However, you can also force such a point at any time during dynpro processing using the method CL_GUI_CFW=>FLUSH. For performance reasons, this should only be done when data must absolutely be exchanged between the presentation and application servers at this point, such as after processing of a control event.

Automation queue

User actions on GUI controls trigger control events. In contrast to user actions on conventional screen elements, control events are not associated with function codes in the OK field and do not directly result in the PAI event. Instead, control events are handled by the CFW and are passed on to the ABAP program. A control class contains the events that are triggered on the control and can be handled. In order to be able to respond to the events in the ABAP program, you must use event handler methods from other classes, which you typically create locally in the program of the dynpro or, if reuse is a consideration, store in the library.

Control events

For performance reasons, for many controls, the events of the corresponding class are not activated automatically, and are not sent from the presentation server to the application server when the corresponding user action takes place. You must activate the events that you want to react to using the method SET_REGISTERED_EVENTS, which is provided in every control class. You pass an internal table of type CNTL_SIMPLE_EVENTS, which contains a line for every event that you want to activate. You identify the events in the first column EVENTID using matching constants of the control classes like EVENTID_NODE_DOUBLE_CLICK in the CL_GUI_SIMPLE_TREE class.

After this kind of activation, the CFW triggers an event on the application server after the corresponding user action. If you want to handle this event with methods, you must register the event handler methods with SET HANDLER, as usual in ABAP Objects, and link the handler object with the proxy object of the control.

There are two types of control events, namely, *system events* and *application events*. You specify the type of event handling when activating an event with the SET_REGISTERED_EVENTS method. If you leave the APPL_EVENT component initial in the internal table passed, the event is a system event. If you fill the component with "X", it is an application event. You use the selection of event handling to control the interplay between control processing and conventional screen processing. This is particularly important if you are using both GUI controls and conventional dynpro fields on the screen. Figure 9.36 shows the processing of control events.

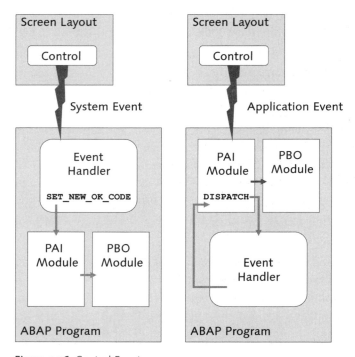

Figure 9.36 Control Events

System events   If the APPL_EVENT component is initial, an event is handled as a system event. This means that this type of event is sent to the application server without initiating PAI, and all the handler methods are triggered there that were registered with SET HANDLER. After executing the handler methods, the system returns to the screen display without initiating PBO. The advantage of this type of handling is that no conflicts can occur with the automatic input check for the conventional dynpro fields.

On the other hand, the contents of any conventional dynpro fields are not transported. If you use conventional dynpro fields along with the GUI controls, and want to be able to evaluate their contents during the event handling of controls, you need to call the static CFW method CL_GUI_CFW=>SET_NEW_OK_CODE within a handler method, and pass it a function code. This method triggers the PAI event including all checks and field transport. After the conventional PAI processing is executed, the PBO event of the next dynpro is triggered. Consequently, the system only returns to the same screen if the next dynpro is set accordingly.

System events are therefore always suitable if you aren't using conventional dynpro fields along with your controls.

If the content of APPL_EVENT is "X", an event is handled as an application event. This means that the event is sent to the application server and the conventional PAI for the dynpro flow logic is triggered there, not the ABAP event handler methods. If you want to call the event handler methods registered with SET HANDLER, you need to call the CFW method CL_GUI_CFW=>DISPATCH in an appropriate PAI module. This triggers ABAP event handling, after which the program execution resumes in the PAI module.

Application event

The advantage of this type of handling is that the contents of conventional dynpro fields are transported before event handling and can be checked, and that you can determine when a control event will be processed during conventional dynpro processing. The disadvantage of this type of handling is that user actions on controls may not be handled at all due to automatic input check.

If you want to use conventional dynpro fields along with controls, application events are always a good means of determining the order of data transport and event handling.

Lifetime of GUI Controls

By default, the lifetime of GUI controls on the presentation server and their proxy objects on the application server is dependent on the lifetime of the internal session of the ABAP program. All objects and associated administrative entries in the CFW are destroyed when the ABAP program ends or, for instance, is exited completely with LEAVE TO TRANSACTION (see Section 3.3).

Deleting In order to delete a GUI control programmatically, you must do more than just delete all references to the proxy object in the ABAP program. In addition to the references in the ABAP program, the CFW also points to all proxy objects for which controls exist on the presentation server (see Figure 9.34). Consequently, automatic garbage collection has no effect after all the reference variables in the ABAP program have been initialized. The proxy objects live on, and you can obtain references to all controls on the current dynpro using the method GET_LIVING_DYNPRO_CONTROLS in the CL_GUI_CFW class.

Every proxy object, however, inherits the FREE method from the class CL_GUI_OBJECT. By calling this method, you delete the associated GUI control on the presentation server and all object references in the CFW. If you then delete all the object references in the ABAP program as well, the proxy object can finally be collected by the Garbage Collector. If you execute the FREE method, but then attempt to access the proxy object again, a runtime error will occur.

When deleting the object references to the proxy object in the ABAP Program, you should not forget to deregister any event handlers. If, for instance, you call the FREE method when you close a dialog box and delete all the associated reference variables, but forget to deregister any event handlers for the controls, the proxy object will still be kept alive. Opening the dialog box again creates a new object, which can quickly add up to a memory bottleneck if the contents are large. For this reason, we recommend[18] that you always test applications that work with GUI controls with the Memory Inspector (see Section 13.4).

Wrapping of Controls

The processing of GUI controls described here shows that their processing can not really be called easy. For this reason, the AS ABAP provides encapsulations for a few frequently used controls, which are easy to use and make the direct use of the proxy object unnecessary. Furthermore, these encapsulations guarantee standardized interfaces, which automatically meet requirements like accessibility.

---

18 This recommendation is the result of painful experience.

The most important encapsulation is that for ALV Controls. SAP pro- ALV
vides the three following classes:

▶ **CL_SALV_TABLE**
for the display of non-hierarchical tabular lists

▶ **CL_SALV_HIERSEQ_TABLE**
for the display of hierarchical sequential lists (two-level hierarchical data)

▶ **CL_SALV_TREE**
for the display of hierarchical tabular lists

These classes are documented and are recommended instead of the direct use of CL_GUI_ALV_GRID and CL_GUI_ALV_TREE. Their usage eliminates the need to create a field catalog. The AS ABAP includes many executable sample programs, which all start with the prefix "SALV_DEMO_". In this book, we use the CL_SALV_TABLE class exclusively.

For the browser control CL_GUI_HTML_VIEWER, there is an encap- Dynamic
sulation called "dynamic documents." The corresponding classes all documents
start with the "CL_DD_" prefix and are documented in the SAP Library under the Control Framework.

You can use dynamic documents to display your own texts formatted in the browser control. They are perfectly adequate for most purposes and are therefore usually preferred over the direct generation of HTML files.[19]

Listing 9.24 shows a direct comparison of the different ways in which to display two text lines in the browser control. On the screen of dynpro 100, there is a custom control called CUSTOM_CONTROL, and the next dynpro is 0. The method ctrl1 uses a dynamic document, while ctrl2 uses an HTML file in an internal table. The formatting of the dynamic document (e.g., font size, background color, etc.), in contrast to the HTML file, automatically adapts to changes to the local GUI layout. For the HTML file, the format is statically specified and adaptations—if desired—must be programmed specifically.

---

19 Exceptions may be applications, which create standardized HTML themselves.

Listing 9.24 Different Uses of the Browser Control

```
REPORT z_gui_controls.

CLASS demo DEFINITION.
  PUBLIC SECTION.
    CLASS-METHODS main.
  PRIVATE SECTION.
    CLASS-DATA container
              TYPE REF TO cl_gui_custom_container.
    CLASS-METHODS: ctrl1, ctrl2.
ENDCLASS.

CLASS demo IMPLEMENTATION.
  METHOD main.
    ctrl1( ).
    ctrl2( ).
  ENDMETHOD.
  METHOD ctrl1.
    DATA oref TYPE REF TO cl_dd_document.
    CREATE OBJECT container
      EXPORTING container_name = 'CUSTOM_CONTROL'.
    CREATE OBJECT oref.
    oref->add_text( text        = 'Header'
                    sap_emphasis = cl_dd_area=>strong ).
    oref->new_line(   ).
    oref->add_text( text = 'Text' ).
    oref->display_document( parent = container ).
    CALL SCREEN 100.
    container->free( ).
  ENDMETHOD.
  METHOD ctrl2.
    DATA oref TYPE REF TO cl_gui_html_viewer.
    DATA html TYPE w3htmltab.
    DATA url  TYPE c LENGTH 255.
    CREATE OBJECT container
      EXPORTING container_name = 'CUSTOM_CONTROL'.
    CREATE OBJECT oref
      EXPORTING parent = container.
    APPEND '<html>'                    TO html.
    APPEND '<body>'                    TO html.
    APPEND '<font face="arial" size="2">' TO html.
    APPEND '<b>Header</b>'             TO html.
    APPEND '<br>'                      TO html.
    APPEND 'Text'                      TO html.
    APPEND '</font>'                   TO html.
    APPEND '</body>'                   TO html.
```

```
   APPEND '</html>'                          TO html.
   oref->load_data( IMPORTING assigned_url = url
                    CHANGING data_table = html ).
   oref->show_url( url = url ).
   CALL SCREEN 100.
   container->free( ).
 ENDMETHOD.
ENDCLASS.
START-OF-SELECTION.
 demo=>main( ).
```

Unfortunately, there are currently no additional user-friendly encapsulations of other important controls. For the Picture Control, we have created our own rudimentary encapsulation in the following example (class ZCL_PICTURE in Listing 9.36). For simple text output, we've created the ZCL_TEXT class shown in Appendix A.6.

Sample Application with GUI Controls

In the following sample application, we will show you the function group Z_AIRLINES. A call to its function module Z_SHOW_AIRLINES (for instance, in the executable program Z_AIRLINES) results in the screen in Figure 9.33.

The function group consists of the usual include programs (see Listing 9.10). It incorporates LZ_AIRLINESO01 for PBO modules, LZ_ AIRLINESP01 for PAI modules, and LZ_AIRLINESP01 for implementations of local classes as additional includes. The function module calls dynpro 100. On the screen of dynpro 100, we have created a custom control in the Layout Editor named CUSTOM_CONTROL, which covers the entire screen. Listing 9.25 shows the dynpro flow logic, which contains nothing that would be new to you (i. e., it is the same as for conventional dynpros without controls).

Listing 9.25 Dynpro Flow Logic   Dynpro 100

```
PROCESS BEFORE OUTPUT.
  MODULE status_0100.

PROCESS AFTER INPUT.
  MODULE cancel AT EXIT-COMMAND.
```

List 9.26 shows the implementation of the dialog modules.

Listing 9.26 Dialog Modules

```
*&--------------------------------------------------------*
*&  Include           LZ_AIRLINESO01
*&--------------------------------------------------------*

MODULE status_0100 OUTPUT.
  SET TITLEBAR  'TITLE_100'.
  SET PF-STATUS 'SCREEN_100'.
  screen_handler=>create_screen( ).
ENDMODULE.
*&--------------------------------------------------------*
*&  Include           LZ_AIRLINESI01
*&--------------------------------------------------------*
MODULE cancel INPUT.
  LEAVE PROGRAM.
ENDMODULE.
```

In the GUI status SCREEN_100, the usual symbols in the standard toolbar are occupied with function codes of type "E". Thus the PAI module `cancel` only serves to exit the program. Dynpro 100 and the associated dialog modules are the conventional framework for our programming with GUI controls. The most important action of the PBO module is the call to the static method `create_screen` in the local class `screen_handler`, which we have declared in the TOP include of the function group as shown in Listing 9.27. No global data is required for the function group.

screen_handler   **Listing 9.27** Declaration of the Class screen_handler in the TOP Include

```
FUNCTION-POOL z_airlines.

CLASS screen_handler DEFINITION CREATE PRIVATE.
  PUBLIC SECTION.
    CLASS-METHODS create_screen.
    METHODS constructor.
  PRIVATE SECTION.
    CLASS-DATA screen TYPE REF TO screen_handler.
    DATA: container_html
            TYPE REF TO cl_gui_custom_container,
          container_box
            TYPE REF TO cl_gui_dialog box_container,
          picture      TYPE REF TO cl_gui_picture,
          tree         TYPE REF TO cl_gui_simple_tree,
          html_viewer TYPE REF TO cl_gui_html_viewer,
          alv          TYPE REF TO cl_salv_table.
```

```
METHODS: fill_tree,
         fill_picture,
         fill_html
           IMPORTING carrid TYPE spfli-carrid,
         fill_list
           IMPORTING carrid TYPE spfli-carrid
                     connid TYPE spfli-connid,
         handle_node_double_click
           FOR EVENT node_double_click
           OF cl_gui_simple_tree
           IMPORTING node_key,
         close_box
           FOR EVENT close
           OF cl_gui_dialog box_container.
ENDCLASS.
```

The public static method `create_screen` serves to instantiate the class, which can only be instantiated privately. All instance attributes except `alv` are reference variables based on CFW classes. You recognize two classes for container controls and three classes for application controls. The static type of reference variable `alv` is the encapsulation class CL_SALV_GRID for the ALV Grid Control. We've declared four instance methods to populate the application controls and two event handler methods for reaction to user actions.

The implementation part of the class is found in the include program LZ_AIRLINESP01. In the following section, we'll examine the implementation of each method.

Listing 9.28 shows the implementation of the static method `create_screen`. It uses the static attribute `screen` to create an object of class `screen_handler`. In this process, the instance constructor `constructor` is executed.

create_screen

Listing 9.28 Method create_screen

```
METHOD create_screen.
  IF screen IS INITIAL.
    CREATE OBJECT screen.
  ENDIF.
ENDMETHOD.
```

Listing 9.29 shows the instance constructor. First, we create a docking control with the local reference variable `docking`. Passing the constant `dock_at_left` of the class CL_GUI_DOCKING_CONTAINER

constructor

to the `side` parameter creates a new area with a width of 135 pixels (`extension` parameter) on the left edge of the screen.

Listing 9.29 Instance Constructor

```
METHOD constructor.
  DATA: event_tab TYPE cntl_simple_events,
        event     LIKE LINE OF event_tab,
        docking   TYPE REF TO cl_gui_docking_container,
        splitter  TYPE REF TO cl_gui_splitter_container,
        container_top
                  TYPE REF TO cl_gui_container,
        container_bottom
                  TYPE REF TO cl_gui_container.

  CREATE OBJECT container_html
    EXPORTING container_name = 'CUSTOM_CONTROL'.
  CREATE OBJECT docking
    EXPORTING side  = cl_gui_docking_container=>dock_at_left
              extension = 135.
  CREATE OBJECT splitter
    EXPORTING parent  = docking
              rows    = 2
              columns = 1.
  splitter->set_border( border = cl_gui_cfw=>false ).
  splitter->set_row_mode( mode = splitter->mode_absolute ).
  splitter->set_row_height( id  = 1 height = 180 ).
  container_top =
    splitter->get_container( row = 1 column = 1 ).
  container_bottom =
    splitter->get_container( row = 2 column = 1 ).
  CREATE OBJECT picture
    EXPORTING parent = container_top.
  CREATE OBJECT tree
    EXPORTING parent = container_bottom
              node_selection_mode =
                cl_gui_simple_tree=>node_sel_mode_single.
  event-eventid =
    cl_gui_simple_tree=>eventid_node_double_click.
  event-appl_event = ' '.
  APPEND event TO event_tab.
  tree->set_registered_events( events = event_tab ).
  SET HANDLER me->handle_node_double_click FOR tree.
```

```
  me->fill_picture( ).
  me->fill_tree( ).
ENDMETHOD.
```

We split this screen area into two horizontal sections by using the local reference variable `splitter` to create an object of class CL_GUI_ SPLITTER_CONTAINER and use the `parent` parameter to pass the reference to the docking control. The sizing is governed by the `rows` and `columns` parameter. By calling methods of the splitter control, we specify that no frame will be drawn and that the height is specified in absolute terms, and will be 180 pixels.

We use the functional method `get_container` to read the references to the two areas of the splitter control into the local reference variables `container_top` and `container_bottom`. Then we create a picture control and a tree control using the `picture` and `tree` instance attributes, passing the `parent` parameter of each constructor one of the references to the splitter control sections.

So that our event handler method `handle_node_double_click` can react to double clicks on nodes of the tree control, we have to activate this event and register the event handler. The `set_registered_ events` method is called for this activation. It is available in every application control. The actual parameter is the internal table `event_ tab`, which we declared locally with type `cntl_simple_events`. We specify the double-click event in the `eventid` column. By not entering an "X" in the `appl_event` column, we determine that the event should handled as a system event and not as an application event. Then we register the event handler.

After calling the `fill_picture` and `fill_tree` methods, we leave the constructor, whereby all the local reference variables of the constructor are deleted. The control objects created with such local reference variables, however, are not collected by the Garbage Collector, because they are kept alive by references from the CFW.

Listing 9.30 shows the `fill_picture` method. Since there is no suitable encapsulation for this GUI control,[20] we have created an auxiliary class ZCL_PICTURE, which at least wraps the technical preparation of an image file for the Picture Control (we describe this class at

fill_picture

---

20 At least, we don't know of any.

the end of this section.) The `factory` method of the ZCL_PICTURE class expects the address of an image file in the MIME Repository, returning a reference to an object enabling the display of the image in a picture control. The `display` method is used to display it, and it is passed a reference to a Picture Control.

Listing 9.30 Method fill_picture

```
METHOD fill_picture.
    DATA pict TYPE REF TO zcl_picture.
    TRY.
        pict = zcl_picture=>factory(
          mime_file =
            '/SAP/PUBLIC/BC/ABAP/Sources/PLANE.GIF'
          pict_type = 'GIF' ).
      CATCH zcx_no_picture.
        RETURN.
    ENDTRY.
    pict->display( picture ).
ENDMETHOD.
```

MIME Repository The MIME Repository is a part of the Repository in the database of an AS ABAP in which multimedia files can be stored as though in a file system (the term MIME refers to *Multipurpose Internet Mail Extension*, which describes a method for packing multimedia content into SMTP email). These files, like all Repository objects, are connected to the transport system. You can call up the MIME Repository in the Object Navigator using the **MIME Repository** button in order to store and manage the files there. We use the image of an airplane in GIF format, which we have loaded for this purpose into the MIME Repository of our trial version of AS ABAP.[21] The browser-based interfaces BSP and Web Dynpro, by the way, have a much more direct access to the MIME Repository than do the classical dynpros.

fill_tree Listing 9.31 shows the `fill_tree` method. The `fill_tree` method generates the tree structure of the tree control. To do this, we have to populate an internal table of a specific structure. For this purpose, we use the predefined MTREESNODE structure from the ABAP Dictionary. If this structure doesn't meet your needs, you can also use self-defined structures, which include TREEV_NODE at the beginning.

---

21 Starting with the next SAP NetWeaver release, the image will be available by default at this path, since it will also be used by examples in the ABAP documentation.

Listing 9.31 Method fill_tree

```abap
METHOD fill_tree.
  DATA: node_table TYPE TABLE OF mtreesnode,
        node       TYPE mtreesnode,
        spfli      TYPE spfli,
        spfli_tab  TYPE zcl_airlines=>tspfli_tab.
  spfli_tab = zcl_airlines=>get_spfli_tab( ).
  node-isfolder = 'X'.
  LOOP AT spfli_tab INTO spfli.
    AT NEW carrid.
      node-node_key = spfli-carrid.
      CLEAR node-relatkey.
      CLEAR node-relatship.
      node-text = spfli-carrid.
      CLEAR node-n_image.
      CLEAR node-exp_image.
      APPEND node TO node_table.
    ENDAT.
    AT NEW connid.
      CONCATENATE spfli-carrid spfli-connid
        INTO node-node_key.
      node-relatkey = spfli-carrid.
      node-relatship = cl_gui_simple_tree=>relat_last_child.
      node-text = spfli-connid.
      CALL FUNCTION 'ICON_CREATE'
        EXPORTING
          name   = 'ICON_FLIGHT'
          info   = text-con
        IMPORTING
          result = node-n_image
        EXCEPTIONS
          others = 4.
      IF sy-subrc <> 0.
        node-n_image = '@AV@'.
      ENDIF.
      node-exp_image = node-n_image.
    ENDAT.
    APPEND node TO node_table.
  ENDLOOP.
  tree->add_nodes( table_structure_name = 'MTREESNODE'
                   node_table           = node_table ).
ENDMETHOD.
```

We've created an internal table `node_table` with the line structure from MTREESNODE. Every line in the table describes a node in the tree structure, and has to have a unique node key in `node_key`.[22] The components `relatkey` and `relatship` describe the relationships between the nodes. Other components make it possible to change the standard icons or create node texts, etc.

In our example, we create the node table from the content of an internal table `splfi_tab`, which, to adhere to the separation of concerns, we don't populate directly in the function group but rather in a service class ZCL_AIRLINES, using data from the database table SPFLI. Using the control level processing statements AT−ENDAT, we populate the node table in a LOOP with rows representing a two-level hierarchy. Before the LOOP, some general node properties are set for all the rows in the working area `node`.

CREATE_ICON
For the subnodes, we replace the standard icons for collapsed and expanded nodes with airplane icons by assigning the components n_ image and `exp_image` the internal representation for these icons, which we create with the standard function module CREATE_ICON. This function module is of general use for the creation of icons on dynpros and allows you to enter additional texts and tooltips. The latter are even a requirement for accessible programs. You find the icon names needed by executing the program SHOWICON. For exception handling, we specify the internal code for the "@AV@" icon, without a tooltip text.

fill_html
Listing 9.32 shows the `fill_html` method. The `fill_html` method creates an object of the CL_GUI_HTML_VIEWER class when it is first called, and binds the associated HTML control to the area of the container control pointed to by the reference in `container_html`, namely the custom control on the dynpro. Note that without the IF statement a new HTML control will be created every time the method is called. All these controls would be active in the ABAP program and present on the presentation server, even though only the last one would be visible. So you can bind multiple application controls to a single container control. You can then control the visibility of the controls with the SET_VISIBLE method.

---

22 This key is limited to 12 characters; however, there is also a class CL_SIMPLE_
TREE_MODEL, which encapsulates CL_GUI_SIMPLE_TREE and removes this
limitation. For our simple example, however, usage of that encapsulation is not
necessary.

Listing 9.32 Method fill_html

```
METHOD fill_html.
  DATA url TYPE zcl_airlines=>turl.
  IF html_viewer IS INITIAL.
    CREATE OBJECT html_viewer
           EXPORTING parent = container_html.
  ENDIF.
  url = zcl_airlines=>get_url( carrid ).
  html_viewer->show_url( url = url ).
ENDMETHOD.
```

We use the ZCL_AIRLINES service class to obtain the URL address of an airline, and pass this to the show_url method of our HTML control, so that it can show the airline's home page.

Listing 9.33 shows the fill_list method. The fill_list method creates a dialog box container if there isn't already one available. For the dialog box container, we register the close_box event handler. Activation with the SET_REGISTERED_EVENTS method is not necessary in this case, since the CLOSE event of the CL_GUI_DIALOGBOX_CONTAINER class is activated in the class itself as a system event. We've programmed the dialog box container ourselves here as a demonstration. In it, you can display any arbitrary GUI controls. If, as in our example, only the display of an ALV list is needed, the SET_SCREEN_POPUP method of the ALV class could be used as well (see the example in Listing 9.51).

fill_list

Listing 9.33 Method fill_list

```
METHOD fill_list.

  DATA flight_tab TYPE zcl_airlines=>tflight_tab.
  DATA settings   TYPE REF TO cl_salv_display_settings.
  DATA list_title TYPE lvc_title.

  IF container_box IS INITIAL.
    CREATE OBJECT container_box
           EXPORTING width  = 300
                     height = 200
                     top    = 100
                     left   = 400
                     caption = text-fli.
    SET HANDLER close_box FOR container_box.
  ENDIF.
```

```
flight_tab = zcl_airlines=>get_flight_tab(
                carrid = carrid
                connid = connid ).
CONCATENATE carrid ` ` connid INTO list_title.
TRY.
    IF alv IS INITIAL.
      cl_salv_table=>factory(
        EXPORTING r_container  = container_box
        IMPORTING r_salv_table = alv
        CHANGING  t_table       = flight_tab ).
      alv->display( ).
    ELSE.
      alv->set_data( CHANGING t_table = flight_tab ).
    ENDIF.
    settings = alv->get_display_settings( ).
    settings->set_list_header( list_title ).
    alv->refresh( ).
  CATCH cx_salv_msg cx_salv_no_new_data_allowed.
    MESSAGE text-alv TYPE 'I' DISPLAY LIKE 'E'.
ENDTRY.
ENDMETHOD.
```

CL_SALV_TABLE   We use the ZCL_AIRLINES service class to read a few details on the selected nodes into an internal table flight_tab, and create a title for an ALV list. If no object is available yet for the ALV list, we create one and pass the internal table with the data to this object. By assigning the reference to the dialog box container, the ALV list is bound to it, and displayed by calling its DISPLAY method. Without the EXPORTING clause on the CREATE OBJECT statement, the ALV list would be displayed in its own dynpro in the entire current window. IF the ALV list is already present, we simply pass it new data. The title of the ALV list is set using a configuration object referenced by settings. The call to the REFRESH method passes the title and any newly written data to the display. If you have the previous edition of this book, compare the use of the ALV grid control described there with the use of the CL_SALV_TABLE encapsulation shown here. You will see that we are now largely liberated from the internal details of list display.

handle_node_   Listing 9.34 shows the method handle_node_double_click. The
double_click   handle_node_double_click method is declared as an event handler for double clicks on nodes in the tree structure and was registered for that purpose in the constructor. It is thus called by any such user

action. The method imports the `node_key` parameter of the `node_double_click` event in the CL_GUI_SIMPLE_TREE class, which contains the key of the selected node. We break the key into the parts we used to build it in the `fill_tree` method, and, depending on that, we call either `fill_html` or `fill_list`.

Listing 9.34 Listing 9.34 Method handle_node_double_click

```
METHOD handle_node_double_click.

  DATA: carrid TYPE spfli-carrid,
        connid TYPE spfli-connid.
  carrid = node_key(2).
  connid = node_key+2(4).
  IF connid IS INITIAL.
    fill_html( carrid = carrid ).
  ELSE.
    fill_list( carrid = carrid
               connid = connid ).
  ENDIF.
ENDMETHOD.
```

The method calls are stored in the automation queue until the next synchronization point between the application and presentation servers. After handling system events, the CFW receives an automatic synchronization point, so that methods are executed during event handling.

Synchronization point

Listing 9.35 shows the `close_box` method. The `close_box` method enables the user to close the dialog box with the usual icon. To do this, the `close_screen` method of the ALV list and the `free` method of the dialog box container are called in succession and then the corresponding reference variables are cleared.

close_box

Listing 9.35 Method close_box

```
METHOD close_box.
    alv->close_screen( ).
    container_box->free( ).
    CLEAR: alv, container_box.
ENDMETHOD.
```

Listing 9.36 shows the ZCL_PICTURE class, which we introduced for the encapsulation of images for the Picture Control. The FACTORY

ZCL_PICTURE

method creates an object containing as its attributes an internal table with an image file and a URL for the table.

Listing 9.36 Class ZCL_PICTURE

```abap
CLASS zcl_picture DEFINITION PUBLIC
  FINAL CREATE PRIVATE.
  PUBLIC SECTION.
    TYPES: tpict_line TYPE x LENGTH 1022,
           tpict_tab  TYPE TABLE OF tpict_line.
    METHODS constructor
      IMPORTING
        mime_file TYPE csequence
        pict_type TYPE c
      RAISING
        zcx_no_picture.
    CLASS-METHODS factory
      IMPORTING
        mime_file TYPE csequence
        pict_type TYPE c
      RETURNING
        value(picture) TYPE REF TO zcl_picture
      RAISING
        zcx_no_picture.
    METHODS display
      IMPORTING
        picture_control TYPE REF TO cl_gui_picture.
  PRIVATE SECTION.
    DATA pict_tab TYPE tpict_tab.
    DATA url TYPE char255 .
ENDCLASS.

CLASS zcl_picture IMPLEMENTATION.
  METHOD constructor.
    DATA  mime_api   TYPE REF TO if_mr_api.
    DATA  pict_wa    TYPE xstring.
    DATA  strl       TYPE i.
    mime_api = cl_mime_repository_api=>get_api( ).
    mime_api->get(
      EXPORTING i_url = mime_file
      IMPORTING e_content = pict_wa
      EXCEPTIONS OTHERS = 4 ).
    IF sy-subrc <> 0.
      RAISE EXCEPTION TYPE zcx_no_picture.
    ENDIF.
```

```
    strl = xstrlen( pict_wa ).
    WHILE strl >= 1022.
      APPEND pict_wa(1022) TO pict_tab.
      SHIFT pict_wa BY 1022 PLACES LEFT IN BYTE MODE.
    strl = xstrlen( pict_wa ).
    ENDWHILE.
    IF strl > 0.
      APPEND pict_wa TO pict_tab.
    ENDIF.
    CALL FUNCTION 'DP_CREATE_URL'
      EXPORTING
        type    = 'IMAGE'
        subtype = pict_type
      TABLES
        data    = pict_tab
      CHANGING
        url     = url.
  ENDMETHOD.
  METHOD factory.
    CREATE OBJECT picture
      EXPORTING mime_file = mime_file
                pict_type = pict_type.
  ENDMETHOD.
  METHOD display.
    picture_control->load_picture_from_url( url = url ).
    picture_control->set_display_mode( display_mode =
      picture_control->display_mode_stretch ).
  ENDMETHOD.
ENDCLASS.
```

In the instance constructor, the requested MIME Repository is read through the appropriate API.[23] Since the result is a byte string, but the Picture Control only works with an internal table, we have to read the content of the pict_wa byte string into the pict_tab internal table. To set the URL to the image in the table, we use the function module DP_CREATE_URL.

The DISPLAY method passes the URL to the load_picture_from_url method of the Picture Control, sending the image into the control's

---

23 If you're familiar with the last edition of this book, you will remember that we then—horror of horrors—threw together a kind of self-defined MIME storage for the image file. It may well be that five years from now, we won't even need to write the encapsulation for the picture control any more.

area on the screen. We use the `set_display_mode` method to specify that the image should always fill the size of the area.

ZCL_AIRLINES   Listing 9.37 shows the ZCL_AIRLINES class for the sake of completeness, which we created to generate the data for the example. Every method has a corresponding `SELECT` statement. A user of the class does not need to know anything about the database tables. All that is required are the data types declared in the public visibility section of the class.

Listing 9.37 Class ZCL_AIRLINES

```
CLASS zcl_airlines DEFINITION PUBLIC
  FINAL CREATE PUBLIC.
  PUBLIC SECTION.
    TYPES:
      tspfli_tab TYPE SORTED TABLE OF spfli
                 WITH UNIQUE KEY carrid connid,
      turl TYPE scarr-url,
      tflight_tab TYPE STANDARD TABLE OF demofli
                  WITH NON-UNIQUE DEFAULT KEY.
    CLASS-METHODS get_spfli_tab
      RETURNING
        value(spfli_tab) TYPE tspfli_tab.
    CLASS-METHODS get_url
      IMPORTING
        carrid TYPE scarr-carrid
      RETURNING
        value(url) TYPE turl.
    CLASS-METHODS get_flight_tab
      IMPORTING
        carrid TYPE sflight-carrid
        connid TYPE sflight-connid
      RETURNING
        value(flight_tab) TYPE tflight_tab.
ENDCLASS.

CLASS zcl_airlines IMPLEMENTATION.
  METHOD get_spfli_tab.
    SELECT carrid connid
           FROM spfli
           INTO CORRESPONDING FIELDS OF TABLE spfli_tab.
  ENDMETHOD.
  METHOD get_url.
    SELECT SINGLE url
           FROM    scarr
```

```
                   INTO    url
                   WHERE   carrid = carrid.
        ENDMETHOD.
        METHOD get_flight_tab.
          SELECT fldate seatsmax seatsocc
                 INTO CORRESPONDING FIELDS OF TABLE flight_tab
                 FROM sflight
                 WHERE carrid = carrid AND connid = connid
                 ORDER BY fldate.
        ENDMETHOD.
      ENDCLASS.
```

The process in our GUI control example can be summarized in the **Summary** following steps, which are generally valid for any work with controls:

1. Create container controls and bind them to screen areas on dynpros.

2. Create application controls or objects in encapsulation classes, and bind them to the container controls.

3. Provide data to fill the controls, usually in internal tables with special types.

4. Send data to the application controls or encapsulation objects.

5. React to user events via implementation and registration of suitable handler methods.

9.2   Selection Screens

Selection screens are special dynpros defined with ABAP statements without needing to use the Screen Painter. When an ABAP program with selection screens is activated, the ABAP runtime environment generates these dynpros with all their components, including flow logic. In the ABAP program, no dialog modules need to be created for selection screens. Instead, user actions on selection screens result in special selection screen events, which can be handled in event blocks.

The historical origin of selection screens can be traced to the follow- **Origin** ing division of classical ABAP programs, which was introduced in Section 7.1:

▶ Reports started with SUBMIT

▶ Dialog programs were called through dialog transactions

While a dialog programmer had to know how to create and operate dynpros, a report programmer should be able to get by without using the Screen Painter. With selection screens, it was very easy to implement a user interface that met the requirements of reporting. That is, selection criteria were primarily used to query selection criteria for database selects, hence the name "selection screen."

Logical database

Even logical databases, which could be bound to executable programs in classical reporting, can contain selection screens as components. If such a logical database is bound to an executable program, the program uses the selection screen of the logical database. Then, even the need to define a selection screen in the program was eliminated.

Standard selection screen

Until Release 4.0, selection screens could actually be defined only in executable programs. Until that time, only a single selection screen (the standard selection screen) was possible per program, which was automatically called with SUBMIT at the start of the program (see Figure 7.1).

As far back as Release 4.0, however, selection screens could be defined in all programs, which can also include dynpros (i. e., in function groups, executable programs, and module pools), and every program can contain multiple selection screens. The selection screens of a program are nothing more than additional dynpros for the program. They have a unique dynpro number and can be called very similarly to dynpros.

Scope of function

The screen elements of selection screens are a subset of all the elements possible on dynpros, including:

▶ Text fields and frames

▶ Input/output fields, checkboxes, and radio buttons

▶ Pushbuttons

▶ Subscreens

▶ Tabstrip Controls

Table controls and custom controls are not possible.[24] The support of automatic input help and checks is similar to that in general dynpros.

---

24 If absolutely necessary, however, general subscreen dynpros can be integrated, which can contain any possible screen elements.

However, no dynpro sequences can be formed by defining a subsequent dynpro.

Use

In many places where the complete functionality of dynpros is not needed, selection screens can have the following advantages:

▶ Fast implementation of small queries without the Screen Painter.

▶ The user can store frequently used entries for each selection screen in so-called *selection variants* and reuse them.

▶ Selection criteria are stored in special internal tables and can be evaluated in logical expressions.

Separation of Concerns

All the notes and suggestions we made in the last section for the use of dynpros apply equally to selection screens. In the context of "separation of concerns," selection screens should only be created in programs that contain exclusively presentation logic and no application logic. As with dynpros, function groups are available here, and Figure 9.20 applies just as well for selection screens if the dialog modules are extended with the event blocks for selection screen events. In our practical introduction, we used selection screens in Section 2.7 in just this way.

9.2.1 Creating Selection Screens

Selection screens can be created with the following statements in the global declaration part of function groups, executable programs, and module pools:

SELECTION-SCREEN BEGIN OF SCREEN

```
SELECTION-SCREEN BEGIN OF SCREEN dynnr
                 [TITLE title] [AS WINDOW].
...

SELECTION-SCREEN END OF SCREEN dynnr.
```

These two statements define a selection screen numbered `dynnr`. Between these statements, the screen elements of the selection screen are defined. Only the standard selection screen of an executable program, for historical reasons, is not declared between the two statements above. We will take a brief look at standard selection screens in Section 9.2.8.

Dynpro number

During program generation, the selection screen is generated in the program as a dynpro with dynpro number `dynnr`. The specified dynpro number must therefore be unique with respect to all selection screens and all general dynpros in the program. The TITLE clause can be used to define a selection screen title title; it is best to specify title as a text symbol. The AS WINDOW clause can be used to prepare the selection screen for display in a modal dialog box.[25]

To define the screen elements of a selection screen, the following statements are used:

▶ PARAMETERS defines a single input field for a so-called *parameter*, which can also be displayed as a checkbox or radio button.

▶ SELECT-OPTIONS defines two related input fields and additional functions for a so-called *selection criterion*.

▶ Additional variants of the SELECTION-SCREEN statement define the other screen elements and influence their arrangement.

We'll cover these statements briefly in the following sections.

9.2.2 Parameters

A parameter is a component of a selection screen, for which an input field on the selection screen and a global variable of the same in the ABAP program are created. The declaration is done using the PARAMETERS statement, for which we will show only a few of the possible clauses:

PARAMETERS

```
PARAMETERS para
    {TYPE type LENGTH len}|{LIKE dobj} [DECIMALS dec]
    [OBLIGATORY]
    [AS CHECKBOX]
    [RADIOBUTTON GROUP group]
    [DEFAULT val]
    [LOWER CASE]
    [VALUE CHECK]
    ...
```

This statement, like DATA, creates a variable named para of a certain data type.[26] At the same time, an input field with this name and a descriptive text are created on the selection screen. The contents of the variable is transported into the input field during PBO in the

25 However, this will only affect the form of error messages and warnings.
26 The name can be only eight characters in length.

selection screen, and adopt its current value during PAI. The data type must be elementary. Strings and the numerical type f are not allowed. If a parameter is declared by reference to a data type in the ABAP Dictionary, the corresponding automatic field and input help are available to the user on the selection screen (see Sections 9.1.13 and 9.1.14). The input help can also be offered as a dropdown list box.

The text is a part of the text elements of a program as a so-called selection text and must be maintained using **Go to • Text elements** from the ABAP Editor or **Show • Text elements** in the context menu of the program in the Object Navigator. If the data type is a dictionary type, the use of texts from the ABAP Dictionary is also possible. Without maintaining the selection text, the name of the parameter is used.

Selection text

The clauses that aren't used to determine the data type—like TYPE and LENGTH—specify the properties of the associated dynpro field, or regulate the handling of input values. The examples we've chosen have the following effects:

- OBLIGATORY makes the input field a required field.

- AS CHECKBOX creates the input field as a checkbox of type c of length 1.

- RADIOBUTTON GROUP defines a radio button in a radio button group group.

- DEFAULT defines a starting value.

- LOWER CASE causes a distinction to be made between uppercase and lowercase letters in user input. Otherwise, all characters in character fields are passed as uppercase letters.

- VALUE CHECK, for fields declared by reference to a data type in the ABAP Dictionary, activates automatic input check (see Section 9.1.12).

Examples for parameters with normal input fields are shown in Listing 2.6 of the practical introduction. Listing 9.38 shows an example with checkboxes and radio buttons.

Listing 9.38 Selection Screen with Parameters

```
FUNCTION-POOL z_selection_screens.

* Selection Screen with Parameters
SELECTION-SCREEN BEGIN OF SCREEN 100
                AS WINDOW TITLE text-100.
PARAMETERS p_input TYPE c LENGTH 16 DEFAULT 'Parameter'.
SELECTION-SCREEN: SKIP,
                  BEGIN OF BLOCK b1
                  WITH FRAME TITLE text-110.
PARAMETERS: p_check1 AS CHECKBOX,
            p_check2 AS CHECKBOX,
            p_check3 AS CHECKBOX.
SELECTION-SCREEN: END OF BLOCK b1,
                  SKIP,
                  BEGIN OF BLOCK b2
                    WITH FRAME TITLE text-120.
PARAMETERS: p_radio1 RADIOBUTTON GROUP rad,
            p_radio2 RADIOBUTTON GROUP rad,
            p_radio3 RADIOBUTTON GROUP rad.
SELECTION-SCREEN: END OF BLOCK b2,
                  END OF SCREEN 100.

...

FUNCTION z_parameters.
*"----------------------------------------------------
*"*"Local Interface:
*"  EXPORTING
*"     REFERENCE(CHECK1) TYPE  CHAR1
*"     REFERENCE(CHECK2) TYPE  CHAR1
*"     REFERENCE(CHECK3) TYPE  CHAR1
*"     REFERENCE(INPUT) TYPE   CHAR16
*"     REFERENCE(SELECTION) TYPE  I
*"----------------------------------------------------
  CALL SELECTION-SCREEN 100 STARTING AT 10 10.

  input = p_input.

  check1 = p_check1.
  check2 = p_check2.
  check3 = p_check3.

  IF p_radio1 = 'X'.
    selection = 1.
  ELSEIF p_radio2 = 'X'.
    selection = 2.
  ELSEIF p_radio3 = 'X'.
```

```
      selection = 3.
   ENDIF.
ENDFUNCTION.
```

In the TOP include of the function group Z_SELECTION_SCREENS, a selection screen numbered 100 is created. The selection screen contains one normal parameter, three checkboxes, and three radio buttons, which are grouped together into a common group rad. Checkboxes and radio buttons are organized into their own blocks (see Section 9.2.4). The selection texts are created as selection texts in the function group, as in Figure 9.37. Note that the selection screen shows up as dynpro 0100 in the object list in the Object Navigator. You can also look at it in the Screen Painter, but you are not allowed to change anything.

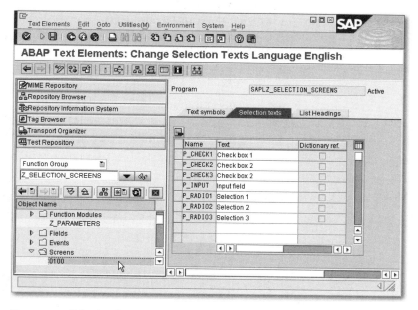

Figure 9.37 Selection Texts

The selection screen is called in the function module Z_PARAME-TERS with the CALL SELECTION-SCREEN statement (see Section 9.2.5). If you execute the function module in the Object Navigator with **Test/Execute**, the selection screen is displayed as shown in Figure 9.38.

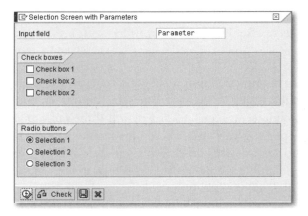

Figure 9.38 Selection Screen with Parameters

After selecting **Execute** (see Section 9.2.6), the inputs are evaluated in the function module and assigned to its output parameters.

9.2.3 Selection Criteria

The possibility of defining selection criteria is the main advantage of the selection screen over a general dynpro. With a single statement, you can define screen elements that offer a wide range of input options to the user. The selections entered by the user are passed to the ABAP program as the content of a special internal table, which can be directly used in a logical expression or in the WHERE clause of an Open SQL statement.

Selection table
A selection criterion is a component of a selection screen for which two input fields are created on the selection screen for interval selection and one button for multiple selection. In the ABAP program, a selection criterion is represented by a special internal table, a so-called *selection table*. The declaration is done using the SELECT-OPTIONS statement, for which we will show only two of the many possible clauses:

SELECT-OPTIONS
```
SELECT-OPTIONS selcrit FOR dobj
    ...
    [NO INTERVALS]
    [NO-EXTENSION]
    ...
```

This statement creates an internal table named `selcrit` with the special structure of a selection table.[27] At the same time, two input fields are created on the selection screen named SELCRIT-LOW and SELCRIT-HIGH, along with a descriptive text and the **Multiple selection** button. When this button is clicked, a dialog box appears with four tabstrip pages on which input fields are shown in table controls. The text, as for a parameter, is a selection text in the text elements of the program.

Instead of the usual `TYPE` or `LIKE` clause, `SELECT-OPTIONS` has a clause `FOR dobj`, in which a global elementary data object of the program must be specified whose data type will be taken for the selection criterion. The data type of `dobj` must be elementary and flat, and the numeric type `f` is not allowed. If the data type of `dobj` is determined by reference to the ABAP Dictionary, its automatic help is available on the selection screen as well.[28]

FOR

The reason that only a global data object can be specified here and not a type is that in the past, the assumption was that a selection criterion would be evaluated only in the same program and only for a global data object in a logical expression or a `WHERE` condition. Today, the exact opposite is true. To comply with the "separation of concerns," selection tables should be passed from the presentation logic to the application logic for processing, so that the declaration of a data object in the presentation logic is actually no longer needed.

A selection table is a four-column internal table (with a header line, unfortunately). Selection tables represent a logical condition, which can be composed of the conditions of multiple lines. All selection tables have the following components:

Components of the selection table

- **sign**
  The data type is `c` with length 1. Possible values are "I" and "E". These values determine whether the result of the condition formulated in the line should be included in or excluded from the overall result.

- **option**
  The data type is `c` of length 2. Possible values are "EQ", "NE", "GE", "GT", "LE", "LT", "CP", and "NP" for single values, or "BT"

---

27 The name can be only eight characters in length.
28 The automatic input checks are not available for selection criteria, however.

and "NB" for intervals. These values are the logical operators of each individual line.

▶ **low, high**
The data type of these components is determined by the FOR dobj clause. These fields are bound to the input fields on the selection screen. Either only low is filled for a single value selection, or low and high contain values for an interval selection. If you use the SELECT-OPTIONS statement with the NO INTERVALS clause, the second input field will not be shown on the selection screen.[29]

The individual results of all lines in a selection table are combined into the final selection when the table used in a logical expression. The NO-EXTENSION clause of the SELECT-OPTIONS statement can be used to define that the user can only fill in a single line in the selection table. Then there will be no button for multiple selection. The SELECT-OPTIONS statement has a variety of additional clauses, which largely correspond to those of the PARAMETERS statement for the determination of properties of screen elements for the handling of input values.

Listing 9.39 shows an example with a selection criterion on a selection screen.

Listing 9.39 Selection Screen with Selection Criterion

```
FUNCTION-POOL z_selection_screens.

...

* Selection Screen with Selection Criterion
DATA g_carrid TYPE scarr-carrid.
SELECTION-SCREEN BEGIN OF SCREEN 200 TITLE text-200.
SELECT-OPTIONS s_carrid FOR g_carrid.
SELECTION-SCREEN END OF SCREEN 200.

...

FUNCTION z_selection_criterion.
*"----------------------------------------------------------
*"*"Local Interface:
*"  EXPORTING
*"     REFERENCE(SELTAB) TYPE  STANDARD TABLE
*"     REFERENCE(RC) TYPE  SYST-SUBRC
*"----------------------------------------------------------
  CALL SELECTION-SCREEN 200.
  IF sy-subrc = 4.
```

---

29 But it will still show up in the window for multiple selection.

```
      rc = sy-subrc.
    RETURN.
  ELSE.
    seltab = s_carrid[].
  ENDIF.
ENDFUNCTION.
```

In the TOP include of the function group Z_SELECTION_SCREENS, a selection screen numbered 200 is created. The selection screen contains one selection criterion, for whose type a global data object g_carrid has been created with data type SCARR-CARRID from the ABAP Dictionary. In the selection texts, **Dictionary ref.** is checked. The selection screen is called in the function module Z_SELECTION_CRITERION and the selection table (without its header line!) is passed to its output parameter SELTAB. In addition, the return value of the selection screen is also passed, which is used to determine whether a user has selected **Cancel** (see Section 9.2.6). Listing 9.40 shows a program Z_SELECTION_CRITERION, which calls the function module.

Listing 9.40 Use of a Selection Criterion

```
REPORT z_selection_criterion.

CLASS demo DEFINITION.
  PUBLIC SECTION.
    CLASS-METHODS main.
ENDCLASS.

CLASS demo IMPLEMENTATION.
  METHOD main.
    DATA: selection TYPE RANGE OF scarr-carrid,
          scarr_tab TYPE TABLE OF scarr,
          alv       TYPE REF TO cl_salv_table,
          subrc     TYPE syst-subrc.
    CALL FUNCTION 'Z_SELECTION_CRITERION'
      IMPORTING seltab = selection.
    IF subrc = 4.
      RETURN.
    ENDIF.
    SELECT *
           FROM scarr
           INTO TABLE scarr_tab
           WHERE carrid IN selection.
    TRY.
```

```
            cl_salv_table=>factory(
              IMPORTING r_salv_table = alv
              CHANGING  t_table = scarr_tab ).
            alv->display( ).
        CATCH cx_salv_msg.
          MESSAGE 'ALV display not possible' TYPE 'I'
                  DISPLAY LIKE 'E'.
      ENDTRY.
    ENDMETHOD.
ENDCLASS.

START-OF-SELECTION.
    demo=>main( ).
```

During program execution, the selection screen appears with two input fields and one button, as shown in Figure 9.39, as the contents of the entire current window.

Figure 9.39 Selection Screen with Selection Criterion

In the input fields, interval selections can be entered. If the user selects the button for **Multiple selection**, another dialog box opens. Here, individual values and more intervals can be entered on the first two tabs. On the last two tabs, individual values or intervals can be excluded from the selection. The assignment to the tabs is determined by the content of the `sign` column in the selection table. A double-click on an individual value or an interval boundary opens another dialog box to maintain the selection options. Here, the type of selection, that is, the contents of the `option` column in the selection table, can be determined.

So a single `SELECT-OPTIONS` statement allows the user to enter a lengthy logical condition. To evaluate such a condition, there is a very simple logical expression:

```
... dobj IN seltab ...
```

IN seltab

This expression can be specified as a normal logical expression or in the `WHERE` condition of an Open SQL statement. The result is true if the content of `dobj` satisfies the condition in the `seltab` selection table. Any internal table can be given as `seltab` if its line structure corresponds to that of a selection criterion. You can create a suitable table either with the `SELECT-OPTIONS` statement or with the following statement:

```
DATA seltab {TYPE|LIKE} RANGE OF {type|dobj}.
```

RANGE OF

This creates an internal table with the structure of a selection table, which is not assigned to a selection criterion of a selection screen and also has no header line.[30] In the Z_SELECTION_CRITERION program, we've created such a table to take over the selection table from the function module, and evaluate its contents in the `WHERE` condition of a `SELECT` statement.

The `SELECT` statement reads the airlines, which correspond to the boundaries in the selection criterion from the SCARR database table into an internal table `scarr_tab`. If the selection table is empty, all the rows of the database table are read. We display the result in an ALV list. So our program Z_SELECTION_CRITERION implements a report that reads and displays data according to a selection criterion.

Report

9.2.4 Additional Elements on Selection Screens

The `SELECTION-SCREEN` statement has additional variants that don't create a selection screen, but rather create additional screen elements

---

30 In the ABAP Dictionary, you can create such a table using **Edit • Define as ranges table type** in the maintenance dialog of table types.

on a selection screen, or influence the structure of a selection screen. These variants include:

SELECTION-
SCREEN

▶ `SELECTION-SCREEN SKIP ...`
  Creates vertical spacing.

▶ `SELECTION-SCREEN ULINE ...`
  Creates horizontal lines.

▶ `SELECTION-SCREEN COMMENT ...`
  Creates output fields.

▶ `SELECTION-SCREEN PUSHBUTTON ...`
  Creates buttons.

▶ `SELECTION-SCREEN BEGIN|END OF LINE ...`
  Arranges multiple elements on a line.

▶ `SELECTION-SCREEN BEGIN|END OF BLOCK ...`
  Organizes multiple elements into a block, optionally with frame and title.

▶ `SELECTION-SCREEN BEGIN|END OF TABBED BLOCK ...`
  Creates a tabstrip control.

Furthermore, a selection screen can be defined during creation as a subscreen dynpro as follows:

`SELECTION-SCREEN BEGIN OF SCREEN` dynnr `AS SUBSCREEN.`

Listing 9.41 shows with a tabstrip example how some of the variants of the `SELECTION-SCREEN` statements can be used.

Listing 9.41 Selection Screen with Tabstrips

```
FUNCTION-POOL z_selection_screens.

...

* Selection Screen with Tabstrips and Subscreens
SELECTION-SCREEN: BEGIN OF SCREEN 300 TITLE text-300,
                 BEGIN OF TABBED BLOCK mytab FOR 10 LINES,
                 TAB (20) button1 USER-COMMAND push1
                          DEFAULT SCREEN 310,
                 TAB (20) button2 USER-COMMAND push2
                          DEFAULT SCREEN 320,
                 END OF BLOCK mytab,
                 END OF SCREEN 300.

SELECTION-SCREEN: BEGIN OF SCREEN 310 AS SUBSCREEN,
                 SKIP 3,
```

```
                     COMMENT /1(30) text-310,
                     END OF SCREEN 310.
SELECTION-SCREEN: BEGIN OF SCREEN 320 AS SUBSCREEN,
                     SKIP 3,
                     COMMENT /1(30) text-320,
                     END OF SCREEN 320.

...

FUNCTION z_tab_strip.
  button1 = text-bu1.
  button2 = text-bu2.
  CALL SELECTION-SCREEN 300.
ENDFUNCTION.
```

In the TOP include of the function group Z_SELECTION_SCREENS, a selection screen numbered 300 is created, which contains a tabstrip control. The tabs are defined with TAB, and tabstrip pages are assigned to them. We use two selection screens, 310 and 320 of the same function group that are defined as subscreens. We could also integrate general subscreen dynpros. The arrangement of tabstrip pages to tabs shown here is static; however, there is also a dynamic variant.

If you execute the function module Z_TAB_STRIP in the Object Navigator with **Test/Execute**, the selection screen is displayed as shown in Figure 9.40.

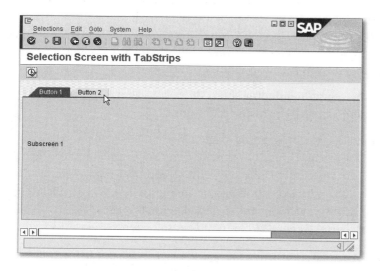

Figure 9.40 Selection Screen with Tabstrips

Compare the effort with that for tabstrips on general dynpros (see Section 9.1.16). Programming of the dynpro flow logic and the use of the `CONTROLS` statement are unnecessary here. You only need to prepare the desired subscreen dynpros, either with the Screen Painter or as selection screens, and integrate them with relatively simple `SELECTION-SCREEN` statements.

9.2.5 Calling Selection Screens

The ABAP statement to call a selection screen is:

CALL SELECTION-
SCREEN

```
CALL SELECTION-SCREEN dynnr
    [STARTING AT x1 y1]
    [ENDING   AT x2 y2].
```

This statement is the counterpart to `CALL SCREEN` for general dynpros. It calls the selection screen with the dynpro number specified in dynnr, starting selection screen processing (see Section 9.2.6).[31] With `STARTING AT` and `ENDING AT`, there is the option of displaying a selection screen in a modal dialog box. In that case, we recommend using the `AS WINDOW` clause when defining the selection screen.

After the conclusion of selection screen processing, the program continues after the `CALL SELECTION-SCREEN`. If the user leaves the selection screen with **Back**, **Exit**, or **Cancel**, the value of sy-subrc is 4; otherwise, it's zero.

Calling with `CALL SELECTION-SCREEN` is the recommended way to call a selection screen. Particularly when selection screens are encapsulated in function groups for "separation of concerns", they should only be called from function modules in this way.

Besides the recommended method, there are other methods of calling selection screens, for historical reasons:

SUBMIT VIA
SELECTION-
SCREEN

▶ If an executable program is started with `SUBMIT`, the `VIA SELECTION-SCREEN` can be used to specify that the runtime environment should automatically call a selection screen of the program at the point of program execution shown in Figure 9.4. Which selection screen is displayed can be specified with the `USING SELECTION-SCREEN` clause. Generally, the standard selection screen is used for

---

31 For selection screens, don't use the `CALL SCREEN` statement; otherwise, selection screen process cannot be started properly.

this (see Section 9.2.8).

▶ For executable programs, a special transaction type called a report transaction can be defined. The transaction code of a report transaction is associated with a selection screen of the executable program. When a report transaction is called, a SUBMIT VIA SELECTION-SCREEN is executed internally.

Report Transaction

▶ A selection screen can even be specified as the initial dynpro of a dialog transaction. If no suitable subsequent dynpro is called during selection screen processing, the program will exit afterwards. If an executable program is called via such a transaction, SUBMIT will not be called, and consequently, the program flow from the lower part of Figure 9.4 will not be started.

Dialog Transaction

9.2.6 Selection Screen Processing

Selection screen processing is performed by the selection screen processor of the ABAP runtime environment. It encapsulates the dynpro flow logic and the sending of the selection screen. No dialog modules in the program are called. Instead, the selection screen process triggers a series of selection screen events for which event blocks can be programmed. During PBO processing, the AT SELECTION-SCREEN OUTPUT event is triggered. During PAI processing, a series of AT SELECTION-SCREEN events are triggered, which reflect the different situations of the general PAI processing of a general dynpro. In particular, self-defined input checks can be executed in the PAI event blocks. As for general dynpros, error messages and warnings can be sent with the MESSAGE statement for this purpose.

Selection screen events

For selection screen events that you want to handle, you must implement the corresponding AT SELECTION-SCREEN event blocks in the ABAP program of the selection screen. For selection screens encapsulated in function groups, this is generally done in the corresponding include program ending in "E..". In the event blocks, you can distinguish between the different selection screens in the program using the system field sy-dynnr. The selection screen events are displayed in the following list:

AT SELECTION-SCREEN

▶ AT SELECTION-SCREEN OUTPUT.
This event is triggered at the time of occurrence of PBO of the selection screen. Here, the selection screen can be prepared by

OUTPUT

assigning values to the data objects of parameters and selection criteria, and making dynamic screen modifications.

ON ▶ AT SELECTION-SCREEN ON para|selcrit.

This event is triggered during PAI of the selection screen when the contents of the input fields of a parameter para (except for radio buttons) or a line of a selection criterion selcrit were passed to the ABAP program. Here, you can implement an input check for individual fields.

ON END OF ▶ AT SELECTION-SCREEN ON END OF selcrit.

This event is triggered during PAI of the selection screen when, after a user action in the dialog box for multiple selection, the entire selection table selcrit was passed to the program. Here, you can implement an input check for the entire table.

ON BLOCK ▶ AT SELECTION-SCREEN ON BLOCK block.

This event is triggered during PAI of the selection screen, when all input fields in a block block of the selection screen were passed to the ABAP program. Here, you can implement an input check for all the input fields in the block.

Radio buttons ▶ AT SELECTION-SCREEN ON RADIOBUTTON GROUP group.

This event is triggered during PAI of the selection screen, when all input fields in a radio button group group on the selection screen were passed to the ABAP program. Here, you can implement an input check for the entire radio button group.

AT SELECTION- ▶ AT SELECTION-SCREEN.
SCREEN

This event is triggered during PAI of the selection screen, when all input fields in the selection screen were passed to the ABAP program. Here, you can implement an input check for the entire selection screen.

ON HELP-, ▶ AT SELECTION-SCREEN ON HELP-REQUEST FOR ...
VALUE-REQUEST   AT SELECTION-SCREEN ON VALUE-REQUEST FOR ...

These two events are triggered for the dynpro events POH and POV of a selection screen, when field help F1 or input help F4 is called for the input field of a parameter or of one of the input fields of a selection criterion. Other selection screen events are not triggered. Here, you can program a self-defined field or input help.

ON EXIT- ▶ AT SELECTION-SCREEN ON EXIT-COMMAND.
COMMAND

This event is the only event triggered at PAI time in a selection screen if the user selects one of the functions **Back**, **Exit**, or **Cancel**. You can take care of any clean-up tasks in the event block.

The creation of self-programmed input checks or field or input help is analogous to how you would perform these tasks for general dynpros, and selection screen processing reacts accordingly. From a technical viewpoint, the only difference is that the FIELD and CHAIN statements of the dynpro flow logic are being encapsulated by appropriate selection screen events.

Listing 9.42 shows a self-defined input check for a selection screen.

Listing 9.42 Selection Screen with Authority Check

```
FUNCTION-POOL z_selection_screens.

...

* Selection Screen with Authority Check
SELECTION-SCREEN BEGIN OF: SCREEN 400 TITLE text-400,
                           BLOCK block WITH FRAME.
PARAMETERS: p_carrid TYPE demo_conn-carrid,
            p_connid TYPE demo_conn-connid.
SELECTION-SCREEN END OF: BLOCK block,
                         SCREEN 400.
...

FUNCTION z_authority_check.
  CALL SELECTION-SCREEN 400.
ENDFUNCTION.

...

AT SELECTION-SCREEN ON BLOCK block.
  CASE sy-dynnr.
    WHEN 400.
      AUTHORITY-CHECK OBJECT 'S_CARRID'
        ID 'CARRID' FIELD p_carrid
        ID 'ACTVT'  FIELD '03'.
      IF sy-subrc <> 0.
        MESSAGE e045(sabapdocu) WITH p_carrid.
      ENDIF.
  ENDCASE.
```

In the TOP include of the function group Z_SELECTION_SCREENS, a selection screen numbered 400 is created, which contains two parameters. We have implemented the AT SELECTION-SCREEN ON BLOCK event block in the include program LZ_SELECTION_

SCREENSE01. The event is triggered after both input fields have been passed to the ABAP program. In the event block, an authority check (see Section 10.5) is performed—a frequent application of selection screen events. If a user does not have authorization to read an airline, we send a message prepared for this purpose as an error message (see Section 9.4.2) and all the input fields of the block are again ready for input (see Figure 9.41).

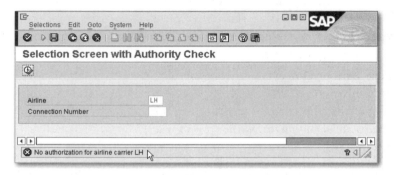

Figure 9.41 Selection Screen with Authority Check

9.2.7 Functions of Selection Screens

Regarding the user interface of selection screens, you should note that in comparison to general dynpros, you have very little way, if any, to modify them. Every selection screen has a single-purpose, standardized GUI status, which you cannot replace with the SET PF-STATUS statement.[32] This GUI status allows the user to confirm inputs with ⌈Enter⌉ or ⌈F8⌉, or to cancel editing with one of the usual keys. There are also a few other predefined functions, such as saving selection screen contents as variants.

GUI status It is not possible for you to define your own function codes in the predefined GUI status of a selection screen. You can, however, define some screen elements with function codes and activate predefined buttons in the application toolbar of the GUI status. The user can then select these functions along with the predefined ones, and you can evaluate them during selection screen processing. If you want to use specific selection screen properties like selection criteria

---

32 To define your own GUI status for a selection screen or to deactivate functions of the GUI status, in exceptional cases the function modules RS_SET_ SELSCREEN_STATUS or RS_EXTERNAL_SELSCREEN_STATUS can be used.

together with a freely configurable GUI status, you can create selection screens as subscreens and then integrate them into general dynpros.

To quit the processing of a selection screen, the following predefined functions are available:

▶ **Execute**
The selection screen events, except for `AT SELECTION-SCREEN ON EXIT-COMMAND`, are triggered. Afterwards, the current program resumes after the `CALL SELECTION-SCREEN` statement, while `sy-subrc` is assigned the value 0.

▶ **Back**, **Exit**, or **Cancel**
Only the event `AT SELECTION-SCREEN ON EXIT-COMMAND` is triggered. Afterwards, the current program resumes after the `CALL SELECTION-SCREEN` statement, while `sy-subrc` is assigned the value 4.

For all other functions—predefined, like `Enter`, or self-defined—a selection screen called with `CALL SELECTION-SCREEN` is automatically called again after the selection screen processing ends. From a technical viewpoint, the resumption of the program is based on the function code in the UCOMM component of the predefined SSCRFIELDS interface work area at the end of selection screen processing.[33]

You can associate checkboxes, radio buttons, dropdown list boxes, and buttons on the selection screen with custom function codes. The corresponding clause for the `PARAMETERS` abd `SELECTION-SCREEN` statements is:

```
... USER-COMMAND ucom ...
```

If the user selects one of these screen elements, the selection screen event `AT SELECTION-SCREEN` is triggered, and the function code can be evaluated in the corresponding event block in the UCOMM component of the SSCRFIELDS interface work area declared with `TABLES`. After the conclusion of the event block, the system returns by default to the display of the selection screen, unless the UCOMM component of the SSCRFIELDS structure contains a function code, indicating exit at the end of selection screen processing. This means that by default function codes on selection screens are only of limited use, that is, for screen modification.

---

33 To access this in the program, it must be declared with `TABLES sscrfields`.

Application toolbar The GUI status of a selection screen contains five inactive buttons in the application toolbar to which the function codes FC01 to FC05 are assigned. You can activate these buttons with the following statement:

FUNCTION KEY `SELECTION-SCREEN FUNCTION KEY n.`

The individual buttons are selected using n between 1 and 5. The text of the buttons must be assigned before calling the selection screen to the component FUNCTXT_0n of the interface work area SSCRFIELDS declared with TABLES. When a button activated in this way is clicked, the system acts as though a screen element with a function code was clicked.

Listing 9.43 shows the use of custom function codes on selection screens.

Listing 9.43 Selection Screens with Self-Defined Functions

```
FUNCTION-POOL z_selection_screens.

...

* Selection Screens with Function Codes
TABLES sscrfields.
DATA    ucomm TYPE sscrfields-ucomm.
SELECTION-SCREEN BEGIN OF SCREEN 500
                    AS WINDOW TITLE text-500.
PARAMETERS: p_alter1 RADIOBUTTON GROUP grp
                    USER-COMMAND selected,
            p_alter2 RADIOBUTTON GROUP grp,
            p_alter3 RADIOBUTTON GROUP grp.
SELECTION-SCREEN END OF SCREEN 500.

SELECTION-SCREEN:
  BEGIN OF SCREEN 510 AS WINDOW TITLE text-510,
  COMMENT 1(40) text-512,
  BEGIN OF LINE,
  PUSHBUTTON 1(10)  text-514 USER-COMMAND yes,
  PUSHBUTTON 11(10) text-516 USER-COMMAND no,
  END OF LINE,
  END OF SCREEN 510.

...

FUNCTION z_user_command.
*"----------------------------------------------------------
*"*"Local Interface:
*"  EXPORTING
```

```
*"      REFERENCE(BUTTON_1) TYPE   CHAR1
*"      REFERENCE(BUTTON_2) TYPE   CHAR1
*"      REFERENCE(BUTTON_3) TYPE   CHAR1
*"-------------------------------------------------------
  CALL SELECTION-SCREEN 500 STARTING AT 10 10.
  IF sy-subrc = 0.
    button_1 = p_alter1.
    button_2 = p_alter2.
    button_3 = p_alter3.
  ENDIF.
ENDFUNCTION.

...

AT SELECTION-SCREEN.
  CASE sy-dynnr.
    WHEN 500.
      CASE sscrfields-ucomm.
        WHEN 'SELECTED'.
          CALL SELECTION-SCREEN 510 STARTING AT 30 12.
          IF ucomm = 'YES'.
            sscrfields-ucomm = 'CRET'.
            MESSAGE text-518 TYPE 'S'.
          ENDIF.
        WHEN 'CRET'.
          MESSAGE text-518 TYPE 'S'.
      ENDCASE.
    WHEN 510.
      CASE sscrfields-ucomm.
        WHEN 'YES'.
          ucomm = sscrfields-ucomm.
          sscrfields-ucomm = 'CRET'.
        WHEN 'NO'.
          ucomm = sscrfields-ucomm.
          sscrfields-ucomm = 'CRET'.
      ENDCASE.
  ENDCASE.
```

In the TOP include of the function group Z_SELECTION_SCREENS, a selection screen number 500 is created with three radio buttons and a selection screen number 510 with two pushbuttons. The USER-COMMAND clause on the first button causes the function code SELECTED to be assigned to all the radio buttons in group grp. The pushbuttons each get their own YES or NO function codes. The associated event handling is implemented in the include program LZ_SELECTION_SCREENSE01.

If you execute the function module Z_USER_COMMAND in the Object Navigator using **Test/Execute** and select a radio button on selection screen 500, selection screen 510 appears immediately with the two pushbuttons, on which you can confirm or reject the selection (see Figure 9.42).

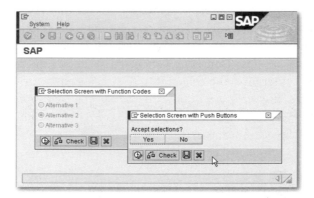

Figure 9.42 Selection Screens with Function Codes and Pushbuttons

For a selection screen called by `CALL SELECTION-SCREEN`, the standard function **Execute** is associated, with the predefined function code CRET. After saving the function code of the selected pushbutton, we set the `ucomm` component of the `sscrfields` interface work area declared with `TABLES` to this value in order to exit the selection screen as if **Execute** were selected. In the processing of selection screen 500, the function code buffered in global field `ucomm` is evaluated and a status message (see Section 9.4.3) is sent when the selection is accepted.

9.2.8 Standard Selection Screens

Standard selection screens are a specialty of executable programs (and also of logical databases). Every executable program—but no other type of program—has a predefined standard selection screen with dynpro number 1000, which need not be defined with `SELECTION-SCREEN BEGIN OF SCREEN 1000`, and, in fact, cannot be self-defined. In an executable program, no other dynpro or selection screen can have the number 1000.[34]

---

34 In function groups and module pools, you have free access to dynpro number 1000.

All PARAMETERS, SELECT-OPTIONS, and SELECTION-SCREEN statements located in an executable program, which are outside the explicit definition of a selection screen, define the screen elements of the standard selection screen. With CALL SELECTION-SCREEN 1000, the standard selection screen can also be called like a standalone selection screen..

During the execution of an executable program via SUBMIT, the standard selection screen is automatically called between the report events INITIALIZATION and START-OF-SELECTION (see Figure 9.43). If the clause VIA SELECTION-SCREEN is used when calling, the selection screen is displayed; otherwise, the selection screen processing runs transparently to the user (i.e., without displaying the selection screen, between INITIALIZATION and START-OF-SELECTION). In either case, the selection screen events are triggered.

SUBMIT

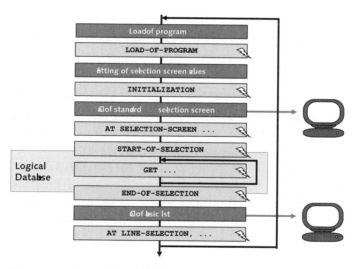

Figure 9.43 Events After SUBMIT

If the standard selection screen is displayed, an executable program is automatically restarted at the end of its program execution. The parameters and selection criteria of the selection screen are then assigned the user input from the previous execution as start values between the events INITIALIZATION and AT SELECTION-SCREEN OUTPUT.

Listing 9.44 shows the declaration of a selection criterion in the standard selection screen of an executable program. When the program is executed, it automatically shows the standard selection screen, selects values according to the selection entered, and displays them in an ALV list. The program basically corresponds to Listing 9.40, except that here the selection screen is defined in the same program. The reason for this breach of separation of concerns will be clear in the next section.

Listing 9.44 Standard Selection Screen in an Executable Program

```abap
REPORT z_submitable.

* Standard Selection Screen
DATA g_carrid TYPE scarr-carrid.
SELECT-OPTIONS s_carrid FOR g_carrid.
CLASS demo DEFINITION.
  PUBLIC SECTION.
    CLASS-METHODS main.
ENDCLASS.
CLASS demo IMPLEMENTATION.
  METHOD main.
    DATA: scarr_tab TYPE TABLE OF scarr,
          alv       TYPE REF TO cl_salv_table,
          subrc     TYPE syst-subrc.
    SELECT *
           FROM scarr
           INTO TABLE scarr_tab
           WHERE carrid IN s_carrid.
    TRY.
        cl_salv_table=>factory(
          IMPORTING r_salv_table = alv
          CHANGING  t_table = scarr_tab ).
        alv->display( ).
      CATCH cx_salv_msg.
        MESSAGE 'ALV display not possible' TYPE 'I'
                DISPLAY LIKE 'E'.
    ENDTRY.
  ENDMETHOD.
ENDCLASS.
START-OF-SELECTION.
  demo=>main( ).
```

9.2.9 Selection Screens as Program Interfaces

Besides their role as user interfaces, selection screens are also useful as parameter interfaces to executable programs. When an executable program is started using SUBMIT, the silent processing of the selection screen is even the standard setting. The display of the selection screen must therefore be forced by specifying VIA SELECTION SCREEN.

Silent selection screen processing is particularly significant for background processing of executable programs, since there can of course be no screen display of the selection screen. To execute a program in the background, it can be scheduled as follows as a background task num in a background request job.

Background processing

```
SUBMIT ... VIA JOB job NUMBER num ...
```

SUBMIT VIA JOB

The SUBMIT statement has a number of clauses to supply values for the parameters and selection criteria of the selection screen of the program called. When the selection screen is processed silently, SUBMIT works like a program call with parameter passing. As an example, we show the following variant:

```
SUBMIT prog WITH selcrit IN seltab.
```

If the selection screen of the program executed includes a selection criterion selcrit, it is passed through the seltab table without the need to display the selection screen. For seltab, you can specify an internal table with a line structure that is that of a suitable selection table.

Listing 9.45 shows the scheduling of the executable program from Listing 9.44 for background processing. The central point of the program is the SUBMIT statement. For the selection criterion s_carrid on the selection screen of the executable program, the table selection is passed, which we fill with the function module Z_SELECTION_CRITERION from Listing 9.39. Since the program is to be run in the background, the output list must be directed to the SAP spool system, which is done by the TO SAP-SPOOL clause. The necessary print parameters are supplied using the GET_PRINT_PARAMETERS function module. The context for the background task and background request (job) is created using the JOB_OPEN and JOB_CLOSE function modules, and we specify GET_FLIGHT_LIST as the job name.

Listing 9.45 Execution of Background Processing

```
REPORT z_submit_job.

CLASS demo DEFINITION.
  PUBLIC SECTION.
```

```abap
      CLASS-METHODS main.
ENDCLASS.
CLASS demo IMPLEMENTATION.
  METHOD main.
    DATA: selection   TYPE RANGE OF scarr-carrid,
          subrc       TYPE syst-subrc,
          number      TYPE tbtcjob-jobcount,
          name        TYPE tbtcjob-jobname
                      VALUE 'GET_FLIGHT_LIST',
          pripars     TYPE pri_params,
          valid_flag TYPE c LENGTH 1.
    CALL FUNCTION 'Z_SELECTION_CRITERION'
      IMPORTING seltab = selection
                rc     = subrc.
    IF subrc = 4.
      RETURN.
    ENDIF.
    CALL FUNCTION 'GET_PRINT_PARAMETERS'
      IMPORTING
        out_parameters      = pripars
        valid               = valid_flag
      EXCEPTIONS
        invalid_print_params = 2
        others               = 4.
    IF sy-subrc <> 0 OR valid_flag <> 'X'.
      RETURN.
    ENDIF.
    CALL FUNCTION 'JOB_OPEN'
      EXPORTING
        jobname  = name
      IMPORTING
        jobcount = number
      EXCEPTIONS
        others   = 4.
    IF sy-subrc = 0.
      SUBMIT z_submitable WITH s_carrid IN selection
                          TO SAP-SPOOL
                          SPOOL PARAMETERS pripars
                          WITHOUT SPOOL DYNPRO
                          VIA JOB name NUMBER number
                          AND RETURN.
      IF sy-subrc = 0.
        CALL FUNCTION 'JOB_CLOSE'
          EXPORTING
```

```
        jobcount   = number
        jobname    = name
        strtimmed  = 'X'
    EXCEPTIONS
        others     = 4.
   IF sy-subrc = 0.
     MESSAGE 'Job submitted' TYPE 'I'.
   ENDIF.
  ENDIF.
 ENDIF.
 ENDMETHOD.
ENDCLASS.

START-OF-SELECTION.
 demo=>main( ).
```

If you execute the program Z_SUBMIT_JOB, first the selection screen **Print parameters**
from Figure 9.39 appears, and then a request for print parameters
from GET_PRINT_PARAMETERS displays, which we fill in as shown
in Figure 9.44.[35]

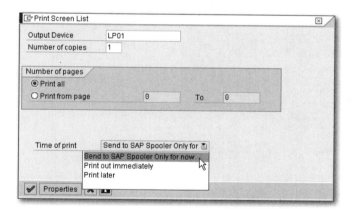

Figure 9.44 Print Parameters

If the scheduling of the background task is successful, a message
appears. Now you can call **System • Services • Jobs • Job Overview**
and select **Execute**. In the job overview, you should see the entry
GET_FLIGHT_LIST (see Figure 9.45).

The icon in the **Ln** column indicates that a spool request was created, **Spool request**
which you can view here with **Spool** or anywhere with **System • Own**

---

35 We showed the input window for the **Time of print** using **Properties**.

Spool Requests. In the overview of spool requests, if you select the respective spool request and select **Display contents**, the ALV list is shown converted into a print list, which is filled in corresponding to the boundaries in the selection table passed (see Figure 9.46).

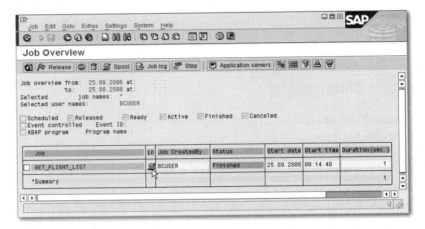

Figure 9.45 Job Overview

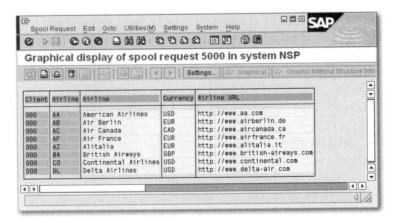

Figure 9.46 Spool Request

The programmed scheduling of a background task shown here was intended as a demonstration of parameter passing to a selection screen and its silent processing. Of course, the Z_SUBMITABLE program can also be scheduled directly in a background task using **System · Services · Reporting** and selecting **Background**. Then the selection screen must be supplied by specifying a selection screen variant. The specification of a start date and periodic execution is also possible here. After an executable program is started in the foreground, its final execution can still be scheduled for background processing from the display of the standard selection screen using **Program** • **Execute in Background**. For general job scheduling and administration, finally, the Transaction SM36 is available (**System** • **Services** • **Jobs** • **Job definition**). Technically, all these options end up doing nothing more than executing SUBMIT VIA JOB that we used directly.

9.3   Classical Lists

Classical lists, in classical ABAP, were the means for structured and formatted output of data. By default, list output is written to a memory area called the *list buffer*. However, you can also send it directly to the SAP spool system as a print list. A list stored in the list buffer can be called up either implicitly or explicitly and is then displayed as a screen list in a list dynpro. During the display of screen lists, interactions are possible, which may lead to the display of additional lists—so-called *details lists*.

In ABAP Objects, classical lists are no longer necessary. We recommend that you don't use the list statement in self-defined classes for various reasons; instead, we suggest that you use suitable controls (see Section 9.1.17). Since in many existing programs classical lists are still in use, however, in this section we will briefly examine the basics of classical list programming, and also show you why they no longer fit into the world of ABAP Objects. For details on classical list creation and processing, we refer you to the *The ABAP Reference* book, which covers this topic in great detail.

9.3.1   List Creation

To create a classical list, there are a series of special ABAP statements, which can be used at any point in any processing block. The writing of data into a list can be compared with output on a roll of continuous paper in a teletype. The most important output statement for lists is:

```
WRITE [AT /pos(len)] dobj ... .
```
WRITE

This statement formats the content of a data object, but unlike WRITE dobj TO, it doesn't assign the content to another data object (see Section 5.2.3). Instead, this statement writes it to a position pos and in an output length len into a list. The position of the list cursor is changed during this process.

Using list statements like POSITION, SKIP, or BACK, the list cursor can also be set explicitly.

Formatting Besides the formatting of the WRITE statement, which corresponds to that of the WRITE TO statement, list segments can also be formatted using the FORMAT statement, which can set foreground and background colors, for example.

Lines and frames On classical lists, you can use the ULINE statement to produce horizontal lines and special characters ("|") to produce vertical lines. Lines can also be connected to form frames.

List width and page layout Other properties that can be specified when creating the list are the list width and the division into pages of a specific length. During the creation of lists with pages, the ABAP runtime environment triggers the events TOP-OF-PAGE and END-OF-PAGE. In the corresponding event blocks, the page header and footer can be defined.

9.3.2 Screen List

List dynpro A screen list is displayed in a list dynpro. The entire screen of a list dynpro is an output area in which the list contents are displayed and which can be scrolled if necessary. Besides formatted texts, there can also be lines, input-ready fields, checkboxes, icons, and symbols. For list displays, you can set special GUI statuses that contain predefined list functions leading to so-called *list events*, which can be handled in the program. The standard list status is set using SET PF-STATUS space.

List processor In contrast to a selection screen, however, the list dynpro is not a dynpro of the ABAP program in which the list is written. Instead, the list dynpro is a component of the so-called *list processor*, a system program for classical list processing. When list processing is called, the list processor displays the screen list that is currently in the list buffer in its list dynpro.

List buffer The list buffer is a storage area on the application server. If printing is not switched on (see Section 9.3.6), every list statement processes a screen list in the list buffer, which is always assigned to the current dynpro sequence. The list buffer of a dynpro sequence is organized into list levels. For every dynpro sequence, there is exactly one basic list in the list buffer, on which, during the processing of list events like line selection by double-clicking, up to 20 details lists can be stacked. The lists stored in the list buffer can also be edited after writing, using statements like READ LINE and MODIFY LINE.

9.3.3   Lists in Executable Programs

Classical lists are closely related to classical reporting using executable programs, as we demonstrated in Section 7.1.1. Just as the standard selection screen (see Section 9.2.8) is automatically processed at the beginning of an executable program started with SUBMIT, at its end, as shown in Figure 9.4, list processing automatically takes place (i. e., after the last reporting event, the list processor is automatically called, which displays the basic list written to the list buffer during program execution). Note that all list statements that are executed during the program write to the same basic list, as long as no new dynpro sequence is opened with CALL SCREEN.

Consequently, the WRITE statement during the execution of an executable program started with SUBMIT is akin to System.out. println(...) in Java or printf in C. This is even the case if you use WRITE in a method of a global class, which is called in an executable program.

WRITE

You must always keep in mind, however, that WRITE is not simply a statement for text output on the screen, although it often gives one this impression, which is why we deliberately misused it in our first "Hello, World!" program in Section 2.5.4.[36] The WRITE statement always writes to a list, which is either a screen list in the list buffer or a print list in the SAP spool system. Without a call to list display, the contents of the list buffer are not displayed. We demonstrate with the example in Listing 9.46.

Listing 9.46 List Output in an Executable Program

```
REPORT z_submit_write.

CLASS demo DEFINITION.
  PUBLIC SECTION.
```

---

[36] Aside from the current section, however, we have kept the examples in this book as WRITE-free as possible.

```
    CLASS-METHODS main.
ENDCLASS.
CLASS demo IMPLEMENTATION.
  METHOD main.
    WRITE 'List output ...'.
  ENDMETHOD.
ENDCLASS.
START-OF-SELECTION.
  demo=>main( ).
```

If you execute the program in such a way that it is internally started with SUBMIT, for example, by executing it in the Object Navigator, it shows a screen list. But, if you associate an OO transaction (e. g., with the transaction code Z_NO_WRITE) with the method main and execute the transaction, you won't receive any output. Although you are able to observe that the list buffer is filled using **Display list** in the (classical) ABAP Debugger, however, there is no automatic call to the list processor.

Therefore, only in programs started with SUBMIT, the WRITE statement and the other list statements actually work like statements for screen output, without additional measures.

9.3.4 Lists and Transactions

If a screen list stored in the list buffer is displayed automatically only in programs started with SUBMIT, the question arises as to how a list is displayed for other types of program execution, such as via transactions. This is the reason for the following statement:

LEAVE TO LIST-
PROCESSING

LEAVE TO LIST-PROCESSING ...

This statement binds the call of the list processor with the current dynpro. The effect of this action is that, at the end of the dynpro, the current dynpro sequence is interrupted and the list processor displays the basic list from the list buffer (see Figure 9.47). The basic list consists of the list output of all output statements executed during the current dynpro sequence. When we return to dynpro processing with LEAVE LIST PROCESSING, or when the list display is exited, the entire list system is reinitialized, and following output statements are writing to an empty basic list.

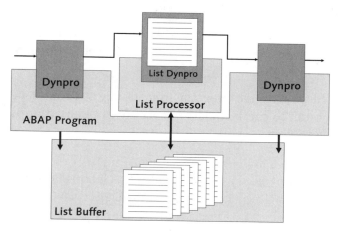

Figure 9.47 List Processing

The encapsulation unit of a list buffer is therefore not the program, but the current dynpro sequence, which often is not yet determined during program creation. The latter applies particularly to list statements in procedures (methods), which are called from other programs. Therefore, to use the creation of lists in a meaningful way in transactions, they should be encapsulated in a single dynpro called with CALL SCREEN, which has no other application. For such a dynpro, we recommend the following properties:

Dynpro sequence

1. The screen of the dynpro isn't necessary and must not be maintained. The flow logic must only call a single PBO module. No PAI modules or dynpro fields are necessary.

2. The first statement of the PBO module should look like this:

    LEAVE TO LIST-PROCESSING AND RETURN TO SCREEN 0.

    This statement calls list processing at the end of the dynpro, and then returns to the point of call of the dynpro.

3. A suitable GUI status should be set for a list.

4. The entire basic list should be written to the buffer with list statements during PBO processing.

5. Finally, one of the statements

    SUPPRESS DIALOG.

    or

    LEAVE SCREEN.

is used to suppress the display of the empty screen content and to end the dynpro immediately. The ABAP runtime environment then branches to the list display, and returns to the point of call of the dynpro afterwards.

Listing 9.47 shows how the program from Listing 9.46 must be extended if the call to the method `main` via an OO transaction is going to start list output.

Listing 9.47 List Output in a Transaction

```
REPORT z_transaction_write.

CLASS demo DEFINITION.
  PUBLIC SECTION.
    CLASS-METHODS main.
ENDCLASS.
CLASS demo IMPLEMENTATION.
  METHOD main.
    CALL SCREEN 100.
  ENDMETHOD.
ENDCLASS.
START-OF-SELECTION.
  demo=>main( ).
MODULE status_0100 OUTPUT.
  LEAVE TO LIST-PROCESSING AND RETURN TO SCREEN 0.
  SET PF-STATUS space.
  SUPPRESS DIALOG.
  WRITE 'List output ...'.
ENDMODULE.
```

This program displays a list both when executed with SUBMIT or via a Transaction Z_LIST associated with `main`. This list is the basic list of the dynpro sequence, which consists of dynpro 100 alone.

According to the "separation of concerns" that we are striving for, the dynpro used to create the list should be encapsulated in a function group and not be part of an application as shown in Listing 9.47. But, due to the way in which lists are created, this soon leads to big problems if you have to program such a function group yourself for arbitrary data. This is because there is the question of how both the data to be displayed and the layout desired could be passed from an application program to a module for list display in order to create the list you want in the format you want.

For exactly this reason, SAP offers the SAP List Viewer (ALV), which handles this for you. In earlier releases, the classical ALV was actually still based on the encapsulation of WRITE statements in function groups. Today, it is based on the encapsulation of GUI controls in classes that are specially provided for tabular list output (see Section 9.1.17).

ALV

9.3.5 Functions on Lists

In the last few sections, we've seen that when the list process is called automatically in executable programs, or if an explicit call occurs during a transaction, the basic list of the current list buffer is displayed in a list dynpro for which a GUI status can be set.

As for selection screens, PAI handling, after the selection of a function in a window of a displayed list, is encapsulated in the list processor and is passed from the ABAP runtime environment to the ABAP program, which is assigned to the list in the form of events. This is either an executable program started with SUBMIT, or the program to which the dynpro sequence belongs, whose list buffer is displayed.

List events

We distinguish primarily between two types of functions:

Double-click

▶ The double-click F2 on a list line, to which by default function code PICK is assigned.

▶ Other functions of the GUI status, to which other function codes can be assigned.

The function code PICK always results in an AT LINE-SELECTION event. Other function codes generally result in an AT USER-COMMAND event. The exception is a set of predefined function codes like P+ or P++, which are handled directly by the ABAP runtime environment. P+ and P++, for example, scroll in the displayed list.

The function code can be obtained from the system field sy-ucomm during handling in the corresponding event blocks. A set of system fields and special statements enables to determine the position selected by the user. In addition, a so-called HIDE mechanism, that is based on global data, makes it possible to store additional data invisibly to a list line in the list buffer, and to evaluate it during the handling of list events.

Details lists

During the handling of a list event, if list output occurs in an associated event block, the output does not continue to write to the basic list, but instead creates so-called *details lists*, which, at the end of the event block, are automatically displayed, either in the current list dynpro or as a modal dialog box (`WINDOW` statement). Details lists are stacked on the basic list in the current list buffer, dividing it into list levels. Every list level is identified by its list index (system field `sy-lsind`), and the list index of the basic list has the value 0. Every selection of a function on a displayed list generates a new list level, thereby increasing the list index by one. In this way, up to 20 details lists can be created in a list buffer for one basic list.

Interactive reporting

Details lists were the technical basis for the classical interactive reporting, in which, instead of a complete, detailed list, one creates a compacted basic list, from which the user can call up detailed information in details lists. Today, interactive reporting is, for instance, possible by the handling of user actions on ALV lists. Listing 9.48 shows a typical example for classical interactive reporting with an executable program.

Listing 9.48 Reporting with Classical Lists

```abap
REPORT z_classic_reporting LINE-SIZE 80.

DATA: carrid TYPE scarr-carrid,
      url    TYPE scarr-url.

CLASS demo DEFINITION.
  PUBLIC SECTION.
    CLASS-METHODS:
      main,
      detail  IMPORTING carrid TYPE scarr-carrid,
      browser IMPORTING url    TYPE csequence.
ENDCLASS.

CLASS demo IMPLEMENTATION.
  METHOD main.
    DATA scarr_wa TYPE scarr.
    SET PF-STATUS space.
    ULINE (80).
    SELECT *
           FROM scarr
           INTO scarr_wa.
      WRITE: / '|', (36) scarr_wa-carrname
                         COLOR COL_HEADING,
             40 '|', (36) scarr_wa-url
```

```
                      COLOR COL_TOTAL, 80 '|'.
    carrid = scarr_wa-carrid.
    url    = scarr_wa-url.
    HIDE: carrid, url.
  ENDSELECT.
  ULINE (80).
  CLEAR: carrid, url.
ENDMETHOD.
METHOD detail.
  DATA spfli_wa TYPE spfli.
  WINDOW STARTING AT 10 10
         ENDING   AT 60 20.
  NEW-PAGE LINE-SIZE 50.
  FORMAT COLOR COL_NORMAL.
  SELECT carrid connid cityfrom cityto
         FROM spfli
         INTO CORRESPONDING FIELDS OF spfli_wa
         WHERE carrid = carrid.
    WRITE: /(3)  spfli_wa-carrid,
           (4)   spfli_wa-connid,
           (20)  spfli_wa-cityfrom,
           (20)  spfli_wa-cityto.
  ENDSELECT.
  IF sy-subrc <> 0.
    MESSAGE e007(sabapdocu).
  ENDIF.
ENDMETHOD.
METHOD browser.
  CALL FUNCTION 'CALL_BROWSER'
    EXPORTING url = url.
ENDMETHOD.
ENDCLASS.

START-OF-SELECTION.
  demo=>main( ).

AT LINE-SELECTION.
  IF carrid IS NOT INITIAL.
    IF sy-cucol < 40.
      demo=>detail( carrid ).
    ELSEIF sy-cucol > 40.
      demo=>browser( url ).
    ENDIF.
    CLEAR: carrid, url.
  ENDIF.
```

653

When executing the program, a classical list is displayed with the names and web addresses of airline carriers (see Figure 9.48). A double-click on the name causes a flight list to be displayed in a details list. A double-click on the web address calls the web browser of the presentation server.

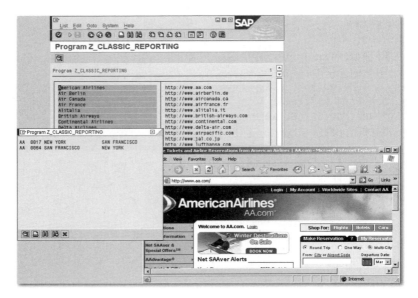

Figure 9.48 Reporting with Classical Lists

We don't want to go into detail on the function of the list statements in this example. If you're interested, you can use the [F1] help for all language elements.

However, you can clearly see that there is no separation of the application logic from the presentation logic. Furthermore, it would hardly be feasible to do so with little effort either, since the formatting of the lists is closely related to the nature of the data. Note that even the program introductory statement REPORT is associated with list output, because it determines the width of the basic list.

9.3.6 Print Lists

SAP spool system   Classical list output can also be sent to the SAP spool system as print lists, instead of being stored in the current list buffer as screen lists. The SAP spool system enables print lists to be output to a printer or stored as archived documents with the so-called *ArchiveLink*.

A print list is sent page by page directly from the main memory to the SAP spool system, and is associated with exactly one spool request during its creation. When the spool request is opened, print parameters must be determined, which can no longer be changed during output.

Printing can be switched on as follows, after which the first output statement will create a new spool request:[37]

▶ **Use of the statement** `NEW-PAGE PRINT ON`
This is the only way to switch on printing during program execution. Only this print procedure can (and should) be switched off again with `NEW-PAGE PRINT OFF`.

▶ **Selection of the function Execute and Print on the standard selection screen of an executable program**
Printing is switched on from the start of program execution on and cannot be switched off in the program.

▶ **Calling an executable program with the clauses** `VIA JOB` **and** `TO SAP-SPOOL` **of** `SUBMIT`
Generally, `VIA JOB` is specified with `TO SAP-SPOOL` in order to specify the print parameters explicitly (see Section 9.2.9). Printing is switched on from the start of program execution on and cannot be switched off in the program. This applies to every ABAP program executed in background.

Print lists can be stacked in up to 20 print list levels. Every time printing is switched on, a new print list level is opened.[38] A print list opened with `NEW-PAGE PRINT ON`, however, cannot be stacked in another print list opened with this statement, only in one opened at the start of program execution.

A spool request must be passed print parameters, which may be extended with archive parameters. Within a program, a set of valid print and archive parameters can only be created with the function module GET_PRINT_PARAMETERS. This function module, which also has an optional interactive user interface, fills structures with all

---

37 When **Print** is selected during the display of a classical screen list, the list processor generates a print list from the already completely formatted screen list, which, in general, is not perfectly formatted.

38 In addition, a call to a dynpro sequence with `CALL SCREEN` also opens a new print list level if printing is switched on.

the values needed, like the name of the printer, the print format, the number of copies, the storage time in the spool system, and so on. These structures are then used in the NEW-PAGE PRINT ON or SUBMIT TO SAP-SPOOL statements.

Listing 9.49 shows how classical list printing works. This time, the print dialog box from Figure 9.44 is not shown.

Listing 9.49 Classical List Printing

```
REPORT z_classic_printing.

CLASS demo DEFINITION.
  PUBLIC SECTION.
    CLASS-METHODS main.
ENDCLASS.

CLASS demo IMPLEMENTATION.
  METHOD main.
    DATA: scarr_wa   TYPE scarr,
          pripars    TYPE pri_params,
          valid_flag TYPE c LENGTH 1.
    CALL FUNCTION 'GET_PRINT_PARAMETERS'
      EXPORTING
        destination        = 'LP01'
        immediately        = ' '
        no_dialog          = 'X'
      IMPORTING
        out_parameters     = pripars
        valid              = valid_flag
      EXCEPTIONS
        invalid_print_params = 2
        others             = 4.
    IF sy-subrc <> 0 OR valid_flag <> 'X'.
      RETURN.
    ENDIF.
    NEW-PAGE PRINT ON
      NO DIALOG PARAMETERS pripars.
    SELECT *
        FROM scarr
        INTO scarr_wa.
      WRITE: /(3) scarr_wa-carrid,
             (30) scarr_wa-carrname,
             (40) scarr_wa-url.
    ENDSELECT.
    ULINE.
    NEW-PAGE PRINT OFF.
```

```
    ENDMETHOD.
  ENDCLASS.

  START-OF-SELECTION.
    demo=>main( ).
```

When the Z_CLASSIC_PRINTING is executed, nothing visible happens. After selecting **System · Own spool requests**, however, you will find the print list as the most recent spool request in the Output Controller (see Figure 9.49).

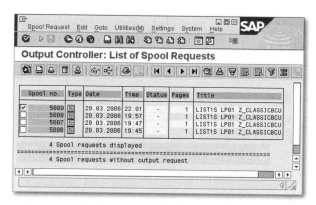

Figure 9.49 List of Spool Requests

The list contents can be displayed for checking here (see Figure 9.50) and sent to a printer. If the input parameter IMMEDIATELY in the function module GET_PRINT_PARAMETERS is assigned the value X, print output takes place immediately and without the list being stored in the spool system.

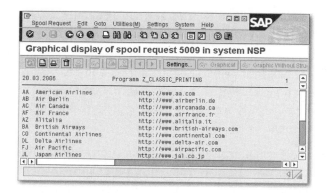

Figure 9.50 Print List

9.3.7 Lists in ABAP Objects

In classical ABAP programming, classical lists were the most important output medium as such. The overview in the last few sections shows that classical lists were also a very powerful tool and could be used for many different purposes. For the following reasons, however, the use of list statements in application programs in the context of ABAP Objects is no longer recommended:

Recommendation:
no lists!

▶ The processing of lists is based on global data and events in the runtime environment. This argument also applies to general dynpros and selection screens, but in those cases, it can be circumvented by application programmers via encapsulation in function groups (see Figure 9.20). At least in application programs, this kind of encapsulation is nearly impossible for classical lists, which is also supported by the following reasons.

▶ The storage of lists in a list buffer is incompatible with the concept of classes and objects. A list buffer (or a print list) is bound to an executable program or a dynpro sequence, and not to the classes and objects using the list buffer. To encapsulate a list buffer in a function group, a special dynpro would have to be provided whose screen is not displayed and during whose processing a list would be written into the list buffer.

▶ For self-defined lists, separation of presentation and application logic is nearly impossible. Due to the very nature of a list as a freely writable, non-standardized interface, list creation is much more closely interwoven with application programming than that of dynpros and general selection screens. In the latter case, data are exchanged only with static input masks. The format of a list, on the other hand, is completely arbitrary and generally always depending on the properties of the current data.

▶ The interface of a freely programmed list is not standardized, and thus generally not handicapped accessible. Accessibility is a product standard, which guarantees that, for instance, blind users can also get to all the necessary information using help technologies like text- reading tools.

Today other technologies can be used for all application areas of classical list programming, which satisfy current requirements for user interfaces, like separation of concerns, standards compliance, accessibility, and so on. As a replacement for the various applications of lists, there are:

► The textedit control for short console output (in the style of `Sys-tem.out.println(...)` in Java or `printf` in C). In Appendix A.6, we show what an encapsulation of this control might look like.

► The tree control for purely tree-like views.[39]

► The browser control or its encapsulation in dynamic documents for formatted output of non-tabular content.

► ALV lists for all presentations of tabular or hierarchical content and associated functions.

► Smart forms for all types of forms and form printing (see the book *SAP Smart Forms* by Werner Hertleif and Christoph Wachter, 2nd Edition, SAP PRESS 2003).

Replacements for lists

Since classical lists are mainly used for the display of tabular data, ALV lists are their most important successor technology. The use of ALV doesn't even mean that classical lists disappear completely from the interface, since ALV can also still create classical lists if necessary. The big difference between the use of ALV and custom list programming, however, is that the actual creation of the list is decoupled from the application logic, and that an application program is therefore independent of the actual technology.

In the following examples, we show you how the most important applications of classical lists can be handled by successor technologies.

Simple Text Output

Listing 9.50 shows how the simple list output from Listing 9.46 can be replaced by the use of a textedit control. Figure 9.51 shows the result.

Listing 9.50 Simple Text Output

```
REPORT z_simple_text.

CLASS demo DEFINITION.
  PUBLIC SECTION.
```

---

39 Before the introduction of the tree controls, tree-like views were still implemented using classical lists, and even in current AS ABAP, there are still some examples of this.

```
    CLASS-METHODS main.
ENDCLASS.
CLASS demo IMPLEMENTATION.
  METHOD main.
    DATA text TYPE REF TO zcl_text.
    text = zcl_text=>get_handle( ).
    text->add_line( 'Text output ...' ).
    text->display( ).
  ENDMETHOD.
ENDCLASS.
START-OF-SELECTION.
  demo=>main( ).
```

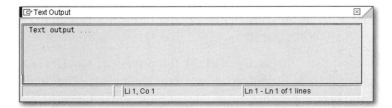

Figure 9.51 Simple Text Output

Interactive reporting

Listing 9.50 implements the reporting with ALV lists implemented in Listing 9.48 with classical lists. Instead of handling the AT LINE-SELECTION ABAP runtime environment event, an event handler method is registered here for the DOUBLE_CLICK event of the ALV class CL_SALV_EVENTS_TABLE. Since there is no HIDE mechanism, the data needed is stored in the internal table but not displayed. The details list is replaced by a second ALV list, which is displayed in a dialog box. The implicit use of a list system in the list buffer is replaced by explicit handling of list objects, which is in accordance with the concept of ABAP Objects. Both programs fulfill the same purpose. The lists in Figure 9.52, in comparison with Figure 9.48, however, look better and automatically have column headings, which can be used to move, select, and change the width of the columns. Additional functions of an ALV list can be defined easily by setting a GUI status with the SET_SCREEN_STATUS method of the CL_SALV_TABLE class or by using an object of the ALV class CL_SALV_FUNCTIONS.

Listing 9.51 Reporting with ALV Lists

```abap
REPORT z_alv_reporting.

CLASS demo DEFINITION.
  PUBLIC SECTION.
    CLASS-METHODS main.
  PRIVATE SECTION.
    CLASS-DATA    scarr_tab TYPE TABLE OF scarr.
    CLASS-METHODS: handle_double_click
                    FOR EVENT double_click
                    OF cl_salv_events_table
                    IMPORTING row column,
                  detail
                    IMPORTING carrid TYPE scarr-carrid,
                  browser
                    IMPORTING url   TYPE csequence.
ENDCLASS.

CLASS demo IMPLEMENTATION.
  METHOD main.
    DATA: alv     TYPE REF TO cl_salv_table,
          events  TYPE REF TO cl_salv_events_table,
          columns TYPE REF TO cl_salv_columns,
          col_tab TYPE salv_t_column_ref.
    FIELD-SYMBOLS <column> LIKE LINE OF col_tab.
    SELECT *
        FROM scarr
        INTO TABLE scarr_tab.
    TRY.
        cl_salv_table=>factory(
          IMPORTING r_salv_table = alv
          CHANGING  t_table = scarr_tab ).
        events = alv->get_event( ).
        SET HANDLER handle_double_click FOR events.
        columns = alv->get_columns( ).
        col_tab = columns->get( ).
        LOOP AT col_tab ASSIGNING <column>.
          <column>-r_column->set_output_length( 40 ).
          IF <column>-columnname = 'CARRNAME' OR
            <column>-columnname = 'URL'.
            <column>-r_column->set_visible( 'X' ).
          ELSE.
            <column>-r_column->set_visible( ' ' ).
          ENDIF.
        ENDLOOP.
        alv->display( ).
```

```
        CATCH cx_salv_msg.
          MESSAGE 'ALV display not possible' TYPE 'I'
                    DISPLAY LIKE 'E'.
      ENDTRY.
  ENDMETHOD.
  METHOD handle_double_click.
    FIELD-SYMBOLS <scarr> TYPE scarr.
    READ TABLE scarr_tab INDEX row ASSIGNING <scarr>.
    IF sy-subrc <> 0.
      RETURN.
    ENDIF.
    IF column = 'CARRNAME'.
      demo=>detail( <scarr>-carrid ).
    ELSEIF column = 'URL'.
      demo=>browser( <scarr>-url ).
    ENDIF.
  ENDMETHOD.
  METHOD detail.
    DATA: alv         TYPE REF TO cl_salv_table,
          BEGIN OF alv_line,
            carrid   TYPE spfli-carrid,
            connid   TYPE spfli-connid,
            cityfrom TYPE spfli-cityfrom,
            cityto   TYPE spfli-cityto,
          END OF alv_line,
          alv_tab     LIKE TABLE OF alv_line.
    SELECT carrid connid cityfrom cityto
           FROM spfli
           INTO CORRESPONDING FIELDS OF TABLE alv_tab
           WHERE carrid = carrid.
    IF sy-subrc <> 0.
      MESSAGE e007(sabapdocu).
    ENDIF.
    TRY.
        cl_salv_table=>factory(
          IMPORTING r_salv_table = alv
          CHANGING  t_table = alv_tab ).
        alv->set_screen_popup( start_column = 1
                               end_column   = 60
                               start_line   = 1
                               end_line     = 12 ).
        alv->display( ).
      CATCH cx_salv_msg.
        MESSAGE 'ALV display not possible' TYPE 'I'
                  DISPLAY LIKE 'E'.
```

```
        ENDTRY.
    ENDMETHOD.
    METHOD browser.
        CALL FUNCTION 'CALL_BROWSER'
            EXPORTING url = url.
    ENDMETHOD.
ENDCLASS.

START-OF-SELECTION.
    demo=>main( ).
```

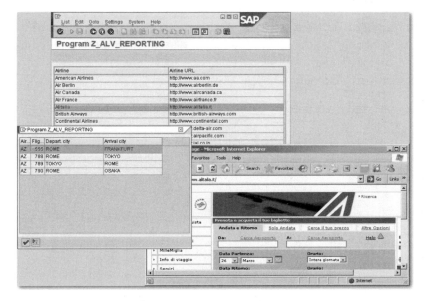

Figure 9.52 Reporting with ALV Lists

ABAP Objects and SAP Spool

At this point, we must point out that classical print lists are—from a technical standpoint—the only way to send ABAP data from ABAP programs directly to the SAP spool system. So how are we going to print and archive if we no longer recommend using list statements in ABAP Objects?

The answer is simple. The SAP List Viewer (ALV), the official AS ABAP tool for tabular list output, takes care of it for you. In the example in Section 9.2.9, we already saw that the ALV in background processing automatically outputs a print list. The same thing happens when you switch on printing using **Execute and Print** on the selec-

Printing via ALV

tion screen. On a later call to an ALV list, it is automatically converted into a print list. As a replacement for NEW-PAGE PRINT ON, you can use the method SET_PRINT_ONLY of the class CL_SALVE_PRINT.[40] To print, the ALV calls classical list processing internally, which is, however, fully separate from your application logic. Lastly, the printing of a list can, of course, also be started by the user from a displayed ALV list.[41]

The example in Listing 9.52 replaces the example in Listing 9.49. The commented-out parts of Listing 9.52 are used for the explicit passing of the print parameters to the ALV. This option is not yet available in the version of AS ABAP used in this book, but should be included in no later than Support Package 6. Figure 9.53 shows the print list of a spool request generated by ALV.

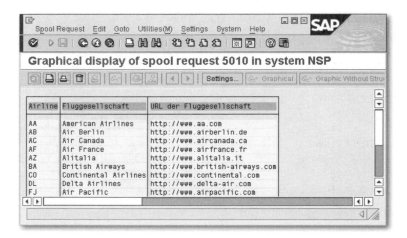

Figure 9.53 ALV Print List

---

40 The call to an ALV list after NEW-PAGE PRINT ON also results in printing, but would require the use of a classical list statement in the application logic.

41 For classical print lists, the data is sent directly, page by page, to the spool system, without the need to build large internal tables. The size of a classical print list is therefore only limited by the capacity of the spool system, not by the storage space of the current internal session. When printing through an ALV, internal tables must be built, which for very large lists may lead to memory bottlenecks. In this case, a list must currently be broken down by the application into multiple lists for printing via ALV. For lists exclusively intended for printing, therefore, an encapsulation by an ALS (SAP List Spooler) would be a possibility, which could compose the data provided into arbitrarily long print lists and forward them to the spool system.

Listing 9.52 ALV List Printing

```
REPORT z_alv_printing.

CLASS demo DEFINITION.
  PUBLIC SECTION.
    CLASS-METHODS main.
ENDCLASS.

CLASS demo IMPLEMENTATION.
  METHOD main.
    TYPES: BEGIN OF scarr_wa,
             carrid   TYPE scarr-carrid,
             carrname TYPE scarr-carrname,
             url      TYPE scarr-url,
           END OF scarr_wa.
    DATA:  scarr_tab  TYPE TABLE OF scarr_wa,
           pripars    TYPE pri_params, "TYPE alv_s_pctl,
           valid_flag TYPE c LENGTH 1,
           alv        TYPE REF TO cl_salv_table,
           print      TYPE REF TO cl_salv_print.
    CALL FUNCTION 'GET_PRINT_PARAMETERS'
      EXPORTING
        destination          = 'LP01'
        immediately          = ' '
        no_dialog            = 'X'
      IMPORTING
        out_parameters       = pripars "-pri_params
        valid                = valid_flag
      EXCEPTIONS
        invalid_print_params = 2
        others               = 4.
    IF sy-subrc <> 0 OR valid_flag <> 'X'.
      RETURN.
    ENDIF.
    SELECT *
        FROM scarr
        INTO CORRESPONDING FIELDS OF TABLE scarr_tab.
    TRY.
        cl_salv_table=>factory(
          IMPORTING r_salv_table = alv
          CHANGING  t_table = scarr_tab ).
        print = alv->get_print( ).
        print->set_print_only( 'X' ).
        "print->set_print_control( pripars ).
        alv->display( ).
      CATCH cx_salv_msg.
```

```
          MESSAGE 'ALV output not possible' TYPE 'I'
                  DISPLAY LIKE 'E'.
     ENDTRY.
   ENDMETHOD.
ENDCLASS.
START-OF-SELECTION.
  demo=>main( ).
```

9.4 Messages

Messages are short, single-line texts, which can be displayed from an ABAP program using the MESSAGE statement in dialog boxes, or in the status line of the current window of the SAP GUI. Using messages, you can inform the user about program flow, carry out an error handling in the context of a self-defined input check for general dynpros or selection screens, or exit the program.

9.4.1 Creating Messages

Message maintenance
Messages are generally Repository objects connected to the Change and Transport System (CTS) and translation, which are edited using the message maintenance tool (Transaction SE91 or call from the object list of the Object Navigator of the ABAP Workbench). Exceptions to this rule are free texts that can be sent as messages using special forms of the MESSAGE statements.

T100
Messages are stored in the database table T100. This table has the following columns:

- A one-character language key
- A twenty-character message class, which assigns its messages to a work area or package
- A three-character message number, where the range from 900 to 999 is reserved for customer development
- A short text of no more than 73 characters as the actual message text

Short and long text
If the message text is not self-explanatory, every message can have a long text defined, which the user can consult when the message is displayed. Placeholders are possible in short and long texts, which can then be dynamically supplied with texts in the MESSAGE statement.

For production ABAP programs, the use of reusable and standardized messages in message classes of the corresponding package is recommended, not the use of free texts.

9.4.2 Sending messages

The statement to be used for sending a message is MESSAGE. You can either select a message from table T100 by specifying the message class and message number or you can specify an arbitrary text. In addition, one of the message types "A", "E", "I", "S", "W", or "X" must be given. The message type determines the form in which the message is sent and how the program continues after the message is sent (see Section 9.4.3).

The static form of the MESSAGE statement to specify a message from table T100 is:

`MESSAGE tn(id).`

MESSAGE

Here, t is the message type, n is the message number, and id is the message class.[42] The dynamic form is:

`MESSAGE ID mid TYPE mtype NUMBER num.`

Here, mid, mtype, and num are fields, which contain the message class, message number, and message type in capital letters.

A form particularly well suited for the use of messages as exception texts (see Section 8.2.1) is:

`MESSAGE oref TYPE mtype.`

Exception texts

If oref is an object reference variable pointing to an exception object whose exception class implements the system interface IF_T100_MESSAGE, the message class will be taken from the component MSGID and the message number will be taken from the component MSGNO of the T100KEY interface attribute (see the example in Figure 8.8).

Lastly, free texts from character fields text can be sent as messages as follows:

---

42 This statement also has a short form MESSAGE tn, which assumes that the message class id is given after the program's introductory statement in the clause MESSAGE-ID.

Free texts   `MESSAGE text TYPE mtype.`

This variant should only be used in cases where the identification of the message by message class and number is not important.[43]

If a message text from table T100 or a long text contains the placeholders &i or &Vi& (i = 1 to 4), these can be replaced by the contents of character fields using the `WITH` clause of the `MESSAGE` statement.

Placeholder   `MESSAGE ... WITH text1 ... text4.`

To change the type of display, the following clause can be used:

Display type   `MESSAGE ... DISPLAY LIKE dtype.`

However, this has no influence on behavior defined by the message type alone.

9.4.3 Message Type

The form of message display and the following processing depend on the type of program execution and the specified message type. Possible types of program execution are dialog processing of dynpros, event handling of GUI controls, batch input,[44] background processing, and update tasks (see Section 10.1.3).

Dialog processing   The most important type of program execution for messages is dialog processing. In this section, we will take a brief look at the role of the different types of message for the individual stages of dynpro processing. All other details can be found in the ABAP keyword documentation. The DEMO_MESSAGES program on the AS ABAP demonstrates the behavior of the different message types in the different stages of dialog processing.

Informative Messages

With the following two message types "I" and "S", you can inform the user about program status with texts like "Action complete" or "Data was read".

---

43 If messages are not displayed on the screen, but only logged—as for instance in background processing—often only the ID is stored.

44 This is a data transfer technique, which makes it possible to pass data automatically to the dynpros of transactions and therefore to AS ABAP in a controlled way.

▶ **Information Messages**

Information messages of type "I" are largely independent of the state of dialog processing. The message is displayed in a dialog box and the program resumes after the MESSAGE statement after the user confirms. Only in PBO modules are information messages handled like messages of type "S".

▶ **Status Messages**

Status messages of type "S" are displayed in the status line of the screen of the next dynpro. Program processing resumes directly after the MESSAGE statement.

Messages for Input Checks on Dynpros

With the following two message types "E" and "W", you can perform a self-defined input check on dynpros (see Section 9.1.12).[45] They are primarily intended for PAI processing, and they otherwise almost always result in program termination.

▶ **Error Messages**

Error messages of type "E" interrupt the current PAI processing and the screen of the dynpro is redisplayed without PBO processing being executed. The message is displayed in the status line by default. On the screen, all the input fields associated in the flow logic with the current PAI module using FIELD or CHAIN are again ready for input. After a user action, PAI processing resumes at the first dynpro statement FIELD or CHAIN. During the handling of selection screen events (see Section 9.2.6), the behavior is similar. For classical list events (see Section 9.3.5), execution returns to the previous list level.

▶ **Warnings**

Warnings of type "W", in principle, behave like error messages of type "E". They differ in the type of display and by the fact that the user can confirm a warning with ⌈Enter⌋ without entering anything else. Program processing then resumes directly after the MESSAGE statement.

---

45 This includes selection screens and, to a certain extent, list dynpros.

Program Terminations with Messages of Type "A" and "X"

With the following two message types "A" and "X", you can terminate ABAP programs. While exits with type "A" may make sense, for instance, in case of missing permissions, exits of type "X" should be thought of as absolute emergency brakes, which should only be sent if the system has hang up in a way that cannot be treated otherwise.

Termination message

▸ **Termination Messages**
Termination messages of type "A" are displayed in a dialog box. Then, the program is stopped and execution resumes after the call point of the first program in the current call chain.

Exit message

▸ **Exit Messages**
Exit messages of type "X" terminate the program with runtime error MESSAGE_TYPE_X. The associated short dump (see Section 8.2.5) contains the message type.

9.4.4 Use of Messages

PAI processing

Messages are primarily for use during PAI processing in classical dynpros. Therefore, messages should only be used during PAI processing. This is particularly true for message types "E" and "W".

Exceptions

Messages should not be misused to trigger exceptions. The classical exception handling in function modules (see Section 8.2.2) offers a mechanism to handle messages as exceptions: a predefined classical exception named error_message. If this exception is handled, messages of types "S", "I", and "W" are simply not sent while messages of types "E" and "A" trigger this exception.

However, this mechanism should no longer be used to send a message with the goal of triggering an exception. There are class-based exceptions for this purpose, which take their exception text from table T100 (see Section 8.2.1). The handling of messages as exceptions can still be used if existing function modules send messages in the wrong context. During handling, a class-based exception should be raised instead, with an appropriate exception text.

Assertions

Exit messages of type "X" should be avoided as far as possible. This applies particularly for coding, which is to be reused. In most cases, exceptions or assertions (see Section 8.3) are better suited. An assertion that leads to a runtime error due to a condition is a direct replacement for the sending of an exit message in an IF control structure. Exit messages should only be used to prevent database inconsistency or in case of fatal errors in the presentation layer, for instance, where it is important to see information about the error situation in the short dump.

9.5   Web Dynpro ABAP

Up to this point, the user interfaces presented so far in this chapter were based on classical dynpros, which are components of ABAP programs and are processed by the ABAP runtime environment. The use of these dynpros assumes that the SAP GUI has been installed on every single computer of every single user. Developments in the user interface area in the past few years at SAP have therefore focused on using standardized technologies for the display of SAP applications. Because most computers today are equipped with an HTTP-compatible browser, it was reasonable to develop support for this protocol as the first step in striving for real web capability for SAP applications.[46]

An initial programming model for this purpose was already presented with the SAP Web Application Server 6.10: Business Server Pages (BSP). In the context of BSP, HTML-based interfaces can be created, which can be augmented by special ABAP scripting and connected with existing functionality on the application server. BSPs already support the separation of presentation logic and application logic better than classical dynpros.

HTML

Web Dynpro for ABAP is a new technology for HTML-based interfaces, which enables a still stronger structuring of programming. In comparison with BSP (see the books *Web Programming in ABAP with the SAP Web Application Server* by Frédéric Heinemann and Christian Rau, 2nd Edition, SAP PRESS 2005, and *Advanced BSP Programming* by Brian McKellar, SAP PRESS 2006), Web Dynpro for ABAP is much more declaratively oriented. While you still have a great leeway of

Web Dynpro vs. BSP

---

46 We have left aside the Internet Transaction Server (ITS) at this point. The ITS is an interface between ABAP and the Internet, which must be installed in addition to an AS ABAP. It allows users on the Internet to communicate with an AS ABAP based on the data interface between ABAP programs and dynpros. The ITS has now been replaced by the Internet Communication Manager (ICM), which is integrated into AS ABAP.

freedom in the arrangement of web pages with BSP, Web Dynpro for ABAP has the advantage that you can rely on a large number of pre-implemented layout elements. This means you can build your web pages with minimum programming effort and a stronger separation of layout and implementation of application logic. BSP, on the other hand, does not offer this preimplementation. There, all visible areas must be completely implemented by the application developer as HTML pages. The higher development effort, of course, also results in a higher implementation flexibility. A decision for one or the other technology therefore depends on the current requirements in each case. But in general, we prefer to recommend Web Dynpro for ABAP for future development.

MVC   The larger and more costly software projects become, the more the question arises as to the general structuring of the components involved. The Model-View-Controller principle (MVC) breaks programs into three areas:

▶ The Model area represents the application data, which will be accessed during the running application. The technical implementation of a model depends greatly on the system landscape in which the project is being implemented.

▶ The Controller area includes the processing of the data at runtime. Here is where all classes and methods are implemented with which the data will be displayed or processed.

▶ The View area provides the visible portion of the application. In this area, the layout of a (browser) window is implemented and all necessary elements, like images, buttons, or data display elements, are attached.

The Web Dynpro framework offered by SAP for the creation of web applications is based on the MVC principle.

Web Dynpro for ABAP and Java   The Web Dynpro technology for user interfaces implements the Model-View-Controller principle used for all NetWeaver-based applications. With SAP NetWeaver 2004s, Web Dynpro is available for both the Java programming languages on the AS Java, and for ABAP on the AS ABAP. Both variants are based on the same metamodel, that is, concepts and terms are largely identical. However, some differences necessarily arise from the very different architectures of the two languages.

The following sections give you an overview of programming with Web Dynpro for ABAP, and are intended to complement this book on ABAP Objects. Based on a simple example, the basic principles of the programming model are explained. Moreover, you will get useful tips on the creation of your own projects. For more information on Web Dynpro, we refer you to the book *Web Dynpro for ABAP* by Ulli Hoffmann (SAP PRESS 2006).

9.5.1 First Steps with Web Dynpro ABAP

We want to approach the Web Dynpro ABAP programming model using simple examples. The first example we want to examine here is again a very simple "Hello World" application.

The framework for any project with Web Dynpro ABAP is the so-called *Web Dynpro component*, which is created in the first step of the example.

Web Dynpro components are the ordering units of all elements that are needed in the context of a Web Dynpro ABAP-based application. Within a component, all Web Dynpro views, windows, and controllers, which belong in a content unit together, are created and managed. Every existing Web Dynpro component can be embedded and used in other components. In practice, this means that both components of largely generic character and those with very concrete purposes can exist. For repeating subtasks of a business application, such as creation of an order or the maintenance of an address, you can create a generic component, which is then embedded into the concrete application components as a reusable building block. However, from a technical standpoint, generic and concrete components do not differ.

Web Dynpro component

In the object selection list of the Object Navigator in the ABAP Workbench, the entry **Web Dynpro Comp./Intf.** is available (see Figure 9.54). You can use this entry to find the tools for creating and editing components and their subcomponents. Alternatively, you can use the menu path **Create · Web Dynpro · Web Dynpro Component (Interface)** in the object list of a package.

A Web Dynpro component is a Repository object and is fully integrated into the ABAP Workbench. As usual, simply enter the name of the new object and answer the following dialog. You need to decide whether you want to create a component or a so-called *component interface* (see Figure 9.55). Since work with component interfaces only becomes relevant in the context of more complex applications, however, select the predefinition for the component type. A name will also be suggested for the *Web Dynpro window* associated with the component, which you can also accept.

Figure 9.54 Introduction to Development with Web Dynpro ABAP

Figure 9.55 Creating a Web Dynpro Component

Web Dynpro Explorer

Save the component to the desired package. The selection of the component opens the tool Web Dynpro Explorer. The Web Dynpro Explorer is the tool in the ABAP Workbench for Web Dynpro ABAP (see Figure 9.56). For the new component, a few subordinate elements have automatically been created, which are needed in the context of a real project: the component controller, a node for the elements of the component interface, and a node for all Web Dynpro windows of this component.[47] However, since these three elements of the component aren't initially required, we will only cover them later (see Section 9.5.2).

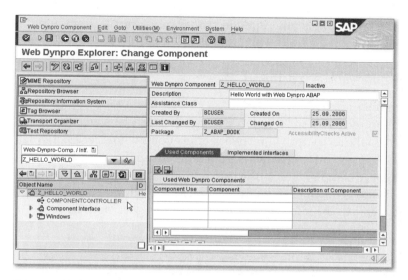

Figure 9.56 Elements of a New Web Dynpro Component

First, we must create another element, which is vital, namely, the first *view*.

The view represents the visible part of a Web Dynpro component. It is graphically designed in the View Designer, and rendered at runtime as a unit in the user's browser. Besides the layout, every view has a view controller, to whose methods and context elements (see Section 9.5.2) only the view itself has access. This is typically where functionality is implemented that has a direct relationship with the view's layout, like event handler methods that react to a user's action (i. e., clicks on a button). Methods that read current values from input fields and pass them on to processing logic is another different example that illustrates where functionality can be directly tied to the view's layout. As a third element, every view has so-called *plugs*. Plugs enable navigation between different views by connecting them together using navigation links.

Web Dynpro view

---

47 Note also the checkbox **Accessibility Checks Active**. In Web Dynpro ABAP, accessibility is supported automatically.

View Designer

To create a view, select **Create • View** in the context menu of the Web Dynpro component, and specify a name and a description. The View Designer then appears with the **Layout** tab of the Web Dynpro Explorer.[48] Save the component. Then the new subnode **Views** will also appear with the new view in the object list. Since this "Hello, world" example is only intended to create a callable application as quickly as possible, we will postpone using the view controller until the next application example, which will focus on how to work with the different controller types.

View layout

The interface of a web application can, in many cases, be designed using a relatively small number of standardized UI elements. Therefore, the Web Dynpro Framework offers you a whole series of different libraries with UI elements from different application areas. In the **Standard Simple** library, for instance, you can find the UI element **TextView**. This UI element can be dragged and dropped into the preview area in the middle part of the View Designer (see Figure 9.57).

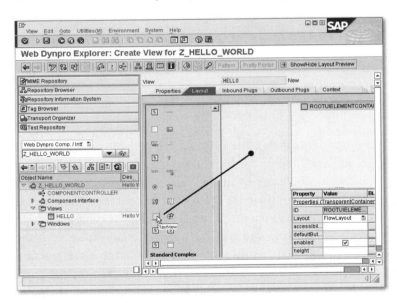

Figure 9.57 Insertion of a UI Element into the Layout

The UI element is displayed in the element hierarchy below the **RootUIelementContainer**. Since it is also automatically marked as an

---

48 You may need to log on once at this point at the ICM using your username and password for AS ABAP.

active element, you can now edit the properties of this UI element in the table below it. In this very simple example, the UI element should only display the static text "Hello World" on the screen. Enter this text in the line in the table provided and select **Continue**. Then the UI element will be indicated in the preview area by a dotted rectangle. If you select **Save**, the text itself will also appear.

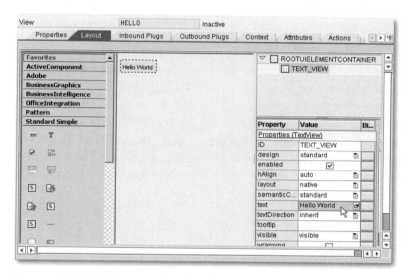

Figure 9.58 Text in Layout and in the Property Table

A view is an object with no interfaces with the world outside the component. In order to use the view in a browser-suitable application, it must first be embedded in a *Web Dynpro window*. The window of a Web Dynpro component is a container for all views, which should be displayed in the browser when a Web Dynpro application is called. In other words, a window, unlike a view, has an interface through which it can be called from outside of a component. This interface is called the *interface view*. It is automatically created for every window and is always uniquely assigned to it. The interface view includes so-called *plugs*, which can be used to open or exit a window. A simple component generally has exactly one Web Dynpro window, but, in the context of large projects, components with multiple windows and components with no windows at all can be created.

Web Dynpro window

When the Web Dynpro component was created, a window was already created with it, which can now be used. If you select the window in the object list, the Window Editor of the Web Dynpro

Embed view in window

Explorer opens on its central tab **Window**. On this tab, the structure of the window is shown as a tree. The root of this structure is the window itself. Every window needs at least one inbound plug to be called in the first place. This plug (**DEFAULT**) is thus automatically generated when the window is created, and is displayed in the structure of the Window Editor as the only existing element. To embed the previously designed view into the window, use drag-and-drop to pull the view's entry out of the object list onto the root node of the window structure (see Figure 9.59).

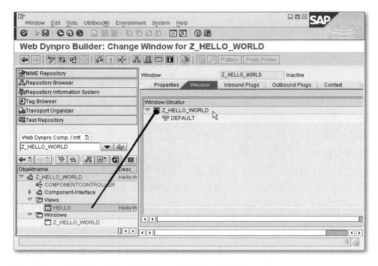

Figure 9.59 Embedding the View into the Window

Default
The embedded view is now shown as a node in the window structure and can be selected there. In the accompanying property table, the **Default** checkbox is checked and cannot be changed (see Figure 9.60).

The property **Default** must be given for exactly one view of the window structure. The view that is marked in such a way is always the first view to be displayed when the window is called in the browser. Because only a single view is embedded in our simple example, it must automatically also be the default view.

Activating a component
When the window is laid out and saved, all the necessary elements of our example component are created. As with (nearly) all Repository objects, all its parts must now be activated using **Activate** before the component can be used.

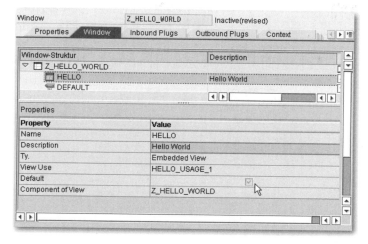

Figure 9.60 Property Table of the Embedded View

The outwardly visible interface of a Web Dynpro component is implemented by the interface views of the window of the component. These interface views, however, cannot be called directly from a client. As a last step, therefore, a so-called *Web Dynpro application* must be created. A Web Dynpro application is an independent Repository object, which connects an interface view of a Web Dynpro component with a URL that can be used in a browser.

Web Dynpro application

Since it only makes sense to use a Web Dynpro application with components, there is no separate category for it in the object list of the Object Navigator; it is always created through the context menu of a Web Dynpro component with **Create · Web Dynpro Application**. If you do this for our component, after confirmation of the creation dialog box, the web application editor of the Web Dynpro Explorer appears (see Figure 9.61).

Since our hello-world component has only a single interface view and this in turn only one inbound plug **Default**, both of these rows in the **Properties** tab are already correspondingly populated, and the Web Dynpro application must simply be saved.

Now the Web Dynpro application can be executed, either through the **Test** option in the context menu or by direct entry of the generated URL in a browser. After entry of a username and password for AS ABAP, the view shown in Figure 9.62 is displayed in the browser.

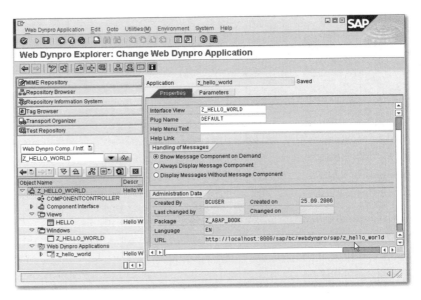

Figure 9.61 Web Dynpro Application

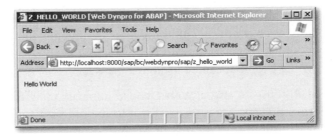

Figure 9.62 Web Dynpro View in the Browser

Summary During the creation of the hello-world component and application, you have already encountered a number of basic concepts of the Web Dynpro framework, and a first kind of executable application could be created. However, we deliberately avoided using any controller functionality, as we wanted the focus to be on the purely static display of a Web Dynpro view in a browser.

The programming part of a Web Dynpro component, that is, the use of different controllers, will be the focus of the next sample application. All the steps we have already taken will be needed there as well. To complete the following example, you will need to create a component, embed one or more views in a window, and create a Web Dynpro application to be called. In addition, however, you will work with different controllers and their contexts, and navigate between two views embedded in the window.

9.5.2 Query with Web Dynpro ABAP

The last example may have left you with the impression that a great deal of effort went into producing such a simple result as it is shown in Figure 9.62. So, this time we'll channel our energy into a more rewarding task: the query and display of data from the AS ABAP for requesters on the Internet.

Web Dynpro is a programming model for the creation and design of web interfaces for business applications. The introductory question in development is therefore the following: What data should be made accessible to the end user, in what form, and to what purpose?

In a browser window, we will display a dialog for the listing of flight connections. In two appropriately designed input fields, the user can enter a departure city and a destination, before starting the search procedure using a button. The names of the two cities are then read from the input fields of the browser window and passed to the processing logic. This then ensures that the data for all available flight connections between the two cities are read using a BAPI[49] from a database table. In the last step, all matching flights are displayed in a table on the screen.

Flight data table

The model in this application is implemented by the BAPI, which obtains the data required from the database table.

Model

In the view, all the graphical elements are arranged and laid out, like the input fields, the output table, and the button to start the search process.

View

Controllers will contain the logic needed to read the input fields, call the BAPI, and prepare the data provided for display. In the context of

Controller

---

49 Business Application Programming Interface. Predefined interface to data and processes in an SAP application, which is stored in the Business Object Repository of AS ABAP. BAPIs are implemented by remotely enabled function modules with the naming convention BAPI_<business_object_name>_<method_name>, which must not engage in user dialog. Using the BAPI transaction code, the BAPI Explorer can be called to display the function modules for every application.

the example, we will examine the distribution of the individual tasks over the different controllers provided by the Web Dynpro framework.

Web Dynpro Component

First, as we did in the previous "Hello World" example, we will create a Web Dynpro component named Z_FLIGHTDATA. For the current example, we need the Web Dynpro component controller that we left aside in the last example. When creating a Web Dynpro component, the ABAP Workbench automatically creates such a controller (see Figure 9.63).

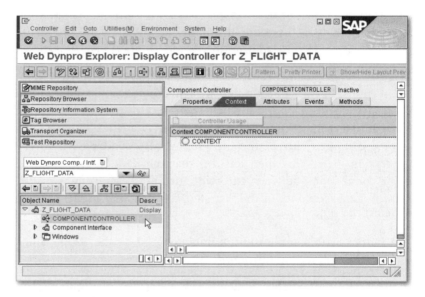

Figure 9.63 Web Dynpro Component Controller

Web Dynpro Component Controller

Controllers are the areas in a Web Dynpro component in which the processing logic of the application is stored. In Web Dynpro ABAP, this logic is implemented in methods of ABAP Objects on the AS ABAP. In Web Dynpro Java, Java and the Java environment are used. The central controller of a component is the *component controller*. Here is where all methods, which are to be visible and accessible for the whole component, are implemented. A typical example is the selection of data from database tables and the storage of data after user editing.

Every controller always has a *Web Dynpro context*. The context is a buffer where processed data is stored and can be prepared for the methods of the controller. A context is always structured in nested nodes and individual attributes.

In our example, we'll use the predefined component controller to retrieve the flight data from a database table in AS ABAP and display the data in the Web Dynpro view. After creating the Web Dynpro component, the context of the component controller is empty (see Figure 9.63) and can be designed on the **Context** tab by creating nodes and attributes. In our example, we leave the design of the component controller context to a wizard, which automatically adapts the context structure to the BAPI used. To do this, select the entry **Create • Service Call** from the context menu of the component, after which the Web Dynpro Wizard appears, which you can execute by repeatedly selecting **Continue** (see Figure 9.64). The individual steps are described exactly in the wizard, and we will only briefly note here what is needed for our example:

1. Specify the controller in which the service call will take place. Then, select the **Existing controller** COMPONENTCONTROLLER.

2. As **Service Type**, currently you can only select "Function module".

3. For the **Function module**, specify the name of the BAPI BAPI_FLIGHT_GETLIST and leave the **Destination** blank.

4. Select the required controller context element, as shown in Figure 9.64.

5. Select the method of the function module that you want to call in the component controller to obtain data. The BAPI we are using has only a single method, which is why the corresponding input field is prepopulated with its name.[50]

6. Click on **Finish**.

After the steps of the wizard have been completed, the Controller Editor shows the generated context of the component controller. Below the root node, there is a node with the name of the BAPI, and under that node are two more nodes—**IMPORTING** and **CHANGING** (see Figure 9.65).

---

50 A BAPI provides so-called *methods*, but these are not methods in classes of ABAP Objects.

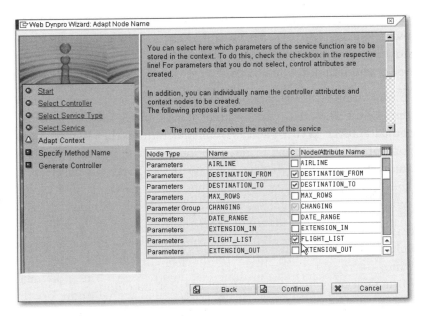

Figure 9.64 Web Dynpro Wizard

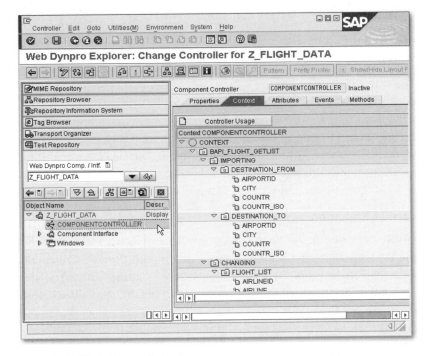

Figure 9.65 Web Dynpro Context

The node **IMPORTING** contains the two nodes **DESTINATION_FROM** and **DESTINATION_TO** in which the values of the attributes are stored describing the departure and destination airports. These two nodes will be needed later when we design two input fields on the view.

Nodes and attributes

The node **CHANGING**, on the other hand, contains only one node named **FLIGHT_LIST**, in which all information on the selected flight route are stored. This node is later associated with a table in the layout of the view.

If you switch to the **Methods** tab of the Controller Editor, you will see that the list of methods for this controller, in addition to the predefined methods, now also contains the method EXECUTE_BAPI_FLIGHT_GETLIST. You can select the method to see it in the ABAP Editor (or to edit it). You will see that this is a method of a class of ABAP Objects, which calls the BAPI function module.

Methods

The classes and interfaces needed, that is, the entire object-oriented environment, is automatically generated by Web Dynpro Explorer when a component is generated. Unlike the case with classical dynpros, here, you don't have to worry about generating programs and their organization yourself. This automatically ensures compliance with the MVC concept.

Programs

The state of the component controller is now sufficient for the purpose of our simple example, and can be saved. The component controller can use the BAPI to obtain the necessary data from the current AS ABAP and to provide it to the component. This data can be consumed by the controllers of the views. Next, we need to create the necessary view and its controller.

Web Dynpro View

Besides the two input fields for departure and destination airports, the Web Dynpro view should provide a table that contains all corresponding flight connections. It also will need a button to start the search function. Follow the procedure in the "Hello World" example to create a view named Z_FLIGHT_DATA_VIEW. Then, select the **Context** tab, opening the Context Editor of the view.

The Context Editor of the view is divided into two parts. On the right side, the context of the component controller from Figure 9.65 is

View context

shown. On the left side of the editor, you see the context of the view, which is empty for the view just created. To structure the view context with reference to the component controller context, the Web Dynpro framework provides the extremely practical *context mapping*.

Context mapping Context editor In context mapping, the context nodes of a view controller can be mapped onto the nodes of a component-wide visible controller context, such as the component controller context. The Web Dynpro framework then ensures that the contents of the two nodes are identical at all times. If the value of an attribute changes in the view controller context, for instance, because the user enters a value, this new value is automatically forwarded to the component controller context. On the other hand, if the value of a node in the component controller context changes, this change is automatically propagated to the corresponding nodes of the view context, if a mapping onto the nodes of the component controller has been defined. The prerequisite here is that both nodes have the same substructure.

Copying context nodes Now drag the node **DESTINATION_FROM** of the component controller context and drop it on the root node of the view context (see Figure 9.66). This step generates copies of context nodes present in the component controller context. The copies are generated in the context of the view and a context mapping to the original nodes is defined.

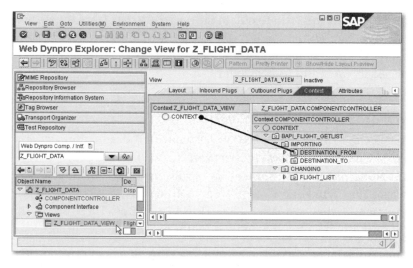

Figure 9.66 Generating Context Nodes and Context Mapping

After confirmation of a prompt, the selected nodes are copied from the component controller and created in the view controller context. At the same time, a mapping of these nodes onto the underlying nodes in the component controller context is defined. In the same way, copy the two nodes **DESTINATION_TO** and **FLIGHT_LIST** of the component controller context, and save the component.

The view controller context now contains three nodes, which are related through the context mapping to the nodes of the component controller that have the same name. The principle of the mapping can be extended to arbitrary subnodes. It is therefore unnecessary to replicate the entire context of the component controller in the view context.

Our view context is now complete, and we go to the view layout by switching to the **Layout** tab.

View layout

As the first UI element, insert the **Group** element from the **Standard Container** library. Select the **Caption** element subordinate to the **Group** element in the UI element hierarchy on the right side of the editor. In its properties table, in the **text** line, enter a short title like "From" (see Figure 9.67).

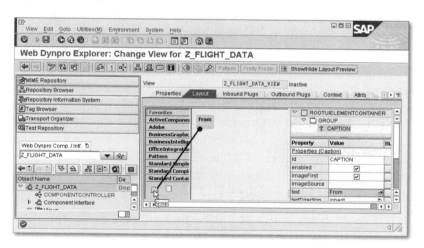

Figure 9.67 Inserting the UI Element Group

Select the **Generate Container Form** in the context menu of the **Group** node in the UI element hierarchy. In the subsequent dialog box, the input field **Standard Cell Editor** is prepopulated with the value **InputField**, which we can accept to create input fields. Click on

Context binding

the **Context** button to show the structure of the view context, and select the **DESTINATION_FROM** node there. Now the attributes of the node appear in a table in the dialog box. Check the checkbox in the **Bind** column as shown in Figure 9.68, so that there is no bind check for the two attributes AIRPORTID and COUNTR_ISO, and then confirm the entries.

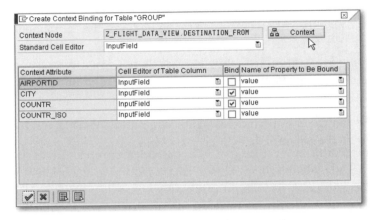

Figure 9.68 Context Binding for Input Fields

Data binding   The context binding just completed means that a data binding exists between UI elements and view context. For many different UI elements in the Web Dynpro framework, certain properties can be bound to attributes of the context belonging to the view controller. Such a binding has the effect that the value of the property of the UI element is always identical to the value of the corresponding context attribute. For the property **value** of an input field, this means that a value entered by a user is automatically written to the view context. Accordingly, for instance, a table field bound over the **value** property will always display the value that the attribute of the context node has at that precise moment.

Figure 9.69 shows the result in the preview window of the View Designer. In the view, two more UI elements of type "InputField" have been generated within the UI element **Group**. If you select one of the two input fields in the UI element hierarchy and look at the **value** line in the property table, you will see that the binding is shown there in the **Binding** column and can also be changed. Each of the two input fields is thus bound through the **value** property to an attribute of the view context node.

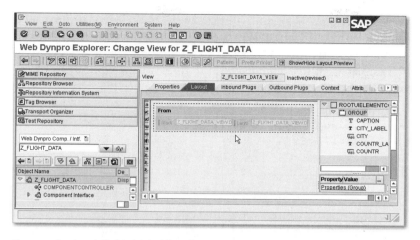

Figure 9.69 Input Fields in the View Designer

To complete the input dialog of this example, we create another input block via which values can be specified for the destination airport. Proceed exactly as you did for the departure airport, and start by embedding another UI element **Group**. In the UI element hierarchy, this new group element will automatically be assigned an order number to ensure uniqueness in the hierarchy. As text for this element's subelement **Caption** enter "To". Create a container form again, and now select the context node **DESTINATION_TO**. Restrict the binding to **CITY** and **COUNTR** of the attributes offered again. After saving, you can check the current design of the layout in the preview of the view designer. The layout now includes two input blocks with two input fields each.

Input dialog

The view can now accept entry from a user. To test this, just as shown in the "Hello World" example, you can embed the view in the generated window of the component, activate all the components involved, create an application, and then display the view in the browser (see Figure 9.70).[51]

Testing Web Dynpro ABAP

As you see, the Web Dynpro framework, like the classical dynpro, also automatically generates an input help for every input field, if the prerequisites are fulfilled. In our case, the connection to the database

Automatic field and input help

---

51 Web Dynpro ABAP is thus solidly in the tradition of Early Prototyping. You can test an application during development without complicated deployment procedures.

table of the ABAP Dictionary on the AS ABAP is created using a BAPI for data retrieval. The input help only offers values present there for the individual fields. The automatic field help, which you should also be familiar with from the classical dynpro and which can be called with the [F1] key, works here as well.

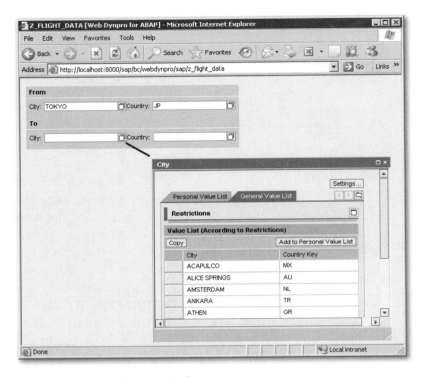

Figure 9.70 Testing the Input Window

Output table

To show the flight data found after entry of the search criteria, we extend the layout of the view with a table element. You can find the UI element **Table** in the **Standard Complex** library. Use drag and drop to move it into the layout preview, and again enter a text like "Result" for the title of the UI element in the **value** line of the properties of the subelement **CAPTION_2**. Then select the **Create binding** entry in the context menu of the UI element **Table** in the hierarchy. In the dialog box, again select **Context** and the node **FLIGHT_LIST** from the list of the view context offered. Now you can select any number of attributes from those offered, or simply select all attributes as bound. After saving, you will find a table column in the layout preview of the View Designer for every selected attribute of the context node.

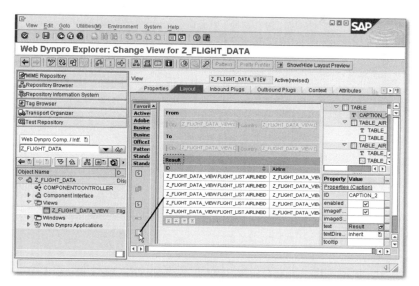

Figure 9.71 Table in the View Designer

As the last UI element, we now insert the button with which a user can start the search for flight data. You can find the predefined element **Button** in the **Standard Simple** library. If you drag and drop it in the layout preview, it is initially automatically inserted at the end of the previously inserted UI elements. However, you can change the position of individual UI elements by selecting the element in the hierarchy and dragging it around the structure. In this manner, simply pull the **Table** element to the end of the structure, placing the button between the input fields and the result list (see Figure 9.72). After you have entered a text for the button in the **text** line of the property list, we can turn our attention to the topic of actions on Web Dynpro views.

Button

The button enables the user to start a search for flight data. The selection of the button thus sets a program flow in motion. In ABAP Objects, this happens via the triggering of an event, which results in a call to a handling method registered for it (see Section 6.5.3). For that reason, we need to ensure that the selection of the button by the user triggers such an event.

Events

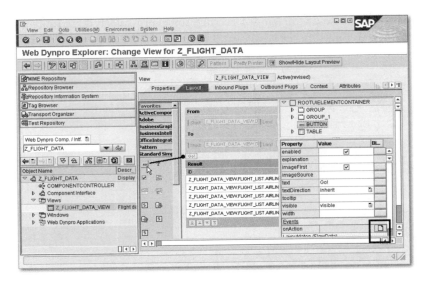

Figure 9.72 Button in the View Designer

Actions

We name events triggered by user action on the interface of a web application action.[52] Actions are generated with the View Designer directly for a UI element of the layout and are linked to an event handler method in the controller of the view.

To create an action, select the icon highlighted at the lower right in Figure 9.72 in the line **onAction**. In the dialog box, which then appears, give the new action a new name, like "SEARCH",[53] leave the input field **Outbound plug** empty for our example, and confirm this action with **Continue**. The **Actions** tab of the View Editor lists all actions of the current view.

Web Dynpro code wizard

Forward navigation takes you from an action to the ABAP Editor for the event handler method, which handles the action's event (see Figure 9.73). This method is still blank and must be implemented. If a user selects the button, the BAPI BAPI_FLIGHT_GETLIST should be called. The call of the BAPI, however, is already encapsulated in the method EXECUTE_BAPI_FLIGHT_GETLIST of the component controller (see above), so that the event handler can simply call this method. The Web Dynpro framework supports you at this point

---

52 In the classical dynpro, actions are implemented by functions, which are connected to function codes.

53 Here, you can also assign already existing functions to a UI element.

with another wizard, which you start with **Edit • Web Dynpro Code Wizard** or by using the application toolbar icon highlighted in Figure 9.73.

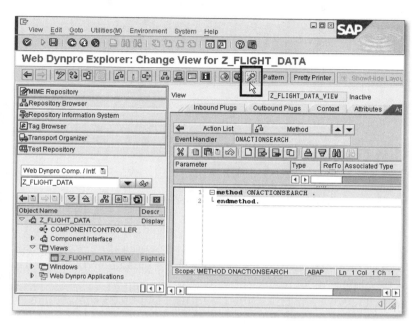

Figure 9.73 Implementation of the Event Handler

In the following dialog box, select the option **Method call in controller used** and then, for **Component Name**, use the input help to select the value Z_FLIGHT_DATA. In the same way, supply the field **Controller Name** with the value COMPONENTCONTROLLER. For **Method name**, you can select EXECUTE_BAPI_FLIGHT_GETLIST. After confirmation of the dialog box, the event handler method of the action, as shown in Listing 9.53, is completely implemented and the view can then be activated.

Event handler

Listing 9.53 Event Handler for an Action

```
METHOD onactionsearch.
  wd_comp_controller->execute_bapi_flight_getlist( ).
ENDMETHOD.
```

If you have not yet embedded the view in a window, do it now. If it hasn't yet been done, create a Web Dynpro application and test the event.

Web Dynpro application

Figure 9.74 shows the display of flight data found for the input data of a user. If no data has been found, the table stays empty.

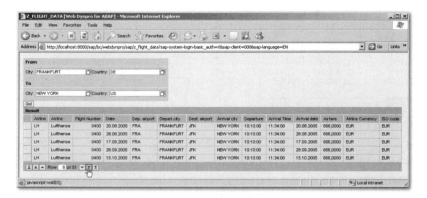

Figure 9.74 Output of Flight Data on the Web Dynpro

Summary The first example, the "Hello World" application was a simple introduction to the creation of a Web Dynpro application with a static interface. In the second example, the flight data table, the interplay of the different controller contexts, and the editing of the methods needed to solve the task, were the focus. Figure 9.75 shows an overview of these relationships again.

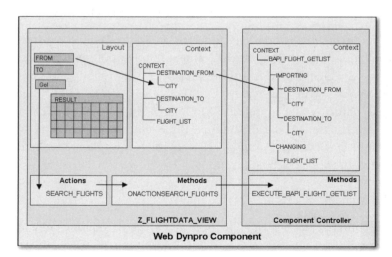

Figure 9.75 Contexts, Actions, and Methods of a Component

The input field FROM is bound to the context attribute CITY in the context of the view controller. At the same time, a mapping is

694

defined between the node **DESTINATION_FROM** of the component controller context and the node in the view controller context that have the same name.

The action of the **Go!** button triggers the event handler method ONACTIONSEARCH_FLIGHTS, which, in turn, calls a method of the component controller. When the BAPI is executed, the data needed from the database table is imported into the Web Dynpro component.

On the first call to the application, the context of the component controller is blank, since the input fields still don't contain values for the search criteria. As a result, the table contains no entries. With the next request/response cycle, the original view is displayed on the screen a second time, but now with the values, which were read from the database table based on the search criteria entered. Therefore, the same view is displayed in the browser twice. This will suffice for a simple example, but not for most applications. In many cases, a different view must be displayed as a reaction to a user action.

View Navigation

Now we'll extend the flight data example so that a second view named Z_NO_FLIGHT_DATA is created in the component (see Figure 9.76). This view should output an appropriate message to the screen if no flight connection exists between two cities entered. We implement this using a simple TextView element with a static text, just as in the "Hello World" example. What's new here is that we equip the view with a button, which allows us to navigate back to the first view in order to start a new search.

The button is again of type **BUTTON** and must therefore be associated with an action; however, here, the event handler of the action must now perform navigation. For this purpose, so-called *plugs* must first be created.

Plugs are interfaces via which the user can navigate from one view to another within a window. Navigation links within a window always start at an *outbound plug* and end at an *inbound plug* of a next view. Every inbound plug, which is targeted by a navigation link, triggers an event. A corresponding event handler method is called before the next view is rendered.

Plugs

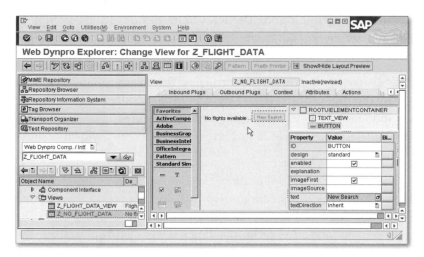

Figure 9.76 Additional View of the Component

Outbound plug | We need a total of four plugs, starting with an outbound plug for the output view Z_FLIGHT_DATA_VIEW. To do this, we enter a name on the **Outbound plugs** tab of this view, as shown in Figure 9.77.

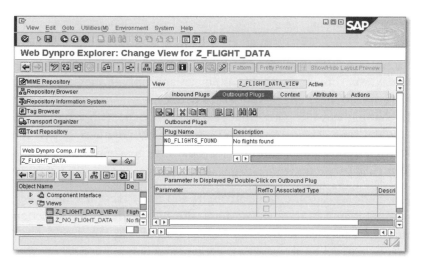

Figure 9.77 Outbound Plugs

This defines the starting point of the navigation. As an end point, an inbound plug (e. g., NO_FLIGHTS_IN) is needed in the view NO_FLIGHTS_AVAILABLE, which is created on the **Inbound plugs** tab. This automatically creates an empty event handler method. This can then be filled with suitable code as needed, but is left empty here. On the **Outbound plugs** tab in the view, the starting point named GOTO_FLIGHT_DATA needed for the return navigation is created.

Finally, we create another inbound plug for the starting view, which can accept the return navigation (see Figure 9.78).

Inbound plug

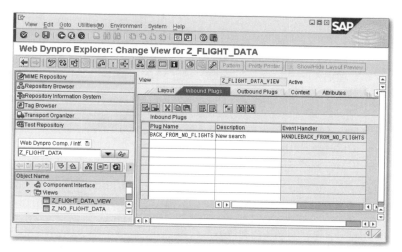

Figure 9.78 Inbound Plug with Event Handler

Figure 9.79 illustrates the principle of navigation between Web Dynpro views. For every view, outbound and inbound plugs can be defined. For a navigation, an outbound plug is connected to an inbound plug of a different view, for which an event handler can be implemented. This is a significant difference from the navigation between classical dynpros, in which arbitrary subsequent dynpros from the same program can be called, but only a single PBO processing can be implemented for each dynpro.

To implement navigation between plugs, navigation links must be defined. This happens in the window in which the views with plugs are embedded. So embed the view Z_NO_FLIGHT_DATA in the window Z_FLIGHT_DATA. In the structure of the window, the plugs created for each view are displayed as its subnodes.[54] The context menu of an outbound plug can be used to create a navigation link (see Figure 9.80).

Navigation links

---

54 A window can have its own plugs independent of the plugs of the views, of which we are already familiar with DEFAULT.

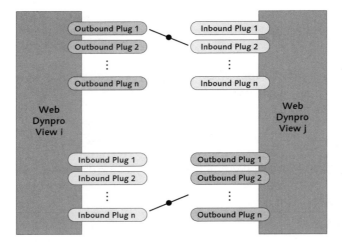

Figure 9.79 Navigation Using Plugs and Navigation Links

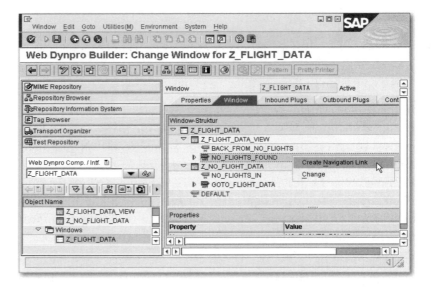

Figure 9.80 Creating a Navigation Link

In the following dialog box, you can use the input help to select the target view and one of its inbound plugs. After confirmation of the dialog box, the navigation link is displayed as a subnode of the outbound plug in the structure. We create the navigation links shown in Figure 9.81. Note that the view Z_FLIGHT_DATA_VIEW is not necessarily the default view of the application after the embedding of a second view in the window, but can be set as the default view.

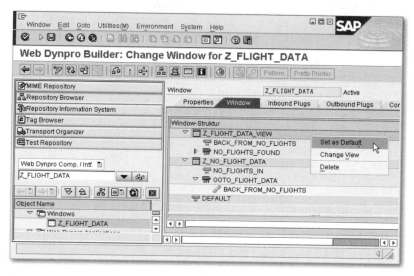

Figure 9.81 Navigation Links and Default View

The navigations of our example are thus completely defined. Now we only need to implement the triggering of navigation—that is, the calls to outbound plugs—within each view.

In the Z_FLIGHT_DATA_VIEW view, to trigger navigation, we have to engage methods, which trigger the population process of the view context, namely, the event handler method ONACTIONSEARCH.[55] To determine whether data is available for display, we must read the context node in this method, which contains the list of flights after the call to the BAPI. If the BAPI found no flights for the values given, this node is empty. In this case, navigation to the second view must be triggered.

Triggering navigation

Since the reading of a context node is a standardized step, the Web Dynpro Code Wizard offers a suitable statement pattern (see Figure 9.82).

Reading the context

The Web Dynpro Code Wizard includes the necessary source code lines at the point marked by the cursor in the method implementation. In addition, some lines are inserted, which are not needed in this example and must be deleted. These are the last lines in the method under the comment line * `get all declared attributes`:

---

[55] You can find the method on the **Methods** tab of your view.

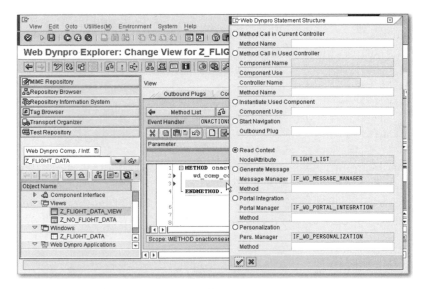

Figure 9.82 Template Statement to Read Context

The method then appears as shown in Listing 9.54.[56]

Listing 9.54 Extended Event Handler for an Action

```
METHOD onactionsearch.
  DATA:
   node_flight_list TYPE REF TO if_wd_context_node,
   elem_flight_list TYPE REF TO if_wd_context_element,
   stru_flight_list TYPE
      if_z_flight_data_view=>element_flight_list.

  wd_comp_controller->execute_bapi_flight_getlist( ).
  node_flight_list =
    wd_context->get_child_node( name = `FLIGHT_LIST` ).
  IF ( node_flight_list IS INITIAL ).
  ENDIF.
  elem_flight_list = node_flight_list->get_element(  ).
  IF ( elem_flight_list IS INITIAL ).
  ENDIF.
ENDMETHOD.
```

Navigation   In the last IF control structure, we want to trigger the navigation. To do this, we call up the Web Dynpro Code Wizard again and select the

---

56 Of course, we have placed the inserted declarations at the start of the method.

template statement **Start navigation**. The only outbound plug that can be selected in our example is the plug NO_FLIGHTS_FOUND. This changes the control structure as shown in Listing 9.55.

Listing 9.55 Starting Navigation

```
IF ( elem_flight_list IS INITIAL ).
  wd_this->fire_no_flights_found_plg( ).
ENDIF.
```

For the return navigation, we have already created a button **New Search** in the Z_NO_FLIGHT_DATA view. For this button, we now create an action NEW_SEARCH and specify the outbound plug GOTO_FLIGHT_DATA directly in the dialog box (see Figure 9.83).

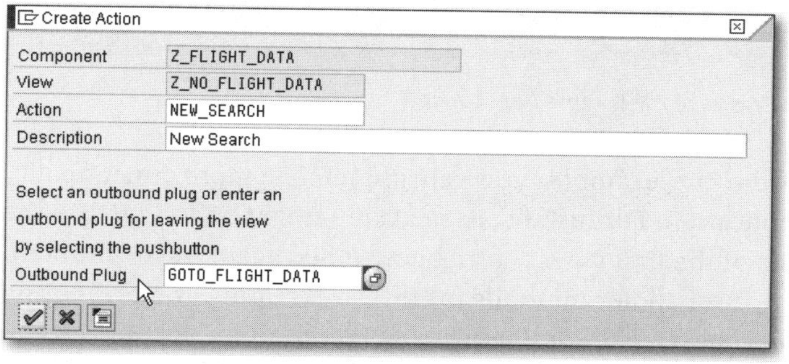

Return navigation

Figure 9.83 Action for Return Navigation

This also implements the associated event handler, as shown in Listing 9.56. You could also leave the input field **Outbound Plug** empty, instead using the code wizard in the event handler method with the statement pattern **Start navigation**.

Listing 9.56 Starting Navigation

```
METHOD onactionnew_search.
  wd_this->fire_goto_flight_data_plg( ).
ENDMETHOD.
```

If you now save and activate all the components of the application, you can test the application again. You will see that in case that no flight connections exist between the two cities given, the application navigates to the second view (see Figure 9.84).

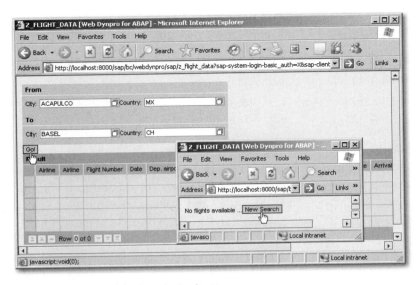

Figure 9.84 Views of the Sample Application

Starting from the example, you can implement more functionality for the application. For instance, a next step might be to initialize the input fields of the first view before being called again by the inbound plug. There are handler methods for this. By creating and presenting a suitable context and designing a corresponding mapping, you could also pass on the names of the missing flight connection to the second view and display them there.

9.5.3 Summary

This section introduced you to Web Dynpro for ABAP. It described the most important terms and concepts based on an executable application, which displays data according to a query from an Internet user, thus a database query requested from the web. Note that we did almost no coding in this example. The Web Dynpro framework created the greater part of the ABAP code needed. This ensures compliance with the MVC concept. Although it still holds true that you can place any language elements allowed in ABAP Objects into the methods accessed by forward navigation, you should always adhere to the MVC principle. A direct database access generally does not belong in methods, which belong to the Web Dynpro.

Our introduction makes no claim to completeness. Topics that were not addressed here include:

- Complete overview of the architecture of Web Dynpro
- Handling of texts and messages
- Dynamic changes during runtime
- ALV for Web Dynpro
- Integration into the SAP Portal

If you would like to get more intensively involved with this topic, we refer you again to *Web Dynpro for ABAP* (SAP PRESS 2006) and the SAP documentation for Web Dynpro ABAP in the SAP Help Portal (*http://help.sap.com*).

"We consider the creation of information to be a sign of intelligence, though in truth the reverse applies: the reduction, the selection of information, is by far the greater feat."
—Heinz Zemanek

10   Working with Persistent Data

ABAP programs generally work with data that is read out from persistent storage media. This data is retained for processing in the memory of the internal session, which can be extended for storage beyond the program runtime or for access from several programs by the shared memory (see Section 6.6).

Various formats and storage media are available for the persistent storage of data:

- Relational database tables of the AS ABAP database
- Data clusters in special database tables
- Binary or text files on an AS ABAP application server
- Binary or text files on the current presentation server

You must always think carefully about where you save your data and how you transport it. We recommend the following for the persistent storage of data:

1. On an AS ABAP, saving data in relational database tables should always be your first choice. ABAP supports this with Open SQL, which is integrated into the language. An object-oriented access is possible via Object Services. **Database tables**

2. In some cases, it may be advantageous to save in data clusters. Examples of saving data in data clusters would be preferable if you include the storage of results of extensive analyses; data that is not suitable for relational databases because it doesn't exist in the first normal form (e.g., nested internal tables); and object networks that can be saved in a data cluster after a serialization to XML (see Section 12.5). **Data clusters**

3. Files on the application or presentation server are the least suitable for the persistent storage of data of an AS ABAP. Instead, they could potentially be used as an interface for data transports from and to third-party systems. The reason for this is that for such files, unlike data in database tables and data clusters, there is no built-in support for the different code pages or byte sequences, which can even differ for the application servers of a single AS ABAP.

In the following sections, we will examine these three types of data storage in ABAP. Of course, the scope of the explanations provided will vary according to the importance of the storage.

10.1 Database Accesses

Relational database table

By far, the largest share of all of the persistent data of an AS ABAP is stored in the relational database tables of its central database. The relational data model maps the real world through the relationships between tables. A database table is a two-dimensional matrix of rows and columns. Each of the smallest possible combinations of columns that can uniquely identify a row of a table is called a *key*. For each table in a relational database, there must be at least one key, and for each table a key is fixed as a primary key. The dependencies between the tables are realized using *foreign key dependencies*.

Some of the database tables of the database of an AS ABAP are delivered prepopulated with values. These database tables contain many components of AS ABAP itself, for example, the repository objects or control data for customer-specific application setting. However, most of the database tables of applications that are based on AS ABAP are delivered empty. They are intended for the business management data of the customer systems and are filled on the customer's side via external data transfer or ABAP programs.

SQL

Each relational database has a programming interface that allows access to the tables of the database using a query language called SQL (*Structured Query Language*) that is standardized to a large extent. Unfortunately the SQL statements of these programming interfaces are not completely uniform, and have vendor-specific characteristics.

Database interface

To make an AS ABAP independent of the database used, it contains a *database interface* (for the overall architecture of the AS ABAP, see

Figure 3.2). ABAP programs only access the database through the database interface. The database interface converts all ABAP statements that access the database into vendor-specific standard SQL statements.

In the sections that follow, we'll address the following topics:

► **Definition of Database Tables**   DDL
  In standard SQL, there is a subarea called DDL (*Data Definition Language*) containing statements such as CREATE, ALTER, or DROP that allow you to define or change database tables. ABAP does not contain any such statements. Instead, these statements are implicitly executed by the ABAP Dictionary tool.

► **Access to Database Tables**   DML
  In standard SQL, there is a subarea called DML (*Data Manipulation Language*) containing statements such as SELECT, INSERT, UPDATE, and DELETE that process the data in database tables. In ABAP, there is a set of statements (each with the same name) that fall under the umbrella of *Open SQL*. Open SQL allows you to use DML statements in ABAP programs, independently of their platform.

► **Control of Database Tables**   DCL
  In standard SQL, there is a subarea called DCL (*Data Control Language*) that allows you to define user views and execute access controls. ABAP does not contain any such statements. The consistency of data is ensured by the SAP-LUW (Logical Unit of Work) concept and SAP locks. The AS ABAP authorization concept checks access rights.

The direct access to database tables remains ABAP's characteristic strength. Even if today, database accesses are increasingly wrapped in services such as BAPIs or web services and a developer needs to become more familiar with using these services, the foundation of these services should be acknowledged. Ultimately, we still need to have developers who can provide such services.

10.1.1 Definition of Database Tables in the ABAP Dictionary

ABAP does not contain any statements from the DDL part of standard SQL. Normal application programs are not supposed to create any database tables or change their attributes. Instead, the ABAP Dictionary tool of the ABAP Workbench, which we have already become familiar with in Section 5.1.7 for creating general global types, also allows database tables to be created. Open SQL statements can only access database tables that have been created with the ABAP Dictionary tool.

We have already provided you with a very comprehensive description of how to use this tool to create database tables in Section 2.4. Generally, as a developer of modules that access database tables, you usually work with existing tables of your application's relational data model. Therefore, you usually use the ABAP Dictionary tool to display existing tables and their structure.

Structure For each database table, the ABAP Dictionary tool creates a structured global data type of the same name. The database table is an instance of this type on the database. From the point of view of the ABAP program, this structure is a global data type of the ABAP Dictionary. You use this type to declare appropriate data objects as work areas for the database accesses in ABAP programs (see Figure 10.1).

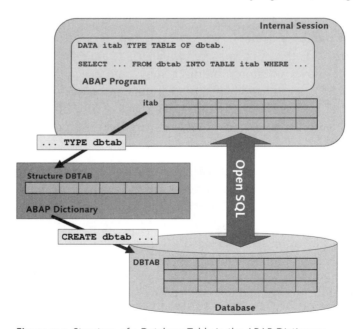

Figure 10.1 Structure of a Database Table in the ABAP Dictionary

Figure 10.1 shows the role of the ABAP Dictionary in defining database tables: In the ABAP Dictionary, DBTAB is a structure that can only contain elementary components (data elements) and has special technical attributes. The table DBTAB is created on the database from this meta description. In the ABAP program, you can use the data type DBTAB to create an internal table to include data from the database table, for example. Data is transported between the database and ABAP data objects with the Open SQL statements. Since data types and data objects have separate namespaces in ABAP, you can create data objects with the same name as a database table. Nevertheless, you should always avoid doing so to avoid confusion.

You can also combine the columns of one or several existing database tables in the ABAP Dictionary to form a *database view* or *view* for short. A view defines an application-specific view for particular data by grouping the columns involved to form a new structure. Like a flat structure, a view can act as a data type, and can be used like a database table in Open SQL statements that read data. If several database tables make up a view, it works like a static predefined join, so to speak.

View

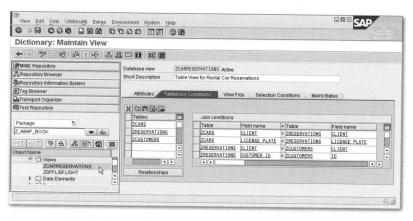

Figure 10.2 Join Conditions of a View

Figure 10.2 shows the definition of the tables that make up a view and the corresponding join conditions. Figure 10.3 shows the layout of the fields of the view. The tables are those of the rental car example from Chapter 2. In the program from Listing 2.14, you can now replace the table name `zreservations` with `zcarreservations` and get the output of the view fields, which includes data from all three tables involved (see Figure 10.4).

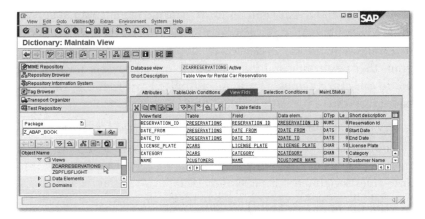

Figure 10.3 Fields of a View

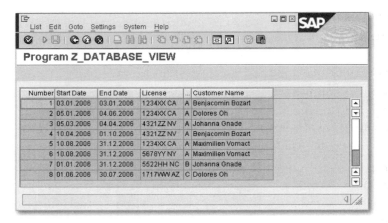

Figure 10.4 Output of a View

Accordingly, if we speak about database tables in the following sections that cover Open SQL statements for read accesses, views will also be meant.

10.1.2 Open SQL

Open SQL is a subset of standard SQL that is fully implemented by ABAP statements. Open SQL comprises the DML part of the standard, and thus allows data to be read (SELECT) and changed (INSERT, UPDATE, MODIFY, DELETE). However, Open SQL also goes beyond the standard by offering variants of the statements that only work in ABAP programs and can simplify or accelerate database accesses.

If you access the database in an ABAP program with Open SQL, you must always monitor the program's performance. It is primarily determined by the database accesses. In a worst-case scenario, a program that performs database accesses in an acceptable time in test mode can cause a system to stand still in live operation, if the database accesses are not programmed properly.

Performance

In the following description of Open SQL, we will indicate how you can obtain a high level of efficiency using the Open SQL statements. In doing so, we will essentially adhere to the following five performance rules for efficient database accesses:

1. **Keep the number of hits low.**
   The amount of selected data burdens the memory of the database system and the network connection between the database and the application server.

2. **Keep the amount of data transferred low.**
   The amount of transported data strains the network connection between the database and the application server.

3. **Keep the number of database accesses low.**
   Each individual database access puts additional workload on the network connection and the database system, because the corresponding administration must be provided on the latter.

4. **Keep the required search effort low.**
   Selection conditions should be formulated in such a way that they only place a minimal workload on the database system and produce a result in the shortest possible time.

5. **Keep the database load generally low.**
   Since there is generally only one database system available for many different application programs, you should always minimize the database workload as much as possible.

The rule that will ensure the best performance usually depends on the data to be processed and the evaluation you want. You must decide on a case-by-case basis what rule is applicable for your application and what rules are less suitable. For more advanced tests to determine which rule would be most beneficial, there are corresponding tools available, such as the runtime analysis (see Section 13.5). However, for specific tests, you can also use the statement GET RUN TIME FIELD. For more information on optimizing database accesses, we recommend the *SAP Performance Optimization Guide* by Thomas Schneider (4th Edition, SAP PRESS 2005).

Reading Data from Database Tables

The Open SQL statement for importing data from database tables into data objects of an ABAP program is SELECT. The functions of SELECT range from simply reading individual rows to programming very complex database queries. The basic form of the SELECT statement is as follows:

SELECT

```
SELECT result
       FROM source
       INTO target
       WHERE cond.
```

The SELECT statement is composed of several so-called *clauses*. Each clause fulfills a different task when the database is accessed. In order to deal efficiently with the SELECT statement, you must understand the function and interplay of the individual clauses:

Clauses

1. The SELECT clause result determines the result set, that is, what columns are read and whether the data of one or several rows is read.

2. The FROM clause source determines the database tables or views from which the data is read.

3. The INTO clause target determines the data objects of the ABAP program into which the data is read.

4. The WHERE clause cond specifies the conditions under which the data is read.

In addition to these four basic clauses, the SELECT statement can contain three additional clauses for special requirements when data is read:

1. A GROUP BY clause to aggregate several rows when importing into one row

2. A HAVING clause to specify conditions for aggregated rows

3. An ORDER BY clause to sort the rows of the result set

All clauses depend on each other. The interaction between all clauses is always important for the syntactically correct formulation of a SELECT statement. If you fully utilize all of the functions of the SELECT statement, it becomes a very powerful statement that enables you to run complex database queries with a single access. A useful tool for determining what the database actually does when you execute an Open SQL statement is SQL Trace (Transaction ST05).

SQL Trace

All clauses have static forms for which the tokens are specified directly, and dynamic forms for which the tokens are specified dynamically as the content of character-like data objects. We will discuss the dynamic forms in Section 11.3.2.

Dynamic SQL

Like every Open SQL statement, the SELECT statement provides the two system fields sy-subrc and sy-dbcnt with return values. Each successful database access sets sy-subrc to the value 0 and sy-dbcnt to the number of selected table rows.

sy-dbcnt

We will begin our description of the clauses of the SELECT statement with access to a single database table. The simplest form of the FROM clause is used for this:

Access to a single
database table

```
SELECT ...
       FROM dbtab [UP TO n ROWS]
       ...
```

FROM clause

For dbtab, you can specify the name of a database table such as spfli, sflight, or the name of a view. Optionally, you can limit the number of rows to be imported using the addition UP TO n ROWS to the number you specify. With this simple form of the FROM clause, we will explore the various combinations that are possible between the SELECT clause and the INTO clause, and the most important forms of the WHERE clause, before we look at accessing multiple database tables. We will begin with the SELECT clause.

The SELECT clause determines the result set, that is, whether one or several rows are read and what columns are read.

SELECT clause

If the SELECT clause is introduced with the word SINGLE, the result set will always have one row:

```
SELECT SINGLE ...
```

SELECT SINGLE

The condition of the WHERE clause should uniquely specify the row you want using conditions for all columns of the table key, because only then is the primary table index used for the access. Otherwise, the system will search linearly for the first suitable entry.

If SINGLE has not been specified, the result set is automatically regarded as having multiple rows, even if it contains only one row. This has a corresponding impact on the INTO clause. If duplicate rows appear in the selection because of a non-unique WHERE clause, a DISTINCT addition can be specified in the SELECT clause to eliminate this duplication.

To import all columns of a database table, use:

`SELECT [SINGLE] * ...`

For a matching INTO clause, we recommend that you specify either the addition CORRESPONDING FIELDS or a data object that is typed with reference to the database table specified in the FROM clause. Otherwise, it is not possible to access the individual components. Listing 10.1 shows an example of how all columns of a row are read into an appropriate work area.

Listing 10.1 Reading All Columns of a Row into a Structure

```
REPORT z_select_single_all_columns.

PARAMETERS: p_carrid TYPE spfli-carrid,
            p_connid TYPE spfli-connid.

CLASS demo DEFINITION.
  PUBLIC SECTION.
    CLASS-METHODS main
      IMPORTING i_carrid TYPE spfli-carrid
                i_connid TYPE spfli-connid.
ENDCLASS.
CLASS demo IMPLEMENTATION.
  METHOD main.
    DATA: spfli_wa TYPE spfli,
          msg      TYPE string.
    SELECT SINGLE *
           FROM spfli
           INTO spfli_wa
           WHERE carrid = i_carrid AND
                 connid = i_connid.
```

```
      msg = sy-subrc.
      CONCATENATE `sy-subrc: ` msg INTO msg.
      MESSAGE msg TYPE 'I'.
    ENDMETHOD.
  ENDCLASS.

START-OF-SELECTION.
  demo=>main( i_carrid = p_carrid
              i_connid = p_connid ).
```

Because of the second performance rule, only the data that is actually required should be read. If you don't need all columns, specify in the SELECT clause a list of the columns that you want to import:

```
SELECT [SINGLE] col1 [AS a1] col2 [AS a2] ...
```

SELECT
col1 col2 ...

You can use the AS addition to set an alternative column name for each column, under which the column can then be addressed in other additions (CORRESPONDING FIELDS OF and ORDER BY). The use of alternative column names is particularly interesting with the so-called *aggregate expressions*. Instead of specifying a column directly as col, an aggregate function can also be listed:

```
SELECT [SINGLE] ... aggregate( col ) [AS a1] ...
```

SELECT aggregate

Aggregate functions are MAX, MIN, AVG, SUM, and COUNT. These functions already calculate a single result in the database from the column contents and only return this result. If the SELECT clause also contains normal column specifications, in addition to aggregate expressions, these must be listed in the GROUP BY clause to form groups for which the result is determined (see Section 10.11).

When you specify individual columns, the INTO clause must, of course, also fit the result set. We will discuss this now.

The INTO clause determines the ABAP data objects into which the result set is written. The INTO clause must fit the result set. If the result set has one row because of the addition SINGLE, the data objects specified in the INTO clause can then also only have one row, that is, they cannot be internal tables:

INTO clause

```
SELECT SINGLE ...
       FROM dbtab
       INTO [CORRESPONDING FIELDS OF] wa ...
```

INTO wa

A suitable structure is usually specified for `wa` (see Listing 10.1). If the result set without the addition `SINGLE` has multiple rows, the data object to be specified after `INTO` is of course an internal table:

INTO TABLE

```
SELECT ...
       FROM dbtab
       INTO [CORRESPONDING FIELDS OF] TABLE itab ...
```

The result set is copied to the internal table and replaces the previous content. If the result set is to be appended to an internal table that is already filled, instead of `INTO TABLE`, you can use the following form of the `INTO` clause:

APPENDING
TABLE

```
SELECT ...
       FROM dbtab
       APPENDING [CORRESPONDING FIELDS OF] TABLE itab ...
```

If you need the imported data several times in a program, importing the data table only once into an internal table is how best to avoid the duplicate reading of data. In this way, you can also ensure that the imported data remains consistent throughout the program runtime. Listing 10.2 shows an example for reading multiple rows into an internal table.

Listing 10.2 Reading All Columns of Multiple Rows into an Internal Table

```
REPORT z_select_table_all_columns.

...

CLASS demo IMPLEMENTATION.
  METHOD main.
    DATA: spfli_tab TYPE TABLE OF spfli,
          msg        TYPE string.
    SELECT *
           FROM spfli
           INTO TABLE spfli_tab
           WHERE carrid = i_carrid.
    msg = sy-dbcnt.
    CONCATENATE `sy-dbcnt: ` msg INTO msg.
    MESSAGE msg TYPE 'I'.
  ENDMETHOD.
ENDCLASS.

...
```

The table category of a table specified in the `INTO` clause is arbitrary. During import, a sorted table is sorted according to its key. However, you must be careful with internal tables with a unique key! The SELECT statement would cause an exception if duplicate entries appeared during the import.

Besides specifying an internal table for result sets containing multiple rows (i. e., without SINGLE), ABAP also offers a variant for specifying single-row data objects as their target area—the SELECT loop:

```
SELECT ...
       FROM dbtab
       INTO [CORRESPONDING FIELDS OF] wa ...
    ...
ENDSELECT.
```

SELECT—
ENDSELECT

Each row in the result set triggers exactly one loop pass. During the loop pass, the data of this row is available in the target area. Listing 10.3 shows the conversion of Listing 10.2 to a SELECT loop.

Listing 10.3 Reading All Columns of Multiple Rows in a Loop

```
REPORT z_select_endselect_all_columns.

...

CLASS demo IMPLEMENTATION.
  METHOD main.
    DATA: spfli_wa TYPE spfli,
          msg      TYPE string,
          cnt      TYPE string.
    msg = `sy-dbcnt: `.
    SELECT *
           FROM spfli
           INTO spfli_wa
           WHERE carrid = i_carrid.
      cnt = sy-dbcnt.
      CONCATENATE msg ` ` cnt INTO msg.
    ENDSELECT.
    MESSAGE msg TYPE 'I'.
  ENDMETHOD.
ENDCLASS.

...
```

When we look at the SELECT loop, the question of the third performance rule arises. According to this rule, frequent database accesses must in principle be avoided. Does a SELECT loop not mean a database access for each row read? This is not the case. Against the data-

Performance of SELECT loops

base interface, a SELECT loop like any other SELECT statement only represents a single access, for which a database cursor is implicitly opened. However, under no circumstances should you nest SELECT loops, unless only very few rows are read in the external loop.

Importing multiple rows into an internal table does not provide you with better performance than using a SELECT loop per se. However, if the SELECT loop is used to fill an internal table row by row, direct importing into the internal table is generally preferable. You use SELECT loops if you want to format the result set during the import, and if this operation occurs only once.

If you specify an internal table as the target area, you can also process the imported data in a SELECT loop by using the addition PACKAGE SIZE in the INTO clause:

PACKAGE SIZE
```
SELECT ...
       FROM dbtab
       INTO TABLE itab PACKAGE SIZE n ...
   ...
ENDSELECT.
```

This addition means that the internal table is supplied in packages of n rows. Only the package that is currently being read is available in the loop. This allows program terminations to be avoided if the data set to be imported is too large for the memory capacity of an internal table.

Now let's consider the effect of the column specifications in the SELECT clause on the INTO clause. Until this point, we have supplied the INTO clause via the column specification * with all the columns of a row and structured the results area accordingly by reference to the database table.

CORRESPOND-
ING FIELDS
You can use the CORRESPONDING FIELDS OF addition to ensure, in all variants shown so far, that only the content of columns for which there are components of the same name in the structure of the target area is read from the result set. This addition is possible with the same effect, in particular, also when you specify individual columns in the SELECT clause. Here, any alternative column names are considered, which allows aggregate expressions and multiple columns (if more than one database table has been specified) to be assigned to the components of the target area. Listing 10.4 shows an example for

reading particular columns into the components of a structure with the same name.

Listing 10.4 Reading Particular Columns of a Row into a Structure

```
REPORT z_select_single_some_columns_1.

...

CLASS demo IMPLEMENTATION.
  METHOD main.
    DATA: BEGIN OF spfli_wa,
            cityfrom TYPE spfli-cityfrom,
            cityto   TYPE spfli-cityto,
          END OF spfli_wa,
          msg TYPE string.
    SELECT SINGLE cityfrom cityto
           FROM spfli
           INTO CORRESPONDING FIELDS OF spfli_wa
           WHERE carrid = i_carrid AND
                 connid = i_connid.
    CONCATENATE `From ` spfli_wa-cityfrom ` to `
                       spfli_wa-cityto INTO msg.
    MESSAGE msg TYPE 'I'.
  ENDMETHOD.
ENDCLASS.

...
```

As a target area for individual columns, the INTO clause has a variant besides the addition CORRESPONDING FIELDS OF, that can only be specified when individual columns or aggregate expressions are specified:

```
SELECT [SINGLE] ... col ... aggregate( col ) ...        INTO (dobj1,
       FROM dbtab                                        dobj2, ...)
       INTO (dobj1,dobj2,...) ...
  [...
ENDSELECT.]
```

This is a list of elementary data objects dobj1, dobj2, ... in parentheses and separated by commas. You must specify just as many data objects dobj as the result set contains columns. The content of the columns is assigned to the data objects according to the sequence specified in the SELECT clause from left to right. If the result set has multiple rows (i. e., there is no addition SINGLE), this will open a loop that must be completed with ENDSELECT. Listing 10.5 shows an example for reading two columns of a row.

Listing 10.5 Reading Particular Columns of a Row in Elementary Fields

```
REPORT z_select_single_some_columns_2.

...

CLASS demo IMPLEMENTATION.
  METHOD main.
    DATA: cityfrom TYPE spfli-cityfrom,
          cityto   TYPE spfli-cityto,
          msg      TYPE string.
    SELECT SINGLE cityfrom cityto
           FROM spfli
           INTO (cityfrom,cityto)
           WHERE carrid = i_carrid AND
                 connid = i_connid.
    CONCATENATE `From ` cityfrom ` to ` cityto INTO msg.
    MESSAGE msg TYPE 'I'.
  ENDMETHOD.
ENDCLASS.

...
```

Especially when you are reading a single row, you will find that specifying a list of elementary data objects is more efficient than using CORRESPONDING FIELDS OF, because no name comparison must be made. However, for internal tables, there is no equivalent for this list in the INTO clause; instead, you must use the addition CORRESPONDING FIELDS OF. We recommend that you construct the internal table only from the required components in order to avoid any unnecessary memory requirement.

Assignment rules For the combinations described here between the SELECT clause and the INTO clause, you should observe the following rules:

▶ When importing all columns (*) without the addition CORRESPONDING FIELDS OF, the target area should be declared with reference to the structure of the database table. If the result set contains strings, this rule is mandatory.

▶ When assigning individual columns or aggregate expressions to individual components through CORRESPONDING FIELDS OF or to a list of elementary data objects, the data types must fit each other in pairs. Conversions are possible to a certain extent, but we recommend that you specify compatible data objects.

When you follow these basic rules, the SELECT statement will work as expected, without any unwanted surprises. For additional—generally not recommended—combinations between the SELECT clause and the INTO clause, and for the precise assignment rules, please refer to *The Official ABAP Reference* book (2nd Edition, SAP PRESS 2004).

As the last of the basic clauses of a SELECT statement, we will now turn our attention to the WHERE clause. The WHERE clause uses conditions to limit the number of rows that are included in the selection from the database, and it is therefore the most important method for fulfilling the first performance rule:

WHERE clause

```
SELECT ...
      FROM dbtab
      INTO ...
      WHERE cond ...
```

WHERE cond

The condition cond is specified by logical expressions, which can be combined with AND and OR and negated with NOT. These logical expressions are similar, but not identical to the logical expressions introduced in Section 5.2.5 for the control structures of the remaining ABAP. This is because within Open SQL, syntax and semantics follow the SQL standard. For example, the placeholder for any character strings in SQL is a percent symbol (%), but otherwise in ABAP, it is an asterisk (*).

The result of a condition can be true, false, or unknown. A row is placed in the result set if the condition is true. A condition is unknown if one of the columns involved contains the null value. To specifically query the null value, you have the special condition IS NULL, which is true if the column contains the null value.[1]

---

1 A null value is an initial value of an empty column. This value can be processed using Native SQL statements, but there are no corresponding statements in ABAP. ABAP does know type-related initial values, but no specific null value. The changing Open SQL statements such as INSERT, UPDATE, or MODIFY usually don't generate any null values in databases, except when a view is addressed instead of a database and that view doesn't contain all columns of the database. However, some database systems represent empty strings as null values. In addition, null values can be created in databases if a table that already contains data is complemented with additional columns in the ABAP Dictionary. During reading, null values can be created in the selection by using aggregate functions of the SELECT clause and by using the FROM clause with a left outer join. During a transfer of values to the ABAP program using the INTO clause, null values are always converted into the type-related initial values.

Comparison   As for the normal logical expressions, the simplest conditions are formed by comparisons with operators =, <, >, <>, <=, >=, such as :

```
... WHERE carrid = 'UA' ...
```

The left operand must always be a column of a database table from the FROM clause; the right operand can be a suitable data object of the ABAP program or a column of a database table of the FROM clause. A column of a database table on the right-hand side must be specified in the form dbtab~col, where ~ is the so-called *column selector*.

Predicates: As for normal logical expressions, in the WHERE condition, it is also
WHERE BETWEEN,   possible to specify the following predicates:
WHERE IN seltab

```
... col [NOT] BETWEEN dobj1 AND dobj2 ...
```

```
... col [NOT] IN seltab ...
```

These expressions have the same meaning here as they do in normal logical expressions; in particular, they allow the evaluation of a selection table directly in the SELECT statement.[2] See also the example in Section 9.2.3.

Further predicates include:

```
... col [NOT] IN (dobj1, dobj2 ...) ...
```

WHERE LIKE   `... col [NOT] LIKE dobj ...`

Here, the IN operator allows comparison with a value list, while LIKE is the SQL equivalent to the character string operator CP (see Section 5.4.5). In the dobj pattern of LIKE, "%" symbols represent an arbitrary including an empty character string and "_" an arbitrary single character.

Optimizing   The conditions of the WHERE clauses directly determine the search
the search   workload that the database must endure in order to find the selected row, and which must be minimized for the fourth performance rule. The correct formulation of the WHERE condition can be the critical factor in a SELECT statement. The execution times of a well formulated and a poorly formulated WHERE condition may differ considerably for the same result set.

---

2 This explains the name "selection table" as well.

Since the rows of a database table are not stored in sorted form, the time involved in searching for a particular row will, on average, increase linearly with the number of rows in the database table. To reduce this time allotted for searching for a particular row in a table, each database table has at least one index, consisting of selected columns of the database table and which is stored in sorted form as a copy in the database system. On a sorted index, it is possible to perform a selective search (i. e., a search for which only parts of the index are searched and whose average time taken increases no more than logarithmically with the number of rows).

Index

In the database of an AS ABAP, the primary key fields of a database table always form a unique *primary index*. Furthermore, in the ABAP Dictionary, you can use the **Indices ...** function to create *secondary indices*.[3] The database tries during database accesses to access the optimal index for the search.[4] Note, however, that with change accesses the secondary index must also be adjusted so that these are more suited for tables for which read accesses are more common than change accesses. You should also avoid creating more than approximately five indices per database table, and these indices should not contain too many common columns, so that the system can find the correct index easier. If a secondary index is not unique, it should be as selective as possible. An index entry should generally refer to less than 5 % of the rows.

Primary index, secondary index

You can therefore minimize the search load on the database by formulating the conditions for the WHERE clause appropriately for one of the indices of the database table, so that only these indices are searched and not the entire table. If you must select by columns that are not yet contained in any index, and the response times are very poor, we recommend that you create an appropriate index. To guarantee an optimal interplay between the WHERE clause and index, you should note the following tips:

Hints on WHERE

▶ In the WHERE clause, if possible, you should enter logical comparisons for all fields of the index with the equals operator (=), which are linked with AND.

---

3 This also holds true for database tables provided by SAP. Only the index must be located within the customer namespace.
4 You can use the SQL Trace tool (Transaction ST05) to determine which index is used.

▸ In the WHERE clause, you should only use positive operators for the index fields such as = instead of <> and you should also avoid the language element NOT, because these are not supported by indices.

▸ If you only specify part of an index in the WHERE clause, the sequence of the index fields plays an important role. An index field in a WHERE clause generally only results in an evaluation of the index if all fields that appear before it in the index definition are fully specified in the WHERE condition.[5]

▸ In selecting and applying an index, the system generally does not utilize any operands linked with OR, unless the operator OR appears in the logical condition at the highest level. So you should use, for example:

```
... WHERE (CARRID = 'LH' AND CITYFROM = 'FRANKFURT') OR
          (CARRID = 'LH' AND CITYFROM = 'NEW YORK').
```

instead of:

```
... WHERE carrid = 'LH' AND
          (cityfrom = 'FRANKFURT' OR cityfrom = 'NEW YORK').
```

▸ Do not query any index column with the condition IS NULL, because some databases don't support these conditions for indices.

You can also boost efficiency if all columns of a SELECT clause are part of an index, because then only the index must be read.

Selection tables and performance

The use of selection tables in the WHERE clause is a very direct way of sending complex delimitations to the database. However, the unrestricted use of this function contradicts the rules for efficient WHERE conditions to a certain extent, because particularly when you enter interval selections in a selection screen, complicated conditions can arise that are not supported by indices. You must therefore compare the ease of using selection tables with any loss of performance on a case-by-case basis. The NO INTERVALS and NO-EXTENSION additions of the SELECT-OPTIONS statement allow you to restrict the freedom of a selection screen user to prevent inefficient selections as far as possible.

---

5 You can compare the evaluation of an index to doing a search in a telephone directory. If you search for an entry for which you know the first name and the street but not the last name, the sort order of the telephone directory by last names will be of no help to you. Consequently, you will have to search all the entries, starting with the first entry of the telephone directory.

Now that we have shown you the basics of the `SELECT` statement using access to a single database table, we will look at accessing multiple database tables.

Access to multiple database tables

A frequent application scenario here is to amalgamate data from different mutually-dependent database tables into one target area. While this task could be accomplished by lots of individual accesses to all of the relevant databases, this would contradict the third performance rule. The number of database accesses often increases in leaps and bounds, especially if, for each imported row in a table, you need additional data from one or several other tables. We will now use the example of database tables SFLIGHT and SPFLI linked through a foreign key dependency to show you the options that Open SQL offers you for accessing both tables, in order to read the flight data from SFLIGHT for a particular departure location from SPFLI.

For demonstration purposes, we will begin in Listing 10.6 with what is absolutely the least favorable solution, namely a nested `SELECT` loop. After that, we will discuss the more efficient options.

SELECT loop

Listing 10.6 Nested SELECT Loops

```
REPORT z_select_nested.

PARAMETERS p_cityfr TYPE spfli-cityfrom DEFAULT 'Frankfurt'.
CLASS demo DEFINITION.
  PUBLIC SECTION.
    CLASS-METHODS main
      IMPORTING i_cityfrom TYPE spfli-cityfrom.
  PRIVATE SECTION.
    TYPES: BEGIN OF flight,
             carrid TYPE spfli-carrid,
             connid TYPE spfli-connid,
             cityto TYPE spfli-cityto,
             fldate TYPE sflight-fldate,
           END OF flight.
    CLASS-DATA flight_tab TYPE TABLE OF flight.
  CLASS-METHODS display.
ENDCLASS.

CLASS demo IMPLEMENTATION.
  METHOD main.
    DATA: flight_wa TYPE flight,
          t0        TYPE i,
          rt        TYPE i,
```

```
        msg          TYPE string.
GET RUN TIME FIELD t0.
SELECT carrid connid cityto
        FROM spfli
        INTO CORRESPONDING FIELDS OF flight_wa
        WHERE cityfrom = i_cityfrom.
    SELECT fldate
        FROM sflight
        INTO CORRESPONDING FIELDS OF flight_wa
        WHERE carrid = flight_wa-carrid AND
              connid = flight_wa-connid.
    APPEND flight_wa TO flight_tab.
    ENDSELECT.
ENDSELECT.
GET RUN TIME FIELD rt.
rt = rt - t0.
msg = rt.
CONCATENATE `Runtime: ` msg INTO msg.
MESSAGE msg TYPE 'I'.
display( ).
ENDMETHOD.
METHOD display.
...
ENDMETHOD.
ENDCLASS.
START-OF-SELECTION.
demo=>main( i_cityfrom = p_cityfr ).
```

The nested SELECT statements read three columns from the rows of Table SPFLI, which match the WHERE condition, and for each of these three columns they read one column from Table SFLIGHT. There is therefore a database access to SPFLI and for each row that is then read, there is an additional database access on SFLIGHT. To combine the data that is read in an internal table, here each work area read must be individually attached to the internal table.

GET RUN TIME   The GET RUN TIME statement measures the time required in order to give you a sense for the performance of such a program. This statement determines the runtime of the program since the program start, in units of microseconds. To obtain a reliable result that avoids individual load-dependent fluctuations, we would actually have to perform the measurement several times in a loop and add up the number of times.

To avoid the multiple database access, Open SQL provides two options for combining the data from several database tables with a single database access: You can either define a corresponding static database view in the ABAP Dictionary and access it, or join several database tables in the FROM clause using a join.

We have already introduced views in Section 10.1.1. For the following example, in Package Z_ABAP_BOOK we create an additional view ZSPFLISFLIGHT, in which the columns CARRID and CONNID of the two tables SPFLI and SFLIGHT are linked together, and which contains all of the columns of both tables. **View**

Listing 10.7 SELECT on View

```
REPORT z_select_view.

...

CLASS demo IMPLEMENTATION.
  METHOD main.
    ...
    SELECT carrid connid cityto fldate
           FROM zspflisflight
           INTO CORRESPONDING FIELDS OF TABLE flight_tab
           WHERE cityfrom = i_cityfrom.
    ...
  ENDMETHOD.
  ...
ENDCLASS.

...
```

The SELECT statement in Listing 10.7 replaces the nested SELECT loops from Listing 10.6. It reads exactly the same data, but its performance is better. It is useful to define a view in the ABAP Dictionary if, in different programs, you always need to have the same links between the rows of different database tables.

However, the SELECT syntax also allows you to link several database tables in a statement by defining a join in the FROM clause: **Join**

```
SELECT ...
       dbtab_left [INNER] JOIN dbtab_right ON cond ...
```

A join in a FROM clause corresponds to the local program implementation of a globally-defined view in the ABAP Dictionary. In the basic form of a join expression shown here, two database tables are linked together using the conditions specified after ON. An ON condition can consist of one or several comparisons that must be linked with AND. Listing 10.8 shows an example of this.

Listing 10.8 SELECT with Inner Join

```
REPORT z_select_inner_join.

...

CLASS demo IMPLEMENTATION.
  METHOD main.
    ...
    SELECT p~carrid p~connid p~cityto f~fldate
           FROM spfli AS p
                INNER JOIN sflight AS f
                ON p~carrid = f~carrid AND
                   p~connid = f~connid
           INTO CORRESPONDING FIELDS OF TABLE flight_tab
           WHERE p~cityfrom = i_cityfrom.
    ...
  ENDMETHOD.
  ...
ENDCLASS.

...
```

Listing 10.8 again reads the same data as Listings 10.6 and 10.7 and performs just as well as Listing 10.7. You can see that you must use the column selectors ~ mentioned earlier to set the columns; otherwise, the database table to which the column belongs would be undefined.

To save space, we have defined *alternative table names* for each database table after AS,[6] which then should be used instead of the complete table name in the SELECT statement.

Linking joins   The left-hand part of a join expression can itself be a join expression, which means that more than two database tables (or views) can be joined together. Currently, a maximum of 25 database tables or views can be linked together. To structure the program better, the involved join expressions can also be enclosed by parentheses.

---

6 This should not be confused with the alternative column names of the SELECT clause that are also defined after an AS addition.

In the inner join shown previously, the columns of each row on the left are joined with the columns of all the rows on the right that meet the ON condition. Consequently, the number of resulting rows in the selection depends on the right-hand side, while the content on the left is duplicated in each additional row. If no row meets the ON condition, no row on the left-hand side will be selected.

INNER JOIN

In addition to the inner join, there are also left outer joins, which are specified using LEFT OUTER JOIN. With the left outer join, the columns of each row on the right-hand side that does not meet the ON condition are filled with null values and linked with the columns of the left-hand side. When the conditions of the WHERE clause have been met, each row on the left-hand side of the left outer join produces at least one row in the selection, irrespective of the ON condition.

LEFT OUTER JOIN

In addition to combining data from several database tables, there is another application scenario, which is also very common, whereby you want to import data from a table that depends on the content of other tables, without needing the data from the other table in your program. If you want to evaluate the table on which the data to be imported depends several times, you can import the relevant data into an internal table and evaluate it. To do this, Open SQL provides the language element FOR ALL ENTRIES with which, in a SELECT statement, you can include data that has already been imported from another table. You can insert this language element before the word WHERE into the WHERE clause:

```
... FOR ALL ENTRIES IN itab WHERE ... col op itab-comp ...
```

FOR ALL ENTRIES

The condition uses one of the usual relational operators op to compare the value of a column col with the value of a component comp of an internal table itab. The condition is evaluated for each individual line of the internal table itab and the result set, minus any duplicate rows, is compiled from the single-row results. If the internal table itab is empty, all rows from the database are placed into the result set. Listing 10.9 shows the conversion of the previous examples for cases where the column CITYTO from SPFLI is not required in the result set. The system reads data from SFLIGHT only, but that depends on SPFLI.

Listing 10.9 SELECT with FOR ALL ENTRIES

```
REPORT z_select_for_all_entries.

...

CLASS demo DEFINITION.
  ...
  PRIVATE SECTION.
    TYPES: BEGIN OF flight,
             carrid TYPE spfli-carrid,
             connid TYPE spfli-connid,
             fldate TYPE sflight-fldate,
           END OF flight.
    ...
ENDCLASS.
CLASS demo IMPLEMENTATION.
  METHOD main.
    DATA: cond_tab TYPE TABLE OF flight,
    ...
    SELECT carrid connid
           FROM spfli
           INTO CORRESPONDING FIELDS OF TABLE cond_tab
           WHERE cityfrom = i_cityfrom.
    SELECT carrid connid fldate
           FROM sflight
           INTO CORRESPONDING FIELDS OF TABLE flight_tab
           FOR ALL ENTRIES IN cond_tab
           WHERE carrid = cond_tab-carrid AND
                 connid = cond_tab-connid.
    ...
  ENDMETHOD.
  ...
ENDCLASS.

...
```

The data on which the final result depends is read in Listing 10.9 in the first SELECT statement into a condition table cond_tab.[7] The result set of the second SELECT statement contains the same rows as in the previous examples without the column CITYTO. Since there are only two database accesses, this type of programming is obviously more efficient than a SELECT inside a loop over the condition table, which would also achieve the same objective. However, here

---

7 We also could have used flight_tab instead of cond_tab; however, we couldn't have reused flight_tab after the second SELECT.

you can usually also improve the performance if you again, access both tables at the same time, with a single SELECT statement.

To read the data from one or several database tables with a single database access depending on the data of another database table, you can use *subqueries*. A subquery is a SELECT statement in parentheses without an INTO clause that you can evaluate using the special operators EXISTS, IN, or using relational operators in the WHERE clause. The WHERE clause of a subquery can contain a subquery and subqueries can be nested a maximum of nine times. Listing 10.10 shows Listing 10.9 converted to a SELECT statement with a subquery.

Subquery

Listing 10.10 SELECT with subquery

```
REPORT z_select_subquery.

...

CLASS demo IMPLEMENTATION.
  METHOD main.
    ...
    SELECT carrid connid fldate
          FROM sflight AS f
          INTO CORRESPONDING FIELDS OF TABLE flight_tab
          WHERE EXISTS
                ( SELECT carrid
                      FROM spfli
                      WHERE carrid  = f~carrid AND
                            connid  = f~connid AND
                            cityfrom = i_cityfrom ).
    ...
  ENDMETHOD.
  ...
ENDCLASS.
...
```

The result set from Listing 10.10 corresponds to the result set in Listing 10.9; however, it is obtained through a single database access. The example shows the simplest query of a subquery using the EXISTS operator. The condition is true if the selection of the subquery contains at least one row. If the subquery, as shown here, contains columns in the SELECT statement above it, we refer to it as a *correlated subquery*.

If the selection of a subquery contains only one column, its values can be queried using the IN operator. The condition is true if the

ALL, ANY, SOME

value of the column that is checked is contained in the subquery's result set. Furthermore, single-column subqueries may also appear as operands in logical relational expressions. If the selection of the subquery has multiple rows, one of the additions ALL, ANY, or SOME must be included before the subquery. With the prefix ALL before the subquery, the condition is true if the comparison is true for all rows of the scalar subquery; otherwise, the condition is true if the comparison is true for at least one row in the selection of the subquery.

Grouping rows and aggregating columns

An application scenario that frequently occurs is that you only need several rows from one or several database tables to derive aggregated information, such as the total for a column or the number of rows. If you import the rows into the ABAP program and evaluate them there, you copy too much data, contradicting the second performance rule. Instead, you can use the aggregate functions of the SELECT clause mentioned above in conjunction with the GROUP BY clause and the HAVING clause, to copy only the results you want:

GROUP BY clause

```
SELECT ... col ... aggregate( col ) ...
       ...
       GROUP BY col1 col2 ...
       HAVING cond ...
```

The GROUP BY clause causes all rows that have the same content in the directly specified columns to be aggregated in one row. The aggregate function is calculated for such a group, and the result is placed in the corresponding column of the aggregated row. The aggregate functions of a SELECT clause and the GROUP BY clause influence each other as follows:

► If a GROUP BY clause is specified, individual columns must be specified in the SELECT clause, and a single value must be calculated using aggregate functions from the values of all of the columns that are not listed in the GROUP BY clause.

► If the SELECT clause contains both aggregate functions and normal column specifications, the latter must be listed in a GROUP BY clause.

HAVING clause

To restrict the rows grouped with the GROUP BY clause using conditions, instead of the WHERE clause, you must use the HAVING clause. This can also only be listed in conjunction with the GROUP BY clause.

The possible conditions of a HAVING clause are the same as those of the WHERE clause; however, you can only specify those columns directly that are also listed in the GROUP BY clause. For all other columns of the database tables listed in the FROM clause, however, you can set aggregate expressions in the HAVING clause. To specify normal conditions on columns not listed in the GROUP BY clause, you additionally use the WHERE clause.

Listing 10.11 SELECT with GROUP BY and HAVING

```
REPORT z_select_group_by.

CLASS demo DEFINITION.
  PUBLIC SECTION.
    CLASS-METHODS main.
  PRIVATE SECTION.
    TYPES: BEGIN OF flight,
             carrid  TYPE sflight-carrid,
             minimum TYPE sflight-price,
             maximum TYPE sflight-price,
             avg     TYPE f,
           END OF flight.
    CLASS-DATA flight_tab TYPE TABLE OF flight.
    CLASS-METHODS display.
ENDCLASS.

CLASS demo IMPLEMENTATION.
  METHOD main.
    SELECT carrid MIN( price ) AS minimum
                  MAX( price ) AS maximum
                  AVG( price ) AS avg
           FROM   sflight AS s
           INTO CORRESPONDING FIELDS OF TABLE flight_tab
           GROUP BY carrid
           HAVING carrid LIKE '%L%'
                  AND MIN( s~price ) <> MAX( s~price ).
    display( ).
  ENDMETHOD.
  METHOD display.
    ...
  ENDMETHOD.
ENDCLASS.

START-OF-SELECTION.
  demo=>main( ).
```

In the SELECT statement in Listing 10.11, all rows that have the same content in the carrid column are grouped in a row. The remaining columns of the result set are calculated as the minimum, the maximum, and the average of the flight price of the summarized rows. The HAVING clause demonstrates the specification of the carrid column from the GROUP BY clause and of another column in the form of aggregate expressions. Note also the definition of the alternative column names for the aggregate expressions in the SELECT clause. These are assigned in CORRESPONDING FIELDS OF to the corresponding components of the internal table.

Sorting rows of the result set
Finally, you can sort the rows of the result set of the SELECT statement using the ORDER BY clause, according to the content of its columns. Without the ORDER BY clause, the sorting of the result set is undefined and may also vary if the same SELECT statement is executed several times. The ORDER BY clause has two variants:

ORDER BY clause

```
SELECT ...

    ...
    ORDER BY {PRIMARY KEY}
           | {col [ASCENDING|DESCENDING] ...}
```

For the variant with PRIMARY KEY, in the SELECT clause all columns must be specified with an asterisk (*), and sorting is done in ascending order according to the primary key. In the second variant, the column specifications in the SELECT clause are arbitrary and you can sort according to particular columns. Here you can also sort according to the result of aggregate functions if an alternative column name is specified. ASCENDING and DESCENDING sorts in ascending and descending order.

However, keeping in mind the fifth performance rule (i. e., keeping the general database workload small), you should only use the ORDER BY clause if the database system uses the same index for sorting as for reading. Otherwise, it is more efficient to import into an internal table and then sort within the program.[8]

Explicit cursor handling
When a database table is read, a *database cursor* is opened that is always assigned to one row of the result set. With SELECT, this happens implicitly. With a SELECT loop, for example, the database cursor

---

8 You can use the SQL Trace tool (Transaction ST05) to determine which index is used for reading or sorting purposes.

is set to the current row for each loop pass. Furthermore, you can also read the result set of a selection through an *explicit cursor handling*.

With an explicit cursor handling, you can use so-called *cursor variables* to open cursors for selections and then read these using the cursor variable. Cursors in cursor variables can be understood as references. That means, cursors can be assigned or transferred between cursor variables and many different cursor variables can point to the same selections.

Cursor variable

Explicit cursor handling is always an option if the remaining options of the SELECT statement—such as joins, subqueries, or the FOR ALL ENTRIES addition—are insufficient for a particular task. Examples of this scenario include:

- Reading multiple database tables in parallel
- Reading a database table using different cursors in parallel
- Passing the database cursor to procedures
- Wanting the database cursor to remain open beyond the scope of a explicitly completed database LUW (see Section 10.1.3)

You may also be able to further reduce the number of database accesses using an explicit cursor handling, to support the third performance rule (i. e., keep the number of database accesses low). But, you should always bear in mind that the explicit cursor handling is not always straightforward and can at times be prone to errors, so that you need to decide for yourself, on a case-by-case basis, whether preference should be given to the performance or the robustness of a program.

You must perform the following steps for an explicit cursor handling:

1. Open a cursor for a selection.

   `OPEN CURSOR dbcur FOR SELECT ...`

   OPEN CURSOR

   This statement opens a database cursor for the selection defined after FOR. For the cursor variable dbcur, you must specify a variable declared with the special data type cursor. The selection is defined by a normal SELECT statement, which can contain all clauses except for the INTO clause. Furthermore, the selection must have multiple rows, so that the SELECT clause cannot contain the SINGLE addition.

2. Read the selection.

FETCH NEXT CURSOR dbcur INTO ...

Depending on the target area of the INTO clause, the statement reads one or several rows of the result set referenced by the database cursor in dbcur and moves the cursor to the next row to be read. All INTO clauses of the SELECT statement can be used. If at least one row has been read, sy-subrc is set to zero; otherwise, it is set to four. After FETCH, the system field sy-dbcnt contains the number of rows that have been read up to that point for the cursor. The FETCH statement is the only way of moving the cursor. Therefore, the program cannot place it onto particular rows of the selection.

3. Close the cursor.

CLOSE CURSOR dbcur.

This statement closes the cursor in dbcur and initializes the cursor variable. As a result, other cursor variables that have pointed to the same selection after an assignment also become invalid.

The explicit cursor handling separates the definition of the selection from that of the target area, which occur united in a normal SELECT statement. Listing 10.12 shows an example that should rather act as a deterrend, in which the nested SELECT loops from Listing 10.6 are mapped through an explicit handling of parallel cursors.

Listing 10.12 Explicit Cursor Handling

```
REPORT z_select_cursor.

...

CLASS demo IMPLEMENTATION.
  METHOD main.
    DATA: cursor1    TYPE cursor,
          cursor2    TYPE cursor,
          flight_wa1 TYPE flight,
          flight_wa2 TYPE flight,
          ...
    OPEN CURSOR cursor1 FOR
      SELECT carrid connid cityto
             FROM spfli
             WHERE cityfrom = i_cityfrom
```

```
            ORDER BY carrid connid.
    OPEN CURSOR cursor2 FOR
      SELECT carrid connid fldate
             FROM sflight
             ORDER BY carrid connid.
    DO.
      idx = sy-index.
      FETCH NEXT CURSOR cursor1
        INTO CORRESPONDING FIELDS OF flight_wa1.
      IF sy-subrc <> 0.
        CLOSE CURSOR cursor1.
        EXIT.
      ENDIF.
      IF flight_wa1-carrid = flight_wa2-carrid AND
         flight_wa1-connid = flight_wa2-connid.
         flight_wa2-cityto = flight_wa1-cityto.
        APPEND flight_wa2 TO flight_tab.
      ENDIF.
      DO.
        FETCH NEXT CURSOR cursor2
          INTO CORRESPONDING FIELDS OF flight_wa2.
        IF sy-subrc <> 0.
          CLOSE CURSOR cursor2.
          EXIT.
        ENDIF.
        IF flight_wa1-carrid = flight_wa2-carrid AND
           flight_wa1-connid = flight_wa2-connid.
           flight_wa2-cityto = flight_wa1-cityto.
          APPEND flight_wa2 TO flight_tab.
        ELSE.
          IF flight_wa1-carrid > flight_wa2-carrid OR
             ( flight_wa1-carrid = flight_wa2-carrid AND
               flight_wa1-connid > flight_wa2-connid ).
            CONTINUE.
          ELSE.
            EXIT.
          ENDIF.
        ENDIF.
      ENDDO.
    ENDDO.
    ...
  ENDMETHOD.
  ...
ENDCLASS.
...
```

Because when you read a row using the database cursor, you get no information other than the content of the row that is read, you must program the evaluation of the mutual dependency of the two selections yourself. Here, we take advantage of the fact that both tables have the same key fields, and sort the selection in the OPEN CURSOR statements accordingly. Both selections are then read in parallel in two nested DO loops and the data is combined. The selection of the inner loop is then searched for rows with the same key fields as the row that is read in the external loop. Since a database cursor cannot be reset, we must also evaluate the last row read of the inner DO loop prior to the entry into the loop.[9]

The result from Listing 10.12 is the same as in Listing 10.6. Prior to the introduction of joins in the SELECT statement, this procedure was also a quite a method to avoid nested SELECT statements. Today, however, explicit cursor handling in such scenarios is no longer required and can be limited to all those situations that cannot be addressed using the SELECT statement.

Changing Data in Database Tables

The Open SQL statements for changing data in database tables are INSERT, UPDATE, MODIFY and DELETE. This section briefly discusses how to program these statements, which are considerably less complex than the SELECT statement. Note, however, that Open SQL statements do not verify authorizations or ensure data consistency in the database. The basics of consistent data storage in an AS ABAP are introduced in Section 10.1.3. At this stage, it is only important to know that changes to table contents are only stored permanently in the database table when the next database commit is executed. Up until that point, the changes can be undone with a database rollback.

Inserting table rows: INSERT dbtab

You use the INSERT statement as shown below to insert individual rows into a database table:

```
INSERT INTO dbtab VALUES wa.
```

or

```
INSERT dbtab FROM wa.
```

---

9 What we do here can be compared to an explicit control level processing on the selections (see also Section 5.5.2).

These two statements are equivalent. Both insert the contents of the wa work area into the dbtab database table. The work area should have the same structure as the database table. The operation is only performed if the database table does not yet contain an entry with the same primary key or unique secondary key. Otherwise, sy-subrc is set to four, rather than zero.

To insert several rows at once, use:

```
INSERT dbtab FROM TABLE itab.
```

INSERT FROM TABLE

This statement tries to insert all lines from the itab internal table into dbtab. If a single line from the internal table cannot be inserted because the same primary key is already in the database table, an exception occurs. You can avoid the exception by using the addition ACCEPTING DUPLICATE KEYS. With this addition, the relevant line of the internal table is simply rejected, and sy-subrc is set to four. The number of rows that are actually inserted is indicated in sy-dbcnt. Listing 2.5 in Chapter 2 shows an example of the insertion of several rows.

In accordance with the third performance rule, you should, wherever possible, use block operations with internal tables, rather than maintaining several individual rows. This applies both to the INSERT statement and to all subsequent statements used to change database contents.

Block operations or single row access

You use the UPDATE statement to change the contents of existing rows. You can either modify specific columns, or overwrite the entire row with a work area. To change individual columns, use:

Changing table rows: UPDATE SET

```
UPDATE dbtab
      SET [col1 = f1 col2 = f2 ... ]
          [col1 = col1 + f1 col2 = col2 + f2 ...]
          [col1 = col1 - f1 col2 = col2 - f2 ...]
      WHERE ...
```

This statement changes the columns specified after SET in all rows of the dbtab database table that satisfy the conditions specified in the WHERE clause. The values in the columns can either be overwritten, or values can be added with + or subtracted with −. Columns in the same table can also be specified for these values. Without the WHERE clause, all rows in the table are changed. The sy-subrc and sy-dbcnt system fields are set as normal.

To replace an entire row, use:

```
UPDATE dbtab FROM wa.
```

To replace several rows, use:

```
UPDATE dbtab FROM TABLE itab.
```

The data type of `wa` or the line type of the `itab` internal table should be declared as usual with reference to the database table. The first statement replaces the row that has the same contents as `wa` in the primary key fields with the contents of `wa`, while the second statement does the same for all lines in the internal table. Both statements set `sy-subrc` to zero if all rows can be replaced. Otherwise, they set `sy-subrc` to four. Once again, you will find the number of rows that are actually inserted in `sy-dbcnt`. Note: If the internal table is empty, both system fields are 0.

Note that replacing entire rows often means that the rows must first be read with the `SELECT` statement. Check whether you can use the `WHERE` clause to avoid unnecessary multiple access (third performance rule). You can also reduce the volume of data transferred by changing only the relevant columns with the `SET` additions, instead of transporting the entire row (second performance rule).

If you don't know whether a row with the relevant primary key already exists before a database change, that is, whether you should insert or change a row, you can use the `MODIFY` statement. For individual rows, use:

```
MODIFY dbtab FROM wa.
```

For several rows, use:

```
MODIFY dbtab FROM TABLE itab.
```

These statements work the same way as `INSERT` if a row does not yet exist with the same contents in the primary key fields as in `wa` or in a line of the `itab` internal table. Otherwise, they work the same way as `UPDATE`. However, even with `MODIFY`, it may not be possible to process a row. For example, the database table may already contain a row with the same unique secondary index. `sy-subrc` and `sy-dbcnt` are always set accordingly.

You use the DELETE statement to delete table rows. You can either use a WHERE clause to select the lines to be deleted, or use work areas. In the first case, the syntax is as follows:

```
DELETE FROM dbtab WHERE ...
```

This statement deletes all rows in the dbtab database table that satisfy the conditions specified in the WHERE clause. Program the conditions very carefully to avoid inadvertently deleting the wrong rows. If you don't specify a WHERE clause, all rows are deleted.[10] An example of the deletion of all rows is provided in Listing 2.5 in Chapter 2.

To specify the rows to be deleted by work area, use the same syntax used in the previous change statements, specifically:

```
DELETE dbtab FROM wa.
```

for individual rows, or

```
DELETE dbtab FROM TABLE itab.
```

for several rows. These statements delete all rows with the same contents in the primary key fields as in wa or in a line of the itab table, and set sy-subrc and sy-dbcnt based on the result. In this case, the work area or the internal table only needs to contain the columns of the primary key.

As with the UPDATE statement, it may be more efficient to use the WHERE clause in order to avoid multiple access when using the DELETE statement.

10.1.3 Consistent Data Storage

Consistent data storage on an AS ABAP is a complex subject, one that we can merely sketch a brief outline for in this book. The basic concepts of consistent data storage are determined more by the architecture of the AS ABAP than by the ABAP programming language. Two concepts play an integral role: the *Logical Unit of Work* (LUW) concept, which regulates the chronological transition from one consistent status to another, and the lock concept, which prevents unwanted access to data during an LUW.

---

10 Specifying a dynamic WHERE condition could also be dangerous here. If it is empty, all rows will be deleted as well.

The SAP LUW Concept for the AS ABAP

The data in an AS ABAP application, which is distributed among various database tables, must normally exist in a consistent status. However, when an application program is executed, the data is often temporarily in an inconsistent status. In the case of a credit transfer, for example, this inconsistent status exists for the interval between the time at which the money is debited from one account and the time at which it is credited to another account. This corresponds, at a minimum, to the interval between two successive UPDATE statements. As a rule, however, the period of inconsistency is much longer, because other tasks must also be completed. Therefore, a consistent data status is not restored until the last relevant statement has been completed. If, however, an error occurs during this period of inconsistency, the database must on under no circumstances remain in this inconsistent status, and an option for restoring the initial status must be available.

LUW
The time that elapses between two consistent statuses, or rather the mechanism that operates during this time, is referred to as the LUW (*Logical Unit of Work*). An LUW always ends with a *commit*, whereby the changes made are committed to the database, or with a *rollback*, whereby all changes are undone. How does this work? In order to understand how LUWs work in the AS ABAP, we must first examine database LUWs in more detail.

Database LUW
A database LUW is the database mechanism responsible for maintaining consistent data statuses in the database, independently of the AS ABAP. The database system either executes a database LUW completely or not at all. Database changes within a database LUW are only written permanently to the database after a database commit. If an error occurs, the changes can be undone with a database rollback.

Commit and rollback
For that reason, the most important question that ABAP programmers must ask themselves is how these database commits and rollbacks are triggered. Of course, ABAP statements can be used for this purpose. But, to gain a better understanding of what is going on, we must first turn instead to the implicit commits and rollbacks that result from the software architecture of the AS ABAP.

Work process
As mentioned in Section 3.3.2, an AS ABAP has one or multiple application servers and these, in turn, have work processes. Every ABAP program that is currently active requires a work process, and

each work process is logged on to the database system as a user. A work process cannot execute more than one database LUW in parallel and, conversely, more than one work process cannot influence a single database LUW.

However, an ABAP program is frequently linked with more than one work process over the course of its total runtime. At all times during which a program is inactive (e. g., because it is waiting for the user to make an entry, or it is waiting, as a client, for a task on a server to be completed), it is normally rolled out of the work process, together with its data,[11] and the work process is otherwise occupied.

As a result, a work process must always end an LUW and execute an implicit database commit when its responsibility for a program changes. Activities that result in a rollout or change of the work process within a program, and thus also cause a database commit to be executed, include the following:

Database commit

▶ Ending a dialog step (see Section 9.1.9). This is by far the most common scenario in which a work process change takes place in conventional dialog processing with dynpros. The program waits for a user action and does not occupy any work process in the meantime. In the next dialog step, the next free work process is assigned to the program.

▶ Sending error messages, information messages, and warnings (see Section 9.4). These messages end the current dialog step.

▶ Calling a function module using a synchronous or asynchronous remote function call (see Section 12.2). The current work process transfers control to another work process or to another system.

▶ Executing the `RECEIVE` statement in a callback routine specified by asynchronous RFC (see Section 12.2.3). The current work process is interrupted in order to receive the data from the other application server.

▶ Executing HTTP/HTTPS/SMTP communication using the Internet Communication Framework (ICF) (see Section 12.3). The current work process is ended with each call of a service in an ICF client program, and after each response is sent in an ICF server program.

▶ Interrupting the program with the `WAIT` statement.

---

11 Hence the name "roll area," see Section 3.3.1.

When you execute the actions listed above, you must always consider that these commit the database changes that have been made up to this point, which means that a database rollback is no longer possible. Just as there are implicit database commits, implicit database rollbacks occur in the following cases:

▶ When a runtime error occurs (see Chapter 8)

▶ When a termination or exit message is sent (see Section 9.4)

In these situations, the status from before the start of the database LUW is restored. The start of the database LUW was either the assignment of a work process, or the ending of the previous LUW by a database commit or rollback.

Therefore, until the current work process ends, you must always try to ensure consistent statuses in the database. This means that you cannot, for example, debit an account in one work process and then credit the amount to another account in a separate work process because, after the work process changes, you no longer have the option of executing a database rollback if an error occurs. In this case, you must log the changes and undo them yourself. A typical example from conventional dialog programming is Process After Input (PAI) processing of dynpros. Once you reach the PAI event of a subsequent dynpro, you are no longer in the database LUW of the previous dynpro.

From the perspective of the application program, however, it is essential that an LUW can extend across several work process changes. This applies equally to dialog processing and to the provision of services. Even though a program execution extends across several work process changes, and therefore several database LUWs, the changes made should not be committed until the program ends, as, for example, by selecting a function such as **Save**. This is exactly what is provided by *SAP LUWs*.

An SAP LUW refers to a logical unit in ABAP programs that behaves like an LUW; in other words, it produces a consistent database status when it ends. While an SAP LUW may extend across several work process changes, the database changes are executed within a single database LUW.

The required database changes are not executed directly in this case. Instead, they are collected over the course of various work process changes, and then executed as a bundle in the database in the final work process of the SAP LUW. This means that only the bundle of collected database changes is subject to the LUW mechanism of the database.

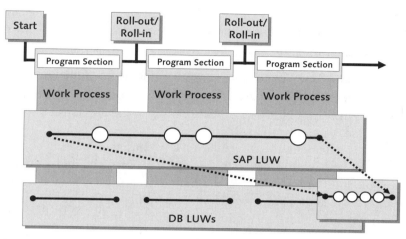

Figure 10.5 Bundling of Database Changes in an SAP LUW

The ABAP language provides three mechanisms for bundling database changes in a work process. Each of these mechanisms is based on classical procedures, namely, bundling by:

► update function modules
► subroutines
► transactional Remote Function Call (tRFC)

In the next section, we briefly discuss the concepts of updating with function modules and bundling using subroutines. We discuss tRFC in Section 12.2.3.

ABAP Objects provides the Transaction Service of Object Services for object-oriented implementation of LUWs (see Section 10.2.4). From a technical point of view, this is based on the procedure of updating with update function modules.

Function modules can be defined as **update modules** in the Function Builder. These update function modules provide a basis for updating. They encapsulate change accesses to the database, and can be registered for delayed execution as follows:

Updating

IN UPDATE TASK `CALL FUNCTION ... IN UPDATE TASK.`

The `CALL FUNCTION` statement does not call a function module with the `IN UPDATE TASK` addition. Instead, it registers the function module, including the actual parameters passed, for execution in a special update work process. To end an SAP LUW, you must ensure that all update function modules collected are processed or, if an error occurs, rejected.

To end an SAP LUW with the execution of the update function modules, use:

COMMIT WORK `COMMIT WORK [AND WAIT].`

With this statement, the current SAP LUW ends and updating begins in the update work process. In this work process, the update function modules are executed in a single database LUW in the same order in which they were registered. Depending on the priority specified when the function modules are defined, and on whether the `AND WAIT` addition is specified when they are called, the update may be either synchronous or asynchronous. `COMMIT WORK` also triggers a database commit. To end an SAP LUW without executing the update function modules, use:

ROLLBACK WORK `ROLLBACK WORK.`

This statement similarly completes an SAP LUW. In this case, however, the registered update modules are not executed, and the registrations are deleted. The `ROLLBACK` statement therefore allows you to do on a logical level exactly what the database does in error scenarios, namely undo all changes or avoid executing these changes in the first place. `ROLLBACK WORK` also triggers a database rollback.

Limits of an SAP LUW — The `COMMIT WORK` and `ROLLBACK WORK` statements determine the limits (start and end) of an SAP LUW. An ABAP program may extend across any number of SAP LUWs; however, the end of an ABAP program is always also the end of the last SAP LUW. By calling ABAP programs with `CALL TRANSACTION` or `SUBMIT ... AND RETURN`, SAP LUWs can be nested.

Database commit and rollback — Although the `COMMIT WORK` and `ROLLBACK WORK` statement always also trigger an explicit database commit or rollback (in addition to handling the SAP LUW), they should not be used solely for this purpose, due to their side effects. The *Official ABAP Reference* book specifies the exact effects of using these statements. If you only want to execute database commits, you can use the DB_COMMIT function module.[12]

Like function modules, subroutines can also be registered:

`PERFORM ... ON COMMIT|ROLLBACK.`

The execution of all registered subroutines is delayed until the next `COMMIT WORK` or `ROLLBACK WORK` statement. However, since the subroutines used cannot have a parameter interface, the data must be stored in the program or transferred using external interfaces, such as the ABAP memory. Subroutine that are executed with `COMMIT WORK` or `ROLLBACK WORK` are therefore better suited to administrative tasks, such as cleanup operations at the end of an SAP LUW, than to the execution of database changes.[13]

This concludes our short discussion of data consistency and LUWs, even though we haven't mentioned transactions, despite the fact that the topics discussed often fall under the category of *Transaction Programming*. The term *transaction* as used in that sense refers to the result of a business-related action, which accesses and manipulates data, and, when finished, produces a consistent data status. In the AS ABAP, in contrast, a transaction refers to the execution of a program using a transaction code (see Section 3.1.2). This term is used because, in the past, such programs (in particular dialog transactions) effected database changes, while executable programs were merely read reports.[14] To avoid confusion, we therefore don't refer to transactions in connection with SAP LUWs. In the case of Object Services, where this potential for confusion does not arise, the relevant service is always referred to as a Transaction Service (see Section 10.2.4).

Subroutines

PERFORM ON COMMIT, ON ROLLBACK

Transaction

---

12 If necessary, you can also use the corresponding Native SQL statements as an exception.

13 Sometimes, it is common practice to register the function modules in such a subroutine. This is possible, because the registered subroutines are called before the registered update function modules when using `COMMIT WORK`. This allows you to collect the necessary parameters during the complete program execution.

14 In the past, the term "transaction programming" used to be a synonym for the programming of module pools.

The AS ABAP Lock Concept

In the previous section, we introduced the concept of SAP LUWs as a basis for consistent data stored in the AS ABAP. Until now, we didn't examine the subject of locks, which is also closely associated with the subject of data consistency. While an ABAP program is making changes to the database, it must be ensured, as a minimum requirement, that a second ABAP program cannot gain write access to the same data.

Database locks

We will begin, once again, at database level. The database system automatically provides a lock mechanism for a database LUW. This mechanism ensures that conflicting changes to data do not result in inconsistencies. All changed data records are physically locked. These locks are bound to the duration of a database LUW. A different lock mechanism is therefore required for SAP LUWs, which are defined independently of database LUWs.

SAP locks

Locks for SAP LUWs must remain in place until the end of an SAP LUW and must be visible to all programs of the AS ABAP. To make this possible, the AS ABAP provides a logical lock mechanism based on entries in a central lock table on a single application server.[15]

Lock table

This lock mechanism does not set any physical locks in the database table. Instead, an ABAP program sends the keys of the table entries it wants to lock to the lock table, and all other programs must check, before accessing the lock table, whether the required entries are locked. However, there is no mechanism to force this behavior. The entire concept is based on the cooperative behavior of application programs. Furthermore, the logical locks are only loosely connected with SAP LUWs. A lock can be set or released at any time.

Lock object

To set an SAP lock, you must create a *lock object* in the ABAP Dictionary or use a *where-used list*, for example, to find out which lock objects already exist for a database table.[16] One or more database tables and key fields for one or more rows can be specified in a lock object. When you activate a lock object, two function modules called ENQUEUE_<lockobject> and DEQUEUE_<lockobject> are generated

---

15 An AS ABAP can contain only one application server with an *enqueue work process*. This server manages the central lock table of the entire system in its memory. The function modules to set and delete locks are executed in this work process.

16 A lock object is a repository object, but not an object of ABAP Objects.

automatically. Calling these function modules sets or deletes an SAP lock for all database rows specified in the lock object.

Figure 10.6 shows a lock object for the ZRESERVATIONS database table from Chapter 2. Lock objects should start with the letter E before the possible prefix of a customer namespace. The lock mode is predefined as a write lock, but it can be overwritten when the relevant function module is called. On the **Lock parameter** tab page, you specify the key fields of the table, for which values can be transferred when the function module is called. If suitable foreign key relationships exist between tables, a lock object can also lock several tables at the same time.

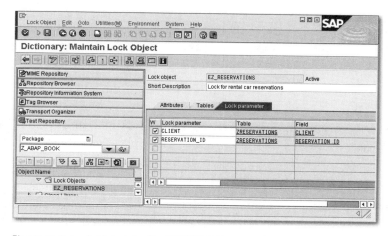

Figure 10.6 Lock Object for the ZRESERVATIONS Table

The ENQUEUE_<lockobject> sets an SAP lock by writing entries into the central lock table of the AS ABAP. Parameter passing can inform the function module whether a read or write lock should be set. While a read lock is set for a lock object, no other ABAP programs can set a write lock for the same lock object; however, additional read locks may be set. To check whether a lock is set, simply try to lock an object with this function module. If the lock cannot be set, the function module triggers an exception.

ENQUEUE

Listing 10.13 shows how to set an SAP lock with the EZ_RESERVATIONS lock object by calling the relevant function module.[17]

---

17 To call such a function module, it is advantageous to use the **Pattern** function of the ABAP Editor.

Listing 10.13 Setting an SAP Lock

```abap
REPORT z_enqueue.

PARAMETERS p_resid TYPE zreservations-reservation_id.
CLASS demo DEFINITION.
  PUBLIC SECTION.
    CLASS-METHODS main.
ENDCLASS.
CLASS demo IMPLEMENTATION.
  METHOD main.
    DATA msg TYPE string.
    CALL FUNCTION 'ENQUEUE_EZ_RESERVATIONS'
      EXPORTING
        mode_zreservations      = 'X'
        reservation_id          = p_resid
      EXCEPTIONS
        foreign_lock            = 1
        system_failure          = 2
        OTHERS                  = 3.
    CASE sy-subrc.
      WHEN 0.
        MESSAGE `Enqueue successful!` TYPE 'I'.
      WHEN 1.
        CONCATENATE `Record already locked by `
                    sy-msgv1 INTO msg.
        MESSAGE msg TYPE 'I' DISPLAY LIKE 'E'.
      WHEN OTHERS.
        MESSAGE `Error in Enqueue!` TYPE 'I'
                DISPLAY LIKE 'E'.
        RETURN.
    ENDCASE.
    CALL TRANSACTION 'SM12'.
  ENDMETHOD.
ENDCLASS.
START-OF-SELECTION.
  demo=>main( ).
```

By transferring "X" (exclusive) to `mode_zreservations`, a write lock is set for all rows in ZRESERVATIONS with keys that match the values transferred to `reservation_id`. The success of the lock is evaluated by the exceptions of the function module. Note also the use of `sy-msgv1` (see Section 8.2.3). After the lock is set, Transaction SM12 (lock management) is called, where the lock entries are displayed in the lock table. If you simultaneously execute the program in several main sessions of the AS ABAP, you can also test the failure of a lock request with this program.

SAP locks can be released either implicitly or explicitly. When an ABAP program ends or, at least when the update task of an SAP LUW ends, the relevant SAP locks are automatically released. SAP locks are explicitly released when you call DEQUEUE_<lockobject>. The call for unlocking a lock object is similar to the call for locking it.

DEQUEUE

10.1.4 Special Sections Relating to Database Accesses

Now that we have introduced the fundamental characteristics of database accesses in the AS ABAP, we can turn our attention to the following more specific topics:

- Client handling, which is a special feature of the AS ABAP, whereby data from different business areas can be stored in the same databse table
- Buffering of database tables, which is a special service of the AS ABAP for improving performance
- Native SQL, which enables (almost) direct access to the programming interface of the database system

Clients and Client Handling

In Chapter 2, you saw that the first column in the structure of a database for application data is usually a client column of the MANDT type (see, for example, Figure 2.20).[18] However, we have not yet used this column in any of our Open SQL statements. And, even though this column belongs to the key of a table, we have not set any corresponding condition in our WHERE clause.

Client column

This leads us to the automatic client-handling mechanisms of Open SQL. Open SQL statements, which access client-specific application tables, always work as standard with the data of the current client. The client is determined when you log on to an AS ABAP, and are prompted to enter a three-digit client ID.[19] This means that a single

Client

---

18 There are also client-independent database tables whose data is equally available to all clients. Usually, it is the system tables of the technical infrastructure that are client-independent.

19 The user ID and password are also client-dependent.

AS ABAP can manage the application data of several independent clients. Therefore, several different companies could, in theory, use a single AS ABAP as an application server.

Client handling Automatic client handling works as follows:

► An explicit condition for the client column cannot be specified in the WHERE clause of Open SQL statements. An equality condition for the current client is instead implicitly added to each WHERE condition by the runtime environment.

► If rows are identified by the key fields of work areas when the database contents are changed, the runtime environment ignores the contents of the client column and uses the current client instead.

If you need to explicitly specify the client in an Open SQL statement because the data of another business area in the same AS ABAP is to be accessed, you can deactivate automatic client handling by using the following addition:

CLIENT SPECIFIED ...dbtab CLIENT SPECIFIED ...

This addition must be specified directly after the name of the database table or a join. When you use this addition, the client column can be specified in the WHERE clause, or the client column is taken into account when the key is specified using a table work area.

Buffering of Database Tables

Every access to a database table places a load on the database system. If tables are read many times but few changes are made to them, you can reduce the database load by buffering the data that is read during the first access in a shared memory of the application server. Then, the data can be accessed from there by all applications on the same server. In Section 6.5, we explained how you can store and manage data in the shared memory with Shared Objects. This section describes SAP buffering, which has been in existence far longer than explicit Shared Objects programming.

SAP buffering SAP buffering refers to the buffering of data from a database defined in the ABAP Dictionary in a table buffer in the shared memory of the current application server. When you define a database table, you also define whether it is to be buffered, and if so, how. You can use fully buffering, whereby the entire table is buffered; generic area buffering, whereby certain areas are buffered; or single records buffering, which buffers individual records. Buffering usually improves performance dramatically (i. e., by a factor of between 50 and 500). It is effective during access with most of the Open SQL statements, but is also bypassed by certain variants.

If a table is buffered, Open SQL read statements first access the buffer before accessing the database. Synchronization between the various buffers, or between the buffers and the database, is controlled by the database interface. As a rule, SAP buffering should be activated if a table is frequently read but rarely changed, and if it is acceptable that a change to the data in the table will not be available on the other application servers until after a delay of approximately 60 seconds.

Buffer synchronization

If, for any reason, data is to be read from the database directly rather than from the SAP buffer, you can specify the following addition in the FROM clause of the SELECT statement:

... BYPASSING BUFFER ...

BYPASSING BUFFER

However, buffering is also implicitly bypassed by a number of other variants of SQL statements for technical reasons. Examples include the DISTINCT addition or aggregate functions in the SELECT clause, joins in the FROM clause, subqueries in the WHERE clause, and use of the GROUP BY clause or the ORDER BY clause in SELECT statements. In all Open SQL statements, the CLIENT SPECIFIED addition bypasses SAP buffering if the client ID is not also specified in a WHERE condition. You should therefore avoid using these syntax variants for buffered tables. If you need to use them, you should also specify the BYPASSING BUFFER addition to make the implicit behavior explicit.

Native SQL

The database interface converts the Open SQL statements into platform-specific SQL commands and passes them on to the database. ABAP programs that use Open SQL are therefore independent of the database used.

In special cases, however, you may need to access the database-programming interface directly with platform-specific SQL statements.

These statements can be specified between the following ABAP statements:

EXEC SQL,
ENDEXEC

```
EXEC SQL.
  ...
ENDEXEC.
```

All statements that can be specified between the EXEC SQL and ENDEXEC statements are referred to as *Native SQL*. These may be database-specific SQL statements or some SAP-specific statements. Native SQL statements are not checked in full by the syntax check and, with the exception of SAP-specific statements, they are transferred unchanged to the database by a special part of the database interface. Note, in particular, that automatic client handling is not performed in this case.

Host variable   To transfer data from ABAP programs to the database, data objects of the ABAP program can be specified as host variables in the Native SQL statements, preceded by a colon (:). Other SAP-specific language elements of Native SQL are used for cursor processing, calling database procedures, and defining database connections.

A program that uses Native SQL is specific to the database system installed. When developing general applications for the AS ABAP, you should therefore avoid using Native SQL where possible. However, Native SQL is used to good effect in certain technical components of the AS ABAP, for example, it is used in the ABAP Dictionary to create or change database tables. You can also use Native SQL in your own programs to create database tables. However, these tables are not subject to AS ABAP administration and can only be maintained with Native SQL.

Listing 10.14 shows an example of the use of Native SQL. From a selection screen, you can create a database table in the MaxDB of the SAP NetWeaver 2004s ABAP Trial Version, fill it with 100 square numbers, import a row from the database table, and delete the database. If exceptions occur (e. g., if you try to create the same database twice), they are handled by displaying the relevant exception text.

Listing 10.14 Native SQL

```
REPORT z_native_sql.

PARAMETERS: p_create RADIOBUTTON GROUP grp,
            p_insert RADIOBUTTON GROUP grp,
```

```abap
                p_select RADIOBUTTON GROUP grp,
                p_drop   RADIOBUTTON GROUP grp.
SELECTION-SCREEN SKIP.
PARAMETERS  p_key TYPE i DEFAULT 1.

CLASS demo DEFINITION.
  PUBLIC SECTION.
    CLASS-METHODS main.
  PRIVATE SECTION.
    CLASS-DATA: wa1 TYPE c LENGTH 10,
                wa2 TYPE c LENGTH 10,
                err TYPE REF TO cx_sy_native_sql_error.
    CLASS-METHODS: create RAISING cx_sy_native_sql_error,
                   insert RAISING cx_sy_native_sql_error,
                   select RAISING cx_sy_native_sql_error,
                   drop   RAISING cx_sy_native_sql_error.
ENDCLASS.
CLASS demo IMPLEMENTATION.
  METHOD main.
    TRY.
        IF p_create = 'X'.
          create( ).
          MESSAGE 'Create was successful' TYPE 'S'.
        ELSEIF p_insert = 'X'.
          insert( ).
          MESSAGE 'Insert was successful' TYPE 'S'.
        ELSEIF p_select = 'X'.
          select( ).
          MESSAGE 'Select was successful' TYPE 'S'.
        ELSEIF p_drop   = 'X'.
          drop( ).
          MESSAGE 'Drop was successful' TYPE 'S'.
        ENDIF.
      CATCH cx_sy_native_sql_error INTO err.
        MESSAGE err TYPE 'I' DISPLAY LIKE 'E'.
    ENDTRY.
  ENDMETHOD.
  METHOD create.
    EXEC SQL.
      CREATE TABLE mytab (
              val1 char(10) NOT NULL,
              val2 char(10) NOT NULL,
              PRIMARY KEY (val1)        )
    ENDEXEC.
  ENDMETHOD.
  METHOD insert.
```

```
DO 100 TIMES.
  wa1 = sy-index.
  wa2 = sy-index ** 2.
  EXEC SQL.
    INSERT INTO mytab VALUES (:wa1, :wa2)
  ENDEXEC.
ENDDO.
ENDMETHOD.
IF sy-subrc <> 0.
  RAISE EXCEPTION TYPE cx_sy_native_sql_error
    EXPORTING
    textid = cx_sy_native_sql_error=>key_already_exists.
ENDIF.
METHOD select.
  DATA: msg TYPE c LENGTH 30,
        key TYPE c LENGTH 10.
  key = p_key.
  EXEC SQL.
    SELECT val1, val2
         INTO :wa1, :wa2
         FROM mytab
         WHERE val1 = :key
  ENDEXEC.
  IF sy-subrc <> 0.
    RAISE EXCEPTION TYPE cx_sy_native_sql_error
      EXPORTING
      textid = cx_sy_native_sql_error=>key_not_found.
  ENDIF.
  WRITE: 'Result:' TO msg,
          wa1 TO msg+10,
          wa2 TO msg+20.
  MESSAGE msg TYPE 'I'.
ENDMETHOD.
METHOD drop.
  EXEC SQL.
    DROP TABLE mytab
  ENDEXEC.
ENDMETHOD.
ENDCLASS.

START-OF-SELECTION.
  demo=>main( ).
```

10.2   Database Access with Object Services

If you use ABAP Objects to develop object-oriented applications, you must consider how you are going to store the application data from objects in the database. You can, of course, create a database table for each class whose instances contain data that is to be stored, and implement methods that access these database tables with Open SQL statements.

Or, you can let Object Services do this for you. Object Services comprises a framework implemented in ABAP Objects, which provides you with a Persistence Service, a Transaction Service, and a Query Service.

The mapping of ABAP Objects classes to relational database tables is referred to as *object-relational mapping*, or *O/R mapping* for short.   O/R mapping

O/R mapping defines how classes are mapped to database tables, and how attributes are mapped to columns. Classes with O/R mapping are referred to as *persistent classes*. Attributes that are mapped to columns in the database table are called *persistent attributes*.

To create a persistent class in the Class Builder, you must execute   Persistent class
O/R mapping there. The Object Services Framework uses this O/R mapping to create the persistent class and a corresponding class actor (or agent).

The class actor is itself a class and provides you with methods for   Class actor
managing instances of persistent classes. Persistent classes can have both persistent and transient instances. Persistent instances mirror persistent objects in the database, and are loaded by class actors into the memory if required. Transient instances exist only in memory and are not mirrored in the database.

Every persistent object has a unique identity, with which it can be   Object identity
accessed. There are two types of object identity: Business key (semantic key) and GUID (Global Unique Identifier) (technical key).

10.2.1   Creating Persistent Classes

As an introduction to the Persistence Service, we have provided the following example, in which we use Object Services to implement the rental car application from Chapter 2. To do this, we create a persistent class with a business key object identity for each database table. We start with the ZCL_CUSTOMER_ENTITY class for the ZCUSTOMERS table.

To create the persistent class ZCL_CUSTOMER_ENTITY, follow the same steps used to create a regular class, with the exception that the **Persistent class** radio button must be selected in the **Create Class** dialog box. The instantiability is automatically changed to **Protected** (see Figure 10.7). All settings are accepted by saving.

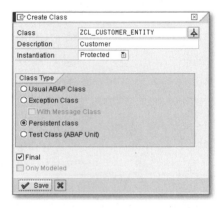

Figure 10.7 Creating Persistent Classes

On the main screen of the Class Builder, you can then choose the **Persistence** function to execute O/R mapping. If you specify the ZCUSTOMERS table in the dialog box that appears, the tool for persistence mapping opens. The fields of the ZCSUTOMERS table are shown in the lower half of the tool screen. Double-click in the **ID** field. This fills the attribute editing area in the center of the screen with default values. For example, the name of the table column is proposed as the attribute name. You can change these default values, or simply press [Enter] to confirm. The new attribute ID, which is linked with the **ID** field of the table, is now displayed at the top of the screen. Accept the value in the **NAME** field in the same way. The persistence mapping display should then appear as shown in Figure 10.8, and can be saved.

GET/SET methods   When you return to the main screen of the Class Builder, you can see that *GET/SET methods* have been generated for the attributes of the persistent classes. These allow you to read and, if necessary, change attributes. The visibility of the GET/SET methods depends on the visibility of the attributes as defined in persistence mapping. The actual visibility of the attributes is internally restricted in order to ensure that they can only be read or changed using the GET/SET methods.

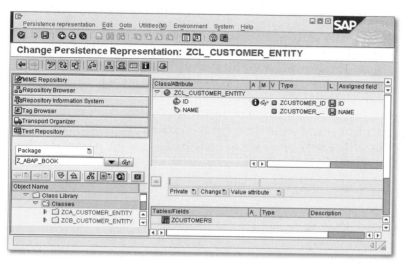

Figure 10.8 Persistence Mapping in the Class Builder

The attributes of a persistent class that are mapped to the key fields of a database table are referred to as *key attributes*. The key attributes of a persistent class form the business key. No SET methods are generated for key attributes because the business key cannot change.

Key attributes

When you activate persistent classes for the first time, you must also confirm the activation of the *class actor*. The class of the class actor has already been created with the creation of the persistent class (see the ZCA_CUSTOMER_ENTITY class in Figure 10.8). However, its methods are only generated during persistence mapping. The methods are created in the class actor's superclass (in this case, ZCB_CUSTOMER_ENTITY, see Figure 10.8), rather than in the class actor itself. This *basic class actor* can only be changed by the Object Services Framework, whereas you can add components or redefine methods in the actual class actor.

Class actor

To complete our example, you must now create the persistent classes ZCL_CAR_ENTITY and ZCL_RESERVATION_ENTITY for the ZCARS and ZRESERVATIONS database tables. To do this, simply copy all columns as attributes during O/R mapping, and activate these, together with their class actors.

10.2.2 Managing Persistent Objects

The following sections explain how you can use the class actor to manage persistent objects.

Using a Query to Load Persistent Objects

Just as you could import data from database tables into ABAP data objects with the Open SQL SELECT statement, so can you use the GET_PERSISTENT_BY_QUERY method of the IF_OS_CA PERSISTENCY interface implemented in the class actor to load persistent objects from the database that match certain conditions. A persistent instance[20] is created for each persistent object in the internal session. A persistent instance is assigned to each row in a database table, in other words, to each persistent object.

GET_PERSISTENT_BY_QUERY

The condition under which a persistent object is to be loaded must be transferred to the GET_PERSISTENT_BY_QUERY method in the form of a query. In this case, a query is represented by a query object, which can be accessed using interface reference variables of the type IF_OS_QUERY. To create a query, use the CREATE_QUERY method of the IF_OS_QUERY_MANAGER interface, which is implemented by a query manager.

Query Manager

The Query Manager is an object that can be accessed with an interface reference variable of the type IF_OS_QUERY_MANAGER, and which is created with the static method GET_QUERY_MANAGER of the CL_OS_SYSTEM system class.

When you create a query with the Query Manager, a filter condition and possibly also a sort condition must be transferred as a string. When you execute a query, a WHERE clause is determined from the filter condition, and an ORDER BY clause is determined from the sort condition, taking into account O/R mapping. A selection is then executed in the database using the Open SQL SELECT statement. The result of a query is a table with object references to the persistent instances that satisfy the filter condition. The sequence of instances in that table is defined by the sort condition.

Filter condition

The filter condition is constructed in a similar way to the WHERE condition of the SELECT statement; however, you must use the names of

---

20 A persistent instance is an instance managed by Object Services. Technically speaking, it is, of course, a transient object.

the attributes of a persistent class instead of the name of the column in a database in this case. You can use the following operators:

`=, <, >, <>, <=, >=`

`LIKE, IS NULL`

These operators can be negated with the logical operator `NOT`, and joined with `AND` and `OR`. For example:

`` `DATE_FROM <= '20060517' `` **`AND`** `DATE_TO >= '20060517'` ``

The operators have the same meaning here as they do in the Open SQL `WHERE` clause.

You can also use parameters instead of attributes on the right of the operators. You can use both the predefined parameters `PAR1`, `PAR2`, and `PAR3`, as well as any other parameter of your choice. You can create user-defined parameters when you generate a query. When you execute a query, the parameters are linked to ABAP data objects, which are transferred to the I_PAR1, I_PAR2, and I_PAR3 parameters when the GET_PERSISTENT_BY_QUERY method is called, or to the I_PARAMETER_TABLE in the case of user-defined parameters. **Parameters**

If the filter condition is empty, or if no filter condition was specified, all persistent objects are loaded into the main memory.

The sort condition simply specifies a list of attributes, together with the direction in which they are to be sorted, as in the following example: **Sort condition**

`` `DATE_FROM ASCENDING DATE_TO DESCENDING` ``

The result of a query is transferred as a table of the type OSREFTAB with row type `REF TO object`. The complete table is populated in the query. It is not possible to iterate over the result in a loop, whereby the result is placed step by step in the result area, as with a `SELECT` loop or explicit cursor processing. To restrict the dataset, you can use the I_UPTO parameter to specify the maximum number of objects to be loaded. If no persistent object that satisfies the filter condition is found in the database, an initial table is returned. **Result of a query**

To illustrate this, we can create a static method called SELECT_BY_CATEGORY in the ZCL_CAR_ENTITY class in our rental car example. This method finds the vehicles that exist within a certain category.

Figure 10.9 shows the interface and the implementation of this method.

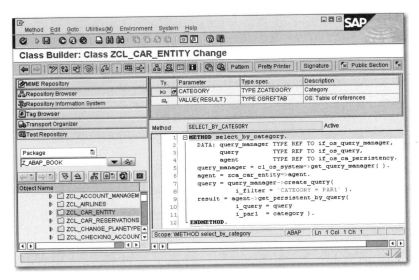

Figure 10.9 Generating and Executing a Query

First, references to the Query Manager and the class actor are retrieved. Both objects are singletons, in other words, they exist only once for each internal session. While the reference to the Query Manager is obtained using an explicit call of a GET method, the reference to the class actor can be taken from the static AGENT attribute of the corresponding class.

A query object with the filter `CATEGORY = PAR1` is generated with the Query Manager. This query is transferred to the class actor for execution. The CATEGORY input parameter of the SELECT_BY_CAT-EGORY method is bound to the PAR1 query parameter using the pre-defined I_PAR1 input parameter of the GET_PERSISTENT_BY_QUERY method.

Listing 10.15 shows a short program for testing the query. The number plates of the two rental cars found in a certain category are output. The result table is only structured because it is output as an ALV list and there no elementary row types are permitted. Note that the `oref` reference variables are typed with the `object` root class. Therefore, a Down Cast to `car`, is required in order to call the GET_

LICENSE_PLATE method statically. Without a Down Cast, only a dynamic method call would be possible.

Listing 10.15 Testing a Query

```
REPORT z_test_os_query.

PARAMETERS category TYPE zcars-category.
CLASS demo DEFINITION.
  PUBLIC SECTION.
    CLASS-METHODS: main,
                   display.
  PRIVATE SECTION.
    CLASS-DATA:
      BEGIN OF license_plate_line,
        license_plate TYPE zcars-license_plate,
      END OF license_plate_line,
      license_plate_tab LIKE TABLE OF license_plate_line.
ENDCLASS.
CLASS demo IMPLEMENTATION.
  METHOD main.
    DATA: reftab          TYPE osreftab,
          oref            TYPE REF TO object,
          car             TYPE REF TO zcl_car_entity.
    reftab = zcl_car_entity=>select_by_category( category ).
    LOOP AT reftab INTO oref.
      car ?= oref.
      license_plate_line-license_plate =
        car->get_license_plate( ).
      APPEND license_plate_line TO license_plate_tab.
    ENDLOOP.
    display( ).
  ENDMETHOD.
  METHOD display.
    ...
  ENDMETHOD.
ENDCLASS.
START-OF-SELECTION.
  demo=>main( ).
```

To determine whether a rental car is available during a certain period, we can create another instance method called CHECK_AVAILABILITY with another query in ZCL_CAR_ENTITY. Figure 10.10 shows the parameter interface, while Listing 10.16 shows the implementation of this method.

Ty.	Parameter	Type spec.	Description
▸◻	FROM	TYPE ZDATE_FROM	Start Date
▸◻	TO	TYPE ZDATE_TO	End Date
◻	VALUE(RESULT)	TYPE ABAP_BOOL	

Figure 10.10 Parameters of the CHECK_AVAILABILITY Method

Listing 10.16 Generating and Executing a Query

```
METHOD check_availability.
  DATA: query_manager TYPE REF TO if_os_query_manager,
        query         TYPE REF TO if_os_query,
        agent         TYPE REF TO if_os_ca_persistency,
        filter        TYPE string,
        license_plate TYPE zlicense_plate,
        reservations  TYPE osreftab.
  query_manager = cl_os_system=>get_query_manager( ).
  agent = zca_reservation_entity=>agent.
  filter = `LICENSE_PLATE = PAR1 ` &
           `AND NOT ( DATE_FROM > PAR3 OR DATE_TO < PAR2 )`.
  query = query_manager->create_query(
          i_filter = filter ).
  license_plate = me->get_license_plate( ).
  reservations = agent->get_persistent_by_query(
                 i_query = query
                 i_par1  = license_plate
                 i_par2  = from
                 i_par3  = to
                 i_upto  = 1 ).
  IF LINES( reservations ) = 0.
    result = abap_true.
  ELSE.
    result = abap_false.
  ENDIF.
ENDMETHOD.
```

Since we only want to know whether at least one reservation exists in this period, we can use the i_upto parameter to restrict the result to a maximum of one hit.

Using the Business Key to Load Persistent Objects

When a query is used to load persistent objects, the objects whose attributes satisfy the filter condition are loaded. Since a persistent object is uniquely identified by its key attributes, you can also load an individual object by specifying its business key if this is known. To do this, you use either the GET_PERSISTENT or GET_PERSISTENT_BY_KEY method of the class actor.

▶ The GET_PERSISTENT method is a method of the class actor whose interface was generated with the O/R mapping. Each key attribute of the persistent class has a corresponding input parameter. For example, the GET_PERSISTENT method of the ZCL_CUSTOMER_ENTITY class has a single parameter, I_NAME, for the NAME key attribute.

GET_PERSISTENT

▶ The GET_PERSISTENT_BY_KEY method is a method of the IF_OS_CA_PERSISTENCY interface, which is implemented in the class actor. It has a predefined interface and expects to receive the key attributes as components of a structure in a defined sequence.

GET_PERSISTENT_BY_KEY

If no persistent object with the business key is found in the database, the CX_OS_OBJECT_NOT_FOUND exception is triggered. Loading with the business key is naturally more efficient than loading with a query.

To load several persistent objects by specifying business keys, use the GET_PERSISTENT_BY_KEY_TAB method of the IF_OS_CA_PERSISTENCY interface. This method uses the SELECT statement internally with FOR ALL ENTRIES to load the persistent object with a single database access, while the Open SQL statement SELECT SINGLE is used to load a single object.

GET_PERSISTENT_BY_KEY_TAB

Creating Persistent Objects

To create a new persistent object with a business key object identity, use either the CREATE_PERSISTENT or CREATE_PERSISTENT_BY_KEY method of the class actor. The latter is also a method of the IF_OS_CA_PERSISTENCY interface.

You must specify the business key in the same way as when loading a persistent object. You can also specify the remaining attributes of the persistent class with CREATE_PERSISTENT. With CREATE_PERSISTENT_BY_KEY, these must be set with the relevant SET methods after the object is created.

CREATE_PERSISTENT, CREATE_PERSISTENT_BY_KEY

If an instance with this business key already exists in the main memory when you try to create it, the CX_OS_OBJECT_EXISTING exception is triggered. No check is performed to determine whether the database already contains a persistent object with this business key. When the current SAP LUW is ended with COMMIT WORK (see Section 10.1.3), the Persistence Service tries to write the persistent object to the database as part of an update. If the object already exists in the database, the update terminates. To ensure that a persistent object with this business key does not already exist, you must load an object with this business key before you create the object. If the CX_OS_OBJECT_NOT_FOUND exception is triggered, an object with this business key does not yet exist.

For example, we can create a static method called MAKE_RESERVATION in the ZCL_RESERVATION_ENTITY class. We can then use the SELECT_BY_CATEGORY and CHECK_AVAILABILITY methods of the ZCL_CAR_ENTITY class to search for an available car in the method, in order to generate and return a reservation for this car with the CREATE_PERSISTENT method of the class actor. The reservation key is determined in the NEW_RESERVATION_ID method. You normally use a number range or a GUID to determine the key. In our example, we generate a eight-digit key that comprises the number of days that have elapsed since the start of the year up to the current date, and the number of seconds that have elapsed since the start of the day up to the time of creation. Figure 10.11 shows the parameter interface, while Listing 10.17 shows the implementation of the method.

Ty.	Parameter	Type spec.	Description
▶□	CUSTOMER	TYPE ZCUSTOMER_ID	Customer Id
▶□	CATEGORY	TYPE ZCATEGORY	Category
▶□	FROM	TYPE ZDATE_FROM	Start Date
▶□	TO	TYPE ZDATE_TO	End Date
▣,	VALUE(RESULT)	TYPE REF TO ZCL_RESERVATION_ENTITY	Rental Car Reservation
▨	ZCX_NO_CAR_AVAILABLE		No car available

Figure 10.11 Parameters of the MAKE_RESERVATION Method

Listing 10.17 Creating a Persistent Object

```
METHOD make_reservation.
  DATA: cars            TYPE osreftab,
        car             TYPE REF TO zcl_car_entity,
        reservation_id  TYPE zreservation_id,
        license_plate   TYPE zlicense_plate.
```

```
  FIELD-SYMBOLS <car>  TYPE osref.
cars = zcl_car_entity=>select_by_category(
        category = category ).
LOOP AT cars ASSIGNING <car>.
  car ?= <car>.
  IF available = car->check_availability(
                      from = from
                      to   = to ) = abap_true.
    license_plate = car->get_license_plate( ).
    reservation_id = new_reservation_id( ).
    result =
      zca_reservation_entity=>agent->create_persistent(
        i_reservation_id = reservation_id
        i_customer_id    = customer
        i_license_plate  = license_plate
        i_date_from      = from
        i_date_to        = to ).
    RETURN.
  ENDIF.
ENDLOOP.
RAISE EXCEPTION TYPE zcx_no_car_available.
ENDMETHOD.
```

The classes in the rental car example are now complete, and the application program shown in Listing 10.18 can now be written.

Listing 10.18 Rental Car Reservation with the Persistence Service

```
REPORT z_os_rental_car_reservation.

CLASS demo DEFINITION.
  PUBLIC SECTION.
    CLASS-METHODS main.
ENDCLASS.

CLASS demo IMPLEMENTATION.
  METHOD main.
    DATA: customer_id  TYPE zcustomer_id,
          car_category TYPE zcategory,
          date_from    TYPE zdate_from,
          date_to      TYPE zdate_to,
          agent        TYPE REF TO zca_customer_entity,
          customer     TYPE REF TO zcl_customer_entity,
          reservation  TYPE REF TO zcl_reservation_entity.
    CALL FUNCTION 'Z_INPUT_CUSTOMER'
      IMPORTING customer_id = customer_id.
    agent = zca_customer_entity=>agent.
```

```
TRY.
    customer =
      agent->get_persistent( i_id = customer_id ).
  CATCH cx_os_object_not_found.
    MESSAGE 'Customer does not exist' TYPE 'I'
            DISPLAY LIKE 'E'.
    RETURN.
ENDTRY.
CALL FUNCTION 'Z_INPUT_RESERVATION'
  IMPORTING car_category = car_category
            date_from    = date_from
            date_to      = date_to.
TRY.
    reservation =
      zcl_reservation_entity=>make_reservation(
        customer = customer_id
        category = car_category
        from     = date_from
        to       = date_to ).
        COMMIT WORK.
  CATCH zcx_no_car_available .
    MESSAGE 'No car available' TYPE 'I'
            DISPLAY LIKE 'E'.
    RETURN.
  ENDTRY.
ENDMETHOD.
ENDCLASS.
START-OF-SELECTION.
  demo=>main( ).
```

When you try to load a customer object with the specified customer ID, a check is performed to determine whether the customer exists.[21] The program then tries to make a reservation with the data entered. If this attempt does not terminate with the ZCX_NO_CAR_AVAILABLE exception, the current SAP LUW is ended with COMMIT WORK, and the persistent reservation object is written to the database. You can verify that this has been successful in Transaction SE16 (Data Browser, see Figure 10.12).

---

21 *See Section 2.7 for more information on these function modules.*

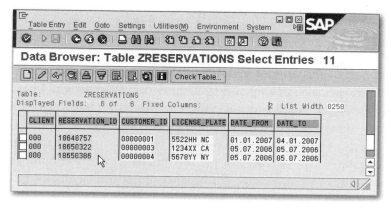

Figure 10.12 Persistent Objects in the Database

Changing Persistent Objects

Persistent objects are only changed when the SET method is called for the relevant attribute. The persistent object is flagged as changed by the Persistence Service, and the changes are written to the database when the SAP LUW ends with COMMIT WORK.

SET methods

In addition to the persistent attributes that can be stored in the database, a persistent object may also have transient attributes, which are not saved persistently, and are only available in the internal session. While persistent attributes must have either an elementary type or a reference type (see Section 10.2.3), transient attributes can have any type.

Transient attributes

Deleting Persistent Objects

To delete a persistent object, you can use the DELETE_PERSISTENT method of the IF_OS_FACTORY interface in the class actor. You must transfer the object reference to this method instead of the business key. Before you can do this, the object to be deleted must have already been loaded.

DELETE_ PERSISTENT

The persistent object is not deleted from the database until the SAP LUW is ended with COMMIT WORK. However, if you try to access it before then, the CX_OS_OBJECT_NOT_FOUND exception is triggered.

Persistent Objects and the SAP LUW

When an SAP LUW is ended with the ABAP command COMMIT WORK, the Persistence Service transfers all changes to persistent objects to the update in the form of update function modules. They are then written to the database, together with other data from the SAP LUW. With the ABAP command ROLLBACK WORK, on the other hand, all changes to persistent objects are undone. This also means, however, that changes to persistent objects cannot be written to the database without the COMMIT WORK statement. The implicit database commit as it occurs with a screen change, for instance, is not sufficient. This relatively simple procedure can be extended to incorporate use of the Transaction Service (see Section 10.2.4).

10.2.3 GUID Object Identity

GUID In our rental car example, we have exclusively used the business key as the object identity, because the underlying tables have semantic keys. Often, however, technical keys in the form of a Global Unique Identifier (GUID), rather than semantic keys are required. The GUID object identity can be used for this purpose. Unlike the business key object identity, the GUID is not an attribute of the persistent class. Instead, it exists only as a key field in the database table. The Persistence Service manages the GUIDs and recognizes the assignment of GUIDs to persistent instances. When a persistent object is created, the Persistence Service automatically generates a GUID and assigns it to the persistent object.

If you want to create a persistent class with a GUID object identity, you must define a key field with the type OS_GUID in the database table and chose the GUID mapping type for this field.

Persistent Object References

Just as you can use references in ABAP Objects to refer to an object from another object, so can you use persistent object references to refer to one persistent object from another. If you use a persistent object reference, the referenced object is automatically loaded from the database into the internal session.

Creation To create a persistent object reference, you must provide two fields of the OS_GUID type in the database table of the referencing class.

You must then map these two fields to an attribute of the persistent class. One of these fields contains the instance GUID, while the other contains the class GUID of the referenced persistent object. Together, these fields make up an Object Identity (OID). Persistent object references can therefore refer only to persistent objects with a GUID object identity. You must assign both fields to the same attribute in persistence mapping. The first field has the mapping type **object reference**, while the second has the mapping type **class identifier**.

With persistent object references, 1:1 relations, 1:N relations, and N:M relations can be realized between objects, in the same way that foreign key relationships exist between relational databases.

10.2.4 Transaction Service

The Transaction Service is an object-oriented wrapper of the SAP LUW, and also offers the concept of nested transactions.

An Object Services transaction is represented by a transaction object, which implements the IF_OS_TRANSACTION interface. Transactions are controlled by the following interface methods:

IF_OS_ TRANSACTION

▶ START starts a transaction.

▶ END ends a transaction and retains the changes made to persistent objects during the transaction, or writes them to the database.

▶ UNDO ends a transaction and rejects the changes made to persistent objects during the transaction.

A transaction manager is required to handle transactions. This is an object (singleton) that implements the IF_OS_TRANSACTION_MANAGER interface. The transaction manager must generate a transaction object for each transaction by calling the CREATE_TRANSACTION method.

IF_OS_ TRANSACTION_ MANAGER

Executing Transactions

We will now use our rental car example to demonstrate how a transaction is executed. To use the Transaction Service, we recommend that you execute a program using an OO transaction where **OO-transaction model** is selected for the transaction code.

We use the **Import** function in the Class Builder to convert the local demo class from the program in Listing 10.18 into a global class called ZCL_RENTAL_CAR_RESERVATION. We then delete the COMMIT WORK statement from the MAIN method, and add an instance method (HANDLE_TRANSACTION) to this class, with which we link an appropriately flagged OO transaction, namely, Z_OS_RENT_A_ CAR.[22] Figure 10.13 shows the methods in the class; Figure 10.14 shows the definition of the transaction code; and Listing 10.19 shows the implementation of the HANDLE_TRANSACTION method.

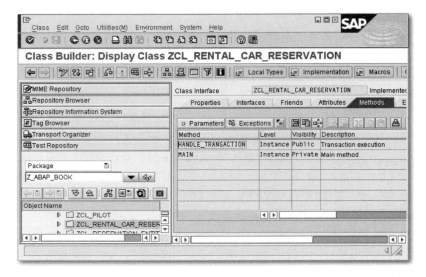

Figure 10.13 Application Class for an OO Transaction

Listing 10.19 Rental Car Reservation with the Transaction Service

```
METHOD handle_transaction.
  DATA: tx_manager TYPE REF TO if_os_transaction_manager,
        tx         TYPE REF TO if_os_transaction.
  tx_manager = cl_os_system=>get_transaction_manager( ).
  tx         = tx_manager->create_transaction( ).
  TRY.
      tx->start( ).
      me->main( ).
      tx->end( ).
    CATCH cx_os_error.
```

---

22 The reason why we need a global class here is that OO transactions using **OO transaction model** cannot be linked to methods of local classes.

```
      tx->undo( ).
    ENDTRY.
  ENDMETHOD.
```

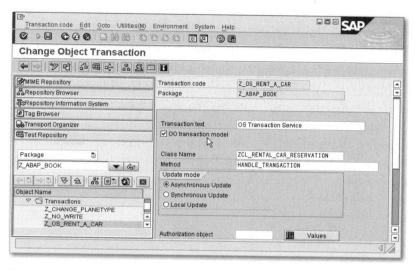

Figure 10.14 Transaction Code for an OO Transaction

The HANDLE_TRANSACTION method generates a transaction manager, together with a transaction object. The transaction object is used to start a transaction, call the MAIN method, and then end the transaction or, if an exception occurs, roll it back.

When you call the OO transaction Z_OS_RENT_A_CAR, a rental car reservation is executed without COMMIT WORK being used explicitly in the class. The transaction in our example is a top-level transaction (see below), whereby the current SAP LUW is ended by the implicit execution of the COMMIT WORK statement when the END method is called. During a Transaction Service transaction, the explicit use of COMMIT WORK is even forbidden, and would trigger an exception. Therefore, remember to delete the statement from the MAIN method. Once again, you can view the result in the Data Browser (Transaction SE16).

Nesting Transactions

If a transaction is started before another transaction has ended, it automatically becomes a subtransaction of the transaction that is still

Subtransactions

running. When a subtransaction is ended with END, the SAP LUW is not also ended, and the changes to persistent objects are transferred to the current transaction. With a rollback with UNDO, on the other hand, all changes made to persistent objects in the subtransaction are undone, and the status of the objects before the subtransaction started is restored.

With subtransactions, you can separate the transactional behavior of a called service from the caller of the service. If the service called also starts a transaction, it can undo its changes to persistent instances by rolling back the transaction it started, without affecting the caller in any way. When the service ends its transaction, control is returned to the caller. The caller can then decide whether to end or to roll back the higher-level transaction. This also affects the changes made by the service called.

Transaction Mode

You can use the Transaction Service in two different ways:

▶ Compatibility mode

▶ Object-oriented transaction mode

Compatibility mode

Compatibility mode allows you to use the Persistence Service in conventional SAP LUWs. This mode is automatically active when the Persistence Service is used without the explicit use of the Transaction Service. In the compatibility mode, the runtime system implicitly starts a transaction, which must be ended with COMMIT WORK and can be rolled back with ROLLBACK WORK. This transaction is called the *top-level transaction*. Our example in Listing 10.18 uses the compatibility mode.

Object-oriented transaction mode

Object-oriented transaction mode is activated when:

▶ an OO transaction with a selected **OO transaction model** is used

▶ the static method CL_OS_SYSTEM=>INIT_AND_SET_MODES is called when the LOAD-OF-PROGRAM event is triggered, whereby the value OSCON_FALSE is passed to the I_EXTERNAL_COMMIT parameter

In both cases, you can determine whether an asynchronous, local, or synchronous update is used, where asynchronous is the standard form.

In object-oriented transaction mode, there is no implicit top-level transaction. Instead, the top-level transaction is the first transaction started. Our example in Listing 10.19 uses the object-oriented transaction mode.

Locks

If you use the Transaction Service, you should note that Object Services currently does not provide a locking service. This means that, as with conventional SAP LUWs, you must use standard lock objects and the corresponding function modules (see Section 10.1.3) to encapsulate your LUWs. You can do so, by offering methods in the class actor, which encapsulate the use of lock function modules.

10.3   File Interfaces

The persistent data that is used by ABAP programs is primarily stored in the central database of the AS ABAP. But ABAP programs can also access the file system of the other two layers of the client-server architecture of AS ABAP. This means you can also store or read persistent data in files that are managed by the operating system of the current application server or presentation server.

A frequently used method for these options is the transfer of data into the AS ABAP. You can import files that are available in a file system in any format into an ABAP program, then process the files in that program, and store them in the database. Vice versa, you can also write data from the database into those file systems to further process them, for example, using desktop applications for presentation purposes.

File system

Because the names of files and directory paths vary among operating systems, programs that access files directly are usually not platform-independent. For this reason, you can use Transaction FILE to create logical file names and logical paths that can be linked with actual identifiers for each required platform. You can then read the correct name that is linked to a logical name for the current platform in your ABAP program using function module FILE_GET_NAME.

File names

10.3.1 Files of the Application Server

ABAP file interface

To process files of the operating system of the current application server, you can use the statements of the ABAP file interface. The statements enable you to open, read, change, close, and delete files.

Opening Files

To use a file of the application server, you must open the file using the following statement:[23]

OPEN DATASET

```
OPEN DATASET dset FOR ...
                  IN {BINARY MODE}
                   |{TEXT MODE ENCODING DEFAULT}
                  [AT POSITION pos].
```

In addition to the basic form shown here, this statement has many variants that enable you to access files of different formats and character presentations. We will focus on the recommended variant here. You must define one of the following types of access to the file specified in dset after FOR:

FOR ...
- INPUT
  Opens the file for reading. The file must already exist.

- OUTPUT
  Opens the file for overwriting. If the file does not exist, it will be created.

- APPENDING
  Opens the file for appending. If the file does not exist, it will be created.

- UPDATE
  Opens the file for changing. The file must already exist.

The AT POSITION addition is used to set the file pointer, which determines from which point onwards the file should be read or changed. If elements are appended to the file, this always occurs after the current file end.

The IN BINARY MODE and IN TEXT MODE additions define that the file is treated as a binary or text file. For text files, you must specify the

---

23 You can still use certain abbreviated forms of OPEN DATASET outside of Unicode programs; however, we strongly recommend that you don't use those forms.

code page in which the contents are to be handled. The recommended code page is the 8-bit Unicode code page UTF-8 that can be specified in a Unicode system using the `DEFAULT` statement. If you specify UTF-8 explicitly, you can also specify how to handle the byte order mark (BOM):

`... ENCODING UTF-8 [SKIPPING|WITH BYTE-ORDER MARK]`

When opening a UTF-8 file for reading or changing purposes, you should specify the `SKIPPING BYTE-ORDER MARK` addition to avoid treating an existing BOM as file content. When opening a UTF-8 file for writing purposes, you should specify the `WITH BYTE-ORDER MARK` addition.

Reading and Changing Files

To read data from a file that has been opened, you can use the following statement:

`READ DATASET dset INTO dobj.`   READ DATASET

In addition to reading a file that has been opened for reading, you can also read files that have been opened for writing, appending, or changing purposes. Text files are read from the current position of the file pointer to the next end-of-line mark. With binary files, the system reads as many data as can be stored in data object `dobj`.

To write data to a file that has been opened, you can use the following statement:

`TRANSFER dobj TO dset.`   TRANSFER

The file must have been opened for writing, appending, or changing. In text files, an end-of-line mark[24] is appended to the contents of `dobj`, and the result is transferred to the file from the current file pointer onwards. For binary files, the contents of `dobj` are simply transferred.

The data object `dobj` can have an elementary data type or it can be a flat structure. It must be character-like if you want to process text files.

---

24 You can use the `NO END OF LINE` addition to avoid having to append an end-of-line mark.

The following additional statements can be used for handling opened files:

GET|SET DATASET ...

These statements enable you to read the properties of files and, to a certain extent, reset those properties. For example, you can set the file pointer and change some specifications that were made when the file was opened, such as the code page used for conversions.

Closing Files

After processing a file, it should be closed again:

CLOSE DATASET dset.

If you don't close a file, it is closed implicitly when the program terminates.

Deleting Files

Lastly, you can also delete a file:

DELETE DATASET dset.

As with all file accesses, you must pay attention to the file access authorizations here. These are checked at three different levels:

▶ Operating system checks
▶ Checks of entries in system table SPTH
▶ Check of authorization object S_DATASET in the case of accesses for changing purposes

Please refer to *The Official ABAP Reference* book for more information.

Example for Files of the Application Server

Listing 10.20 shows how the ABAP file interface works. Using a selection screen, you can open, write, read, close, and delete a file. If you use the SAP NetWeaver 2004s ABAP Trial Version, you can find the file in the following directory: *...\sap\NSP\DVEBMGS00\work*. The *work* directory is the default directory if you specify the file name without a path. Note that we call the selection screen in a loop instead of using the mechanism for executable programs, as we did in Listing 10.14 (see also Section 7.1.1), which automatically restarts the program. The reason for this is that the opened file would be closed at the end of each program execution.

Listing 10.20 ABAP File Interface

```
REPORT z_dataset.

SELECTION-SCREEN BEGIN OF SCREEN 100.
PARAMETERS: p_open    RADIOBUTTON GROUP grp,
            p_transf  RADIOBUTTON GROUP grp,
            p_read    RADIOBUTTON GROUP grp,
            p_close   RADIOBUTTON GROUP grp,
            p_delete  RADIOBUTTON GROUP grp.
SELECTION-SCREEN END OF SCREEN 100.

CLASS demo DEFINITION.
  PUBLIC SECTION.
    CLASS-METHODS: class_constructor,
                   main.
  PRIVATE SECTION.
    CLASS-DATA: scarr_tab TYPE TABLE OF scarr,
                scarr_wa  TYPE scarr.
    CONSTANTS   dset      TYPE string VALUE `myfile.dat`.
    CLASS-METHODS: open     RAISING cx_sy_file_access_error,
                   transfer RAISING cx_sy_file_access_error,
                   read     RAISING cx_sy_file_access_error,
                   close    RAISING cx_sy_file_access_error,
                   delete   RAISING cx_sy_file_access_error,
                   display  IMPORTING value(result_tab)
                            LIKE scarr_tab.
ENDCLASS.

CLASS demo IMPLEMENTATION.
  METHOD class_constructor.
    SELECT *
           FROM scarr
           INTO TABLE scarr_tab
           ORDER BY carrid.
  ENDMETHOD.
  METHOD main.
    DATA err TYPE REF TO cx_sy_file_access_error.
    DO.
      CALL SELECTION-SCREEN 100.
      IF sy-subrc <> 0.
        RETURN.
      ENDIF.
```

```
      TRY.
          IF p_open = 'X'.
            open( ).
          ELSEIF p_transf = 'X'.
            transfer( ).
          ELSEIF p_read = 'X'.
            read( ).
          ELSEIF p_close = 'X'.
            close( ).
          ELSEIF p_delete = 'X'.
            delete( ).
          ENDIF.
        CATCH cx_sy_file_access_error INTO err.
          MESSAGE err TYPE 'I' DISPLAY LIKE 'E'.
      ENDTRY.
    ENDDO.
  ENDMETHOD.
  METHOD open.
    OPEN DATASET dset FOR OUTPUT IN BINARY MODE.
    IF sy-subrc = 0.
      MESSAGE 'File opened' TYPE 'S'.
    ELSE.
      MESSAGE 'File not opened' TYPE 'S'
              DISPLAY LIKE 'E'.
    ENDIF.
  ENDMETHOD.
  METHOD transfer.
    DATA msg TYPE string.
    LOOP AT scarr_tab INTO scarr_wa.
      TRANSFER scarr_wa TO dset.
    ENDLOOP.
    msg = LINES( scarr_tab ).
    CONCATENATE msg ` lines transferred` INTO msg.
    MESSAGE msg TYPE 'S'.
  ENDMETHOD.
  METHOD read.
    DATA result_tab LIKE scarr_tab.
    SET DATASET dset POSITION 0.
    DO.
      READ DATASET dset INTO scarr_wa.
      IF sy-subrc <> 0.
        EXIT.
      ENDIF.
      APPEND scarr_wa TO result_tab.
    ENDDO.
```

```
      display( result_tab ).
  ENDMETHOD.
  METHOD close.
    CLOSE DATASET dset.
    MESSAGE 'File closed' TYPE 'S'.
  ENDMETHOD.
  METHOD delete.
    DELETE DATASET dset.
    IF sy-subrc = 0.
      MESSAGE 'File deleted' TYPE 'S'.
    ELSE.
      MESSAGE 'File not deleted' TYPE 'S'
              DISPLAY LIKE 'E'.
    ENDIF.
  ENDMETHOD.
  METHOD display.
    ...
  ENDMETHOD.
ENDCLASS.
START-OF-SELECTION.
  demo=>main( ).
```

10.3.2 Files of the Presentation Server

There are no ABAP statements available for processing files on the presentation server. Instead, the CL_GUI_FRONTEND_SERVICES class of the class library contains corresponding methods such as the following:

CL_GUI_
FRONTEND_
SERVICES

▸ GUI_DOWNLOAD for writing files

▸ GUI_UPLOAD for reading files

▸ DIRECTORY_CREATE, DIRECTORY_DELETE for creating and deleting a directory

▸ FILE_DELETE, FILE_COPY, FILE_EXIST, etc., for file operations

You can also use the function modules GUI_DOWNLOAD and GUI_UPLOAD to write and read files.

Listing 10.21 shows an example of processing files on the presentation server. Using a selection screen, you can write, read, and delete a file. The file directory is created if necessary.

Listing 10.21 Data on the Presentation Server

```abap
REPORT z_gui_download_upload.

PARAMETERS: p_downld RADIOBUTTON GROUP grp,
            p_upload RADIOBUTTON GROUP grp,
            p_delete RADIOBUTTON GROUP grp.
SELECTION-SCREEN SKIP.
PARAMETERS: p_direct TYPE c LENGTH 30
                     DEFAULT 'C:\GUI_Download_Upload\'
                     LOWER CASE,
            p_fname  TYPE c LENGTH 30
                     DEFAULT 'myfile.dat'
                     LOWER CASE.

CLASS demo DEFINITION.
  PUBLIC SECTION.
    CLASS-METHODS: class_constructor,
                   main.
  PRIVATE SECTION.
    CLASS-DATA: scarr_tab TYPE TABLE OF scarr,
                fname     TYPE string.
    CLASS-METHODS: download,
                   upload,
                   delete,
                   create_directory,

                   display IMPORTING value(result_tab)
                           LIKE scarr_tab.
ENDCLASS.

CLASS demo IMPLEMENTATION.
  METHOD class_constructor.
    SELECT *
           FROM scarr
           INTO TABLE scarr_tab
           ORDER BY carrid.
    CONCATENATE p_direct p_fname INTO fname.
  ENDMETHOD.
  METHOD main.
    TRY.
        IF p_downld = 'X'.
          download( ).
        ELSEIF p_upload = 'X'.
          upload( ).
        ELSEIF p_downld = 'X'.
          download( ).
        ELSEIF p_delete = 'X'.
```

```abap
        delete( ).
      ENDIF.
    ENDTRY.
  ENDMETHOD.
  METHOD download.
    DATA: table_line LIKE LINE OF scarr_tab,
          size       TYPE i.
    create_directory( ).
    DESCRIBE FIELD table_line LENGTH size IN BYTE MODE.
    size = size * LINES( scarr_tab ).
    cl_gui_frontend_services=>gui_download(
      EXPORTING  bin_filesize = size
                 filename     = fname
                 filetype     = 'BIN'
      CHANGING   data_tab     = scarr_tab
      EXCEPTIONS OTHERS       = 4 ).
    IF sy-subrc = 0.
      MESSAGE 'File was saved' TYPE 'I'.
    ELSE.
      MESSAGE 'File could not be saved' TYPE 'I'
              DISPLAY LIKE 'E'.
    ENDIF.
  ENDMETHOD.
  METHOD upload.
    DATA result_tab LIKE scarr_tab.
    cl_gui_frontend_services=>gui_upload(
      EXPORTING  filename     = fname
                 filetype     = 'BIN'
      CHANGING   data_tab     = result_tab
      EXCEPTIONS OTHERS       = 4 ).
    IF sy-subrc = 0.
      display( result_tab ).
    ELSE.
      MESSAGE 'File could not be loaded' TYPE 'I'
              DISPLAY LIKE 'E'.
    ENDIF.
  ENDMETHOD.
  METHOD delete.
    DATA rc TYPE i.
    cl_gui_frontend_services=>file_delete(
      EXPORTING  filename = fname
      CHANGING   rc       = rc
      EXCEPTIONS OTHERS   = 4 ).
    IF sy-subrc <> 0 OR rc <> 0.
      MESSAGE 'File could not be deleted' TYPE 'I'
```

```
                  DISPLAY LIKE 'E'.
          LEAVE PROGRAM.
        ELSE.
          MESSAGE 'File was deleted' TYPE 'I'.
        ENDIF.
    ENDMETHOD.
    METHOD create_directory.
      DATA: directory TYPE string,
            rc        TYPE i.
      directory = p_direct.
      CONCATENATE directory '\' INTO directory.
      REPLACE ALL OCCURRENCES OF '\\' IN directory WITH '\'.
      IF cl_gui_frontend_services=>directory_exist(
            directory ) IS INITIAL.
        cl_gui_frontend_services=>directory_create(
              EXPORTING directory = directory
              CHANGING  rc        = rc
              EXCEPTIONS OTHERS   = 4 ).
        IF sy-subrc <> 0 OR rc <> 0.
          MESSAGE 'Directory could not be created' TYPE 'I'
                  DISPLAY LIKE 'E'.
          LEAVE PROGRAM.
        ELSE.
          MESSAGE 'Directory was created' TYPE 'I'.
        ENDIF.
      ENDIF.
    ENDMETHOD.
    METHOD display.
      ...
    ENDMETHOD.
ENDCLASS.
START-OF-SELECTION.
  demo=>main( ).
```

10.4 Data Clusters

A data cluster is an aggregation of data objects for the purpose of storing those objects in a storage medium that can be freely selected. The storage medium can be persistent or transient. In contrast to the storage formats described in the preceding sections, such as relational databases and files, data clusters have an SAP-proprietary format that can only be processed using the associated ABAP statements.

10.4.1 Storing Data Clusters

You can use the following statement to store a data cluster:

```
EXPORT p1 = dobj1 p2 = dobj2 ...
     TO medium
     [COMPRESSION ON|OFF].
```

This statement stores the specified data objects, dobj1, dobj2, ..., under the IDs p1, p2, ..., in a cluster and saves the cluster in the medium specified. A compression function can be switched on or off when doing this. You can store all data objects except for reference variables in data clusters. If you want to store reference variables, you must first serialize them to XML (see Section 12.5).

The following specifications can be made for the storage medium:

▶ **DATA BUFFER** xstr or **INTERNAL TABLE** itab
For storage within a byte string or internal table of the current program. A data cluster stored in this way can, for instance, be transferred to procedures or stored persistently in a database table or file.

▶ **MEMORY ID** id
For storage in the ABAP memory of the current call sequence (see Section 3.3.2). You can access a data cluster stored in this way in all programs of the call sequence. A data cluster is kept within the ABAP memory until the first program of the call sequence terminates.

▶ **SHARED MEMORY** dbtab(ar) **ID** id or
SHARED BUFFER dbtab(ar) **ID** id
For storage in the cross-transaction application buffer in the shared memory of the current application server (see Section 3.3.2). The two types differ in the displacement mechanism in the case of memory bottlenecks. The storage of data clusters in the cross-transaction application buffer represents the predecessor technology of shared objects (see Section 6.5). Because it does not provide a copy-free access to the data stored in the application buffer, you should no longer use this technology.

▶ **DATABASE** dbtab(ar) **ID** id
For storage in a specially structured database table of the database. A data cluster stored in this way allows you to store processed data persistently in the database, independent from the relational model.

The ID addition defines the identifier of the data cluster in the storage media. If you store clusters in database tables, you must use dbtab to specify the database table and ar to specify an area that serves as an additional identifier. Although the cross-transaction application buffer has nothing to do with database tables, you must make the dbtab(ar) specification here as well because the data has been stored in a correspondingly structured storage table.

INDX-like   The database tables in which you can store the data clusters directly using the EXPORT statement must have a specific structure.[25] This structure contains components that contain administrative information and a CLUSTR component that stores the actual data. A database table that has the structure required for storing data clusters in database tables and in the shared memory is referred to as *INDX-like*. This term refers to database table INDX provided by SAP. The database table INDX has the required structure and can be used as a template for the creation of your own database tables as well as for testing purposes. However, we strongly recommend that you use your own INDX-like database tables in production programs. In particular, you can then customize the columns containing administrative information per your own requirements. Please refer to *The Official ABAP Reference* book for more detailed information on the structure of an INDX-like database table.

10.4.2 Reading Data Clusters

The following statement for reading a data cluster is the counterpart to the EXPORT statement:

IMPORT   **IMPORT** p1 = dobj1 p2 = dobj2 ...
          FROM medium
          [conversion_options].

The specified storage media is searched for a data cluster with the ID id, and the data stored under p1, p2, ... is assigned to data objects dobj1, dobj2, ... For this purpose, compatibility of the data types is strictly required, with a few exceptions. However, you can use some conversion_options additions to mitigate this rule, which can be

---

25 This structure is not necessary if you first export to a byte string, for example, and then save to a database. But, this also means that you must handle all of the administrative tasks yourself.

particularly important when importing data from previous releases—especially those from the pre-Unicode era. You can evaluate `sy-subrc` in order to determine whether the import was successful. In addition, it is recommended to catch all possible exceptions.

10.4.3 Deleting Data Clusters

Finally, you can also delete data clusters of a certain ID:

```
DELETE FROM medium.
```

DELETE FROM

Here you can specify the medium in the same way as for export and import with the exception that you cannot specify DATA BUFFER and INTERNAL TABLE. For those two media, you can simply use a CLEAR statement.

In addition to the statements listed here, you can also process data clusters using the methods of the subclasses of CL_ABAP_EXPIMP. In particular, these methods enable generic deletions.

10.4.4 Example for Data Clusters

In Listing 5.18, we already introduced a real-life example with program Z_STRING_OPERATOR.[26] In that example, we analyzed the subject list for the ABAP keyword documentation. This subject list is stored as a relational database table in the database, because a direct relationship exists between subjects and documents.

With the ABAP index that links the ABAP language elements with documents of the ABAP keyword documentation, things look a bit different. In this case, there can be several documents for one index entry. This fact is reflected internally by a nested internal table. Because it takes a lot of time to create this table, it makes sense to create it once and store it as a persistent data cluster.

Listing 10.22 shows how you can read the table in a program. First, the system tries to import it from the mx area of the INDX-like database table ABAPHTML. Only if this attempt fails will the function module be called to newly generate the index. The result of this is then exported as a data cluster in order to be available for import during the next program execution.

---

26 Well, at least from the real life of this author.

Listing 10.22 Data Cluster

```abap
REPORT z_import_export.

TYPE-POOLS abdoc.
CLASS demo DEFINITION.
  PUBLIC SECTION.
    CLASS-METHODS main.
  PRIVATE SECTION.
    CLASS-DATA index_tab TYPE abdoc_man_index_tab.
    CLASS-METHODS: get_index,
                   display_index.
ENDCLASS.
CLASS demo IMPLEMENTATION.
  METHOD main.
    get_index( ).
    display_index( ).
  ENDMETHOD.
  METHOD get_index.
    DATA: abaphtml_wa TYPE abaphtml,
          abaphtml_id TYPE abaphtml-srtfd,
          langu       TYPE sy-langu,
          subrc       TYPE sy-subrc.
    IF sy-langu <> 'D'.
      langu = 'E'.
    ELSE.
      langu = 'D'.
    ENDIF.
    CONCATENATE 'MAN_INDEX.' langu INTO abaphtml_id.
    TRY.
        IMPORT man_index_tab = index_tab
               FROM DATABASE abaphtml(mx)
               ID   abaphtml_id
               TO   abaphtml_wa.
        subrc = sy-subrc.
      CATCH cx_sy_import_mismatch_error.
        subrc = 8.
    ENDTRY.
    IF subrc <> 0.
      CALL FUNCTION 'ABAP_DOCU_MAN_INDEX_TABLE'
        EXPORTING langu     = langu
        CHANGING  index_tab = index_tab.
      DELETE FROM DATABASE abaphtml(mx) ID abaphtml_id.
      abaphtml_wa-aedat = sy-datum.
      abaphtml_wa-aetim = sy-uzeit.
```

```
      EXPORT man_index_tab = index_tab
             TO    DATABASE abaphtml(mx)
             ID    abaphtml_id
             FROM  abaphtml_wa.
    ENDIF.
  ENDMETHOD.
  METHOD display_index.
    ...
  ENDMETHOD.
ENDCLASS.
START-OF-SELECTION.
  demo=>main( ).
```

The example also shows the use of the FROM and TO additions with EXPORT and IMPORT, which we haven't mentioned yet. These additions enable you to export the application-specific administrative data of an INDX-like table from a correspondingly structured work area or to import the data into that work area. The example shown here involves two columns containing date and time information for the last new index generation.

10.5 Authorization Checks

To conclude our chapter on accessing external data, we have to briefly mention the extremely important subject of authorizations, which is closely linked to processing persistent data but not automatically supported by the corresponding ABAP statements. The only exception is the automatic authorization check of the ABAP file interface.

Each application of an AS ABAP usually works with data that cannot be accessed by every user, i.e., there are certain restrictions imposed. Consequently, because the ABAP statements are not linked to automatic authorization checks, you must not write a program that accesses critical data without having any security mechanism in place, as this would enable any user to access this data. Instead, you must explicitly verify whether all users and clients that may call the program do indeed have the authorization to access the data processed in this program.

10.5.1 Authorization Objects and Authorizations

Authorization object

An authorization object is a repository object in which the basic information regarding authorizations is defined. For this purpose, an authorization object contains up to 10 authorization fields that represent data such as key fields of database tables and activities such as reading or changing data. The authorization fields are used to assign authorizations and to perform authorization checks. You can maintain authorization objects in the context menu of a package in the Object Navigator via **Create • More... • Authorization Object**, or by using Transaction SU21 (authorization object maintenance). Figure 10.15 shows an example of an authorization object that has been generated in package Z_ABAP_BOOK.

Authorization

An authorization is an entry in the user master record of a user as part of an authorization profile. During the assignment of authorizations in the user master record, each user is assigned values for the fields of authorization objects. In the example displayed in Figure 10.15, the authorization object contains a field called TESTFIELD into which generic values can be entered during the assignment of authorizations to a user. If you want activities to be checked, the authorization object must contain a field called ACTVT. The abbreviations for possible activities are stored in tables TACT and TACTZ. The latter is relevant for custom developments.

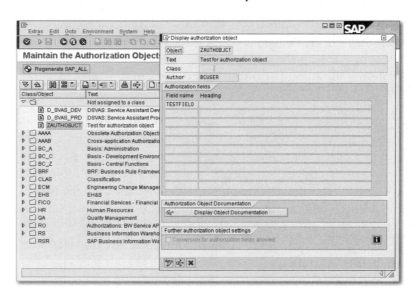

Figure 10.15 Authorization Object

You don't need to maintain each authorization object for each individual user when assigning authorizations to users. Instead, you can assign one or several predefined authorization profiles to a user. These profiles contain specific default values for all authorization objects of an AS ABAP. You can generate profiles using the profile generator from role maintenance (Transaction PFCG).

Authorization profile

10.5.2 Authorization Check

During an authorization check, for each authorization field of an authorization object a comparison is made between a value to be checked and the corresponding entries in the user master record. For your own developments, you can either draw back on the existing authorization objects, or you must create such objects by yourself and make them known to system administration so that the objects are entered into the authorization profiles.

To check the authorizations for executing entire ABAP programs or parts of ABAP programs, you have the options described in the following section. For these checks, a so-called *Check Indicator* controls whether an authorization object is actually checked. In an SAP environment, check indicators for authorization objects are set using Transaction SU22, and in customer systems, they are set using Transaction SU24. In customer systems, you must use Transaction SU25 to import the settings made in Transaction SU22 into Transaction SU24 so that they can take effect.

Check Indicator

Authorization to Execute Transactions

When creating a transaction code (see Figure 2.75 in Chapter 2, for example), you can specify the name of an authorization object in the **Authorization Object** field and click on the **Values** button to enter values for the fields of the authorization object. If a user wants to execute the transaction, the runtime environment compares those values with the values in the user master record. The transaction starts only if the user has the appropriate authorization. Otherwise the system will output a corresponding message.

If a transaction is called using the LEAVE TO TRANSACTION statement, the authorization of the current user to execute the called transaction is checked automatically. However, if a transaction is called using the

AUTHORITY_ CHECK_TCODE

791

CALL TRANSACTION statement, the authorization is not checked automatically. If no authorization check is performed within the program that has been called, you will have to call function module AUTHORITY_CHECK_TCODE in the calling program to do so.

Authorization to Execute ABAP Programs

The properties of executable programs, module pools, and subroutine pools contain the **Authorization group** input field where you can enter any name. The authorization group is linked to the P_GROUP field of authorization objects S_DEVELOP and S_PROGRAM. By combining values in this field of the program properties with values in the user master record, you can assign authorizations for individual ABAP programs. When the SUBMIT statement is executed, an automatic authorization check is performed for the authorization group specified in the program properties.

Authorization Check Within ABAP Programs

If an ABAP program cannot be protected by automatic authorization checks at program startup, or if not all the users that are authorized to execute the program are allowed to perform every action in it, you must implement an authorization check at all critical parts of your programs in the following manner:

```
AUTHORITY-CHECK OBJECT auth_obj [FOR USER user]
                ID id1 {FIELD val1}|DUMMY
                ...
                ID id10 {FIELD val10}|DUMMY.
```

This statement checks the authorization of the current user, or of another user specified optionally after USER with regard to an authorization object auth_obj. You must use id1 through id10 to specify at least one and maximally all 10 authorization fields of the authorization object. After FIELD you must specify a value to be checked; alternatively, you can specify DUMMY here. The combination of values specified after FIELD is then compared with the authorizations assigned in the user master record. If you specify DUMMY as a value, you can explicitly avoid the checking of a field. Fields of the authorization object that are not specified are not checked.

If the authorization check is successful, sy-subrc is set to 0. If the authorization check is not successful, various reasons may account for it. Either there was no authorization, the authorization object could not be found, or the authorization fields were specified incorrectly. Make sure you evaluate sy-subrc accordingly.

Listing 10.23 shows an example of a program-internal authorization check that uses the authorization object from Figure 10.15.

Listing 10.23 Authorization Check

```
REPORT z_authority_check.

PARAMETERS p_name TYPE c LENGTH 30 LOWER CASE.
CLASS demo DEFINITION.
  PUBLIC SECTION.
    CLASS-METHODS main IMPORTING i_name TYPE clike.
ENDCLASS.
CLASS demo IMPLEMENTATION.
  METHOD main.
    AUTHORITY-CHECK OBJECT 'ZAUTHOBJCT'
             ID 'TESTFIELD' FIELD i_name.
    IF sy-subrc = 0.
      MESSAGE 'Authorized' TYPE 'S'.
    ELSEIF sy-subrc = 4.
      MESSAGE 'Not authorized!' TYPE 'S'
             DISPLAY LIKE 'A'.
      RETURN.
    ELSE.
      MESSAGE 'Problem with authority check!' TYPE 'S'
             DISPLAY LIKE 'E'.
      RETURN.
    ENDIF.
    ...
  ENDMETHOD.
ENDCLASS.

START-OF-SELECTION.
  demo=>main( p_name ).
```

Figure 10.16 displays how you can create an authorization ZAU-THORIZE in the authorization profile ZPROFILETEST for authorization object ZAUTHOBJECT in Transaction SU01 (user maintenance). This authorization grants access to all fields that begin with letters between H and K.

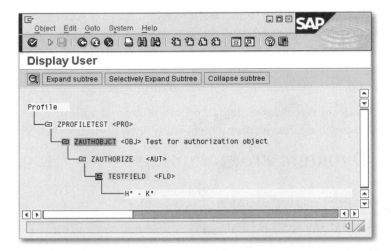

Figure 10.16 Profile of a User

If a user that is assigned this profile enters a name within the range between H and K in the selection screen of Listing 10.23, the user is accepted; otherwise, the user is rejected (see Figure 10.17).

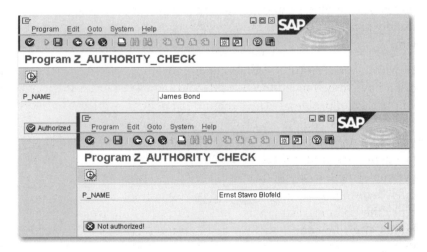

Figure 10.17 Authorization Check

"There is something static about beauty. Charm reveals itself in fleeting movement."
—Sigmund Graf

11 Dynamic Programming

Usually, a software module is developed to solve a particular problem. In general, the problem is already known when the code is compiled, and is solved by a specially implemented algorithm. A program that displays the content of a particular database table, for instance, can solve this specific problem, which has already been identified prior to the code's compilation time. This essentially involves static programming. Although such programs can also be controlled by user entries and execute different actions, depending on certain variable values or database states, nevertheless, these are usually programs that execute a specific algorithm for a specific problem.

However, for reasons of economy and efficiency, software modules often have to be much more flexible and capable in order to solve a whole class of problems. The dynamic and generic software development methods come into play here. For example, if you want to develop a program that can display the content of any table, only the problem class, and not the specific problem, is known. The precise parameters and basic conditions that must be taken into account are only determined during the program runtime. The table, its row type, the column restrictions, and a line selection are only determined after the code is compiled, when the service is requested by the user.[1]

Flexible software

In this chapter, we will present the various language tools that ABAP offers for dynamic and generic program development.

---

1 For the listing output in this book, we use, for example, the class CL_SALV_TABLE, which offers exactly this type of generic service.

11.1   Field Symbols and Data References

Field symbols and data references are used to dynamically access data objects in ABAP programs. While a data object can always be statically accessed through the name of the data object, field symbols and data references allow access to data objects whose name and attributes are only known at runtime.

With the declaration of a data object, you statically determine the data object's name and technical properties while the program is being created. These settings will apply for the entire runtime of an ABAP program and can no longer be changed. Such a data object is instantiated automatically when the program is loaded into internal mode or when the corresponding procedure is called. But what happens if your program can only decide at runtime with what data object it even wants to work? In such a case, you can dynamically address data objects with field symbols or even create them dynamically through data references.

Value semantics
You can think of field symbols as symbolic names for data objects. You work with field symbols under *value semantics*. When field symbols are accessed, solely the content of the assigned data object is addressed. Field symbols are handled in expressions like dereferenced pointers.

Reference semantics
Data references are addresses of data objects. You work with data references under *reference semantics*. Data references are the content of data reference variables, and the data reference itself is addressed when you access reference variables. To access the content of the data object to which a data reference variable refers, it must be dereferenced.

Field symbols vs. data references
When to use field symbols and when to use data reference variables depends entirely on their intended purpose. Generally, we recommend that you use data reference variables, because they embody the more modern concept and fit better into the world of ABAP Objects. Furthermore, field symbols are insufficient for certain tasks, such as mapping complex data structures in the memory. Nevertheless, there are situations where field symbols are still necessary:

▶ For dynamic access to the components of structures (see Section 11.1.1)

▶ For the casting of data objects (see Section 11.1.1)

▶ For dereferencing data reference variables with a generic data type (see Section 11.1.2)

11.1.1   Field Symbols

Field symbols are placeholders or symbolic names for existing data objects or parts of existing data objects. A field symbol does not reserve any physical space for a field; instead, it is a kind of dynamic label for a memory area, where a particular data object or a part thereof is stored.

Dynamic labels

Field symbols can point to almost any data objects.[2] The data object to which a field symbol points is assigned to it dynamically during the program's runtime. A field symbol can be compared to a data reference variable that is dereferenced with "->*". Access to a field symbol is like an access to the assigned data object, or a part of it. Although ABAP also has real pointers with data reference variables, field symbols still remain important because they allow you to work directly with memory areas to which data references cannot always be directed.

First, field symbols allow you to work generically with data objects, that is, you can program operations without knowing the data objects with which the program will actually work at runtime. Secondly, you can use field symbols for the casting of data objects. This means that you handle the content of a data object not according to the type of the data object, but rather according to another type. For dynamic programming, it is therefore important that field symbols can be typed with generic types.

To make you familiar with the principles of how field symbols work, we'll start with a brief example in Listing 11.1.

Listing 11.1 Field Symbols

```
REPORT z_field_symbols.

CLASS demo DEFINITION.
  PUBLIC SECTION.
    CLASS-METHODS main.
ENDCLASS.
```

---

2 A field symbol, however, cannot point to sections of reference variables.

```
CLASS demo IMPLEMENTATION.
  METHOD main.
    FIELD-SYMBOLS <fs> TYPE ANY.
    DATA: city    TYPE string,
          zipcode TYPE n LENGTH 5,
          output  TYPE string.
    ASSIGN city TO <fs>.
    <fs> = 'Walldorf'.
    ASSIGN zipcode TO <fs>.
    <fs> = '69190'.
    CONCATENATE zipcode city INTO output
      SEPARATED BY space.
    MESSAGE output TYPE 'I'.
  ENDMETHOD.
ENDCLASS.
START-OF-SELECTION.
  demo=>main( ).
```

In Listing 11.1 we have declared two data objects of different types and a field symbol using the FIELD-SYMBOLS statement. We use the ASSIGN statement to assign the field symbol the data object city. After this assignment, it no longer makes any difference whether we execute an operation with the field symbol or directly with city. The assignment of the character string "Walldorf" to the field symbol <fs> therefore writes into the field city. With the zipcode field, we proceed in the same way, using the same field symbol. The output with MESSAGE shows that the correct assignments of city and zip code have been made to the two data objects.

From this short example, you can already deduce what the two important elements for working with field symbols are:

▶ Declaration of a field symbol
▶ Assignment of a data object to a field symbol

We will deal with these topics in some more detail in the following sections.

Declaration and Typing of a Field Symbol

For the declaration of field symbols, you use the FIELD-SYMBOLS statement, whose basic form is:

```
FIELD-SYMBOLS <fs> {TYPE type}|{LIKE dobj}.
```

For the name of the field symbol, the angled brackets are part of the name, and must therefore be specified in the program. You must type the field symbol using the addition TYPE or LIKE. The typing is similar to the typing of interface parameters (see Section 6.1.1) and defines what data objects can be assigned to the field symbol. Generic and fully-qualified type specifications are possible. You can look up the generic types in Table 5.3 in Chapter 5. All other types, with the exception of self-defined generic table types, are complete.

All data objects whose respective properties conform to the typing can be assigned to a generically-typed field symbol. Since it is statically unknown what values of the missing properties will be transferred to the field symbol through the assignment of a data object, the system can either only dynamically access these attributes, or not access them at all. For example, a field symbol that is typed with ANY can never be handled as an internal table, while a field symbol that is typed with ANY TABLE can be handled as an internal table. Listing 11.2 shows another example.

Generic typing of a field symbol

Listing 11.2 Generically Typed Field Symbol

```
REPORT z_field_symbols_generic.

...

CLASS demo IMPLEMENTATION.
  METHOD main.
    TYPES: BEGIN OF t_address,
             street TYPE string,
             no     TYPE n LENGTH 5,
           END OF t_address.
    DATA: wa_address  TYPE t_address,
          address_tab TYPE HASHED TABLE
                      OF t_address WITH UNIQUE KEY no,
          key TYPE c LENGTH 4 VALUE 'no'.
    FIELD-SYMBOLS <fs> TYPE ANY TABLE.
    ASSIGN address_tab TO <fs>.
    "Syntax Error
    "READ TABLE <fs> WITH
    "  TABLE KEY no = '1' INTO wa_address.
    READ TABLE <fs> WITH
      TABLE KEY (key) = '1' INTO wa_address.
  ENDMETHOD.
ENDCLASS.

...
```

The deactivated READ TABLE statement would lead to a syntax error, because the system cannot statically access the no component. However, if you dynamically specify the name of the key column as the content of the key field, there is no syntax error. The system only analyzes key at runtime. If the field contains an existing column, reading will work; otherwise, an exception will occur.

Complete typing of a field symbol

Provided there is no casting, only data objects that have exactly the same type can be assigned to a fully-typed field symbol. Contrary to working with generically-typed field symbols, here all of the technical properties of the field symbol are already statically known. Each access to the field symbol is identical to an access to the data object itself, and all operations that can be performed with the data object can also be performed with the field symbol.

Assigning a Data Object to a Field Symbol

In the examples shown so far, you have already seen that we can assign a data object to a field symbol using the following statement:

ASSIGN

```
ASSIGN dobj TO <fs>.
```

The assignment can be performed either statically or dynamically.

Static ASSIGN and subfield addressing

We always refer to a static ASSIGN if the name of the data object that is being assigned to the field symbol is already known when the program is created. Here, not only can you assign entire data objects to a field symbol, but also you can assign subfields of byte- or character-type data objects, which you specify using offset- and length specifications. The syntax is the same here as it is in the subfield addressing that we already saw in Section 5.4.3:

```
ASSIGN dobj[+off][(len)] TO <fs>.
```

The subfield assignment to field symbols therefore allows us to operate on parts of byte- or character-type data objects using symbolic names. If an offset/length is specified, the data type of dobj must not be string or xstring in this case. Let's look at the example in Listing 11.3.

Listing 11.3 Static ASSIGN with Subfield Addressing

```
REPORT z_assign_static.

...
```

```
CLASS demo IMPLEMENTATION.
  METHOD main.
    DATA:
      BEGIN OF address,
        street TYPE c LENGTH 20
               VALUE 'Dietmar-Hopp-Allee',
        no     TYPE c LENGTH 3  VALUE '15a',
        zip    TYPE c LENGTH 5  VALUE '69190',
        city   TYPE c LENGTH 20 VALUE 'Walldorf',
      END OF address.
    FIELD-SYMBOLS: <street_no> TYPE c,
                   <zip_city>  TYPE c.
    ASSIGN: address(23)    TO <street_no>,
            address+23(25) TO <zip_city>.
    MESSAGE <street_no> TYPE 'I'.
    MESSAGE <zip_city>  TYPE 'I'.
  ENDMETHOD.
ENDCLASS.

...
```

Here we assign two subfields of a character-type structure to two field symbols. With `<street_no>`, the first two components are referenced, and with `<zip_city>`, the last two components are referenced. Below, we will show you an even more elegant variant of the `ASSIGN` statement that you can use to assign field symbols to components of structures.

If the name of the data object that you want to assign to a field symbol is not known until runtime, you can use the following variant of the `ASSIGN` statement:

Dynamic ASSIGN

```
ASSIGN (name) TO <fs>.
```

ASSIGN (name)

As a result of using the above statement, the data object whose name is contained in the `name` field in brackets is assigned to the field symbol `<fs>`. If the assignment is successful, `sy-subrc` is set to 0 here, as is also the case with the following dynamic variants. If no data object with the right name is found, there is no assignment to the field symbol and `sy-subrc` is set to the value four. Following a dynamic assignment, you must always check `sy-subrc` before you access the field symbol, so that no runtime error exception occurs.

We call the following variants of the dynamic assign *Dynamic Access*. With Dynamic Access, you can access the attributes of objects or classes dynamically.

Dynamic Access
```
ASSIGN oref->(attr_name)          TO <fs>.
ASSIGN (class_name)=>(attr_name)  TO <fs>.
ASSIGN (class_name)=>attr         TO <fs>.
ASSIGN class=>(attr_name)         TO <fs>.
```

Here you can specify the names of the attributes, and for static attributes, you can also specify the class name dynamically as the content of character-type data objects attr_name and class_name. Listing 11.4 shows an example in which both the class name and the attribute name are specified in the form of a character-type data object enclosed in brackets. Note that the names are not case-sensitive (i. e., there is no differentiation between uppercase and lowercase). Otherwise, in many other dynamic operand positions, ABAP generally requires that you use all uppercase (i. e., all capital letters).

Listing 11.4 Example for Dynamic Access

```
REPORT z_assign_dynamic_access.

CLASS demo DEFINITION.
  PUBLIC SECTION.
    CLASS-METHODS main.
ENDCLASS.

CLASS other_class DEFINITION.
  PUBLIC SECTION.
    CLASS-DATA: attr TYPE string
                VALUE 'Dynamic Access'.
ENDCLASS.

CLASS demo IMPLEMENTATION.
  METHOD main.
    DATA: attr_name  TYPE string VALUE `attr`,
          class_name TYPE string VALUE `other_class`.
    FIELD-SYMBOLS <attr> TYPE ANY.
    ASSIGN (class_name)=>(attr_name) TO <attr>.
    IF sy-subrc = 0.
      MESSAGE <attr> TYPE 'I'.
    ENDIF.
  ENDMETHOD.
ENDCLASS.

START-OF-SELECTION.
  demo=>main( ).
```

In the example in Listing 11.4, in the main method we dynamically access the attribute attr of the class other_class. Here, both the name of the class and the name of the attribute are given in the character-type fields `class_name` and `attr_name`.

Another form of the `ASSIGN` statement allows you to dynamically address the components of structures :

```
ASSIGN COMPONENT comp OF STRUCTURE struc TO <fs>.
```

ASSIGN
COMPONENT

The component `comp` of the structure `struc` is then assigned to the field symbol `<fs>`. If `comp` is a data object of the type `c` or `string`, its content is interpreted as the name of the component. If `comp` has a different type and if the content is a number, this specifies the number of the component. Listing 11.5 shows an example.

Listing **11.5** Assigning Structures by Component

```
REPORT z_assign_component.

CLASS demo DEFINITION.
  PUBLIC SECTION.
    CLASS-METHODS main.
  PRIVATE SECTION.
    CLASS-METHODS display_any_table
                  IMPORTING any_table TYPE ANY TABLE.
ENDCLASS.
CLASS demo IMPLEMENTATION.
  METHOD main.
    DATA scarr_tab TYPE TABLE OF scarr.
    SELECT * FROM scarr INTO TABLE scarr_tab.
    display_any_table( scarr_tab ).
  ENDMETHOD.
  METHOD display_any_table.
    DATA: text      TYPE REF TO zcl_text,
          text_line TYPE zcl_text=>t_line,
          tlen      TYPE i,
          olen      TYPE i,
          nlen      TYPE i,
          offset    TYPE i.
    FIELD-SYMBOLS: <wa>   TYPE ANY,
                   <comp> TYPE ANY.
    text = zcl_text=>get_handle( ).
    DESCRIBE FIELD text_line OUTPUT-LENGTH tlen.
    LOOP AT any_table ASSIGNING <wa>.
      CLEAR text_line.
      offset = 0.
      DO.
```

```
        ASSIGN COMPONENT sy-index
          OF STRUCTURE <wa> TO <comp>.
        IF sy-subrc <> 0.
          EXIT.
        ENDIF.
        DESCRIBE FIELD <comp> OUTPUT-LENGTH olen.
        nlen = offset + olen.
        IF nlen > tlen.
          EXIT.
        ENDIF.
        WRITE <comp> TO text_line+offset.
        offset = offset + olen + 1.
      ENDDO.
      text->add_line( text_line ).
    ENDLOOP.
    text->display( ).
  ENDMETHOD.
ENDCLASS.
START-OF-SELECTION.
  demo=>main( ).
```

A filled internal table is passed to the method `display_any_table`. This method has no knowledge of the line type of the table, but nevertheless is able to output the content of the table in tabular form. Two field symbols are used for this. A line from the passed table is assigned to the field symbol `<wa>` for each `LOOP` pass. In the `DO` loop, the individual components of a line are then assigned to the field symbol `<comp>` through their position. Provided enough space is available, the field symbols are output in calculated positions in a text line that is attached to the output table of the ZCL_TEXT class from Appendix A.6. Figure 11.1 shows the output.

Figure 11.1 Output of Components

Finally, there is also the possibility within a structure to incrementally access subfields of the structure:

ASSIGN dobj INCREMENT inc TO <fs> [RANGE range].

ASSIGN
INCREMENT

A memory area is assigned to the field symbol that is exactly as long as the data object dobj and is offset inc times this length of dobj.

With RANGE, for the ASSIGN statement you can generally specify the area within which an assignment is possible. Here, range is a data object that comprises the subareas. Without specifying RANGE, you can only access the memory area within dobj itself. The example in Listing 11.6 shows how within a character-type structure text, starting from the two-character component comp1, subfields of the component comp2 are accessed that are just as long.

RANGE

Listing 11.6 Incremental Assignment

```
REPORT z_assign_increment.

...

CLASS demo IMPLEMENTATION.
  METHOD main.
    DATA: BEGIN OF text,
            comp1 TYPE c LENGTH 2
                  VALUE 'xx',
            comp2 TYPE c LENGTH 10
                  VALUE 'aabbccddee',
          END OF text,
          result TYPE string.
    FIELD-SYMBOLS <fs> TYPE c.
    DO.
      ASSIGN text-comp1 INCREMENT sy-index
             TO <fs> RANGE text.
      IF sy-subrc <> 0.
        EXIT.
      ENDIF.
      CONCATENATE result <fs>
        INTO result SEPARATED BY space.
    ENDDO.
    MESSAGE result TYPE 'I'.
  ENDMETHOD.
ENDCLASS.

...
```

Checking the Assignment

You can use the logical expression

IS ASSIGNED   ... <fs> IS ASSIGNED   ...

to check whether a data object is assigned to a field symbol. The expression will be true if the field symbol <fs> points to a data object. We recommend that this expression be evaluated prior to using any field symbol for which it has not been otherwise ensured that the field symbol points to a data object. This is because when you access a field symbol to which no data object is assigned, an untreatable exception will occur.

Initializing Field Symbols

You can use the statement

UNASSIGN   UNASSIGN <fs>.

to ensure that no more data objects are assigned to a field symbol. After UNASSIGN, the field symbol will have the same status as it does directly after its declaration, and the above logical expression will be false.

On the other hand, the statement CLEAR <fs> does not mean that the field symbol will be initialized, but rather the memory area that was assigned to the field symbol.

Casting of Data Objects

When you assign data objects to field symbols, a cast can be performed on any data types. This means that the assigned memory area can be handled assuming a particular type. In this way it is possible, for example, to access a purely character-type structure in the same way as a single elementary field or e. g. to consider a text field under a date perspective. The explicit casting of data objects is an important attribute of field symbols and is only enabled by these.

Typing   A cast is performed with the addition CASTING of the statement ASSIGN. Furthermore, the addition CASTING allows you to assign data objects to field symbols whose type is not compatible with the typing of the field symbol. Without explicit casting with the addition CASTING, the field symbol always takes over the type of the specified data object, which must then be compatible with the typing of the field symbol.

We differentiate between a cast with an implicit type specification and a cast with an explicit type specification.

If the field symbol is typed either fully or with one of the built-in generic ABAP types c, n, p or x, the following form of the ASSIGN statement can be used :

Cast with implicit type specification

```
ASSIGN dobj TO <fs> CASTING.
```

ASSIGN CASTING

The assigned memory area is cast to the type of the field symbol. Listing 11.7 shows an example in which the content of the character-type system field sy-datum is interpreted as a structure. You can access subfields of the system field through the fully-typed field symbol, component by component.

Listing 11.7 Casting with Implicit Type Specification

```
REPORT z_assign_casting.

...

CLASS demo IMPLEMENTATION.
  METHOD main.
    TYPES: BEGIN OF t_date,
             year  TYPE n LENGTH 4,
             month TYPE n LENGTH 2,
             day   TYPE n LENGTH 2,
           END OF t_date.
    DATA msg TYPE string.
    FIELD-SYMBOLS <date> TYPE t_date.
    ASSIGN sy-datum TO <date> CASTING.
    CONCATENATE <date>-year
                <date>-month
                <date>-day INTO msg SEPARATED BY '/'.
    MESSAGE msg TYPE 'I'.
  ENDMETHOD.
ENDCLASS.

...
```

If the field symbol is typed generically, rather than completely, you can use the following form of the ASSIGN statement:

Cast with explicit type specification

```
ASSIGN f TO <fs> CASTING {TYPE type|(name)}
                        |{LIKE dobj}
                        |{TYPE HANDLE handle}.
```

ASSIGN CASTING TYPE

The assigned memory area is cast to the specified type. Behind TYPE, you can also specify a name of a data object enclosed in round brackets; this then specifies the data type dynamically. Finally, you can also use the addition TYPE HANDLE to specify a reference to a type object of the *Run Time Type Services* (RTTS, see Section 11.2), which allows an entirely dynamic casting, because such a type object can be created through the definition of a new data type.

You cannot specify any types with which an explicit casting of data objects does not make sense, such as a cast of a standard table onto a sorted table or a cast of an object reference onto a data reference.

The specified data type must be compatible with the generic typing of the field symbol. It can preserve or specialize the generic typing, but it cannot overwrite an already known technical property of the field symbol. The explicit type specification is forbidden for a fully typed field symbol.

Listing 11.8 shows an example in which the numerical content of a text field is interpreted once as a date and once as a number value. This interpretation occurs when the field symbol is assigned to an integer field, where the data type of the field symbol determines the conversion rule.

Listing 11.8 Casting with Explicit Type Specification

```
REPORT z_assign_casting_type.

CLASS demo DEFINITION.
  PUBLIC SECTION.
    CLASS-METHODS: main,
                   assign_casting
                     IMPORTING text  TYPE csequence
                               dtype TYPE csequence.
ENDCLASS.

CLASS demo IMPLEMENTATION.
  METHOD main.
    DATA: text TYPE c LENGTH 8 VALUE '20061001'.
    assign_casting( text = text dtype = 'D' ).
    assign_casting( text = text dtype = 'N' ).
  ENDMETHOD.
  METHOD assign_casting.
    DATA: int4 TYPE i,
          msg  TYPE c LENGTH 40.
    FIELD-SYMBOLS <fs> TYPE ANY.
```

```
      ASSIGN text TO <fs> CASTING TYPE (dtype).
      int4 = <fs>.
      WRITE int4 TO msg NO-GROUPING.
      MESSAGE msg TYPE 'I'.
    ENDMETHOD.
ENDCLASS.
```

. . .

11.1.2   Data References

A data reference is a reference that points to a data object in the memory. In addition to field symbols, a data reference offers an alternative access option to existing data objects, but it can also be used to dynamically create anonymous data objects. In ABAP, a data reference appears as the content of a data reference variable, which can be declared as follows (see Section 5.1.6):

```
DATA dref TYPE|LIKE REF TO data|dtype|dobj.
```

Data reference variables

As for object references, with the data reference variables we distinguish between a static and a dynamic type. The static type must be either fully typed or fully generic. You can therefore only specify complete types using `dtype` and `dobj`, or using `data` for the only complete generic data type.

The dynamic type, that is, the type of data object to which a reference variable points, is always more special than or equal to the static type (golden rule for reference variables, see Section 6.4.1). For data reference variables, there are just two cases:

Golden rule

► A fully typed data reference variable points to a data object of exactly this type.

► A data reference variable typed with `data` points to a data object of any type.

After its declaration, a data reference variable is initial, that is, it does not point to any object. There are three options for supplying a data reference variable with a data reference:

► A data reference is obtained on an existing data object.

► An anonymous data object is created through the data reference variable.

► The data reference variable is assigned an existing data reference from another data reference variable.

The content of a referenced object is accessed by dereferencing the corresponding data reference variables.

Obtaining References to Data Objects

With the following statement, you can place data references to existing data objects in data reference variables:

GET REFERENCE

```
GET REFERENCE OF dobj INTO dref.
```

Here, `dobj` is any data object that, as always, can be specified using its name, as a field symbol or as a dereferenced data reference. After the statement, `dref` points to `dobj`. Listing 11.9 shows an example for obtaining such references.

Listing 11.9 Obtaining a Data Reference

```
REPORT z_get_reference.

...

CLASS demo IMPLEMENTATION.
  METHOD main.
    TYPES char1     TYPE c LENGTH 1.
    DATA: dref      TYPE REF TO char1,
          dref_tab  LIKE TABLE OF dref,
          text      TYPE c LENGTH 10 VALUE '0123456789',
          off       TYPE i.
    DO 10 TIMES.
      off = sy-index - 1.
      GET REFERENCE OF text+off(1) INTO dref.
      APPEND dref TO dref_tab.
    ENDDO.
    LOOP AT dref_tab INTO dref.
      MESSAGE dref->* TYPE 'I'.
    ENDLOOP.
  ENDMETHOD.
ENDCLASS.

...
```

In the example, a data reference is obtained by specifying an offset/length for each individual character of the data object `text` and stored in an internal table. The data references are read again in the LOOP and dereferenced. Figure 11.2 shows the situation of the internal session of the ABAP program after the internal table is filled. The figure is the equivalent to Figure 4.12 in Chapter 4 for object references.

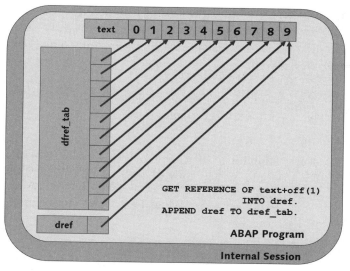

Figure 11.2 Data References in an Internal Table

Dereferencing

In Listing 11.9, you have already seen a dereferencing. It is performed through the dereferencing operator `->*`:

`... dref->* ...`   `dref->*`

If the data reference variable is fully typed, it can be specified in this form like a field symbol at all operand positions for which the referenced data object is also possible, and the statement then works with the content of the data object. If the data reference in `dref` is initial or invalid, no dereferencing is possible and an untreatable exception occurs.

If the data reference variable is typed generically with `data`, `dref->*` cannot be specified at any operand positions, but only in a special variant of the dynamic `ASSIGN`:

`ASSIGN dref->* TO <fs>.`   `ASSIGN dref->*`

Here, the memory area of the data object to which `dref` points is assigned to the field symbol, and it can then be used at any suitable operand positions. `sy-subrc` contains the value 0 following a successful assignment. If the field symbol is completely generic, it takes over the data type of the data object. In the event of a partial or complete typing of the field symbol, the compatibility of the data types will be checked. If the data reference in `dref` is initial or invalid, the field symbol is not changed and `sy-subrc` is set to four. By using `ASSIGN`, you can avoid the untreatable exception for fully typed data reference variables as well.

If the data object is a structure, you can access the entire structure with `dref->*`. With

dref->comp

```
... dref->comp ...
```

You can also access individual structure components `comp` in the same way that you would access the components of objects with object reference variables.

Anonymous Data Objects

All data objects that are declared in the declaration part of a program or a procedure are created by the runtime environment and already exist when the program or procedure starts. Such data objects have a name and can be accessed using this name. They are called *named data objects*. In addition, we also already know literals as data objects determined through their value in the source text (see Section 5.1.10). In this section, you will get to know the third type of data object that is possible in ABAP—the *anonymous data object*.

An anonymous data object is created dynamically when it is needed during program execution and receives a type corresponding to the requirements. To do so, you use the following statement:

CREATE DATA

```
CREATE DATA dref TYPE|LIKE ...
```

This statement creates an anonymous data object and assigns the reference to the data object to the `dref` reference variable. An anonymous data object cannot be addressed using a name, but rather only using a data reference variable. A dereferencing must be performed to access the contents.

Anonymous data objects are very closely related to objects that are created as instances of classes using `CREATE OBJECT`. While an object represents the instance of a class, an anonymous data object is the instance of a data type.[3]

---

3 Ultimately, a data object is an object without methods; conversely, an instance of a class without methods can be regarded as a structured data object. Furthermore, syntactically there is no difference between `dref->comp` and `oref->attr`.

The latter of course applies to every data object. What anonymous data objects and objects have in common, however, is that they can only be instantiated explicitly by using CREATE and they can only be addressed using reference variables.

By default, the data object is created in the internal session of the current program and resides there for as long as it is needed.[4] Just like the objects of a class, anonymous data objects are deleted from the memory by the Garbage Collector if they are no longer referenced by a reference variable.

Garbage Collector

To define the data type of an anonymous data object, that is, of the dynamic type of the reference variables, the statement CREATE DATA behind TYPE and LIKE offers the same possibilities as the statement DATA and also an additional feature, namely the reference to a type object of the RTTS:

Data type of anonymous data objects

- If neither the addition TYPE nor LIKE is specified behind CREATE DATA, the data object is created with the static type of the data reference variables, which must be complete for this action to take place.

- Behind TYPE and LIKE, you can use the same language elements as for DATA, to create elementary fields, reference variables, or internal tables anonymously. Behind TYPE, you can also define the type here dynamically by specifying a bracketed character-type data object (name). You cannot construct a new structure, as it is possible for DATA with BEGIN OF ... END OF. This gap is closed by the RTTS.

- The addition

  ... **HANDLE** handle ...

  behind TYPE allows you to specify a reference to a type object of the RTTS (*Run Time Type Services*, see Section 11.2). This type object can be obtained through the RTTI (*Run Time Type Information*), or may have been generated dynamically through the RTTC (*Run Time Type Creation*).

TYPE HANDLE

---

4 With certain restrictions, some of which have been relaxed as of the next SAP NetWeaver release, anonymous data objects can also be stored as shared objects (see Section 6.6) in the Shared Object Memory.

Using anonymous
data objects

Generally, anonymous data objects are used if the required data type is statically unknown (i. e., at the time of compilation), or if complex dynamic data structures, such as trees, linked lists, or the like, are to be mapped.[5] We are therefore concluding this topic in Listing 11.10 with an example in which we dynamically build and output a basic linked list.

Listing 11.10 Dynamic Data Structure in the Form of a Linked List

```abap
REPORT z_create_data.

CLASS zcl_text DEFINITION LOAD.

CLASS demo DEFINITION.
  PUBLIC SECTION.
    CLASS-METHODS main.
  PRIVATE SECTION.
    TYPES: BEGIN OF t_item,
             content TYPE zcl_text=>t_line,
             next    TYPE REF TO data,
           END OF t_item.
    CLASS-DATA: dref_start TYPE REF TO t_item,
                dref_new   TYPE REF TO t_item.
    CLASS-METHODS: create_list,
                   append_item,
                   show_list.
ENDCLASS.

CLASS demo IMPLEMENTATION.
  METHOD main.
    create_list( ).
    show_list( ).
  ENDMETHOD.
  METHOD create_list.
    DATA ncontent TYPE n LENGTH 3.
    DO 10 TIMES.
      ncontent = sy-index.
      CREATE DATA dref_new.
      CONCATENATE 'List element:'
                  dref_new->content ncontent
        INTO dref_new->content SEPARATED BY space.
      IF sy-index = 1.
        dref_start = dref_new.
      ENDIF.
```

---

5 On the other hand, the typical usage of occupying only disk space if it is needed carries less weight in ABAP, because there are dynamic data objects for this in the form of internal tables.

```
      append_item( ).
    ENDDO.
  ENDMETHOD.
  METHOD append_item.
    DATA dref_cur TYPE REF TO t_item.
    IF dref_start = dref_new.
      EXIT.
    ENDIF.
    dref_cur = dref_start.
    WHILE dref_cur->next IS BOUND.
      dref_cur ?= dref_cur->next.
    ENDWHILE.
    dref_cur->next = dref_new.
  ENDMETHOD.
  METHOD show_list.
    DATA: text      TYPE REF TO zcl_text,
          text_line TYPE zcl_text=>t_line,
          dref_cur  TYPE REF TO t_item.
    text = zcl_text=>get_handle( ).
    dref_cur = dref_start.
    WHILE dref_cur IS BOUND.
      text->add_line( dref_cur->content ).
      dref_cur ?= dref_cur->next.
    ENDWHILE.
    text->display( ).
  ENDMETHOD.
ENDCLASS.
START-OF-SELECTION.
  demo=>main( ).
```

The list contains elements of the type t_item. Each element contains **Linked list**
a value (running number) and a reference to the next list element in
the chain. The reference of the last element is always a null reference. In addition, we always include a reference to the first element
and the new element of a list to be added. The reference to the start
of the list keeps the whole list alive.

We create 10 elements in a loop. At the beginning of each loop run,
we create an element of the type t_item, to which the data reference
variable dref_cur points. We assign to the component content a
character string with the running number of the current list element.

The append_item method attaches the data object to which dref_new
points to the list. If the reference variables for the start element and

815

new element point to the same data object, it is the first list element and the method is immediately exited. Otherwise, the entire list is processed when we move through `dref_cur->next` from one element to the next. If the `next` component does not contain any valid reference, we have reached the end of the list. This is the point at which we must attach a new element, so we assign to the component `next` a reference to the new list element.

Figure 11.3 shows how the linked list is implemented in the memory. The data reference variable `dref_start` references the first dynamic data object of the list, which points to the next list element, and so on.

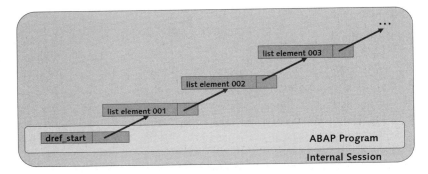

Figure 11.3 Linked List with Anonymous Data Objects

The `show_list` method runs through the complete list. In each loop pass, the data reference variable `dref_cur` is assigned the reference to the current list element. It is dereferenced, and the value of the `content` component is output.

This example already contains two operations with data reference variables that we have not mentioned so far—checking the dereferencability and assigning data references.

Checking the Dereferencability

You can use the following logical expression to check whether a data reference variable contains a valid reference or is dereferencable:

IS BOUND   `... dref IS BOUND ...`

Unlike object reference variables, for which IS BOUND is also possible, a query for the null reference with IS INITIAL is not sufficient with data reference variables. An object reference variable that contains a reference other than the null reference is always valid, because it keeps the object alive. While a data reference variable keeps anonymous data objects alive, it does not do so for named data objects to which a reference has been obtained. A data reference variable that contains a reference other than the null reference can therefore become invalid if the referenced data object is removed from memory; for example, because its context (procedure, object) is deleted. The same also applies to field symbols.

Assigning Data References

An assignment between data reference variables functions in just the same way as the assignment between object reference variables (see Section 6.4.2). You must always adhere to the golden rule that the static type is always more general than or equal to the dynamic type:

▶ If the static type of the source variables is more special than or equal to the static type of the target variables, the golden rule is fulfilled and you can use the statement MOVE or the assignment operator =. This is an Up Cast.   Up Cast

▶ If the static type of the source variables is more general than the static type of the target variables, the golden rule must be checked at runtime, and you can only use the statement MOVE ?TO or the casting operator ?=. This type of assignment corresponds to a Down Cast. The Down Cast occurs with data reference variables if the static type of the source variables is data and the static type of the target variables is completely typed. If the golden rule has not been fulfilled, a treatable exception CX_SY_MOVE_CAST_ERROR occurs.   Down Cast

Data reference variables can only be assigned to each other. Assignments to object reference variables or other variables are not possible. After the assignment, the reference in the target variable points to the same data object as the reference in the source variable. Listing 11.11 shows an example for a Down Cast with data reference variables.

Listing 11.11 Down Cast for Data Reference Variables

```abap
REPORT z_dref_down_cast.

PARAMETERS type TYPE c LENGTH 30.
CLASS demo DEFINITION.
  PUBLIC SECTION.
    CLASS-METHODS: main,
                   string_processor
                     IMPORTING dref TYPE REF TO data.
ENDCLASS.
CLASS demo IMPLEMENTATION.
  METHOD main.
    DATA dref TYPE REF TO data.
    TRY.
        CREATE DATA dref TYPE (type).
      CATCH cx_sy_create_data_error.
        MESSAGE 'Wrong data type!' TYPE 'I'
                DISPLAY LIKE 'E'.
        RETURN.
    ENDTRY.
    string_processor( dref ).
  ENDMETHOD.
  METHOD string_processor.
    DATA: sref  TYPE REF TO string,
          xref  TYPE REF TO xstring.
    IF dref IS NOT BOUND.
      RETURN.
    ENDIF.
    TRY.
        sref ?= dref.
        MESSAGE 'Processing string ...' TYPE 'S'.
      CATCH cx_sy_move_cast_error.
        TRY.
            xref ?= dref.
            MESSAGE 'Processing xstring ...' TYPE 'S'.
          CATCH cx_sy_move_cast_error.
            MESSAGE 'Not a string or xstring!' TYPE 'I'
                    DISPLAY LIKE 'E'.
        ENDTRY.
    ENDTRY.
  ENDMETHOD.
ENDCLASS.
START-OF-SELECTION.
  demo=>main( ).
```

In the `main` method, an anonymous data object is created for which the user can enter any type; types from the ABAP Dictionary are also possible. The reference to the anonymous data object is passed to the `string_processor` method, which can process byte strings or text strings. The input parameter is generically typed with `REF TO DATA`, because there is no other generic type for data reference variables.[6] Once the dereferencability is checked, the system checks using two Down Casts, and by handling the corresponding exception, whether the dynamic type of the passed data reference variables is `string` or `xstring`. This could also be determined with the methods of the RTTI, which we will introduce in the next section.

11.2   Run Time Type Services (RTTS)

The ABAP Run Time Type Services (RTTS) is an object-oriented framework that essentially fulfills two tasks:

▶ The *Run Time Type Information* (RTTI) allows type information on existing objects, that is, data objects and instances of classes, to be determined during the program execution.

▶ The *Run Time Type Creation* (RTTC) allows new data types to be defined during the program execution.

To implement these tasks, a hierarchy of system classes is available in the class library. We describe their instances as type objects. Exactly one type object can be created for each available type. New type objects can be constructed for new types. The attributes of a type object contain information on the attributes of the type.

Type object

For each type of the ABAP type hierarchy, such as an elementary type, a table or a class, for example, there is a type class with special attributes for the special type properties. Figure 11.4 shows the class hierarchy of the type classes, which reflects the hierarchy of the ABAP type hierarchy from Figure 5.2 in Chapter 5. All classes and methods of the RTTS are documented in the class library.

Type class

---

6 For `string` and `xstring`, there would be no other common generic type anyway.

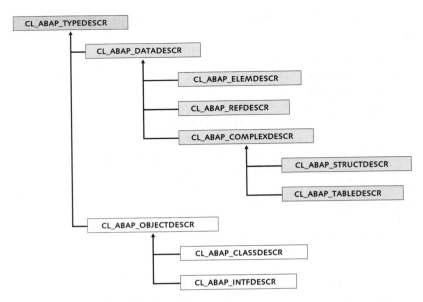

Figure 11.4 Hierarchy of the Type Classes

11.2.1 Run Time Type Information (RTTI)

In particular, during dynamic programming we often need to determine the technical properties of a data object or the instance of a class during the program execution. For instance, you want to know the data type, the length, and the number of decimal places of a generically-typed parameter in a procedure before calculating with it. All of this information can be determined using type objects.

DESCRIBE FIELD · ABAP also offers the statement DESCRIBE FIELD, however, you can only use this statement to determine information on elementary data objects. The DESCRIBE FIELD statement already shows its limitations for information on structures. For elementary data objects, you can certainly still use DESCRIBE FIELD, but for everything else, type objects are more appropriate.

CL_ABAP_ TYPEDESCR · Type objects are created using the methods of type classes. To obtain a reference to a type object of a type, you can use the static methods of the CL_ABAP_TYPEDESCR class or call methods of the special type classes. Listing 11.12 shows an example of creating and evaluating type objects with the methods of the RTTI.

Listing 11.12 Demonstration for Applying the RTTI

```
REPORT z_rtti.

CLASS demo DEFINITION.
  PUBLIC SECTION.
    CLASS-METHODS main.
  PRIVATE SECTION.
    CLASS-DATA: text      TYPE REF TO zcl_text,
                text_line TYPE zcl_text=>t_line.
    CLASS-METHODS analyze_type_object IMPORTING
       type_descr_ref TYPE REF TO cl_abap_typedescr.
ENDCLASS.

CLASS demo IMPLEMENTATION.
  METHOD main.
    TYPES: BEGIN OF my_struc,
             col1 TYPE d,
             col2 TYPE t,
           END OF my_struc.
    DATA: my_data        TYPE my_struc,
          type_descr_ref TYPE REF TO cl_abap_typedescr.
    text = zcl_text=>get_handle( ).
    type_descr_ref =
      cl_abap_typedescr=>describe_by_data( my_data ).
    analyze_type_object( type_descr_ref ).
    text->add_line( space ).
    type_descr_ref =
      cl_abap_typedescr=>describe_by_object_ref( text ).
    analyze_type_object( type_descr_ref ).
    text->display( ).
  ENDMETHOD.
  METHOD analyze_type_object.
    DATA: struc_descr_ref TYPE REF TO cl_abap_structdescr,
          components      TYPE
             cl_abap_structdescr=>component_table,
          class_descr_ref TYPE REF TO cl_abap_classdescr.
    FIELD-SYMBOLS <component> LIKE LINE OF components.
    CONCATENATE `Type name: `
              type_descr_ref->absolute_name
      INTO text_line.
    text->add_line( text_line ).
    CASE type_descr_ref->type_kind.
      WHEN cl_abap_typedescr=>typekind_struct1 OR
           cl_abap_typedescr=>typekind_struct2.
        struc_descr_ref ?= type_descr_ref.
        components = struc_descr_ref->get_components( ).
```

```
          LOOP AT components ASSIGNING <component>.
            CONCATENATE `Name: ` <component>-name
              INTO text_line.
            text->add_line( text_line ).
            CONCATENATE `Type name: `
                        <component>-type->absolute_name
              INTO text_line.
            text->add_line( text_line ).
            CONCATENATE `Type kind:`
                        <component>-type->type_kind
              INTO text_line.
            text->add_line( text_line ).
          ENDLOOP.
        WHEN cl_abap_typedescr=>typekind_class.
          class_descr_ref ?= type_descr_ref.
          class_descr_ref =
            class_descr_ref->get_super_class_type( ).
          CONCATENATE `Super class: `
                      class_descr_ref->absolute_name
            INTO text_line.
          text->add_line( text_line ).
        WHEN OTHERS.
          ...
      ENDCASE.
    ENDMETHOD.
ENDCLASS.

...
```

In this example, type information is determined for a data object that has a self-defined structured data type. Information on an object (instance of a class) is also determined. Figure 11.5 shows an output of the results.

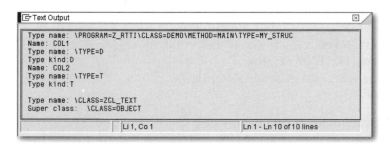

Figure 11.5 RTTI Results

Via the static method DESCRIBE_BY_DATA of the class CL_ABAP_ TYPEDESCR we create a type object that describes the properties of the structured type that the data object my_struc is based on, and pass this to the method analyze_type_object.

DESCRIBE_
BY_DATA

To demonstrate the description of an object, we then use the method DESCRIBE_BY_OBJECT_REF of the class CL_ABAP_TYPEDESCR to create an additional type object that describes the properties of the class ZCL_TEXT, on which the object that we are using for the text output is based (see Appendix A.6), and we pass this to the analyze_ type_object method.

DESCRIBE_
BY_OBJECT_REF

In the method analyze_type_object, we first display the attribute ABSOLUTE_NAME. This contains the absolute type name, which is displayed like a path description. It uniquely specifies the context of a data type, a class or an interface, and can be used in dynamic type specifications. All other type names, as we statically use them, are relative type names, because they are context-dependent, where local types hide more global types of the same name.

Absolute
type name

You can determine the type using the attribute TYPE_KIND by comparing with constants of the class CL_ABAP_TYPEDESCR. In a CASE control structure, we identify the passed type object as a description of a structure or of a class and perform a Down Cast on appropriate reference variables of the type CL_ABAP_STRUCTDESCR or CL_ ABAP_CLASSDESCR, in order to use these reference variables to access the special methods of the type object.[7] The methods can be used to examine the components of the structure or query information on the class.

CL_ABAP_STRUCT-
DESCR, CL_ABAP_
CLASSDESCR

The above example shows two different methods to create a type object: DESCRIBE_BY_DATA for the type of a data object, and DESCRIBE_BY_OBJECT_REF for the type of an object to which an object reference variable points. Other methods to create a type object are DESCRIBE_BY_NAME for a type that can be called using a relative/absolute name, and DESCRIBE_BY_DATA_REF for the type of a data object to which a data reference variable points.

DESCRIBE_BY_
NAME, DESCRIBE_
BY_DATA_REF

As shown in the example by using GET_COMPONENTS of CL_ ABAP_STRUCTDESCR, the subclasses of CL_ABAP_TYPEDESCR have

---

7 If you want to access the special methods using the reference variable of the type CL_ABAP_TYPEDESCR, a dynamic method call is required (see Section 11.4).

special methods to determine references to subtypes of complex types. With these methods, we can navigate through a composite type to all subtypes.

11.2.2 Run Time Type Creation (RTTC)

As shown in Section 11.2.1, the RTTI methods of the RTTS allow us to create a type object for any available data type, containing specific information on this data type. However, conversely, we can also create type objects on the basis of which any new types can be dynamically created while the program is being executed.[8] In this context, we refer to *Run Time Type Creation*.

Application Area of Dynamic Type Creation

The methods of the RTTC are always needed, when the tools of the statement CREATE DATA are insufficient to create a new bound type. As we already mentioned in Section 11.1.2, when creating anonymous data objects, almost all data types can be constructed as if we used the statements TYPES or DATA—with a vital exception: No new structures can be defined. Before the RTTC was introduced, this gap caused many problems for generations of ABAP programmers. Although Open SQL statements such as SELECT have allowed a dynamic token specification for a long time (see Section 11.3.1), it was not possible to dynamically create appropriate structured work areas. Either you had to work with unstructured containers, or you had to generate programs (see Section 11.5).

This gap is closed by the addition TYPE HANDLE of the statement CREATE DATA, which can refer to a type object, and the methods of the RTTC, which means that a program generation is no longer required for this purpose.

---

8 Excluded from this are elementary data types, such as c or p, because these already exist. To address them at runtime, the RTTS provides corresponding GET_... methods, where "..." in this case stands for the name of the elementary data type. See the documentation of the class CL_ABAP_ELEMDESCR.

CreatingType Objects

Type objects can be created with the factory method CREATE of one of the type classes CL_ABAP_REFDESCR, CL_ABAP_STRUCTDESCR, and CL_ABAP_TABLEDESCR.[9] The required information, from which the type is built, is passed to this method. Since the creation of different types requires very different kinds of information, the CREATE methods of the different type classes are also implemented differently. So, for example, CREATE expects a component table to create a structure type, a structure type to create an internal table, and so on.

Dynamically created data types are program-local and only live for the duration of the internal session in which they were created. Furthermore, they are always anonymous; in other words, they have no name. In much the same way that anonymous data objects can be accessed only via a data reference variable, dynamically created data types can be accessed only via their type object.

Since the type description, for example, for a structure (i.e., the component table) may be a very complex matter, it may be beneficial to perform such a type description on the basis of an existing type.

We will show you the procedure in Listing 11.13 with an example that implements a self-written data browser resp. a query for random database tables.

Data browser

Listing 11.13 Data Browser for Random Database Tables

```abap
REPORT z_rttc.

PARAMETERS: p_dbtab TYPE c LENGTH 132,
            p_cols  TYPE c LENGTH 132,
            p_where TYPE c LENGTH 132.
CLASS demo DEFINITION.
  PUBLIC SECTION.
    CLASS-METHODS  main IMPORTING dbtab TYPE csequence
                                  cols  TYPE csequence
                                  where TYPE csequence.
  PRIVATE SECTION.
    CLASS-METHODS display
```

---

9 Starting with the next SAP NetWeaver release, there will be a new GET method, which only creates a type if it doesn't already exist as a type object. It is more beneficial to use this new method rather than the CREATE method.

```abap
         IMPORTING value(result) TYPE STANDARD TABLE.
ENDCLASS.
CLASS demo IMPLEMENTATION.
  METHOD main.
    DATA: type_descr   TYPE REF TO cl_abap_typedescr,
          struct_descr TYPE REF TO cl_abap_structdescr,
          table_descr  TYPE REF TO cl_abap_tabledescr,
          table_ref    TYPE REF TO data,
          components   TYPE
            cl_abap_structdescr=>component_table,
          component    LIKE LINE OF components,
          error        TYPE REF TO cx_root.
    FIELD-SYMBOLS <table> TYPE ANY TABLE.
    cl_abap_typedescr=>describe_by_name(
      EXPORTING  p_name = dbtab
      RECEIVING  p_descr_ref = type_descr
      EXCEPTIONS type_not_found = 4 ).
    IF sy-subrc = 4.
      MESSAGE 'Type not found' TYPE 'I'
              DISPLAY LIKE 'E'.
      RETURN.
    ENDIF.
    TRY.
        struct_descr ?= type_descr.
      CATCH cx_sy_move_cast_error INTO error.
        MESSAGE error TYPE 'I' DISPLAY LIKE 'E'.
        RETURN.
    ENDTRY.
    components = struct_descr->get_components( ).
    LOOP AT components INTO component.
      CONCATENATE '\b' component-name '\b'
        INTO component-name.
      FIND REGEX component-name IN cols.
      IF sy-subrc <> 0.
        DELETE components INDEX sy-tabix.
      ENDIF.
    ENDLOOP.
    TRY.
        struct_descr =
          cl_abap_structdescr=>create( components ).
        table_descr =
          cl_abap_tabledescr=>create( struct_descr ).
      CATCH cx_sy_struct_creation
            cx_sy_table_creation INTO error.
        MESSAGE error TYPE 'I' DISPLAY LIKE 'E'.
```

```
            RETURN.
        ENDTRY.
        TRY.
            CREATE DATA table_ref TYPE HANDLE table_descr.
            ASSIGN table_ref->* TO <table>.
          CATCH cx_sy_create_data_error INTO error.
            MESSAGE error TYPE 'I' DISPLAY LIKE 'E'.
            RETURN.
        ENDTRY.
        TRY.
            SELECT (cols)
                    FROM (dbtab)
                    INTO CORRESPONDING FIELDS OF TABLE <table>
                    WHERE (where).
          CATCH cx_sy_sql_error INTO error.
            MESSAGE error TYPE 'I' DISPLAY LIKE 'E'.
            RETURN.
        ENDTRY.
        display( <table> ).
      ENDMETHOD.
      METHOD display.
        ...
      ENDMETHOD.
    ENDCLASS.
    START-OF-SELECTION.
      demo=>main( EXPORTING dbtab = p_dbtab
                            cols  = p_cols
                            where = p_where ).
```

A large part of the program consists of exception handling—a situation that cannot be avoided in dynamic programming to prevent runtime errors, because a static checking of the dynamic parts is not possible as a matter of principle. Minus the exception handling, the realization of a general data browser is completely straightforward:

▶ A selection screen allows you to enter a database table, the number of columns you want, and the condition for a SELECT statement.

▶ The columns of the entered database table are determined with the DESCRIBE_BY_NAME method and the subsequent GET_COMPONENTS of the RTTI. Unlike RTTC, the RTTI already existed prior to the introduction of the class-based exceptions, so, unfortunately here, we must do a classical exception handling via sy-subrc.

- ► A regular expression is used to remove all lines from the component table whose components were not requested by the user.

- ► Based on the reduced component table, with the RTTC method CREATE of the class CL_ABAP_STRUCTDESCR, a type object is created for a new structure and from this, with CREATE of the CL_ABAP_TABLEDESCR class, a new type object for an internal table of this line type.

- ► With the addition TYPE HANDLE of the CREATE DATA statement, an internal table is created as an anonymous data object on the basis of the new type object. Because the static type of the reference variables used must be generic, the new table is immediately assigned a field symbol <table> through the dereferencing provided especially for this purpose. The field symbol enables the user to access the new table from hereon like a normal data object.

- ► The remainder is a fully dynamic SELECT statement, which we are already using here in anticipation of Section 11.3.2. Thanks to the RTTC, the anonymous data object named by <table> offers a perfectly appropriate target table, which we, in turn, output in the display method entirely dynamically as an ALV list.

This example impressively illustrates the possibilities of dynamic programming in ABAP. It can output the desired columns and rows of any database table defined in the ABAP Dictionary. Just try it yourself! Figure 11.6 shows an example for a possible input into the selection screen, and Figure 11.7 shows the result of this input.

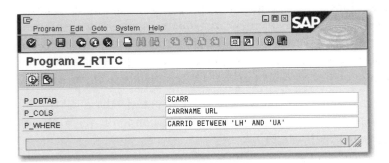

Figure 11.6 Query Input for the Data Browser

Without the RTTC, such results would only be possible via program generation, as described in Section 11.5. For such purposes, at least, a program generation is now no longer needed.

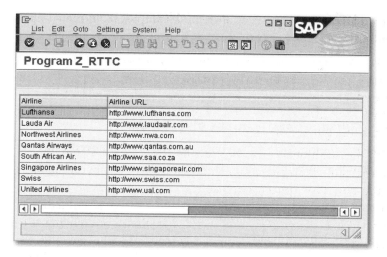

Figure 11.7 Result of the RTTC-Based Data Browser

Basically, the concept of the dynamic creation of types is very simple. The only challenge is to ensure that you give the type object during CREATE the right information. Here, if possible you should work on the basis of existing types and modify their description accordingly, as we did in the example with the component table.

11.3   Dynamic Token Specifications

Many ABAP statements allow you to specifiy individual operands or entire portions of the application dynamically as content of a character-type data object. The content of the data object is evaluated only when the statement is executed and the statement is dynamically assembled. If the statement is then not syntactically correct, a corresponding exception occurs that must be handled to avoid a runtime error.

The syntax for the dynamic token specification is usually such that instead of the static syntax, a bracketed data object is given that contains the actual syntax:

```
... (dobj) ...
```
                                                                        (dobj)

`dobj` usually involves elementary character-type fields. However, there are also statements for which internal tables with a character-type line type can be specified. When an internal table is specified, its lines are combined to form a single expression.

Note that the syntax in dynamic token specifications often must be given in all uppercase. Here, exceptions confirm the rule.

11.3.1 Dynamic Specifications of Operands

The most common form for dynamic tokens is the specification of individual operands. Examples include:

- `SUBMIT` (name) ... for dynamic program calls
- `WRITE` (name) `TO` ... for dynamic formatted assignments
- `READ|SORT|MODIFY|DELETE` ... (name1) ... (name2) ... for the dynamic component specification when editing internal tables
- `ASSIGN` (name) ... for the dynamic `ASSIGN`
- `ASSIGN` ... `CASTING TYPE` (name) or `CREATE DATA dref TYPE` (name) ... for a dynamic type specification

These are statements for which dynamic specifications are an alternative to static specifications. There are also statements for which operands can only be given dynamically, for which there are no static forms. Examples include:

- `CALL TRANSACTION` trans ...
- `CALL FUNCTION` func ...

You must always specify character-type fields for trans and func. You can only achieve a kind of static form here by specifying literals.

11.3.2 Dynamic Specifications of Clauses

The most prominent example for the dynamic specification of entire clauses are Open SQL statements. Here, entire parts of a statement, including the ABAP language elements, are specified as the content of bracketed data objects, without there being any significant restrictions in the syntax. For example, you can even form joins in a dynamic FROM clause. Listing 11.13 has already shown a SELECT statement in which all clauses are specified dynamically.

Starting with the next release of SAP NetWeaver, you will also be able to dynamically specify the WHERE clauses for internal tables.

11.3.3 Special Dynamic Specifications of Clauses

Lastly, there are also dynamic specifications, which are made through special internal tables. Examples include:

▶ Specifying the sort criteria for the statement SORT itab

▶ Specifying the data objects for EXPORT/IMPORT or for CALL TRANS-FORMATION

▶ Parameter transfer for dynamic procedure calls (see Section 11.4)

To demonstrate dynamic token specifications, Listing 11.14 shows a data browser that is simplified compared with Listing 11.13. It works without an RTTC (Run-Time Type Creation), but it can sort the result according to a column.

Data browser without RTTC

Listing 11.14 Simple Data Browser with Sorting

```
REPORT z_dynamic_tokens.

PARAMETERS: p_dbtab TYPE c LENGTH 30,
            p_sort  TYPE c LENGTH 30.
CLASS demo IMPLEMENTATION.
  METHOD main.
    DATA: tref      TYPE REF TO data,
          otab      TYPE abap_sortorder_tab,
          oline     LIKE LINE OF otab,
          error     TYPE REF TO cx_root.
    FIELD-SYMBOLS <table> TYPE STANDARD TABLE.
    TRY.
        CREATE DATA tref TYPE TABLE OF (p_dbtab).
        ASSIGN tref->* TO <table>.
      CATCH cx_sy_create_data_error INTO error.
        MESSAGE error TYPE 'I' DISPLAY LIKE 'E'.
        RETURN.
    ENDTRY.
    TRY.
        SELECT *
            FROM (p_dbtab)
            INTO TABLE <table>.
      CATCH cx_sy_sql_error INTO error.
        MESSAGE error TYPE 'I' DISPLAY LIKE 'E'.
        RETURN.
    ENDTRY.
    TRY.
        IF p_sort IS NOT INITIAL.
          oline-name = p_sort.
```

```
        APPEND oline TO otab.
          SORT <table> BY (otab).
        ENDIF.
      CATCH cx_sy_dyn_table_error INTO error.
        MESSAGE error TYPE 'I' DISPLAY LIKE 'E'.
        RETURN.
    ENDTRY.
    display( <table> ).
  ENDMETHOD.
  METHOD display.
    ...
  ENDMETHOD.
ENDCLASS.

...
```

Since all columns are to be read, the line type of the target table in the statement CREATE DATA can be specified as a dynamic token. In this SELECT statement, only the FROM clause is specified as a dynamic token specification, while the SELECT clause is specified statically. The sorting of the internal table demonstrates the use of the special table otab for the dynamic specification of the sort column.

11.4   Dynamic Procedure Call

The dynamic procedure call is really nothing more than an application of dynamic token specifications. However, because of its major importance, we will look at this now in detail.

11.4.1   Dynamic Method Call

A method call, apart from the static form introduced in Section 6.1.2, is also possible in the following dynamic form:

CALL METHOD
```
CALL METHOD {(meth_name)
            |oref->(meth_name)
            |(class_name)=>(meth_name)
            |class=>(meth_name)
            |(class_name)=>meth}
  [PARAMETER-TABLE ptab]
  [EXCEPTION-TABLE etab].
```

With this form, you must use the language element CALL METHOD. This can also be specified for static calls, but it isn't necessary there. The method to be called can be specified by dynamic token specifications in various forms, which essentially correspond to the dynamic access to attributes (see Section 11.1.1). Correspondingly, we refer to the dynamic call as a *Dynamic Invoke*.

Dynamic Invoke

Behind PARAMETER-TABLE and EXCEPTION-TABLE, we can specify special internal tables for the parameter transfer or the handling of any non-class-based exceptions. Needless to say, the latter is not required for class-based exceptions, which, as always can be handled in a TRY control structure.

PARAMETER-TABLE, EXCEPTION-TABLE

Let's look at the table to be specified behind PARAMETER-TABLE in a little more detail. This is a hash table of the type ABAP_PARMBIND_TAB with the line type ABAP_PARMBIND, both from the type group ABAP. The line type has three components:

▶ **NAME**
Here you must specify the name of the relevant formal parameter.

▶ **KIND**
Here you can specify the kind of parameter from the caller's point of view. You can use the constants of the CL_ABAP_OBJECTDESCR class for this parameter.

▶ **VALUE**
This component is of the type REF TO data and is used as a pointer to an appropriate actual parameter. The data object to which the reference variable in VALUE points is assigned to the formal parameter specified in NAME.

During execution of the CALL METHOD statement, this table must contain exactly one line for each non-optional formal parameter, and can contain exactly one line for each optional formal parameter.

The procedure is best explained using an example such as that provided in Listing 11.15, in which we have rudimentarily implemented an environment for random method tests.

Listing 11.15 Dynamic Method Call

```
REPORT z_dynamic_invoke.

PARAMETERS: p_class TYPE string
            DEFAULT `CL_GUI_FRONTEND_SERVICES`,
```

```
                    p_meth   TYPE string
                       DEFAULT `DIRECTORY_EXIST`,
                    p_in     TYPE string
                       DEFAULT `DIRECTORY`,
                    p_value TYPE string
                       DEFAULT `c:\windows`,
                    p_out    TYPE string
                       DEFAULT `RESULT`.

CLASS demo DEFINITION.
  PUBLIC SECTION.
    CLASS-METHODS main.
    TYPE-POOLS abap.
ENDCLASS.

CLASS demo IMPLEMENTATION.
  METHOD main.
    DATA: out_value  TYPE string,
          parameter  TYPE abap_parmbind,
          parameters TYPE abap_parmbind_tab,
          error      TYPE REF TO cx_root,
          msg        TYPE string.
    parameter-name = p_in.
    parameter-kind = cl_abap_objectdescr=>exporting.
    GET REFERENCE OF p_value INTO parameter-value.
    INSERT parameter INTO TABLE parameters.
    parameter-name = p_out.
    parameter-kind = cl_abap_objectdescr=>returning.
    GET REFERENCE OF out_value INTO parameter-value.
    INSERT parameter INTO TABLE parameters.
    TRY.
        CALL METHOD (p_class)=>(p_meth)
          PARAMETER-TABLE parameters.
        CONCATENATE `Return value: ` out_value
          INTO msg.
        MESSAGE msg TYPE 'I'.
      CATCH cx_sy_dyn_call_error INTO error.
        MESSAGE error TYPE 'I' DISPLAY LIKE 'E'.
    ENDTRY.
  ENDMETHOD.
ENDCLASS.

START-OF-SELECTION.
  demo=>main( ).
```

Input parameter and return value — Our example works for any static methods of global classes that expect exactly one non-optional input parameter and deliver a return value, which are both compatible with the data type `string`. You must enter the names for the class, method, parameter, and the value of the parameter on a selection screen.

These two parameters are each represented by a line in the parameter table `parameters`. While the components NAME and KIND can simply be assigned to the parameter table, in the component VALUE, we must store a data reference to a data object in each case, which then acts as an actual parameter.

With the default values shown, a method is called that determines whether a particular directory exists on the presentation server. After the call, `out_value` contains the method's return value.

As already mentioned, this example is just a brief demonstration of how the Dynamic Invoke works. Hopefully, you can now imagine how you can also write more universal wrappers for any method calls, with parameter tables and information on the methods that you obtain using the RTTI (see Section 11.2.1).

11.4.2 Dynamic Function Module Call

In Section 7.2.1, we explained that the specification of the function module in statement CALL FUNCTION is theoretically always dynamic. However, as long as there is a static parameter transfer, a function module is usually specified as literal and not as the content of a variable. In this case, we can therefore certainly refer to a static call.

But, like dynamic method calls, a real dynamic function module call is also possible:

```
CALL FUNCTION func
  [PARAMETER-TABLE ptab]
  [EXCEPTION-TABLE etab].
```

CALL FUNCTION

Here, the function module is specified as the content of a character-type variable `func`, and the parameters are transferred in just the same way as for the dynamic method calls via special tables PARAMETER-TABLE and EXCEPTION-TABLE. The data types of the tables are the only difference. For function modules, they are of the type ABAP_FUNC_PARMBIND_TAB and ABAP_FUNC_EXCBIND_TAB, but they are handled in almost exactly the same way as they are for dynamic method calls.

Subroutine In the third type of procedure in ABAP—the subroutines—the subroutine can also be specified dynamically during the call, but dynamic parameter transfers are not possible. The dynamic subroutine call still plays a role during transient program generation (see Section 11.5.1).

11.5 Program Generation

In the previous sections, we described dynamic and generic programming, and we explored many different variants of the dynamics involved. Nevertheless, there may be situations in which the actual tasks to be accomplished are so structurally different, or where we are forced to tackle such frequently changing input parameters, that a dynamic control of the program with the development methods shown thus far is no longer sufficient.

The *program generation* is available as a final emergency solution in such cases. It allows complete programs to be fully generated and executed while a program is being executed. For a very specific problem, you would therefore have the program that is currently running generate an appropriate solution module. A program obviously cannot itself actually program, but if you give it the right prerequisites, you can easily use it as a code generator for certain problems.

Transient and persistent generation ABAP gives you two options to create dynamic programs. We distinguish between a *transient program generation* and a *persistent program generation*:

- Transient programs are created temporarily in the main memory and are available only in the current internal session.

- Persistent programs are created in the Repository and can be called throughout the system.

While we do provide you with a brief example of the program generation in the following section, you should note that, in most cases, ABAP—with the tools that you have already seen in this chapter—makes the dynamic program generation superfluous.

Dynamic program generation is the most advanced, but often also the most labor-intensive and error-prone, dynamic programming option:

► Generated programs are hard to test and maintain.

► Generated programs can present serious security risks.

► The program generation performance is poorer than dynamic token specifications. An exception to this rule is the repeated use of the same dynamic parts in a program, where a generation only occurs once, which can be preferable to a repeated evaluation of other dynamic parts.

The bottom line is that dynamic program generation is a tool for real experts. For instance, if a program's source code depends on settings when an entire AS ABAP starts and otherwise remains stable, a generation based on a previously stored template may be very helpful. On the other hand, for these programs, you must then also dynamically perform all of the administrative activities and dynamically connect the programs to test tools.

Expert tool

11.5.1 Transient Program Generation

For the transient program generation, there is the following statement:

```
GENERATE SUBROUTINE POOL itab NAME prog.
```

GENERATE SUB- ROUTINE POOL

This statement generates a temporary subroutine pool. The source code of the subroutine pool is extracted from the character-type internal table `itab`. The generated subroutine pool is stored in the memory of the current internal session, and the variable `prog` is assigned the name of the temporary subroutine pool, through which it can be accessed.

If the source code contained in `itab` has a syntax error, the subroutine pool is not generated. The statement GENERATE SUBROUTINE POOL has further additions for analyzing syntax and generation errors.

Unfortunately, ABAP does not offer any GENERATE CLASS POOL statement to generate class pools instead of subroutine pools. Such a subroutine pool can only be reached from outside through external subroutine calls.[10] Nevertheless, you should also work with ABAP Objects in a generated subroutine pool. An externally called subroutine of a subroutine pool, such as the processing block START-OF-

ABAP Objects in subroutine pools

---

10 In fact, there is a trick to reach a method of local classes with a dynamic method call by using absolute type names, but we won't elaborate on this here.

SELECTION of an executable program, can serve here purely as a point of entry into the program and immediately call a method of a local class.

To generate a program that is as fault-free as possible, we recommend that you store a pre-defined program as a template in the Repository and read it with the statement

READ REPORT

```
READ REPORT INTO itab.
```

into the internal table. There you can modify the parts you want before a temporary subroutine pool is generated from it. Listing 11.16 shows such a template for a small data browser.

Listing 11.16 Template for Transient Program

```
PROGRAM z_data_browser_pattern.

CLASS demo DEFINITION.
  PUBLIC SECTION.
    CLASS-METHODS main.
  PRIVATE SECTION.
    CLASS-METHODS display
      IMPORTING value(result) TYPE STANDARD TABLE.
ENDCLASS.
CLASS demo IMPLEMENTATION.
  METHOD main.
    DATA result TYPE TABLE OF t100.
    SELECT *
          FROM t100
          INTO TABLE result.
    display( result ).
  ENDMETHOD.
  METHOD display.
    DATA alv TYPE REF TO cl_salv_table.
    TRY.
        cl_salv_table=>factory(
          IMPORTING r_salv_table = alv
          CHANGING  t_table      = result ).
        alv->display( ).
      CATCH cx_salv_msg.
        MESSAGE 'ALV display not possible' TYPE 'I'
                DISPLAY LIKE 'E'.
    ENDTRY.
  ENDMETHOD.
ENDCLASS.
```

```
FORM entry.
  demo=>main( ).
ENDFORM.
```

This template is free of errors and the subroutine entry could already be externally called from every other program. To do this, the program accesses the message table T100, which is contained in every AS ABAP.

The program in Listing 11.17 is the generation equivalent to the dynamic data browsers from Listing 11.13 and Listing 11.14. It reads the sample program from Listing 11.16, replaces the name of the database table T100 with the input on the selection screen, generates the modified program, and calls up the entry subroutine.

Generated data browser

Listing 11.17 Transient Program Generation

```
REPORT z_generate_subroutine_pool.

PARAMETERS p_dbtab TYPE string.
CLASS demo DEFINITION.
  PUBLIC SECTION.
    CLASS-METHODS main.
ENDCLASS.
CLASS demo IMPLEMENTATION.
  METHOD main.
    DATA: source TYPE TABLE OF string,
          prog   TYPE string,
          msg    TYPE string.
    READ REPORT 'Z_DATA_BROWSER_TEMPLATE' INTO source.
    IF sy-subrc <> 0.
      MESSAGE 'Template not found' TYPE 'I'
              DISPLAY LIKE 'E'.
      RETURN.
    ENDIF.
    REPLACE ALL OCCURRENCES OF 'T100' IN TABLE source
            WITH p_dbtab IGNORING CASE.
    GENERATE SUBROUTINE POOL source NAME prog
                      MESSAGE msg.
    IF sy-subrc = 0.
      PERFORM entry IN PROGRAM (prog).
    ELSE.
      MESSAGE msg TYPE 'I' DISPLAY LIKE 'E'.
    ENDIF.
```

```
  ENDMETHOD.
ENDCLASS.
START-OF-SELECTION.
  demo=>main( ).
```

This program can also display the content of any database tables of the ABAP Dictionary. We refrained from presenting you with any accesses more complicated than simple read-outs, because then the program generation quickly becomes very complex.

11.5.2 Persistent Program Generation

The persistent program generation functions in a similar way to the transient program generation. You must again create an internal table containing the source code of the new program, and then store this with the following statement under the name `prog`:

INSERT REPORT   `INSERT REPORT` prog `FROM` itab.

The main difference between persistent program generation and transient program generation is that persistent programs are stored, just as it is for manually written programs, in the AS ABAP Repository, where they are available for general use. The program type and the remaining program attributes can be freely selected. However, the new program is not initially assigned to any package. If a package assignment is required, you must do this yourself using suitable means.

TRDIR   Furthermore, it is vital to note that the statement `INSERT REPORT` overwrites existing programs entirely and without warning. You can prevent any unintended overwrites by first checking the system table TRDIR to check whether the name given in `prog` is not already contained in its NAME column.

"The most interesting thing is the inside of the outsider."
—*Jean Genet*

12   External Interfaces

The ABAP environment is not only the functional core of the actual AS ABAP in SAP NetWeaver, it is also the core of an entire ABAP-based SAP system, including its various application components. Using methods, function modules, and complex ABAP programs, processes are controlled, data is extracted, and messages and documents are generated.

Besides the processing of application data, however, one more requirement must be satisfied in order to model business processes universally: the ability to communicate with other systems.

Communication capabilities

After all, what good is an Enterprise Resource Planning (ERP) system that can process business processes within the company without problems, but can't send data to and receive data from the outside and do so consistently? In today's networked world, a customer must be able, for instance, to process invoices from an SAP system directly in his or her non-SAP system; conversely, the offers of external suppliers with non-SAP systems shouldn't have to be hand-fed to a SAP system.

There must be appropriate mechanisms in place that can be used to enable an AS ABAP to communicate freely with the outside word, such as with the ABAP-based system of a business partner, with a non-ABAP-based system, or with the Internet.

The AS ABAP offers a number of communications technologies for this purpose, which make it possible to receive, process, and transmit external data. In this section, we'll concentrate on the basic techniques used by the AS ABAP to support the latest in communications scenarios:

Communications technologies

▶ **Communication via Remote Function Call (RFC)**
This is the classical ABAP communication technology. It allows communication between different AS ABAP systems, between AS ABAP and non-SAP systems, between AS ABAP and AS Java in SAP NetWeaver, and between AS ABAP and external Java systems.

▶ **Communication via the Internet Communication Framework (ICF)**
This technology was introduced in Release 6.10 and turned the earlier SAP Basis into SAP Web Application Server, which today is AS ABAP. The ICF lets an ABAP program have direct access to the Internet and forms the basis of all corresponding applications.

▶ **Communication via Web Services**
These represent a "high-level" interface for the AS ABAP to the Internet. Web services, like the entire web technology of AS ABAP, are based on the ICF, but encapsulate their SAP-specific technology behind a high-level standardized protocol. For a web service client, the actual technology of the web service provider is no longer important.

Data transmission An important feature of any communication is the type of data transmission. Here, XML has gained increasingly more ground in the last decade as a standard for the description of the format of the data transmitted. That's reason enough to examine ABAP's handling of XML as a standard data interface.

Since we can only touch on the most important topics here, for more information, we refer you to the book *SAP Interface Programming* by Johannes Meiners and Wilhelm Nüßer (SAP PRESS 2004).

12.1 Synchronous and Asynchronous Communication

Before we turn our attention to the individual technologies, let's look at the two basic types of communications, since these play an important role, particularly in RFC.

Communications between two systems can be separated into two basic types: *synchronous* and *asynchronous communications*. Both communication forms have specific advantages and disadvantages, which can affect their business applications and system administration.

12.1.1 Synchronous Communication

Synchronous communication (see Figure 12.1) works with a one-time function call. This assumes that at the time of the call (e. g., the sending of a message), the receiving system is also active and can immediately receive the call, and, if necessary, process it.

▶ **Advantage:** Synchronous communication can be used for function calls that require the immediate return of data to the sending system. For example, in the sending system, we want to create an order for an account and execute a budget verification in the central accounting system before saving the order.

One-time call

▶ **Disadvantage:** It must be verified that both systems are active and addressable. Otherwise, there may be serious problems with process flow. Problems may, for instance, arise when the receiving system is unavailable for maintenance reasons (e. g., in the process of a system upgrade) for longer periods of time.

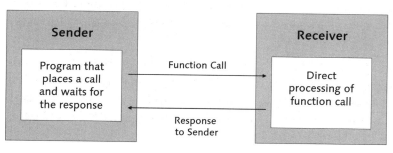

Figure 12.1 Synchronous Communication

12.1.2 Asynchronous Communication

In asynchronous communication (see Figure 12.2), the receiving system does not need to be available when a function call is made by the sending system. The receiving system can take the call at a later time and process it. If the receiving system is not addressable, the function call is placed into the outgoing queue of the sending system. The call is then repeated at regular intervals until it can be processed by the receiving system.

▶ **Advantage:** The receiving system does not need to be available at the time of the function call. If the system is inactive for a longer time, such as for an upgrade, it can also process the data (sent in the meantime) at some later time, without disturbing the proc-

Outgoing queue

esses in the sending system. For instance, let's say that an order is to be sent to a supplier's system. The sending system has no influence on the availability of the receiving system. If the receiving system isn't available, the transmission of the order can be repeated until the supplier's system is available again.

▶ **Disadvantage:** Processes that require an immediate response to the sender system cannot be executed with this method.

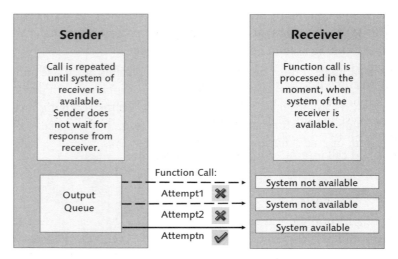

Figure 12.2 Asynchronous Communication

If you use asynchronous communications, you typically have the option to send data (e.g., business documents or master data changes) in packets or even individually (e.g., immediately). (Please note: The option "send immediately" should not be confused with "synchronous communication"!)

Work process | The advantage of sending data packets lies in the better use of system resources, since every external function call is assigned its own work process on an AS ABAP. For example, we want to distribute 100 materials master changes to different systems. If we transmit the changes in packets (of 100 apiece), we need only one work process. If we were to send the same 100 materials master changes individually, we would need 100 separate work processes.

Therefore, if you use asynchronous communication, you should always consider the tradeoff between availability of your system resources and the necessity of immediate data transmission carefully.

Before we explore the possibilities of synchronous and asynchronous communications in AS ABAP, there's one more thing that we want to say: Unfortunately, the term "asynchronous" is sometimes used with a certain degree of ambiguity, which can lead to misunderstandings. In the following sections, therefore—wherever it seemed necessary—we have clarified these ambiguities in order to clarify the actual properties of the two types of communication.

12.2 Remote Function Call (RFC)

Remote Function Call (RFC) is SAP's own standard protocol in AS ABAP to allow functions in remote systems to be called. All communication between two AS ABAP systems, or between an AS ABAP or another system can be implemented using the RFC interface of an AS ABAP. The RFC interface consists of a call interface for ABAP programs and call interfaces for non-ABAP programs.

RFC interface

12.2.1 RFC Variants

Remote Function Calls include different variants that have different features and are correspondingly used for different purposes. All RFC variants are transmitted via CPI-C (*Common Programming Interface for Communication*, a standard IBM interface for intersystem communication of programs) or TCP/IP (Transmission Control Protocol/Internet Protocol). They represent a form of gateway communication.

CPI-C, TCP/IP

Synchronous RFC

A *synchronous RFC* (sRFC) executes a call to an external function from an AS ABAP based on synchronous communication, that is, all systems involved must be addressable at the time of the call. If the target system is not available at the time of the call, a SYSTEM_FAILURE or COMMUNICATION_FAILURE exception is raised, that is, this call fails and is not repeated by the system. This also results in the basic characteristic (*Quality of Service*) of synchronous RFC. It is executed at most one time (*At Most Once*). If the first (and only) communications attempt fails, the call is abandoned.

sRFC

Asynchronous RFC

aRFC As its name implies, *asynchronous RFC* (aRFC) is a form of asynchronous communication. This is only conditionally true, however, since aRFC does not strictly fulfill all the criteria of asynchronous communication (see Section 12.1.2).

As you'll see, the RFC variants still to come—tRFC and qRFC—are the variants that work asynchronously in the stricter sense. It's important to distinguish between the terms: Asynchronous RFC in SAP terminology denotes a standalone RFC type, which should really be called "pseudo-asynchronous." However, it is not the generic term for rRFC or qRFC (which both represent true asynchronous communications.)

The aRFC is similar to tRFC or qRFC in that the calling programming need not wait for the successful execution of the RFC before continuing processing, that is, functional control returns directly to the calling program after the call. However, there are three significant points in which aRFC and trRFC or qRFC differ:

▶ If the caller starts an asynchronous RFC, the called server must be available to accept the request. The parameters of asynchronous RFCs are not buffered, but are passed directly to the server.

▶ During an asynchronous RFC, a user of the calling AS ABAP can engage in a dialog with the remote system.

▶ The calling program can receive results from the asynchronous RFC.

At Most Once Since aRFC, like synchronous communication, assumes the availability of the system called, it does not fulfill the corresponding deciding criterion of asynchronous communication. So aRFC, like sRFC, has the service property *At Most Once*. It is called at most once, and after a failed attempt at calling, it counts as failed.

Asynchronous real-time communication This type of RFC is always used when you need to set up real-time communications with a remote system, but don't need to wait on the results of the function module to continue processing. Just like the other RFC variants, asynchronous RFCs can be sent to a remote system, as well as to the calling system itself.

Transactional RFC

In contrast to aRFC, *transactional RFC* (tRFC) implements true asynchronous communications, which executes the function called on the RFC server exactly once (*Exactly Once*). The remote system need not be available at the moment the RFC client program executes a tRFC. The tRFC component saves the called RFC function, together with the respective data, in the database of the AS ABAP under a unique transaction ID (TID). In the event of communications problems, it is kept there for later transmission. In any case, there is a status indicator on the database, which can be used by the sender for information about the status of processing by the receiver. This status information also ensures that transmission does not occur twice by mistake.

If a call is sent while the receiving system is unavailable, the call remains in a local holding queue. The calling program can continue to run without waiting to see whether or not the function was executed successfully. If the RFC server is not activated within a certain period of time, the call is scheduled as a background request (job).

tRFC is used whenever a function should be executed within one *Logical Unit of Work* (LUW, see Section 10.1.3) of an AS ABAP. Within the LUW, all calls included are:

1. Executed in the order in which they were called
2. Executed in the target system in the same program context
3. Executed in a single transaction, i. e., database modifications are either completely written to the database of the target AS ABAP (COMMIT WORK) or completely rolled back (ROLLBACK WORK)

For the aforementioned reasons, tRFC is recommended when you want to ensure that the transactional sequence of calls within an LUW is preserved.

Queued RFC

To achieve a predefined sequence of multiple LUWs specified by the caller, a serialization of tRFC using *queues* (input or output queues) can be performed. This RFC variant is called *queued RFC* (qRFC).

Margin notes: tRFC · Exactly Once · qRFC

qRFC is an extension of tRFC. In addition to the transactional execution quality, it also ensures that calls are executed or processed in the order in which they were placed into queues by the caller (service property *Exactly Once In Order*). The so-called *dependencies* are another interesting feature of qRFC. Here, the caller can enter an execution unit (multiple function modules within an LUW, which are regarded as an atomic unit for execution) into multiple queues. A synchronization point is set between multiple queues. This is comparable to a lock (enqueue) in an ABAP program. For the recording of queues and their transmission, the infrastructure (data storage and status messages) of tRFC is used.

There are different scenarios for the use of qRFC:

▶ **Outbound Scenario**
In the outbound scenario, the calls are recorded as an output queue on the database of the caller. A scheduler runs asynchronously from the called application to ensure that the calls are executed. This scenario is used to achieve a decoupling of the sender and the receiver and to enable load distribution for the receiver, although a very limited one.[1]

▶ **Inbound Scenario**
In the inbound scenario, the calls are stored in the database of the receiver in an input queue. In most applications, the receiver isn't a remote system, but rather an application server on the sending AS ABAP. Here, too, a scheduler handles asynchronous execution. This scenario is used to parallelize an application and to perform load distribution for that application over the application servers of a system.

▶ **Out/in Scenario**
The out/in scenario is the combination of the outbound and inbound scenarios. It seems to unify all the positive features of these scenarios, but stores the data of the queues in the databases of both the receiver and the sender. This scenario should only be used when there are good reasons to justify this duplicated cost.

▶ **No-send Scenario**
The no-send scenario is actually an aberrant case. While the push principle is used by the scheduler in the two previous scenarios,

---

[1] The status of the receiver is derived from the status of the sender.

that is, the sender tries to reach the receiver, in the no-send scenario there is no scheduler involved, and therefore it implements the pull principle. This scenario is used, for instance, when connecting mobile devices (laptops or PDAs) to CRM middleware. Only the serialization of the RFCs and the persistence layer provided by tRFC/qRFC are used in the database tables. The data from a queue is transmitted to the mobile device when that device requests it, for instance, whenever a sales force employee can dial in from a hotel room.

12.2.2 RFC Communication Scenarios

Communications via RFC can be broken down into five different scenarios. We'll examine these scenarios in order to point out the respective typical properties of RFC.

Scenario 1: Two AS ABAP Systems (ABAP—ABAP)

Data exchange between the AS ABAP of two ABAP-based SAP systems typically takes place over their RFC interfaces (see Figure 12.3). The externally visible functionality of an ABAP RFC server is available in the form of function modules, which are designated as being remote-enabled in their properties (RFMs, see also Section 12.2.3).

Remote-enabled Function Module (RFM)

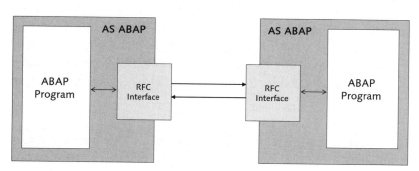

Figure 12.3 Communication Between Two AS ABAP Systems

Every ABAP program on an ABAP RFC client can call the RFM of an ABAP RFC server using the statement

```
CALL FUNCTION ... DESTINATION dest ...
```

CALL FUNCTION DESTINATION

The DESTINATION parameter causes the call to proceed over the RFC interface, and determines the *RFC destination* dest, which specifies the target system.[2] RFC destinations are administered using the SM59 transaction (tool for the configuration of RFC connections).

RFC destination

If both the caller and the program called are ABAP programs of an AS ABAP, communication for both participants takes place through their RFC interfaces. The caller can be any ABAP program, while the function called must be a Remote-enabled Function Module (RFM).

Scenario 2: AS ABAP and Non-SAP System (ABAP—Non-SAP System)

An AS ABAP can also communicate through its RFC interface with a non-SAP system, or with an external program (see Figure 12.4). For this, the non-SAP system must be extended with an external RFC interface (RfcLibrary) and the associated RFC API (RFC Application Programming Interface), which can communicate with the programs of the non-SAP system.

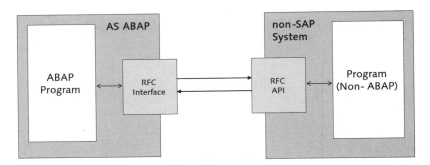

Figure 12.4 Communication Between AS ABAP and a Non-SAP System

RFC SDK

This interface can be implemented using the *RFC Software Development Kit* (RFC SDK) supplied by SAP. The most important components of the RFC SDK are different RFC client and server programs, along with platform-specific RFC libraries, which provide all the functional information for the RFC interface (see Section 12.2.4).

---

2 The specification of the special destination NONE causes a call to an RFM on the current AS ABAP through the RFC interface.

Scenario 3: AS ABAP and AS Java (ABAP—SAP-Java)

Another important application area is communication between the ABAP and Java environments of the Application Server of SAP NetWeaver (see Figure 12.5). The coexistence of these two different environments within a system appearing externally as a single application server (see Section 3.2.2) requires intensive communication options, so that, for example, from the Java environment, an ABAP function can be called, and vice versa, without causing significant performance losses.

The communication between ABAP and Java within an Application Server of SAP NetWeaver, from the point of view of ABAP, also represents a form of remote communication implemented using RFC. To enable a mapping between ABAP and Java data, the RFC communicates with a component named the *SAP Java Connector* (SAP JCo), which acts like an interface to the AS Java.[3] The SAP JCo is based on the RFC library and transforms the ABAP data of an RFC data stream into Java and vice versa. From a technical point of view, therefore, the SAP JCo is also communicating via RFC.

SAP JCo

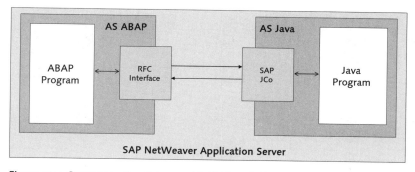

Figure 12.5 Communication Between AS ABAP and AS Java

Scenario 4: AS ABAP and External Java (ABAP—External Java)

The technology of SAP-internal communication between ABAP and Java can also be used to exchange data from an AS ABAP with an external Java environment (see Figure 12.6). Here, too, the RFC interface communicates with the SAP JCo, which, in this case, however, is used as an external (standalone) component, not as an interface to AS Java.

---

3 Actually, SAP JCo is a standalone component.

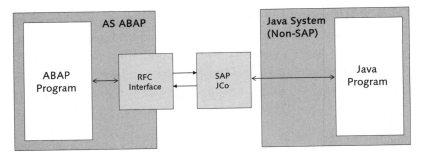

Figure 12.6 Communication Between AS ABAP and External Java

Scenario 5: AS ABAP and SAP Java Resource Adapter (ABAP—SAP-JRA)

If the J2EE system of AS Java from scenario 3 is operated as a pure client, from SAP NetWeaver '04 on instead of SAP JCo, the integrated *SAP Java Resource Adapter* (SAP JRA) can also be used for communication (see Figure 12.7). The SAP JRA is an internal add-on component and functions as an encapsulation for the SAP JCo in AS Java.

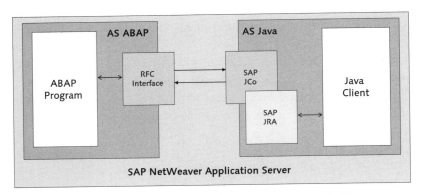

Figure 12.7 Communication Between AS ABAP and AS Java via SAP JRA

SAP JRA   The SAP JRA is based on the J2EE connector architecture. This is a standard architecture, via which a J2EE application server can communicate with different systems when a corresponding adapter is used. The SAP JRA provides a standardized access from AS Java to all externally available functions (RFMs, see below) of an AS ABAP. The use of the SAP JRA for communication between ABAP and Java within the SAP NetWeaver Application Server offers the following advantages:

▶ The SAP JRA can be configured using a user interface.

▶ Thread control, security configuration, transaction management, connection establishment, and synchronization are administered through AS Java and don't require separate settings in SAP JRA.

▶ SAP JRA implements only J2EE standard interfaces. Working with it is significantly simpler for Java developers, since a familiar set of interfaces can be used.

12.2.3 RFC Programming on AS ABAP

In this section and the sections that follow, we'll introduce you to the programming of the various components of RFC and connectors. Due to the variety and multitude of application options, we cannot possibly fully cover each individual area. Instead, we'll examine the structure of important basic functions and work through the particularities of each communication type in order to help you better orient yourself for your own programming activities.

First, we will give you a brief introduction to the programming of remote-enabled function modules in AS ABAP. Then, we'll go over the execution of the different RFC variants in ABAP programs, and finally, we'll review the programming of the external RFC interface and the SAP Java Connector. Actual work with these connectors requires basic C or Java programming knowledge. However, because of their significance for RFC communication between ABAP and the rest of the world, particularly with Java, these connectors also need to be mentioned in this book.

Remote-enabled Function Modules (RFMs)

To create an RFM in Function Builder, the same description applies as for a normal function module (see Section 7.2.1). The significant difference is that an RFM is marked as a **Remote-Enabled Module** in its properties, which automatically publishes the RFM in the RFC interface of the AS ABAP. An RFM can also execute its own RFCs. For synchronous calls, this allows RFMs to call other RFMs in the system that executed the original RFC (callback functionality).

However, there are still some limitations for RFMs, namely:

- All formal parameters must be completely typed.
- No reference variables can be passed.
- No class-based exceptions can be propagated.
- In an RFM, no statements like `LEAVE PROGRAM` can be executed, which close the connection in an uncontrolled manner.

When creating RFMs, you should note that they always pose a certain security risk, since they can be called from any external system that has the appropriate permissions. For that reason, appropriate authorization checks should always be performed in the RFM.

Synchronous RFC (sRFC)

For the synchronous call to a remote function module, we use the statement already mentioned:

`CALL FUNCTION func DESTINATION dest ...`

The `CALL FUNCTION` statement largely corresponds to that for local function modules of the same application server (see Section 7.2.1). With the `DESTINATION` clause, however, a call is carried out via the RFC interface and an RFC destination `dest` is specified. In `dest`, there must be an RFC destination managed with the Transaction SM59 specified, or a predefined value like NONE.

The calling program continues only when the function called remotely has finished. In a called function, specification of a predefined destination BACK makes an RFC back into the calling system possible.

For `func`, a Remote-enabled Function Module (RFM) must be specified. This is either a correspondingly marked function module of an AS ABAP, or a function of a non-ABAP system, which has been made available by RFC API or JCo.

For the passing of actual parameters to the formal parameters of the RFM and the handling of exceptions, there are the usual clauses `EXPORTING`, `IMPORTING`, `CHANGING`, `TABLES`, and `EXCEPTIONS`.[4] In addition to the explicit exceptions of the RFM called, the two predefined

---

4 Only classical exceptions can be handled. An RFM has no `RAISING` clause.

exceptions SYSTEM_FAILURE and COMMUNICATION_FAILURE can be handled. These occur when there is a runtime error during the execution of the function module called remotely, or when there is no connection to the RFC server.

In contrast to the call of local function modules, parameters are only passed by value. This applies specifically to table parameters defined and passed with TABLES.

Value passing

If the RFC server is another AS ABAP, the function module called remotely can be debugged on the remote system with the ABAP Debugger (see Section 13.2). The ABAP Debugger runs on the local system, however, and the values needed are supplied by the RFC server.

RFC debugging

Asynchronous RFC (aRFC)

For an asynchronous RFC, we use the statement

```
CALL FUNCTION func STARTING NEW TASK task
            [DESTINATION dest] ...
```

CALL FUNCTION STARTING NEW TASK

Here, the specification of the RFC destination can even be omitted and is then implicitly set to NONE, that is, to the current AS ABAP. With task, an arbitrary task identifier of no more than eight characters[5] must be specified for the remote function module called.

With asynchronous RFC (aRFC), in contrast to synchronous RFC (sRFC), there are the limitations that no values can be passed with IMPORTING, and that for actual parameters specified with CHANGING values are passed, but not returned. Moreover, aRFC does not support any communication with non-SAP systems or programs in other programming languages.

With a clause

Callback routine

```
... CALLING meth
```

a public method meth can be specified as a callback routine, which is executed after the asynchronously called function module completes.[6] In the callback routine, the statement

---

5 From the next release on, the task identifier will have a maximum of 32 characters.
6 A PERFORMING subr clause is also possible for the use of a subroutine instead of a method.

RECEIVE RESULTS

```
RECEIVE RESULTS FROM FUNCTION func
        IMPORTING ... TABLES ... EXCEPTIONS ...
```

can be used to receive the output parameters of the asynchronous function and handle exceptions.

Parallel processing

The aRFC enables the parallel processing of function modules on different application servers of the current AS ABAP. This is the purpose of the statement:

CALL FUNCTION DESTINATION IN GROUP

```
... DESTINATION IN GROUP group|DEFAULT
```

The IN GROUP clause can only be specified as an alternative to a true RFC destination. You can either use group to specify an RFC server group created with the Transaction RZ12, or DEFAULT (recommended) to specify all application servers of the current AS ABAP. If the function module cannot be executed on any of the application servers, the predefined exception RESOURCE_FAILURE is raised.

Since the IN GROUP clause automatically optimally utilizes all the resources available, it is preferable to using self-defined parallel processing. For parallel processing, you should note the following:

▶ There is no guarantee that functions will be processed in a certain order, or that, at any particular point in time, a certain result will be available. In short, the functions that have to be executed in parallel must be fully independent of one another and cannot assume that any sequential processing will take place.

▶ An application server of the AS ABAP must provide enough resources to support the parallel processing. Among other things, the application server must have at least three dialog work processes.

▶ In an RFM executed in parallel processing, no RFC back into the calling system (destination BACK) is possible.

Function group SPBT

The function group SPBT contains some useful function modules for self-defined parallel processing. Parallel processing of multiple independent tasks can include the following steps:

1. Determine availability of resources with function module SPBT_ INITIALIZE.

2. Execution of one or more suitable aRFCs with the DESTINATION IN GROUP clause.

3. Determine any application servers used with function module SPBT_GET_PP_DESTINATION.

4. Optionally exclude an application server that is raising exceptions, using SPBT_DO_NOT_USE_SERVER.

5. Use RECEIVE in callback routines to gather results.

6. Use of the ABAP statement WAIT UNTIL to wait in the calling program until all functions have been executed.   **WAIT UNTIL**

Listing 12.1 shows an example that contains many of the language elements introduced here, and should give you a feel for the parallel processing of aRFCs.

Listing 12.1 Parallel Processing with Asynchronous RFC

```
REPORT z_parallel_rfc.

CLASS demo DEFINITION.
  PUBLIC SECTION.
    CLASS-METHODS:
      main,
      callback_meth IMPORTING p_task TYPE clike.
  PRIVATE SECTION.
    TYPES: BEGIN OF task_type,
             name TYPE string,
             dest TYPE string,
           END OF task_type.
    CLASS-DATA:
      task_list TYPE STANDARD TABLE OF task_type,
      task_wa   TYPE task_type,
      rcv_jobs  TYPE i,
      mess      TYPE c LENGTH 80.
ENDCLASS.

CLASS demo IMPLEMENTATION.
  METHOD main.
    DATA: snd_jobs TYPE i,
          exc_flag TYPE i,
          indx     TYPE c LENGTH 4,
          name     TYPE c LENGTH 8.
    DO 10 TIMES.
      indx = sy-index.
      CONCATENATE 'Task' indx INTO name.
      CALL FUNCTION 'RFC_SYSTEM_INFO'
        STARTING NEW TASK name
        DESTINATION IN GROUP DEFAULT
        CALLING callback_meth ON END OF TASK
```

857

```
      EXCEPTIONS
        system_failure        = 1  MESSAGE mess
        communication_failure = 2  MESSAGE mess
        resource_failure      = 3.
    CASE sy-subrc.
      WHEN 0.
        snd_jobs = snd_jobs + 1.
      WHEN 1 OR 2.
        MESSAGE mess TYPE 'I'.
      WHEN 3.
        IF snd_jobs >= 1 AND
          exc_flag = 0.
          exc_flag = 1.
          WAIT UNTIL rcv_jobs >= snd_jobs
                UP TO 5 SECONDS.
        ENDIF.
        IF sy-subrc = 0.
          exc_flag = 0.
        ELSE.
          MESSAGE 'Resource failure' TYPE 'I'.
        ENDIF.
      WHEN OTHERS.
        MESSAGE 'Other error' TYPE 'I'.
    ENDCASE.
  ENDDO.
  WAIT UNTIL rcv_jobs >= snd_jobs.
  LOOP AT task_list INTO task_wa.
    WRITE: / task_wa-name, task_wa-dest.
  ENDLOOP.
ENDMETHOD.
METHOD callback_meth.
  DATA info TYPE rfcsi.
  task_wa-name = p_task.
  rcv_jobs = rcv_jobs + 1.
  RECEIVE RESULTS FROM FUNCTION 'RFC_SYSTEM_INFO'
    IMPORTING
      rfcsi_export = info
    EXCEPTIONS
      system_failure        = 1 message mess
      communication_failure = 2 message mess.
  IF sy-subrc = 0.
    task_wa-dest = info-rfcdest.
  ELSE.
    task_wa-dest = mess.
  ENDIF.
```

```
      APPEND task_wa TO task_list.
  ENDMETHOD.
ENDCLASS.
START-OF-SELECTION.
  demo=>main( ).
```

The remote-enabled function module RFC_SYSTEM_INFO is called 10 times in a loop as aRFC with different task identifiers. The callback routine `callback_meth` counts the finished function modules and receives the output values.

The `GROUP DEFAULT` clause distributes processing over all application servers of the current system. If, after at least one successful call, no more free work processes are available, the execution of the program is interrupted for a maximum of five seconds, until all function modules started have finished. After all the function modules are started, the program waits until all the callback routines have been executed. Then, the internal table `task_list` filled there is output as a classical list. The output shows the order in which the individual tasks finished and on which application server each was executed.[7]

Transactional RFC (tRFC)

For a transactional RFC, we use the following statement:[8]

```
CALL FUNCTION func IN BACKGROUND TASK
              [DESTINATION dest] ...
```

CALL FUNCTION IN BACKGROUND TASK

As with asynchronous RFC, the explicit specification of the destination is optional. To pass actual parameters, only `EXPORTING` and `TABLES` can be executed, and no exceptions can be handled.

In tRFC, the function called is registered with the destination and actual parameters passed in a database table of the current AS AP, with a unique transaction id (TID) for the current SAP LUW (see Sec-

SAP LUW

---

7 Since on a locally installed SAP NetWeaver 2004s ABAP Trial Version, there is only one application server, no true parallel processing can occur there. Instead, an attempt is made to execute as many functions as possible in sequence.

8 As of the next SAP NetWeaver release, this statement will be replaced by the so-called bgRFC, which is implemented by the statement `CALL FUNCTION func IN BACKGROUND UNIT oref`. The transactional RFC is controlled by an object that implements the IF_BGRFC_UNIT interface. The new statement includes and extends the tRFC shown here.

tion 10.1.30), and the calling program continues afterwards. Here, you should note that even tRFCs with different destinations are assigned a single TID. To work with different destinations (i. e., distributed system environments), the qRFC described in the next section is available, which assigns each destination a TID.

When the SAP LUW ends with COMMIT WORK, the registered function modules are started in the order they were registered. The statement ROLLBACK WORK, on the other hand, deletes the registrations for the current SAP LUW. The AS SEPARATE UNIT clause can also be used to execute a tRFC in such a way that the function called is registered with its own TID and is executed in its own context.

If the specified destination is not available at the end of the SAP LUW, a background process is started, which continues to attempt to start the registered function modules in this destination. Settings for this are made in the Transaction SM59. Only when the calls are not successful after a given number of attempts the tRFC is considered to have failed, and this failed transactional RFC is marked in the database table.

Asynchronous Communication

This means that, as we already mentioned, tRFC implements true asynchronous communication. In the function called, no RFC back into the calling system (destination BACK) is possible. The tRFC ensures that the function module called is executed in the RFC server exactly once, regardless of its current availability.

In tRFC, you should note the following:

▶ All functions are executed in the order in which they were registered.

▶ All functions are executed in the same context.

▶ All functions are executed within one SAP LUW.

Transaction

Therefore, if update functions are located on a remote system and the changes to the database tables don't need to be executed before the calling program continues, it is suitable for the transactional processing of data in database tables, and provides an alternative to update function modules (see Section 10.1.3).

To reset an LUW executed with tRTC under program control, you can call the function module RESTART_OF_BACKGROUNDTASK, which executes a rollback and ensures that the LUW is executed again at a later time. Moreover, the execution of the registered function modules can also be decoupled from the COMMIT WORK statement by using the function module START_OF_BACKGROUNDTASK to determine an execution time after the first tRFC.

The status of the functions registered with tRFC can be determined **tRFC status** in the program using the function module STATUS_OF_BACK-GROUNDTASK. To do this, you must retrieve the TID after the first tRFC with the function module ID_OF_BACKGROUNDTASK, and pass that to STATUS_OF_BACKGROUNDTASK. The latter then supplies different information on the current LUW.

You can also monitor and control functions registered with tRFC, independent of the program using the Transaction SM58 (tool for transactional RFC).

Queued RFC (qRFC)

For qRFC, there is no separate ABAP statement. Instead, this is an extension of tRFC with an administration enabling control of execution order (serialization) and a proper distribution of the calls to different systems of a distributed system environment (see qRFC scenarios in Section 12.2.1).

To convert a normal tRFC into a qRFC, before registration with CALL FUNCTION IN BACKGROUND TASK, call the following function module:

```
CALL FUNCTION 'TRFC_SET_QUEUE_NAME'.
  EXPORTING qname  =
            nosend = ...
            ...
```

This function module ensures that the processing of the following **qRFC manager** tRFCs does not simply occur on COMMIT WORK, but are serialized according to the scenario desired into an output queue, an input queue, or both. The actual processing is the responsibility of the *qRFC manager*. The qRFC manager includes the QOUT and QIN schedulers.

To manage qRFCs, there is an extensive qRFC API, which is provided **qRFC API** by function modules with the prefix TRFC as well as with transactions for administration like SMQE (tool for qRFC administration), SMQS (tool for QOUT scheduler), or SMQR (tool for QIN scheduler).

Coming soon:
bgRFC In the context of this book, however, we don't want to delve deeper into today's programming and features of qRFC, because the future replacement of tRFC with bgRFC (Background RFC) will mean significant changes, particularly for qRFC. The current concepts of qRFC will be included and replaced by the new object-oriented control of bgRFC. Thus the details of today's qRFC will only be relevant for existing applications, while new development from the next SAP NetWeaver release and beyond will be using bgRFC.

12.2.4 RFC Programming of an External RFC Interface

With the external RFC interface (*RfcLibrary*) and the associated RFC API (*RFC Application Programming Interface*), SAP provides a tool that can be installed on a non-ABAP system to be able to communicate with an AS ABAP through RFC. The programming language used for this is C. For the Java programming language, there is a separate API, the *Java Connector* (JCo, see Section 12.2.5).

RFC API   The RFC API consists of a collection of C routines, which handle the appropriate communication tasks. Thus it enables the call of ABAP function modules from a C program and vice versa, and asynchronous communication is also possible.

The external RFC interface includes the following three main components:

- ▶ The include file *saprfc.h* contains data type and structure definitions, along with prototypes (declarations) of the functions of which the API consists.

- ▶ The include file *sapitab.h* defines an interface for the processing of internal tables of ABAP.

- ▶ A platform-specific RFC library (e. g., *librfc32.dll* for MS Windows) contains the actual functions of the API.

Communication
functions   Figure 12.8 shows the functions of the API, which play a role in a typical RFC communication.[9] Figure 12.8 extends Figure 12.4. The functions shown in Figure 12.8 primarily appear in both of the RFC

---

9   For simplicity's sake, we show the function names RfcOpen, RfcCall, RfcReceive, etc. here. To use the full functionality of the RFC API, the functions RfcOpenEx, RfcCallEx, RfcReceiveEx, etc. are used, which are essentially the same, but extended.

interfaces shown in Figure 12.4, but are already encapsulated on the AS ABAP by the runtime environment. So we only need to concern ourselves with the RFC API of a non-SAP system with the call of these functions.

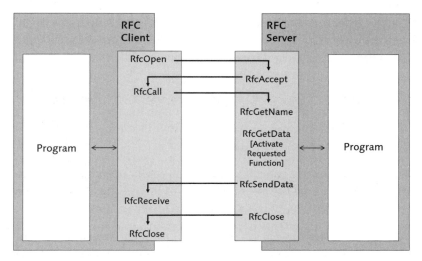

Figure 12.8 Functions of the RFC Interface

To implement the RFC API on a non-SAP system, the RFC SDK (*RFC Software Development Kit*) is used, which is available for download from the SAP Service Marketplace (*http://service/sap.com/patches*).

RFC SDK

In the following section, we'll first look at the functions of the API that you'll need when a non-SAP system is to function as an RFC client for an AS ABAP, and then at the programming of a non-SAP system as an RFC server for an AS ABAP.

Non-SAP System as RFC Client

An RFC client program is an external program that uses functions of the RFC API to call function modules of an AS ABAP. According to Figure 12.8, these are the following functions:

- ▶ RfcOpen to establish a connection to AS ABAP
- ▶ RfcCall to call a function module (RFM)
- ▶ RfcReceive to receive output parameters
- ▶ RfcClose to close the connection

Opening
a connection

The RfcOpen function opens the connection to the AS ABAP and registers the client there as a user. The required connection parameters, like destination, application server, message server, and login data[10] can either be taken from the *saprfc.ini* file, or passed directly from the client program. Using the *saprfc.ini* file has the advantage that it can be maintained independently of the client program. If it is not in the same directory, the environment variable RFC_INI must be set to its complete name including the path. An example file for *saprfc.ini* can be found in the RFC SDK as *\rfcsdk\text*. The configuration for different application scenarios is also described there in detail. For security reasons, however, it is always recommended that you supply the password as a parameter only when the connection is established, and not to store it in *saprfc.ini*.

While opening the connection, either an application server can be specified directly or the message server of the AS ABAP (see Section 3.5.2). The latter has the advantage that fewer parameters must be passed, that we're independent of any certain application server, and that, as usual, the optimal available application server is found for the current load distribution.

If the function module called uses interface elements from the SAP GUI (see Chapter 9), it must be installed in the calling system and the connection must be called with the extended function RfcOpenEx, giving a nonzero value for the use_sapgui parameter. This makes it possible to integrate entire SAP GUI screen sequences into the applications of non-SAP systems. Moreover, there are also ways to activate the ABAP Debugger for the call in order to debug the RFM called.

Calling a
function module

The RfcCall function calls a Remote-enabled Function Module (RFM) of the AS ABAP and passes parameters to it, and the RfcReceive function receives its output parameters. In the synchronous call handled here first, RfcReceive waits until the function module call finishes. Normally, you don't have to execute anything else between the function calls in the client program, so both calls can be bundled using the RfcCallReceive function.

Closing the
connection

Finally, the connection must be closed again with RfcClose. Typical examples of RFC client programs can be found in the RFC SDK in the *sapinfo.c*, *startrfc.c*, and *srfctest.c* programs.

---

10 The login to the AS ABAP can occur as a dialog or a communications user.

Non-SAP System as RFC Server

An RFC server program is an external program that provides functions in the RFC API, which can be called from the ABAP programs of an AS ABAP. According to Figure 12.8, the RFC server program provides the following functions:

- `RfcAccept` to accept a connection from the AS ABAP
- `RfcGetName` to receive the function name
- `RfcGetData` to accept the input parameters and the call to the function
- `RfcSendData` to pass the output parameters
- `RfcClose` to close the connection

As an alternative to direct use, instead of the sequence `RfcGetName`, `RfcGetData`, then `RfcSendData`, the following recommended sequence can be used:

- `RfcInstallFunction` to register all callable functions
- `RfcDispatch` to call a requested function in a loop

In this case, the RFC server program registers all functions, which can be called within this server program, and then waits on incoming calls and distributes them using `RfcDispatch` in a loop. Every function called must then call `RfcGetData` and `RfcSendData` itself.

So that an RFC server program can be addressed from an incoming RFC call, it must be registered with the *SAP Gateway*. The SAP Gateway is a server that must be installed and started on any non-SAP system, which is to function as an RFC server. In an AS ABAP, there is always a gateway server active.

SAP Gateway

Registration of an RFC server program is done using constants in the RFC server program itself, or using the configuration file *saprfc.ini* that you should already be familiar with from our discussion of RFC client programs. The registration is independent of any particular AS ABAP. An RFC server program can execute functions from different clients.[11]

---

11 Alternatively, there is also the option of directly addressing an RFC server program on a non-SAP system without registration before every use from AS ABAP. Here, too, the communication takes place through the SAP Gateway.

On an AS ABAP, which wants to use the non-SAP system as an RFC client, the Transaction SM59 must be used to create a matching RFC destination. In contrast to ABAP/ABAP connections, which use CPI-C, these connections use the TCP/IP connection type. Furthermore, the destination must include sufficient information on the SAP Gateway of the server.

An RFC from the client is passed by the SAP Gateway to the server functions registered there. After execution of a function, the RFC connection is closed. If the server program, as recommended, is working by calling RfcDispatch in a loop, it will automatically reregister on the SAP Gateway and can wait on more RFC calls from the same or different AS ABAP.

Parameter Passing

The API functions RfcCall, RfcReceive, RfcCallReceive, RfcGet-Data, and RfcSendData pass data between the non-SAP system and the AS ABAP, and vice versa. So that data transfer between the C program and the ABAP function module can work, on the C side a description of the respective formal parameter must be passed with each actual parameter, including its name and a series of technical properties. Structures of the predefined types RFC_PARAMETER and RFC_TABLE are provided for these descriptions. The above API functions expect arrays of these structures as parameters.

Elementary ABAP types For the description of elementary ABAP types, the C structure RFC_PARAMETER is used, which is defined in *saprfc.h* as follows:

```
typedef struct {
  void * name;
  unsigned nlen;
  RFC_TYPEHANDLE type;
  void * addr;
} RFC_PARAMETER;
```

For every elementary ABAP type, *saprfc.h* defines a mapping to a C type, which can be specified in the type column. For example, for the ABAP type c, you must specify the C type RFC_CHAR, and for the ABAP type i, you must specify the C type RFC_INT.

Structures For the description of structures, the C structure RFC_TYPE_ELEMENT2 is used, which must contain appropriate information for every component of an ABAP structure. This structure must be constructed in the C program and then registered using the function RfcInstallStructure2. The structure description can be created manually, but the API also provides functions for automatic creation. Using RfcGetStructureInfoAsTable, information on structures in the ABAP Dictionary[12] can be referred to, and from that, RfcExid-ToRfcType can then create the actual C type.

For the description of internal tables, the C structure RFC_TABLE is **Internal Tables** used, which is defined in *saprfc.h* as follows:

```
typedef struct {
  void * name;
  unsigned nlen;
  RFC_TYPEHANDLE type;
  unsigned leng;
  ITAB_H ithandle;
  RFC_ITMODE itmode;
  int newitab;
} RFC_TABLE;
```

The data in an internal table is managed on the C side by a control structure of type ITAB_H.[13] Such an internal table is created using the function ItCreate. The RFC API includes more functions for the processing of this kind of internal tables to insert, read, or delete lines. For ITMODE, the value RFC_ITMODE_BYREFERENCE should be specified, since the internal table is then addressed from C more efficiently.

An RFC server program can also raise exceptions using the functions **Raising exceptions** RfcRaise or RfcRaiseTables, which can be handled by the caller on the AS ABAP.

Transactional RFC on non-SAP systems

Up until now, we have assumed synchronous RFC (sRFC) in the introduction of the RFC API. An asynchronous RFC (aRFC), which is possible when communicating between two AS ABAP systems, is not possible between an AS ABAP and a non-SAP system. True asynchro-

---

12 Structured formal parameters of a Remote-enabled Function Module (RFM) always refer to a structure in the ABAP Dictionary.

13 This corresponds to the table header used in the ABAP kernel for the administration of internal tables.

nous communication, however, is supported with certain limitations using transactional RFC (tRFC), which can be extended with queued RFC (qRFC).

The following functions of the RFC API support tRFC:

- `RfcCreateTransID` for the creation of a transaction ID (TID) in an RFC client program

- `RfcIndirectCallEx` to group functions together with one TID in an RFC client program and to send them as tRFC to the AS ABAP

- `RfcInstallTransactionControl` for transaction control in an RFC server program. This function itself must call the following four functions:

  - `OnCheckTidEx`
    to check whether the TID sent by the AS ABAP has not yet been used

  - `OnCommitEx`
    to perform a database commit on the database on the non-SAP system after a successful conclusion of all functions

  - `OnRollbackEx`
    to perform a database rollback on the database on the non-SAP system after an unsuccessful conclusion of all functions

  - `OnConfirmtidEx`
    to delete everything associated with a TID after a successful conclusion of a local transaction

On an AS ABAP acting as a tRFC server for a non-SAP system, there are no adaptations necessary. A non-SAP system acting as a tRFC server for an AS ABAP receives a tRFC call from the internal tRFC administration of the AS ABAP. The RFC API confirms the successful execution of all the associated functions. Until the confirmation is received, the tRFC administration of the AS ABAP tries to repeat the call as often and as long as is specified in the SM58 transaction.

Similar to the way in which a tRFC in ABAP/ABAP communication can be converted into a qRFC, this is also possible in the communication between an AS ABAP and a non-SAP system.

In an RFC client program, the call to the `RfcIndirectCallEx` function must be replaced by calls to `RfcQueueInsert`. The latter inserts the function module called and the parameters passed into an output queue. After successful execution, this is available as an input queue on the AS ABAP, and can be processed by its QIN scheduler. In contrast to qRFC between two AS ABAP systems, an input queue from an RFC client program on a non-SAP system can contain at most one function call. If the AS ABAP does not support qRFC with input queues, it processes the incoming queue immediately, that is, like a normal tRFC.

In an RFC server program, which receives an output queue from an AS ABAP, on the other hand, no modifications are necessary. The functions in the queue are processed immediately. The advantage of this procedure lies in the improved resource control on the part of AS ABAP. Because the qRFC manager checks available resources before execution and executes them at a later time if necessary, better performance of the overall distributed system can be achieved.

12.2.5   RFC Programming with JCo

The SAP Java Connector (SAP JCo) connects the ABAP and the Java worlds. It constitutes the interface in three of the five scenarios presented in Section 12.2.2. The JCo, or its encapsulation by the SAP JRA, make it possible to call ABAP functions from Java and vice versa. A significant task here is to execute the mapping of the datatypes between ABAP and Java.

If communication takes place between AS ABAP and AS Java within SAP NetWeaver (Figure 12.5 and Figure 12.7), then JCo and its use are part of the overall system, so that generally no separate programming effort is required. In the case of communication between an AS ABAP and a non-SAP Java system (Figure 12.4), the JCo is a standalone component, which can be downloaded from the web page *http://service.sap.com/connectors*, and whose use in the non-SAP system must be programmed specifically, just as with an external RFC interface for C programs (see Section 12.2.4). From a technical point of view, a standalone JCo doesn't communicate directly with an AS ABAP; instead, it addresses the AS ABAP through the external RFC interface of the non-SAP system, and vice versa. The Rfc Library required is a part of the installation of a standalone JCo. Within SAP NetWeaver, however, the JCo communicates directly with the AS ABAP.

In the following section, we'll introduce you to a few central elements of JCo programming. We won't go into the SAP Java Resource Adapter (SAP JRA) here any further.

JCo Client Programming

First, let's look at the SAP JCo from the point of view of a client application, and introduce the basic steps.

Establishing a connection to an AS ABAP

If we want to use the SAP JCo to establish a connection to an AS ABAP, there are two different programming models available to us: direct connections and connection pools.

► Direct connections can be kept open as long as possible after they are opened.

► A connection pool manages connections and provides them upon request. Once a connection is released back to the connection pool, it can be assigned to a different requester.

These two models can be used in parallel in a Java application. If you are building web server applications, you should always use pools, but even in the case of desktop applications, connection pools can often be the more sensible solution.

Direct connections

First, let's use some excerpts from an example program to look at the creation of a direct connection. The complete example program Connect1 can be found in the documentation for the Java Connector on the SAP Help Portal (*http://help.sap.com*).

To create a direct connection, we need the following three classes:

► JCO is the main class of the SAP JCo. It contains many useful static methods.

► JCO.Client is a connection to AS ABAP.

► JCO.Attributes contains the attributes of a connection, like information about the AS ABAP system.

You use these classes with the following `import`:

```
import com.sap.mw.jco.*;
```

To address an AS ABAP, you need a connection variable:

```
JCO.Client mConnection;
```

To create JCo client objects, use the factory method `createClient()` of the JCO class, to which the connection data is passed:

```
mConnection = JCO.createClient
    ("<client>", "<userid>", "<password>", "<language>",
    "<hostname>", "<system-number>");
```
JCO.createClient

There are different versions of this method to allow specification of the connection parameters in different ways. The example above implements a connection by specifying login data and the address of the AS ABAP. The actual connection is created with the following call to `connect`:

```
try {
    mConnection.connect();
}
catch (Exeption ex) {
    ex.printStackTrace();
    System.exit (1)
}
```
JCO.connect

Now you can call the connection's methods, like:

```
mConnection.getAttributes()
```

to get information about the connection, or

```
mConnection.ping()
```

to test the connection. Other methods allow calls to functions on the AS ABAP (see below). Finally, the connection is closed again:

```
mConnection.disconnect();
```
JCO.disconnect

In contrast to the use of a connection pool, for direct connections, we don't recommend closing a connection between calls to methods. A direct connection should only be closed when no use is anticipated for a longer time.

All the connections in a connection pool have the same information for the system, user, and account. When using generic user names, as is usually the case for web server applications, we recommend that you use connection pools, for the following reasons:
Connection pools

▶ Since a connection from a connection pool stays open for reuse after the first login, you avoid having too many logins.

▶ You can limit the maximum number of concurrent logins to avoid using too many resources on the AS ABAP. You should select the maximum number of concurrent logins to avoid login delays for the users.

The greatest advantage of connection pools can be achieved when all pools use the same user name, which cannot always be the case for security reasons.

Based on excerpts from an example program, we now examine the use of a connection pool. The complete example program Connect2 can be found in the documentation for the Java Connector on the SAP Help Portal (*http://help.sap.com*).

Creating a
connection pool

We need the following classes:

▶ JCO.Pool is a connection pool.

▶ JCO.PoolManager manages all the connection pools in one Java Virtual Machine (JVM).

When creating a connection pool, you must assign it a name, which must first be defined:

```
static final String POOL_NAME = "Pool";
```

Because connection pools are global within a JVM, a naming convention should be followed. Before each use, it can be checked whether there is already a connection pool with this name.

```
JCO.Pool pool
    = JCO.getClientPoolManager().getPool (POOL_NAME);
if (pool == null) { ... }
```

Now you can create a connection pool using the factory method add-ClientPool:

JCO.addClientPool

```
OrderedProperties logonProperties =
    OrderedPropertiess.load("/logon.properties");
JCO.addClientPool(POOL_NAME,
                  <no_of_connections>,
                  logonProperties);
```

There are different versions of the addClientPool method to allow specification of the connection parameters in different ways. The example above uses a properties object of the utility class Ordered-

Properties, whose attributes are loaded from the *logon.properties* file. The maximum number of connections, specified with <no_of_ connections>, can no longer be increased later on, so you must specify a sufficiently large number.

If you use connections from a connection pool, you don't use the connect or disconnect methods from the JCO.Client class. These methods are encapsulated in the classes for connection pools. To request a connection from a connection pool, use:

```
mConnection = JCO.getClient(POOL_NAME);
```

JCO.getClient

If all connections in a pool have been assigned, SAP JCo waits a certain amount of time, which can be determined with setMaxWaitTime. If there is still no connection available during that period of time, the exception JCO.Exception.JCO_ERROR_RESOURCE is raised. After the successful request of a connection, you can execute one or more method calls to access the AS ABAP (see below), and then return the connection to the connection pool:

```
JCO.releaseClient(mConnection);
```

JCO.releaseClient

We recommend performing the release in a finally block, so that the method will be executed in any case, regardless of whether or not an exception is raised. Otherwise, the connections of the connection pools might be used up incorrectly.

On the AS ABAP, the context of a call from the connection pool is opened by calling JCO.getClient and then closed with JCO.release-Client. If you want to execute different RFMs in one context, you should keep the connection until the entire sequence has been performed.

The SAP Java Connector must have the signatures (name, interface parameters, and exceptions) of all RFMs of an AS ABAP that are to be used by a Java client, so that they can be properly called. For this purpose, a JCo repository object is created in a JCo client program. The signatures for the RFMs of a current connection are automatically retrieved by the AS ABAP system and are available in this object.

SAP JCo
Repository

For the JCo repository, we need the class JCO.Repository as a template for the JCo repository object. The attributes contain information on the RFMs.

A JCo repository object is created directly with `new`, and the constructor is given a name for the object and the connection for which the repository is going to be constructed. As a connection, either a `JCO.Client` object or the name of a connection pool can be passed:

JCO.Repository
```
JCO.Repository mRepository;

mRepository = new JCO.Repository(
  "<repository_name>", mConnection|POOL_NAME);
```

Function call objects
After a repository object has been created for a connection, so-called *function call objects* can be created for the RFMs of the corresponding AS ABAP, through which they can be called. The following interfaces and classes are needed for this:

▶ IfunctionTemplate describes the signature of an RFM.

▶ JCO.Function is the call of an RFM in the repository with all its associated parameters.

To create a JCo function call object, you must perform the following steps:[14]

```
IFunctionTemplate mFT =
  mRepository.getFunctionTemplate("<RFM>");
```

With the `getFunctionTemplate` method of the JCo repository object, a so-called *function template* is created for the specified RFM, implementing the `IFunctionTemplate` interface. The function template then contains the signature of the RFM:

JCO.Function
```
JCO.Function mFunctionCall = new JCO.Function(mFT);
```

A function call object of the `JCO.Function` class is created with `new`, the constructor being passed the function template. Alternatively, a function call object can also be created with the `getFunction` method of the function template.

```
JCO.Function mFunctionCall;
mFunctionCall = mFT.getFunction();
```

A function call object is used to call the RFM on the AS ABAP and to pass the associated parameters. Since a function call object repre-

---

14 We describe the recommended procedure here. Instead of using a function template, the signature could also be given directly when creating a function call object.

sents exactly one call with certain parameter values, we recommend that a new function call object be created for each new call.

Before calling an RFM, the input parameters of the RFM in the function call object must be set to the desired values. To do that, we need the following classes:

Parameter Passing

▶ JCO.ParameterList is the parameter interface of an RFM.

▶ JCO.Structure is an ABAP structure.

▶ JCO.Table is an internal table from ABAP.

A function call object contains methods to read lists of various types from parameters of an RFM in parameter lists, that is, in the objects of the class JCO.ParameterList:

```
JCO.ParameterList mImportParameterList;
JCO.ParameterList mTableParameterList;
mImportParameterList =
  mFunctionCall.getImportParameterList();
mTableParameterList =
  mFunctionCall.getTableParameterList();
```

JCO.ParameterList

The parameter list object contains methods to assign values to the input parameters. After the filling of the parameter lists with values, they can be passed back to the function call object using the corresponding set methods.

The setting of elementary input parameters is simply done with set-Value. To access structured parameters, you must obtain references to structure objects using the getStructure methods of the parameter lists:

```
JCO.Structure mStructure;
mStructure = mImportParameterlist.getStructure();
```

JCO.Structure

The procedure for tabular parameters is similar; there are table objects in the parameter list, to which references can be obtained in the same way:

```
JCO.Table mTable;
mTable = mTableParameterlist.getTable();
```

JCO.Table

To access structure components and table rows, the structure and table objects themselves contain methods such as type-specific methods for the elementary components of a structure, or setRow, set-

Value, and appendRow for table rows. We won't go into any more detail here, however.

Just as for parameter passing through an external RFC interface (see Section 12.2.4), in JCo there is a mapping defined for every elementary ABAP type onto a predefined Java type. For example, for the ABAP type c, you must specify the JCo type JCO.TYPE_CHAR, and for the ABAP type i, there is the JCo type JCO.TYPE_INT.

Function call To call an RFM of a connection, finally, you pass a function call object in which the values for the input parameters of the RFM have already been set using the parameter lists to the execute method of the JCo client object:

```
mConnection.execute(mFunctionCall);
```

After a successful remote call, the output parameters of the RFM can be extracted by reading out the corresponding parameter lists from the function call object, and analyzed using its methods:

```
JCO.ParameterList mExportParameterList;
JCO.ParameterList mTableParameterList;
mExportParameterList =
  mFunctionCall.getExportParameterList();
mTableParameterList =
  mFunctionCall.getTableParameterList();
```

For the handling of exceptions, the class JCO.Exception is used with its subclasses JCO.ConversionException and JCO.AbapException.

JCo Server Programming

The JCo also allows a Java system to act as a server for calls from an AS ABAP. In a standalone JCo, the call goes through the external RFC interface, and a JCo server program, like a server program written in C, must be registered with the SAP Gateway (see Section 12.2.4). As with the external RFC interface, sRFC, tRFC, and qRFC can be handled.

For the programming of a JCo server, you must primarily do the following:

▶ Define a subclass of the JCO.Server class as your own JCO server implementation.

▶ Implement a constructor in this subclass that sets the connection parameters needed for the registration with the SAP Gateway.

▶ Override the `handleRequest(JCO.Function function)` method and implement the code there, which is executed when a call is received.

▶ Create one or more server objects from the subclass, and start them with the `start()` method.

For an example of a JCo server and everything else you need to know about JCo programming, see the documentation for the Java Connector in the SAP Help Portal (*http://help.sap.com*).

12.3 Internet Communication Framework (ICF)

For many years, all SAP communications technology was primarily based on RFC. With the explosive development of the Internet from a manageable server landscape to the global marketplace and communications center that it is today, the significance of the underlying HTTP communication has naturally been enhanced for the SAP system environment as well. The logical consequence is that a communication channel has also been developed for the AS ABAP, which allows HTTP-based applications to exchange data with ABAP programs.

The result of this development is the Internet Communication Manager (ICM) of the SAP NetWeaver Application Server, which can be operated from ABAP programs via the Internet Communication Framework (ICF). The ICF is an object-oriented layer of AS ABAP implemented with interfaces and classes, which allows the handling of HTTP requests within the ABAP environment. Besides HTTP, the ICF also enables ABAP programs to communicate with the Internet through HTTPS and SMTP.

ICM

The ICF is the technological basis for all application-oriented SAP technologies that use the HTTP(S) protocol to provide ABAP functions to the outside, or to access them from outside. Examples of these technologies include ABAP Web Services, Web Dynpro ABAP, and Business Server Pages.

HTTP

In comparison with RFC, communications through the ICF have some significant extensions:

▶ The user can establish a connection to an SAP system from any arbitrary location in the Internet, without being bound to a specially programmed API.

▶ The HTTP protocol allows the use of web-based services and therefore the flexible integration of cross-system business processes independent of the ERP system used.

12.3.1 ICF in AS ABAP

Figure 12.9 shows a schematic diagram of the integration of the ICF into the AS ABAP.

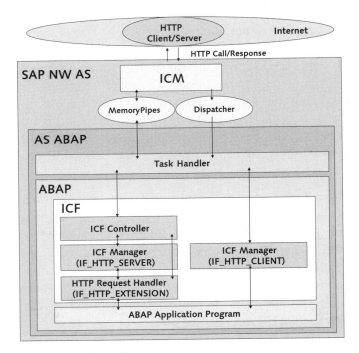

Figure 12.9 ICF Architecture

Communication Flow

In ICF communications, the AS ABAP has both server and client functions. Responding to a request from the Internet, the ICM checks whether an HTTP call is directed to the ABAP or the Java environment of the SAP NetWeaver AS, and, if required, forwards the call to a work process on the AS ABAP. In AS ABAP, the Task Handler of the work process starts the associated components of the ICF, which execute a suitable ABAP program to process the data in the call and pass the corresponding response back to the ICF. For a request from ABAP to the Internet, the ICF supports communication in the reverse direction.

In the following sections, we'll take a brief look at the programming of custom-developed servers and clients using the ICF. When using the SAP-provided technologies—ABAP Web Services, Web Dynpro ABAP, or Business Server Pages—you will generally have no contact with this layer (i. e., the ICF).

12.3.2 ICF Server Programming

The ICF provides the infrastructure for the processing of HTTP requests in the ABAP runtime environment of an AS ABAP. The principle of this communication is actually rather simple: An HTTP request calls a service in the ICF server. This service contains one or more HTTP request handlers, which are responsible for the execution of the corresponding ABAP functionality. SAP provides appropriate ICF services and request handlers for many standard functions. By defining your own HTTP request handlers and services, however, the ICF can also be used for custom-developed applications.

HTTP request to
SAP service

The HTTP Request Handler

An HTTP request handler is a class that implements the interface IF_ HTTP_EXTENSION. Every HTTP request handler is identified by a URL and processes the corresponding incoming HTTP requests. To be able to perform this task, the HTTP request handler must have access to the data of the request and be capable of sending a response back to the client. The ICF provides that infrastructure.

IF_HTTP_
EXTENSION

The HTTP request handler is the central component of the ICF, which implements the processing of an HTTP call in an ABAP program. If you want to use your own functionality in ABAP through HTTP calls, you need to program a suitable HTTP request handler and then register it in ICF as a handler for a service.

Creating an HTTP request handler

To implement an HTTP request handler, create a normal global class in the Class Builder, and specify "IF_HTTP_EXTENSION" on the **Interfaces** tab. The significant task is then just to implement the single method HANDLE_REQUEST of the interface.

Let's look at a simple example. We'll define a global class ZCL_HTTP_SERVICE, bind the interface IF_HTTP_EXTENSION, and implement its method HANDLE_REQUEST as follows:

```
METHOD if_http_extension~handle_request.
  WAIT UP TO 1 SECONDS.
ENDMETHOD.
```

External breakpoint

At first, this method won't do anything. We just want to show that it can be called via HTTP. To do that, we activate the class and set an *external breakpoint* on the WAIT statement in the ABAP Editor of the Class Builder. Unlike a session breakpoint, an external breakpoint also works in programs acting as HTTP servers.

Registering the HTTP request handler as a service

Now we just need a service for which we can register the HTTP request handler. To provide a class, which is implemented as an HTTP request handler, as a service, you must link it in the Transaction SICF (Maintain service) to a service in a service path, for which task a Service Wizard is available. We create such a service as follows:

1. Call the SICF transaction and select **Execute** on the starting screen.

2. In the lower half of the service tree, select the top-most node and then select the function **Wizard: Create service**.

3. Under **Select data**, select **Service**.

4. Under **General data**, enter the name Z_HTTP_SERVICE into the **Service name** field, and enter a suitable description under that.

5. Under **Handler list data**, enter the name of our class, ZCL_HTTP_SERVICE, into the **Handler** field. Note that multiple classes can also be registered.

6. After **Finish**, you will see the new service in the tree (see Figure 12.10), which you can activate by selecting **Activate Service**.

7. You can use the **Display Service** function to jump to the properties of the service, which you can further edit if you want.

To test the service, you can now select **Test Service**, which opens the browser at the service address. You can also enter the address directly into the browser; when accessing the address on the same system it might look something like *http://localhost:8000/z_http_ service*. When accessing it from another system, the network name of the computer must be specified in place of *localhost*.

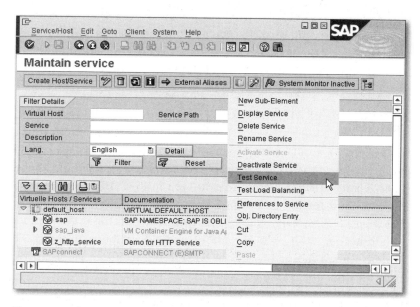

Figure 12.10 Creating an HTTP Service

After entering the user name and password for AS ABAP, the ABAP Debugger opens at the previously defined external breakpoint. Our interface method is really handling an HTTP request (see Figure 12.11).

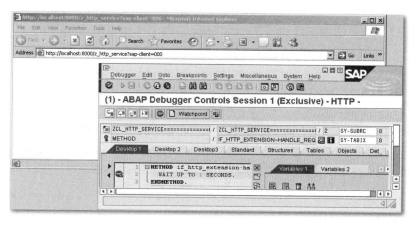

Figure 12.11 Debugging the HTTP Request Handler

Implementing
an HTTP request
handler

In the following, we will look at a few more details of how an HTTP request handler can be implemented more usefully.

The method HANDLE_REQUEST has an input parameter SERVER of type IF_HTTP_SERVER, to which is passed from ICF a reference to the ICF_MANAGER through whose components the request and response data can be accessed. For this purpose, IF_HTTP_SERVER has the attributes REQUEST and RESPONSE of type IF_HTTP_REQUEST and IF_HTTP_RESPONSE, respectively.

Header fields For instance, IF_HTTP_REQUEST contains the methods GET_HEADER_FIELD(S) and SET_HEADER_FIELD(S) of the interface IF_HTTP_ENTITY as aliases in order to provide read or write access to the attributes of the HTTP header. Constants for the names of general HTTP header attributes are found in the IF_HTTP_HEADER_FIELDS interface, and for the names of SAP-specific attributes in IF_HTTP_HEADER_FIELDS_SAP. Names starting with a tilde (~) denote pseudo-header fields, which are not true field attributes of the HTTP header, but are derived from the HTTP request line (e. g., "~query_string" for the query string of a URL).

Body If you know that IF_HTTP_RESPONSE contains the methods GET_CDATA and SET_CDATA that gain direct access to the character data in the HTTP body, you can already write a small application. Listing 12.2 shows the implementation of a small "web report" in an HTTP request handler named ZCL_HTTP_REPORT.

Listing 12.2 HTTP Request Handler as Report

```
METHOD if_http_extension~handle_request.
  DATA: header_data TYPE string,
        html_body   TYPE string,
        fldate      TYPE sflight-fldate,
        planetype   TYPE sflight-planetype,
        seatsocc    TYPE sflight-seatsocc,
        seatsmax    TYPE sflight-seatsmax,
        line        TYPE tline,
        flight      TYPE tflight.
  header_data = server->request->get_header_field(
              if_http_header_fields_sap=>query_string ).
  FIND REGEX '(\D+)(\d+)' IN header_data
    SUBMATCHES flight-carrid flight-connid.
  SELECT SINGLE cityfrom cityto
         FROM spfli
```

```
               INTO (flight-cityfrom,flight-cityto)
               WHERE carrid = flight-carrid AND
                     connid = flight-connid.
     SELECT fldate planetype seatsocc seatsmax
               FROM sflight
               INTO (fldate,planetype,seatsocc,seatsmax)
               WHERE carrid = flight-carrid AND
                     connid = flight-connid.
               WRITE fldate TO line-datestr.
               line-planetypestr = planetype.
               line-seatsfreestr = seatsmax - seatsocc.
         APPEND line TO flight-table.
     ENDSELECT.
     CALL TRANSFORMATION z_flight_to_html
                          SOURCE flight = flight
                          RESULT XML html_body.
     server->response->set_header_field(
               name  = if_http_header_fields=>content_type
               value = 'text/html' ).
     server->response->set_cdata( data = html_body ).
ENDMETHOD.
```

The data types `tline` and `tflight` used are defined as follows in the public visibility area of the class:

```
TYPES: BEGIN OF tline,
          datestr       TYPE c LENGTH 10,
          planetypestr TYPE string,
          seatsfreestr TYPE string,
       END OF tline,
       BEGIN OF tflight,
         carrid    TYPE spfli-carrid,
         connid    TYPE spfli-connid,
         cityfrom TYPE spfli-cityfrom,
         cityto    TYPE spfli-cityto,
         table     TYPE STANDARD TABLE OF tline
                       WITH NON-UNIQUE DEFAULT KEY,
       END OF tflight.
```

If you create a service named "z_http_report" for this request handler in the SICF transaction under the node **default_host** and enter "http://localhost:8000/z_http_report?LH0400" into the address field of your browser, you will get the result shown in Figure 12.12.

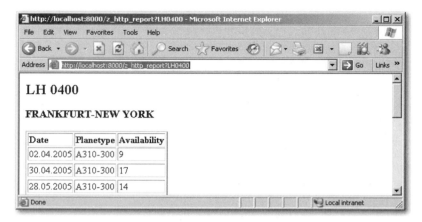

Figure 12.12 Results of the "Web Report"

The HTTP request handler uses exactly three methods of the ICF: GET_HEADER_FIELD, SET_HEADER_FIELD, and SET_CDATA. The rest is usual ABAP: The query string of the URL is evaluated using a regular expression; then the associated data is read from the database and an HTML page is built from it, which is then sent as the response. So ABAP brings its old name[15] new glory!

Simple transformation

> **Insertion: Simple Transformations**
>
> For the construction of the HTML page, we could have easily used statements for character string processing like CONCATENATE, but instead, as foreshadowing for Section 12.5.4, we chose to introduce a simple transformation, which we can call using CALL TRANSFORMATION. The exchange of data (serialization/deserialization) between ABAP and (XML) data structures suitable for the Internet is, after all, exactly the application area of such transformations. The transformation used can be seen in Listing 12.3.
>
> **Listing 12.3** Simple Transformation Z_FLIGHT_TO_HTML
>
> ```
> <?sap.transform simple?>
> <tt:transform
>   xmlns:tt="http://www.sap.com/transformation-templates">
>   <tt:root name="FLIGHT"/>
>   <tt:template>
>     <html><body>
>       <h2><tt:value ref=".FLIGHT.carrid"/>
> ```

---

15 **A**llgemeiner **B**erichts-**A**ufbereitungs **P**rozessor, the General Report Preparation Processor in the original German.

```
              <text> </text>
              <tt:value ref=".FLIGHT.connid"/></h2>
      <h3><tt:value ref=".FLIGHT.cityfrom"/>
          <text>-</text>
          <tt:value ref=".FLIGHT.cityto"/></h3>
      <table border="2">
        <tr>
          <td><b>Date</b></td>
          <td><b>Planetype</b></td>
          <td><b>Availability</b></td>
        </tr>
        <tt:loop ref=".FLIGHT.table">
          <tr>
            <td><tt:value ref="$ref.datestr"/></td>
            <td><tt:value ref="$ref.planetypestr"/></td>
            <td><tt:value ref="$ref.seatsfreestr"/></td>
          </tr>
        </tt:loop>
      </table>
    </body></html>
  </tt:template>
</tt:transform>
```

Without delving into the syntax of simple transformations, you can already see that the element tt:template defines a pattern for an HTML page that contains variable parts, which can be associated with ABAP data objects in the CALL TRANSFORMATION statement. In particular, note the tt:loop statement for the direct serialization of the internal table. The simple transformation used is particularly interesting, because we will use it again for a deserialization in Listing 12.4.

Of course, the example in Listing 12.2 is not intended as a template for a real application. It is only intended to show you how easy it is to connect the AS ABAP to the Internet. We know that this example violates the principle of "separation of concerns," which we introduced in Chapter 9 in the context of the programming of user interfaces, and which should naturally be adhered to when programming services. A service like the report shown here should therefore only be provided as a true ABAP Web Service (see Section 12.4), and should not be implemented directly in the request handler.

Separation of concerns

The evaluation of the URL shown here, too, and even the formatting of the HTML page itself, is essentially just an example and is not intended for imitation. In its interfaces, the ICF has many other methods for the creation of services for the Internet.

Form fields ▸ The methods GET_FORM_FIELD(S) and SET_FORM_FIELD(S) in the IF_HTTP_ENTITY interfaces allow access to the form fields in the URL. For instance, in Listing 12.2, instead of using GET_HEADER_FIELD and the following regular expression, the following calls could also have been used:

```
carrid = server->request->get_form_field( 'carrid' ).
connid = server->request->get_form_field( 'connid' ).
```

If the associated class (ZCL_HTTP_QUERY in the package Z_ABAP_BOOK) is then assigned to a service z_http_query, the URL *http://localhost:8000/z_http_query?carrid=LH&CONNID=0400* returns the same result as shown in Figure 12.12.

Cookies ▸ The methods GET_COOKIE(S) and COOKIE(S) in the IF_HTTP_ENTITY interface allow access to cookies that were sent with the HTTP request.

Stateful, Stateless ▸ You can use the methods SET_SESSION_STATEFUL and SET_SESSION_STATEFUL_VIA_URL in the IF_HTTP_SERVER interface to define whether the communication with a URL is stateless (has no context) or stateful (contains a context) by using a cookie or a URL. The standard setting is stateless. In stateful communication, the internal session of the request handler is retained for the duration of the communication as a context. At the end of communication, the state must explicitly be set to stateless, so that the internal session can be deleted after the last execution of the handler.

In the SICF transaction, you can find a service sap/bc/icf/demo/example_1 provided by SAP, whose request handler CL_HTTP_EXT_DEMO demonstrates the use of these methods.

12.3.3 ICF Client Programming

HTTP request to the Internet

The ICF, through its interface IF_HTTP_CLIENT, supports the option of sending an HTTP request from an ABAP program to the Internet. Without going into details, let's look at this option in Listing 12.4. A program should call the z_http_report created for the example above. In this case, our AS ABAP acts as both the client and the server; however, the program from Listing 12.4 can be executed on any arbitrary AS ABAP with access to the Internet, just by adapting the name for the HTTP server.

Listing 12.4 ABAP Program as HTTP Client

```abap
REPORT z_icf_client.

CLASS demo DEFINITION.
  PUBLIC SECTION.
    CLASS-METHODS: main,
                   display_list
                     IMPORTING value(html) TYPE string.
ENDCLASS.

CLASS demo IMPLEMENTATION.
  METHOD main.
    DATA: client    TYPE REF TO if_http_client,
          path      TYPE string
                    VALUE '/z_http_report?LH0400',
          errortext TYPE string,
          html_body TYPE string.
    cl_http_client=>create(
      EXPORTING  host    = 'localhost'
                 service = '8000'
      IMPORTING  client  = client
      EXCEPTIONS argument_not_found = 1
                 internal_error     = 2
                 plugin_not_active  = 3 ).
    IF sy-subrc <> 0.
      MESSAGE 'Client object not created' TYPE 'I'
              DISPLAY LIKE 'E'.
      RETURN.
    ENDIF.
    cl_http_utility=>set_request_uri(
      request = client->request
      uri     = '/z_http_report?LH0400' ).
    client->send(
      EXCEPTIONS http_communication_failure = 1
                 http_invalid_state         = 2
                 http_processing_failed     = 3
                 OTHERS                     = 4 ).
    IF sy-subrc <> 0.
      client->get_last_error(
        IMPORTING message = errortext ).
      MESSAGE errortext TYPE 'I'
              DISPLAY LIKE 'E'.
      RETURN.
    ENDIF.
    client->receive(
      EXCEPTIONS http_communication_failure = 1
```

```
                        http_invalid_state          = 2
                        http_processing_failed      = 3
                        OTHERS                       = 4 ).
      IF sy-subrc <> 0.
        client->get_last_error(
          IMPORTING message = errortext ).
        MESSAGE errortext TYPE 'I'
                DISPLAY LIKE 'E'.
        RETURN.
      ENDIF.
      html_body = client->response->get_cdata(  ).
      client->close( ).
      display_list( html_body ).
    ENDMETHOD.
    METHOD display_list.
      DATA: flight TYPE zcl_http_report=>tflight,
            alv    TYPE REF TO cl_salv_table.
      CALL TRANSFORMATION z_flight_to_html
                          SOURCE XML html
                          RESULT flight = flight.
      TRY.
          cl_salv_table=>factory(
            IMPORTING r_salv_table = alv
            CHANGING t_table = flight-table ).
          alv->display( ).
        CATCH cx_salv_msg.
          MESSAGE 'ALV display not possible' TYPE 'I'
                  DISPLAY LIKE 'E'.
      ENDTRY.
    ENDMETHOD.
ENDCLASS.

START-OF-SELECTION.
  demo=>main( ).
```

The actual HTTP client is an object of class CL_HTTP_CLIENT, which is generated using its factory method CREATE. The parameters for the desired HTTP server are explicitly passed during this process. Alternatively, you can also call the method shown in Listing 12.5 without changing the program in any other way:

Listing 12.5 HTTP Client over Destination

```
REPORT z_icf_client_via_destination.

...
```

```
CLASS demo IMPLEMENTATION.
  METHOD main.
    ...
    cl_http_client=>create_by_destination(
      EXPORTING  destination = 'HTTP_TEST'
      IMPORTING  client      = client
      EXCEPTIONS destination_not_found    = 1
                 internal_error           = 2
                 argument_not_found       = 3
                 destination_no_authority = 4
                 plugin_not_active        = 5
                 OTHERS                   = 6 ).
    ...
```

To do this, as shown in Figure 12.13, you must use the SM59 transaction to create an **RFC Destination** of connection type **H** (HTTP connection to an ABAP system) that contains the respective parameters.
As with all RFC destinations, parameters for the **Logon & Security**
tab, etc., must be determined. With the login procedure **SAP Standard** or **SAP Trusted System**, the need to supply a user name and password during the login can be eliminated. The use of such a destination is generally recommended.

Destination

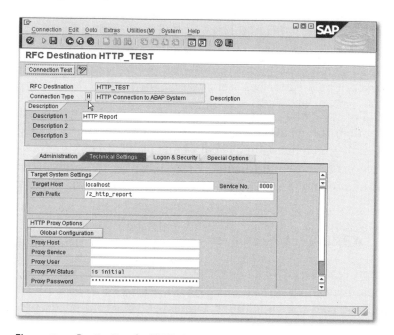

Figure 12.13 Destination for HTTP Connection

After the successful creation of the client object, it is used as follows:

1. The request of the client to the server is determined by using the method SET_REQUEST_URI in the class CL_HTTP_UTILITY.[16]

2. After any necessary adjustments are made to the attributes of the client object, the request is sent to the HTTP server with the SEND method.

3. The result can now be retrieved with the RECEIVE method, and then all the necessary data is available in the client object. For example, there is a RESPONSE attribute of type IF_HTTP_RESPONSE, which can be used, as it was for the HTTP handler, to access request and response data. Here, we simply use the GET_CDATA method to read the entire HTML page into a string.

4. Then the CLOSE method is used to close the connection, after which the data is no longer available in the client object.

In all these steps, we recommend that you perform suitable exception handling.

Deserialization To display the table in an ALV list, we use the `display_list` method to deserialize the HTML file, which we serialized in Listing 12.2 back into local ABAP data, for whose type we refer to the declaration in CL_HTTP_REPORT. Perhaps, this is not all that practical, but it shows ideally how elegantly such a task can be solved using a simple transformation: Our simple transformation from Listing 12.3 is symmetrical, and can be used for both serialization and for deserialization!

As with the implementation of an HTTP server, the ICF also provides many options for clients that greatly exceed the scope of this book. For example, the requests of a client can be parallelized onto different servers. For more information, we refer you to the appropriate documentation in the SAP Help Portal (*http://help.sap.com*).

12.4   ABAP Web Services

In Section 12.3, we got to know the programming interface of the AS ABAP, through which we can access AS ABAP programs via the Internet: the Internet Communication Framework (ICF). After we pro-

---

16 When using a destination, this specification can also be made in the SM59 transaction.

grammed a small "web service" (see Listing 12.2), more or less manually, we now want to take a look at a proper encapsulation of this technology—ABAP Web Services.

Web services form the technological basis of the Enterprise Service-Oriented Architecture (Enterprise SOA). They are the building blocks of modern service-oriented software architectures. By using web services, IT infrastructure can be converted step by step into service-oriented architectures.

In the following sections, you will discover how to create a web service and integrate it into an application.

12.4.1 What Is a Web Service?

A web service is a modularized executable unit, which can be called in a heterogeneous system environment across system boundaries. Based on the input parameters passed, a task is completed, which is then sent back to the caller. Web services can be used, for instance, to perform a credit card verification, to convert a currency, to send a price request to a supplier, or to place an order. Industrial manufacturers can also provide web services to their customers, partners, and suppliers for implementation in their programs to build overall supply-chain solutions. The advantage of web services in comparison with other communications technologies is derived from an internationally accepted standardization.

The creation or extension of business processes without using web services can often be a complicated and time-consuming process, as demonstrated by the following example. An airline would like to enable customers to book rental cars via the airline's Internet portal. So that customers need not have to book the desired rental car themselves, and therefore have to go through a rental car agency's website, the airline's portal should be able to process the booking itself. This assumes that the developer of the portal application not only has access to the data from the rental car agency, but also knows the technical infrastructure of the rental car agency's website, such as the programming language of the application used or different middleware approaches. On the other hand, if the rental car agency offers a web service like *Check availability of a rental car*, this service can be

SOA

Modularized, executable units

used by any application as a sort of black box, without the need to set up complicated development projects.

Solution approaches for the interoperable use of software components have been around for years. None of these solutions, like CORBA (*Common Object Request Broker Architecture*), Java RMI (*Remote Method Invocation*), or DCOM (*Distributed Component Object Model*), however, have experienced the desired success.

Standards Due to the complex work on binding standards for web services and the promise by most software manufacturers, including Microsoft, IBM, Sun Microsystems, SAP, and many others to adhere to those standards, the possibility of having systems of different types and technologies communicate with one another using web services is now a reality.

12.4.2 Web Services and Enterprise SOA

While web services represent a technical concept, the Enterprise Service-Oriented Architecture (Enterprise SOA) enables the design of a complete solution for a business application.

The broader the offering of web services, the more concrete the image of the Enterprise Service-Oriented Architecture is becoming. It is not enough just to provide a technological platform, in this case SAP NetWeaver. Instead, SAP must make its enterprise software (ERP, CRM, SCM, etc.) available bit by bit in the form of services, which is planned for the near future. Customers will thus receive a powerful tool to adapt applications like SCM, CRM, and others to their needs by combining services. In this context, it makes sense when customers and partners also make their own solutions service-capable, in order to leverage all the advantages of the service-oriented architecture.

Enterprise Services With enterprise services, user interfaces can be simplified and standardized. Schematic user interfaces (UI) should also be configurable without programming knowledge by using standardized *UI patterns*. Generic UI patterns should be populated with concrete application services. The nature of these services is oriented to the details of the UIs and differs from message-oriented web services due to additional metadata.

Both types of service, however, have a lot in common (e. g., data types used, implementation aspects). This is the reason that in future releases SAP will extend the Integration Repository of the Exchange Infrastructure into a so-called *Enterprise Services Repository*.

Enterprise
Services
Repository

12.4.3 Standards for Web Services

So that application components, which have been developed in different programming languages on different hardware and operating systems, can be connected into a single business process using web services, the web service technology must be based on generally accepted standards.

The conventional channels and standards of the Internet are used for communication. WSDL (*Web Services Description Language*) is used to specify the interface of a web service, SOAP (*Simple Object Access Protocol*) is used to transmit remote procedure calls, and then UDDI (*Universal Description, Discovery and Integration*) can be used to locate web services.

Even though these standards have largely already been established, there is still work to do for the institutions that establish standards. Some standards are newly created, while others are still developing. Extended standards like security standards or additional protocols will be integrated into its Web Service Framework by SAP step by step.

The following organizations are concerned with the creation of generally binding standards for web services:

▶ The *World Wide Web Consortium* (W3C) is responsible for the core technologies within the web service framework. The W3C consists of a series of provider-independent working groups whose task it is to define standards for certain portions of a technology. SAP is a member of the *Web Services Architecture Working Group* of the W3C.

W3C

▶ The *Organization for the Advancement of Structured Information Systems* (OASIS) is particularly concerned with processes. Here, the interplay of web services and their integration into business applications is in the foreground. Directory services play a large role, as does the security of using web services. SAP supports business-oriented initiatives in the area of web services. Besides

OASIS,
UN/CEFACT

OASIS, the *United Nations Center for Trade Facilitation and Electronic Business* (UN/CEFACT) is also supported. Both organizations are concerned with the development of standards for web services in the business arena, for example, the *Universal Business Language* (UBL) and *WS-Security*.

WS-I ▶ The *Web Service Interoperability Organization* (WS-I) has set itself the task of advancing web service interoperability, independent of platforms, applications, and programming languages. WS-I offers practical help in the form of introductions, recommended procedures, and tools to support the development of interoperable web services. The interoperability of web services is ensured by the definition of WS-I profiles, which each include a number of specifications. If a web service complies with a WS-I profile, it must fulfill all the specifications it contains. Besides profiles, WS-I usage scenarios and supply chain management use cases are also provided by WS-I.

Standards of the Web Service Framework | To summarize, the Web Service Framework of SAP supports the following standards:

W3C (SOAP 1.1, WSDL 1.1, XML Schema, XML Signature, XSL), OASIS, CIM, BPML (SAML, UBL, UDDI 2.0, WSRP, WS-Security, XML.org), Wf-XML, WS-I (Basic Profile 1.0), and many others.

12.4.4 Web Services for AS ABAP

SOAP, WSDL, and UDDI | The AS ABAP can act as both a server for web service providers and also as a web service requester. As we already mentioned, SOAP, WSDL, and UDDI are the core components of the web service approach. SOAP specifies a general, application-independent format for XML messages, which can be exchanged between communication partners over different transport protocols. WSDL adds the application-oriented components: Using this XML-based language, the interface of actual web services is described, consisting of the names of operations, and the input and output messages. These messages are packaged into SOAP messages at runtime, and then transmitted. UDDI enables us to make web services publicly known and to then be able to search for these services.

Figure 12.14 shows the basic architecture of the Web Service Framework of AS ABAP.

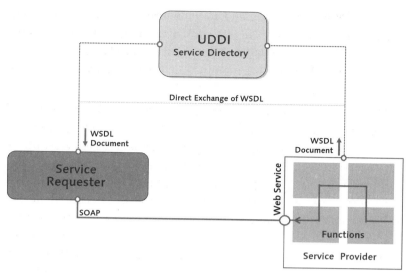

Figure 12.14 Architecture of the Web Service Framework

If the AS ABAP is acting as a service provider, then a web service interface is created for the function implemented, whether it is an Remote-enabled Function Module (RFM), a BAPI, an XI message interface,[17] or an IDoc, which represents the web service for the user. Based on this interface, the web service is configured and can be called at runtime.

Service provider

Published web services can be placed in a UDDI registry. They can be searched in all registries and published in all registries, which correspond to the standard. SAP itself provides a public UDDI business registry at *http://uddi.sap.com*.

Service directory

If the AS ABAP is acting as a service requester, a WSDL file can be used to generate a web service client in a few steps.

Service requester

12.4.5 Role of the Exchange Infrastructure

With SAP NetWeaver Exchange Infrastructure (SAP XI), business processes can be created that span multiple systems. SAP XI can be used to connect systems from different manufacturers (non-SAP and

SAP XI

---

17 An XI message interface is used for the platform-independent description of communications (synchronous or asynchronous) between different application components in WSDL.

SAP) in different versions and implemented in different programming languages (Java, ABAP, etc.). SAP XI is based on an open architecture, uses open standards (particularly those from the XML and Java worlds), and offers services that are indispensable in a heterogeneous, complex system environment, namely:

- Runtime infrastructure for the exchange of messages
- Configuration options for the control of business processes and message flow
- Options for the transformation of message contents between sender and recipient

SAP XI even supports company-internal and intra-enterprise scenarios.

The ABAP proxies of XI and web services follow the same programming model. This has the advantage that both technologies can be used to complement one another. Messages can either be sent or received through the XI runtime or the web service runtime.

Additional services of the proxy runtime can be controlled by protocol. These are requested by a method of the proxy. The scope of functionality depends on whether the Web Service Framework or Exchange Infrastructure is used for communication.

Integration broker

Point-to-point web service calls can be extended by using an integration broker as a mediator between the web service client and the service provider. Figure 12.15 shows how the integration broker can forward web service calls to services on different systems in a heterogeneous system environment.

Proxy

To execute a service on a different system, an application calls a proxy in the application system. The call causes the application system to send a message to the integration broker. The integration broker processes the message according to a central configuration, which determines the routing and, if necessary, any mapping to be performed. The processing of the message by an integration process is optionally possible. The service provider receives the message, calls the service, and sends the answer to the request through the integration broker to the web service client.

In addition to a service, which a provider like an AS ABAP publishes as a web service, you can also call services of a non-SAP system or an older ABAP system, which aren't provided directly as web services (e. g., because they don't support the SOAP protocol) through the integration broker. Using a mapping, the integration broker can also call services whose interface signature doesn't match that of the web service call. To determine the recipient, the routing functions of the integration broker are used.

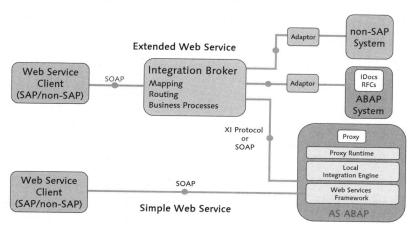

Figure 12.15 Web Service Call Through the Integration Broker

12.4.6 Web Service Framework

Any business standard function that exists independently and in a modular form can be provided as a web service. The standard interfaces used with SAP, like RFMs, BAPIs, and the XI message interfaces of ABAP, can be published without involving any additional programming effort by the Web Service Framework of the AS ABAP as web services.

The Web Service Framework includes parts of the ABAP Workbench, tools for the support of UDDI registration, and the SOAP Runtime (see Figure 12.16).

The processing of SOAP requests is performed through the Internet Communication Framework (ICF, see Section 12.3). The AS ABAP uses the HTTP protocol of the ICF for communication between web service requesters and providers.

ICF

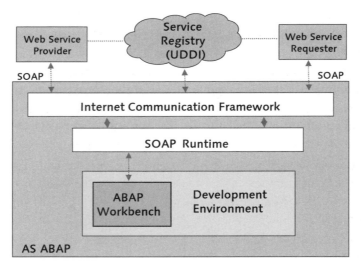

Figure 12.16 Web Service Framework of the AS ABAP

12.4.7 Creating a Web Service

To provide a web service-capable function as a web service, you must create a service definition that represents the web service for the external user.

Service Definition
Wizard

The Web Service Framework includes a Service Definition Wizard in order to create a web service with a few mouse clicks.[18] The wizard contains predefined profiles with predefined settings for the security of web services or the transport protocol used.

In the following procedure, the creation of a simple web service using the Service Definition Wizard will be explained. In the function group Z_WEB_SERVICES, we have prepared a Remote-enabled Function Module (RFM) for this purpose named Z_SQRT, which will be offered as a web service.

Procedure

Proceed as follows:

1. In the Function Builder, select **Utilities • More Utilities • Create Web Service • From the Function Module** (see Figure 12.17). Then the starting screen of the **Service Definition Wizard** appears, on which you click **Continue**.

---

18 This assumes that you have been assigned the role SAP_BC_WEBSERVICE_ ADMIN in the user master record.

2. In the **Create Service** screen, give the name of the service definition and a brief description (see Figure 12.18), and then select **Continue**.

3. In the **Choose Endpoint** screen, enter the name of the function module and select the checkbox **Mapping of Names**. If the checkbox is checked, the name of the end point is used. Underscores, which are often used in AS ABAP for the naming of function modules, will be removed, and the first letters will be capped.

4. In the **Configure Service** screen, select one of the predefined profiles for the configuration of the web service. If you select the profile **Basic Auth SOAP**, the user name and password of the caller of the web service will be requested. With the profile **Secure SOAP**, authentication takes place using client certificates, and data transmitted is encrypted using the Secure Socket Layer (SSL) protocol. In either case, the communication is stateless. Leave the **Release Service for Runtime** checkbox unchecked, since we will perform the release in the WSCONFIG transaction, which is provided for that purpose.

5. In the **Complete** screen, select the corresponding button and assign the service to a package.

You will now find the service definition under the node **Enterprise Services • Service Definitions** in the Repository Browser of the Object Navigator in the package you selected. If necessary, you can continue to use the appropriate tool (Web Service Definition Editor, see Section 12.19) to further edit the service properties defined by the wizard.

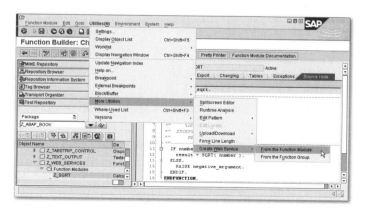

Figure 12.17 Creating a Web Service from an RFM

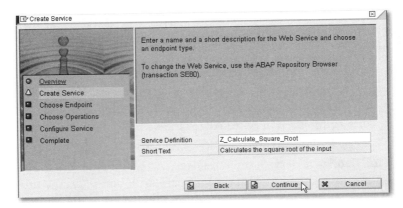

Figure 12.18 Service Definition Wizard

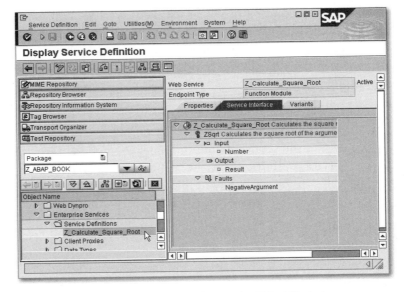

Figure 12.19 Web Service Definition Editor in the Object Navigator

12.4.8 Releasing a Web Service

WSCONFIG After the creation of a web service, it must be released. To do this, we use the Transaction WSCONFIG ("Release Web Services for SOAP Runtime"). This transaction reads the predefined settings, for example, for the security of data transmission, from the service definition, and offers suitable setting options. In this sense, the values of the service definition are considered as suggested values or value ranges.

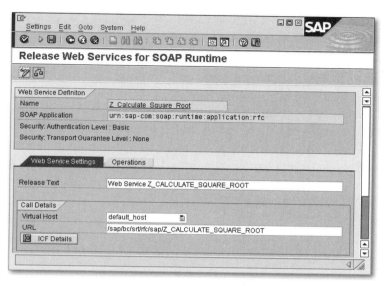

Figure 12.20 Releasing a Web Service

Call the WSCONFIG transaction and proceed as follows:

1. In the entry fields **Service Definition** and **Variants**, enter the name of the service definition and select **Create**. Then the screen shown in Figure 12.20 will appear.[19]

2. In the **Release Text** field, enter the text to be used to publish the web service in a registry. Under **Call Details**, you will find information on the service, like the host and the URL. To generate the corresponding WSDL document, the host and port number must be unique. When specifying **default_host** in the **Virtual Host** field, the values defined in ICM for the current application server will be used. If you want to use the address of a specific application server of the AS ABAP in the WSDL document, you can assign the host name and port number of a new virtual host in the starting screen of the transaction under **Goto • Manage Call Addresses for Virtual Hosts**, and use that.

3. By selecting **ICF Details**, you will go to the display screen of the SICF transaction, which you should already be familiar with from Figure 12.10. There, you can find the new service in an ICF service

---

19 If you are working on the SAP NetWeaver 2004s ABAP Trial Version with client 000, this must first be set to **changeable** in the client maintenance (Transaction SCC4) in the system administration.

path created by the wizard, which you can select and change if you want.[20]

4. Select the **Operations** tab. Using this tab, you can select security profiles (inbound/outbound) for every operation. Security profiles allow you to use the framework of WS Security for the security of the web service. Using WS Security, SOAP messages between the provider of a web service and the web service client are protected by digital XML signatures, XML encryption, timestamping, and security tokens. For simple situations, for example, when a client wants to communicate with exactly one server, HTTPS will suffice as an encryption mechanism.

5. Save your entries. The web service is now displayed on the initial screen of the transaction in the list of web services released for the SOAP runtime.

12.4.9 Testing a Web Service

WSADMIN   For released web services, the Transaction WSADMIN ("Administration of Web Services for SOAP Runtime") can be used to perform additional actions:

Web service   For instance, it allows the Web Service Framework to call a web service home page   home page for every released web service. Using the web service home page, web services can be tested, the WSDL documents of the web service can be displayed, and proxies can be generated.

J2EE server   For the presentation of the web service home page, the Web Service Framework uses the J2EE infrastructure of the AS Java in the application server of SAP NetWeaver. A standalone installation of AS ABAP is not sufficient to perform the following steps. The installation must be extended with an AS Java. For instance, an SAP NetWeaver 2004s Java Trial Version can be used on the same or a different computer on the network.[21] Under **GoTo • Settings Admin-**

---

20 To see all services, you must select the **Reset Filter** function.

21 We recommend installing the ABAP and Java versions of SAP NetWeaver 2004s ABAP Trial Version only together. The additional installation of a Java version in an existing ABAP version can lead to difficulties. In any case, you should save all your development objects before changing your installation. To do this, you can perform a transport through the CTS, or you can carry out a database backup, for example. The latter is possible using the MaxDB database manager, which can be installed separately.

istration of the WSADMIN transaction, the address of an application server must be entered on which a J2EE Engine is running. To test the web service in this book, an existing J2EE demo system within SAP was accessed from the SAP NetWeaver 2004s ABAP Trial Version.

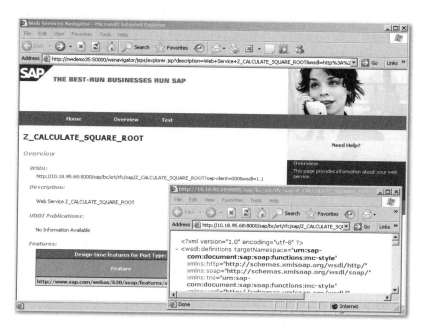

Figure 12.21 Web Service Home Page and WSDL Document

1. To display the web service home page, in the WSADMIN transaction, select the service definition you created under the node **SOAP Application for RFC-Compliant FMS** and select **Web Service Homepage** (with **WSDL** you can show the corresponding WSDL document).

2. In the following dialog window, select **Document Style**. For style definitions in WSDL documents, there is a basic distinction between the *Remote Procedure Call* (RPC) style and the *Document* style. In the RPC style, the SOAP message includes remote procedure calls. Data types are then used in accordance with the SOAP specification. In Document style, XML documents are exchanged. The data types are defined using XML schemata.

3. Enter a user name and password if the web service requests this authentication. Then the web service home page will appear on

the page **Overview** with the properties of the web service. There, you can also select **WSDL** to look at the WSDL document again (*see* Figure 12.21).

4. Select **Test**. Under **Operations**, select **ZSqrt** to send a client request.

5. An input form for the input parameters of the function module appears. Enter a value for **Number** and select **Send**. This displays the results screen shown in Figure 12.22.

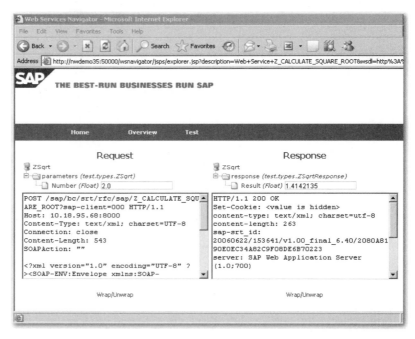

Figure 12.22 Testing a Web Service

12.4.10 Publishing a Web Service

When using web services, there is a distinction made between service providers and service requesters. In the simplest case, the service provider knows the service requester and informs the requester where services can be found. However, this contradicts the idea of web services as a global service platform. What makes the use of web services attractive is that it purports the idea that applications can be built from globally available web services.

To provide this comprehensive global marketplace for web services to providers and consumers as fully and as expediently as possible, there are central directory services. These services are made possible by the development of the UDDI standard (*Universal Description Discovery and Integration*), which was defined by the OASIS standards organizations. Many companies offer public UDDI servers. Examples are: SAP (*http://uddi.sap.com/*), Microsoft (*http://uddi.microsoft.com/*), and IBM (*http://uddi.ibm.com/*).

UDDI allows registrations comparable to the Yellow Pages. UDDI registries contain descriptions of services in the form of WSDL documents, extended with structured specifications of the provider (with contact information), as well as industries and business categories for which the web services are suitable in detail. Web services created in the ABAP Workbench can be published in any registry that corresponds to the UDDI standard.

UDDI

12.4.11 Creating a Client for Web Services

To conclude our brief sojourn through web services, let's also create a client application for our web service:[22]

1. In the WSADMIN transaction, obtain the URL of the WSDL document of the web service created earlier (either the **WSDL** function or on the web service home page).

2. In the Object Navigator on the **Enterprise Services** node, first select the function **Create • Proxy Object**, then **URL/HTTP-Destination**, and copy the URL of the WSDL document into the corresponding field.

Proxy object

3. Assign the name of a package[23] (and a prefix if necessary for the customer namespace) to the client proxy to be generated. This proxy will act as a handler for the server of the web service desired. It encapsulates the entire technical part, like the automatic packagings of calls into a SOAP message and the evaluation of incoming responses.

4. Activate the proxy. Now, all repository objects needed to call a web service are generated. These primarily constitute a proxy class

Proxy class

---

22 The following steps are possible without a connection to a J2EE server again.
23 The package must include a usage declaration for the package interface SAI_TOOLS.

from which the actual proxy objects can be instantiated in programs, and (structured) data types for parameter passing.

Logical port   5. A client proxy needs a so-called *logical port*. This is an SAP-specific concept for the configuration of the runtime features for web service client proxies. Runtime features are properties that must be configured in the runtime environment at the time of activation of the web service client. For instance, they include the URL to call the service. Generally, this URL is generated directly in the proxy object. SAP selected a special path here: runtime features can be changed using an editor. Call the Transaction LPCONFIG to create a logical port for the client. There, enter the name of the proxy class (the client proxy you just created) and a name for the logical port. Select **Default Port** and click **Create**.

6. On the **Call Parameters** tab, the address of the web service must be entered into the **URL** field. On the **Runtime** tab, you must decide whether the web service runtime will be used to call a web service over the Internet for simple services, or the XI runtime for more complicated services. We use the web service runtime and change no other settings. Save and activate the logical port.

Client program   7. Create an ABAP program and drag the client proxy in the Object Navigator into the desired point in the program. The template shown in Figure 12.23 will be inserted.

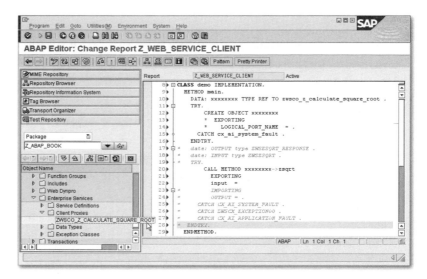

Figure 12.23 Template for Calling a Web Service

8. Replace the placeholder in the template created, as shown in Listing 12.6.

Listing 12.6 ABAP Program as Web Service Client

```abap
REPORT z_web_service_client.

CLASS demo DEFINITION.
  PUBLIC SECTION.
    CLASS-METHODS main.
ENDCLASS.
CLASS demo IMPLEMENTATION.
  METHOD main.
    DATA: ws     TYPE REF TO zwsco_z_calculate_square_root,
          input  TYPE zwszsqrt,
          output TYPE zwszsqrt_response,
          msg    TYPE string.
    TRY.
        CREATE OBJECT ws
          EXPORTING
            logical_port_name = 'Z_LOGICAL_PORT'.
      CATCH cx_ai_system_fault.
        MESSAGE 'Error when creating Web Service Client'
                TYPE 'I' DISPLAY LIKE 'E'.
    ENDTRY.
    TRY.
        input-number = '2.0'.
        CALL METHOD ws->zsqrt
          EXPORTING input  = input
          IMPORTING output = output.
        msg = output-result.
        CONCATENATE `Result of Web Service is ` msg
          INTO msg.
        MESSAGE msg TYPE 'I'.
      CATCH cx_ai_system_fault
            zwscx_exception00
            cx_ai_application_fault.
        MESSAGE 'Error when calling Web Service Client'
                TYPE 'I' DISPLAY LIKE 'E'.
    ENDTRY.
  ENDMETHOD.
ENDCLASS.
START-OF-SELECTION.
  demo=>main( ).
```

The program instantiates a proxy object from the proxy class and calls its `zsqrt` method. Input and output parameters are passed in structures of the data types generated specifically for this purpose. If you have done everything correctly, the square root of 2 will be displayed as the result of the web service. Behind the `zsqrt` method, after all, there is nothing more than a call to the Z_SQUARE_ROOT RFM offered as a web service.

12.5 ABAP and XML

XML (*Extensible Markup Language*), because of its flexible and versatile application possibilities, has emerged in the last few years as a standard format for many applications. Primarily due to the fact that it can be used as a data exchange format for heterogeneous system environments, it has certain advantages over other formats, which has made it the dominant format in this area, just as SQL has become the dominant language for working with relational databases (e. g., see the WSDL file in Figure 12.21).

Enterprise SOA, XI, RFC

In SAP, data exchange using XML forms the technological basis of the Enterprise Service-Oriented Architecture (Enterprise SOA), and SAP NetWeaver Exchange Infrastructure (XI). In RFC, too (see Section 12.2), XML is used internally for parameter passing.[24]

Serialization, deserialization

In this section, you'll learn about ABAP's support for creating and reading XML documents. This primarily involves the direct conversion of ABAP data into the XML format (serialization) and the reading of XML documents into ABAP data objects (deserialization).

The infrastructure provided by AS ABAP to process XML documents in ABAP programs is not the XML-based communication mechanisms themselves, as provided, for instance, by ABAP Web Services, Enterprise Services Infrastructure (ESI), or XML-RPC (*Remote Procedure Call*), but rather the underlying technologies that are needed to use XML as a data format in ABAP. For working with XML, ABAP provides three core technologies with a broad associated infrastructure:

---

24 Only when passing internal tables using the TABLES clause is a binary format used instead of an XML format, and this is for performance reasons.

1. iXML library, which provides a validating XML parser along with the associated Document Object Model (DOM)

2. SAP XSLT processor, which enables complex standardized transformations of XML and ABAP data structures

3. Simple Transformations (ST) for efficient transformation of ABAP data structures into XML and vice versa

After a very brief introduction into the basics of XML, we'll take a closer look at these three technologies in the following sections. As long as you use standardized communication mechanisms, you should rarely encounter the direct processing of XML data in ABAP, since access to XML files is generally encapsulated by the appropriate frameworks. However, there are certainly situations where knowing how ABAP data is serialized/deserialized will help you. The simple example in Section 12.3 already shows how elegantly an internal table can be converted into a displayable form using a Simple Transformation. Another example is the serialization of object references, including the objects they point to, which isn't possible using the normal `IMPORT/EXPORT` mechanism (see Section 10.4).

12.5.1 What Is XML?

XML, the *Extensible Markup Language*, unlike most other languages for the description of data models, did not originate in the database arena. Instead, the roots of XML, like those of the *Hypertext Markup Language* (HTML), on which the documents of the World Wide Web are based, are in the document management. Unlike HTML, however, XML is suitable for the representation of many types of structured data. These include the data from business applications and the representation of data from databases. Since XML can represent data with different structures, it is particularly useful as a data format when an application must communicate with other applications, or information from different applications must be integrated.

The basic principle of markup languages is based on the separation of content, structure, and layout. The term *markup* in the XML world covers anything that isn't a part of the actual data, but which is primarily for the structuring of that data. We use the term *metadata* in this case, that is, data about the data.

Markup Elements and Elements

Tags   In the family of markup languages, including XML and HTML as well, markup is implemented by markup elements (tags), included in angle brackets (`<tag>`). Markup elements are used in pairs, so that `<tag>` and `</tag>` mark the beginning and the end of an element in an XML document. For example, the title of this chapter might be expressed as follows:

```
<title>ABAP and XML</title>
```

Adaptation of tags   Unlike HTML, however, XML does not provide a fixed set of markup elements.[25] This flexibility allows the adaptation of documents to reflect the specific requirements of technical as well as business applications. This viewpoint is vital for the significant role of XML in the exchange and representation of business data, while HTML is primarily used for the formatting of documents.

For instance, let's look at the following XML document, which describes a supply order in an ERP system. If you look at the use of markup elements like `OrderId` or `OrderItem`, you will see that they represent contextual information for the data and allow it to define a semantic logic for the relationships between data. The data itself is represented as elements of the XML document, that is, the content between the beginning and end of markup elements.

```
<SalesOrder>
  <OrderHeader>
    <OrderId> 063418844-2A </OrderId>
    <Delivery> 2000-10-09 </Delivery>
  </OrderHeader>
  <OrderBody>
    <OrderItem>
        <amount> 7 </amount>
        <descr> ABAP Objects Reference </descr>
        <price> 159.00 </price>
    </OrderItem>
    <OrderItem>
        <amount> 2 </amount>
        <descr> ABAP Reporting for Dummys </descr>
        <price> 35.00 </price>
```

---

25 A cleanly formed HTML document, however, can certainly be seen as a special XML document. See using XML in the example of Section Internet Communication Framework (ICF).

```
      </OrderItem>
      <OrderItem>
          <amount> 4 </amount>
          <descr> SAP NetWeaver Application Server </descr>
          <price> 38.00 </price>
      </OrderItem>
    </OrderBody>
</SalesOrder>
```

If you compare the storage of data in XML documents with tabular representation in relational databases, the representation as XML elements appears to be very inefficient at first glance. Each element must have the markup elements added, and these are repeated continuously. Thus they constitute a large part of the document contents, which can even surpass the data content itself. Despite this disadvantage, the XML representation has significant advantages once XML is used as a data exchange format:

Inefficient data storage?

▶ The use of markup elements makes the document self-describing. That means no additional schema information is needed to understand the structure and meaning of the data. The above XML document can be directly read and understood.

▶ The format of an XML document is not predetermined. For instance, a partial step of an application can insert additional information into the document, like information about the last change to a business document. An application processing the document can ignore such information if it's not needed. The capability to recognize and skip unexpected markup elements makes it possible to develop document formats further without making existing applications obsolete.

▶ Elements can be nested within other elements down to any level you choose. Encapsulation of markup elements allows for the representation of complex information in a single document. For example, a customer order can contain markup elements for the supplier, the customer, and all the items of the order. Every one of these elements has subelements. An order position can consist of material number, quantity, description, and price.

Although the nested representation makes it relatively simple to describe nearly any information, it almost always leads to a redundancy of data. For instance, every order item might have its own delivery address as a subelement, which then appears in the docu-

Redundancy

ment many times if multiple order items are to be delivered to the same delivery address. Such redundancies could be avoided by establishing a relationship between elements, but they are often tolerated in order to retain the readability and integrity of all elements in the document, that is, to avoid relationships.

Attributes

In addition to elements between tags, XML also allows the storage of attributes. The following example shows how an attribute can be used to associate currency information with a price specification:

```
<price currency="USD"> 35.00 </price>
```

The attributes of an element are defined with the equals sign (=) as name/value pairs before the terminating bracket (>) of the opening markup element. Attributes are character data and contain no markup. Furthermore, an attribute, unlike a subelement, may not appear more than once within an element.

To distinguish between attributes and subelements is generally only relevant when working with document descriptions like HTML, since the content of attributes is not output by the processing application (the browser), but is used as an additional means for formatting. When using XML for pure data exchange, this distinction is less important. The decision to represent information as attributes or subelements is therefore often arbitrary.

Namespaces

Namespaces are a mechanism that allows you to use markup elements from different contexts together in a single document, without running the risk of name conflicts. Namespaces are therefore especially useful when integrating data from different applications. The following example demonstrates the concept of namespaces:

```
<sd:OrderHeader xmlns:sd="www.sap.com/sd"
                xmlns:fi="www.sap.com/fi">
  <sd:OrderId> 063418844-2A </sd:OrderId>
  <fi:InvoiceId> FI-23243512-20060306 <fi:InvoiceId>
</sd:OrderHeader>
```

To declare a namespace, special `xmlns` attributes are used. Here, a Uniform Resource Identifier (URI) is assigned to a prefix. In the example above, the namespace declaration `xmlns:sd="www.sap.com/sd"` binds the prefix `sd` to the URI `www.sap.com/sd`. Namespaces are used in so-called *Qnames* (qualified names). A qname consists of a namespace prefix and a local name, separated by a colon. The qname `sd:OrderId` thus consists of the local name `OrderId` and the namespace prefix `sd`. The prefix `sd` associates a local name `OrderId`, which may not be unique, with the unique namespace `www.sap.com/sd`, so that naming conflicts can be avoided.

xmlns

Summary

XML provides flexible mechanisms to model self-describing data formats. It supports a series of features like nested structures, multivalued attributes, namespaces, and allows the representation of different types of data in a single document.

The examples thus far can serve only as the briefest overview of XML. As the name Extensible Markup Language implies, there are a variety of additional specifications and standards based on XML. If you seriously want to develop applications with XML, learning more about the concepts of XML can only help you.

12.5.2 The iXML Library

The iXML library provides object-oriented access to the handling of XML documents. It is implemented using global classes in the class library, which can be used through the IF_IXML_... interfaces in the SIXML package. The complete documentation of the iXML library and its interfaces can be found in the SAP Help Portal (*http://help.sap.com*). It provides the following functionality:

▶ A validating XML-1.0 parser including namespaces

Functionality

▶ An event-based XML parser with a pull API (similar to SAX, the *Simple API for XML*, a standard used in Java)

▶ Support of Document Type Definitions (DTD)

▶ An implementation of the Document Object Model (DOM)

▶ An XML renderer

Parsers analyze and process existing HTML documents and can convert them into a DOM representation. The renderer converts a DOM back into an XML document. Furthermore, the iXML library provides input and output streams, which can be bound directly to XSL transformations using the CALL TRANSFORMATION statement.

Document Type Definition

DTD A *document type definition*, or DTD, is a mechanism standardized by the World Wide Web Consortium (W3C) to check XML documents for validity. To do this, the structure of an XML document is determined in a DTD using type declarations for elements, attributes, and entities.

If an XML document is read and corresponds to the rules of the document type definition, we refer to this as a *valid document*—in contrast to a *well-defined* document, which complies with the requirements of the XML specification but does not satisfy the rules of the DTD.

Due to the lack of support of XML namespaces, however, this type of validity checking has lost its significance, and is only occasionally still used.

Document Object Model

DOM The *Document Object Model*, or DOM, which is also standardized by the World Wide Web Consortium, allows you to store an XML document as a logical tree representation. The methods of the iXML library enable you to manipulate these representations in ABAP programs. The advantage of these procedures is that you get very simple access to the individual components of a document. The disadvantage, however, is the relatively high storage requirements, which can take on a truly impressive scale for larger documents (i.e., when using the DOM representation, you should plan for a storage consumption of about 10 times the document's size).[26]

---

26 If you now remember that an XML document generally contains more markup data than actual data, and that the data is often redundant, it will soon become apparent that the design of XML and its scope, as already mentioned earlier, was not particularly influenced by considerations of mass business data processing. Instead, with XML, it is all about brief, well-structured responses to queries.

Example of Parsing with iXML

Instead of covering the components of the iXML library in detail, we'll use the example in Listing 12.7 to show you the parsing of a simple XML document into a DOM representation.

Listing 12.7 Parsing of an XML Document

```abap
REPORT z_ixml_parsing.

CLASS demo DEFINITION.
  PUBLIC SECTION.
    CLASS-METHODS main.
  PRIVATE SECTION.
    CLASS-METHODS:
      process_errors
        IMPORTING parser   TYPE REF TO if_ixml_parser,
      process_dom
        IMPORTING document TYPE REF TO if_ixml_node.
ENDCLASS.

CLASS demo IMPLEMENTATION.
  METHOD main.
    DATA: ixml     TYPE REF TO if_ixml,
          factory  TYPE REF TO if_ixml_stream_factory,
          parser   TYPE REF TO if_ixml_parser,
          istream  TYPE REF TO if_ixml_istream,
          document TYPE REF TO if_ixml_document,
          xmldata  TYPE string.
    CONCATENATE
      '<?xml version="1.0"?>'
      '<order number="4711">'
      '  <head>'
      '    <status>confirmed</status>'
      '    <date format="mm-dd-yyyy">08-15-2006</date>'
      '  </head>'
      '  <body>'
      '    <item units="2" price="17">ABAP Book</item>'
      '    <item units="1" price="10">'
      '                  SAP NetWeaver Book</item>'
      '    <item units="5" price="12">XML Book</item>'
      '  </body>'
      '</order>' INTO xmldata.
    ixml     = cl_ixml=>create( ).
    factory  = ixml->create_stream_factory( ).
    istream  =
      factory->create_istream_string( string = xmldata ).
    document = ixml->create_document( ).
```

```
      parser   = ixml->create_parser( document = document
                                       stream_factory = factory
                                       istream = istream ).
    IF parser->parse( ) <> 0.
      process_errors( parser ).
    ELSE.
      process_dom( document ).
    ENDIF.
  ENDMETHOD.
  METHOD process_errors.
    DATA: error TYPE REF TO if_ixml_parse_error,
          msg   TYPE string,
          count TYPE i,
          index TYPE i.
    count = parser->num_errors( min_severity =
              if_ixml_parse_error=>co_warning ).
    IF count = 0.
      RETURN.
    ENDIF.
    DO count TIMES.
      index  = sy-index - 1.
      error  = parser->get_error(
                  index = index
                  min_severity =
                    if_ixml_parse_error=>co_warning ).
      msg    = error->get_reason( ).
      IF error->get_severity( ) =
           if_ixml_parse_error=>co_warning.
        MESSAGE msg TYPE 'I' DISPLAY LIKE 'W'.
      ELSE.
        MESSAGE msg TYPE 'I' DISPLAY LIKE 'E'.
      ENDIF.
    ENDDO.
  ENDMETHOD.
  METHOD process_dom.
    DATA: iterator TYPE REF TO if_ixml_node_iterator,
          node     TYPE REF TO if_ixml_node,
          nodemap  TYPE REF TO if_ixml_named_node_map,
          attr     TYPE REF TO if_ixml_node,
          name     TYPE string,
          value    TYPE string,
          indent   TYPE i,
          count    TYPE i,
          index    TYPE i,
          output   TYPE c LENGTH 80,
```

```
            name_val TYPE string,
            text     TYPE REF TO zcl_text.
      IF document IS INITIAL.
        RETURN.
      ENDIF.
      text = zcl_text=>get_handle( ).
      text->add_line( 'DOM Tree' ).
      text->add_line( space ).
      iterator  = document->create_iterator( ).
      node = iterator->get_next( ).
      WHILE NOT node IS INITIAL.
        indent = node->get_height( ) * 2.
        indent = indent + 20.
        CASE node->get_type( ).
          WHEN if_ixml_node=>co_node_element.
            name    = node->get_name( ).
            nodemap = node->get_attributes( ).
            WRITE 'ELEMENT   :' TO output.
            WRITE name TO output+indent.
            text->add_line( output ).
            IF NOT nodemap IS INITIAL.
              count = nodemap->get_length( ).
              DO count TIMES.
                index  = sy-index - 1.
                attr   = nodemap->get_item( index ).
                name   = attr->get_name( ).
                value  = attr->get_value( ).
                WRITE 'ATTRIBUTE:' TO output.
                CONCATENATE name ` = ` value INTO name_val.
                WRITE name_val TO output+indent.
                text->add_line( output ).
              ENDDO.
            ENDIF.
          WHEN if_ixml_node=>co_node_text OR
               if_ixml_node=>co_node_cdata_section.
            value  = node->get_value( ).
            WRITE 'TEXT      :' TO output.
            WRITE value TO output+indent.
            text->add_line( output ).
        ENDCASE.
        node = iterator->get_next( ).
      ENDWHILE.
      text->display( ).
    ENDMETHOD.
ENDCLASS.
```

```
START-OF-SELECTION.
  demo=>main( ).
```

In the `main` method, an XML document created there is first converted into an input stream object, and this can then be read into a DOM object using a parser object. After successful parsing, the DOM object is passed to the `process_dom` method, in which the methods of the iXML library are used to merge the nodes of the tree represented by the DOM object into a text for the encapsulation of the textedit control shown in Appendix A.6. The output of the program is displayed in Figure 12.24.

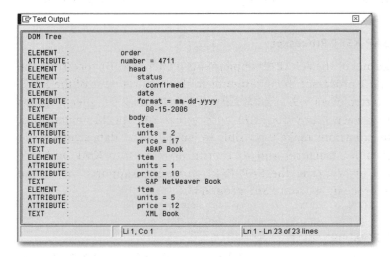

Figure 12.24 Tree Structure of the DOM Object

If you change the program so that the XML document contains errors—for instance, by renaming a closing tag—then the method `process_errors` will be called instead, and the corresponding error message output.

Package SIXML_TEST   Additional example programs that demonstrate the use of more of the iXML library options for the processing of XML can be found in the package SIXML_TEST.

12.5.3 Using XSLT

Transformation of XML documents   XSLT is the abbreviation for *Extensible Stylesheet Language Transformations*. This is a declarative programming language standardized by the World Wide Web Consortium (W3C) for the structural transformation of XML documents. XML documents are treated as logical tree structures. XSLT programs, so-called *XSLT stylesheets*, are themselves coded in a dialect of XML, and allow the definition of transformation rules in so-called *templates*, which are applied to the source tree.

For the navigation and selection of node sets from the source tree, XSLT uses the *XPath* query language. XSLT programs are largely portable and can be developed and used on different platforms. The result of such a transformation does not necessarily have to be an XML document. You can use an XML description to generate HTML, deserialize into ABAP data objects, and generate ABAP programs.

Tree transformation

The SAP XSLT Processor

The kernel of the AS ABAP implements its own XSLT processor—the SAP XSLT processor. It corresponds to the requirements of the XSLT-1.1 (*http://www.w3c.org/TR/xslt*) and XPath-2.0 specifications (*http://www.w3c.org/TR/xpath*) with a few SAP-specific extensions. These extensions make it possible to handle ABAP data structures as logical tree structures and to transform them into XML and vice versa. Furthermore, the SAP XSLT processor supports the call of ABAP procedures from XSLT programs.

XSLT programs

The XSLT programs, which can be executed with the SAP XSLT processor, are just like ABAP programs repository objects of the AS ABAP. They are thus completely integrated into the ABAP Workbench and the change and transport system; all of this brings a series of highly integrated editing possibilities ranging from the creation, editing, and debugging to intersystem transport and delivery.

The XSLT programs of the AS ABAP are not only handled like ABAP programs from the standpoint of administration, but also as far as program generation into byte code and program execution are concerned. The advantages of program generation are the significantly higher execution speeds in comparison to interpreted XSLT processors, as well as better scalability for the repeated execution of programs. The advantages of using a declarative high-level language like XSLT as opposed to the iXML library are:

Byte code

- Higher productivity during development
- Better maintainability of XSLT programs
- Simple adaptability in case of schema changes
- Modularization of transformations using templates
- Reusability of transformations

Since XSLT internally also works on the Document Object Model (DOM), however, it has the same disadvantages from a storage requirement point of view as does direct manipulation of the object tree using the iXML library.

Creating Transformations

As stated earlier, the creation of an XSL transformation is completely integrated into the ABAP Workbench and can, for instance, be performed from the context menu of a package in the Object Navigator using **Create** · **More ...** · **Transformation**. You must then decide between an XSLT program or a Simple Transformation (see Section 12.5.4). Both types of transformation are in the same namespace and appear in the tree display of the Object Navigator at the same level under the node **Transformations**. Of course, the usual Workbench forward navigation, e. g. from an ABAP program, is also possible.

Transformation Editor

The tool in the Workbench for transformations is the Transformation Editor (see Figure 12.31 further below), which can also be called using the transaction code STRANS. In the Transformation Editor, XSLT programs and Simple Transformations can be edited and activated.

Calling Transformations

The ABAP statement to call a transformation is:

CALL TRANSFOR-
MATION

```
CALL TRANSFORMATION trans SOURCE [XML] ...
                          RESULT [XML] ...
```

For `trans`, an XSLT program or a Simple Transformation can be specified. At first, let's just look at XSLT programs.

If the clause XML is specified after both SOURCE and RESULT, an XML document can be transformed into a different XML document using the specified XSL transformation. The XML documents can be specified as strings or as iXML input/output stream objects.

asXML

That takes care of the possibility of XML/XML transformations integrated into AS ABAP, but what about the integration of ABAP data objects? To serialize ABAP data objects or to deserialize into them, then instead of XML a parameter list can be given, similar to that in an ABAP procedure call, which binds the ABAP data objects to XML elements. Since XSLT is a standardized language for the transformation of XML documents, however, during serialization you must ensure that the ABAP data is already in an XML format that is understood by XSLT. This is managed using an implicit intermediate step, which transforms the ABAP data into a canonical XML representation called asXML (*ABAP Serialization XML*). The transformation from ABAP data to XML and back, using XSLT is shown in Figure 12.25.

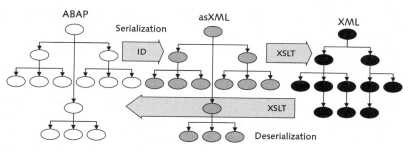

Figure 12.25 Serialization/Deserialization with XSLT

During serialization, the ABAP data is first converted to asXML using a predefined transformation "ID," and this intermediate result is then used as the actual source of the XSL transformation. If the transformation "ID" itself is specified in CALL TRANSFORMATION, the intermediate result is output with no further transformation. During deserialization, the result of the XSL transformation is deserialized directly into the ABAP data.

asXML

You must know the asXML format, because it is the source format for your own XSL transformations of ABAP data. When transforming XML documents into ABAP data, the result of the transformation must be in the asXML format in order to be deserialized by the system into the ABAP data objects.

In the simplest case, you only use the predefined transformation "ID" in CALL TRANSFORMATION, which then allows you to serial-

Transformation "ID"

ize/deserialize arbitrary ABAP data objects[27] to and from asXML. We would like to restrict ourselves only to this case here, as well, and below we will display the asXML format for the different ABAP data types. There is no reason to describe XSLT itself here, since there is sufficient (online) literature on this topic.

Elementary
data objects

The example in Listing 12.8 shows the transformation of an integer number to asXML, and also demonstrates the general structure of an asXML document.

Listing 12.8 asXML for Elementary Data Objects

```
REPORT z_asxml_elementary.

CLASS demo DEFINITION.
  PUBLIC SECTION.
    CLASS-METHODS main.
ENDCLASS.
CLASS demo IMPLEMENTATION.
  METHOD main.
    DATA: num    TYPE i VALUE 111,
          dat    TYPE d VALUE '20060627'
          xmlstr TYPE xstring.
    CALL TRANSFORMATION id
                    SOURCE number = num
                           date   = dat
                    RESULT XML xmlstr.
    CALL FUNCTION 'DISPLAY_XML_STRING'
      EXPORTING xml_string = xmlstr.
  ENDMETHOD.
ENDCLASS.
START-OF-SELECTION.
  demo=>main( ).
```

In the CALL TRANSFORMATION statement, the data objects num and dat are bound to the XML elements number and date. The function module DISPLAY_XML_STRING represents the result of the transformation (see Figure 12.26).

Mapping

The root element of every asXML document is abap in the namespace http://www.sap.com/abapxml. The subelement values of the same namespace contains all elements to which the ABAP data objects in CALL TRANSFORMATION are bound. The text content of these elements

---

27 Particularly reference variables as well, which point to objects or data objects.

is determined by the value of the data objects bound, and a mapping of the elementary ABAP types to XML schema data types is performed.

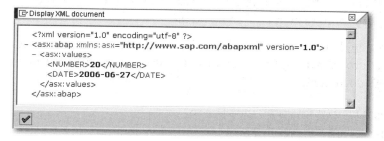

```
 Display XML document                                    ⊠
    <?xml version="1.0" encoding="utf-8" ?>
  – <asx:abap xmlns:asx="http://www.sap.com/abapxml" version="1.0">
    – <asx:values>
        <NUMBER>20</NUMBER>
        <DATE>2006-06-27</DATE>
      </asx:values>
    </asx:abap>
```

Figure 12.26 asXML for Elementary Data Objects

An XML document constructed in this way can also be deserialized back into ABAP data objects with the following statement:

```
CALL TRANSFORMATION id
                SOURCE XML xmlstr
                RESULT number = num
                       date   = dat.
```

Not only can you use XML serialized ABAP data for data exchange with other systems, but you can also store the serialized data persistently, and read it back in later.

The serialization of structures into asXML is very simple, as you **Structures** might have expected, and is shown in the example in Listing 12.9.

Listing 12.9 asXML for Structures

```
REPORT z_asxml_structure.

CLASS demo DEFINITION.
  PUBLIC SECTION.
    CLASS-METHODS main.
ENDCLASS.
CLASS demo IMPLEMENTATION.
  METHOD main.
    DATA: BEGIN OF struct,
            num  TYPE i VALUE 20,
            dat  TYPE d VALUE '20060627',
          END OF struct,
          xmlstr TYPE xstring.
    CALL TRANSFORMATION id
```

```
                              SOURCE structure = struct
                              RESULT XML xmlstr.
        CALL FUNCTION 'DISPLAY_XML_STRING'
           EXPORTING xml_string = xmlstr.
      ENDMETHOD.
    ENDCLASS.

    START-OF-SELECTION.
      demo=>main( ).
```

As Figure 12.27 shows, a structure simply results in a higher-level XML element for its components.

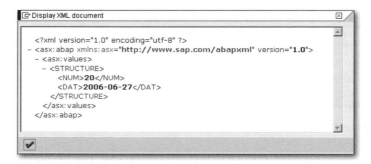

Figure 12.27 asXML for Structures

Internal tables Internal tables, too, are not a major problem for asXML, as shown in the example in Listing 12.10.

Listing 12.10 asXML for Internal Tables

```
REPORT z_asxml_table.

CLASS demo DEFINITION.
  PUBLIC SECTION.
    CLASS-METHODS main.
ENDCLASS.

CLASS demo IMPLEMENTATION.
  METHOD main.
    DATA: itab TYPE TABLE OF i,
          xmlstr TYPE xstring.
    DO 3 TIMES. APPEND sy-index TO itab. ENDDO.
    CALL TRANSFORMATION id
                        SOURCE table = itab
                        RESULT XML xmlstr.
    CALL FUNCTION 'DISPLAY_XML_STRING'
      EXPORTING xml_string = xmlstr.
```

```
  ENDMETHOD.
ENDCLASS.
START-OF-SELECTION.
  demo=>main( ).
```

Every line in an internal table is a subelement item of the table (see Figure 12.28). If the line type is defined in the ABAP Dictionary, instead of item the name from the dictionary is used.

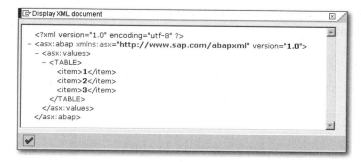

Figure 12.28 asXML for Internal Tables

Finally, asXML also allows the serialization of objects. The prerequisite is only that the class of an object includes the tag interface IF_SERIALIZABLE_OBJECT (see Listing 12.11).

Objects

Listing 12.11 asXML for Objects

```
REPORT z_asxml_object.

CLASS serializable DEFINITION.
  PUBLIC SECTION.
    INTERFACES if_serializable_object.
    DATA attr TYPE string VALUE `Attribute`.
ENDCLASS.

CLASS demo DEFINITION.
  PUBLIC SECTION.
    CLASS-METHODS main.
ENDCLASS.

CLASS demo IMPLEMENTATION.
  METHOD main.
    DATA: oref TYPE REF TO serializable,
          xmlstr TYPE xstring.
    CREATE OBJECT oref.
    CALL TRANSFORMATION id
                    SOURCE object = oref
```

```
                       RESULT XML xmlstr.
      CALL FUNCTION 'DISPLAY_XML_STRING'
         EXPORTING xml_string = xmlstr.
    ENDMETHOD.
  ENDCLASS.

  START-OF-SELECTION.
    demo=>main( ).
```

Figure 12.29 shows that the attributes of an object are serialized as subelements of an element heap. The association between the reference variables in the values element and the object in heap takes place through an XML reference mechanism. By default, all instance attributes of a serializable class are serialized, which can be changed using special auxiliary methods.

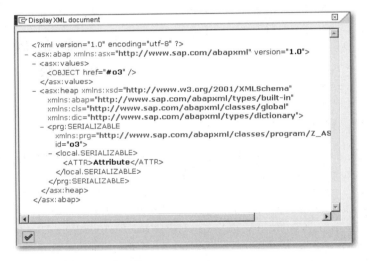

Figure 12.29 asXML for Objects

12.5.4 Use of Simple Transformations

In the last section, we were introduced to XSLT as a very powerful language for general transformations. However, there are a few disadvantages:

Disadvantages of XSLT

▸ If you can't get by with a predefined transformation like ID, you need to learn XSLT to be able to use it.

▸ For simple transformations, XSLT is far too oversized.

▸ There is no static type checking.

▶ XSL transformations are generally asymmetrical. For serialization and deserialization, you need two XSLT programs.

▶ XSLT needs a lot of resources (e. g., for internal construction of the DOM).

That's why SAP also provides Simple Transformations (ST), a separate, easy-to-learn XML-based language for the transformation of ABAP data to XML and back from XML into ABAP. Simple Transformations differ from XSL transformations due to their simpler transformation templates and their consequently less powerful expressiveness.

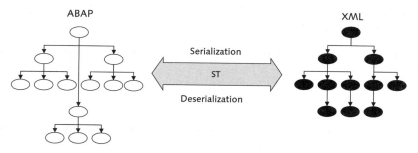

Figure 12.30 Serialization/Deserialization with ST

Figure 12.30 shows the serialization and deserialization with ST. In comparison with XSLT in Figure 12.25, the intermediate step as asXML is eliminated during serialization. The ABAP data objects passed to a Simple Transformation are directly addressable there (i. e., when using ST you need almost no asXML knowledge). Direct access to the ABAP data objects increases both efficiency and the readability of a transformation.

Direct access to ABAP

During deserialization, purely sequential access is made to the XML data stream. This means a certain limitation with respect to XSLT, where navigation within the XML document is arbitrary. On the one hand, this limits the power of the transformations possible; on the other hand, it lays the groundwork for the high-performance processing of large XML documents.

Sequential processing of XML

An important feature of a Simple Transformation is the option for symmetrical transformations, that is, you only need one ST for either serialization or deserialization. The direction of the transformation is determined when the transformation is called. In many cases, two

Symmetry

XSL transformations can be replaced by a simple, much more efficient ST. However, asymmetric transformations can also be written in which an XML document created in a serialization cannot be deserialized back into the same data objects.

The scope of the ST language elements covers about 90 percent of the functionality normally needed by applications. Simple Transformation, among other things, allows for the:

▶ Renaming of structural components

▶ Permutation of structural components

▶ Skipping of subelements

▶ Conditional execution of ST statements

▶ Separate control of serialization and deserialization

Processing of mass data

In comparison with XSLT, ST programs can perform static type checks, and are faster by a factor of about 10. Furthermore, they are more memory-efficient, so that ideally there is no upper limit on the size of data. ST programs are thus particularly well-suited for the processing of mass data, such as occur in communications via the SAP NetWeaver Exchange Infrastructure (XI) or the Enterprise Service-Oriented Architecture (Enterprise SOA)

Contrary to XSLT, however, reference variables and their objects cannot be transformed. So Simple Transformations are not well-suited for the preparation of a persistent storage form for object groups, and that is also not the purpose for using them. The fact that ST provides fewer expression options than XSLT is due to compromises made intentionally, in order to optimize the efficiency of the main purpose of the language, namely data exchange.[28]

ST Programs on the AS ABAP

To create and execute Simple Transformations on AS ABAP, the same procedures apply as for XSLT programs (see Section 12.5.3). They are repository objects; they are created and activated in the Transformation Editor; and they are called using CALL TRANSFORMATION.[29]

---

28 The passing of reference variables and their objects to non-SAP systems is generally not meaningful, since the underlying programming model is generally a different one.

29 As of the next SAP NetWeaver release, there will also be an ST Debugger available.

Elements of a Simple Transformation

Simple Transformations, like XSLT programs, are themselves encoded in XML. A Simple Transformation contains ST statements and literal elements (XML elements, attributes, and text). The literal elements are the structure for the XML document into which the ABAP data is serialized or which is to be deserialized into ABAP. To distinguish the ST statements from other components, they are all in the namespace `http://www.sap.com/transformation-template`. As a convention, we will use the namespace prefix `tt`.

ST statements

Figure 12.31 shows a minimal Simple Transformation in the Transformation Editor of the ABAP Workbench. If you select the Tag Browser of the Object Navigator when editing a Simple Transformation, you can also very conveniently drag the ST statements into the ST program.[30]

Tag browser

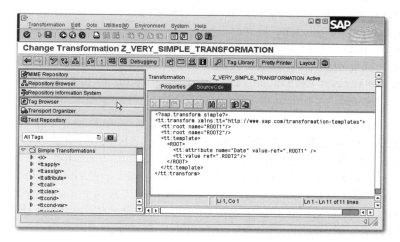

Figure 12.31 Simple Transformation in the Transformation Editor

Before we go into more detail about the structure of an ST program in the next section, look at Listing 12.12 to see a call to this Simple Transformation.

Listing 12.12 Calling a Simple Transformation

```
REPORT z_call_very_simple_trans.

CLASS demo DEFINITION.
  PUBLIC SECTION.
```

CALL TRANSFOR-MATION

---

30 The Tag Browser also works for XSLT, HTML, BSP, etc.

```
      CLASS-METHODS main.
ENDCLASS.
CLASS demo IMPLEMENTATION.
  METHOD main.
    DATA: str    TYPE string VALUE `Hello XML!`,
          dat    TYPE d,
          xmlstr TYPE xstring.
    dat = sy-datum.
    CALL TRANSFORMATION z_very_simple_transformation
        SOURCE root1 = dat
               root2 = str
        RESULT XML xmlstr.
    CALL FUNCTION 'DISPLAY_XML_STRING'
        EXPORTING xml_string = xmlstr.
  ENDMETHOD.
ENDCLASS.
START-OF-SELECTION.
  demo=>main( ).
```

Data root   In Listing 12.12, you will note that there is no significant difference from the XSLT calls in the previous section. This time, however, no asXML is generated; instead, the variables str and dat are bound to so-called *data roots* root1 and root2 of a Simple Transformation. Figure 12.32 shows the result of the program.

Figure 12.32 Result of a Simple Transformation

In direct comparison with Figure 12.31, you can see that the only literal element of the Simple Transformation, ROOT, is kept, and how its attribute and its text content are created by ST statements from the data roots resp. the bound ABAP data objects.

The transformation shown is symmetrical. That is, the following statement reads the data that was just serialized back into data objects of the same type:

```
CALL TRANSFORMATION z_very_simple_transformation
     SOURCE XML xmlstr
     RESULT root1 = dat
            root2 = str.
```

Structure of an ST Program

The principal structure of an ST program is as follows, although the order of the elements within <tt:transform> can vary:

```
<?sap.transform simple?>
<tt:transform [template="tmpl"]
   xmlns:tt="http://www.sap.com/transformation-templates">
  [<tt:type ... />]
  [<tt:root ... />]
  [<tt:parameter ... />]
  [<tt:variable ... />]
  [<tt:include ... />]
  <tt:template [name="tmpl1"]>
    ...
  </tt:template>
  [<tt:template [name="tmpl2"]>
    ...
   </tt:template>]
  ...
</tt:transform>
```

The root element <tt:transform> binds the prefix tt to the namespace for ST statements, and can use the optional attribute template to determine the main template of the transformation. If no main template is given, the unnamed template is by default the main template. Only one unnamed template can exist.

tt:transform

The statement <tt:root name="..." ... > declares data roots. Data roots, which are declared outside a template are the interface of a Simple Transformation to the outside. ABAP data objects are bound to these data roots during the call to CALL TRANSFORMATION, and they can then be accessed within the main template. The statement <tt:root ... />, however, is also possible within subtemplates, and then defines their interface to the calling template.

tt:root

Besides the data roots, the templates defined with <tt:template [name="..."] ... > are the alpha and omega of Simple Transformations. There is exactly one main template and any number of

tt:template

optional subtemplates, all of which must have unique names. The main template is the pattern for the XML document into which the ABAP data will be serialized, or from which data is to be deserialized. The main template can use the `<tt:apply name="..." ... >` statement to call subtemplates, and to pass parameters. In subtemplates, the `<tt:context>` can be used to declare local data roots, parameters, and variables. In the main template, the data roots, parameters, and variables of the ST program implicitly form the context of the template.

tt:type,
tt:parameter,
tt:variable

Using `<tt:type name="..." ... >`, data types can be declared for the typing of data roots. All ABAP data types and global types from the ABAP Dictionary are supported. The statement `<tt:parameter name="..." ... >` allows the creation of additional parameters for the transformation, which are not bound to ABAP data objects. Similarly, `<tt:variable name="..." ... >` does the same thing for normal variables and not for parameters to be passed. In subtemplates, local parameters and variables are possible.

tt:include

Finally, the statement `<tt:include name="..." ... >` allows the integration of type definitions and templates from other ST programs into a Simple Transformation.

Addressing of ABAP Data Objects

The addressing of ABAP data objects takes place via the data roots of an ST program. To do this, the data objects are bound at the time of the execution of CALL TRANSFORMATION to the data roots provided on the left side of the equals sign (=). The ABAP data objects supported by ST programs are elementary data objects, structures, and internal tables.

Data nodes

All data is considered to be nodes of tree structures, which proceed from the data roots. Addressing is done either by accessing the data roots, or by accessing the so-called *current node*, which can be defined at any point in an ST program. The data roots or the current node can then be used to access subnodes.

tt:ref

The current node can be set with the statement `<tt:ref name="node">` or using an attribute in a statement `<tt:... ref="node">`. In all statements in which data is accessed, the explicit addressing of data can be omitted, and then the current node is used implicitly. This must then be set. The current node can also be given explicitly using `$ref`.

All data roots `root` that are connected to an ABAP data object can be addressed at any time using a prefixed dot (`.root`). For structures, the addressing of components is simply through `.root.comp`. In the defined current node, a component is accessed using `$ref.comp`, or simply with `comp` (i. e., for a defined current node, a node specification `node` always implicitly means `$ref.node`).

The typical statement to access the value of an elementary data node, that is, to serialize or deserialize it, is `<tt:value ref="...">` or the corresponding attribute of an statement `<tt:... value-ref="...">`. You've already seen an example of this in the Simple Transformation of Figure 12.31. In Listing 12.13, let's look at the transformation Z_SIMPLE_STRUCTURE for a structure.

tt:value

Listing 12.13 Simple Transformation for a Structure

```
<?sap.transform simple?>
<tt:transform
    xmlns:tt="http://www.sap.com/transformation-templates">
  <tt:root name="structure"/>
  <tt:template>
    <STRUCTURE>
      <tt:ref name=".structure">
        <NUM>
          <tt:value ref="num"/>
        </NUM>
        <DAT>
          <tt:value ref="dat"/>
        </DAT>
      </tt:ref>
    </STRUCTURE>
  </tt:template>
</tt:transform>
```

Here, the `<STRUCTURE>` element creates a context using `<tt:ref ...>` in which the current node is set to the data root `structure`. Thus the components of the structure in `<tt:value ...>` can be given directly as `"num"` and `"dat"`. Alternatively, the full spelling `".structure.num"` and `".structure.dat"` could also be specified. If a template references a component of a structure that is not present, the transformation is aborted with the exception CX_ST_REF_ACCESS.

If you copy the program Z_ASXML_STRUCTURE from Listing 12.9 into Z_ST_STRUCTURE, and simply replace the name of the called transformation "ID" with Z_SIMPLE_STRUCTURE, the structure is serialized as shown in Figure 12.33. So we have written a Simple Transformation that generates the data structure of the asXML shown in Figure 12.27.

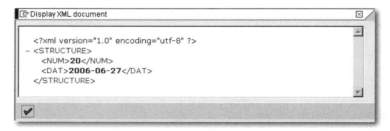

Figure 12.33 Transformed Structure

Now let's turn our attention to internal tables. We want to write another Simple Transformation that generates the same result as the example for the XSL transformation "ID" (see Figure 12.28). Listing 12.14 shows this Simple Transformation Z_ST_TABLE.

tt:loop   **Listing 12.14** Simple Transformation for an Internal Table

```
<?sap.transform simple?>
<tt:transform
    xmlns:tt="http://www.sap.com/transformation-templates">
  <tt:root name="table"/>
  <tt:template>
    <TABLE>
      <tt:loop ref=".table">
        <ITEM>
          <tt:value />
        </ITEM>
      </tt:loop>
    </TABLE>
  </tt:template>
</tt:transform>
```

An internal table is serialized or deserialized in a loop using the <tt:loop ...> statement. Within the loop, the current node is set to the current row of the internal table. For this reason, we can use the implicit form of <tt:value ...> to access the row contents.

Copy the program Z_ASXML_TABLE from Listing 12.10 into Z_ST_
TABLE again, and simply replace the name of the called transformation "ID" by Z_SIMPLE_TABLE. Figure 12.34 shows the expected result.

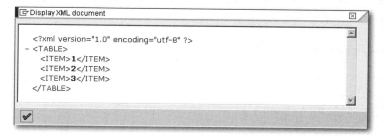

Figure 12.34 Transformed Internal Table

Symmetry of Serialization and Deserialization

All the Simple Transformations presented so far are symmetrical. That is, when serialization and deserialization (or the reverse!) are carried out one after the other, the result is the same as the starting values. This is not automatically the case, however, but rather because we programmed it that way.

For example, the symmetrical Simple Transformation in Listing 12.14 can be turned into an asymmetrical transformation very easily by removing the lines <ITEM> and </ITEM> (see transformation Z_SIMPLE_TABLE_ASYMMETRIC in the package Z_ABAP_BOOK). The call to this transformation in the program Z_ST_TABLE_ASYMMETRIC gives the result shown in Figure 12.35.

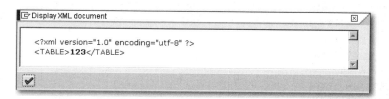

Figure 12.35 Asymmetrically Transformed Internal Table

The content of all table rows is written into the same element. In a reverse transformation in the case shown, only the first row of the internal table will be filled in again. It is clear that in such cases exceptions can also arise fairly easily, if the format of the document to be deserialized no longer fits the ABAP data objects.

If a symmetrical transformation is desired, therefore, you must always be careful when creating the transformation to store the contents of different data objects into different XML elements.

ST Flow Control

Simple Transformations offer some possibilities to set conditions on the content or state of data nodes, and thus to control the data flow within a template. Examples of corresponding ST statements are `<tt:cond .../>` and `<tt:switch .../>`.

Pattern When working with these commands, the concept of the *pattern* is crucial. When deserializing, the data stream is consumed as a sequence of tokens. The current token decides how the processing will proceed. A pattern is a sequence of tokens whose global structure is already determined by the first token. Patterns consist of template contents like single elements, attributes, literal text, and sometimes the empty element (`<tt:empty/>`). The following example should clarify this relationship using the statement `<tt:cond .../>`:

tt:cond `<tt:cond data="bool='X'"> <X>true</X> </tt:cond>`

During the serialization, depending on the value of the field `bool`, the non-empty element `<X>true</X>` is written into the document. During deserialization, depending on the pattern `<X>true</X>`, the variable `bool` is initialized with the value `'X'`. The element `<X>` in combination with the text `true` is a pattern, which is compared during deserialization. The ST command `<tt:cond .../>` can be used to formulate very complex conditions. For instance, in addition to conditions, preconditions and assertions can also be specified. Moreover, there are directional variants for serialization (`<tt:s-cond .../>`) or deserialization (`<tt:d-cond .../>`).

tt:switch Case decisions can be implemented using the ST command `<tt:switch>`. Here, the cases are considered in order. Listing 12.15 shows the transformation Z_SIMPLE_SWITCH as an example.

Listing 12.15 Simple Transformation with Case Decision

```
<?sap.transform simple?>
<tt:transform
    xmlns:tt="http://www.sap.com/transformation-templates">
  <tt:root name="size"/>
  <tt:template>
    <SHIRT>
      <tt:attribute name="SIZE">
        <tt:switch>
          <tt:cond data="size=1"> small  </tt:cond>
          <tt:cond data="size=2"> medium </tt:cond>
          <tt:cond data="size=3"> large  </tt:cond>
        </tt:switch>
      </tt:attribute>
    </SHIRT>
  </tt:template>
</tt:transform>
```

During serialization in this example, the data node `size` is used to make a case decision, and the element `<SHIRT>` and the attribute `size` with the value `"small"`, `"medium"`, or `"large"` is written to the XML document. The program Z_ST_SWITCH of the package Z_ABAP_BOOK calls the transformation once for every possible value of `size` and displays one of the following three lines depending on the size:

```
<SHIRT size="small" />
```

```
<SHIRT size="medium" />
```

```
<SHIRT size="large" />
```

The transformation is symmetrical. During a deserialization, the data node is restored based on the `size` attribute.

12.5.5 Summary

In the context of this book, we don't want to go into transformations between ABAP and XML any more than we did in the last few sections of this chapter. Now you know the relevant tools—iXML library, XSLT, and Simple Transformations—and their significant features. In conclusion, we would like to state one more time why it is important to pay attention to this kind of transformation.

The ABAP data model's primary purpose is for the data processing of relational data. The XML data model is used for data transmission and integration. The transformations shown here act as a bridge between these two worlds, and their areas of application are correspondingly different:

- XML-based middleware
  - Exchange Infrastructure (XI)
  - Enterprise Services Infrastructure (ESI)
- XML-based persistence
  - Import/export of XML
  - SAP Archiving
- Application-specific
  - Structured documents
  - Program generation

"Oh, does one examine what one wishes oneself?"
—Voltaire, The Princess of Babylon

13 Testing and Analysis Tools

Regardless of how good developers are, they will never be able to create software that is free of errors. Errors can occur in all phases of the development process. At worst, they can even appear in production systems. Using efficient tools to analyze ABAP applications is indispensable, particularly in large and complex applications created by several developers.

For that reason, in this chapter we have provided with an overview of the most important testing and analysis tools. In doing so, we turn our attention mainly to the latest tools like ABAP Unit and ABAP Debugger.

In this chapter, we will have a look on the following tools:

Tools described here

- **Syntax Check**
  A syntax check determines the correctness of a program's syntax.

- **Extended Syntax Check**
  An extended program check performs static checks that are too time consuming for a nomal syntax check.

- **Code Inspector**
  The Code Inspector checks repository objects in terms of performance, security, syntax, and adherence to naming conventions.

- **ABAP Debugger**
  The ABAP Debugger is a programming tool that executes ABAP programs by line or by section. You can use the ABAP Debugger to display the contents of data objects and to check the flow logic of programs.

- **ABAP Unit**
  The ABAP Unit is the module-testing tool for ABAP programs. It supports module tests of individual development objects and mass tests.

▶ **Memory Inspector**
The Memory Inspector is a tool to display and analyze memory snapshots.

▶ **ABAP Runtime Analysis**
The ABAP Runtime Analysis measures and analyzes the performance of programs, transactions, function modules, and methods.

▶ **Coverage Analyzer**
The Coverage Analyzer records the number of calls for processing blocks and executable programs, separated by periods of times, users, and subject areas.

▶ **eCATT**
The Extended Computer-Aided Test Tool (eCATT) is used to create and execute functional software tests. It is primarily used for automatic testing of SAP business processes.

Each tool has its own purpose; its importance can vary in different phases of the software lifecycle. It is important to know how the tools interact and when to use the appropriate tool at the appropriate time. Figure 13.1 shows how the tools are used in particular phases of the software lifecycle.

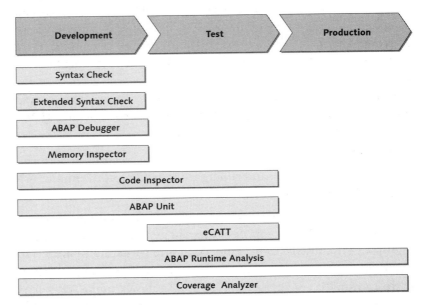

Figure 13.1 Testing and Analysis Tools in the Software Lifecycle

Many of the tools are linked to each other. For example, ABAP Unit is seamlessly integrated with the Code Inspector. Similarly, you can use the functions of the Memory Inspector in the ABAP Debugger. When we discuss the individual tools, we primarily introduce them as independent tools, although we do indicate possible integration options.

Integration of tools

13.1 Static Testing Procedures

Static testing procedures are a type of testing that refers only to known static program characteristics, that is, those characteristics that are related to a program's source code. Therefore, with static testing procedures, no check occurs at program runtime.

Source code

For that reason, static testing procedures are considered to be the simplest method for checking programs; however, you cannot detect all the errors in a program using this method. Static tests primarily check the syntax of the source code. They cannot determine whether a syntactically correct program does what it is intended to do.

The use of dynamic programming techniques is another limitation for the static testing procedure. As you learned in Chapter 11, certain data types or object types become known only at runtime with dynamic programming. For example, tokens are assembled from character strings that result only in a valid statement during the execution of a program. In this case, you can't get very far by using purely static checks, which is why static testing procedures should only be regarded as an initial, self-evident test of a program. Therefore, the following sections address the various options of static tests only briefly.

13.1.1 Syntax Check

As the name implies, syntax checks verify whether a program is syntactically correct. While editing a program, you can call syntax checking via the following menu path: **Program • Check • Syntax**. The check produces a message stating that the syntax of the program is correct or that it contains errors, or it issues a warning. The syntax check refers to the content of the program currently being edited. It also checks the top include, if one is present. Other includes are usually not considered (see Section 3.3.1).

Syntax error A syntax error is a violation of the syntax rules of ABAP. A program that contains syntax errors cannot be executed. Therefore, you must correct it. The check can respond to errors with a suggested correction, if a keyword was written incorrectly, for example.[1]

Syntax warnings If warnings occur, the program is executable, but foreseeable exceptions can appear at runtime. Warnings have a priority of 1–3.

▶ Priority 1 warnings lead to a termination of the program. This category also contains constructs that should not be used because they lead to program errors and semantically incorrect behavior.

▶ Priority 2 warnings refer to constructs that don't necessarily lead to errors, but that might be obsolete and that can be replaced with current constructs. Errors of priority level 2 can lead to errors of priority level 1 or syntax errors in future releases.

▶ We also recommend the correction of priority 3 warnings if at all possible. Their priority level can be increased in future releases.

As a general rule, an ABAP program should not produce any warnings, regardless of their priority.

13.1.2 Extended Program Check

SLIN You can call an extended, static program check using Transaction SLIN or via the following menu path: **Program • Check • Extended Program Check**.

There, you can explicitly switch static tests on and off. The results of an extended program check are divided into three classes: errors, warnings, and messages. Let's look at the example in Listing 13.1.

Listing 13.1 Demo Program for an Extended Program Check

```
REPORT z_slin.

CLASS demo DEFINITION.
  PUBLIC SECTION.
    CLASS-METHODS main.
ENDCLASS.

CLASS demo IMPLEMENTATION.
  METHOD main.
```

---

1 With syntax highlighting and the automatic completion mechanism of the new ABAP Editor, these kinds of incorrect terms should hardly appear at all.

```
    TRY.
        CALL FUNCTION 'STRING_SPLIT'
            EXPORTING
                delimiter = '-'
                text      = 'SLIN-Demo'.
        CATCH cx_sy_dyn_call_error INTO error.
            MESSAGE error TYPE 'I'.
    ENDTRY.
  ENDMETHOD.
ENDCLASS.

START-OF-SELECTION.
  demo=>main( ).
```

When you execute an extended program check for program Z_SLIN, the screen shown in Figure 13.2 displays. You can switch various checks on and off in this screen. The figure shows that the **Character Strings** check has been turned on: the default setting is off. You can call the documentation for each check with the [F1] help.

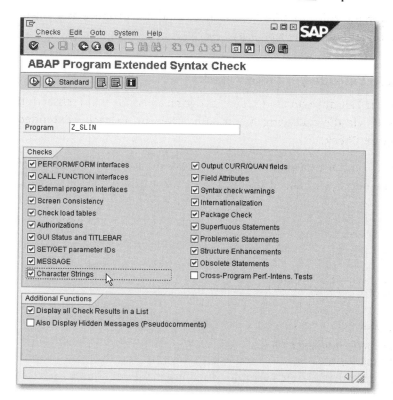

Figure 13.2 Getting Started with an Extended Programming Check

List output   When you activate the first additional function and start an extended programming check, the list shown in Figure 13.3 is generated along with all messages. In this case, it shows that the parameter interface of the function module was handled incorrectly.[2] Although the program is syntactically correct, it will raise an exception when it is executed. Moreover, it is recognized that the function module may no longer be used. Finally, SLIN determines that a literal is used without being linked to a text symbol. You can select a message to navigate directly to the related part of the source code and correct it.

Figure 13.3 Results of an Extended Program Check

The extended program check is an important tool. It ensures that you write a syntactically correct program whose source code is optimized for future compatibility. We strongly recommend that you use this tool. Note that for larger projects or larger sets of source code, an

---

2 To handle a static method call, a syntax check should suffice.

extended program check takes much longer than a normal syntax check, which is why the checks are distinct from each other. At some point before the release of a program, you should ensure that an extended program check of the program does not produce any messages.

You can hide any messages produced by an extended program check if they don't apply in special cases.[3] To hide all the messages produced by an extended program check in a section of a program, use the following statement:

Hiding messages

```
SET EXTENDED CHECK OFF.
...
SET EXTENDED CHECK ON.
```

SET EXTENDED CHECK

If you want to hide only individual statements, you can use *pseudo comments*. A pseudo comment is essentially nothing more than a special line-end comment that begins with #EC. The comment excludes the content of the line in question from testing by the extended program check. For example, if you use "#EC *, the current line is excluded from all tests.

Special pseudo comments are available for messages that must often be turned off. For example, if you enter "#EC NOTEXT, no message appears when the current line contains a literal without an assigned text symbol. This approach is helpful whenever technical context that doesn't appear in the user interface is involved. A typical example would be the following:

#EC

```
APPEND '<html>' TO html. "#EC NOTEXT
```

You can use the F1 help in Transaction SLIN to display a list of all possible pseudo comments.

13.1.3 Code Inspector

The Code Inspector is a tool to check repository objects in terms of performance, security, syntax, and adherence to naming conventions. You can call it using Transaction SCI or from within various applications of the ABAP Workbench via the following menu path: **Program • Check • Code Inspector**.

---

3 Messages that result from a normal syntax check cannot be hidden.

SCI When you call the Code Inspector from the ABAP Workbench, the standard check variant checks only the individual object being currently processed. When you call the Code Inspector using the transaction code, you can define the quantity of repository objects to be checked and the scope of the check in your own check variant. To provide an overview of the tool, we will focus on the second variation here. Listing 13.2 contains the sample program that will be checked.

Listing 13.2 Test Program for the Code Inspector

```
REPORT z_code_inspector.

CLASS demo DEFINITION.
  PUBLIC SECTION.
    CLASS-METHODS main.
ENDCLASS.
CLASS demo IMPLEMENTATION.
  METHOD main.
    DATA scarr_tab TYPE TABLE OF scarr.
    DO 10 TIMES.
      SELECT *
              FROM scarr
              INTO TABLE scarr_tab.
    ENDDO.
  ENDMETHOD.
ENDCLASS.
START-OF-SELECTION.
  demo=>main( ).
```

When you call the Code Inspector via Transaction SCI, the initial screen illustrated in Figure 13.4 appears.

The figure shows that the Code Inspector uses the **Inspection**, **Object Set**, and **Check Variant** elements. You use the icon to the left of the entry fields to change the visibility of elements for one user (local) or for all users (global). The icon used here indicates local visibility.

Check Variant

Individual checks A check variant consists of one or more individual checks. After the inspection starts, the individual checks examine the elements of the object set for errors, warnings, and information. The individual checks are assigned to various categories, such as performance, security, and syntax.

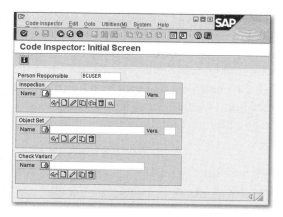

Figure 13.4 Initial Screen of the Code Inspector

You can use an existing check variant[4] or create a new one. When you create a new variant, you can use a tree of check variants to define the exact checks to execute in the context of the variant. Figure 13.5 shows variant MY_CHECK_VARIANT, which we created for this example. We have activated single checks here. Use the **i** button to obtain more information on each single check.

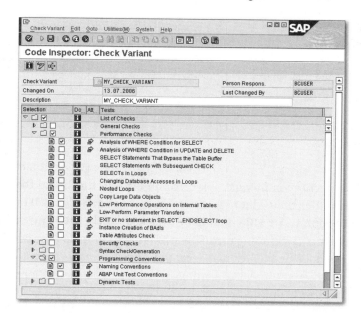

Figure 13.5 Check Variant in the Code Inspector

4   The global check variant **DEFAULT**, for example.

Checking with
parameters A small arrow appears with some individual checks. The arrow
means that you must enter some additional parameters in order to
execute the check. For example, if you select the arrow next to the
Naming Conventions check, you can define the prefix or suffix
required for the name of a specific object. By default, local classes
must begin with the prefix "lcl_".

Object Set

You can use the object set to define the repository objects to be considered by the check. Here, too, you can select an existing object set
or define and store your own object set. Figure 13.6 shows that we
have entered the sample program from Listing 13.2 as the object set.

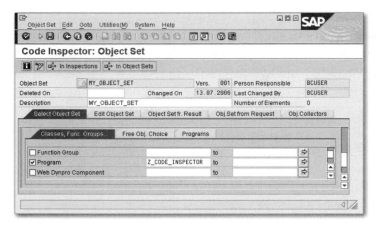

Figure 13.6 Object Set in the Code Inspector

Inspection

During an inspection, individual objects or object sets are checked to
determine whether they adhere to the rules defined in a check variant. An inspection run results in a list of the individual checks that
have been executed, including errors, warnings, and information. As
an ABAP developer or quality manager, you can use inspections to
determine whether static ABAP coding or other object definitions
follow the previously defined rules.

For our example, we create an inspection named MY_INSPECTION
and assign the previously defined check variant and object set to it
(see Figure 13.7).

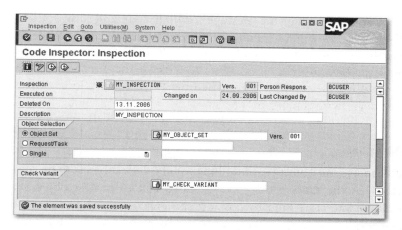

Figure 13.7 Inspection in the Code Inspector

You can now execute the inspection. The result is displayed in a tree that contains all checks and the messages associated with these checks (see Figure 13.8).

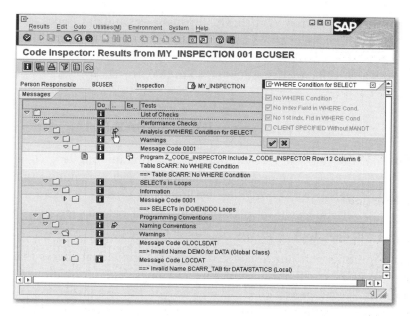

Figure 13.8 Results of the Code Inspector Check

When you select the arrow next to a message, a dialog window displays additional information on the reason for the error message. If you select the **i** icon, you receive detailed documentation on the pos-

Detailed documentation

sible consequences of the message for your code and how you can improve it. We will not examine individual results any further here, because, for our simple example, the Code Inspector messages are self-explanatory.

Quality management Even this brief overview should clarify the potential of this tool. Particularly for large development projects, the Code Inspector enables a quality manager to easily define check variants for static tests that each developer must then use for checking. As a special service, options are available that distribute comprehensive and expensive tests across several servers or that can schedule the tests as a background job.

Open Framework

Finally, we want to emphasize that the Code Inspector is an open framework. Besides receiving a set of tests that are predefined by SAP, which you can execute for your own developments, you can parameterize the checks delivered by SAP as patterns, or develop your own checks from scratch. Quality managers and developers can therefore implement project-specific checks on their own and then use a standard tool of the development environment to make the checks accessible to all those involved in the project.

13.2 Program Analysis with the ABAP Debugger

Like most development environments for programming languages, ABAP has its own debugger. The debugger is a programming tool that can execute ABAP programs by line or by section. You can use the ABAP Debugger to display the contents of data objects and to check the logic flow of programs. The debugger enables you to stop a program at any given point in time and examine the system status at that point in detail. In many cases, only a debugger and a structured approach to searching for errors can uncover semantic errors in a program.

13.2.1 The New ABAP Debugger with Two-Process Architecture

Two types of ABAP debugging are currently available: debugging with the classical debugger for releases earlier than 6.40 and debugging with the new debugger, available as of Release 6.40. The main differences between the classical debugger and the new ABAP Debugger are the following:

Classical and new debugging

▶ The classical ABAP Debugger runs in the same internal session as the application to be analyzed (debuggee). That's why it is displayed in the same window as the application; however, this technology has some restrictions. For example, technical reasons prohibit you from analyzing some ABAP programs (such as conversion exists) in debug mode. Another restriction is that you cannot use any ABAP technology to design the debugger interface, which blocks the path for designing a modern user interface.

▶ However, the new ABAP Debugger is executed in its own external session (debugger); the application to be analyzed (debuggee) occupies a second external session (Figure 13.9). This technology enables you to design the user interface of the debugger with ABAP as you like. The separation of debugger and debuggee into two distinct sessions or processes is referred to as a two-process architecture.

Debugger and debuggee

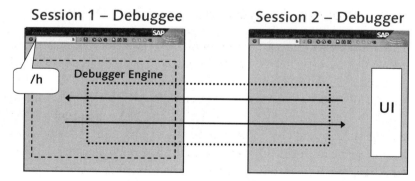

Figure 13.9 Two-Process Architecture of the ABAP Debugger

As of Release 6.40, you can choose the type of debugging. Select **Utilities • Settings** in the ABAP Editor to choose the classical debugger or the new ABAP Debugger. You can also switch between the two technologies at any time during a debugger session.

Because this book deals exclusively with the new ABAP Debugger, we always refer to it as the ABAP Debugger or debugger for the sake of simplicity.

13.2.2 User Interface of the ABAP Debugger

Desktops

The debugger provides users with a flexible and freely configurable user interface with up to 10 desktops. Depending on a user's selection, up to four tools can be placed and arranged, such as the tools to display source code or structures. Users therefore can design the UI of the debugger to meet their own needs.

Structure of the Debugger UI

Figure 13.10 shows the five main components of the user interface of the ABAP Debugger.

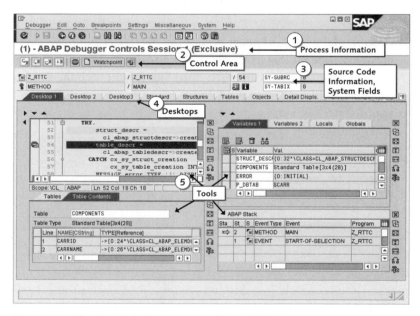

Figure 13.10 The Five Main Components of the ABAP Debugger

1. **Process Information**

   The title area of the window displays information on the debugger or the debuggee. Because several applications can be debugged in parallel, the session number of the debuggee to which the debugger is linked is displayed in parentheses. Depending on which application is being debugged, you can also see here if RFC or HTTP debugging, and so on, is being executed. Information is also displayed on whether or not the application being debugged exclusively occupies a work process of the application server.

2. **Control Area**

   You can select the main functions to control the program flow in this area. For example, here you can determine whether the next program line is executed or whether the program is executed up to the next breakpoint. You can also manage breakpoints, watch points, and the current layout of the debugger user interface here.

3. **Source Code Information and System Fields**

   The current dynpro number, the program name (including line number), and the current processing block are displayed under the control area. The neighboring column lists the current return values of system fields `sy-subrc` and `sy-tabix`. You can display other data objects here, instead of the system fields.

4. **Desktops**

   Desktops take up the largest part of the debugger window. These are the workareas that users can design to meet their needs. A total of 10 desktops are available; you can display them with the respective tabs.

5. **Tools**

   The individual desktops contain various tools, such as those for displaying source code or providing an overview of variables. The debugger provides predefined desktops that cover many typical debugging situations.

Customizing the User Interface for Individual Requirements

Users can modify all 10 desktops individually in terms of the proportions of the tools and their combinations. Up to four tools can be displayed simultaneously in a desktop. Figure 13.11 shows the various configuration options available for the tool windows.

1. You can use the **Close Tool** function to remove tools from a desktop: the last tool is always displayed in full size.

   Configuration options

2. The **New Tool** function enables the insertion of any tool. A tool can also appear multiple times on a desktop.

3. You can use the **Replace Tool** function to replace a previously placed tool with another tool in the same position.

4. The **Full Screen** function enlarges the tool to fill the available space of the desktop.

5. With the **Maximize Horizontally** and **Vertically** functions, you can change the size and position of a tool. You can also use the **Enlarge Size** and **Reduce Size** buttons on the left-hand side of the tool to enlarge or reduce the size step by step.

6. You can use the **Exchange** function to exchange tools horizontally or vertically.

7. You can use the **Services of the Tool** function to configure a tool. Various configuration options are available for each tool.

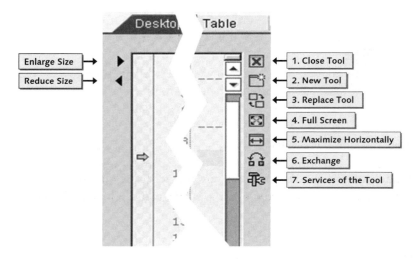

Figure 13.11 Configuration Options of a Tool Window

You can use the **Back** function to undo any modification you have made—those related to setting up a desktop and those related to changing the size of subareas. There is no limit to the number of undo steps.

Debugger variant   You can use the **Save Layout** function to save the configuration of the first three user-specific desktops permanently in a *debugger variant*. The variant named START_UP is used when you start the debugger to define the current layout. Use the menu path **Debugger • Debugger Session • Load** to load variants saved under a different name.

Debugger Tools

When you select a new tool, a selection dialog displays with all the tools provided by the ABAP Debugger. Figure 13.12 shows the selection window for tools of the ABAP Debugger, which is divided into three areas.

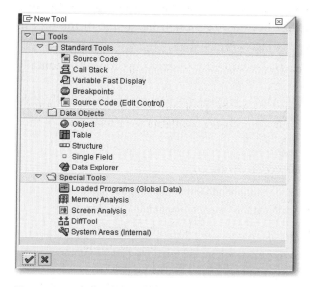

Figure 13.12 Tools of the ABAP Debugger

In addition to the standard tools available to display the source code or to monitor variables, you also have special tools, to analyze memory, for example.[5]

13.2.3   Using the Debugger

Starting and Ending a Debugging Session

You have various options to start the debugger for a program, depending on whether it is an executable program, the call of a method, or a background job:

Start

▶ To start the debugger from a tool of the ABAP Workbench, you can generally use a menu path or a button from the toolbar of the development tool.

---

5 As of the next SAP NetWeaver release, debugger scripting, Web Dynpro debugging, and ST debugging will also be available.

▶ In many cases, you can switch on debugging by entering "/h" in the command field of the standard toolbar in the GUI status of a classical dynpro.

▶ To start the debugger for a background job or for a program that is already running, use Transaction SM50 (process overview) to switch on debugging for the required process using the following menu path: **Program/Mode • Program • Debugging**.

End You have the following options to end a debugging session:

▶ When the debugger is ready for input and the application is also waiting for an entry, you can end the debugger using menu path **Debugger • Exit Debugger**. That closes the debugger, but the application (that was the debuggee) continues to run. You can achieve the same effect by entering and confirming "/hx" in the command field of the standard toolbar.

▶ To close both the debugger and the debuggee, use menu path **Debugger • Exit Application and Debugger** in the debugger.

Note that the debugger is always the controlling unit during a debugging session, not the debuggee. You cannot use the UI of the debuggee to close the debugger.

Breakpoints

A breakpoint is a point in an ABAP program that directs you to the ABAP Debugger at the moment it is reached during program flow. You can set breakpoints with a limited lifespan and breakpoints that are valid only for the current user interactively in the ABAP Editor or the ABAP Debugger. Note the following types of breakpoints:

▶ **Debugger Breakpoints**
Debugger breakpoints are set with a click at the beginning of the line, at which point the program should pause, or are set with the **Create Breakpoint** function in the toolbar. A debugger breakpoint is live only when the debugger is active. If you close the debugger, all the breakpoints that have been set are lost. A stop symbol at the start of the appropriate line of source code indicates a debugger breakpoint.

▶ **Session Breakpoints**
Session breakpoints are generally set in the ABAP Editor. Session

breakpoints are always related to the current logon. That means that the breakpoints are effective in all the main sessions of this logon. Session breakpoints are indicated by a stop symbol overlaid with a screen symbol.

▶ **User Breakpoints**
When you set a breakpoint inside the code of a Web Dynpro or a BSP application, you set a user breakpoint. User breakpoints are stored in the database and are valid for all sessions of this user on the current application server. User breakpoints are indicated by a stop symbol overlaid with a user symbol.

▶ **Checkpoints**
You can use the

`BREAK-POINT ID` group.   BREAK-POINT

statement to define a breakpoint as a *checkpoint* of an ABAP program. The `ID` addition assigns the breakpoint to a *checkpoint group,* `group,` that controls the activation of the breakpoint from outside the program via Transaction SAAB.[6] Without the `ID` addition, the breakpoint is always active, which is why this variant must not be used in production programs and why an extended program check would flag it as an error.

You can set breakpoints in the debugger with a click at the start of a line and with the **Create Breakpoint** function at a specific location (see Figure 13.3). You can set more than one breakpoint at one time.

You can modify, delete, activate, or deactivate existing breakpoints using the breakpoint tool of the debugger.

Watchpoints

A watchpoint forces a program to stop when the value of a specific variable changes, unlike a breakpoint, which forces the program to stop at a specific line. Watchpoints therefore allow you to monitor the content of individual variables.

---

6 The checkpoint created with the `BREAK-POINT` statement is an unconditional checkpoint. On the other hand, a checkpoint created with `ASSERT` is a conditional checkpoint. The latter can also navigate to the debugger when the assertion is set accordingly (see Section 8.3.2). The log points created with the `LOG-POINT` statement are another type of unconditional checkpoint that can be used only for writing log entries.

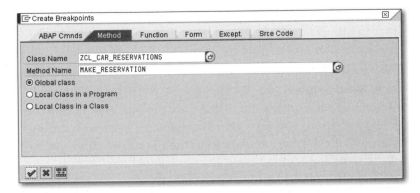

Figure 13.13 Creating Breakpoints

You can create watchpoints with the **Create Watchpoint** function. When you create a watchpoint, the variable that is pointed to by the cursor in the editor or other tools is used as the suggested value for the watchpoint variable. You can only set watchpoints on variables of the current context (program).[7]

Free condition   You can also enter a free condition in the **Condition** section in the watchpoint dialog (see Figure 13.14). The debugger stops the program only when the watchpoint variable changes *and* the condition is met (when a variable has reached a specific value, for example).

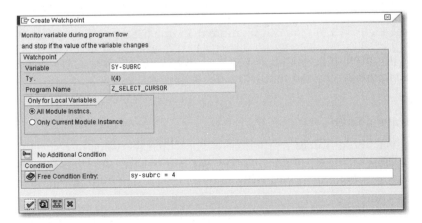

Figure 13.14 Creating a Watchpoint

---

7 For local variables, you can specify if the watchpoint applies only to the current procedure instance or to all instances of the procedure that are called. This difference can be particularly important for recursive calls of the procedure.

Figure 13.14 illustrates how an additional condition can be specified. The debugger does not stop at every modification of sy-subrc; it stops only when sy-subrc has a value of 4.

Additional to breakpoints, you can also use the breakpoint tool to modify, delete, or add new watchpoints (in the **Watchpoints** tab).[8]

Debugging a Sample Program

To conclude, we provide an example of debugging that analyzes the sample program Z_RTTC from Section 11.2. We have already used the program to demonstrate RTTC. The program can write the contents of any database table to an internal table and output only the required columns and rows. We will examine it with the debugger and try out some of the tools.

1. Load the program into the ABAP Editor and set a session breakpoint at the head of the LOOP loop in the main method.

2. Then start the program in the debugger via **Execute • Debugging**. A second session is opened with the ABAP Debugger.

3. Configure the desktop so that the **Source Code, Variable Fast display**, and **Breakpoints** tools are available.

4. Figure 13.15 illustrates how the debugger might appear on the screen. You can see that the Session Breakpoint is already displayed in the breakpoint tool.

5. You can run through the program step by step with ⌐F5⌐ or with the left button on the toolbar. Execute the program until you reach the first statement in the main method.

6. Enter the internal table components in the **Variable Fast Display** and confirm the entry with ⌐Enter⌐. The display indicates that it is an empty standard table with four columns.

7. Double-click on the table name in the **Variable Fast Display** tool. The **Table** tool opens, which displays the structure of the components table.

8. You can use ⌐F8⌐ or the fourth button in the toolbar to continue running the program. The program stops at the breakpoint that has been set. At this point, the internal table components has

---

8 The new debugger scripting in the next release of SAP NetWeaver will be much more powerful than watchpoints.

already been populated, and its contents are displayed in the **Table** tool. The debugger UI should now appear as shown in Figure 13.16.

9. Then click on the **Create Breakpoint** button in the **Breakpoints** tool. Create a breakpoint for the `display` method of the program.

10. Let the program continue to run by pressing [F8]. The program stops at the first statement of the `display` method.

11. Display the contents of the table by double-clicking on `result`. You can select individual fields in the **Table** tool and change their contents in the **Detail Display**. Assign a different value to some columns.

12. Let the program continue to run by pressing [F8]. The output is displayed: you can see the values that you modified.

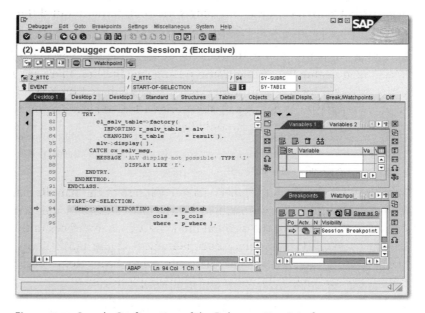

Figure 13.15 Sample Configuration of the Debugger User Interface

Additional debugger tools

This brief example gives you an idea of the options provided by the ABAP Debugger. Examine our own programs or other sample programs with the debugger so you can familiarize yourself with its functions. Try out the various tools, including the **DiffTool**, **Memory Analysis**, and **Screen Analysis**.

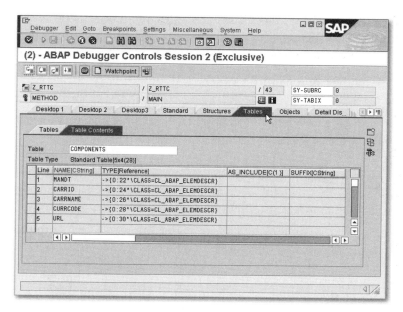

Figure 13.16 Display of the Table Contents in the Table Tool

13.3 Module Tests with ABAP Unit

The execution of functional tests is an essential part of all program development and is indispensable to verify the required behavior of a program. To be able to perform comprehensive tests that can be reused over the long term, automatic testing procedures are required. A tool like the ABAP Debugger is usually used during development or to analyze severe errors. Debugging information is available only interactively and in a step-by-step method, which means that it cannot be used for automated tests. The stored information in logs from assertions (see Section 8.3) is also of limited use for the analysis of comprehensive test runs.

Automatic testing procedures

The requirements of automated testing procedures are met by *module testing tools,* however. ABAP Unit is the module testing tool for ABAP programs. You can use ABAP Unit to handle the following tasks:

- Combining individual tests into test tasks
- Analyzing test results
- Executing test runs automatically

This section examines these tasks and gives you a brief overview of the ABAP Unit features.

13.3.1 What Is a Module Test?

Perhaps you have already encountered the term "module test" in your work as a developer. According to the *IEEE Standard Computer Dictionary*, a *module test* is defined as follows:

Module test
: *The testing of individual hardware or software units or groups of related units*

IEEE defines a *module* as follows:

Module
: *A separately testable element specified in the design of a computer software component*

In the real word, a module test is a test that is defined from the perspective of the developer during development. Ideally, such tests encompass all the components created by a developer and that are not trivial.[9] You should be able to test a component independently, without your having to execute (and test) other components of the software system. In ABAP, such components and modules are procedures like methods and also function modules.

Module tests also offer a variety of advantages. First, the independence of modules from each other means that any module can be tested at almost any point in the development process. Secondly, the area in which the error is looked for is limited to the module, which simplifies the search for errors. Furthermore, trivial parts of the system are omitted from the test, which also saves time during the testing process.

Module test and integration test
: Of course, a module test cannot replace an integration test that tests the correct interplay of all components. Nonetheless, a module test does ensure the reliability of individual parts of the software system at practically every point in the development process.

---

9 A test of trivial components—components that by definition cannot create an error—makes no sense and is therefore excluded from the effort needed for testing.

13.3.2 Organization of ABAP Unit

ABAP Unit is the module testing tool integrated in the ABAP runtime environment for checking the functionality of a program's components. The module tests executed by ABAP Unit are organized in the ABAP Unit test hierarchy (see Figure 13.17).

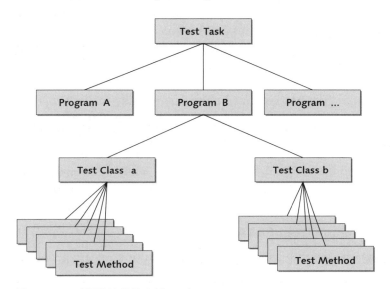

Figure 13.17 ABAP Unit Test Hierarchy

The root of the ABAP Unit test hierarchy is the *test task*. It combines all the tests of one or more ABAP programs that can be executed for a *test run*. A test run is the execution of a test task. You can start test runs for the test tasks of individual programs directly in the appropriate editor with **Test • Module Test**. The Code Inspector enables you to execute more comprehensive test runs. After a test run, the results are displayed in the user interface of ABAP Unit.

Test task

Test classes are the basis of ABAP Unit tests. In general, you can create test classes locally in the programs to be tested or globally in the class library. A local test class combines the related tests for a program. Global test classes can be used only in local test classes and help to enable the reuse of complex test preparations. The actual tests of ABAP Unit are implemented in the test classes as test methods. A test method is a special instance method that contains the test logic and that is executed during a test run of ABAP Unit. The execution sequence is not defined there.

Test class and test method

963

Local test classes are part of the production programs to be tested. This approach avoids problems that arise because the test code is separated from the productive code. Because the test code is part of the production program, it is easy to keep the module tests at the same status as the productive code.

abap/test_
generation

Although the test code is transported through the system landscape with the production programs, ABAP Unit tests don't increase the memory load in the production system. The test class of a program does not belong to its productive code and, by default, is not generated in the production system. That's why a test class and its components cannot be addressed in the productive code of the program, but only in other test classes. To be able to execute an ABAP Unit test, you must set the abap/test_generation profile parameter to the value "on."[10] For the SAP NetWeaver 2004s ABAP Trial Version, you can do so by inserting "abap/test_generation = on" in the profile file ...\sap\NSP\SYS\profile\NSP_DVEBMGS00_P<host>.

13.3.3 Sample Use of ABAP Unit

Creating a
module test

To create and execute a module test, three major steps are generally required:

▶ Identification and possible preparation of the module to be tested

▶ Definition and implementation of a test class

▶ Execution and analysis of the test run

We will illustrate these steps in the subroutine pool in Listing 13.3.

Listing 13.3 Sample Module Test

```
PROGRAM z_abap_unit.

CLASS test_sflight_selection DEFINITION DEFERRED.
CLASS demo DEFINITION
      FRIENDS test_sflight_selection..
  PUBLIC SECTION.
    METHODS get_carrier_flights
              IMPORTING carrier TYPE string.
  PRIVATE SECTION.
```

---

10 After the test, the profile parameter should be reset to "default" or "off" to avoid loading the program memory with test code, because it can occupy more space than the productive code in some instances.

```abap
      DATA sflight_tab TYPE TABLE OF sflight.
ENDCLASS.

CLASS demo IMPLEMENTATION.
  METHOD get_carrier_flights.
    SELECT * FROM sflight
           INTO TABLE sflight_tab
           WHERE carrid = 'LH'.
  ENDMETHOD.
ENDCLASS.

CLASS test_sflight_selection
      DEFINITION    "#AU Risk_Level Harmless
      FOR TESTING. "#AU Duration Short
  PRIVATE SECTION.
    METHODS: test_get_carrier_flights FOR TESTING,
             setup.
    DATA: demo_ref      TYPE REF TO demo,
          test_carrid   TYPE string,
          test_carrids TYPE TABLE OF string.
ENDCLASS.

CLASS test_sflight_selection IMPLEMENTATION.
  METHOD setup.
    CREATE OBJECT demo_ref.
    APPEND 'LH' TO test_carrids.
    APPEND 'UA' TO test_carrids.
    APPEND 'AA' TO test_carrids.
  ENDMETHOD.
  METHOD test_get_carrier_flights.
    DATA: act_carrid TYPE string,
          msg        TYPE string,
          sflight_wa TYPE sflight.
    LOOP AT test_carrids INTO test_carrid.
      CONCATENATE 'Selection of' test_carrid
                  'gives different airlines'
                  INTO msg SEPARATED BY space.
    demo_ref->get_carrier_flights( test_carrid ).
    LOOP AT demo_ref->sflight_tab INTO sflight_wa.
      act_carrid = sflight_wa-carrid.
      cl_aunit_assert=>assert_equals(
          act = act_carrid
          exp = test_carrid
          msg = msg
          quit = cl_aunit_assert=>no ).
      IF act_carrid <> test_carrid.
        EXIT.
      ENDIF.
```

```
      ENDLOOP.
    ENDLOOP.
  ENDMETHOD.
ENDCLASS.
```

Structure of the Program

The program in Listing 13.3 contains two classes, one of which has the FOR TESTING addition. That is a test class. Test classes don't belong to the productive code of the program. That's why a program that contains test classes is made up of a productive part and a test part that consists of test classes. As we already mentioned, the test part is not generated in production systems by default.

Productive code

The productive part of our program is the demo class. Its method get_carrier_flights receives an airline as parameter and it writes all the flights of this airline to an internal table. As you can see in the implementation of the method in Listing 13.3, we have deliberately done so incorrectly so that the module test has something to report.

The module to be tested is therefore the get_carrier_flights method.[11] It is public so that in this case the test class can access it. Although you don't have to change the code to be tested for the testing of public components, it might be advisable for you to take some preparatory steps.

Test class as friend

We want to check the contents of table sflight_tab in the test class, but it is a private attribute of the productive class. That's why the productive class demo must use FRIENDS to offer friendship to the test_sflight_selections test class, which also requires a forward declaration of the test class with DEFERRED. But those aforementioned tasks are actually administrative and therefore don't affect the module to be tested. Because ABAP Unit is a testing tool only for developers and is integrated in the source code, no design problem occurs here.

---

11 For testing the methods of global classes or function modules, what was said about the example of a local class applies here as well. The tests are then simply implemented in the class pool or in the function group.

Definition of the Test Class

ABAP Unit tests are implemented as test methods in test classes. Hardly any additional knowledge is required, except knowing how to inform the ABAP Unit framework of the test results. Global class CL_AUNIT_ASSERT is available for this task.

Both test classes and test methods are defined with the addition of

```
... FOR TESTING ...
```

FOR TESTING

to the CLASS DEFINITION or METHODS statements. Only test classes can contain test methods that are then called by the ABAP Unit framework during the test run.

You use pseudo comments

Test properties

```
... "#AU Risk_Level Critical|Dangerous|Harmless
```

```
... "#AU Duration Short|Medium|Long
```

to assign test properties to a test class. Risk_Level defnes the risk level and Duration defines the expected execution time of a test. Test properties are checked during the execution of the test. Tests with a risk level higher than that allowed in the system are not executed. Tests that last longer than the expected duration are terminated. To specify two test properties for a test class, the CLASS statement must be split across several lines. The pseudo comments take into account uppercase and lowercase. Syntax deviations during the execution of a test will lead to a warning.[12]

Test methods are called only by ABAP Unit and have no other external user. As a general rule, it's best to declare them in the private visibility section of the test class.[13] A declaration in the protected section is only comes into question when you want to use a test method in a subclass of the test class. A declaration in the public section is only comes into question when you want to call the test method from the test method of another test class.

Test method

---

12 These pseudo comments will become obsolete with the next release of SAP NetWeaver. Instead of pseudo comments, you will be able to specify real additions, RISK LEVEL and DURATION, for CLASS ... FOR TESTING.

13 The ABAP unit framework is implicitly a friend of all test classes.

Fixture

Good test data is an important precondition for the effective testing of complex programs. For systematic reasons, you should always test with the same set of initial data. That means that you must have an option to set up test data in your module test. To avoid having module tests affect each other, different test units that work with the same data should always find the data unchanged and in the same form. Consequently, a local test class can contain special private methods that implement a *fixture*[14] for the tests of the class. These methods have predefined names. Instance method `setup` is called before every test of the class; the `teardown` method is called after every test of the class. The static methods `class_setup` and `class_teardown` are called before and after all tests of the test class.

Components of test classes

In addition to the test methods and special methods for the fixture, a test class can also contain other components. Depending on their visibility, these components can be used only in your own test class or in other test classes. That's how you can define auxiliary methods for tests, for example. The test class in our example has some attributes.

Implementing the Test Class

setup

We use the `setup` method to create a test object of the productive class and to define appropriate test data. When you use fixtures, you cannot count on a specific sequence of the test methods. Accordingly, the test methods should not change the predefined test data, especially not those of class-related fixtures.

Test method

The implementations of the test methods execute the actual tests and use service methods of class CL_AUNIT_ASSERT to transfer the results to the ABAP Unit framework.

ASSERT_EQUALS

As an example, we'll take the ASSERT_EQUALS method. It receives an expected value in parameter EXP and an actual value in ACT and compares the two. You can transfer a text to parameter MSG that indicates the task that caused a test to fail. You can also use the QUIT parameter to define what occurs if the test fails. The options include having the test continue to run or terminating the current test session, the entire test class, or all current tests.

---

14 A fixture is a test configuration that results in a unique testing behavior. It usually includes test data, test objects, resources, and connections that are needed for a test behavior that can be reproduced.

You can use the other methods of class CL_AUNIT_ASSERT to perform other checks and transfer the results to the ABAP Unit framework. It's important that you can use the parameters of all these methods to control the presentation of the results and the flow of the entire module test.

CL_AUNIT_ASSERT

In our test method, we call method ASSERT_EQUALS within two loops. In the external loop, we go through all the airlines for which the selection method should be tested. In the inner loop, we check to see if only the airlines that correspond to the transferred ID were actually read. Checking in the inner loop ends as soon as we encounter an airline that we don't want to select.

13.3.4 Execution and Analysis of a Test Run

For security reasons, executing ABAP Unit tests in customers' production systems is prohibited by default, because the tests could produce side effects in the production data. For example, to perform a module test with SAP NetWeaver 2004s Trial Version, you must first set the **Client Role** to **Test** in client maintenance (Transaction SCC4).

Test permission

For individual program units, you can call a test run (the call of all existing test methods) from the ABAP Editor of the corresponding tool via the **Test · Module Test** function. Figure 13.18 illustrates the result for our sample program.

Test run

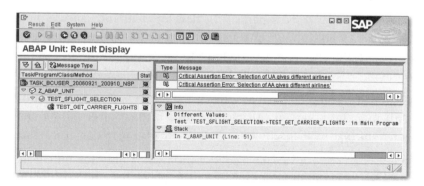

Figure 13.18 Result of a Module Test

All tests are listed as nodes of a **task** on the left-hand side. Our example involves only one test class with one method. Messages that we have transferred to the ASSERT_EQUALS method for the event of an

Test exceptions

error are output on the right-hand side. The type of test exception is also output. ABAP Unit distinguishes between four types of test exceptions:

- **Assertion Error**
  A check assumption that was encountered in a test method was incorrect. That's the case in our example.

- **Exception Error**
  A class-based exception was triggered in the test method without being captured there.

- **Runtime Error**
  A runtime error occurred during execution of the test method (applies only to background processing).

- **Warning**
  A warning does not involve a problem in the code being tested, but incorrect use of the ABAP Unit.

The area in the lower right displays additional details on the test results. Because our productive method "incorrectly" reads only data for airline LH, messages appear when AA and UA are expected.

13.3.5 ABAP Unit in Code Inspector

The execution of test runs of the ABAP Unit is completely integrated with the Code Inspector (see Section 13.1.3). Developers generally implement their tests as part of the development and execute them in the ABAP Editor. But, quality managers or test teams can execute mass tests during the consolidation and integration phase of a development process, thanks to the integration with the Code Inspector.

Essentially, you only have to activate the test **Dynamic Tests • ABAP Unit** in a check variant. All module tests of the object set are executed during the inspection; the results are displayed.

When we create a variant (see Section 13.1.3) only for unit tests, include the program in Listing 13.3 in an object list, and execute the corresponding inspection, we obtain the result shown in Figure 13.19. By selecting result lines, you can navigate to the results presentation of the ABAP Unit framework.

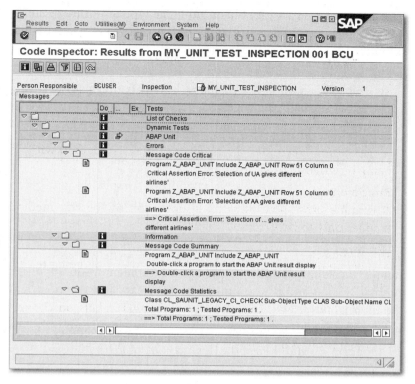

Figure 13.19 Result of ABAP Unit in the Code Inspector

13.4 ABAP Memory Inspector

The Memory Inspector is a tool for displaying and analyzing *memory snapshots*. A memory snapshot contains information regarding the memory usage of all data objects and instances of classes within an internal session.

Memory snapshot

You can analyze and compare memory snapshots to find any *memory leaks* that might exist. The basic question here is if such memory leaks can occur very often in ABAP. Classic ABAP, which has long characterized the perception of ABAP, almost never worked directly in the memory, as is the case with C or C++. But because of the following reasons, memory leaks in today's ABAP can quickly become a source of errors that you should keep an eye on.

Memory leak

▶ Since the introduction of reference variables for object and data references and their increasingly broad use in modern ABAP pro-

Reference variables

gramming, the above statement no longer applies. You can create any objects in the memory that can lead to memory leaks when handled incorrectly and despite garbage collection.

Dynamic
data objects

▶ The data of the deep data objects strings, and internal tables is also dynamically stored in the memory. This data objects collectively are called *dynamic data objects*. Access to these data objects is direct, but they are managed internally with references, which creates administrative costs. Unfavorable use of dynamic data objects can also create memory leaks.

In summary, we can define objects addressed explicitly with reference variables and dynamic data objects managed implicitly with internal references as dynamic memory objects. The memory use of dynamic memory objects cannot be controlled statically. A program can terminate once the available memory is exhausted. How much memory is actually available depends on the memory limits of the internal session and is also limited by the characteristics of strings and internal tables.

The following sections first describe how dynamic memory objects occupy memory and then show how to control memory usage.

13.4.1 Dynamic Memory Objects

Table 13.1 provides an overview of the possible dynamic memory objects in ABAP and the references that can be used to access the memory objects.

Memory Object	References
Table body of an internal table	Internal table reference
Text or byte strings	Internal string reference
Anonymous data objects created using CREATE DATA	Data reference
Instances of classes created using CREATE OBJECT	Object reference

Table 13.1 Memory Objects and Their References

Dynamic
data objects

Dynamic memory objects include anonymous data objects and objects that can actually be addressed only with reference variables. They also include the dynamic data objects strings and internal tables that are addressed with internal references. Assignments between reference variables are subject to reference semantics (see Section

6.4.2), but dynamic data objects use value semantics so that they are ostensibly perceived more as normal data objects and not as referenced memory objects. Internally, however, the sharing based on copy-on-write semantics mentioned in Section 5.1.8 takes place: reference semantics is switched to value semantics at the moment a modifying access occurs.

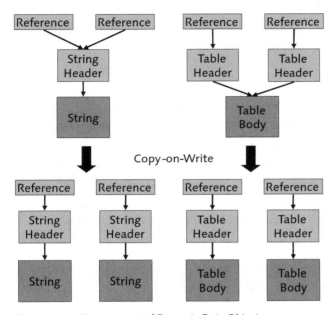

Figure 13.20 Management of Dynamic Data Objects

Figure 13.20 illustrates the internal management of dynamic data objects. The memory requirements of deep data objects consist of a constant memory requirement for the reference, a dynamic memory requirement for the *header*, and the actual objects. The memory requirement for the implicit reference is 8 bytes. As long as no dynamic memory is demanded, the memory requirement for a string or internal table is exactly 8 bytes. The dynamic memory consists of a header (string header or table header) and the actual data (string or table body). The reference points to the header, which contains the address of the actual data and of additional administrative information. The memory requirement of a header is approximately 100 bytes.

Header

The upper part of the figure shows two different strings or internal tables that point to the same data after an assignment (sharing). You

Sharing

can see that the header is also subject to sharing with strings, but not with internal tables. Sharing ends when an access modifies the objects involved: individual data objects are created (copy-on-write).

Internal management of dynamic data objects therefore attempts to use sharing to save memory, despite the value semantics. Nevertheless, memory leaks can occur even with dynamic data objects. First, sharing can be unintentionally turned off. Second, you must know that the reference variables and the header are retained when initializing a dynamic data object. Particularly with the use of nested internal tables, a table that is actually empty can use a great deal of memory.

Reference semantics The upper-left portion of Figure 13.20 also applies to data and object references. An *object header* also lies between references in reference variables and their objects. When assigning reference variables, only references are copied because of the reference semantics. In other words, sharing always applies and it is never removed (there is no "deep copy"). When you initialize all reference variables that point to an object, the Garbage Collector deletes the object and its header.[15] Only the costs for the reference variables actually remain. When dealing with reference variables, memory leaks generally occur because you have forgotten to delete an object that is no longer needed for all references, or because you have inadvertently created identical objects for which sharing would be possible.

This brief excursus shows that the management of dynamic memory objects in large programs can become quite complex and cannot always be understood from the source code or from a flowchart. The latter applies particularly when you mix the use of reference variables and dynamic data objects—when internal references contain objects, or when objects wrap internal tables. An exact analysis of such chains leads to terms like *strongly connected components* (SCC), which we do not address further in this book.

Memory bottlenecks When memory bottlenecks actually occur, you are, of course, interested in learning where they came from. And even when it's difficult to determine the actual cause of a memory bottleneck, which ulti-

---

15 To ensure that an internal table does not occupy any memory after it has been deleted, it might be worthwhile to wrap the internal table in an object and transfer the object to garbage collection to be deleted.

mately depends on how many users are simultaneously logged on to the system, how many data sets they are processing, and so on, you should examine all the programs involved for potential memory leaks and possible options for saving memory—at the latest when they occur. Of course, it would be ideal if memory leaks could be recognized and avoided during development or testing.

To analyze the current memory utilization of a program at any given point, you can use the **Memory Analysis** tool of the ABAP Debugger. With the tool and other functions, you can create memory snapshots that you can then thoroughly examine and compare in the Memory Inspector tool.

Memory analysis

13.4.2 Creating Memory Snapshots

You have the following options to create a memory snapshot:

- ▶ Enter "/hmusa" in the command field in the standard toolbar in the GUI status of a classical dynpro.

- ▶ Follow menu path **System • Utilities • Memory Analysis • Create Memory Snapshot** in the menu bar in the GUI status of a classical dynpro.

- ▶ Use the **Services** menu of the **Memory Analysis** tool in the new ABAP Debugger.[16]

- ▶ Call the static method WRITE_MEMORY_CONSUMPTION_FILE of system class CL_ABAP_MEMORY_UTILITIES in any processing block of the ABAP program.

The memory snapshots are stored in the file system of the application server. You can then analyze and manage them using the Memory Inspector. The name of the memory snapshot begins with a prefix determined by profile parameter abap/memory_inspector_file and continues with a client ID and a sequential number.

We will create memory snapshots for the program given in Listing 13.4 and then examine them with the Memory Inspector.

---

16 Menu path **Development • Memory Analysis • Create Memory Snapshot** in the old ABAP Debugger.

Listing 13.4 Example of a Program with a Memory Leak

```
REPORT z_memory_leak.

SELECTION-SCREEN BEGIN OF SCREEN 100.
PARAMETERS p_dbtab TYPE c LENGTH 30 DEFAULT 'SFLIGHT'.
SELECTION-SCREEN END OF SCREEN 100.

CLASS demo DEFINITION.
  PUBLIC SECTION.
    CLASS-METHODS main.
    CLASS-EVENTS  trigger.
ENDCLASS.

CLASS dbtab_data DEFINITION.
  PUBLIC SECTION.
    METHODS: constructor
                IMPORTING dbtab TYPE csequence
                RAISING cx_sy_create_data_error
                        cx_sy_open_sql_error,
             handle_data
                FOR EVENT trigger OF demo.
  PRIVATE SECTION.
    DATA data_ref TYPE REF TO data.
ENDCLASS.

CLASS demo IMPLEMENTATION.
  METHOD main.
    DATA: oref  TYPE REF TO dbtab_data,
          error TYPE REF TO cx_root.
    DO.
      CALL SELECTION-SCREEN 100.
      IF sy-subrc <> 0.
        RETURN.
      ENDIF.
      TRY.
          CREATE OBJECT oref
            EXPORTING dbtab = p_dbtab.
          RAISE EVENT trigger.
        CATCH cx_sy_create_data_error
              cx_sy_open_sql_error INTO error.
          MESSAGE error TYPE 'I' DISPLAY LIKE 'E'.
          RETURN.
      ENDTRY.
    ENDDO.
  ENDMETHOD.
ENDCLASS.

CLASS dbtab_data IMPLEMENTATION.
  METHOD constructor.
```

```
    FIELD-SYMBOLS <table> TYPE STANDARD TABLE.
    CREATE DATA data_ref
           TYPE STANDARD TABLE OF (dbtab).
    ASSIGN data_ref->* TO <table>.
    SELECT *
           FROM (dbtab)
           INTO TABLE <table>.
    SET HANDLER handle_data.
  ENDMETHOD.
  METHOD handle_data.
    MESSAGE 'Handling data ...' TYPE 'S'.
  ENDMETHOD.
ENDCLASS.

START-OF-SELECTION.
  demo=>main( ).
```

When you execute the program, you can enter the name of database tables in a selection screen; their data is then loaded into an object for processing. The program is intended so that there should be always only one object with the data of one table.

Execute the program, select **Execute** in the selection screen, and create a memory snapshot by entering "/hmusa" or by using the corresponding function. Select **Execute** in the selection screen a few more times and create an additional memory snapshot there.

13.4.3 Working with the Memory Inspector

You can start the Memory Inspector using transaction code S_MEMORY_INSPECTOR. If you have created both memory snapshots for the program in Listing 13.4 as described, they are listed in the upper part of the initial screen. You can load them into the tool by selecting **Open Memory Snapshot**. The Memory Inspector can simultaneously load two memory snapshots named (t_0) and (t_1), display them in various forms, and compare them. Load the first memory snapshot as (t_0) and then the second memory snapshot as (t_1). Select **(t_0) Display** and **Ranked List** in the **View** field to view the screen displayed in Figure 13.21.

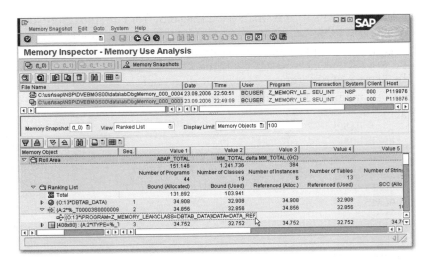

Figure 13.21 Ranked List for a Memory Snapshot

Ranked list The ranked list displays the contents of the memory snapshot, as sorted by the memory used by the memory objects it contains. As expected, the ranked list in our example is led by an object of class `dbtab_data`. The anonymous data object referenced by the object's attribute, `data_ref`, and the internal table are displayed directly below. The memory utilized by these three entries primarily involves the data of one and the same internal table. It is listed multiple times because it is referenced in various ways. The ranked list enables you to identify the items in your program that consume inordinate amounts of memory. We will not explore views other than the ranked list here.

Difference If you want to find out when and why the memory used by a program increases, you can compare two memory snapshots with each other. A comparison of the two memory snapshots requires that they were created in the same internal mode. The following memory objects are displayed when you select (**t_1−t_0**) or **Display Difference**:

- ▶ Recently added memory objects are displayed first. They are identified by a plus sign before the name of the object and appear in red.

- ▶ Memory objects whose use of memory has changed are displayed next. They are displayed without a plus sign and appear in black.

▶ The memory objects that were deleted from memory are displayed at the end. They are identified by a minus sign before the name of the object and appear in blue.

The display of differences does not display memory objects that exist in both memory snapshots and that don't have different memory values.

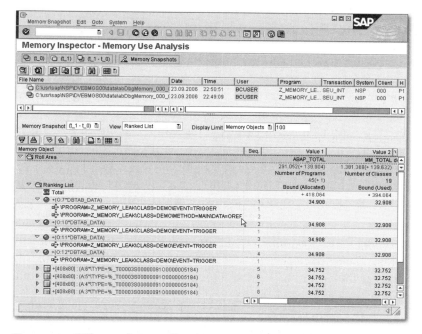

Figure 13.22 Difference Between Two Memory Snapshots

Figure 13.22 shows the difference between the memory snapshots for our example. Four more objects of class `dbtab_data` have been added to the original object. The Memory Inspector shows that only one of the objects is referenced by reference variable `oref` (displayed with its absolute type name). That's the only object that we would have expected. The garbage collector should have deleted the other objects.

Of course, the error can be found in our program. Because the `dbtab_data` class registers its objects in the instance constructor as an event handler for a static event of another class, references to these objects are stored in the system-internal event-handler table. We cannot access this table outside of an object and it keeps the objects alive until the internal session ends.

Strictly speaking, the program also has functional errors, because the event handlers of all the objects registered so far are executed every time the event is triggered. But that doesn't interest us here. We simply wanted to introduce you to memory snapshots and show you how you can use this tool for memory analysis to uncover unexpected memory leaks.

13.5 ABAP Runtime Analysis

Computing time

Computing time is another important resource, right alongside memory.[17] With the ABAP runtime analysis, you can analyze the computing time that affects the performance of ABAP program units. That includes programs, methods, and function modules, for example. The runtime analysis saves the results of your measurements in performance data files on the application server. You can evaluate the files to discover statements that consume a great deal of runtime, combine table accesses, and examine the hierarchy of the program flow.[18] You can discover the following situations that might indicate problems:

▶ Frequent use or unnecessary calls of modularization units

▶ Sections of the program that demand a great deal of computing time

▶ Self-defined functions that can be replaced by ABAP statements

▶ Slow and superfluous accesses to the database

The measurements focus on statements that might prove expensive. Such statements include accesses to the database; calls of program units with CALL SCREEN, CALL METHOD, CALL FUNCTION, and so on; accesses to internal tables; and statements that process external text files.

---

17 It's just like real life, i. e., you never have enough room and there's never enough time.

18 The runtime analysis is primarily intended for runtime measurements of complex programs or transactions. However, if you want to measure the runtime of small parts of a program or of individual ABAP statements, you can also use the GET RUN TIME FIELD statement during development, as used in the sample program in Section 10.1.2.

13.5.1 Calling the Runtime Analysis

You can start the runtime analysis using transaction codes SE30 or ATRA, which display the initial screen shown in Figure 13.23.[19]

SE30, ATRA

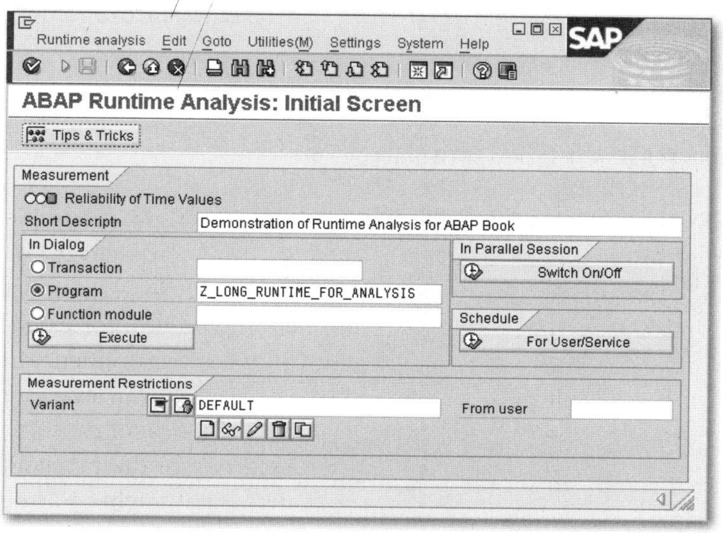

Figure 13.23 Initial Screen of the ABAP Runtime Analysis

In the initial screen, you determine which unit should be measured and what settings should apply. Listing 13.5 shows the sample program that we entered in Figure 13.23.

Listing 13.5 Sample Program for Runtime Analysis

```
REPORT z_long_runtime_for_analysis.

CLASS demo DEFINITION.
  PUBLIC SECTION.
    CLASS-METHODS main.
ENDCLASS.

CLASS demo IMPLEMENTATION.
  METHOD main.
    DATA: sflight_tab TYPE TABLE OF sflight,
          sflight_wa  TYPE sflight.
    DO 10 TIMES.
      SELECT *
             FROM sflight
```

---

19 As of the next release of SAP NetWeaver, Transaction SAT will replace Transactions SE30 and ATRA.

```
                    INTO sflight_wa
                  WHERE carrid LIKE '%A%'.
              APPEND sflight_wa TO sflight_tab.
            ENDSELECT.
*       SELECT *
*               FROM sflight
*               INTO TABLE sflight_tab
*               WHERE carrid LIKE '%A%'.
          ENDDO.
          LOOP AT sflight_tab INTO sflight_wa.
            sflight_wa-carrid = 'XX'.
            MODIFY sflight_tab FROM sflight_wa.
          ENDLOOP.
        ENDMETHOD.
      ENDCLASS.

      START-OF-SELECTION.
        demo=>main( ).
```

Variants Similar to the case with the Code Inspector (see Section 13.1.3), you must use a *variant* to set the measurement limits that should apply. For example, you can exclude specific parts of the program or statements from the measurements. For our example, we use the predefined standard variant, **DEFAULT**, in the **Variant** input field and select **Execute**.

The lower area of the screen then shows the performance data file that was generated. You can analyze it using the **Evaluate** function.

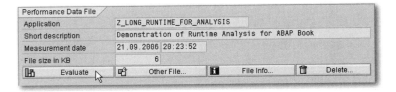

Performance Data File	
Application	Z_LONG_RUNTIME_FOR_ANALYSIS
Short description	Demonstration of Runtime Analysis for ABAP Book
Measurement date	21.09.2006 20:23:52
File size in KB	6

Figure 13.24 Selecting a Performance Data File

13.5.2 Evaluating the Performance Data Files

The evaluation shown in Figure 13.25 is displayed for our example.

Additional evaluation functions You can clearly see that the largest portion of the runtime is devoted to database accesses. Starting from this screen, you can call additional evaluation functions, including various hit lists of the most expensive statements or the call hierarchy with costs of individual calls. The gross and net times of individual calls are given in micro-seconds. The gross time is the total time needed for a call. It also comprises the runtime of all the subunits that have been called. The net time is the gross time minus the runtime of all the subunits that have been called.

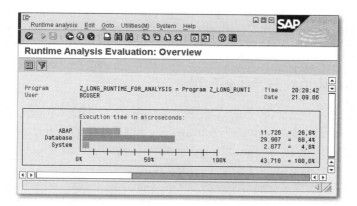

Figure 13.25 Evaluating the Runtime Analysis

When you replace the SELECT loop used in Listing 13.5 with the direct read into the internal table that is commented out and execute the measurement again, you see the result shown in Figure 13.26.

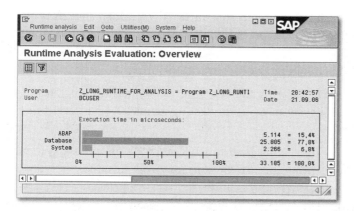

Figure 13.26 Runtime Distribution for an Improved Program

You can clearly see that with better overall performance, the ratio of the time needed by ABAP to the time needed by the database has decreased, because the effort required by the APPEND statement is no longer needed.

13.5.3 Tips & Tricks

The **Tips & Tricks** function of the initial screen of the runtime analysis provides a small collection of source code excerpts on specific topics that shows two different solutions for the same task. This tool allows you to measure the runtime of both variants; we recommend that you use the more efficient alternative. You can even modify the example directly to try out some self-defined variants.

13.6 Additional Testing Tools

Now that we've described some testing tools in detail and with the use of examples in the previous sections, we will finish this chapter by introducing you to two additional testing tools that can also be helpful to ensure the quality of your programs.

13.6.1 Coverage Analyzer

Number of calls The Coverage Analyzer captures the number of calls for processing blocks and executable programs, separated by times, users, and area. This enables the developer or quality manager to collect a variety of useful information, for example:

▶ Developers might be interested in how frequently specific code units like methods or programs are used, so that they can determine where performance-tuning activities might be useful or which code should be processed with priority.

▶ Quality managers are generally interested in the global testing coverage of a system, or in the testing activities of different user groups.

▶ You can also determine how much dead code exists in a system, for example, programs or sections of programs that are never called or called only rarely.

▶ You can also obtain hints on program organization. For example, if a class pool or a function group contains procedures that are seldom used, you should place them in separate service programs to avoid increasing the load on the program memory.

The options of the Coverage Analyzer are multifaceted, even though it's based on a very simple principle.

Functions of the Coverage Analyzer

The Coverage Analyzer simply monitors the execution of all program units throughout the system and stores the related information in the database. It thereby stores information on how often a program unit was executed and changed and on how many runtime errors occurred within a program unit. Program units include the following:

▸ Programs (executable programs and module pools)

▸ Procedures (methods, function modules, and subroutines)

▸ Dialog modules called from the dynpro flow logic

▸ Event blocks for events of the runtime environment

You can start the Coverage Analyzer using transaction code SCOV,   scov
which takes you to the initial screen shown in Figure 13.27.

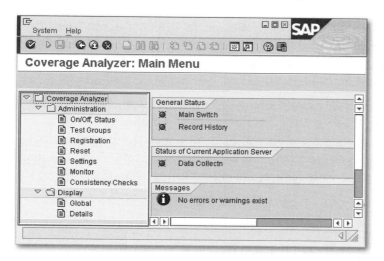

Figure 13.27 Initial Screen of the Coverage Analyzer

In the left half of the screen, you can see a tree that contains a variety of administrative functions under the **Administration** node and that provides the actual analysis functions under the **Display** node. You can use the administrative functions to switch the Coverage Analyzer on and off or to manage test groups.[20]

---

20 Test groups are helpful to combine and display the results of the Coverage Analyzer for a specific group of persons under a common name.

Analysis results The two most important functions of the Coverage Analyzer can be found in the subnodes **Global** and **Details**. You can evaluate the results of the analysis here. Under **Global**, you can display the coverage results at the level of authors or packages, according to criteria that you can select beneath the **Settings** node. Under **Details**, you can display processing blocks individually, according to criteria that you can also select in the **Settings** tab.

13.6.2 Extended Computer-Aided Test Tool (eCATT)

For the sake of completeness, we want to close this chapter by mentioning the Extended Computer-Aided Test Tool (eCATT). This tool is so comprehensive that we can only offer a brief overview here. However, it is one of the most important tools for automating tests of complete applications and therefore must be mentioned here.

CATT eCATT is an enhancement of CATT, which has long been known in the ABAP-based SAP environment; in eCATT, the functionality of CATT has been extended to interfaces that contain GUI controls. CATT test cases can be migrated to eCATT and benefit from the enhanced functions of eCATT.

eCATT provides an environment for the development and execution of functional tests. It is primarily used for automatic testing of SAP business processes on AS ABAP. Every test creates a detailed log that documents the test run and the results of the test. The use of automatic tests greatly reduces the effort needed for testing.

eCATT options In summary, eCATT provides the following options:

- Testing transactions, reports, and scenarios
- Calling BAPIs and function modules
- Testing remote systems
- Checking authorizations (user profiles)
- Testing of upgrades (database, applications, and user interfaces)
- Testing the effects of changed customizing settings
- Checking system messages

Components of eCATT tests eCATT tests are described by various objects. eCATT provides four different object types: The object types, system data container, test data container, and test scripts form the basis of a test and make up a complete test case in a test configuration.

▶ **System Data Container**

The system environment to be tested is described by a system data container in eCATT. This container provides all the information needed to describe the end of the test, the systems to be tested, and the communications connections of the systems. For example, it specifies the required RFC destinations for the target systems.

▶ **Test Scripts**

A test script contains the individual testing actions that should be executed in the context of a test. It normally includes one or more recorded transactions with linked checks and calculations that are then executed in the context of a test.

▶ **Test Data Container**

In eCATT, the majority of the test data is usually stored separately from test scripts in test data containers. The main reasons for this approach are reusability and maintenance. The test data containers and a test script are combined in a test configuration to create an executable test.

▶ **Test Configurations**

Test configurations combine the previously noted object types into a complete test. You can then assign the configurations to individual users for testing. A test configuration outputs its results as a log. The log provides a message about the success or failure of the complete test along with a lasting and detailed record of the test.

You must allow the execution of a CATT or eCATT test in client maintenance (Transaction SCC4).

For more information on eCATT and test automation, see *Testing SAP Solutions* by Markus Helfen et al. (SAP PRESS 2007).

A   Appendix

A.1   Overview of all ABAP Statements

This appendix provides an overview of all statements introduced by ABAP keywords arranged by different subjects.

A.1.1   Statements Introducing a Program

CLASS-POOL	Introduction of a class pool
FUNCTION-POOL	Introduction of a function group
INTERFACE-POOL	Introduction of an interface pool
PROGRAM	Introduction of a module pool or a subroutine pool
REPORT	Introduction of an executable program
TYPE-POOL	Introduction of a type pool

A.1.2   Modularization Statements

Procedures	
FORM ENDFORM	Definition of a subroutine
FUNCTION ENDFUNCTION	Definition of a function module
METHOD ENDMETHOD	Definition of a method

Dialog Modules	
MODULE ENDMODULE	Definition of a dialog module

Event Blocks	
AT LINE-SELECTION	List event
AT PF##	List event
AT SELECTION-SCREEN	Selection screen event
AT USER-COMMAND	List event
END-OF-PAGE	List event
END-OF-SELECTION	Reporting event
GET	Reporting event
INITIALIZATION	Reporting event
LOAD-OF-PROGRAM	Program constructor event
START-OF-SELECTION	Reporting event
TOP-OF-PAGE	List event

Source Code Modules	
DEFINE END-OF-DEFINITION	Definition of a macro
INCLUDE	Integration of an include program

A.1.3   Declarative Statements

Data Types and Data Objects	
CONSTANTS	Declaration of a constant
DATA	Declaration of a variable
FIELD-SYMBOLS	Declaration of a field symbol
INCLUDE	Integration of a structure
NODES	Declaration of a table work area
STATICS	Declaration of a static variable
TABLES	Declaration of a table work area
TYPE-POOLS	Integration of a type pool
TYPES	Definition of an independent data type

Classes and Interfaces	
ALIASES	Declaration of an alias name
CLASS ENDCLASS	Definition of a class
CLASS-DATA	Declaration of a static attribute
CLASS-EVENTS	Declaration of a static event
CLASS-METHODS	Declaration of a static method
EVENTS	Declaration of an instance event
INTERFACE ENDINTERFACE	Definition of an interface
INTERFACES	Integration of an interface
METHODS	Declaration of an instance method
PRIVATE SECTION	Introduction of the private visibility area
PROTECTED SECTION	Introduction of the protected visibility area
PUBLIC SECTION	Introduction of the public visibility area

A.1.4 Object Creation

CREATE DATA	Creation of an anonymous data object
CREATE OBJECT	Creation of an object

A.1.5 Calling and Exiting Program Units

Calling Programs	
CALL TRANSACTION	Calls a transaction
LEAVE TO TRANSACTION	Calls a transaction
SUBMIT	Calls an executable program

Calling Processing Blocks	
CALL FUNCTION	Calls a function module
CALL METHOD	Calls a method
PERFORM	Calls a subroutine
PUT	Triggers a reporting event

Calling Processing Blocks	
RAISE EVENT	Triggers an event
SET HANDLER	Registers an event
SET USER-COMMAND	Triggers a list event

Exiting Program Units	
CHECK	Exits a loop pass
CONTINUE	Exits a loop pass
EXIT	Exits a loop
LEAVE PROGRAM	Exits an ABAP program
REJECT	Exits a processing block
RETURN	Exits a processing block
STOP	Exits a processing block

A.1.6 Program Flow Control

Control Structures	
DO ENDDO	Loop
CASE WHEN ENDCASE	Branch

IF
ELSEIF
ELSE
ENDIF
	Branch

WHILE ENDWHILE	Loop

Program Interruption	
WAIT UP TO	Program interruption for a specific period of time

Exception Handling	
CATCH SYSTEM-EXCEPTIONS	Catches catchable runtime errors
RAISE	Triggers a non-class-based exception
RAISE EXCEPTION	Triggers a class-based exception
TRY CATCH CLEANUP ENDTRY	Handles class-based exceptions

A.1.7 Assignments

Value Assignments	
MOVE	Assignment based on a conversion rule
MOVE-CORRESPONDING	Assignment of structure components
UNPACK	Unpacks a packed number
WRITE TO	Formatted assignment

Setting References	
ASSIGN	Sets a field symbol
UNASSIGN	Initializes a field symbol
GET REFERENCE	Sets a data reference

Initializations	
CLEAR	Initializes a data object
FREE	Initializes a data object
REFRESH	Initializes an internal table

A.1.8 Processing Internal Data

Calculation Expressions	
COMPUTE	Calculates an arithmetic or bit expression

Calculation Statements	
ADD	Adds numerical data objects
DIVIDE	Divides numerical data objects
MULTIPLY	Multiplies numerical data objects
SUBTRACT	Subtracts numerical data objects

Processing Byte and Character Strings	
CONCATENATE	Concatenates byte or character strings
CONDENSE	Condenses a character string
CONVERT TEXT	Converts a character string
FIND	Searches within a byte or character string
GET BIT	Reads single bits within a byte string
OVERLAY	Carries out replacements within a character string
REPLACE	Carries out replacements within a byte or character string
SET BIT	Sets single bits within a byte string
SHIFT	Shifts a byte or character string
SPLIT	Splits a byte or character string
TRANSLATE	Translates a character string

Internal Tables	
APPEND	Appends single lines to an internal table
AT	Control level processing of an internal table
COLLECT	Insertion of collected lines into an internal table
DELETE	Deletes lines from an internal table
FIND IN TABLE	Performs a search run in an internal table
INSERT	Inserts lines into an internal table
LOOP AT ENDLOOP	Loop at an internal table
MODIFY	Modifies lines in an internal table
PROVIDE ENDPROVIDE	Loop at several internal tables

Internal Tables	
READ TABLE	Reads a row of an internal table
REPLACE IN TABLE	Carries out a replacement in an internal table
SORT	Sorts an internal table
SUM	Sums up numerical fields in an internal table

Extracts	
AT	Control level processing of the extract dataset
EXTRACT	Fills the extract dataset
FIELD-GROUPS	Declaration of a field group
INSERT	Builds up a field group
LOOP ENDLOOP	Loop at the extract dataset
SORT	Sorts the extract dataset

Attributes of Data Objects	
DESCRIBE	Determines the attributes of a data object

A.1.9 User Dialogs

General Dynpros	
CALL SCREEN	Calls a dynpro sequence
CONTROLS	Declaration of a control
EXIT FROM STEP-LOOP	Exits a table control or step loop
GET CURSOR	Reads the cursor position
GET PF-STATUS	Determines the GUI status
LEAVE [TO] SCREEN	Exits a dynpro
LOOP AT SCREEN ENDLOOP	Loop at screen elements
MODIFY SCREEN	Modifies a screen element
REFRESH CONTROL	Initializes a table control
SET CURSOR	Sets the cursor position

General Dynpros	
SET HOLD DATA	Switches standard menu items on and off
SET PF-STATUS	Sets the GUI status
SET SCREEN	Sets the next dynpro
SET TITLEBAR	Sets the GUI title
SUPPRESS DIALOG	Suppresses the screen layout

Selection Screens	
PARAMETERS	Defines a parameter
SELECTION-SCREEN	Defines a selection screen or a screen element
SELECT-OPTIONS	Defines a selection criterion

Classic Lists	
BACK	Relative positioning of the list cursor
DESCRIBE LIST	Determines the properties of a list in the list buffer
FORMAT	Formats a list
GET CURSOR	Reads the cursor position
HIDE	Stores a data object in a list level
LEAVE TO LIST-PROCESSING	Calls the list processing
LEAVE LIST-PROCESSING	Exits the list processing
MODIFY LINE	Modifies a list in the list buffer
NEW-LINE	Line break in a list
NEW-PAGE	Page break in a list
POSITION	Positions the list cursor
PRINT-CONTROL	Formats a print list
READ LINE	Reads a list in the list buffer
RESERVE	Relative page break in a list
SCROLL LIST	Scrolls a list
SET BLANK LINES	Controls blank characters in a list
SET CURSOR	Sets the cursor position

Classic Lists	
SET MARGIN	Sets the margin of a print list
SET PF-STATUS	Sets the GUI status
SET LEFT SCROLL-BOUNDARY	Sets the scrollable area of a list
SET TITLEBAR	Sets the GUI title
SKIP	Positions the list cursor
ULINE	Outputs a horizontal line in a list
WINDOW	Outputs a list in a dialog window
WRITE	Outputs data to a list

Messages	
MESSAGE	Sends a message

A.1.10 Processing External Data

Open SQL	
CLOSE CURSOR	Closes a database cursor
DELETE	Deletes rows from a database table
FETCH NEXT CURSOR	Reads rows through a database cursor
INSERT	Inserts rows into a database table
MODIFY	Modifies or inserts rows in a database table
OPEN CURSOR	Opens a database cursor
SELECT ENDSELECT	Reads rows from a database table
UPDATE	Modifies rows in a database table

Native SQL	
EXEC SQL ENDEXEC	Defines a coding area for Native SQL
EXIT FROM SQL	Exits the Native SQL processing

Data Clusters	
DELETE	Deletes data clusters
EXPORT	Exports data objects into a data cluster
FREE MEMORY	Deletes data clusters from the ABAP memory
IMPORT	Imports data objects from a data cluster
IMPORT DIRECTORY	Creates the table of contents of a data cluster

File Interface	
CLOSE DATASET	Closes a file
DELETE DATASET	Deletes a file
GET DATASET	Determines the properties of a file
OPEN DATASET	Opens a file
READ DATASET	Reads a file
SET DATASET	Sets the properties of a file
TRANSFER	Fills a file
TRUNCATE DATASET	Changes the size of a file

Data Consistency	
AUTHORITY-CHECK	Checks an authorization
COMMIT WORK	Completes an SAP LUW
ROLLBACK WORK	Cancels an SAP LUW
SET UPDATE TASK LOCAL	Sets a local update task

A.1.11 Program Parameters

SAP Memory	
GET PARAMETER	Reads an SPA/GPA parameter
SET PARAMETER	Sets an SPA/GPA parameter

Language Environment	
GET LOCALE	Determines the text environment
SET COUNTRY	Sets output formats in lists

Language Environment	
SET LANGUAGE	Loads a text pool
SET LOCALE	Sets the text environment

Date and Time Information	
CONVERT DATE	Converts date and time into a time stamp
CONVERT TIME STAMP	Converts a time stamp into date and time
GET TIME	Fills the system fields for date and time
GET TIME STAMP	Creates a time stamp

A.1.12 Program Processing

Testing and Checking Programs	
ASSERT	Defines an assertion
SET EXTENDED CHECK	Controls the extended program check
BREAK-POINT	Defines a break point
LOG-POINT	Defines a log point
GET RUN TIME	Determines a measurement interval
SET RUN TIME ANALYZER	Controls the runtime analysis
SET RUN TIME CLOCK	Sets the measurement accuracy for measurement intervals

Dynamic Program Development	
EDITOR-CALL FOR REPORT	Calls the ABAP Editor
GENERATE SUBROUTINE POOL	Generates a subroutine pool
INSERT REPORT	Stores an ABAP program
INSERT TEXTPOOL	Stores a text pool
READ REPORT	Reads an ABAP program
READ TEXTPOOL	Reads a text pool
SYNTAX-CHECK	Calls the syntax check

A.1.13 ABAP Data and Communication Interfaces

Remote Function Call	
CALL FUNCTION DESTINATION	Remote Function Call
RECEIVE	Receives parameters for a remote function call
WAIT UNTIL	Waits until a remote function call has finished

ABAP and XML	
CALL TRANSFORMATION	Calls an XSLT program or a simple transformation

OLE Interface	
CALL METHOD	Calls an OLE Automation method
CREATE OBJECT	Creates an OLE Automation object
FREE OBJECT	Releases memory in the OLE Automation
GET PROPERTY	Reads an attribute in the OLE Automation
SET PROPERTY	Sets an attribute in the OLE Automation

A.1.14 Enhancements

Source Code Enhancements	
ENHANCEMENT ENDENHANCEMENT	Implements an enhancement to the source code
ENHANCEMENT-POINT	Defines an enhancement to the source code
ENHANCEMENT-SECTION END-ENHANCEMENT-SEC-TION	Defines an enhancement to the source code

Enhancements via BAdIs	
GET BADI	Creates a BAdI object
CALL BADI	Calls BAdI methods

A.2 ABAP System Fields

The following tables contain all system fields that can be used (see Section 5.1.10). All other components of the SYST structure of the ABAP Dictionary are either reserved for internal use or obsolete. In principle, you should only use read access for the system fields.

Information on the Current AS ABAP	
sy-dbsys	Central database system of AS ABAP, e.g., ORACLE, ADABAS
sy-host	Name of the application server, such as KSAP0001, HS01234
sy-opsys	Operating system of the application server, such as Windows NT, HP-UX
sy-saprl	Release status of AS ABAP, such as 700, 710
sy-sysid	Name of AS ABAP, such as NSP, K99

Information on the Current User Session	
sy-langu	One-digit language key, such as D, E, F. Either logon language of the user or set via the SET LOCALE LANGUAGE statement.
sy-mandt	Client ID used by the user to log on, for example, 401, 800
sy-modno	Indexing of the external sessions. Set to 0 in the first session. Increased by 1 in new sessions created with the **Create Session** function or by calling a transaction with /o in the input field in the standard toolbar.
sy-uname	User's logon name, such as KELLERH, KRUEGERS

Date and Time Information	
sy-datlo	Local date of the user, for example, 19990723, 20000422
sy-datum	Date of the application server, for example, 19990723, 20000422
sy-dayst	Set to "X" during daylight saving time; otherwise, blank
sy-fdayw	Factory calendar weekday, Monday = 1, …, Friday = 5
sy-timlo	Local time of the user, for example, 152557

Date and Time Information	
sy-tzone	Time difference to UTC reference time in terms of seconds, for example, 3600, 10800
sy-uzeit	Time of the application server, for example, 152558
sy-zonlo	User's time zone, such as CET, PST

Information on the Current ABAP Program	
sy-calld	Contains a blank character in the first program of a call sequence; otherwise, set to "X".
sy-cprog	In externally called procedures, the name of the calling program; otherwise, the name of the current program. If an externally called procedure calls another external procedure, sy-cprog retains the name of the first main program and is not set to the main program name of the other calling program.
sy-dbnam	The linked logical database for executable programs
sy-dyngr	Screen group of the current dynpro. You can assign several dynpros to a common screen group in Screen Painter. You can then use the group to modify all the screens in that group, for example.
sy-dynnr	Number of the current dynpro. The current selection screen during selection screen processing. The number of the subscreen container during list processing. During the processing of a subscreen dynpro (also in the case of tabstrip controls), the number of that subscreen dynpro.
sy-ldbpg	The database program of the linked logical database for executable programs
sy-repid	Name of the current ABAP program. For externally called procedures, the name of the main program of the procedure. sy-repid is not a part of the SYST structure, but a predefined constant.
sy-tcode	Name of the current transaction code

Information on Batch and Batch Input Processing	
sy-batch	Set to "X" in ABAP programs running in the background; otherwise, initial.

Information on Batch and Batch Input Processing

sy-binpt	Set to "X" during the processing of batch input sessions and in ABAP programs called via CALL TRANSACTION USING; otherwise, initial.

ABAP Programming—Constants

sy-abcde	Contains the alphabet. Can be used to access specific letters through the offset information, independently of the code page.
sy-uline	Contains a horizontal line of 255 characters length for list outputs.
sy-vline	Contains a vertical line, "|", for list outputs.

ABAP Programming—Loop Processing

sy-index	Contains the number of loop passes, including the current loop, in DO and WHILE loops.

ABAP Programming—Character String Processing

sy-fdpos	Position information in operations with character-type fields

ABAP Programming—Internal Tables

sy-tabix	Line of an internal (index) table that has been addressed last. Is set to 0 when accessing a hashed table.
sy-tfill	During the statements DESCRIBE TABLE, LOOP AT, and READ TABLE, sy-tfill is filled with the number of lines in the addressed internal table.
sy-tleng	During the statements DESCRIBE TABLE, LOOP AT, and READ TABLE, sy-tleng is filled with the line width of the addressed internal table.

ABAP Programming—Database Accesses

sy-dbcnt	SQL statements set the content of sy-dbcnt to the number of processed table rows.

ABAP Programming—Return Value	
`sy-subrc`	Return value that is set by many ABAP statements. In general, 0 means that the statement was executed without problems. Depending on which statement caused `sy-subrc` to be set, you can derive the cause of the error from the corresponding value.

ABAP Programming—Dynpros	
`sy-cucol`	Horizontal cursor position. The count begins at column 2.
`sy-curow`	Vertical cursor position. The count begins at row 1.
`sy-datar`	Set to "X" during PAI if at least one input field of a dynpro was changed due to user action or other data transfer; otherwise, blank.
`sy-loopc`	Number of lines currently displayed in a table control
`sy-pfkey`	GUI status of the current dynpro
`sy-scols`	Number of columns in the current screen
`sy-srows`	Number of rows in the current screen
`sy-stepl`	Index of the current row in a table control. Is set during each loop pass.
`sy-title`	Text that is displayed in the title bar of the dynpro
`sy-ucomm`	Function code that triggered the PAI event

ABAP Programming—Selection Screens	
`sy-slset`	Variant used to fill a selection screen

ABAP Programming—List Creation	
`sy-colno`	Current column during list creation. The count begins at 1.
`sy-linct`	Page length of the list. `sy-linct` is 0 for a standard list of any length and is set to a value other than 0 for lists with a defined page length.
`sy-linno`	Current line during list creation. The count begins at 1 and contains the page header.
`sy-linsz`	Line width of the list. Unless it is changed, this is the standard width of the window.

ABAP Programming—List Creation

sy-pagno	Current page during list creation
sy-tvar0 ... sy-tvar9	You can assign values to these system fields in your programs. During the TOP-OF-PAGE event, the contents of sy-tvar0 to sy-tvar9 replace the placeholders in the list and column headers of the program.
sy-wtitl	Is set to "N" in the REPORT, PROGRAM, and FUNCTION-POOL statements if the addition NO STANDARD PAGE HEADING was used; otherwise, blank.

ABAP Programming—Interactive List Processing

sy-cpage	Page number of the top page from the list in which the list event was triggered. The count begins at 1.
sy-lilli	Line in which the list event was triggered. The count begins at 1 and contains the page header.
sy-lisel	Content of the line in which the list event was triggered (restricted to the first 255 characters)
sy-listi	Index of the list in which the list event was triggered
sy-lsind	Index of the list that is being created (basic list: 0, details lists: > 0). sy-lsind is automatically increased by one during each interactive list event. You can modify sy-lsind in the ABAP program to navigate between details lists.
sy-staco	Number of the first displayed column of the list in which the list event was triggered. The count begins at 1.
sy-staro	Number of the top displayed row in the top page of the list in which the list event was triggered. The count begins at 1. The page header is not included in the count.

ABAP Programming—Printing Lists

sy-callr	Contains a value indicating where the printout was started, such as NEW-PAGE for program-driven printing or RSDBRUNT for printing from the selection screen.
sy-prdsn	Contains the name of the spool file.
sy-spono	Contains the number of the spool file.

ABAP Programming—Printing Lists	
`sy-marow`	Contains the number of rows in the top margin.
`sy-macol`	Contains the number of columns in the left margin.

ABAP Programming—Messages	
`sy-msgid`	Contains the message class after the `MESSAGE` statement.
`sy-msgno`	Contains the message number after the `MESSAGE` statement.
`sy-msgty`	Contains the message type after the `MESSAGE` statement.

`sy-msgv1`
 `...`
 `sy-msgv4`
	Contain the field contents that were used for the placeholders of the message after the `MESSAGE` statement.

A.3 ABAP Program Types

The following table provides an overview of all ABAP program types, as well as the program components and properties supported by those types. All these programs are compilation units that are compiled and loaded separately. In addition, include programs are available that represent source code sections that can be included in compilation units.

	Executable Program	Module Pool	Function Group	Subroutine Pool	Type Group	Class Pool	Interface Pool
Global data types and data objects	x	x	x	x	x	x	
Dynpros	x	x	x				
Dialog modules	x	x	x				
Program constructor event `LOAD-OF-PROGRAM`	x	x	x	x			
Selection screen events	x	x	x				

	Executable Program	Module Pool	Function Group	Subroutine Pool	Type Group	Class Pool	Interface Pool
Classic list events	x	x	x				
Reporting events	x						
Classes	x	x	x	x		x	
Interfaces	x	x	x	x		x	x
Methods	x	x	x	x		x	
Function modules			x				
Subroutines	x	x	x	x			
Executable via SUBMIT	x						
Executable via transaction code	x	x	x	x		x	

The program components and properties indicate the following:

- Whether a program contains a global declaration part for global data types and data objects
- Whether a program supports dynpro-based user interfaces
- Which event blocks are supported by a program in order to respond to the relevant ABAP runtime environment events
- Which procedures can be contained in a program
- How a program can be executed

A.4   ABAP Naming Conventions

The following naming conventions apply to all definable objects within ABAP programs, such as data types, data objects, classes, and procedures:

- A name can contain a maximum of 30 characters.
- You can use the letters A to Z, the numbers 0 to 9, and the underscore (_).
- Names must begin with a letter or an underscore (_).

▶ A name may be preceded by a namespace prefix. A namespace prefix consists of at least three characters enclosed by two slashes (/.../). The total length of the prefix and name combined must not exceed 30 characters.

▶ You cannot use the names of predefined ABAP types or predefined data objects for data types and data objects.

▶ If you use field symbols, you must specify their names in angle brackets (<>).

We do not recommend using denominators that are reserved for ABAP words. Whereas a declaration, such as

```
DATA i TYPE i.
```

can be tolerated, you should never use declarations such as the following:

```
DATA i TYPE f.
```

A.5 Selectors

The following table provides an overview of all selectors that can be used in names:

-	Structure component selector for `struct-comp`
->	Object component selector for `ref->comp`
=>	Class component selector for `class=>comp`
~	Interface component selector for `intf~comp`
~	Column selector for `dbtab~col`

Except for the column selector, which is required in a SELECT statement if the name of a column occurs in several database tables that are accessed simultaneously, you can use all other selectors in concatenations. The requirement for using these selectors is that the complete expression specified on the left-hand side of a selector has the correct type.

A.6   Auxiliary Class for Simple Text Outputs

The class that is used in the following code listing represents a wrapping of the text edit control in a class, which has been carried out specifically for this book. The class can replace the use of the WRITE statement for simple, unformatted text outputs.

Listing A.1 Class ZCL_TEXT

```
CLASS zcl_text DEFINITION PUBLIC
  FINAL CREATE PRIVATE.
  PUBLIC SECTION.
    TYPES: t_line TYPE char80,
           t_text TYPE STANDARD TABLE OF t_line.
    CLASS-METHODS get_handle
      RETURNING
        value(text) TYPE REF TO zcl_text.
    METHODS add_table
      IMPORTING
        text_table TYPE t_text.
    METHODS add_line
      IMPORTING
        text_line TYPE t_line.
    METHODS display.
    METHODS delete.
  PRIVATE SECTION.
    DATA text TYPE t_text.
ENDCLASS.

CLASS zcl_text IMPLEMENTATION.
  METHOD get_handle.
    CREATE OBJECT text.
  ENDMETHOD.
  METHOD add_table.
    APPEND LINES OF text_table TO me->text.
  ENDMETHOD.
  METHOD add_line.
    APPEND text_line TO me->text.
  ENDMETHOD.
  METHOD display.
    CALL FUNCTION 'Z_SHOW_TEXT'
      EXPORTING text = me->text.
  ENDMETHOD.
  METHOD delete.
    CLEAR me->text.
  ENDMETHOD.
ENDCLASS.
```

The following listing contains the function group Z_TEXT_OUTPUT that is used by the class.

Listing A.2 Function Group Z_TEXT_OUTPUT

```
FUNCTION-POOL z_text_output.

DATA: container TYPE REF TO cl_gui_custom_container,
      textedit  TYPE REF TO cl_gui_textedit,
      g_text    TYPE zcl_text=>t_text.

FUNCTION z_show_text.
*"----------------------------------------------------------
*"*"Local interface:
*"  IMPORTING
*"     REFERENCE(TEXT) TYPE  ZCL_TEXT=>T_TEXT
*"----------------------------------------------------------
  g_text = text.
  CALL SCREEN 100 STARTING AT 10 5.
ENDFUNCTION.

MODULE status_0100 OUTPUT.
  SET PF-STATUS 'STATUS_100'.
  SET TITLEBAR  'TITLE_100'.
  IF container IS INITIAL.
    CREATE OBJECT:
      container
        EXPORTING container_name = 'CUSTOM_CONTAINER',
      textedit
        EXPORTING parent         = container.
  ENDIF.
  textedit->set_readonly_mode( 1 ).
  textedit->set_toolbar_mode( 0 ).
  textedit->set_font_fixed( 1 ).
  textedit->set_text_as_r3table( table = g_text ).
ENDMODULE.

MODULE cancel INPUT.
  LEAVE SCREEN.
ENDMODULE.
```

The following listing shows how you can use the ZCL_TEXT class.

Listing A.3 Using ZCL_TEXT

```
REPORT z_text_output.

CLASS demo DEFINITION.
  PUBLIC SECTION.
    CLASS-METHODS main.
ENDCLASS.
CLASS demo IMPLEMENTATION.
  METHOD main.
    DATA: text       TYPE REF TO zcl_text,
          text_table TYPE zcl_text=>t_text,
          text_line  TYPE zcl_text=>t_line.
    text = zcl_text=>get_handle( ).
    text_line = 'First line of text'.
    text->add_line( text_line ).
    text->add_line( ' ' ).
    DO 10 TIMES.
      CLEAR text_line.
      text_line(3) = sy-index.
      CONCATENATE 'Table line' text_line
        INTO text_line SEPARATED BY space.
      APPEND text_line TO text_table.
    ENDDO.
    text->add_table( text_table ).
    text->add_line( ' ' ).
    text_line = 'Last line of text'.
    text->add_line( text_line ).
    text->display( ).

    text->delete( ).
    text->add_line( 'New text' ).
    text->display( ).
  ENDMETHOD.
ENDCLASS.
START-OF-SELECTION.
  demo=>main( ).
```

First it outputs the text displayed in Figure A.1. This text is then replaced by another text.

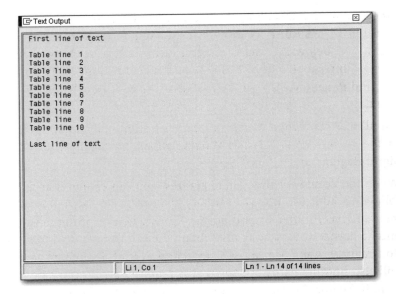

Figure A.1 Output of ZCL_TEXT

A.7 References on the Web

We would like to refer you to two very useful links on the Internet:

▸ **http://sdn.sap.com**
The *SAP Developer Network* contains specific pages and discussion forums for ABAP developers.

▸ **http://help.sap.com**
The *SAP Help Portal* contains the complete SAP online help.

A.8 Installing and Using the SAP NetWeaver 2004s ABAP Trial Version

The SAP NetWeaver 2004s ABAP Trial Version is available for download from the SAP Developer Network and is also contained on the DVD that accompanies this book. For all questions and patches regarding the Trial Version, please visit the respective forum and download area at the SAP Developer Network (*www.sdn.sap.com*).

▸ When installing the application, you should follow the step-by-step instructions included in the delivery.

▶ We recommend installing the latest version of SAP GUI after installing the AS ABAP. With SAP GUI for Windows, Release 6.40, Patch level below 20, there are some issues when used together with MS Internet Explorer 7. If not yet contained on the DVD, you can find Patch level 23 for download at the SAP Developer Network.

▶ For all matters related to system administration you should refer to the book *SAP R/3 System Administration* by Liane Will and Sigrid Hagemann (SAP PRESS 2004).

▶ When the license for the system expires, you can extend it at the following address: *http://service.sap.com/sap/bc/bsp/spn/minisap/minisap.htm*. If, after extending the license, you're prompted to enter a licence key, you can also obtain the key from that address. You manage your license in Transaction SLICENSE, where you will also find the hardware key that is required for license extension. If the initial license has expired, you can still log on using the SAP* user to install a new license.

▶ If you want to import sample programs from transport requests, you can copy the *cofiles* into the ...\sap\trans\cofiles directory, and the data files to ...\sap\trans\data.

Call Transaction STMS and double-click on the line **NSP**. Then select **Extras · Other Requests · Add**. In the dialog window, call the input help (F4) and select the requested order number. Then you can import the order by selecting **Order · Import Request** from the menu.

Attention: HTTP services (e. g., for Web Dynpro, ICF, Web services, etc.) must be explicitly activated in Transaction SICF after an import; otherwise, you cannot use them.

Authors

Horst Keller

Horst Keller received a PhD in physics from the technical university of Darmstadt, Germany, and joined SAP in 1995. He is a member of the SAP NetWeaver Foundation ABAP group where, as a knowledge architect, he is primarily responsible for the documentation and roll-out of ABAP and ABAP Objects, while also developing the programs for formatting and presenting the ABAP documentation including the related search algorithms. He is the author and editor of many ABAP books at SAP PRESS, as well as many other publications and workshops on this subject.

Contribution to this book

All chapters and sections not listed under the other authors; editorial proofing of the manuscripts from all authors; compiling the entire manuscript and all general work required, and creating all examples in the SAP NetWeaver 2004s ABAP Trial Version.

Sascha Krüger

Sascha Krüger has a degree in computer science and business administration. Since 1995, he has worked with complex IT systems on long-term IT strategies. In addition to having written numerous textbooks and publications on ABAP and IT management, he has also lectured at colleges on this subject for a number of years. Today, he is Vice President at SAP for the Business Development EMEA Central (Europe, Middle East, and Africa) area, where he manages the Service Providers industries.

Contribution to this book

Practical checking of the example given in Chapter 2, preparation of the chapter on the fundamental language elements, as well as the chapters on error handling, dynamic programming, and on test and analysis tools.

Stefan Bresch

Stefan Bresch studied computer science at the University of Karlsruhe, Germany, where he completed his degree in 1996. He then worked as an R/3 consultant in a mid-sized corporate consultancy firm and moved to SAP in 2000, where he worked in the area of object persistence in SAP NetWeaver Application Server ABAP (Object Services) and Java (JDO). He was involved in the implementation of simple transformations and is currently working on the XML infrastructure in SAP NetWeaver Foundation ABAP.

Contribution to this book

Section on object services.

Rupert Hieble

Rupert Hieble studied technical informatics at the University of Applied Sciences of Ravensburg-Weingarten, Germany, where he completed his degree in 1996. He initially worked as a consultant in SAP's Technical Core Competence area. He built on this experience by later moving to the system and process analysis area, driving innovative developments in Reverse Business Engineering (RBE). Since April 2000, he has worked in the area of XML processing with the SAP NetWeaver Application Server.

Contribution to this book

Section on ABAP and XML.

Anne Lanfermann

Anne Lanfermann joined SAP in 1992 and initially worked as an instructor in the training department. Since 1996, she has worked in product management, where she focuses primarily on documentation, knowledge transfer, and rollout. She's a member of the Process Integration & Enterprise Services department.

Contribution to this book

Section on ABAP Web Services.

Frank Müller

Having been involved in customer-side SAP implementation projects, Frank Müller joined SAP in 1999 where he first worked as an instructor and coordinator for customer and partner training courses in the area of logistics and e-business. Since 2001, he has worked as an information developer in the ABAP Connectivity area of SAP NetWeaver Foundation ABAP, where he is responsible for Remote Function Call (RFC), Internet Connection Framework (ICF), and connectors.

Contribution to this book

Sections on communication, RFC, and ICF.

Stefanie Rohland

Stefanie Rohland studied physics at Freie Universität Berlin, Germany, where she completed her degree in 1994. In August 2000, she began working in product management for technology development at SAP. Since 2004, she has worked in NetWeaver product management, where her primary focus has been on information development in the area of Web Dynpro for ABAP.

Contribution to this book

Section on Web Dynpro ABAP.

Index

F

M

**Learn to design intuitive
business applications with
SAP Visual Composer for
NetWeaver 2004s**

**Best practices for configuration
settings and advice to master
the development lifecycle**

524 pp., 2007, 69,95 Euro / US$ 69,95
ISBN 978-1-59229-099-4

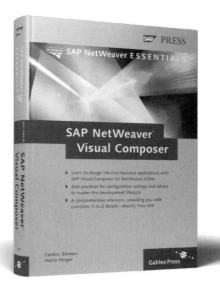

SAP NetWeaver
Visual Composer

www.sap-press.com

C. Bönnen, M. Herger

SAP NetWeaver Visual Composer

Instead of conventional programming and implementation,
SAP NetWeaver Visual Composer (VC) enables you to
model your processes graphically via drag & drop—
potentially without ever having to write a single line of
code. This book not only shows you how, but also serves as
a comprehensive reference, providing you with complete
details on all aspects of VC. You learn the ins and outs of
the VC architecture—including details on all components
and concepts, as well as essential information on model-
based development and on the preparation of different
types of applications. Readers quickly broaden their
knowledge by tapping into practical expert advice on the
various aspects of the Development Lifecycle as well as on
selected applications, which have been modeled with the
VC and are currently delivered by SAP as standard
applications.

Basic principles, architecture, and configuration

Development of dynamic, reusable UI components

Volumes of sample code and screen captures for help you maximize key tools

360 pp., 2006, 69,95 Euro / US$
ISBN 1-59229-078-7

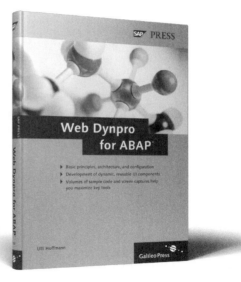

Web Dynpro for ABAP

www.sap-press.com

U. Hoffmann

Web Dynpro for ABAP

Serious developers must stay ahead of the curve by ensuring that they are up-to-date with all of the latest standards. This book illustrates the many benefits that can be realized with component-based UI development using Web Dynpro for ABAP. On the basis of specifically developed sample components, readers are introduced to the architecture of the runtime and development environment and receive highly-detailed descriptions of the different functions and tools that enable you to efficiently implement Web Dynpro technology on the basis of SAP NetWeaver 2004s. Numerous code listings, screen captures, and little-known tricks make this book your indispensable companion for the practical design of modern user interfaces.

Comprehensive guide to end-to-end process integration with SAP XI—from a developer's perspective

Practical exercises to master system configuration and development of mappings, adapters, and proxies

341 pp., 2007, 69,95 Euro / US$ 69,95
ISBN 978-1-59229-118-2

SAP Exchange Infrastructure for Developers

www.sap-press.com

V. Nicolescu, B. Funk, P. Niemeyer, M. Heile

SAP Exchange Infrastructure for Developers

This book provides both experienced and new SAP XI developers with a detailed overview of the functions and usage options of the SAP NetWeaver Exchange Infrastructure. The authors take you deep into the system with a series of practical exercises for the development and configuration of mappings, adapters, and proxies: RFC-to-File, File-to-IDoc, ABAP-Proxy-to-SOAP, and Business Process Management. Each exercise is rounded off by a description of relevant monitoring aspects and is combined in a comprehensive case study.

Examples of dynamic programming, componentization, integration of applications, navigation, and much more

Essential and practical knowledge about installation, configuration, and administration of the Web Dynpro runtime

497 pp., 2006, 69,95 Euro / US$
ISBN 1-59229-077-9

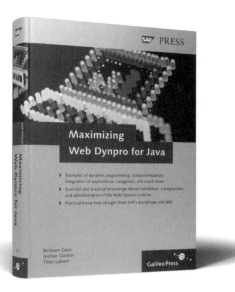

Maximizing
Web Dynpro for Java

www.sap-press.com

B. Ganz, J. Gürtler, T. Lakner

Maximizing Web Dynpro for Java

Standard examples of Web Dynpro applications can leave SAP developers with many questions and severe limitations. This book takes you to the next level with detailed examples that show you exactly what you need to know in order to leverage Web Dynpro applications. From the interaction with the Java Developer Infrastructure (JDI), to the use of Web Dynpro components, to the integration into the portal and the use of its services—this unique book delivers it all. In addition, readers get dozens of tips and tricks on fine-tuning Web Dynpro applications in terms of response time, security, and structure. Expert insights on the configuration and administration of the Web Dynpro runtime environment serve to round out this comprehensive book.

**Improve your Design Process
with "Contextual Design"**

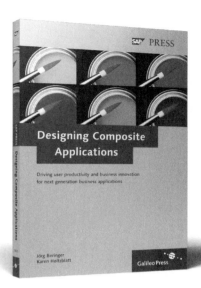

182 pp., 2006, 49,95 Euro / US$ 49,95
ISBN 978-1-59229-065-9

Designing
Composite Applications

www.sap-press.com

Jörg Beringer, Karen Holtzblatt

Designing Composite Applications

Driving user productivity and business innovation for
next generation business applications

This book helps any serious developer hit the ground
running by providing a highly detailed and
comprehensive introduction to modern application
design, using the SAP Enterprise Services
Architecture (ESA) toolset and the methodology of
"Contextual Design". Readers will benefit
immediately from exclusive insights on design
processes based on SAPs Business Process Platform
and learn valuable tricks and techniques that can
drastically improve user productivity. Anybody
involved in the process of enterprise application
design and usability/quality management stands to
benefit from this book.

Detailed comparison of ABAP and JAVA/J2EE concepts

Comprehensive introduction to the SAP NetWeaver Developer Studio

Tutorials on the Java Dictionary, Web Dynpro, Session Beans, Message Driven Beans and much more

495 pp., 2005, 69,95 Euro / US$ 69,95
ISBN 978-1-59229-027-7

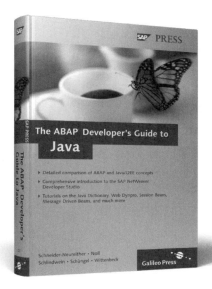

The ABAP Developer's Guide to Java

www.sap-press.com

A. Schneider-Neureither (Ed.)

The ABAP Developer's Guide to Java

Leverage your ABAP skills to climb up the Java learning curve

This all-new reference book is an indispensable guide for ABAP developers who need a smooth transition to Java. The authors highlight each fundamental aspect pertaining to the development of business applications in both languages, and the differences as well as similarities are analyzed in detail. This book helps any developer learn techniques to master development tools and objects, application design, application layers and much more. Learn about Beans, OpenSQL for Java, JDBC, Security, and more.

Get a detailed introduction to
the concept of Design Patterns

Learn how to easily implement
Adapter, Composite, Decorator,
Façade, and MVC

Benefit immediately
from extensively commented
code samples

88 pp., 2006, 68,– Euro / US$ 85,00
ISBN 1-59229-087-6

Design Patterns in Object-Oriented ABAP

www.sap-hefte.de

Igor Barbaric

Design Patterns in Object-Oriented ABAP

SAP PRESS Essentials 15

This new SAP PRESS Essentials technical guide
introduces experienced ABAP programmers to the
detailed concepts of Design Patterns in object-
oriented ABAP. Using real-life scenarios from a fully
functional business application, the author shares key
insights, while showing you proven best practices for
how to implement the most common Design
Patterns in ABAP Objects. Adapter, Composite,
Decorator, Facade, and—probably the most well
known—Model View Controller (MVC), are all
covered extensively.
After reading this exclusive guide, you can quickly
unleash the full potential of Design Patterns to
improve performance and quality, as well as the
robustness of your most critical applications.

Discover all aspects of XML data exchange: software development, specification, and testing

Maximize your use of all XML technologies in ABAP: XML Library, XSLT, and Simple Transformations (ST)

121 pp., 2006, 68,– Euro / 85,– US$
ISBN 1-59229-076-0

XML Data Exchange using ABAP

www.sap-hefte.de

T. Trapp

XML Data Exchange using ABAP

SAP PRESS Essentials 13

This SAP PRESS Essentials technical guide shows you, step-by-step, how to implement XML data exchange processes using ABAP. Based on a variety of interface examples, readers are provided with highly detailed descriptions of all XML technologies including XML Library, XSLT (with a specific focus on XSLT 2.0 extensions), and Simple Transformations. Volumes of code samples enable you to implement your own data exchange scenarios and select the appropriate technologies to support them. In addition, readers benefit from best practices for data exchange and from practical guidance on all aspects of software development—including specification, testing, data validation via Java integration, and more.

The Official ABAP Reference

www.sap-press.com

H. Keller

The Official ABAP Reference

Thoroughly revised and significantly extended, this
all-new edition of our acclaimed reference, contains
complete descriptions of all commands in ABAP and
ABAP Objects, Release 6.40.

Not only will you find explanations and examples of
all commands, you'll also be able to hit the ground
running with key insights and complete reviews of all
relevant usage contexts. Fully updated for the current
Release 6.40, many topics in this new book have
been revised completely. Plus, we've added full
coverage of ABAP and XML, which are now
described in detail for the very first time. The book
comes complete with a test version of the latest
Mini-SAP System 6.20!